# The Handbook of Criminological Theory

## Wiley Handbooks in Criminology and Criminal Justice

**Series Editor**: Charles F. Wellford, University of Maryland College Park.

The handbooks in this series will be comprehensive, academic reference works on leading topics in criminology and criminal justice.

*The Handbook of Law and Society*
Edited by Austin Sarat and Patricia Ewick

*The Handbook of Juvenile Delinquency and Juvenile Justice*
Edited by Marvin D. Krohn and Jodi Lane

*The Handbook of Gangs*
Edited by Scott H. Decker and David C. Pyrooz

*The Handbook of Deviance*
Edited by Erich Goode

*The Handbook of Criminological Theory*
Edited by Alex R. Piquero

# The Handbook of Criminological Theory

*Edited by*

Alex R. Piquero

**WILEY** Blackwell

This edition first published 2016
© 2016 John Wiley & Sons, Inc.

*Registered Office*
John Wiley & Sons, Ltd, The Atrium, Southern Gate, Chichester, West Sussex, PO19 8SQ, UK

*Editorial Offices*
350 Main Street, Malden, MA 02148-5020, USA
9600 Garsington Road, Oxford, OX4 2DQ, UK
The Atrium, Southern Gate, Chichester, West Sussex, PO19 8SQ, UK

For details of our global editorial offices, for customer services, and for information about how to apply for permission to reuse the copyright material in this book please see our website at www.wiley.com/wiley-blackwell.

The right of Alex R. Piquero to be identified as the author of the editorial material in this work has been asserted in accordance with the UK Copyright, Designs and Patents Act 1988.

*Library of Congress Cataloging-in-Publication Data*
The handbook of criminological theory / edited by Alex R. Piquero.
    pages   cm. – (Wiley handbooks in criminology and criminal justice)
Summary: "Provides up-to-date, in-depth summaries of the most important theories in criminology, from classic deterrence theory and social disorganization to modern labeling theory and integrated theory"– Provided by publisher.
    Includes bibliographical references and index.
    ISBN 978-1-118-51238-8 (hardback) – ISBN 978-1-119-11075-0 (paper)
1.  Criminology–Handbooks, manuals, etc.   I.  Piquero, Alex R.
    HV6025.H2783 2015
    364.01–dc23
                                        2015016630
A catalogue record for this book is available from the British Library.

Cover image: © bestdesigns / iStockphoto

Set in 10.5/13pt Minion by SPi Global, Pondicherry, India

Printed in the UK

# Contents

## Contents

# Notes on Contributors

**Robert Agnew** is the Samuel Candler Dobbs Professor of Sociology at Emory University. His research focuses on the causes of crime and delinquency, particularly his general strain theory of delinquency. His recent works include *Criminological Theory: Past to Present* (Oxford, 2015); *Juvenile Delinquency: Causes and Control* (Oxford, 2015); *Toward A Unified Criminology: Integrating Assumptions about Crime, People, and Society* (NYU Press, 2011); *Pressured into Crime: An Overview of General Strain Theory* (Oxford, 2006); and *Why Do Criminals Offend: A General Theory of Crime and Delinquency* (Oxford, 2005). He has served as President of the American Society of Criminology, is a Fellow of that organization, and is on the Southern Sociological Society Roll of Honor.

**Jose R. Agustina** is an Associate professor of Criminal Law and Criminology at Universitat Internacional de Catalunya (Barcelona). He has recently been Visiting Scholar at Texas State University in 2012 where he carried out a research project on juveniles' hangouts. Besides teaching at the Universitat Internacional de Catalunya (UIC), Barcelona, Spain, he has worked as a part-time magistrate at the High Criminal Court in Barcelona. His research interests encompass not only crime theory and crime analysis but also crime policy and legal issues in a variety of fields, from cybercrime, business crime prevention or privacy concerns to youth crime and criminal justice issues.

**Ronald L. Akers**, Ph.D., is Professor Emeritus of Criminology and Sociology at the University of Florida. He is former Chair of the Department of Sociology and Director of the Center for Studies in Criminology and Law. Dr. Akers has authored over 100 journal articles and book chapters.

**Olena Antonaccio** is Associate Professor of Sociology at the University of Miami. Her interests include theory testing and development, and comparative criminology.

**Ashley N. Arnio** is an Assistant Professor in the School of Criminal Justice at Texas State University. Her research interests are primarily in the areas of communities and crime and law and social control. She has explored the first theme in several spatial analyses addressing the link between the contemporary foreclosure crisis and crime rates. More recently, her focus has been on the latter theme, specifically examining aggregate-level racial disparities in imprisonment rates during the period of mass incarceration.

**J.C. Barnes** is an associate professor in the School of Criminal Justice at the University of Cincinnati. He is a biosocial criminologist whose research seeks to understand how genetic and environmental factors combine to impact criminological phenomena.

**Eric P. Baumer** is Professor of Sociology and Criminology at Pennsylvania State University. His research focuses on temporal and spatial dimensions of crime and justice, and especially how structural and cultural features of communities affect crime, social control, and other aspects of human behavior. He has examined these issues empirically in multi-level studies of the influence of community characteristics on individual attitudes and behaviors, macro-level studies of spatial and temporal patterns in crime and social control, and in case studies of crime and justice in Iceland, Malta, and Ireland. Recent publications have appeared in *Criminology*, *American Sociological Review*, and the *American Journal of Sociology*.

**Kevin M. Beaver** is a professor in the College of Criminology and Criminal Justice at Florida State University and Visiting Distinguished Professor in the Center for Social and Humanities Research at King Abdulaziz University. His research focuses on the biosocial underpinnings to antisocial behaviors.

**Joanne Belknap** is a professor of Ethnic Studies at the University of Colorado, and is Past-President of the American Society of Criminology (2013–14). She authored the book, *The Invisible Woman: Gender, Crime, and Justice*, currently in the fourth edition. Her current research focuses on intimate partner abuse, women's pathways to jail, and sexual minority status delinquents.

**Mark T. Berg,** Ph.D. is an assistant professor in the Department of Sociology at the University of Iowa. His current research interests include contextual processes, adolescent development, violence and aggression.

**Ekaterina V. Botchkovar** is Associate Professor of Criminal Justice at Northeastern University. Her interests include comparative criminology and theory development.

**Brian B. Boutwell** is an associate professor of criminology and criminal justice in the School of Social Work and associate professor (secondary appointment) in the Department of Epidemiology at Saint Louis University. His research interests include the evolution of complex outcomes such as violence and chronic criminality, as well as the genetic basis of social behaviors.

**Chester L. Britt** is Professor and Chair of the Department of Sociology at Iowa State University. His research interests include criminological theory, criminal justice decision-making, and quantitative research methods.

**Henry H. Brownstein** is Associate Dean for Research, Professor and Director of the Center for Public Policy at the L. Douglas Wilder School for Government and Public Affairs at Virginia Commonwealth University. Until recently he was a Senior Fellow at NORC at the University of Chicago and prior to that he was a Senior Vice President and Department Director. Previous positions include: Director of the Drugs and Crime Research Division and Executive Director of the Arrestee Drug Abuse Monitoring (ADAM) program at the National Institute of Justice (NIJ), Professor and Director of the Graduate Program in Criminal Justice at the University of Baltimore, Principal Investigator at Narcotic and Drug Research, Inc. (NDRI), and Chief of Statistical Services at the New York State Division of Criminal Justice Services. For more than 30 years he has been conducting research on illicit drugs and drug markets, violence and violent crime, and qualitative research methods. He is the author of books, scholarly articles, essays, and book chapters on these subjects. His latest books are *Contemporary Drug Policy* (2013, Routledge) and *The Methamphetamine Industry in America: Transnational Cartels and Local Entrepreneurs* (2014, Rutgers University Press). He earned his Ph.D. in sociology from Temple University in 1977.

**Elizabeth Cauffman**, Ph.D. is a Professor of Psychology and Social Behavior, Education, and Law at the University of California, Irvine. At the broadest level, Dr. Cauffman's research addresses the intersect between adolescent development and juvenile justice. She has published over 100 articles, chapters, and books on a range of topics in the study of contemporary adolescence, including adolescent brain development, risk-taking and decision-making, parent-adolescent relationships, and juvenile justice.

**Caitlin Cavanagh**, M.A., is a doctoral student in the Department of Psychology and Social Behavior at the University of California, Irvine. Her program of research seeks to produce developmentally sound research that can improve how the juvenile justice system interfaces with adolescent offenders and their families.

**Breanne Cave** is a doctoral candidate in the Criminology, Law and Society Program at George Mason University. Her research interests include crime and place and policing.

**Frances R. Chen** is a doctoral student in criminology at the University of Pennsylvania. She is interested in understanding initiation, maintenance and desistance of antisocial behavior from a developmental and biosocial perspective. She has conducted research on the interaction between life adversity (e.g., harsh parenting) and biological vulnerability (e.g., stress-response systems) on the development of behavior problems among children. Another line of her research attempts to elucidate the role of significant life events (e.g., marriage, cohabitation) in men's desistance from antisocial behavior in early adulthood. Currently she is conducting research on how early versus late puberty timing interplay with peer network to affect substance use and delinquency in adolescence.

**Heith Copes** is a professor in the Department of Justice Sciences at the University of Alabama at Birmingham. He earned his PhD in sociology from the University of Tennessee in 2001. Heith has published over 50 articles and chapters on deviance and crime and several books (e.g., *Identity Thieves: Motives and Methods*) and edited collections (e.g., *Voices from the Criminal Justice*). His research emphasis is on understanding the ways that deviants and offenders make sense of their actions.

**Scott H. Decker** graduated from DePauw University with a BA in Social Justice. He earned a PhD in Criminology from Florida State University in 1976. He is Foundation Professor in the School of Criminology and Criminal Justice at Arizona State University. His main research interests are in the areas of gangs, violence, criminal justice policy, and the offender's perspective. He is a Fellow in the American Society of Criminology and the Academy of Criminal Justice Sciences. He is an active and contributing member of the Eurogang Research Group. He is the co-author of *Confronting Gangs* (Oxford) and co-editor of *The Handbook of Gangs* (Wiley) with David Pyrooz.

**Matt DeLisi** is Professor and Coordinator of Criminal Justice Studies and Affiliate with the Center for the Study of Violence at Iowa State University. The Editor-in-Chief of the *Journal of Criminal Justice*, Dr. DeLisi received the Fellow Award from the Academy of Criminal Justice Sciences in 2012 and is the author of more than 250 scholarly publications.

**Sachiko Donley** is a doctoral student in the Department of Psychology and Social Behavior at the University of California Irvine. Her program of research focuses on adolescent risk-taking and the environmental and social contexts that promote or reduce risk-taking behaviors.

**David P. Farrington** is Emeritus Professor of Psychological Criminology and Leverhulme Trust Emeritus Fellow in the Institute of Criminology, Cambridge University. He received the Stockholm Prize in Criminology in 2013. He is Chair of the ASC Division of Developmental and Life-Course Criminology. His major research interest is in developmental criminology, and he is Director of the Cambridge Study in Delinquent Development, a prospective longitudinal survey of over 400 London males from age 8 to age 56. In addition to over 600 published journal articles and book chapters on criminological and psychological topics, he has published nearly 100 books, monographs and government reports.

**Marcus Felson** has been a leader not only in crime theory (namely, the routine activity theory) but also in applying that theory to reducing crime. His central argument is that everyday legal activities set the stage for the illegal activities that feed on them. Before Texas State University, he was professor at the Rutgers University School of Criminal Justice and the University of Illinois.

**Yu Gao**, Ph.D., is an Assistant professor in Department of Psychology at Brooklyn College and the Graduate Center of City University of New York. Dr. Gao obtained her doctoral degree from University of Southern California, and then worked at the

University of Pennsylvania as a postdoctoral fellow. Her research focuses on the neurobiological and psychosocial bases of antisocial behavior, using psychophysiological methods and longitudinal approaches. In particular, her work on fear conditioning deficits and emotion dysregulation in individuals with aggressive and criminal behavior extends prior literature and is in supportive of the neurodevelopmental perspective of crime.

**Andrea L. Glenn**, Ph.D., is Assistant Professor in the Center for the Prevention of Youth Behavior Problems and the Department of Psychology at the University of Alabama. Her research focuses on understanding the biological correlates of psychopathy and using biological information in the development of interventions for youth with conduct problems.

**Andy Hochstetler** is Professor of Sociology at Iowa State University where he teaches in the Criminal Justice Program. Using wide-ranging methodologies, both quantitative and qualitative, he writes mainly on offender self-concepts and the choice to commit crime, and has published over 50 articles and one book. His work usually emphasizes identity and decision-making. He maintains general interests in recidivism, criminal decision-making, choice, and in examining psychological variables and offending in longitudinal data.

**Wesley G. Jennings**, Ph.D., is Associate Professor, Associate Chair, and Undergraduate Director in the Department of Criminology, has a Courtesy Appointment in the Department of Mental Health Law and Policy, and is a Faculty Affiliate of the Florida Mental Health Institute in the College of Behavioral and Community Sciences at the University of South Florida. In addition, he also has a Courtesy Appointment in the Department of Health Outcomes & Policy and is a Faculty Affiliate of the Institute for Child Health Policy in the College of Medicine at the University of Florida. He received his doctorate degree in criminology from the University of Florida.

**Marv Krohn** is currently a Professor in the Department of Sociology and Criminology & Law at the University of Florida. Professor Krohn has a long-standing interest in the etiology of delinquency and drug use, focusing primarily on social process and life-course approaches. For the past 26 years he has been a Co-Principal Investigator on the Rochester Youth Development Study, a three-generational longitudinal panel study targeting those at high risk for serious crime and delinquency. His book (with co-authors Terence P. Thornberry, Alan J. Lizotte, Carolyn A. Smith and Kimberly Tobin), *Gangs and Delinquency in Developmental Perspective*, was the American Society of Criminology's recipient of the 2003 Michael J. Hindelang Award for Outstanding Scholarship. Professor Krohn also co-authored *Delinquent Behavior* (with Don C. Gibbons) and *Researching Theories of Crime and Delinquency* (with Charis E. Kubrin and Thomas D. Stucky) and has co-edited four compendiums on crime and delinquency. In addition, he has contributed to numerous research articles and book chapters. He is a former Vice President and Executive Counselor of the American Society of Criminology and was recently named a Fellow in the American Society of Criminology.

**Charis E. Kubrin** is Professor of Criminology, Law and Society at the University of California, Irvine. She is also co-director of the Irvine Laboratory for the Study of Space and Crime (ILSSC). Her research focuses on neighborhoods, race, and violence as central to social disorganization theory. Charis is co-author of *Researching Theories of Crime and Deviance* (Oxford University Press 2008) and *Privileged Places: Race, Residence, and the Structure of Opportunity* (Lynne Rienner 2006), and co-editor *of Introduction to Criminal Justice: A Sociological Perspective* (Stanford University Press 2013), *Punishing Immigrants: Policy, Politics, and Injustice* (New York University Press 2012), and *Crime and Society: Crime*, 3rd Edition (Sage Publications 2007). In addition to books, Charis's work has been published in various academic journals including *American Journal of Sociology, Annals of the American Academy of Political and Social Science, City and Community, Criminology, Criminology & Public Policy, Homicide Studies, Journal of Quantitative Criminology, Journal of Research in Crime and Delinquency, Justice Quarterly, Men and Masculinities, Social Forces, Social Problems, Social Science Quarterly, Sociological Perspectives, Sociological Quarterly*, and *Urban Studies*. In 2005, Charis received the American Society of Criminology's Ruth Shonle Cavan Young Scholar Award and recently, she was awarded The Coramae Richey Mann Award from the American Society of Criminology's Division on People of Color and Crime in recognition of her outstanding contributions to scholarship on race, crime, and justice.

**Thomas A. Loughran** is an Associate Professor in the Department of Criminology and Criminal Justice at the University of Maryland. His research interests include offender decision-making and deterrence, illegal markets and quantitative methods.

**Tara Renae McGee** is an Australian Research Council DECRA Research Fellow in the School of Criminology and Criminal Justice at Griffith University. She is a developmental criminologist conducting research on the onset and continuity of antisocial behavior and offending, as well as gender differences in offending. She is founding co-editor of the *Journal of Developmental and Life-Course Criminology*, the vice president of the Australian and New Zealand Society of Criminology and the secretary/treasurer of the ASC Division of Developmental and Life-Course Criminology.

**Sharon Niv** earned her Ph.D. in Clinical Psychology and Brain Cognitive Science at the University of Southern California. Her focus was childhood EEG patterns in prediction of adolescent mood and behavior, and therapeutic neurofeedback. Sharon is interested in developments in neuroscience, and advancing understanding of the brain and mind. Her personal aim is to bring technological approaches to psychotherapy. She is a scientific consultant for several projects surrounding wellbeing, psychological health, and behavior change. Sharon earned her B.A. in molecular and cellular biology at UC Berkeley in 2005 and her M.A. in clinical and brain cognitive psychology at the University of Southern California in 2010. She graduated Singularity University in 2010.

**Ray Paternoster** is a professor in the Department of Criminology and Criminal Justice at the University of Maryland. His research interests are rational choice theory, offender decision-making, criminal desistance and issues related to capital punishment.

**Alex R. Piquero** is Ashbel Smith Professor of Criminology at the University of Texas at Dallas; adjunct professor at the Key Centre for Ethics, Law, Justice, and Governance, Griffith University Australia, and faculty affiliate with the Center for Violence and Injury Prevention, George Warren Brown School of Social Work, Washington University in St. Louis. He has received several research, teaching, and mentoring awards and is a fellow of both the American Society of Criminology and the Academy of Criminal Justice Sciences. In 2014, he received the University of Texas System Regents' Outstanding Teaching Award.

**Jill Portnoy** is a doctoral candidate in criminology at the University of Pennsylvania. Her research examines biological, psychological, and social risk factors for antisocial behavior in children and adolescents. She is particularly interested in how biological and social risk factors interact to predict antisocial behavior. Her current research focuses on interactions between neighborhood disadvantage and reduced biological stress reactivity in predicting adolescent aggression and rule-breaking.

**Travis C. Pratt** is a Fellow at the University of Cincinnati Corrections Institute. His work focuses primarily on criminological theory and correctional policy. He is the author of *Addicted to Incarceration* (Sage 2009), and he has published more than 60 peer-reviewed articles that have appeared in journals such as *Criminology, Journal of Research in Crime and Delinquency, Journal of Quantitative Criminology*, and *Crime and Justice: A Review of Research*.

**Adrian Raine**, D.Phil., is the Richard Perry University Professor of Criminology, Psychiatry, and Psychology at the University of Pennsylvania. He gained his under-graduate degree in Experimental Psychology at the University of Oxford, and his Ph.D. in Psychology from the University of York. His interdisciplinary research focuses on the etiology and prevention of antisocial, violent, and psychopathic behavior in children and adults. He has published 354 journal articles and book chapters, seven books, and given 331 invited presentations in 26 countries. His latest book, *The Anatomy of Violence* (Pantheon and Penguin 2013), reviews the brain basis to violence and draws future implications for the punishment, prediction, and prevention of offending, as well as the neuroethical concerns surrounding this work. He is currently President of the Academy of Experimental Criminology, and received an honorary degree (D. Univ.) from the University of York (UK) in 2015.

**Michael Rocque** is an Assistant Professor in the Department of Sociology at Bates College and the Senior Research Advisor for the Maine Department of Corrections. His research interests include life-course criminology, race and justice, and crime prevention.

**Robert Schug** earned a Ph.D. in psychology from the University Southern California. He is an assistant professor of criminal justice and forensic psychology in the Department of Criminal Justice at California State University, Long Beach.

His area of specialization is the biology and psychology of the criminal mind. His research interests are predominantly focused upon understanding the relationship between extreme forms of psychopathology and antisocial, criminal, and violent behavior from a biopsychosocial perspective – with the application of advanced neuroscience techniques from areas such as neuropsychology, psychophysiology, and brain imaging. He is particularly interested in the etiological mechanisms, risk factors, and developmental progression of antisocial behavior within major mental disorders such as psychopathy and schizophrenia, as well as the ability to predict antisocial behavioral outcomes within mentally ill individuals. A seasoned writer, Dr. Schug has published numerous articles in prominent psychiatric, psychological, criminal justice, and neuroscience journals; and has both authored and co-authored edited book chapters for several successful texts in forensic psychology, criminology, and the neurosciences. He recently (2015) published a textbook on mental illness and crime.

**Martin D. Schwartz**, Ph.D. is Visiting Professor at George Washington University, Professor Emeritus at Ohio University, and the author, co-author or editor of 14 books and over 130 refereed articles, chapters and essays. He is the 2008 Fellow of the Academy of Criminal Justice Sciences (ACJS), and has received distinguished scholar awards from an ACJS section (Critical Criminal Justice) and two divisions of the American Society of Criminology (Women and Crime, and Critical Criminology). A former visiting scholar at the U.S. Dept. of Justice and the British Home Office Research Unit, at Ohio University he was Graduate Professor of the Year, Best Arts and Sciences Professor, and given the title Presidential Research Scholar. A former co-editor of *Criminal Justice*, he has served on the editorial boards of 11 other professional journals, while doing hundreds of manuscript reviews for some 65 journals.

**Eric A. Sevell**, M.A., is a graduate student in the Department of Sociology, and the Department of Criminal Justice at Indiana University. Broadly, his research interests include deviant behavior, social control, and cultural criminology.

**Aiden Sidebottom** is lecturer in the Department of Security and Crime Science at University College London. His main research interests are crime prevention evaluation and evidence-based policing.

**Eric A. Stewart** is a professor in the College of Criminology and Criminal Justice at Florida State University. He is a member of the Racial Democracy, Crime and Justice Network. His research interests include racial inequality and criminal outcomes, crime over the life course, and contextual processes and microprocesses that affect adolescent development.

**April Gile Thomas**, M.S., is a doctoral student in the Department of Psychology and Social Behavior at the University of California, Irvine. Her research examines the biopsychosocial context of adolescent development and risk-taking behavior, with an emphasis on juvenile delinquency and justice system involvement.

**Charles R. Tittle** received his Ph.D. in sociology from the University of Texas, Austin, in 1965. He has served on faculties at Indiana University, Florida Atlantic University, Washington State University, and currently is in the phased retirement program at North Carolina State University, teaching half-time. He is interested in theory building and testing in criminology, studies of deviance, and social control.

**Kyle Treiber** (Ph.D., University of Cambridge) is University Lecturer in Neurocriminology at the Institute of Criminology, University of Cambridge and the Deputy Director of the PADS+ study. Her main research interests include the history of biological theories of crime, and the interaction between neurocriminological factors and social environmental influences, including gene × environment interactions.

**Ruth Triplett** is a Professor in the Department of Sociology and Criminal Justice at Old Dominion University. Along with labeling theory, her current research interests include understanding the role of neighborhood-based institutions in neighborhood crime rates.

**Lindsey Upton** is a Ph.D. candidate and Graduate Teaching Assistant in the Department of Sociology and Criminal Justice at Old Dominion University. Her research interests include criminological theory, crime, media and culture studies, the politics of crime control, and fear of crime and victimization.

**Michael G. Vaughn** is Professor in the School of Social Work at Saint Louis University. Dr. Vaughn is a nationally recognized scholar in the areas of adolescent antisocial behavior, substance abuse, violence, delinquency and chronic offending, and juvenile psychopathy. Current projects funded by federal and foundation sources involve the epidemiology, etiology, and prevention of youth violence, the prediction and prevention of school dropout, testing biosocial models using twin samples, examining problem behavior in national data international data sets.

**Jeffrey T. Ward** is an assistant professor in the Department of Criminal Justice at the University of Texas at San Antonio. His research interests include developmental and life-course criminology, sanction effects, gangs, and quantitative methodology. His work has recently appeared in *Crime & Delinquency*, *Criminal Justice and Behavior*, *Criminology*, and *Journal of Criminal Justice*.

**David Weisburd** is Distinguished Professor of Criminology, Law and Society at George Mason University, and Walter E. Meyer Professor of Law and Criminal Justice at the Institute of Criminology, Faculty of Law, The Hebrew University.

**Douglas B. Weiss** earned his Ph.D. in Criminology and Criminal Justice from the University of Maryland in 2014. He is currently an Assistant Professor at California State University at San Bernardino. His research interests include criminological theory, comparative criminology, substance use and crime, and corrections.

**Per-Olof H. Wikström** (Ph.D., Docent, Stockholm University) is Professor of Ecological and Developmental Criminology at the Institute of Criminology, University of Cambridge, and a Fellow of the British Academy. He is the director of the Peterborough Adolescent and Young Adult Development Study (PADS+), a major ESRC-funded research project which aims to advance knowledge about crime causation and prevention. Professor Wikström's main research interests are developing a unified theory of the causes of crime (Situational Action Theory), its empirical testing and its application to devising knowledge-based prevention policies.

**James C. Wo** is a doctoral student in the Department of Criminology, Law and Society at the University of California, Irvine. His primary research interests include the community context of crime, local institutions/organizations, civic engagement, land use, and quantitative methodology. He is a member of the Irvine Laboratory for the Study of Space and Crime (ILSSC), and his recent research has been published in *Crime & Delinquency* and *Journal of School Violence*.

**Richard Wortley** is Head of the Department of Security and Crime Science and Director of the Jill Dando Institute, University College London. His main research interest concerns situational theories of crime.

**Yaling Yang**, Ph.D., is an Assistant Professor in the Department of Pediatrics at the Children's Hospital Los Angeles/ University of Southern California. She has a broad background in externalizing behavioral problems across the lifespan, from early psychopathic traits and substance exposure to later criminal, violent behavior and substance abuse/dependence. Currently, she leads an NIH-funded project at CHLA on genetic and environmental contributions to brain development and identify how neurobiological precursors interact with psychosocial risk factors in contributing to the development of psychopathology in children. In addition, she is also conducting research using multimodule imaging methods to assess the effect of mild traumatic brain injuries on a developing brain and the long-term behavioral outcome.

# 1

# Introduction: Theory and Contemporary Criminology

## Charles R. Tittle

The word "theory" means different things to different contemporary criminologists, depending on their philosophies about the nature of criminology, what it is attempting to accomplish, and how they think criminology ought to be done. Diversity is evident from the presence of at least seven differing "philosophies of the enterprise," expressed in distinct "models" for doing criminology. The seven approaches include: (1) theoretical science; (2) problem solving; (3) "verstehen" analysis; (4) descriptive approaches; (5) critical work; (6) nihilistic thinking; and (7) amelioration. Yet, there does appear to be a dominant paradigm.

In the following pages, I will briefly describe six of the styles of contemporary criminology and assess the meaning and importance of theory in each. However, my description of theoretical science is far more extensive than it is for the other six because theoretical science seems to be the most widely endorsed, even if not always actually practiced, mode of work in contemporary criminology. While all seven of the models to be discussed have an established place in the criminological landscape, are represented by strong advocates, contain powerful intellectual challenges, have produced important results, and command a degree of influence, most criminology seems to follow, to one degree or another, the model of science. Of course, classifying scholars and/or their products into camps is always somewhat arbitrary, and the relative popularity of the various modes of work may be undergoing change. Nevertheless, for now I will follow the classification scheme outlined above in trying to describe theory and its uses in contemporary criminology.

*The Handbook of Criminological Theory*, First Edition. Edited by Alex R. Piquero.
© 2016 John Wiley & Sons, Inc. Published 2016 by John Wiley & Sons, Inc.

## Theoretical Science

Theoretical accounts within a scientific model are intellectual structures designed to help explain things within given domains of interest (for more detailed descriptions of theoretical science see Reynolds, 1971; Tittle, 1995; Turner, 2003: Chapter 1). That is, scientific theories, and explanations try to provide answers to questions of "why" and "how" that are deemed satisfactory by critical audiences made up of scientists who expect such a theory to provide intellectual satisfaction as well as the means for predicting aspects of the phenomena of interest. However, scientific predictions are quite different from prophecy. A scientific prediction is of the form: "given conditions $x$, $y$, and $z$, one should expect to find $q$," which may be applied to events or phenomena in the past as well as the present. A prophecy, on the other hand, is a projection into the future. Scientifically oriented criminologists do not issue prophecies except in the form of conditional statements, such as: "if conditions $x$, $y$, and $z$ continue or emerge, then $q$ is likely to happen."

Scientific explanations can be free-standing, applying to specific phenomena, often at a particular time and place, with quite concrete elements. But, the most useful explanations are embedded in general theories setting forth abstract principles from which explanations of many separate phenomena can be derived. Science strives for such general theories because they are more efficient than myriad specific explanations. In addition, if organized in a deductive way (from general abstract statements or ideas down to more and more concrete phenomena), general theories make it possible to synthesize large bodies of knowledge as well as to derive explanations of phenomena that previously have not been explained. Finally, general theories serve the ends of science because they rest on common causes of various phenomena, thereby guiding the identification of the unity in nature on which science is built.

Theories, however, are intellectual accounts with no necessary connection to the real world they purport to explain. Theories may be intellectually excellent – providing convincing-sounding explanations and being well-structured, logical, comprehensive, and the like – at the same time that the predictions they suggest about the empirical world may be incorrect. Science strives to produce theories that are good intellectual products and that are also empirically faithful. Ultimately, the point is to explain (answer questions of "why" and "how"; establish the causes of) aspects of the domain covered by the theory. To determine if a theory is empirically correct, and to provide the means for improving it when evidence shows that it is not fully correct, scholars must assess how well it accommodates appropriate data about the real world. Research is mainly about testing the match between the intellectual world of a theory with the empirical world supposedly being explained.

In advanced fields the research process first requires derivation of specific, reality-oriented hypotheses from existing theories, the validity of which can be assessed with concrete, empirical information. Hypotheses are statements about relationships among two or more variables, each of which has a direct empirical reference. Statements of relationship contained within, or implied by, a general theory cannot be tested directly because they are in the form of abstract notions about "concepts" rather than variables. Moreover, general theories typically cannot be tested in their entirety because (1) they are composed of many potential causal parts that must fit together in particular specified ways; and (2) because some theoretical propositions in general theories are usually of such high levels of abstraction that it is impractical to attempt to reduce them to concrete form. Checking the "real world" applicability of a general theory, then, inevitably involves substantial theoretical manipulation prior to the technical procedures required for empirical test.

For instance, a given theory may suggest that $A$ (a general, abstract concept) causes $B$ (another general, abstract concept) and that $C$ (a general, abstract concept) causes $D$ (a general, abstract concept), as well as many other relationships and causal connections. In addition, that theory might imply that $A$ indirectly affects $D$ because $A$ affects $C$, which in turn, affects $D$. As long as these implied relationships concern abstract phenomena they stand simply as intellectual puzzles. An empirical test, however, requires that the general, abstract concepts of $A$ and $B$ be reduced to concrete instances of the general categories of $A$ and $B$, that the theoretical relationship between those general categories be specified in more specific empirical terms, and that those empirical terms be accurate reflections of the concepts of the theory. Sometimes, many hypotheses from a given general theory can be assessed simultaneously by estimation of an entire set of causal relationships. But, usually, for a variety of technical and theoretical reasons, the whole set of relationships implied by a theory cannot be tested at once. Instead, scientifically oriented criminologists usually focus on more limited empirical statements (as noted above, called hypotheses). By testing a large number of such hypotheses derived from a theory (not necessarily all at once, but through many research projects by many different scholars, using many samples or social contexts), scholars can indirectly test the accuracy of the entire theory – but only if the theory lends itself to deductive reasoning so that very general notions can lead logically to more concrete specifications of relationships among variables.

Thus, because the same abstract principles can yield many hypotheses, and because abstract concepts can be expressed in many concrete variables, no particular test of a hypothesis provides all, or even a substantial amount, of the information needed to evaluate a theory. Correct evaluation requires many tests of many hypotheses in many different circumstances, using various operationalizations (the term used to refer to the translation of abstract concepts into concrete empirical variables). Certainly, no single study makes a science or permits firm conclusions about the nature of reality or the validity of a given theory. At any given time the status of a theory depends on the weight of evidence compiled up to that point. No theory is ever completely proven, because even if all prior tests have been supportive, there is no guarantee that the next test, with different variables, different samples, and in different parts of the world, will also be supportive. Further, when a theory enjoys numerous successful tests it is likely to provoke closer attention to detail that reveals other possibilities needing testing or that call for refinements of the theory to accommodate previously ignored possibilities. For the same reasons, no theory is ever completely discredited, though substantial negative evidence (provided the evidence is correctly applicable to the theory) may place a theory in low regard in the community of scholars.

Hence, the adequacy of a theory is always tentative, resting on the collective judgment of the community of scientists who express various degrees of confidence in it at any given point in time. Theories are not deemed to be right or wrong; they simply enjoy different amounts of support. Of course, as noted above, theories with little or no empirical support may hold peripheral status, depending on whether their lack of support comes from unsupportive tests or simply from the absence of adequate tests. Though scientifically oriented criminologists ideally downplay theories lacking empirical support, they rarely reject any theories altogether. This is partly because many tests of criminological theories are deemed to be weak, often with the measured variables having poor correspondence with the theoretical concepts at the center of the theories. But, it is also because the culture of criminology, which views theories as the property of their makers rather than as collective endeavors, promotes themes of professional politeness. The ethic of professional politeness leads most scholars to interpret results of research in a generally positive light, so that negative evidence is softened by researchers' calling attention to various counter-possibilities. Indeed, the culture of criminological research calls for authors of papers reporting research results to try first to convince readers that the evidence is relevant and useful for the purpose at hand and then within the same paper to caution readers by detailing reasons why the research should be questioned. Consequently, definitive studies are rare.

In the practice of theoretical science in criminology, theory is the central focus – it is the point of the enterprise. Research is merely a handmaiden to theory-building. If criminologists could explain everything about crime, criminal behavior, and efforts to prevent or channel it, and could do so in an efficient, general, and completely accurate way, there would be no need for research. Criminologists would have achieved their collective goals. Of course, the probability of ever reaching this goal is extremely low, especially since, without research, we cannot ascertain the accuracy of explanations. So, for science, whose guiding goal is theory, research is typically the beginning, the constant helpmate, and the ultimate arbiter.

The process of theoretical criminology, then, is a constant interaction between efforts to build or improve theory and testing of theory as it exists at any given point in time. The process begins with establishing, or perhaps sometimes imagining, regularities in behaviors or social arrangements that seem to bear on crime or crime-related phenomena. Such observations or perceptions sometimes inspire attempts at *ad hoc* explanation (aimed at the specific regularities observed or documented). Once an *ad hoc* explanation has been formulated, it must then be tested in other circumstances where the *ad hoc* phenomenon potentially exists. Such testing requires statement of some logical expectations (hypotheses) based on the previously formulated explanation. If the results of a series of such tests are unfavorable, then scientists are not likely to continue to entertain that explanation (though, as noted before, social scientists are, and must be, cautious in abandoning explanations or theories, even in the face of seemingly strong contrary evidence). If some of the tests are favorable and some are not, theorists are challenged to modify the *ad hoc* explanation to help it accommodate the evidence. If all of the tests are favorable, theorists and researchers are likely to try to expand the argument to include more situations and more variables.

The early stages of a discipline striving to become a theoretical science will spawn numerous observations of regularities, formulations of *ad hoc* explanations, testing of hypotheses, and feedbacks to produce alterations of original *ad hoc* explanations. Thus, at a certain point in the development of a science, the field will contain a number of limited explanations of specified phenomena. Such a situation challenges theorists to recognize or discover the commonality or kinship of underlying causal processes which can be incorporated within a more general formulation. And so begins the enterprise of building general theory (a comprehensive, abstract account) from disparate-appearing, limited explanations.

But, general theories, like free-standing explanations before them, must be squared with the empirical world through derivation and testing of hypotheses. Some scholars/theorists contend that the results of such theory testing should be used to modify theories to make them more consistent with the evidence (see Tittle, 1995, 1985, 1989). Other scholars/theories, however, regard theories as more or less fixed in their original form (see Hirschi, 1979, 1989). To them, empirical tests are simply to confirm or contradict specific theoretical statements, with the whole enterprise consisting of competition among various theories to see which ones fare better. Presumably, the theory that prevails in this competitive struggle will be accepted as true and correct – at least until a rival arises to pose a new challenge. Hence, criminologists pursuing theoretical science disagree as to whether theory is to be accommodative or defensive in the face of contrary evidence.

Criminologists also disagree about the next step after testing initial theoretical formulations. Some believe that theoretical science requires efforts to tie limited theories together into still more general and encompassing accounts that explain more phenomena more accurately. If such higher-level formulations are created, they, in turn, are expected to lead to empirical testing through hypothesis derivation, translation of concepts into variables, and empirical testing. Results from such tests also provide a basis for forming various degrees of confidence in these "integrated" theories. And, for those who embrace an "accommodative" approach to contrary evidence, challenging evidence is ideally used to alter theories in order to more adequately account for the empirical facts. Theoretical alterations of this type are long-range and collective, with an aim toward developing more effective general theories in the face of challenging research evidence. Such theoretical refinements are far different from situational maneuvering by researchers who sometimes modify theories on the spot to more effectively square with the evidence, thereby giving a false impression of strong support.

But, just as criminologists disagree about how theorists should deal with non-supportive evidence, they also disagree about whether various limited theories should be fused through an "integrative process." Some regard integration disapprovingly, allegedly because it compromises one or more of the original theories that are integrated. More importantly, theoretical integration is sometimes condemned as a fool's errand because different explanatory formulations are alleged to be based on specific assumptions that may be contradictory or incompatible across theories, rendering integration impossible or impractical. For instance, it is said that the general class of theories relying on weak or inadequate "control" to explain why individuals commit crime assume that motivation for misconduct can be taken for granted because misconduct is inherently gratifying. Yet, many other theories attempt to explain criminal behavior by referring to the strength of motivation as a key element (see Tittle & Paternoster, 2000). To some, this means that integration of control-type and motivation-type theories makes no sense because, presumably, motivation for crime cannot be both a constant and a variable.

The advocates for theoretical integration, however, do not accept the inherent incompatibility notion, viewing it as posing a false conflict, stemming from a failure to distinguish fundamental assumptions from assumptions of convenience. Many assumptions made by theorists are idiosyncratic to that theorist and are not necessary within the parameters of the basic ideas incorporated within the theory. Moreover, theorists sometimes deliberately make assumptions in order to "hold constant" certain elements relevant to their theory until the theoretical consequences of other elements are explored and developed.

When assumptions associated with specific theories simply reflect biases of the theorist or involve deliberate maneuvers to assist in efficient theory-building, they are "assumptions of convenience" and in no way represent barriers to theoretical integration. Sometimes, of course, seemingly there are incompatible assumptions between various theories, or even within specific theories that may raise questions about the possibility of integration. Integrationists, however, maintain that such "incompatibilities" can be accommodated with the addition of contingency statements within integrated theories. Contingencies are statements of the "scope" of causal arguments, representing conditions under which a causal process operates with more or less force. Thus, if some condition or process is an assumption of a given theory that is integrated into a more general formulation along with a second theory with a different fundamental assumption, the larger, integrated theory can take those differing assumptions into account by specifying that some causal process (presumably the main one set forth by the integrated theory) is theorized to work better or perhaps work at all only when the terms of the contingency have been met.

Therefore, despite differences among theoretical scientists about technicalities, the ideal agreed end-product is general theory that specifies causal processes and which has been shaped and/or confirmed by empirical test. It is important to note, however, that theory is not evaluated only by empirical test. Besides being empirically accurate; theories in scientifically oriented criminology also must be satisfying to critical audiences, they must be "internally" well structured, and they must do certain things. To satisfy critical audiences theories must reflect what is currently (at whatever time the theory is being assessed) thought to be known (that is, they must be sensible and reasonable), and they must actually answer causal questions in a way that is convincing to those who have struggled extensively with the issues relevant to the theory. To qualify as "well-structured" theories must be logically organized, systematic (in that all the parts fit together without inconsistencies, illogicalities, or tautologies, and without loose ends) and manipulable in ways that will yield specific applications (this is usually in the form of a deductive system in which general abstract principles lead to more concrete outcomes through sequential reasoning).

In addition, to qualify as fully adequate theory, formulations must exhibit certain features. Although various scholars uphold somewhat different standards concerning the characteristics of good theory, scientifically-oriented work mandates at least five desirable characteristics: (1) actual explanations that satisfactorily answer questions of why and how; (2) breadth; (3) comprehensiveness; (4) precision; and (5) depth.

*Explanation*    The first, and most important criterion of good theory within the framework of theoretical science is whether the theory answers questions of "why" and "how." This means that a formulation must, above all, help satisfy intellectual curiosity as to the causes of phenomena of interest. However, since audiences for theories differ in sophistication, scientifically oriented theories primarily aim to satisfy professional audiences that are knowledgeable about the subject matter and who employ an acute critical and demanding perspective. Clearly, many intellectual endeavors, some called "theory," do not in fact provide explanations. Such formulations include: perspectives that provide broad paradigms for analyzing or thinking about crime-relevant phenomena; moral philosophies; classification systems for crime-relevant analyses or understanding; descriptions of crime-relevant features of societies, groups, or individuals; and conceptualizations involving development of names and ideas about the parts of social situations or societies that seem to bear on crime. As astute, interesting, and important as many of these efforts are, they do not fulfill the needs of theoretical science and so do not qualify as "theory" within that framework.

*Breadth*    A second desirable trait of good theory is the capacity to explain a variety of specific instances within a given domain of phenomena. Ideally, criminological theories should encompass all forms of crime, no matter what is included within the criminal code of various societies, and provide explanations of all aspects of crime-relevant phenomena. Of course, breadth is a matter of degree and it is likely that no criminological theory will ever achieve total coverage. Nevertheless, with its general theories, theoretical science strives to explain as wide a range of phenomena as possible, and increasing degrees of success along those lines are usually highly regarded.

*Comprehensiveness*    This feature of theory refers to inclusivity of causal processes; that is, the explanatory mechanism or mechanisms must accommodate, in one way or another, all of the operative causes of the phenomena in question. It is unrealistic to imagine that crime-relevant phenomena have one and only one cause, so an adequate theory for scientific purposes must take that complex reality into account.

This can be achieved in several ways. One way is to feature a central causal process that incorporates within itself various causal streams. Another way is to identify and bring into the formulation various contingencies (discussed earlier) for the operation of a main causal process. Still a third way is to integrate various causal processes through a structural arrangement of theoretical elements, showing how each element comes to bear on various other processes and outcomes.

*Precision*   The fourth desirable feature of good scientifically oriented theory is especially difficult to achieve. It refers to three different aspects of theory. The first is specification of when and to what degree the causal forces laid out in the theory operate with greater or less force – in other words, good theories spell out the contingencies under which causal forces unfold with greater or less strength or completeness.

The second aspect of precision relevant to adequate scientifically oriented theory has to do with the form of theorized causal effects. Most criminological theories are interpreted as proposing linear effects only (many suspect this is because our methods of analyzing linear effects are more easily employed and better known than are those concerning other forms of relationships). However, many existing theoretical statements actually imply curvilinear or even more complicated forms of effects among relevant variables. Moreover, it does not take much imagination to expect many crime-relevant phenomena to involve complicated causal effects not yet detailed in theories. So, a strong but frequently ignored feature of adequate scientific theories is to spell out the various forms of likely effects.

Finally, precision calls for specification of casual intervals. An ideal theory according to theoretical science details the amount of time that must transpire before a causal variable produces the theorized outcome. Some effects may be instantaneous; some may be short-term (perhaps a few hours or days); and others may not unfold until years later. For adequate explanation (and appropriate empirical assessment), such differences must be recognized and the correct causal interval specified. Current theoretical formulations in criminology rarely do this, though some general causal lags are sometimes implicit in the argument. For example, theories about the effects of childhood experiences on adolescent or adult crime inherently suggest a causal interval of several years.

*Depth*   A fifth feature of adequate theory in the service of theoretical science is specification of how the concepts of the formulation fit together in sequences of effects and/or interactions. Many of the causes of crime no doubt involve feedback effects, and no cause of crime exists without a history and roots in other features of social life. One goal of adequate theory, then, is specification of complete causal chains that show the prior influences on all variables and how the operative causal variables mesh with each other in causally ordered sequences.

*Parsimony*   An additional feature that some expect of good theory is parsimony. However, it is not always regarded as highly desirable, depending on the definition of parsimony one uses. According to this criterion, theories should be as simple as possible. This is, of course, easy to endorse because unnecessary complexity is burdensome, but there is a catch – the phrase "as possible." Many scholars contend that crime-relevant phenomena are not, in reality, very simple so theories to account for them must necessarily be more complicated. In other words, it is "not possible" to be simpler because simplicity is often bought at the price of accuracy or adequacy. In fact, many dictionary definitions of parsimony describe it as "excessive" simplicity. Overall, most scholars agree that there is no advantage to making theories more complicated or complex than is required for the theoretical job, but at the same time, if theories are to account for inherently complicated phenomena, they must also be complex. The notion of parsimony is usually invoked when comparing two or more theories purportedly explaining the same thing. If all explain equally well, then the more acceptable theory would be the one that does the job in the most straight-forward way, using the fewest variables and qualifications. Again, however, there is a catch – it is unlikely that all contending theories explain specific phenomena equally well. So, the issue of parsimony will rarely emerge as a relevant criterion for adequate theory. But when it does, theorists must be alert to the possibility of sacrificing accuracy in search of simplicity.

*Formalization*   A final feature of good theory according to some is formalization (see Gibbs, 1972, 1994; Hage, 1994). Formalization refers to the way in which the various propositions of a theory are arranged and expressed relative to each other. A fully formalized theory is one in which all of the causal relationships among concepts are arranged tightly into a clear deductive system from which one can derive lower-level causal statements indirectly from higher-level statements. Ideally, these theoretical relationships are expressed mathematically so that the theory appears as a series of equations. The advocates for formalization argue that it should be the goal of scientific theory because anything less leads to massive disagreements among scholars about the implications of various theoretical accounts. Indeed, it is common to find criminologists arguing about whether certain evidence supports or challenges one theory or another, or even about whether specific outcomes are predicted from various theories. However, most criminologists do not think that formalization, especially full formalization through mathematical statement, is desirable or even possible. Most are more comfortable with a discursive mode of reasoning, though deduction through logical sequences of specific causal statements from more general abstract principles to more specific outcomes is favored.

*Summary*   Theoretical science, which seems to be the dominant approach to contemporary criminology, ideally demands much of its theory. However, in actual practice the criminological community is tolerant and forgiving. Though completed theory that explains everything we want explained, does so with breadth and precision, and shows adequate depth, does not currently exist and probably never will, the enterprise of scientifically driven criminology forges ahead, recognizing that science is ongoing. It is the striving for the ideal that inspires and guides our work. The more we learn, the more questions we have. And the more often a general statement is upheld empirically, the more scientists look for limits of applicability. Our knowledge at any given level of theoretical development then depends on theory development and verification, with greater verification generating more confidence and with refinement of internal structure bringing about greater intellectual satisfaction. Rarely, however, do theoretical scientists in the various realms of social inquiry uniformly endorse a given theory. Science is always in process, and theory, which is the end-product of that process, is always incomplete.

At this point in theoretical development of criminology as science, no theory has achieved the ideal, or even come close to achieving it. Yet, there are many contenders that include some of the desirable characteristics of scientific theory, and most theoretical scientists believe that the main causal processes concerning crime-relevant processes have been identified. Thus, for most theoretical scientists, the remaining tasks are to refine the theories we have and to find ways to bring them together to fulfill the features specified above as desirable for science work. It would take a very large book to detail all, or even most, such efforts, but suffice it to say that theory in the scientific tradition in criminology is quite viable.

## Theory Within Other Philosophies of the Enterprise

While theory in theoretical science has a particular meaning and is crucial, representing the ultimate goal of criminological work, theory does not have the same meaning for all criminologists, nor is it necessarily of great import to the work of many. Indeed, for some criminologists, theory, regardless of how it is conceptualized, is irrelevant or of only tangential significance. In the following paragraphs I will briefly describe the essence of the other contemporary camps of criminology, with an emphasis on the meaning and uses of theory. These descriptions are necessarily attenuated and may not fully represent the various approaches in ways acceptable to their practitioners. After all, practitioners within any given camp of criminology are less acquainted with and have less understanding of the intricacies of alternative styles of work than do those more deeply involved in specific modes. While one may acknowledge the viability and legitimacy of various approaches to criminology, balanced understanding of the place of theory for each style of work is challenging.

### Problem-solving criminology

A substantial number of criminologists, perhaps even a majority (though theoretical science seems to be the dominant approach, there are no hard data to establish that judgment), aim their work toward finding solutions to crime or crime-related problems (for examples, see any issue of journal *Criminology and Public Policy*, or Kleiman, 2009). Such problems range all the way from international threats of terrorism to very focused concerns with how best to prevent littering on public streets in particular towns or cities, and may even involve efforts to assess all manner of collateral damage for crime-linked activities. Problem-solving criminology includes *ad hoc* explanatory efforts as well as evaluations of existing programs designed to achieve specific purposes. Some problem-solving criminologists define their efforts as policy-oriented, designed to help public officials formulate approaches to managing crime or crime-related problems. Others think of themselves as providers of information to enable any responsible party (whether parents and school officials, bureaucratic functionaries, or private citizens) to fashion their crime-relevant actions.

Problem-solving (practical) criminologists usually follow scientific mandates in collection, analysis, and interpretation of data. However, they do not necessarily formulate their research issues from theories, nor do they attempt to judge the import of their findings for theories. In fact, some think that theory is irrelevant to their work; sometimes problem-solving scholars do invoke "theory" but turn out to be classifying actions such as identifying potential predictive variables based on prior research as "theory." At times, practical criminologists aim to develop explanations concerning the specific situation or problem they are investigating without concern as to whether that explanation or explanations might generalize to other issues in other circumstances. Moreover, problem-solving criminologists typically approach their work from a focused perspective – concentrating on specific locales or specific instances of the problems in question. Within this *ad hoc* orientation, variables to be measured and studied are those that seem to have particular relevance to the instant situation, with such variables and concepts often being based on the "folk" understandings and statements of local participants.

Theory for problem-solving criminologists, then, may correspond roughly to theory for theoretical scientists or it may be as crude as a "hunch" about some variable, process, or outcome. To problem-solving criminologists, theory, no matter its meaning, may or may not be important, but it is seldom crucial. Many such scholars, having been trained as researchers in the science tradition, are acquainted with general theories, and they do recognize that solutions may depend on understanding of causes. However, they tend to believe that such understanding can be achieved by direct study of the situations exhibiting the problems at issue without reference to larger theoretical accounts or confirmation by a large number of diverse investigations. The theoretical outcomes of problem-solving criminology, therefore, are typically *ad hoc* explanations.

Still, theoretical science and problem-oriented criminology share some commonality. The results of investigations aimed toward problem-solving can sometimes help identify and document regularities that call for explanation. *Ad hoc* explanations derived to account for those regularities can sometimes then be tied to other *ad hoc* explanations and become embedded within more general, abstract theories. In addition, the research of problem-oriented criminologists sometimes provides tests of hypotheses from larger general theories, though such service is usually inadvertent. Nevertheless, given the number of criminologists who try to solve problems and in the process collect data relevant to some general theories, and given the relative dearth of pure theory-driven research, it may be that inadvertent theory testing is actually the main source of data for assessing some general theories.

## Verstehen analysis

This approach to criminology features efforts to "understand" the actions and thoughts of participants. (*Verstehen* is the German word for "to understand"; its use as the name for this process became popularized in sociology and criminology by the writings of Max Weber.) The verstehen researcher usually tries to put himself psychically in the positions of the research subjects in order to see and interpret the world as the subjects see it and interpret it. This emphatic process is often assisted by careful ethnographic research and sometimes it is aided by comparative analyses designed to isolate differences between subjects exhibiting different outcomes or exposures. In recent times there has been a strong emphasis in criminology on exploring the active part that individuals play in their crime-relevant behavior or in escaping from criminal pasts (sometimes called human agency), and the verstehen approach is especially useful in pursuing that theme (see for example: Giordano, Cernkovich, & Rudolph, 2002; Maruna, 2001).

Studies of crime or crime-relevant issues from a verstehen perspective typically have a narrow focus, involving individuals and/or local settings. Moreover, research is normally aimed at producing a "grounded" (rooted in the immediate circumstances in which actors find themselves) interpretation of whatever is being studied. That interpretation, which presumably takes into account numerous causal influences as they are interpreted and acted upon by the subject, is sometimes called theory. Such theory, however, is emergent and as such applies only to the immediate situation. These interpretations, while regarded as theory by those who practice this approach to criminology, bear little resemblance to theory as it is understood by practitioners of theoretical science. Grounded theory makes little effort to identify general causal processes that might operate in other circumstances, for other individuals, or at different points in time and it studiously avoids abstract notions in favor of folk narratives.

Though verstehen criminology is usually narrowly focused on the individual or a few individuals, there is a related, larger analog that attempts to understand or interpret entire social situations. "Case studies," often employing in limited sense the methods of verstehen criminology, allow scholars to appreciate how various social arrangements fit together, the various influences that shape how functionaries and other participants understand their world, and what forces, as interpreted by the participants, seem to be operative in everyday activities. As with problem-solving criminology, the theoretical work of verstehen criminologists, while quite different from the theoretical work of science-oriented criminology, is nevertheless potentially useful for theoretical science. Many times various studies in a verstehen tradition contain common elements not obvious to the researchers concentrating on their particular research foci and often the products of such work exhibit insightful interpretations that actually have larger implications. Therefore, theoretical scientists can and sometimes do "glean" the field, picking up such commonalities and incorporating insightful observations within the more abstract notions contained within general theories. And case studies have always been important in mainstream criminology, having provided crucial material for theoretical scientists in their quest for general theory.

## Descriptive criminology

A fourth style of work in contemporary criminology attempts to describe crime-relevant phenomena, situations, and relationships among variables, or to offer conceptual distinctions with which to classify, think about, or analyze crime-relevant aspects of social life. The objective is to identify the relevant variables empirically, and show how they actually mesh together in various circumstances. Once accurate description has been achieved, many descriptive criminologists are ready to move on to other research issues. In other words, the bulk of descriptive work is atheoretical – neither inspired by nor answerable to theory (see, for example: Farrington, 1997; Loeber, Slot, & Stouthamer-Loeber, 2006).

Though most descriptive criminologists show little interest in interpreting situations or in answering questions of why or how, some do pursue theory in the form of organizational schemes or designation of dimensions by which empirical patterns can be arranged in an orderly or recurrent manner. Some products of conceptual efforts are classification schemes, or taxonomies (see, as examples, Cooney, 2009; Gibbs, 1981). Such intellectual products are sometimes highly insightful and useful. However, they do not qualify as theory within a theoretical science approach because they do not identify or explicate the causes of phenomena. Indeed, for descriptive criminologists, classification schemes are the "explanations," and demonstration that the classification schemes actually accommodate aspects of the empirical world proves that the "theories" are correct.

While the notion of theory employed in theoretical science is foreign to that embraced by most descriptive criminologists, the work of description is nevertheless important to theory-building within a theoretical science model. Description is, after all, the first step in science – identifying empirical regularities in similar circumstances or disparate regularities across sets of circumstances. But, while science-oriented scholars attempt to develop abstract notions or conceive of processes that assimilate those similarities or differences in ways that permit abstract constructs to be integrated into general causal schemes, descriptive scholars are content to paint pictures of reality or to classify parts in such a way as to bring conceptual order to what is being portrayed. Interestingly enough, theoretical scientists can sometimes provide the causal mechanisms to actually explain what descriptive "theorists" claim has already been explained by their showing that the "theoretical" descriptions are accurate. Hence, descriptive work may inadvertently serve as a handmaiden to theoretical science.

## Critical work

A substantial number of criminologists define their work roughly as spelling out social conditions that they believe are responsible for human suffering, injustice, or inequality, which, in turn, are thought by many to be linked with criminal behavior and crime-relevant phenomena (cf. Bonger, 1916 (1969); Daly & Chesney-Lind, 1988; Gove, 1980; Quinney, 1970, 1974). Within this camp, any argument that logically or meaningfully connects a social situation or condition with a negative outcome that is assumed to be associated with crime or crime-relevant outcomes is called "theory." Often the identified culprits are capitalism, mal-distribution of economic resources, patriarchy, racism, or other large structural arrangements. Scholars working in this vein share with theoretical science the goals of showing why and how the particular problem-generators operate. However, critical work differs from theoretical science in several crucial ways.

First, critical theorists usually start with a belief, often a commitment to a particular ideology or interpretation, that some particular social phenomena are inherently destructive or immoral, being responsible for violations of human rights, justice, and ultimately crime-relevant phenomena. The critical scholar, or theorist, therefore deliberately sets out to expose the operations and influence of these societal flaws. Skeptics contend that such *a priori* commitments almost inevitably incline scholars to avoid a search for evidentiary challenges or to ignore contrary evidence. Theoretical scientists, by contrast, supposedly remain open to contrary possibilities. Thus, theories in scientifically oriented criminology are presumably answerable to empirical research, which is undertaken specifically to test or challenge those theories, and scientific theorists are expected to either alter their theories in light of such negative evidence or at least to confront the possibility. Further, critical theorists rely mainly on select historical case studies to illustrate their arguments, exposing themselves to charges of "cherry picking" the evidence. Theories in the theoretical science tradition, by contrast, are presumably open to all evidence, with their validity resting on the relative balance of positive and negative findings.

Thus, critical theory, though often insightful and revealing, and sometimes indistinguishable from scientifically oriented theory, has a different focus than do theories in theoretical science. Some criminologists regard critical theories as no more than ideology, partly because the stated project of many critical theorists is to "save" or rescue their argument from hostile forces. Further, the resistance to empirical accountability except for illustrative case studies generates suspicion. Yet, it is possible to treat at least some critical theory just as scientific theory is treated, though it is often heavily laden with the theorist's moral judgments. In this respect, it is instructive to remember that some theories in theoretical science are also vulnerable to the same kind of suspicion as is critical theory. "Science" theories sometimes seem to reflect their author's ideological biases, sometimes remain popular in the face of nonsupportive evidence, and are invoked as moral imperatives.

## Nihilistic thinking

A relatively small, yet vocal, segment of criminologists embrace the notion that it is impossible to build theories or explanations, and they are highly critical of science as a model for crime studies (cf. Arrigo, 2003; Einstadter & Henry, 1995; Taylor, Walton, & Young, 1973). Such scholars essentially contend that nothing can be known except that nothing can be known. For them, theory is simply the collection of arguments, many of which are based on obvious biases evident in mainstream criminology, purportedly showing that humans are incapable of general understanding of human behavior or social structure and are utterly unable to study social life objectively. So, the idea of theory as a set of explanatory principles setting out the causes of things relevant to crime is far-fetched. To the nihilist, one can only document human attempts to understand each other or situations through narratives, or stories, shared and reacted to by members of local communities.

Nihilistic thinking appears to contradict almost every other type of criminological work. Yet, the purveyors of nihilism in criminology provide an important service. Above all, they force us to confront questions we would ordinarily never consider. The nihilists, to the extent that they are taken seriously, make us pause to demonstrate things we ordinarily take for granted. Moreover, they make us aware of generally unrecognized biases to which all of our activities are subject. But, according to nihilistic thinking, theory as normally understood by other camps of criminological inquiry is a sham.

## Amelioration

A final style of criminology bears much in common with critical work in that it attempts to identify sources of human suffering or injustice, but it goes a step further and offers a prescription for overcoming those forces (cf. Pepinsky & Quinney, 1991). Theory for such criminologists, then, consists of the arguments specifying or asserting particular forces leading to human distress, which are thought to be connected with the probability of criminal behavior or the construction of legal rules artificially constraining various segments of the population, along with the remedies to be followed in overcoming those forces. Such scholars often reject legal notions of crime, redefining it in terms of behaviors or social structures producing suffering or injustice. Such theory differs from that central to theoretical science in that it is not subject to test except through practical application and its aim is action not explanation.

## Summary

Theory takes many forms in contemporary criminology because criminological scholars endorse and follow various philosophies of the enterprise, each involving specific notions about the value of theory and/or the form it should take. The dominant philosophy appears to be that of theoretical science in which theory to *explain* (answer questions of why and how about phenomena within its domain) is the ultimate goal. Desirable theory within that philosophical camp follows a deductive framework, is subject to empirical test, admits the possibility of negative evidence, and reflects demanding characteristics. Problem-solving criminology, probably the second-most popular style of criminology may or may not draw on theory and usually produces at best *ad hoc* causal explanations applying to specific problems or situations. Verstehen analysis aims to permit scholars and consumers of verstehen work to see the world through the eyes of the subjects of investigation, to vicariously experience the things the subjects experience, and to appreciate, from the point of view of the subjects, why they did or do various things linked to crime or crime-related phenomena. Descriptive scholars frequently eschew theory altogether, focusing instead on accurate portrayal of patterns of behavior, though sometimes they produce conceptual schemes that organize recurrent patterns of crime-relevant factors. Critical scholars try to identify the social conditions producing human injustice or suffering, often asserting favorite villains and attempting to persuade audiences of the validity of their arguments rather than testing their ideas. Accounts of how those structures or forces seem to operate is the essence of critical theory. Nihilistic criminologists question the whole project of other styles of work, claiming that nothing can be known, particularly scientifically, except that nothing can be known. To them, "theory" consists of such arguments, often complicated and insightful, along with admonitions to key into folk narratives to appreciate how people interpret their own worlds. Finally, amelioration usually combines critical analysis with prescriptions for remedying structures or situations that produce injustice or destructive criminal behavior.

# References

Arrigo, B. (2003). Postmodern justice and critical criminology: Positional, relational, and provisional science. In M.D. Schwartz & S.E. Hatty (Eds.), *Controversies in Critical Criminology* (pp. 43–55). Cincinnati, OH: Anderson.

Bonger, W. (1916[1969]). *Criminality and Economic Conditions*. Bloomington, IN: Indiana University Press.

Cooney, M. (2009). *Is Killing Wrong?* Charlottesville, VA: University of Virginia Press.

Daly, K., & Chesney-Lind, M. (1988). Feminism and criminology. *Justice Quarterly, 5*, 497–535.

Einstadter, W.J., & Henry, S. (1995). *Criminological Theory: An Analysis of Its Underlying Assumptions*. Fort Worth, TX: Harcourt and Brace.

Farrington, D.P. (1997). Early prediction of violent and non-violent youthful offending. *European Journal on Criminal Policy and Research, 5*, 51–66.

Gibbs, J.P. (1972). *Sociological Theory Construction*. Hinsdale, IL: Dryden.

Gibbs, J.P. (1981). *Norms, Deviance, and Social Control*. New York, NY: Elsevier Scientific.

Gibbs, J.P. (1994). Resistance in sociology to formal theory construction. In J. Hage (Ed.), *Formal Theory in Sociology: Opportunity or Pitfall?* (pp. 90–104). Albany, NY: State University of New York Press.

Giordano, P.C., Cernkovich, S.A., & Rudolph, J.L. (2002). Gender, crime, and desistance: Toward a theory of cognitive transformation. *American Journal of Sociology, 107,* 990–1064.

Gove, W.R. (Ed.) (1980). *The Labeling of Deviance: Evaluating a Perspective,* 2nd edition. Beverly Hills, CA: Sage.

Hage, J. (Ed.) (1994). *Formal Theory in Sociology: Opportunity or Pitfall?* Albany, NY: State University of New York Press.

Hirschi, T. (1979). Separate and unequal is better. *Journal of Research in Crime and Delinquency, 16,* 34–37.

Hirschi, T. (1989). Exploring alternatives to integrated theory. In S.F. Messner, M.D. Krohn, & A.E. Liska (Eds.), *Theoretical Integration in the Study of Deviance and Crime: Problems and Prospects* (pp. 37–49). Albany, NY: State University of New York Press.

Kleiman, M.A.R. (2009). *When Brute Force Fails: How to Have Less Crime and Less Punishment.* Princeton, NJ: Princeton University Press.

Loeber, R., Slot, N.W., & Stouthamer-Loeber, M. (2006). A three-dimensional, cumulative developmental model of serious delinquency. In P.-O.H. Wikström & R.J. Sampson (Eds.), *The Explanation of Crime: Context, Mechanisms, and Development* (pp. 153–194). New York: Cambridge University Press.

Maruna, S. (2001). *Making Good: How Ex-Convicts Reform and Rebuild Their Lives.* Washington, DC: American Psychological Association.

Pepinsky, H., & Quinney, R. (Eds). (1991). *Criminology as Peacemaking.* Bloomington, IN: Indiana University Press.

Quinney, R. (1970). *The Social Reality of Crime.* Boston, MA: Little, Brown.

Quinney, R. (1974). *Critique of the Legal Order: Crime Control in Capitalist Society.* Boston, MA: Little, Brown.

Reynolds, P.D. (1971). *Primer in Theory Construction.* Boston, MA: Allyn & Bacon.

Taylor, I., Walton, P., & Young, J. (1973). *The New Criminology: For a Social Theory of Deviance.* London: Routledge & Kegan Paul.

Tittle, C.R. (1985). The assumption that general theories are not possible. In R.F. Meier (Ed.), *Theoretical Methods in Criminology* (pp. 93–121). Beverly Hills, CA: Sage.

Tittle, C.R. (1989). Prospects for synthetic theory: A consideration of macro-level criminological activity. In S.F. Messner, MD. Krohn, & A.E. Liksa (Eds.), *Theoretical Integration in the Study of Deviance and Crime: Problems and Prospects* (pp. 161–178). Albany, NY: State University of New York Press.

Tittle, C.R. (1995). *Control Balance: Toward a General Theory of Deviance.* Boulder, CO: Westview Press.

Tittle, C.R., & Paternoster, R. (2000). *Social Deviance and Crime: An Organizational and Theoretical Approach.* Los Angeles, CA: Roxbury.

Turner, J.H. (2003). *The Structure of Sociological Theory,* 7th edition. Belmont, CA: Wadsworth/Thomson.

# 2

# Correlates of Crime

## Matt DeLisi and Michael G. Vaughn

## Introduction

All humans engage in some form of antisocial behavior during their life. Ironically, much of this antisocial behavior occurs during the first years of life and is poorly recalled by memory. Early childhood is characterized by instinctual needs for food, hydration, sleep, security, and nurturing and these needs are pursued with a brute self-interest. Infants cry and flail to get what they want, and this behavioral repertoire is largely effective. In other words, humans recognize early in life that aggressive, self-interested acts tend to be successful. As infants become toddlers, however, they are faced with the inevitable truth that the world is greater than their immediate self-interest, and includes others. This necessitates social interaction. Aggressive self-interest is no longer tolerated, nor is it viewed favorably. Fortunately, by approximately age 2 years, as expressed language and receptive language skills proliferate, children are able to communicate in more sophisticated and socially appropriate ways. For most people, the days of crying, flailing, and aggressing are mostly over.

Across childhood and adolescence, the complexities of social development continue toward a central goal of an individual's ability to regulate his or her behavior in the midst of environmental contingencies. In other words, human development necessitates the capacity to control oneself in order to function appropriately and successfully with societal demands. Krueger and his colleagues (1996: 108) captured this sentiment well:

> Society is predicated on the notion that its members can delay gratification in the service of cooperative living. Yet it is for precisely this reasons that all societies are precarious. There are always some persons so driven by the prospect of immediate

*The Handbook of Criminological Theory*, First Edition. Edited by Alex R. Piquero.
© 2016 John Wiley & Sons, Inc. Published 2016 by John Wiley & Sons, Inc.

rewards that they pursue these with little regard for the collective consequences of their actions. What sets these antisocial persons apart from the rest of society? How do they differ from others who manage to wait?

Antisocial behavior still occurs, but it is often episodic, usually involves more trivial forms of noncompliance or rule violations, and is very responsive to reproach, sanction, or punishment. Thus, while some will occasionally shoplift candy from a corner store, or get into a physical fight with a schoolmate during an argument, or drink beer before the legal age-limit, these transgressions are usually a one-off occurrence.

The take-away point is that the opportunities to engage in antisocial behavior – or more directly, to commit crime – are ubiquitous. But one should not conclude that crime occurs evenly across social strata and that everyone is equally likely to become a recurrent criminal offender (see DeLisi & Piquero, 2011; Fox & Piquero, 2003; Jennings & Reingle, 2012; Piquero, Farrrington, & Blumstein, 2003). Moreover, one should not conclude that very little separates criminal offenders from nonoffenders. Epidemiological research is helpful to illustrate this point. In a study of more than 43,000 participants selected from the National Epidemiologic Survey on Alcohol and Related Conditions (NESARC), Vaughn and his colleagues (2011) identified four latent groupings or classes of offenders based on 34 types of externalizing or problem behaviors. About 66% of the sample were characterized as normative and had very low – essentially zero – involvement in various externalizing behaviors. The next largest group, which was nearly 21% of the total sample, contained individuals who displayed high levels of externalizing behaviors but low levels of substance use. A third group that was 8% of the sample was the opposite: they exhibited high levels of substance use but moderate other antisocial behaviors. The smallest group – just 5% of the sample – were severe, and were characterized by across-the-board high levels of externalizing behaviors (Vaughn, DeLisi, Gunter, Fu, *et al.*, 2011).

Compared to the normative individuals, the other three groups were noteworthy not only for their antisocial, externalizing, or criminal behaviors, but also for their psychiatric problems. The drug users, criminal offenders, and severe 5% were significantly likely to have mood disorders, bipolar disorder, dysthymia, panic disorder, social phobia, specific phobia, and psychotic disorders. In short, compared to their essentially noncriminal peers, criminals are behaviorally, emotionally, and psychiatrically impaired. Even greater distinctions are made between those who abstain from even low levels of antisocial behavior during adolescence and everyone else. Based on the same NESARC data, abstainers have been shown to be more well-adjusted, functional, and healthy than those who use alcohol, experiment with drugs, or engage in delinquency (Vaughn, Fu, Wernet, DeLisi, Beaver, *et al.*, 2011). Overall, the focus of this chapter is on *bona fide* offenders, not those whose antisocial conduct (beyond the first years of life) is close to zero.

In the interest of providing the most exhaustive and panoramic statement about the correlates of crime, the discussion depends almost entirely on systematic reviews, large-scale epidemiological studies, meta-analyses, and research overviews.

In addition, the focus is on individual-level correlates of crime and thus does not examine structural or macro characteristics of society, such as cultural and economic factors that are associated with offending at the community or nation level.

## Sex

The fundamental correlate of crime is sex. In an overview and critique of mainstream criminological theories, Harris (1977:14) forcefully captured this idea:

> That the sex variable in some form has not provided the starting point of all theories of criminal deviance has been the major failure of deviance theorizing in this century. In all, it appears to provide the single most powerful predictor of officially and unofficially known criminal deviance in this society and almost certainly in all others.

Studies based on data from North America, South America, Europe, Asia, Africa, and Australia revealed that males display higher levels of problem behaviors than females.

That there are sharp differences between males and females in terms of their liability for and engagement in antisocial behaviors is also seen in various behavioral disorders and other antisocial conditions. For example, the sex ratio (the number of males to females in a sample or population) for antisocial conditions such as conduct disorder, antisocial personality disorder, psychopathy, life-course-persistent offending, career criminality, and other typologies of serious crime show a clear asymmetry where boys are significantly more likely to display impairments compared to girls. There is evidence that for serious, lifelong forms of criminal behavior, for example, the ratio is in the range of 15–20:1 (Eme, 2010), and for extreme psychopathology, such as multiple homicide offending, sexual homicide, and sexual sadism, the incidence is almost entirely perpetrated by males (DeLisi, 2013). Indeed, the paucity of female offenders among the most violent offenders and among the most severe criminal justice sanctions (e.g., capital punishment, civil commitment, and supermax confinement) is so low that it is conventional for researchers to utilize exclusively male samples. In sum, when crime is pathological, it is almost exclusively perpetrated by males.

The significant sex differences in criminal behavior reflect an array of genetic, hormonal, neurological, and psychosocial differences between males and females. The evidence for this is overwhelming. In a review of biological influences on sex differences in serious conduct problems, Eme (2007) suggests that differences in the sex chromosomes create genetic sex differences in various biological mechanisms that manifest in multiple risk factors for conduct problems among males versus females. Specifically, males display greater and more extreme signs of aggression, greater impairments in effortful control and self-regulation, greater impairments in language development and cognitive control of emotional impulses, and greater resistance to behavioral modulation (e.g., punishment) than females.

Sex differences in antisocial behavior and crime not only reflect core biological and physiology variation by gender, but also psychological differences that are found among males and females. This is particularly seen in personality functioning. There is ample evidence that males are more impulsive, more resistant to punishment, have greater sensation-seeking, and are more risk-taking in their behaviors than females. Indeed, Cross, Copping, & Campbell (2011) performed a meta-analysis of 741 effect sizes from 277 studies that examined sex differences in impulsivity. Many features favored females in terms of their personality functioning, and thus buffered them from crime. Girls had better effortful control, were more sensitive and responsive to punishment, were less risk-taking, and had less sensation-seeking. Another meta-analysis of over 150 studies showed that males are much more prone to risk-taking than females, one facet of the enormous gender differences in antisocial behavior (Byrnes, Miller, & Schafer, 1999). In other words, there are sharp differences in the ways that males and females approach the environment, respond to the environment, and behaviorally interface with others in the environment.

Despite the extraordinary evidence of psychosocial differences between males and females, there is still widespread belief that sex differences in criminal offending are primarily the product of differential socialization practices. From this sociological perspective, sex differences are actually gender differences whereby boys are socialized according to a culturally and gender-specific template and girls are socialized according to a culturally and gender-specific template. For example, boys are encouraged to be aggressive and competitive in the context of rough-and-tumble play and sports, and sometimes these behaviors spill over to society in the form of aggressive criminal behavior. Meta-analytic research indicates however that the notion of differential gender socialization as an explanation of sex differences in behavior is mostly a myth. In a landmark review of 172 studies, Lytton and Romney (1991) found that most parenting practices did not vary by gender of their children. For example, among studies conducted on participants selected from North America, 18 of 19 socialization effects were not significant. Overall, they advised that there was scant evidence that differential socialization by gender produces differences in diverse behaviors and abilities.

There are forms of antisocial behavior where data indicate that females are more involved than males or comparably involved (see Archer, 2000). Girls tend to engage in more relational aggression that uses gossip and social ostracism to isolate and aggress against victims. In terms of arrest data and in many correctional samples, female arrests are disproportionately for theft, forgery/fraud, prostitution, and drug crimes. Compared to their male delinquent peers, female offenders also tend to have significantly worse victimization histories, including sexual abuse victimization and comorbid psychiatric problems (Archer, 2004; Collins, 2010; Eagly & Steffen, 1986). Taken as a whole; however, these are mere exceptions to the rule that male sex or gender is a primary correlate of antisocial conditions and crime.

# Age

Another central correlate of crime, one that denotes important social, biological, and psychological development is age. Generally, age is inversely related to criminal behaviors, which means that younger people, especially adolescents and young adults, are disproportionately involved in crime as offenders and victims compared to older adults. In terms of aggression and antisocial behavior, it is important to note that there are two age–crime curves to consider. The first occurs in the first years of life. During infancy and toddlerhood, a cascade of developmental processes occur where children develop increased communication skills and self-regulation skills that result in a sharp decrease in aggressive acts, such as hitting parents, hitting siblings, biting, screaming, and crying. It is during this period that the near-universal use of aggression nearly disappears with the onset of expressed language.

A second curve emerges – commonly known as the age–crime curve – where involvement in antisocial behavior emergences during middle to late adolescence, explodes into the first years of adulthood, and then dramatically declines thereafter. The crime-prone years spanning ages 15–20 or so are recurrently seen across data sources and historical eras. The inverse age effect on crime is so robust that it figures prominently in epidemiological conceptual models of antisocial behavior. The most influential approach is Moffitt's developmental taxonomy (1993) that articulates three behavioral prototypes: a large group whose antisocial conduct traces the age–crime curve (adolescence-limited offenders), a small pathological group who display severe and lifelong behavioral problems (life-course-persistent offenders), and a small, healthy/functional group that does not experiment with delinquency (abstainers). Essential to the trajectory of antisocial behavior is the age of the individual.

An assortment of meta-analyses provides support for the strong inverse relationship between age and diverse manifestations of crime. What is important to consider is the consistent effect of age across samples and variations in offender groups. In a meta-analysis of 35 predictors of general recidivism and 27 predictors of violence recidivism among 64 samples of mentally disordered offenders, Bonta, Law, & Hanson (1998) reported that young age was importantly related to both forms of criminal conduct. A meta-analysis of 61 studies of sex offenders including more than 23,000 participants, Hanson & Bussière (1998) found that young age was significantly predictive of sexual recidivism, nonsexual violent recidivism, and general recidivism. Similarly, Cottle, Lee, & Heilbrun's (2001) meta-analysis of 23 studies using 30 predictors of delinquency among more than 15,000 juveniles found that the two strongest predictors of recidivism – age at first police contact and age at first commitment – related to the inverse age effect. A common refrain across these meta-analyses is that youthfulness is a potent risk factor for antisocial behavior.

It is important to recognize that age is a multifactorial risk factor that denotes social risk factors, such as the intense association with peers that typify adolescence, biological risk factors, such as physical and hormonal development, and psychological changes, such as personality development. As a result, the brute age effect on crime can also be interpreted as reflecting some other biological, physiological, or psychological development. For example, Blonigen (2010) has noted the codevelopment of personality and antisocial conduct across adolescence and into adulthood. During this period of the life-course, there are significant declines in novelty-seeking or sensation-seeking that correspond to maturity in decision-making generally. In other words, impulsive adolescents mature into more prudent, responsible adults. Thus the age–crime curve can be superimposed on the ascendancy of constraint and the decline of rash teenage behavior. Irrespective of how one views age, as a direct measure or a proxy of some other form of development, it is a core correlate of crime.

## Race

In terms of criminal offending, criminal victimization, and criminal justice system involvement, there are significant and often large differences by racial status. The preponderance of the criminological literature has focused on whites and blacks, due mostly to data availability, and the bulk of research studies have shown that blacks are overrepresented in crime data and offend at a rate several times that of whites. Using nationally representative US data from the Uniform Crime Reports and National Crime Panel, Hindelang (1978) found large race differences for rape, robbery, aggravated assault, and simple assault. Whereas both data sources indicated that whites were involved in crime at levels far beneath their proportion of the population, the opposite was true for blacks. For these crimes, blacks were overrepresented among violent crimes by a factor of between two and six. In a subsequent study using national data from the National Crime Survey (a forerunner of the National Crime Victimization Survey), Hindelang (1981) revealed large demographic differences by race, sex, and age, with crime prevalence significantly higher among blacks, males, and youth. Young black males, for instance, displayed an incidence of offending that was more than 300 times higher than the incidence of offending among white, female adults.

More recent analyses of national data sources including the Uniform Crime Reports, National Crime Victimization Survey, and prisoner data continue to show dramatic racial and ethnic differences in criminal violence, with blacks committing the highest levels, Hispanics committing medium levels, and whites committing the lowest levels among these three groups. In addition, the black disproportionate involvement in murder, rape, robbery, assault, and other violence has remained high over the past three decades (Steffensmeier, Feldmeyer, Harris & Ulmer, 2011). It should be noted that crime among Hispanics reveals a multifaceted and sometimes conflicting picture (cf., Rennison, 2010; Salas-Wright, Olate, & Vaughn, 2013; Salas-Wright & Vaughn, 2014). In terms of gang delinquency and associated violence, Hispanics have generally high criminal involvement and commensurate victimization. However, new immigrants to the United States, who are disproportionately Hispanic, have lower involvement in crime than would be expected based on their socioeconomic circumstances (Vaughn, Salas-Wright, DeLisi, & Maynard, 2013). In addition, the measurement of Hispanic crime is not consistent across jurisdictions. In many places, Hispanics are classified as white, and some Hispanic groups, such as persons from the Dominican Republic, are classified as black. These measurement discrepancies cloud the understanding of Hispanic involvement in offending vis-à-vis the extant data for whites and blacks.

Race differences are the most extreme for the most extreme forms of crime, especially homicide. For example, based on national data from the National Center for Health Statistics, O'Flaherty & Sethi (2010) found that the homicide offending and victimization ratios (black to white) have ranged from 6.6:12.4 for men and 3.3:7.9 for women since 1950. Fox & Zawitz (2006) studied homicide offending and homicide victimization among white and black males aged 14–24 as a proportion of the total United States population, homicide victim population, and homicide offender population spanning 1976 to 2004. During this time period, young white males constituted about 10% of the total population in 1976 to about 6% in 2004. Across the time period, young white males comprised about 10% of homicide victims and this rate was consistent. Young white males comprised about 18% of homicide offenders and this rate fluctuated between approximately 16 and 20%. For African American males ages 14–24 the proportions are quite different. While young African American males comprised about 1% of the total population, they accounted for significant numbers of homicide victims and offenders. For victims, the rate hovered at 10% before escalating in 1985 to a peak of nearly 20% in 1995 and leveling off to about 15% in 2004. For offenders, a similar slope is observed, albeit with about twice the magnitude. Young African American males ages 14–24 accounted for about 20% of homicide offenders – 20 times their proportion of the population – from 1976 to 1985. This rate peaked in about 1993 at nearly 35% – 35 times their proportion in the population – and leveled off to about 28% in 2004.

The association between race and crime is an exceedingly sensitive and controversial area in criminology in the United States, but it does not need to be. The offending and victimization that demonstrate racial differences in crime converge, which means that these data sources are presenting the same information and telling the same empirical story. Given the large race differences in crime, the large race differences in arrest, judicial, and correctional data make sense because the criminal justice system responds empirically to the processing of known criminal offenders. In this way, these first three correlates – sex, age, and race are the "big three" in terms of understanding crime and criminal justice processing. They also are helpful for developing theory, as Hindelang indicated decades ago: "If sociological theorists of crime and delinquency were to use the 'clues' provided by known correlates of criminal behavior – in this instance, sex, race, and age group – as a basis for generating and modifying theory, theory and research might be able to advance more steadily" (Hindelang, 1981:473). The remaining correlates depart from demographic characteristics and constitute individual-level constructs that are importantly related to behavior.

## Temperament

Temperament is the stable, heritable, usual ways that an individual regulates his or her emotions and behavior and interacts with environmental stimuli, including other people. In many respects, temperament is the physiological foundation upon which personality emerges. Temperament has been studied since antiquity and was a major area of study by Hippocrates and Galen. In this Greco-Roman model, there are four archetypal temperaments found in the population. The melancholic person is one who is described as moody and anxious, with a predominance of black bile. The sanguine person is one who is described as cheerful, spirited, and good-natured, with a predominance of blood. The choleric person is one who is described as angry and irritable, with a predominance of yellow bile. The phlegmatic person is one who is described as slow to arousal, with predominance of phlegm (see Kagan, 1998, 2010).

Of these types, two clearly correspond to the temperament profile of antisocial individuals. The melancholic person, for example, presents as introverted and unstable in mood or emotion. Melancholic individuals are characterized as quiet, unsociable, reserved, pessimistic, sober, rigid, anxious, and moody. It is believed that such a temperament is consistent with symptoms of internalizing conditions and is prone to alcohol and drug abuse. The choleric temperament is the one that most clearly embodies a temperament that appears prone to antisocial behavior. Choleric individuals are extraverted and highly neurotic, and are characterized as touchy, restless, aggressive, excitable, changeable, impulsive, optimistic, and active. Some of these traits – particularly aggressiveness, impulsivity, and activity level – are associated with behavioral disorders and criminal behaviors.

Temperamental facets are relatively stable and enduring and thus show continuity from childhood through adulthood. For example, De Pauw & Mervielde (2010) merged childhood temperament models with the five-factor model of personality in attempt to explain internalizing and externalizing disorders. Persons with anxiety disorders would have high scores on neuroticism, characterized by high levels of fear and anxiety. They would have low scores on extraversion, evidenced by high levels of social inhibition and low scores on conscientiousness based on low levels of attentional control. For externalizing disorders, similar translations can be made. For example, attention deficit hyperactivity disorder (ADHD) is characterized by high extraversion based on hyperactivity levels and low conscientiousness based on reduced attentional control and reduced inhibitory control. Antisocial conduct characterized by reactive aggression would be captured by high extraversion (e.g., high activity level), low conscientiousness (e.g., low inhibitory control), and low agreeableness (e.g., high anger and high antagonism). This represents the general temperamental risk profile for antisocial youth. Antisocial conduct characterized by proactive aggression would be captured by very low neuroticism (e.g., reduced fear) and very low agreeableness (e.g., very low empathy). This represents the general temperamental risk profile for psychopathic youth.

In addition to the clinical disorders, temperamental features are broadly related to psychopathology generally. Research based on data from over 8,000 participants selected from the 2000 British Psychiatric Morbidity Survey produced several key findings that suggest the importance of temperament (Markon, 2010). First, internalizing disorders characterized by anxiety, fear, depression, and emotional lability (e.g., moodiness) can broadly be understood as negative emotionality. Second, externalizing disorders including antisocial behaviors, drug problems, and alcohol abuse are closely connected with feelings of anger, hostility, and attention-seeking. These traits encompass both negative emotionality and difficulty with reactivity to others and self-regulation (which is discussed later in the chapter). Third, pathological introversion included factors such as social anxiety, unassertiveness, and dependence, which is somewhat of a blend of a phlegmatic and melancholic temperament. An important point to consider with the latter temperamental features is these emotional states often serve to motivate substance use which can culminate in substance dependence. Meta-analytic research has indicated that substance users are three to four times more likely to commit crime than nonusers (Bennett, Holloway & Farrington, 2008).

Finally, temperament represents the biological basis of personality and denotes important physiological characteristics that differentiate the ways that individuals respond to the environment. One-half of the peripheral nervous system, the autonomic nervous system, controls smooth muscle, glands, the heart, and other organs. It contains two subsystems. The sympathetic nervous system activates the body to cope with emotional and physical stressors, and is commonly known as the "fight or flight" system. The parasympathetic nervous system acts as a brake, slowing organ activity, and is commonly known as the "rest and digest" system. Heart rate is affected by both the sympathetic and parasympathetic nervous systems. Other autonomic indicators, such as electrodermal activity (EDA), are controlled by the sympathetic nervous system. Electrodermal activity is the electrical changes at the surface of the skin that are a response to emotional arousal, physical exertion arousal, and cognitive arousal. All of these stimuli increase skin conductance or sweating.

The evidence is considerable that an underaroused or hypoactive autonomic nervous system is associated with aggression, crime, and related constructs. Meta-analyses indicated that resting heart rate was a robust predictor of antisocial behavior, with effect sizes in the moderate to large range (Raine, 1996; Ortiz & Raine, 2004). Lorber (2004) meta-analyzed 95 studies published between 1957 and 2001 and found that resting heart rate, task heart rate, heart-rate reactivity, resting EDA, task EDA, and EDA reactivity were associated with aggression, psychopathy, and conduct problems among children, adolescents, and adults. These data are helpful toward understanding the physiological foundation upon which temperament and later personality are built.

## Personality

Personality is the relatively consistent and stable ways that a person behaves, thinks, and feels. Personality has been a major area of research in the psychological study of behavioral problems and social functioning. It also has a long history in criminology, and has been a particular research focus in the last two decades. A major reason why is that personality functioning is an important correlate of antisocial behavior, one with profound social implications. Criminological epidemiologists recently examined the social welfare burden of personality disorders in the United States, drawing on data from the National Epidemiologic Survey on Alcohol and Related Conditions, a nationally representative sample of more than 43,000 adults (Vaughn, Fu, Beaver, DeLisi, Perron, & Howard, 2010). They found that diagnoses for any personality disorder significantly predicted receipt of Medicaid, Supplementary Security Income, and Food Stamps. Moreover, persons who were diagnosed with Antisocial Personality Disorder – the personality disorder that most directly corresponds to a criminal personality – were significantly likely to receive Medicaid, Food Stamps, and Women Infant and Children (WIC) assistance.

Some of the most compelling evidence for the personality–crime link stems from birth cohort research in New Zealand. Caspi and his colleagues (Caspi, Elder & Bem, 1987; Caspi, 2000; Caspi & Silva, 1995) identified an undercontrolled type of child – 10% of the sample –impulsive, restless, negativistic or disagreeable, and emotionally labile at age 3 years. Between ages 5 and 11, the undercontrolled children were consistently and significantly rated by parents and teachers to have externalizing problems. By ages 13 to 15, the undercontrolled at age 3 group continued to be noteworthy for their externalizing behaviors in addition to internalizing problems. By 18, undercontrolled children had low constraint, were admittedly reckless and careless, enjoyed dangerous and exciting activities, scored high on negative emotionality, were aggressive, and felt alienated and mistreated by others. At 21, formerly undercontrolled children reported employment difficulties and conflicts with family and romantic partners. They were described as conflict-prone, unreliable, and untrustworthy. They had problems with alcohol and often had extensive criminal records.

Several meta-analyses have illuminated the importance of personality as a correlate of crime, and specified the particular personality features that are most commonly seen among offenders. For instance, Miller & Lynam (2001) examined four structural models of personality (the five-factor model, Eysenck's PEN model, Tellegen's three-factor model, and Cloninger's temperament model) among 59 studies and found the strongest evidence linking low agreeableness and low conscientiousness to crime. In their meta-analysis, Samuel & Widiger (2008) investigated the five-factor model and its facets among the personality disorders using data from 16 samples. Although there were many significant effects among the personality disorders, the most pertinent were for antisocial personality disorder. It is characterized most strongly by low levels of agreeableness and low levels of conscientiousness.

Jones, Miller, & Lynam (2011) reviewed 53 studies to explore the association between the five-factor model and outcome measures for antisocial behavior and aggression. Overall, effect sizes for three of the five factors were significantly associated with antisocial behavior. There was a positive link between neuroticism and antisocial behavior, indicating that people who experience greater levels of negative emotionality, such as anger and hostility, are likely to commit crime. Larger effect sizes were found for agreeableness and conscientiousness, with more antagonistic and less conscientious domains associated with antisocial behavior. All five factors were significantly associated with aggression. The direction for neuroticism, agreeableness, and conscientiousness was the same for aggression. In addition, extraversion and openness to experience were negatively correlated with aggression. In sum, meta-analyses make clear that personality features are significantly related to crime, aggression, and delinquency.

In a meta-analytic review of 194 studies on conscientiousness and health-related behaviors, Bogg & Roberts (2004) reported strong evidence that conscientiousness is associated with behaviors implicated by self-control. Specifically, more conscientious individuals were less likely to drink alcohol to excess, were less likely to use drugs, were less likely to have unhealthy eating habits, were less likely to engage in risky driving, were less likely to engage in risky sexual behaviors, were less likely to be suicidal, were less likely to use tobacco, and were less likely to commit violence crime. Ruiz, Pincus, & Schinka (2008) meta-analyzed 63 samples of 15,331 participants and reported significant associations between conscientiousness and all of its facets to antisocial pathology, substance abuse pathology, and the comorbidity of antisocial and substance pathology.

## Self-Control/Self-Regulation

A construct that relates to temperament and personality, and is an indispensible correlate of crime, is self-control, or as it is known more generally in the social and behavioral sciences, self-regulation (the terms are used interchangeably here). Self-control refers to the broad ability to modify one's emotions and behaviors in the face of social demands. It is an umbrella term that spans additional constructs relating to neurocognition and social behavior. Perhaps the most famous criminological theory of self-control is Gottfredson & Hirschi's (1990) self-control theory. In *A General Theory of Crime*, Gottfredson and Hirschi advanced that self-control was the quintessential individual-level predictor of crime and analogous behaviors that relate to maladaption and reduced social functioning. In their theory, low self-control was characterized by self-centeredness/narcissism, impulsivity, temper/reactive aggression, short gratification delay, action as opposed to verbal/cognitive orientation, and preference for easy, quick returns as opposed to long-term investments. As can be seen, self-control displays convergent validity with temperamental and personality constructs that were examined earlier.

Across the social sciences, self-control has emerged as a potent correlate of crime. For example, drawing on birth cohort data from the Dunedin Multidisciplinary Health and Development Study, Caspi and his associates (1996) conducted a longitudinal–epidemiological study where 3-year-old children were classified into groups based on their behavioral disposition or self-regulation and reassessed at age 21. Those who were described as undercontrolled or impulsive at age 3 were about three times more likely than non-impulsive children to be diagnosed with antisocial personality disorder at age 21. Moreover, they were more than two times as likely to be repeat offenders and nearly five times more likely to be convicted of a violent crime. Compared to a control group, formerly impulsive children were also more likely to attempt suicide and have alcohol problems. In this sense, serious adult psychopathology was the outcome of readily observable self-regulation problems at age 3.

Also using the Dunedin data, Moffitt and her colleagues (2011) recently evaluated the predictive validity of childhood self-control on a range of life outcomes during adulthood. The findings were startling. Persons who displayed low self-control during childhood reported a range of difficulties at age 32. These included worse physical health, greater depression, higher likelihood of drug dependence, lower socioeconomic status, lower income, greater likelihood of single-parenthood, worse financial planning, more financial struggles, and most importantly for a criminological audience, more criminal convictions. Indeed, 45% of participants with low self-control during childhood had criminal convictions at age 32, a level that is nearly fourfold higher than the prevalence of criminal convictions for persons who had high childhood self-control. In fact, self-control was as important a predictor of life outcomes as intelligence and social class.

In a meta-analysis of the first decade of tests of Gottfredson and Hirschi's self-control theory, Pratt & Cullen (2000) reviewed 21 studies that included 17 independent data sets. They examined the effect-size estimates of 126 self-control measures to crime-related dependent variables and found a consistent effect size that exceeded 0.20. A more recent and expansive meta-analysis of 102 studies found significant associations between various measures of self-control and a wide range of outcome behaviors (de Ridder, Lensvelt-Mulders, Finkenauer, Stok, & Baumeister, 2012). The overall message was that when self-control was high, it corresponded to functional, adaptive, pro-social behaviors, and when self-control was low, it corresponded to dysfunctional, maladaptive, antisocial behaviors.

An allied construct to self-control is religiousness. Religiousness is the belief and involvement in a religion that specifies a particular god and attitudinal and behavioral precepts that are consistent with the god's teachings. Religiousness is a continuously measured construct, and theory and research indicate that individuals with greater religiousness display lower involvement in crime. There are several explanations for this effect. In their systematic review, McCullough & Willoughby (2009) identified six propositions that show protective mechanisms by which religiousness enhances self-regulation/control. These include (1) religion promotes self-control; (2) religion influences self-regulation by influencing people's goals; (3) religion influences self-regulation by promoting self-monitoring; (4) religion influences self-regulation by building self-regulatory strength; (5) religion influences self-regulation by prescribing and promoting mastery with specific outputs for self-change (which in a criminological context could mean desisting crime substance use, changing antisocial thinking styles, etc.); and (6) religion affects health, wellbeing, and social behavior through its emphasis on self-regulation.

Empirically, an individual's religiousness is positively associated with self-control and negatively associated with crime. In addition, self-control is inversely related to crime. Thus, to the extent that an individual is characterized by high religiousness and high self-regulation, there is a double insulation effect against antisocial conduct. In their meta-analysis of 60 studies, Baier & Wright (2001) found that religiousness exerted a moderate, significant deterrent effect against crime.

It is also important to recognize that most theories of self-control explicitly implicate neurocognitive factors, or more accurately, neurocognitive deficits that are part and parcel of the deficits in self-control. Indeed, Moffitt's influential developmental taxonomy makes this connection clearly. In other words, a main reason why some individuals have difficulty suppressing their behavioral impulses and regulating their emotion relates to neurocognition. Meta-analytic research has demonstrated the importance of neurocognition. Morgan & Lilienfeld (2000) conducted a meta-analysis of 39 studies that encompassed 4,589 participants and found that antisocial groups performed 0.62 standard deviation units worse on executive functioning tests than their control groups. This is a medium to large effect size. Participants included those with antisocial personality disorder, conduct disorder, psychopathy, delinquent status, or offender status. The effect sizes were largest for groups whose criminal behavior had attracted the attention of the criminal justice system and resulted in a correctional or judicial status. Ogilvie, Stewart, Chan, and Shum (2011) conducted a significantly larger meta-analysis of studies that explored the linkages between neuropsychological deficits, executive functioning, and antisocial behavior. Ogilvie and his colleagues examined 126 studies that involved 14,784 participants. They reported a grand mean effect size of $d = 0.44$ – which is medium in size – indicating that antisocial individuals have greater neuropsychological deficits than their conventional peers. Additionally, largest effects were found when comparing criminality and externalizing behavior disorders. Overall, they concluded that the relationship between executive dysfunction or neuropsychological deficits is robust.

## Family/Parenting Factors

One of the most widely-studied, and to the general public, most obvious, correlates and potential causes of antisocial behavior centers on early-life family characteristics. Family effects figure prominently in many of the leading theoretical explanations of crime. In the social learning tradition, parents and older siblings who engage in antisocial conduct serve as models of deviant behavior for younger children. In families where crime is openly committed, there are numerous opportunities to learn antisocial behavior, such as drug use and interpersonal violence, and numerous reinforcements of that behavior. In the social control tradition, children who are poorly bonded to their parents, which in turn often coincides with weaker bonding to school responsibilities, have greater opportunities to run afoul of the law. Since their attachment, commitment, involvement, and belief in conventional forms of behavior is lacking, they are susceptible to engage in alternative modes of conduct, such as delinquency. In the self-control tradition, parents who inadequately socialize their children and fail to inculcate a sense of self-control produce children who do not understand or appreciate long-term consequences of behavior, and instead prefer easy gratification of impulsive desires (DeLisi, 2013).

Another reason that family and parent effects on crime are strong is genetics. Children receive half their genes from their father, half from their mother, and also inherit family environments in the home. Consider the main findings from a recent study using participants from over 1,000 families consisting of 11-year-old twins and their parents. It was discovered that parent–child resemblance in terms of criminal behavior was accounted for by a general susceptibility to externalizing disorders, and this general susceptibility was mostly genetic in origin. For example, 73% of the variance in oppositional defiant disorder was heritable, that is attributable to genetic factors, with 24% attributable to nonshared environmental factors unique to the child, and just 4% attributable to shared environmental factors within the family. Similar effects were found for ADHD: 73% of the variance was attributable to genetic factors, 27% was attributable to nonshared environmental factors, and interestingly, zero variance was attributable to family factors. For conduct disorder, the most severe of these three conditions, 51% was genetic, 30% was shared environmental, and 19% was attributable to nonshared environmental factors (Bornovalova, Hicks, Iacono, & McGue, 2010). In short, genes and family environments contribute significantly to antisocial conditions.

Myriad parenting factors occur during the early life-course that increase the likelihood of antisocial conduct. In their widely-cited systematic review, Loeber & Stouthamer-Loeber (1986) conducted an early meta-analysis of the parenting/family factors associated with conduct problems and delinquency in youth. The three most important factors in their review were parental supervision, which was negatively associated with behavioral problems, parental rejection, which was positively associated with delinquency, and parent–child involvement, which was negatively associated with conduct problems. In addition, Loeber & Stouthamer-Loeber found that parental marital relations were also moderately predictive of crime. The latter finding is consistent with meta-analytic research on the behavioral outcomes of children of divorce. Aside from poor father–child relations, child-conduct or behavioral problems are the largest empirical consequence of divorce (Amato & Keith, 1991).

Hoeve and colleagues (2009) conducted a meta-analysis of 161 studies of the linkages between parenting and delinquency. Their study examined an array of parenting categories. Parental support includes affection toward children, involvement in their activities, open communication with them, and negative features such as neglect, rejection, hostility, and negative support. Authoritative control includes rewarding and inductive techniques where parenting lessons are "taught" as they occur in the natural home environment. Authoritarian control includes the use of physical punishment, punishment, and verbal aggression. Behavioral control includes the use of discipline, whether the discipline is consistently or inconsistently applied, rules setting, decision making, permissiveness, and monitoring.

Psychological control includes overprotection and other forms of psychological coercion, such as guilt trips. Many of these parenting features were predictive of delinquency in children.

What is the parenting background of an antisocial individual? Criminal offenders are raised by parents (usually just one parent is present) who express low affection, display little involvement, and are generally unsupportive. Their parents are disproportionately neglectful, rejecting, hostile, and use psychological, verbal, and physical aggression against them. Behaviorally, offenders are generally raised in homes with few rules, little or inconsistent discipline, and low monitoring. Antisocial youth also tend to be reared in neighborhoods that are severely disadvantaged, with neighbors who are socioeconomically very similar to them. Disadvantaged neighborhoods are characterized by high levels of poverty, low levels of home ownership or vehicle ownership, frequent residential turnover, meager and few business and cultural amenities, high levels of physical disorder and environmental decay (e.g., graffiti, dilapidated and burnt buildings, abandoned vehicles and appliances, trash and litter), and high levels of social disorder (e.g., open and flagrant drug sales and drug use, prostitution, unemployed persons loitering for much of the day and night, etc.).

Meta-analytic studies have shown that "bad" neighborhoods and the pervasive material and behavioral poverty that plagues them are significantly associated with crime (Hsieh & Pugh, 1993; Pratt & Cullen, 2005). For example, Hsieh & Pugh (1993) reviewed 34 studies that produced 76 estimates of the effects of poverty and income inequality on violent crime and found that all but two studies, or 97% of study findings, significantly linked these socioeconomic conditions to violence. Bad neighborhoods also tend to have low collective efficacy, which is the degree of togetherness, informal social controls, and social networks that allow residents to overcome crime and other local problems (see Sampson, Raudenbush, & Earls, 1997).

From these core crime correlates, many others emerge. The temperamental, personality, and self-regulation deficits set into motion contexts where individuals are generally rejected by conventional peers and accepted by antisocial ones. Over time, their antisocial development takes precedence over their pro-social development, and along the way the entire pantheon of criminological theories becomes relevant (social learning, social disorganization, general strain, labeling, deterrence, and others) as the contextual framework in which to explain and understand crime. But it all stems from these basic correlates.

# References

Amato, P.R., & Keith, B. (1991). Parental divorce and the well-being of children: A meta-analysis. *Psychological Bulletin, 110*(1), 26–46.

Archer, J. (2000). Sex differences in aggression between heterosexual partners: A meta-analytic review. *Psychological Bulletin, 126*(5), 651–680.

Archer, J. (2004). Sex differences in aggression in real-world settings: A meta-analytic review. *Review of General Psychology, 8*(4), 291–322.

Baier, C.J., & Wright, B.R. (2001). "If you love me, keep my commandments." A meta-analysis of the effect of religion on crime. *Journal of Research in Crime and Delinquency, 38*(1), 3–21.

Bennett, T., Holloway, K., & Farrington, D. (2008). The statistical association between drug misuse and crime: A meta-analysis. *Aggression and Violent Behavior, 13*(2), 107–118.

Blonigen, D.M. (2010). Explaining the relationship between age and crime: Contributions from the developmental literature on personality. *Clinical Psychology Review, 30*(1), 89–100.

Bogg, T., & Roberts, B.W. (2004). Conscientiousness and health-related behaviors: A meta-analysis of the leading behavioral contributors to morality. *Psychological Bulletin, 130*, 887–919.

Bonta, J., Law, M., & Hanson, K. (1998). The prediction of criminal and violent recidivism among mentally disordered offenders: A meta-analysis. *Psychological Bulletin, 123*(2), 123–142.

Bornovalova, M.A., Hicks, B.M., Iacono, W.G., & McGue, M. (2010). Familial transmission and heritability of childhood disruptive disorders. *American Journal of Psychiatry, 167*, 1066–1074.

Byrnes, J.P., Miller, D.C., & Schafer, W.D. (1999). Gender differences in risk taking: A meta-analysis. *Psychological Bulletin, 125*, 367–383.

Caspi, A. (2000). The child is father of the man: Personality continuities from childhood to adulthood. *Journal of Personality and Social Psychology, 78*, 158–172.

Caspi, A., Elder, G.H., & Bem, D.J. (1987). Moving against the world: Life-course patterns of explosive children. *Developmental Psychology, 23*, 308–313.

Caspi, A., Moffitt, T.E., Newman, D.L., & Silva, P.A. (1996). Behavioral observations at age 3 years predict adult psychiatric disorders: Longitudinal evidence from a birth cohort. *Archives of General Psychiatry, 53*, 1033–1039.

Caspi, A., & Silva, P.A. (1995). Temperamental qualities at age 3 predict personality traits in young adulthood: Longitudinal evidence from a birth cohort. *Child Development, 66*, 486–498.

Collins, R.E. (2010). The effect of gender on violent and nonviolent recidivism: A meta-analysis. *Journal of Criminal Justice, 38*(4), 675–684.

Cottle, C.C., Lee, R.J., & Heilbrun, K. (2001). The prediction of criminal recidivism in juveniles: A meta-analysis. *Criminal Justice and Behavior, 28*(3), 367–394.

Cross, C.P., Copping, L.T., & Campbell, A. (2011). Sex differences in impulsivity: A meta-analysis. *Psychological Bulletin, 137*(1), 97–130.

DeLisi, M. (2013). *Criminal psychology*. San Diego, CA: Bridgepoint Education.

DeLisi, M., & Piquero, A.R. (2011). New frontiers in criminal careers research, 2000–2011: A state-of-the-art review. *Journal of Criminal Justice, 39*(4), 289–301.

De Pauw, S.S.W., & Mervielde, I. (2010). Temperament, personality and developmental psychopathology: A review based on the conceptual dimensions underlying childhood traits. *Child Psychiatry and Human Development, 41*, 313–329.

de Ridder, D.T.D., Lensvelt-Mulders, G., Finkenauer, C., Stok, M., & Baumeister, R.F. (2012). Taking stock of self-control: A meta-analysis of how trait self-control relates to a wide range of behaviors. *Personality and Social Psychology Review, 16*(1), 76–99.

Eagly, A.H., & Steffen, V.J. (1986). Gender and aggressive behavior: A meta-analytic review of the social psychological literature. *Psychological Bulletin, 100*(3), 309–330.

Eme, R.F. (2007). Sex differences in child-onset, life-course-persistent conduct disorder: A review of biological influences. *Clinical Psychology Review, 27*(3), 607–627.

Eme, R.F. (2010). Male life-course-persistent antisocial behavior. *Archives of Pediatrics and Adolescent Medicine, 164*(5), 486–487.

Fox, J.A., & Piquero, A.R. (2003). Deadly demographics: Population characteristics and forecasting homicide trends. *Crime & Delinquency, 49*(3), 339–359.

Fox, J.A., & Zawitz, M.W. (2006). *Homicide trends in the United States.* Washington, DC: U.S. Department of Justice, Office of Justice Programs, Bureau of Justice Statistics.

Gottfredson, M.R., & Hirschi, T. (1990). *A General Theory of Crime.* Stanford, CA: Stanford University Press.

Hanson, R.K., & Bussière, M.T. (1998). Predicting relapse: A meta-analysis of sexual offender recidivism studies. *Journal of Consulting and Clinical Psychology, 66*(2), 348–362.

Harris, A.R. (1977). Sex and theories of deviance. *American Sociological Review, 42,* 3–16.

Hindelang, M.J. (1978). Race and involvement in common law personal crimes. *American Sociological Review, 43*(1), 93–109.

Hindelang, M.J. (1981). Variations in sex–race–age-specific incidence rates of offending. *American Sociological Review, 46*(4), 461–474.

Hoeve, M., Dubas, J.S., Eichelsheim, V.I., Van Der Laan, P.H., Smeenk, W., & Gerris, J.R. (2009). The relationship between parenting and delinquency: A meta-analysis. *Journal of Abnormal Child Psychology, 37*(6), 749–775.

Hsieh, C.C., & Pugh, M.D. (1993). Poverty, income inequality, and violent crime: a meta-analysis of recent aggregate data studies. *Criminal Justice Review, 18*(2), 182–202.

Jennings, W.G., & Reingle, J.M. (2012). On the number and shape of developmental/life-course violence, aggression, and delinquency trajectories: A state-of-the-art review. *Journal of Criminal Justice, 40*(6), 472–489.

Jones, S.E., Miller, J.D., & Lynam, D.R. (2011). Personality, antisocial behavior, and aggression: A meta-analytic review. *Journal of Criminal Justice, 39,* 329–337.

Kagan, J. (1998). *Galen's Prophecy: Temperament in Human Nature.* Boulder, CO: Westview.

Kagan, J. (2010). *The Temperamental Thread: How Genes, Culture, Time, and Luck Make Us Who We Are.* New York: The Dana Press.

Krueger, R.F., Caspi, A., Moffitt, T.E., White, J., & Stouthamer-Loeber, M. (1996). Delay of gratification, psychopathology, and personality: Is low self-control specific to externalizing problems? *Journal of Personality, 64,* 107–129.

Loeber, R., & Stouthamer-Loeber, M. (1986). Family factors as correlates and predictors of juvenile conduct problems and delinquency. *Crime & Justice: An Annual Review of Research, 7,* 29–149.

Lorber, M.F. (2004). Psychophysiology of aggression, psychopathy, and conduct problems: A meta-analysis. *Psychological Bulletin, 130*(4), 531–552.

Lytton, H., & Romney, D.M. (1991). Parents' differential socialization of boys and girls: A meta-analysis. *Psychological Bulletin, 109*(2), 267–296.

Markon, K.E. (2010). Modeling psychopathology structure: A symptom-level analysis of Axis I and Axis II disorders. *Psychological Medicine, 40,* 273–288.

McCullough, M.E., & Willoughby, B.L. (2009). Religion, self-regulation, and self-control: Associations, explanations, and implications. *Psychological Bulletin, 135*(1), 69–93.

Miller, J.D., & Lynam, D.R. (2001). Structural models of personality and their relation to antisocial behavior: A meta-analytic review. *Criminology, 39,* 765–798.

Moffitt, T.E. (1993). Adolescence-limited and life-course-persistent antisocial behavior: A developmental taxonomy. *Psychological Review, 100*(4), 674–701.

Moffitt, T.E., Arsenault, L., Belsky, D., Dickson, N., Hancox, R.J., Harrington, H., *et al.* (2011). A gradient of childhood self-control predicts health, wealth, and public safety.

*Proceedings of the National Academy of Sciences of the United States of America, 108,* 2693–2698.

Morgan, A.B., & Lilienfeld, S.O. (2000). A meta-analytic review of the relation between antisocial behavior and neuropsychological measures of executive function. *Clinical Psychology Review, 20,* 113–136.

O'Flaherty, B., & Sethi, R. (2010). Homicide in black and white. *Journal of Urban Economics, 68*(3), 215–230.

Ogilvie, J.M., Stewart, A.L., Chan, R.C. K., & Shum, D.H.K. (2011). Neuropsychological measures of executive function and antisocial behavior: A meta-analysis. *Criminology, 49,* 1063–1107.

Ortiz, J., & Raine, A. (2004). Heart rate level and antisocial behavior in children and adolescents: A meta-analysis. *Journal of the American Academy of Child & Adolescent Psychiatry, 43*(2), 154–162.

Piquero, A.R., Farrington, D.P., & Blumstein, A. (2003). The criminal career paradigm. *Crime and Justice, 30,* 359–506.

Pratt, T.C., & Cullen, F.T. (2000). The empirical status of Gottfredson and Hirschi's general theory of crime: A meta-analysis. *Criminology, 38,* 931–964.

Pratt, T.C., & Cullen, F.T. (2005). Assessing macro-level predictors and theories of crime: A meta-analysis. *Crime and Justice, 32,* 373–450.

Raine, A. (1996). Autonomic nervous system activity and violence. In D.M. Stoff & R.B. Cairns (Eds.), *Aggression and Violence* (pp. 145–168). Mahwah, NJ: Lawrence Erlbaum.

Rennison, C.M. (2010). An investigation of reporting violence to the police: A focus on Hispanic victims. *Journal of Criminal Justice, 38*(4), 390–399.

Ruiz, M.A., Pincus, A.L., & Schinka, J.A. (2008). Externalizing pathology and the five-factor model: A meta-analysis of personality traits associated with antisocial personality disorder, substance use disorder, and their co-occurrence. *Journal of Personality Disorders, 22,* 365–388.

Salas-Wright, C.P., Olate, R., & Vaughn, M.G. (2013). The protective effects of religious coping and spirituality on delinquency results among high-risk and gang-involved Salvadoran youth. *Criminal Justice and Behavior, 40*(9), 988–1008.

Salas-Wright, C.P., & Vaughn, M.G. (2014). A "refugee paradox" for substance use disorders? *Drug and Alcohol Dependence, 142,* 345–349.

Sampson, R.J., Raudenbush, S.W., & Earls, F. (1997). Neighborhoods and violent crime: A multilevel study of collective efficacy. *Science, 277*(5328), 918–924.

Samuel, D.B., & Widiger, T.A. (2008). A meta-analytic review of the relationships between the five-factor model and DSM-IV-TR personality disorders: A facet level analysis. *Clinical Psychology Review, 28,* 1326–1342.

Steffensmeier, D., Feldmeyer, B., Harris, C.T., & Ulmer, J.T. (2011). Reassessing trends in black violent crime, 1980-2008: Sorting out the "Hispanic Effect" in Uniform Crime Reports Arrests, National Crime Victimization Survey offender estimates, and US prisoner counts. *Criminology, 49*(1), 197–251.

Vaughn, M.G., DeLisi, M., Gunter, T., Fu, Q., Beaver, K.M., Perron, B.E., *et al.* (2011). The severe 5%: A latent class analysis of the externalizing behavior spectrum in the United States. *Journal of Criminal Justice, 39*(1), 75–80.

Vaughn, M.G., Fu, Q., Beaver, K.M., DeLisi, M., Perron, B., & Howard, M. (2010). Are personality disorders associated with social welfare burden in the United States? *Journal of Personality Disorders, 24,* 709–720.

Vaughn, M.G., Fu, Q., Wernet, S.J., DeLisi, M., Beaver, K. M., Perron, B. E., *et al.* (2011). Characteristics of abstainers from substance use and antisocial behavior in the United States. *Journal of Criminal Justice, 39*(3), 212–217.

Vaughn, M.G., Salas-Wright, C.P., DeLisi, M., & Maynard, B.R. (2014). The immigrant paradox: Immigrants are less antisocial than native-born Americans. *Social Psychiatry and Psychiatric Epidemiology, 49*(7), 1129–1137.

## Further Readings

Ellis, L., Beaver, K., & Wright, J. (Eds.) (2009). *Handbook of Crime Correlates.* San Diego, CA: Academic Press/Elsevier.

Gibson, C.L., & Krohn, M.D. (Eds.) (2013). *Handbook of Life-Course Criminology: Emerging Trends and Directions for Future Research.* New York: Springer.

# 3

# Theory Testing In Criminology

## Travis C. Pratt

We seem to be facing a virtual embarrassment of riches with respect to contemporary criminological theory. To be sure, it appears that we have as many varieties of explanations as to why people break the law as ways that Wile E. Coyote has used to try to snuff out the Roadrunner. We have control theories (social control, self-control, power-control, control balance, see Gottfredson & Hirschi, 1990; Hagan, Gillis, & Simpson, 1985; Hirschi, 1969; Tittle, 1995), learning theories (Akers, 2009; Bandura, 1978), strain theories (classic strain, revised strain, general strain, see Agnew, 1985, 1992; Merton, 1938), rational-choice theories (from deterrence to Bayesian updating, see Anwar & Loughran, 2011; Nagin & Pogarsky, 2001), theories of support and theories of coercion (Colvin, 2000; Cullen, 1994), as well as those from feminist camps (Daly & Chesney-Lind, 1988), the Marxian tradition (Quinney, 1974), those aimed at the macro level (Pratt & Cullen, 2005) and those that focus on individuals (Andrews & Bonta, 2010), and integrated theories (Braithwaite, 1989), mid-range theories (Currie, 1997), general theories (Gottfredson & Hirschi, 1990), and the list goes on. Clearly, we are not suffering from a shortage of ideas.

The problem is that we have arguably reached a point where the production of new theoretical explanations is outpacing the production of empirical tests of the core propositions of the theories that we already have. Empirical tests – particularly those conducted under a wide variety of methodological conditions – are necessary if we are, as a field, ever going to know which of our theories are better than others. Ideally, enough tests of a theory's core statements would accumulate to the point where a meta-analysis could be undertaken – something that has already occurred to a limited extent in criminological theory (Braga & Weisburd, 2012; Hoeve *et al.*, 2012; Nivette, 2011; Pratt & Cullen, 2000, 2005; Pratt *et al.*, 2006; Pratt *et al.*, 2010),

*The Handbook of Criminological Theory*, First Edition. Edited by Alex R. Piquero.
© 2016 John Wiley & Sons, Inc. Published 2016 by John Wiley & Sons, Inc.

but we still have much more work to do. Put simply, we need more empirical tests of criminological theories.

The purpose of this chapter is to provide the field with a set of guidelines for how to go about testing criminological theories. I must offer the caveat, however, that these guidelines are certainly not foolproof. Nevertheless, through my own trial and error, and in talking with a number of scholars who are incredibly good at this (much better than I am), these guidelines should help those doing theory testing to more consistently get their work published in peer-reviewed outlets. And unlike most lists like this that typically only go to 10, this list, out of respect for *Spinal Tap*, goes to 11.

## Guidelines for Testing Criminological Theories

### 1.  Learn some skills

This may seem a bit too general, but its importance cannot be overstated. If one is to go about the important yet difficult task of testing any criminological theory, a certain skill-set must first be in place. At minimum, these skills must include writing well and understanding a wide array of research methods. And gaining these skills is likely to entail engaging in a rather painful process of honest self-reflection. You need to take a good, hard look at your abilities and then critically evaluate what things you do well and which ones you do not. And with respect to writing and methodological prowess, we all have room for improvement.

So how do we improve our skills? Most of us received some form of methodological training in our graduate programs, but new methods are being produced rapidly – far more quickly than graduate curricula can accommodate them into the classroom. Thus, scholars who wish to be at the top of their theory-testing game over the course of their career will have to continue to educate themselves as new methods emerge. And another good reason to have a strong – and more importantly, eclectic – methodological skill-set is so that you will not have to define (and therefore confine) yourself as either a quantitative or qualitative criminologist (although some people enthusiastically embrace such labels). You can instead call yourself a criminologist and be safe in the knowledge that you have command of whatever methodological "tool" you will need to answer whatever criminological question you have decided to ask.

And how do you become a better writer so that your theory tests will actually be read and understood? First of all, care about writing – treat it as a priority. Then, read the work of those authors whose writing you respect and admire (we all have our favorites). And do not limit your roster of favorite authors to criminologists! Do your best to deconstruct what they do, what kind of language they use, what their transitions look like, and how they structure their arguments. Become intimately familiar with this work and then do your best to "reverse engineer" what they do. The best writers in our discipline have been doing this very thing for years with the work that they themselves admire.

## 2. Become familiar with the datasets used in the field

There is a lot of secondary data analysis that goes on in theory testing in criminology. This is not surprising given the central role that life-course perspectives play in the discipline. Thus, a handful of longitudinal datasets have become critically important to those who wish to do theory testing. Accordingly, scholars should familiarize themselves with all of the "usual suspects" here – as well as how they have been used. Important studies include the National Longitudinal Study of Adolescent Health (Add Health; see, e.g., Daigle, Beaver, & Turner, 2010; Haynie, Weiss, & Piquero, 2008), along with the National Youth Survey (NYS; see, e.g., Lee, Menard, & Bouffard, 2014; Pogarsky, Kim, & Paternoster, 2005), the Gang Resistance, Education, and Training data (GREAT; see, e.g., Esbensen *et al.*, 2012; Turanovic & Pratt, 2013), and the National Longitudinal Study of Youth (NLSY; see, e.g., Piquero, Brezina, & Turner, 2005; Shulman, Steinberg, & Piquero, 2013). There are, of course, several others, including those coming out of Cambridge, Rochester, and Chicago just to name a few. And becoming familiar with the measures these datasets contain, their apparent advantages and disadvantages, and how they have been used in prior literature, will make for a much stronger theory-tester.

## 3. Know the literature

I have reviewed hundreds of manuscripts submitted to peer-reviewed journals – some of which focused on testing criminological theories, others tackling other topics. But a common thread that runs through nearly every article that receives my recommendation of rejection is that the coverage of the research literature fell short. The importance of reading everything you can get your hands on is critical. And I mean *everything*. To be sure, to know what the next logical contribution to a body of literature should be requires first knowing what has already been done. And not just those studies confined to our discipline's journals – criminology is inherently interdisciplinary, and scholars coming out of psychology, sociology, economics, political science, public health, social work, and genetics/biology all have something to say about criminal behavior. It is important to know this work as well. This is not to say that every single study that has ever been conducted in a particular theoretical tradition needs to be cited and discussed in a manuscript's front end, but it does require you to know the literature well enough to know which pieces do, in fact, need to be cited and discussed. And the only way to really know that is to have covered the full set of literature. Just keep reading.

## 4. Ask a good question

Of course, asking a good question can only be done if you know the literature! And in criminology, asking a good question means asking a good *research* question – one that is answerable. Such a question need not be asked in a way that demands a yes or no answer (although questions framed in such a way are typically good ones), but rather it needs to be asked in such a way that the set of potential answers is evident. Perhaps the best way to illustrate this point is with some examples of what might be termed "bad" and "good" research questions.

Bad: What are the direct and indirect effects of strain on delinquency? Good: Is the effect of strain on delinquency conditioned by social support? (or some other conditioner that you might be focusing on empirically). Bad: Do online routine activities predict victimization? Good: Does risky online purchasing predict identity theft? Bad: Why do most caregivers of children of incarcerated parents experience negative outcomes but not all? Good: What are the social processes responsible for variation in the experiences of caregivers of children of incarcerated parents? In each of these examples the "bad" questions are not necessarily terrible – I have reviewed (and rejected) many manuscripts from journals where the question was far less clear and some manuscripts where I could never figure out what the question was. The key for the "good" questions, however, is specificity. What, exactly, are you trying to uncover in this test of a criminological theory? Be precise.

And there is a larger lesson to be conveyed here in terms of asking the right question, and it concerns how to go about communicating that question to some important people – journal editors and reviewers. Keep in mind that the people who will be evaluating your test of a criminological theory are not nearly as invested in your study as you are. They are busy people who are cramming this review into their already packed schedules. Thus, you will want to establish your research question and its importance to them as quickly as possible, and that should be done in your manuscript's introduction. And while scholars differ in terms of how they tend to go about doing this, I have found that all good introductions have three primary parts, and often times those three parts can be handled in three paragraphs.

The first part entails demonstrating to the reader the broad context in which you are locating your study. Is it a self-control paper? Or a life-course paper? Whatever it is, the first part of the introduction is where the reader will be clued into the broad body of literature that you are proposing to make a contribution to with your empirical test. The second part of the introduction concerns identifying some tangible "problem" in the literature. This part is critical and can often be the most difficult part of a manuscript to write, since in this section you must identify some significant gap in the literature (please, never refer to it as a "lacuna"; please, just don't) and convince the readers that this gap is consequential. It is not enough in this section to merely point out that "research has not yet addressed this issue." There are lots of issues that have not been addressed, many for good reason. The key here is to avoid the lazy method of justifying your study on the basis that it has not been done; move to the more intellectually rigorous model of justifying it on the basis that it *needs* to be done. Finally, the third part of the introduction, after the problem has been identified, is where you will introduce your research question that is intended to address that very problem. In this section it is also useful to map out what data you will be using and what methodological approach you will be taking.

The key here is that in relatively quick fashion you are communicating to the readers (1) the broad theoretical area the paper is rooted in; (2) the problem in the literature that needs to be addressed; and (3) how you are planning to address it. And with that in mind, for those of you planning on becoming criminological theory-testers, I have one final note of caution concerning asking a good research question: ask the *right* question. By this I mean that it is not uncommon for me to see tests of criminological theories that have up to five or six (or more) different hypotheses that are being proposed. I think this is typically done under the mistaken assumption that more is better. But what this generally indicates is that the five or six questions are being specified only because the authors do not know which one is the right question (a problem that often stems from not knowing the literature very well). Maybe five or six hypotheses are actually warranted in your study, but carefully evaluate if that is actually the case. Often it is not. In any event, several examples of tests of criminological theories that take this approach to asking their research question(s) can be found in the literature (see Hay & Forrest, 2008; Reisig & Pratt, 2011; Xie & McDowall, 2008).

## 5.  Get the right data

Getting the right data to test your research question is not an easy task. Depending on the question, there may be data publicly available or maybe there is not. For life-course theory testing, for example, there are really only a few datasets that researchers can use. For other research questions, however, far more options exist. The key here is to use a dataset that contains good measures of the key concepts you are specifying. And if there are data that are already available to you then great; if not, the task will be to collect your own.

It is understandable that collecting original data is not always the first resort. So much data is already available to the public and these data sources are well-known in the field. There is, however, a lingering (and understandable) bias present in the field against using secondary datasets to answer certain criminological questions. The problem, critics cite, is that those data were not collected with our research questions in mind so they are of limited use to us because the measures they contain are often not very good (Maxfield & Babbie, 2010). Collecting original data would therefore be preferable since measures could be constructed solely for the study's purpose, yet doing so is often resource-intensive. One option is to use data drawn from samples of college students, who are typically available to criminologists. Yet, there is also a bias present in the field against this as well, where problems such as range restriction on key variables of interest and generalizability are noted (Payne & Chappell, 2008). Nevertheless, studies typically find plenty of variation among college student samples (Reisig, Wolfe, & Pratt, 2012) and most large, publicly available datasets contain so much missing data that they cannot be assumed to be representative of the population from which they are drawn. Thus, it is arguably preferable to use data drawn from student samples and to sacrifice the false promise of generalizability for the benefit of precision in measurement. Either way, when going about testing criminological theories, finding the right data is critical.

## 6. Answer empirically the question you asked

Studies that get submitted to peer-reviewed journals often contain a series of unnecessary analyses that seem to have been conducted not because there was a good reason to, but rather simply because they could be. These "supplemental" analyses are not necessarily tied to the primary research question (i.e., "robustness checks" – see point 8 below), but instead appear like disconnected models that are intended to fill up space. These typically come in two forms: split-sample analyses and examining interaction effects. If, for example, your research question is whether a particular form of risky behavior is related to a particular form of victimization, it is not necessary to split the sample by race or gender to see if the same patterns exist (unless, of course, you have made a strong theoretical case for doing so and it is integrated into your research question). Neither is it necessary to specify a number of interaction terms to "explore" whether some "interesting" conditioning effects pop up (again, unless you've already made a strong case up front for estimating them). These additional analyses – which are rarely if ever tied to the research question at hand – should be avoided whenever possible. This may also mean making a case to a journal editor that they are unnecessary if a reviewer on your manuscript asks you to do them (which they do all the time). Just ask your research question, answer it, and stay focused!

## 7. Rule out methodological artifacts

So this is the part where a careful reader might accuse me of contradicting myself. Having just advised you to simply "answer empirically the question you asked" and to avoid unnecessary supplemental analyses, there are additional analyses that probably still need to be done. We refer to these sometimes as "robustness checks" or "sensitivity analyses." The purpose of these analyses is to ensure that the results you obtained (i.e., the answer to your question) are not a methodological artifact. For example, if it is questionable whether the models should have been estimated with a Poisson or negative binomial specification, it may be important to estimate both to see if the results change in any substantive way. In addition, if it is theoretically plausible to specify a model with a different set of covariates, those models should be estimated as well to ensure that the results you get are not sensitive to a particular way of producing them methodologically. Studies that have asked the right question and have gotten the right data to answer it almost invariably survive these additional analyses, and reviewers and editors tend to have much more confidence in the validity and reliability of the results. Several good examples of this practice can be found in the criminological literature (see Apel *et al.*, 2008; Sampson & Raudenbush, 1999; Turanovic & Pratt, 2014).

## 8. Understand the implications of your work

This tip is directed toward writing the Discussion section to your test of a criminological theory – the last chance you will get to make an impression on the reviewers that your test is an important contribution to the literature. Once again, doing this well requires a firm understanding of the full body of literature that you are drawing from for your empirical test, whatever that may be. And there is a good way of approaching this section and one very, very bad way. The bad way tends to entail some version of re-stating the major findings from the analyses. Stating the study's findings should be done in the Results section so stating them once again in the Discussion section is redundant and treats the reader as if they are incapable of remembering something they just read two pages ago. I assure you, they remember. The key here is not to let the reader know what you found, but rather to communicate to them what the findings *mean*.

And doing so requires that you do, in fact, know what they mean! For example, what if you conducted a study that found that the causal mechanisms that lead from victimization to offending are not the same as those that lead from offending to victimization. What are the implications of this finding? What are its theoretical ramifications (i.e., which theoretical perspective is supported by this finding and which ones might be undermined by it)? What are its policy implications? What are its implications for future research? These are the kinds of questions that a good Discussion section does in tests of criminological theories.

This is also where you will want to be careful in discussing the limitations of your study. No study is perfect and there are always problems that can (and should be) pointed out – even in really good studies. The sample could be more representative, the measures could be more precise, the models could be specified differently but the data lacked certain variables, and so on. What is curious is that many authors will end their manuscripts with a full paragraph about their study's limitations! Why do that? You have just spent an entire manuscript justifying your research question and answering it methodologically with sufficient care that you are confident that the results you obtained are "real" and not a methodological artifact, and therefore your study represents a contribution to the field of criminology, and then you are going to end the paper with the whimper of why the results may be of limited value? There is a better way to acknowledge your study's potential limitations.

First, since such limitations are always methodological, they can first be addressed in your study's Methods section. If there is a limitation with the representativeness of your sample, for example, you can offer up statistical comparisons between your sample and the population from which it was drawn to determine whether your results are likely to be biased in favor of a particular outcome. If a scale that is used to measure a key concept is less than ideal, you can discuss its psychometric properties and relationships with other variables to give the reader confidence that even if it is not perfect it seems to be "behaving" the way it should. And when these limitations are addressed in the Discussion section it is much better to frame them so that they represent *opportunities* for future research. Put differently, you can use these limitations as a way to guide future research on the subject by cluing the field in to how they might build off of your work. That's not a whimper – it's a call to action that you are directing! Good examples of how to do this are certainly at your disposal (see Kubrin & Stewart, 2006; Matsueda, Kreager, & Huizinga, 2006; Piquero *et al.*, 2013).

## 9.  Seek advice and listen to it

When a reviewer gets the manuscript containing your test of a criminological theory, that should not be the first time a pair of eyes from someone not included in the author roster has seen it. Prior to the manuscript's submission seek advice from trusted colleagues. If you are a graduate student, this could include your faculty advisors as well as your fellow students (who may also give you more detailed feedback than anyone else). Whatever substantive theoretical area you are working in there are people who are able and willing to help you.

But seeking advice, of course, comes with a cost: you will get it. And you will not always like it. You have spent perhaps months (maybe even longer) preparing this manuscript and your test of a criminological theory has become your intellectual progeny. You want to protect it with bear-like ferocity. And when someone reads your paper and offers up some constructive criticism it might not initially feel so constructive. My advice is to put away your ego and listen to the advice that has been given to you. This does not mean that you need to do exactly what they say, but if they have raised an issue of concern it is likely something that you will somehow need to address. The people who you have asked to read your work want to help you. Let them.

## 10.  Select the right journal

So you have your test of a criminological theory written up in a clean and error-free (as much as possible) manuscript that has been revised according to the comments of those whose wise counsel you have sought. Now is the time to make sure that you send your paper to the *right* journal. There is a perception in the field – at least according to my admittedly nonscientific method of listening to the anecdotes of colleagues – that the best course of action is to send the paper to one of the top journals in the field, regardless of the paper's quality or content. The idea is expressed in this way: "Sure, it doesn't have a snowball's chance in Hell of being accepted at *Criminology* but at least we will get good reviews so we can revise it and send it somewhere else." While authors are free to pursue this strategy at their discretion, it is potentially problematic for three reasons.

First, you should already have received good reviews from those colleagues who have read your work and have offered their suggestions for making it better. Second, if you already have a pretty good idea that your criminological test is not going to pass muster at *Criminology*, waiting for the review process to merely confirm your suspicions represents a loss of time that you do not get back. And if you are in the early stages of your career on the tenure track, that loss of time may be more consequential than you think, since the tenure clock is unforgiving. Third, if your paper truly has no shot at such an outlet you are wasting not only your own time but that of the editor and reviewers as well, so avoid voluntarily relinquishing your social capital in this way.

Instead, there are two reliable ways to know which journal you should submit your study to, the most straightforward of which is to look to your own reference list to see where the work you are citing most heavily came from. That will be a good quick and dirty indicator of where yours should go too. Second, and even more reliable but also more labor-intensive, if you truly know the literature in the area you are conducting your test within, you will know what kinds of journals will be a good fit. Even further, if you know the literature well enough you could even have a target journal in mind before you ever start writing. Either way, finding the right journal is critically important when it comes to exposing your test of a criminological theory to the academic world.

## 11.  Expect to make revisions

Theory testing in criminology is an iterative process. Ideas take a while to form and scholars are constantly wrestling with themselves over what the right question is and what the best methodological approach is for answering it. So if you are going through those same struggles you have plenty of very talented company. What this also means is that you should expect to make revisions constantly until your study ultimately appears in print.

And to that end, every study tends to go through three versions of itself. The first version is the one that exists in your head (or perhaps in a detailed outline). This is the genesis of the idea itself and how you are thinking about approaching it. The next version is the one that you submit to the journal – sometimes it closely resembles the first version but more often than not, once you have completed your study and have written it up, key substantive differences often emerge. And finally, the third version of the paper is the one that exists after you have addressed the concerns raised by the reviewers. And of course, we always tend to think that the version we submitted to the journal is perfect as it is, the final version that has addressed the reviewers' concerns is always better. Sometimes it just takes us a while to realize that. Either way, accept the fact that undertaking constant revisions is a good thing and that your work will get better and better as a result of doing so.

## Conclusion

Theory testing in criminology is not for the faint of heart. Mastering the literature, carving out a question that the field will view as necessary, getting the right data, conducting the appropriate analyses, and writing it all up are all challenging tasks in and of themselves. But this process is necessary so that new knowledge can be produced and our theoretical perspectives can either be supported or refuted. And as that happens, we need to recognize how theory and methods are fundamentally intertwined. We cannot move theory forward without developing new and better methods of getting after our key theoretical constructs, nor can we develop such methods without theoretical guidance. And as we move forward, the future of theory-testing in criminology lies primarily in tackling two challenges.

First, we need to do a much better job of specifying theoretically and measuring directly the intervening processes that lead to our outcomes of interest. The common practice in theory-testing is to focus on a particular independent variable – for example, associating with deviant peers – and see if it predicts some outcome (e.g., engaging in delinquent behavior) after controlling for a bunch of other stuff in a multivariate model. The problem with this approach is that it tells us nothing about *why* something like associating with deviant peers matters – indeed, whatever causal processes are at work typically go unmeasured. This empirical approach, which has been used repeatedly by criminologists for decades, is rapidly reaching its expiration date. Theory testing in the future will be of most value when it is focused on highlighting these intervening social processes.

And, second, theory testers in the future should concentrate their efforts on developing better measures of the key concepts in the field, which may entail cutting some ties with our criminological past. A couple of examples may be of help here. When Travis Hirschi (1969) attempted to pit social bond, cultural deviance, and strain theories against one another, he was faced with the daunting task of attempting to measure individuals' levels of strain. Using survey data from youths, he did so by asking kids what they aspired to be and what they expected to be. This was done under the assumption that youths – particularly those of lower socioeconomic status – would be sufficiently aware of the social and structural impediments they would face in the future that would eventually squash their aspirations. A larger gap between one's aspirations and expectations would thus indicate greater levels of strain. It turned out in Hirschi's data that these youths did not really experience any strain (i.e., there was no notable aspirations–expectations gap), which he took as evidence of the weakness of strain theory.

But was it? Might it have instead been the case that children do not see much (if any) difference between the words aspirations and expectations, and that the absence of an identifiable gap merely indicates that this was not a very good measure of strain? Strangely enough, however, criminologists embraced this measure and tested it repeatedly in the following years, with studies consistently revealing that strain and crime/delinquency were unrelated (see Burton & Cullen, 1992). Things remained this way until Eric Baumer and Regan Gustafson took a different approach and measured strain according to the differential cultural emphasis on economic success relative to using legitimate means to secure it – a much stronger and theoretically-faithful measure than the aspirations–expectations gap. And in the process, Baumer & Gustafson (2007) found support for strain theory in what some (myself included) might contend is the only true test of strain theory in the published literature. It took a major departure from the measurement strategy of the past to bring us this new knowledge. We need more studies like it.

Another example of this problem can be found in the criminological literature on routine activity theory. Early tests of the theory (Cohen & Felson, 1979) used the household activity ratio – an index primarily of female participation in the labor force – as a macro-level proxy to capture the possible interactions of motivated offenders and suitable targets in the absence of capable guardianship. This was all well and good as a start, but the problem really emerged when scholars started to test the theory at the individual level. In these tests, the macro-level household activity ratio was translated primarily into individual-level measures of employment, under the assumption that leaving the home to go to one's job is "risky" when it comes to victimization. But is having a job really risky? Is leaving the home – in and of itself – risky? Probably not, at least according to Pratt *et al.* (2014:1.4), who stated that "it is not simply going outside of the house that matters, but it is instead the differential risks associated with *what one is actually doing outside* – such as planting flowers in a garden versus selling drugs on a street corner – that influence one's susceptibility to victimization" (emphasis in the original). And yet studies continue to fail to make this distinction in favor of weak measures such as having a job or going shopping. Routine activity theory will continue to languish as long as such measures are allowed to populate our knowledge base. It will be up to the next generation of theory-testers to do better.

In the end, good theory-testing in criminology means creative theory-testing. Major contributions come when scholars take risks and improve the way we measure key theoretical constructs. This is not easy and will likely require much in the way of original data collection – something that can be done without much cost in a university setting through student surveys. In doing so, the key will be to develop original measures as opposed to reifying those gleaned from publicly available datasets simply because they have been used in prior research. We need better measures of social control, peer influence, risky routines, coping strategies, and the list goes on. This is the future of theory testing in criminology that we need to embrace.

# References

Agnew, R. (1985). A revised strain theory of delinquency. *Social Forces, 64*, 151–167.

Agnew, R. (1992). Foundation for a general strain theory of crime and delinquency. *Criminology, 30*, 47–88.

Akers, R.L. (2009). *Social Learning and Social Structure: A General Theory of Crime and Deviance*. New Brunswick, NJ: Transaction.

Andrews, D.A., & Bonta, J. (2010). *The Psychology of Criminal Conduct*, 5th edition. New Provence, NJ: Matthew Bender and Company.

Anwar, S., & Loughran, T.A. (2011). Testing a Bayesian learning theory of deterrence among serious juvenile offenders. *Criminology, 49*, 667–698.

Apel, R., Bushway, S.D., Paternoster, R., Brame, R., & Sweeten, G. (2008). Using state child labor laws to identify the causal effect of youth employment on deviant behavior and academic achievement. *Journal of Quantitative Criminology, 24*, 337–362.

Bandura, A. (1978). Social learning theory of aggression. *Journal of Communication, 28,* 12–29.

Baumer, E.P., & Gustafson, R. (2007). Social organization and instrumental crime: Assessing the empirical validity of classic and contemporary anomie theories. *Criminology, 45,* 617–663.

Braithwaite, J. (1989). *Crime, Shame and Reintegration.* Cambridge: Cambridge University Press.

Braga, A.A., & Weisburd, D.L. (2012). The effects of focused deterrence strategies on crime: A systematic review and meta-analysis of the empirical evidence. *Journal of Research in Crime and Delinquency, 49,* 323–358.

Burton, V.S., & Cullen, F.T. (1992). The empirical status of strain theory. *Journal of Crime and Justice, 15,* 1–30.

Cohen, L.E., & Felson, M. (1979). Social change and crime rate trends: A routine activity approach. *American Sociological Review, 44,* 588–608.

Colvin, M. (2000). *Crime and Coercion: An Integrated Theory of Chronic Criminality.* New York: St. Martin's Press.

Cullen, F.T. (1994). Social support as an organizing concept for criminology: Presidential Address to the Academy of Criminal Justice Sciences. *Justice Quarterly, 11,* 527–559.

Currie, E. (1997). Market, crime and community: Toward a mid-range theory of post-industrial violence. *Theoretical Criminology, 1,* 147–172.

Daigle, L.E., Beaver, K.M., & Turner, M.G. (2010). Resiliency against victimization: Results from the National Longitudinal Study of Adolescent Health. *Journal of Criminal Justice, 38,* 329–337.

Daly, K., & Chesney-Lind, M. (1988). Feminism and criminology. *Justice Quarterly, 5,* 497–538.

Esbensen, F., Peterson, D., Taylor, T.J., & Osgood, D.W. (2012). Results from a multi-site evaluation of the G.R.E.A.T. program. *Justice Quarterly, 29,* 125–151.

Gottfredson, M.R., & Hirschi, T. (1990). *A General Theory of Crime.* Palo Alto, CA: Stanford University Press.

Hagan, J., Gillis, A.R., & Simpson, J. (1985). The class structure of gender and delinquency: Toward a power-control theory of common delinquent behavior. *American Journal of Sociology, 90,* 1151–1178.

Hay, C., & Forrest, W. (2008). Self-control theory and the concept of opportunity: The case for a more systematic union. *Criminology, 46,* 1039–1072.

Haynie, D.L., Weiss, H.E., & Piquero, A.R. (2008). Race, the economic maturity gap, and criminal offending in young adulthood. *Justice Quarterly, 25,* 595–622.

Hirschi, T. (1969). *Causes of Delinquency.* Berkeley, CA: University of California Press.

Hoeve, M., Stams, G.J.J.M., van der Put, C.E., Dubas, J.S., van der Laan, P.H., & Gerris, J.R.M. (2012). A meta-analysis of attachment to parents and delinquency. *Journal of Abnormal Child Psychology, 40,* 771–785.

Kubrin, C.E., & Stewart, E.A. (2006). Predicting who reoffends: The neglected role of neighborhood context in recidivism studies. *Criminology, 44,* 165–197.

Lee, J., Menard, S., & Bouffard, L.A. (2014). Extending interactional theory: The labeling dimension. *Deviant Behavior, 35,* 1–19.

Matsueda, R.L., Kreager, D.K., & Huizinga, D. (2006). Deterring delinquents: A rational choice model of theft and violence. *American Sociological Review, 71,* 95–122.

Maxfield, M.G., & Babbie, E. (2010). *Research Methods for Criminal Justice and Criminology,* 6th edition. Belmont, CA: Wadsworth.

Merton, R.K. (1938). Social structure and anomie. *American Sociological Review, 3,* 672–682.

Nagin, D.S., & Pogarsky, G. (2001). Integrating celerity, impulsivity, and extralegal sanction threats into a model of general deterrence: Theory and evidence. *Criminology, 39,* 865–892.

Nivette, A.E. (2011). Cross-national predictors of crime: A meta-analysis. *Homicide Studies, 15,* 103–131.

Payne, B.K., & Chappell, A. (2008). Using student samples in criminological research. *Journal of Criminal Justice Education, 19,* 175–192.

Piquero, A.R., Brezina, T., & Turner, M.G. (2005). Testing Moffitt's account of delinquency abstention. *Journal of Research in Crime and Delinquency, 42,* 27–54.

Piquero, A.R., Connell, N.M., Piquero, N.L., Farrington, D.P., & Jennings, W.G. (2013). Does adolescent bullying distinguish between male offending trajectories in late middle age? *Journal of Youth and Adolescence, 42,* 444–453.

Pogarsky, G., Kim, K., & Paternoster, R. (2005). Perceptual change in the National Youth Survey: Lessons for deterrence theory and offender decision-making. *Justice Quarterly, 27,* 1–29.

Pratt, T.C., & Cullen, F.T. (2000). The empirical status of Gottfredson and Hirschi's general theory of crime: A meta-analysis. *Criminology, 38,* 931–964.

Pratt, T.C., & Cullen, F.T. (2005). Assessing macro-level predictors and theories of crime: A meta-analysis. *Crime and Justice: A Review of Research, 32,* 373–450.

Pratt, T.C., Cullen, F.T., Blevins, K.R., Daigle, L.E., & Madensen, T.D. (2006). The empirical status of deterrence theory: A meta-analysis. In F.T. Cullen, J.P. Wright, & K.R. Blevins (Eds.), *Taking Stock: The Empirical Status of Criminological Theory – Advances in Criminological Theory* (pp. 367–395). New Brunswick, NJ: Transaction.

Pratt, T.C., Cullen, F.T., Sellers, C.S., Winfree, L.T., Madensen, T., Daigle, L., *et al.* (2010). The empirical status of social learning theory: A meta-analysis. *Justice Quarterly, 27,* 765–802.

Pratt, T.C., Turanovic, J.J., Fox, K.A., & Wright, K.A. (2014). Self-control and victimization: A meta-analysis. *Criminology, 52,* 87–116.

Quinney, R. (1974). *Critique of the Legal Order: Crime Control in Capitalist Society.* Boston, MA: Little, Brown.

Reisig, M.D., & Pratt, T.C. (2011). Low self-control and imprudent behavior revisited. *Deviant Behavior, 32,* 589–625.

Reisig, M.D., Wolfe, S.E., & Pratt, T.C. (2012). Low self-control and the religiosity-crime relationship. *Criminal Justice and Behavior, 39,* 1172–1191.

Sampson, R.J., & Raudenbush, S.W. (1999). Systematic social observation of public spaces: A new look at disorder in urban neighborhoods. *American Journal of Sociology, 105,* 603–651.

Shulman, E.P., Steinberg, L.D., & Piquero, A.R. (2013). The age-crime curve in adolescence and early adulthood is not due to age differences in economic status. *Journal of Youth and Adolescence, 42,* 848–860.

Tittle, C.R. (1995). *Control Balance: Toward a General Theory of Deviance.* Boulder, CO: Westview.

Turanovic, J.J., & Pratt, T.C. (2013). The consequences of maladaptive coping: Integrating general strain and self-control theories to specify a causal pathway between victimization and offending. *Journal of Quantitative Criminology, 29,* 321–345.

Turanovic, J.J., & Pratt, T.C. (2014). "Can't stop, won't stop": Self-control, risky lifestyles, and repeat victimization. *Journal of Quantitative Criminology, 30*(1), 29–56.

Xie, M., & McDowall, D. (2008). Escaping crime: The effects of direct and indirect victimization on moving. *Criminology, 46,* 809–840.

# 4

# Deterrence

## Thomas A. Loughran, Ray Paternoster, and Douglas B. Weiss

## Introduction

The workings of the criminal justice system are guided by a number of different, and somewhat contradictory, philosophies of punishment, both deontological and utilitarian. For example, we enforce the law and punish criminal offenders in part for purely retributive reasons. One who has violated the law has done a moral wrong; we deem it important to cancel that moral wrong by making the offender "pay for" their crime. In retributive punishment, then, there is no expectation for crime reduction or any other instrumental goal – one who commits a crime simply deserves to forfeit something through punishment, and that punishment is allocated in proportion to the magnitude of the offender's moral wrong. However, the criminal justice system is also at the same time guided by more utilitarian philosophies. For example, "habitual offender" laws were passed because society was deemed to have the right to be protected from repeat criminal offenders and a clear way to ensure that society is protected from these predators is through incapacitation (incarcerating offenders to deny them the opportunity to commit crime). Although both retribution and incapacitation are recognized philosophical foundations of the criminal justice system, it can reasonably be argued that its primary purpose is deterrence.

In a nutshell, deterrence occurs in one instance when someone who has committed a criminal offense in the past and has been caught and punished for it refrains from doing so in the future because they fear being apprehended and punished again. This type of deterrence is typically referred to in the criminological literature as *specific deterrence* (Andenaes, 1974). Another type of deterrence occurs when a would-be offender (someone who has not yet committed a crime but is contemplating one) refrains from committing a crime because they fear apprehension and

*The Handbook of Criminological Theory*, First Edition. Edited by Alex R. Piquero.
© 2016 John Wiley & Sons, Inc. Published 2016 by John Wiley & Sons, Inc.

punishment. This is *general deterrence* (Andenaes, 1974). Although it is sometimes difficult to disentangle the two (Stafford & Warr, 1993), both specific and general deterrence are utilitarian justifications for law enforcement and punishment. The logic is that a system of punishment produces harm for people, and under a deterrence schema this harm can only be justified if the harm which is prevented by punishment (by inhibiting crime) is greater than the harm it produces (by punishing offenders). In other words, to be justified, punishment must produce a utility or net gain. Whether it is specific or general, deterrence theorists talk about three basic properties of punishment – its certainty, severity, and celerity. The basic idea regarding these properties of punishment is that deterrence happens when punishment is certain, moderately severe, and arrives without much delay.

This notion of crime inhibition through deterrence is very old. We perhaps see it first in an Enlightenment-era treatise, *On Crimes and Punishment* written by the Italian, Cesare Beccaria, in 1764; an essay very likely read by every undergraduate and graduate criminology student. In this tiny essay Beccaria rails against what he and other Enlightenment philosophers saw as the abuses of existing legal and penal practices, including forced confessions and torture, laws that were not codified, and capricious punishments, among other things. Beccaria's objection to these practices was that they were not rational and were, therefore, inefficient. His essay consisted of a series of proposed reforms of existing criminal justice practices based on Enlightenment assumptions about the rationality of (most) human beings. He argued that punishment by authorities is necessary in order to counteract self-interest, which he describes as "the despotic spirit which is in every man", a self-interest which leads to the commission of crime because it is beneficial (1985: 12). One would not be far off to say that Beccaria's *Essay* was essentially the deterrence theorists' *primitus opus.*[1] For example, in Chapter 15 he explicitly states that "The purpose [of punishment] can only be to prevent the criminal from inflicting new injuries on its citizens and to deter others" (1985: 42). Further, in various chapters Beccaria clearly laid out the three propositions which remain even to this day at the heart of deterrence theory, a discussion of the empirical tests of which will cover the better part of this chapter. For example, with respect to the severity of punishment he noted that while severe punishment deters because it involves the infliction of pain, and therefore increases the cost of crime, it must be moderate in magnitude: "For a punishment to attain its end, the evil which it inflicts has only to exceed the advantage derivable from the crime…" (1985: 43). In addition to being of moderate severity, to be an effective deterrent a punishment should swiftly follow the commission of the crime (1985: 55–56):

> The more promptly and the more closely punishment follows upon the commission of a crime, the more just and useful it will be … because when the length of time that passes between the punishment and the misdeed is less, so much the stronger and more lasting in the human mind is the association of these two ideas, *crime and punishment*; they then come insensibly to be considered, one as the cause, the other as the necessary inevitable effect (emphasis in original).

Finally, what has virtually become dogma among deterrence theorists and researchers today, Beccaria (1985: 58) argued that the certainty of punishment is more important than its severity:

> One of the greatest curbs on crimes is not the cruelty of punishments but their infallibility … [t]he certainty of a punishment, even if it be moderate, will always make a stronger impression than the fear of another which is more terrible but combined with the hope of impunity; even the least evils, when they are certain, always terrify men's minds....

There have been some notable changes to the theoretical model of deterrence over the ensuing 250-plus years since Beccaria, such as the addition of informal sanction threats and the perceived benefits of offending (Matsueda, Kreager, & Huizinga, 2006; Piliavin *et al.*, 1986; Williams & Hawkins, 1986), however, for the most part, when deterrence researchers conduct empirical tests they continue to be deeply interested in the three basic hypotheses laid out below, with one notable exception.

There has been a great asymmetry in the attention given to these hypotheses: deterrence researchers have paid very little attention to the idea of the celerity or swiftness of punishment. In part this reflects some ambiguity with respect to the notion as to how swiftness acts to deter crime. So for instance, Gibbs (1975: 131)[2] argued that since the celerity hypothesis may be presumed to be based on Pavlovian conditioning where even a minimal delay between stimulus (crime) and response (punishment) prevents learning, its relevance for the criminal justice system, where delays of months and even years is modus operandi, is virtually nil. In fact, Gibbs questions the entire celerity premise that punishment must be swiftly delivered in order to be effective, suggesting that rather than weakening the effectiveness of punishment a delay may actually strengthen it, since people come to dread the delay itself: "Even the supposition that immediate punishment is more dreaded that delayed punishment is questionable, for it could be that some individuals view the delay in legal punishment as no less discomforting than the punishment itself" (for more on this idea, see Loewenstein, 1987).

In the remainder of this chapter we will review the empirical evidence on deterrence. Since there has in the past been more than adequate reviews of the earlier research literature (Chalfin & McCrary, 2014; Cook, 1980; Nagin, 1998, 2013; Nagin, Cullen, & Johnson, 2009; Paternoster, 1987, 2010;), we will place much greater emphasis on the literature published since 2000. Further, the literature will be reviewed in three distinct sections – that pertaining to (1) perceptual studies of deterrence, (2) deterrence and the police, and (3) deterrence and imprisonment.

## Effect of Sanction Threat Perceptions on Crime

What most people, lay and academic, know about the deterrence doctrine are the hypothesized relationships between the perceived certainty, severity, and celerity of punishment and crime. In words they are:

*H1: There is an inverse relationship between the perceived certainty of punishment of an individual and their offending.*

*H2: There is an inverse relationship between the perceived severity of punishment of an individual and their offending.*

*H3: There is an inverse relationship between the perceived celerity of punishment of an individual and their offending.*

One of these hypotheses, the certainty hypothesis, has spawned a great deal of research, which has covered more than 40 years by now. Over this time, certainty research has gone through several eras: cross-sectional research, panel research, multivariate panel research, and vignette/scenario designs. As we will discuss in more detail below, more recent research on the certainty hypothesis has employed experimental designs. For the most part, this line of research has shown inverse but very modest relationships between the perceived certainty of punishment and various measures of self-reported offending or intentions to offend. The most generous statement that could be made about the perceived severity of punishment is that evidence in support of a deterrent effect has been inconsistent; perhaps a more accurate statement is that supportive evidence has been weak. The third hypothesis, the celerity hypothesis, unlike the other hypotheses, never really had its day in the sun, as until very recently deterrence scholars were stymied both by how to operationalize the perceived swiftness of punishment as well as to easily predict what the sign of the relationship to crime should be.[3] In recent years, however, deterrence researchers have shown renewed interest in examining the effect of perceived swift vs. delayed punishment. In testing these deterrence hypotheses, researchers have employed either a survey methodology based on self-reported offending or one where hypothetical crime scenarios are used. As with the research on police and deterrence and incarceration and deterrence discussed below, since there are excellent reviews of the perceptual deterrence literature, our review in this section will only cover research published since 2000.[4]

Using the Dunedin cohort study, Wright and colleagues (2004) asked approximately 1,000 adolescents and young adults about their perceptions of the risk of "getting caught" for seven different criminal offense types, the risk of informal sanctions (social censure), as well as their self-reported involvement in those crimes (shoplifting, car theft, burglary, using stolen credit cards, using marijuana, hitting someone in a fight, and driving while drunk). Consistent with perceptual deterrence theory, they found that, net of background factors such as gender, social class, and childhood self-control, there was a significant inverse relationship between the perceived risk of getting caught and the self-reported variety and frequency of criminal behavior, as well as for the certainty of social censure and crime. This deterrent effect was particularly pronounced among those with the highest criminal propensity, and in fact, there was no deterrent effect at all observed at the lowest levels of criminal propensity. It was argued that those with very low criminal propensity may be immune to sanction threats because they simply do not contemplate committing antisocial acts, rendering such threats moot. This finding is consistent with a great deal of prior perceptual deterrence research which has shown that those inhibited from offending by strong moral beliefs against crime are unaffected by perceptions of sanction threats. Wright *et al.*'s finding of a more substantial deterrent effect of sanction threats on those high in criminal propensity is, however, inconsistent with the Pogarsky (2002) study to be discussed below.

A study by Matsueda *et al.* (2006) examined the relationship between the perceived certainty of arrest and subsequent delinquency using adolescents in the Denver Youth Study. They found that net of such factors as age, race, gender, impulsivity, risk preference and other background factors, perceptions of the certainty of arrest were related to self-reported theft and violence. Further, those who perceived that there were opportunities to commit theft and violence and get away with it were more likely to report both acts of theft and violence. There was also support for the view that the anticipated gains or benefits of crime are influential, as those who perceived theft as "exciting" were more likely to report theft (a comparable effect for violence was not found), and those who thought that they would be seen as "cool" if they were to steal and commit acts of violence were more likely to commit both offenses. Finally, although the costs of crime were expected to be delayed, and therefore discounted some, Matsueda *et al.* found that the relative effects of the costs and rewards of crime were roughly comparable in magnitude.

In a similarly specified model, Lochner (2007) examined the relationship between perceived sanction threat and offending in two data sets with nationally representative samples, the National Longitudinal Survey of Youth (NLSY97) and the National Youth Survey (NYS). As predicted from deterrence theory, he found that the perceived probability of arrest was significantly and inversely related to both self-reported auto theft and minor theft. The effect, however, was modest – a 10% increase in the perceived risk of arrest was estimated to reduce self-reported auto theft by 8% and theft by only 3%, with only the former being significantly different from zero. In his analysis of the NYS, Lochner estimated the relationship between the probability of arrest for two different magnitudes of theft (something worth less than $5 and something worth more than $50), breaking and entering, and attacking someone and self-reported involvement in each offense. He found that, consistent with perceptual deterrence theory, net of control factors the estimated coefficients for the perceived risk of arrest on self-reported offending were negative, but again the magnitude of the deterrent effect was modest – a 10% increase in the perceived probability of arrest for each offense reduced participation by from 7 to 12%, with only the effects for minor theft and attacking someone statistically significant.

Loughran *et al.* (2012) employed the Pathways to Desistance data, a longitudinal dataset comprised of a sample of juvenile offenders who had been convicted of a serious felony. Each youth was asked how likely it was that they would be arrested for the following seven offenses: fighting, robbery with a gun, stabbing someone, breaking into a store or home, stealing clothes from a store, vandalism, and auto theft, as well as their self-reported involvement in 17 different criminal offenses. They found a significant inverse effect between perceived sanction certainty and self-reported offending for a summary scale of perceptions on an index of self-reported offending, but this relationship did not exist across all levels of certainty. At low levels of perceived certainty (below a probability of 0.30) there was no relationship with self-reported offending, at a mid-range of arrest probability from 0.30 to 0.70, a 10% increase in the perceived probability of arrest was associated with a statistically significant average decrease of 0.5 offenses, while beyond the 0.70 risk probability area there was an inverse relationship between perceived risk and arrest that was not significantly different from zero. Consistent with some research at the aggregate level, then, this study seemed to suggest that perceived certainty had to reach a certain threshold or "tipping point" before the threat was credible to create a deterrent effect.

An early scenario-type study was devised by Nagin & Pogarsky (2001) who offered the following expected utility model of crime:

$U$(Benefits) > $p$ $U$(Legal Costs + Extralegal Costs)

Where the benefits of crime include both the direct gains (such as money, property, the vanquishing of a rival) and indirect gains (ex: social prestige), the legal costs include formal sanction threat certainty and severity, while the extralegal costs include the possibility of informal sanctions such as social censure and guilt, and $p$ is the perceived probability of each outcome. This utility model did not directly include a parameter for the celerity of punishment, but Nagin & Pogarsky (2001: 872) did include a discount factor or "intertemporal exchange rate" to reflect the fact that the costs of crime usually are delayed while the benefits are immediate:

$U$(Benefits) > $\delta_t$ $p$ $U$(Legal Costs + Extralegal Costs)

The value of the discount factor $\delta_t$ is defined as a function of the individual's discount rate ($r$) and time ($t$):

$$\delta_t = \frac{1}{(1+r)^t}$$

Notice that for a given individual the discount factor varies over $t$, or the number of time periods over which punishment is delayed (the celerity of punishment). Using the intention to drink and drive in response to a hypothetical scenario as the outcome variable, Nagin and Pogarsky found evidence for both a certainty and severity effect for perceived sanction threats, but a statistically insignificant effect for celerity. As is typical for deterrence studies, the magnitude of the certainty effect was greater than that for severity, and the deterrent effect of extralegal sanctions was at least as large as that for legal sanctions.

In a subsequent study also with drinking and driving, Pogarsky (2002) found that, net of background control factors, both the perceived certainty and severity of punishment were inversely related to self-reported intentions to drink and drive in response to a hypothetical scenario. Consistent with a great deal of other prior research, he also found that informal sanctions, in this case self-disapproval or shame, had an even stronger inhibiting effect than did formal sanction threats. Interestingly, Pogarsky stratified the sample into three groups in terms of how "deterrable" they were. The "acute conformists" stated that they would not drink and drive even if they probability of getting caught was nil, the "deterrable" respondents who stated that they would drink and drive but the probability would be reduced by the threat of punishment, and the "incorrigible" respondents who were impervious to the threat of sanctions in that they were more likely to drink and drive in the face of punishment. Contrary to the results of Wright *et al.*'s (2004) survey study reported above, Pogarsky found that deterrence works best in the mid-range of criminal propensity. Future research will have to sort out this inconsistency.

Nagin & Pogarsky (2003) conducted a randomized experiment with 256 college students in which they completed a survey that asked them difficult trivia questions and allowed them to cheat in order to earn extra money. Students were told that they were to complete an eight-item trivia quiz and that if they answered at least six questions correctly they would be given a $10 bonus. The questions were designed so that it would be almost impossible to earn the bonus, but students were told that the correct answers were on the back of the trivia question sheet and students could, after they finished the survey, look at the answers to satisfy their curiosity. In one of the conditions the subjects were aware that the experimenter would be in the room during the survey (high certainty) while in a second condition the experimenter would be absent (low certainty). In a high-severity condition students were told that if caught cheating they would have all earned money taken away, a threat that was not given in the low-severity condition. Nagin and Pogarsky found that a significantly greater proportion of students in the low-certainty condition received the trivia bonus, but severity had no effect on cheating, nor did an interaction between the perceived certainty and severity of punishment.

While many survey/vignette studies seem to show strong support for at least the perceived-certainty hypothesis of deterrence theory, a note of caution is perhaps called for. In a recent paper, Loughran, Paternoster, & Thomas (2014) presented college student respondents with a hypothetical scenario involving drinking and driving. There were three different conditions under which the survey was administered: (1) a typical paper and pencil instrument given in a large class (a frequent, if not the most frequent, data-collection environment in perceptual-deterrence research), (2) a computer-based instrument given in a small computer lab under conditions otherwise similar to most prior studies, where subjects were given incentives for their honesty and accuracy, (3) a computer-based instrument also given in a small computer lab where subjects were given incentives according to the Bayesian Truth Serum (BTS). The BTS is a scoring rule designed to elicit accuracy in the reporting of survey items such as perceived probability distributions by means of an incentive structure which induces respondents to be thoughtful and accurate in reporting their subjective beliefs. The purpose of this incentivized scoring rule is simply to get subjects to put in the mental effort necessary to accurately provide their estimates, rather than give easy-to-mentally-access, intuitive responses.

Loughran and his two colleagues provide compelling evidence that the elicitation of subjective probability estimates of sanction threat risks and self-reported involvement in illegal acts are two areas where respondents may be disinclined or unable to recall information accurately and thoughtfully. They found that respondents spent more time completing the data-collection instrument under the BTS condition compared with the other two (perhaps indicating more thoughtfulness), and that under incentivized conditions estimates of the perceived risk of arrest were generally lower than when subjects were given no incentive. Those in the BTS incentive condition were also more likely to be in the lower perceived-certainty categories than those in the regular incentive condition. Finally, for three of four offenses the observed correlation between perceived certainty and self-reported intentions to offend in response to the scenarios were substantially higher under the non-incentive condition, a condition characteristic of most previous perceptual-deterrence research, than under the BTS condition. This finding does two important things: (1) it suggests that criminologists in general should consider paying more attention to the advantage of incentivized scoring rules in their survey research; and (2), if replicated, these results suggest that correlations between perceived certainty and offending reported in previous perceptual deterrence research may be exaggerated.

## Deterrence and the Police

Twenty years ago, policing scholar David Bayley (1994:3) made this statement about the ability of police to prevent crime: "The police do not prevent crime. This is one of the best kept secrets of modern life. Experts know it, the police know it, but the public does not know it." The body of research on the ability of the police to prevent crime that has since accumulated over the past 20-plus years has cast some doubt on Bayley's statement. There is now moderately strong evidence that the police can contribute to crime prevention both through their presence and through the strategies they employ (Durlauf & Nagin, 2011). Research on the deterrent effect of police has focused on the relationship between crime and either (a) police numbers/resources or (b) specific policing strategies.

### Size of police force and resources

One line of research on the deterrent effect of police examines the relationship between police numbers or resources and crime rates in a jurisdiction. Greater police numbers/resources are believed to deter criminal offending by increasing the objective certainty of arrest and punishment. Research in this area has been based on either (a) natural experiments during which there is a shock to the size of the police force or (b) panel studies that relate police force size to crime rates.

Some of the best evidence for the deterrent effect of police comes from studies of the effect of police strikes on crime rates. Andeneas (1974) described an immediate increase in crime rates following the arrest of the entire Danish police force by occupying German forces during World War II. The greatest increases were observed for street crimes that would most likely be deterred by police presence rather than crimes, such as fraud, which are less likely to be affected by police presence. Sherman & Eck (2002) identify five other studies of the effect of police strikes on crime rates; four of which found large increases in crime during police strikes. While these studies employ weak research designs, they do provide good evidence for the absolute deterrent effect of police. That is, going from a complete absence of police to even a small force seems to have a large deterrent effect.

While the mere presence of a police force may exert considerable deterrent effects compared to a complete absence of police, the more interesting and policy-relevant question pertains to the marginal deterrent effect of police. The marginal effect of police concerns the crime prevention that is bought with each additional police officer. There is a large body of research on the relationship between police size and crime rates, although much of this research is correlational and fails to adequately control for the simultaneity problem (Eck & Maguire, 2005). According to the simultaneity problem, the relationship between police and crime rates can operate in two directions: either police hiring can decrease crime rates through deterring potential offenders, or high crime rates may prompt departments to hire more police officers. Researchers have addressed this problem by using either natural experiments or panel designs that relate crime rates to policing resources. Natural experiments on the deterrent effect of police size take advantage of naturally occurring shocks to police presence. Since these shocks are exogenous to the relationship between police and crime, they influence levels of police presence, but should have no effect on crime rates. Two recent studies take advantage of shocks to police presence due to threats of terrorism. Di Tella & Schargrodsky (2004) examined the influence of changes in police protection following a terrorist bombing of a Jewish center in Argentina in 1994. Following the bombing, authorities increased police presence around every Jewish and Muslim building in the country. They found that rates of auto theft declined by 75% when extra police were deployed. This effect, however, was localized to city blocks that received extra presence, and may have resulted in crime displacement rather than crime prevention (Donohue & Ho, 2005). Even if the extra police deployment only served to displace crime to other areas, this finding still suggests greater police presence deters crime, as offenders were dissuaded from offending in the areas with the extra presence.

In another natural experiment, Klick & Tabarrok (2005) took advantage of changes in the terror alert level to study the influence of police deployment on DC crime rates. When the terror alert level rose from "elevated" (yellow) to "high" (orange), DC police responded by increasing police deployments around the city. They found the change in terror alert level was associated with a 7% drop in police daily crime reports. Further, this effect was limited to property crimes, such as auto theft and burglary, which are most likely to be affected by police presence due to their public nature.

Several studies have used panel designs to estimate the impact of police resources on crime rates (Levitt, 1997, 2002; Marvell & Moody, 1996; McCrary, 2002). Marvell & Moody (1996) used Granger causal models to estimate the relationship between the number of police officers per capita and felony crime rates in 49 US states and 56 large cities from 1973 to 1992. They found a significant inverse relationship between police officers per capita and homicide, robbery, and burglary crime rates at both state and city levels.

Panel studies have also used instrumental variable (IV) analysis to address the simultaneity problem. Levitt (1997) examined the relationship between police officers per capita and felony crime rates in 59 U.S. cities from 1970 to 1992 using election cycles as an instrument. Levitt reasons that police hiring increases during election years as politicians desire low crime rates or seek to appear tough on crime in an effort to maximize their chances of reelection. He finds evidence of a deterrent effect, with an increase in the number of police resulting in a 5–8% reduction across different crime types. Levitt estimated an elasticity between the number of police and crime rates around $-1.0$ for violent crime and $-0.3$ for property crime. McCrary (2002) later pointed out two errors in Levitt's (1997) analysis which, when corrected, rendered the estimate of police on crime nonsignificant. Levitt (2002) responded by proposing an alternate instrument, the number of firefighters per capita, and found a slightly larger effect for property crimes, although the impact of police levels on violent crime was about half as large as his original estimate. The elasticity between the number of police officers and crime rates was $-0.4$ for violent crime and $-0.5$ for property crime.

Evans & Owens (2007) used funding from the Community Oriented Policing Services (COPS) program as an instrument to estimate the effect of police force size on crime rates from 1990 to 2001 in 2,074 U.S. cities. They find additional officers were associated with declines in rates of burglary, auto theft, robbery, aggravated assault and murder. Consistent with the studies reviewed above, the strongest effects were observed for property crimes. Thus, there appears to be good support for the notion that increasing the number of police in a jurisdiction will reduce crime rates.

As stated earlier, an increase in police resources is expected to result in reduced crime rates by increasing the objective certainty of punishment. However, as discussed in some detail above, deterrence is a perceptual theory based on individuals' perceived risks of punishment rather than objective risks. If the objective increase in certainty of apprehension fails to affect individuals' risk perceptions, then it is unlikely that the increased police presence is affecting crime rates through the mechanism of deterrence. Although few studies have explored the link between the objective risk of punishment and subjective risk perceptions, a recent study by Kleck & Barnes (2010) finds no relationship between the number of police officers per capita and perceived risk of arrest or punishment in a survey of 1,500 adults in 54 large urban counties in the United States. The failure to establish a link between the objective certainty of punishment as measured by police resources and individual risk perceptions casts some doubt on the deterrent effect of police force size on crime rates.

## Policing strategies

The police may also deter crime through the use of specific strategies. There is a large body of research on the effectiveness of various police strategies in regards to crime prevention. This research has primarily been conducted using either (1) quasi-experimental designs which compare crime rates before and after an intervention or (2) randomized experiments. This body of research suggests policing strategies that are focused on particular geographic areas or offenders are effective in deterring crime, while strategies that lack a clear crime-control focus have little impact on crime rates.

Early research on the effectiveness of policing strategies focused on what has been termed the "standard model" of policing (Weisburd & Eck, 2004). The standard model of policing was generally thought to deter crime by increasing the certainty of punishment through increasing the odds of apprehension. The standard model of policing includes strategies such as random preventative patrol, rapid response to 911 calls, and reactive arrest policies.

The initial empirical test of the deterrent effect of police strategies involved random preventive patrol (Kelling *et al.*, 1974). Random preventive patrol assumes that the presence or potential presence of police officers will deter individuals from offending. In the Kansas City Preventive Patrol experiment, 15 beats of the southern police district of Kansas City were randomly assigned to receive one of three treatments: no police presence, normal presence (control), or increased police presence (up to 4× normal). The results of the evaluation indicated that random preventive patrol had no impact on reported crime or victimization. This strategy may have failed to deter as, according to the citizen survey, citizens did not even notice a change in police presence in treatment areas.

Rapid response is another strategy associated with the "standard model" of policing that was thought to deter crime. Quick responses to calls for service were thought to result in more arrests and an increased certainty of apprehension and punishment. Rapid response, however, appears to be ineffective in increasing the probability of apprehension and punishment as individuals either delay in calling police or don't discover the crime until long after the offender has fled the scene (Kansas City Police Department, 1977; Spelman & Brown, 1984).

There is also a lack of evidence supporting the deterrent effect of reactive arrest policies. Whereas the strategies of preventive patrol and rapid response pertain to general deterrence, reactive arrest policies are an example of specific deterrence as they seek to reduce the probability of repeat offending among arrestees. Much of the research on the specific deterrent effect of arrest has focused on its impact in cases of misdemeanor domestic violence. The initial Minneapolis experiment suggested a strong deterrent effect of arrest (Sherman & Berk, 1984), although the results of the replication studies were mixed and sometimes depended on the employment status of offenders (Sherman, 1992).

While the strategies associated with the "standard model" of policing appear to have little deterrent effect on crime or repeat offending, there are several policing strategies that have been shown to be effective deterrents. These strategies include police crackdowns, hot-spot policing, problem-oriented policing and focused deterrence. Whereas the strategies associated with the "standard model" of policing lack a clear crime-control focus, these effective strategies focus on particular crimes, specific geographic areas, or particular offenders.

Police crackdowns focus police resources on specific crimes that occur in particular geographic areas. This tactic is presumed to deter offending by increasing the objective certainty of arrest and punishment through increased police presence. Sherman (1990) reviewed 18 case studies of police crackdowns and concluded crackdowns produce short-term deterrent effects that decay over time. Both Sherman (1990) and Nagin (1998) suggest this "initial deterrence decay" may reflect ambiguity aversion such that potential offenders may have greater uncertainty about the risk of apprehension shortly following a police crackdown. Even though the initial deterrent effect decays over time, Sherman (1990) notes that it takes some time for crime to return even after the crackdown is over. Sherman adopts the term "residual deterrence" to describe the lingering effect of police crackdowns on crime and goes on to suggest the police may prevent more crime through residual deterrence rather than initial deterrence as offenders are unaware of when "it is once again 'safe' to offend" (p. 10).

Police crackdowns are related to another policing strategy, hot-spots policing, that has been shown to be effective at crime prevention. Whereas crackdowns involve temporary concentrations of police resources, hot-spots policing focuses police patrols on particular geographic locations, known as crime "hot spots," where a substantial amount of crime occurs. The rationale behind this patrol strategy is based on Sherman, Gartin, & Buerger's (1989) finding that just 3% of addresses in Minneapolis accounted for 50% of all calls to the police. Sherman & Weisburd (1995) first tested this strategy in a randomized experiment which doubled police patrols at "hot spots." Total crime calls in "hot spots" receiving extra police patrols decreased between 6% and 13%.

Braga and colleagues (2012) conducted a systematic review of 25 hot-spot policing studies and concluded that concentrating police resources in high-crime areas can be effective in reducing crime. Twenty of the 25 tests indicated that hot spots which received increased police patrols experienced greater reductions in crime compared to hot spots that received usual police attention. This patrol strategy, however, allows for the possibility that crime will be displaced to other areas. Even though there is limited evidence for crime displacement in studies of hot-spots policing, any displacement that may result from this strategy is still consistent with deterrence, as offenders are avoiding those areas in which they perceive a heightened risk of apprehension.

Problem-oriented policing (POP) is another policing strategy that has been shown to prevent crime. Problem-oriented policing focuses police resources on the specific problems that contribute to crime. Whereas the policing strategies discussed thus far rely primarily on traditional police functions such as patrol and arrest, problem-oriented policing does not solely rely on traditional police powers. Instead, police who adopt a POP strategy may try a variety of approaches to combat crime problems such as working with landlords on shutting down abandoned properties. Since problem-oriented policing may involve a variety of approaches to address situations conducive to crime, any crime prevention that is a result of such strategies may not be entirely due to the deterrent effect of police.

A subset of problem-oriented policing strategies termed "focused deterrence" or "pulling levers" strategies appear to be particularly effective at deterring crime. This strategy was first developed as part of Boston's Operation Ceasefire, which was law enforcement's response to the increasing problem of youth gun violence in the early 1990s (Kennedy *et al.*, 2001). Operation Ceasefire involved a working group of local, state, and federal law enforcement agencies that adopted a problem-oriented approach to youth violence. Their response to the problem of youth gun violence involved two strategies, both of which are based on deterrence. The first strategy targeted enforcement efforts towards those supplying weapons to youth gangs. The second strategy targeted youth gang members themselves. Youth gang members were assembled into community forums and notified that any further violence would result in the working group "pulling every lever" possible to punish the responsible gang. The purpose of these notification meetings was to communicate a strong message of deterrence by promising punishment will be certain, severe, and swift for those who disregard their message. The credibility of this message was enhanced by providing an example of a gang that disregarded their message and the actions that law enforcement proceeded to take against them. These notification meetings were also attended by community members who spoke about the effect of the violence on their neighborhood and representatives of social service agencies who offered to provide services.

An evaluation of Operation Ceasefire suggested it produced a statistically significant reduction in youth homicides, gun assaults and "shots fired" calls for service (Kennedy *et al.*, 2001). The success of Operation Ceasefire led other cities to adopt this focused deterrence strategy to combat youth violence and open-air drug markets. Braga & Weisburd (2012) reviewed 11 evaluations of focused deterrence strategies and find this strategy is associated with a statistically significant, moderate reduction in crime. It is important to note, however, that the strongest deterrent effects were observed in those evaluations that employed the weakest research designs.

While "focused-deterrence" strategies emphasize deterrence, it is also important to note that these strategies usually consist of multiple components which may contribute to their effectiveness. For instance, the involvement of community members in notification meetings and other elements of this strategy often serve to increase police legitimacy. It is possible that at least part of the "success" of these interventions is due to this increased legitimacy rather than creating a credible threat of deterrence. Although one study has found that the offender-notification meetings are one of the most important components of these strategies (Papachristos *et al.*, 2007), more research is needed to evaluate the effect of the various components of these strategies.

In sum, there is good evidence to suggest that both police presence and deployment strategies can effectively reduce crime, although it is not clear that this is entirely due to deterrence. Studies of police strikes provide strong evidence for an absolute deterrent effect of the police, while panel studies and natural experiments involving shocks to police presence both suggest a marginal deterrent effect as well. However, while police presence may raise the objective certainty of punishment, research has yet to establish the link between the objective risk of punishment and individuals' risk perceptions. Police strategies that focus on crime hot spots or particular crime problems have also been shown to be effective at crime prevention. The success of some of these strategies, however, may not be entirely due to deterrence since they involve multiple components that also contribute to crime prevention.

## Deterrence and Imprisonment

While deterrence research focused on perceptions of punishment likelihood through either individual-level perceptual changes or macro-level policing strategies, Becker's (1968) economic model of crime allows for deterrence to also operate through an increased severity in punishment. This presumption of the responsiveness of offenders to harsher sanctions, which is typically thought of in terms of either custodial sanctions (instead of probation) or increased sentence length, but can also include the narrowing of the jurisdiction of the juvenile court through adult waiver mechanisms (Fagan, 2008; Feld, 1999; Zimring, 1998), is a necessary element for specific deterrence to operate as hypothesized. It is important to emphasize the distinction between general and specific deterrence here, as studies which attempt to solve a version of the generic problem of studying the effect of certain experienced sanctions on post-sanctioning recidivism using individual-level data are concerned with the latter. In this section, we consider what we know about the specific deterrent effects of harsher sanctions, including both the effect of imprisonment on reoffending and the effect of adult waiver policies, and we reiterate some arguments about the methodological difficulties in studying this problem.

### Imprisonment and reoffending

There have been several recent reviews of the literature on imprisonment and reoffending which provide an excellent overview of the state of our knowledge on this topic.[5] Rather than describe specific studies included in these reviews, here we summarize their conclusions before considering several more recent studies not included. First, Villettaz, Killias, & Zoder (2006) conducted a systematic review of the evidence on custodial versus noncustodial sanctions as part of the Campbell Collaboration. The authors reviewed 27 studies, more than half of which (14) showed no statistically significant difference in rates of reoffending between individuals receiving custodial versus noncustodial sanctions. In the rest of the comparison, the rate of reoffending was significantly lower for the noncustodial group in 11 comparisons, yet lower for the custodial group in the other two. This set of findings led the authors to conclude that there was no systematic evidence for either deterrence or for a criminogenic effect of placement.

A second series of studies was conducted by Gendreau and colleagues (Gendreau, Goggin, & Cullen, 1999; Gendreau, Goggin, & Fulton, 2000; Gendreau *et al.*, 2001). The authors here conducted meta-analyses of 117 prior studies, which accounted for 442,471 offenders in total. The net conclusion of these was that increased sanctions did not suppress future criminality and were perhaps even criminogenic. It is worth noting that others have reached similar conclusions regarding the criminogenic effect of sanctions (e.g., Andrews *et al.*, 1990; Lipsey & Cullen, 2007).[6]

Building on these two prior reviews, Nagin, Cullen, & Johnson (2009) offer perhaps the most comprehensive review of the literature on imprisonment and reoffending. Nagin *et al.* considered the included studies based on the methodology employed. First, they reviewed five studies which used random assignment, the totality of which they concluded pointed to a weak, criminogenic effect of imprisonment. Second, they considered 11 studies which employed matching designs, which were matched on relevant confounders either directly or using propensity scores. The conclusions of this set of studies were mixed, and often did not yield statistically significant estimates. Finally, Nagin *et al.* considered 31 regression-based studies, which essentially controlled for relevant confounders.[7] Though the largest set of studies, Nagin *et al.* found this set to be the most difficult from which to draw useful conclusions, due to methodological questions. The primary concern identified by the authors in this set of studies was the tendency to simply control for age, as opposed to directly match on it.[8]

Herein lies a key issue with the literature on imprisonment and reoffending – the methodological quality of the evidence. Nagin *et al.* (2009: 177) provide perhaps the most compelling commentary on our knowledge of the specific deterrent effect of imprisonment, when they note "a remarkable fact is that despite the widespread use of imprisonment across democratic nations and the enormous expansion of the prison system in the United States, rigorous investigations of the effect of incarceration on reoffending are in short supply." More specifically, the problem of selection bias is a monumental hurdle which researchers must overcome to identify effects of formal sanctions on future reoffending. We are in full agreement with the conclusion offered by Nagin *et al.* that simply controlling for possible confounders in a regression-based model is insufficient to identify the important result. Below, we consider some more recent studies that have used more rigorous methods to assess this relationship.

A common assumption used in recent studies to combat the selection problem is the so-called "selection on observables," which usually allows the researcher to employ propensity score methods to compare placement and probation cases.[9] Several recent studies not included in the Nagin *et al.* review have employed this approach. First, Snodgrass *et al.* (2011) find a flat dose–response relationship after eliminating criminal history and crime type as potential confounders in a study of Dutch adults. The authors concluded a null effect of placement on future recidivism. Conversely, Meade *et al.* (2013) matched individuals in a sample from Ohio using different sentence lengths as "treatment," observing that offenders with longer lengths of confinement had recidivated at a lower rate, though the dosage effect was not great except for the longest-serving group. This finding led them to conclude that the specific deterrent effect, if any, was limited. Finally, using a large sample of offenders from Florida, Bales & Piquero (2011) compared three methods – one regression-based and two matching – and observed a criminogenic effect of imprisonment which was robust to method specification. In summary, while the sum of the conclusions tends to be murky, these studies nonetheless provide very little evidence in support of the specific deterrent effects of imprisonment, similar to conclusions reached by Nagin *et al.* (2009).

Several other studies, mainly outside of criminology, have employed instrumental variables as a means of dealing with the selection issue. The idea behind this approach is to take advantage of exogenous variation which predicts differences in treatment (e.g., placement or sentence length) but is otherwise uncorrelated with the error term. For instance, several recent studies have been able to exploit the fact that, in some jurisdictions, defendants are assigned randomly to judges who vary in sentencing inclinations (e.g., Berube & Green, 2007; Green & Winik, 2010). Results generally tend to find little support for a relationship between sentence length and recidivism. Using data from Pennsylvania, Nagin & Snodgrass (2013) employed a judge instrumental variable to look at the effect of incarceration on recidivism rates after one, two, five and ten years. They concluded there was little evidence that incarceration was linked with recidivism. Turner (2009) and Abrams (2011) both used data from Clark County, Nevada and random assignment to attorney and heterogeneity in attorney skill as an instrument for sentence length. Turner's analysis again revealed little relationship between sentence length and recidivism. In contrast, Abrams (2011) found heterogeneous effects of sentence length on recidivism, in which individuals sentenced to 0 to 2 months were actually *more* likely to recidivate than probationers.[10]

Taken together, this body of studies find little to no evidence for a specific deterrent effect. While there is certainly variability in the methodological quality of the wide array of studies that have attempted to address this issue, and it is incumbent on the consumer of these studies to critically assess the potential value of the evidence of any one study, it is difficult to find much evidence for specific deterrence. Nagin *et al.* (2009:178) summarize this point as follows:

> a key finding of our review is that the great majority of studies point to a null or criminogenic effect of the prison experience on subsequent offending. This reading of the evidence should, at least, caution against wild claims – at times found in "get tough" rhetoric voiced in recent decades – that prisons have special powers to scare offenders straight.

## Adult waiver

Another class of "get tough" policies has been aimed at dramatically strengthening the laws governing prosecution and sentencing of juveniles (Griffin, 2003). This waiver, or transferring, of individuals from rehabilitation-oriented juvenile court system to a more punitively oriented adult court was seen as a means to better deal with juvenile crime (Feld, 1999), and the expansion of provisions which allow for transfer of juveniles has created a larger pool of juvenile offenders who are waived to adult court. While there has been a considerable amount of debate about the transfer debate regarding the proper role of the juvenile court (Bishop & Frazer, 2000; Fagan & Zimring, 2000; Feld, 1999), including adolescents' culpability and amenability to treatment (e.g., Fagan, 1995; Mulvey & Leistico, 2008; Steinberg & Scott, 2003), there is considerably less evidence regarding any specific deterrent effect of adult waiver.[11] In an earlier review of the evidence on adult waiver across multiple locations, Bishop & Frazier (2000) concluded that, when compared to individuals retained in the juvenile court system, transferred youth were more likely to "recidivate, recidivate at a higher rate, and be rearrested for more serious offenses, on average, than those retained in the juvenile system." Nonetheless, there are again important methodological considerations which must be accounted for to properly summarize the evidence.

Loughran *et al.* (2010: 477) offer the following caution as a counterpoint:

> It is debatable whether this research has fully addressed the issue of sample selection when assessing the impact of being transferred to adult court or retained in juvenile court. Several factors, including but not limited to age, offense, and number of prior petitions, may influence the likelihood that an individual's case is transferred to criminal court. Furthermore, some of these same factors associated with transfer may also be associated with higher levels of future recidivism. A comparison of offenders who do and do not get transferred to adult court thus involves a contrast of two groups that are inherently different in important, preexisting ways.

In other words, selection bias is again a particularly problematic issue in studying the specific deterrent effect of adult waiver, which is compounded by the fact that the volume of literature is relatively thin as compared to the larger body of work on imprisonment and reoffending to begin with. Furthermore, the nature of certain transfer provisions makes it difficult to properly define a good counterfactual outcome for many transferred individuals.[12]

That said, there have been several studies which have attempted to directly confront the selection issue in creative ways. Fagan, Kupchick, & Liberman (2003) took advantage of a natural experiment due to differences in state laws between New York and New Jersey governing transfer as an opportunity to study recidivism among 15- and 16–year-olds charged with robbery and burglary. The differences in the state laws could be thought of as representing exogenous variation which could perhaps reveal a treatment effect. The authors found robbery offenders who were transferred were more likely to recidivate and recidivate more quickly than retained juveniles, though they observed no such effect for burglary offenses. A few studies also utilized matching estimators to address selection. Bishop, Frazier, Lanza-Kaduce, & Winner (1996) and Winner, Lanza-Kaduce, Bishop, & Frazier (1997) matched a sample of Florida transfer cases to nontransfer cases on several factors, including number and seriousness of charges, number and seriousness of priors, age, race, and gender. Again, results revealed transferred youth tended to reoffend more quickly than their retained juveniles. Finally, Myers (2003) considered a sample of Pennsylvania transfer cases, using regression-based controls. Again, the result revealed transferred youth had higher rates of recidivism.

Along with the issue of selection bias, Loughran *et al.* (2010) introduce another important methodological consideration when considering the effects of adult waiver – heterogeneity among transferred youth, which must be considered when describing a treatment effect of waiver. This argument centers on the fact that, due to the increasing pool of youth being transferred, some of the less serious or chronic offenders may react very differently to harsher sanctions than typical offenders. Using propensity score matching on a sample of serious juvenile offenders in Arizona, Loughran *et al.* found an overall null effect of transfer on rate of re-arrest. However, in a subsequent, descriptive analysis (in which the authors were constrained to use regression instead of matching due to sample-size limitations), transferred youth who were charged with more serious person crimes displayed lower rates of re-arrest, even after controlling for relevant differences, as compared to those charged with property crimes. Using the same sample of transferred youth, Schubert *et al.* (2010) uncovered an important amount of variability within the transferred sample in both legal and certain risk-need factors, and in terms of adjustment following waiver. In other words, there may be important heterogeneity in the effect of adult waiver, which may perhaps reveal itself to yield specific deterrent effects for a subset of youth, yet could also turn out to be criminogenic for others. Overall, this issue requires more empirical attention before drawing firmer conclusions.

In summary, the literature on the treatment effect of adult transfer, while limited by important methodological issues, has not managed to uncover strong evidence of a specific deterrent effect of youth being waived. In conjunction with the parallel literature on imprisonment and deterrence, it can be argued there is at best very limited evidence for the specific deterrent effect of harsher sanctions. A final point worth emphasizing is the nature of *heterogeneity* in response to sanctions, which could imply that even despite an overall null or criminogenic effect, for a subset of individuals harsher sanctions may in fact have a specific deterrent effect. We thus advocate this topic for future research.[13]

## Conclusions

In large measure the philosophical foundation of the US criminal justice system is deterrence – the prevention or inhibition of crime through enforcement of the laws and punishment either among offenders who are punished (specific deterrence) or would-be offenders (general deterrence). Deterrence theory is essentially a social psychological theory, since punishment practices by authorities are presumed to affect offenders or would-be offenders through their perceptions of the certainty, severity, and swiftness of punishment. In this chapter we have been able to only briefly review the empirical literature with respect to three parts of deterrence, the extent to which: (1) perceived sanction threats deter, (2) the activities and policies of the police affect crime, and (3) the effect of imprisonment or enhanced sanctions through adult waiver deters crime. The perceptual deterrence literature generally (though not consistently and not strongly) shows that certain punishment is an effective deterrent to crime, as is enhanced law enforcement. A major stumbling block to making clear policy recommendations, however, is that there seems to be little relationship between what law enforcement officials do and people's perceptions of sanction threats. In addition, the literature with respect to enhanced severity via either imprisonment or increased sentence length indicates that getting tougher on crime may not do much to protect the public, and may in fact make things worse. While we know much more about how the deterrence process works and does not work than we did 40 years ago, there is much we still are in the dark about. Recent attempts within rational choice theory to incorporate insights from cognitive psychology, decision sciences, and behavioral economics provide opportunities to learn more about the inhibition of crime in order to better inform public policy.

## Notes

1  We hasten to add that Jeremy Bentham (1988), who first developed the utilitarian maxim of "the greatest good for the greatest number" as well as the notion of utility, certainly could be given co-credit for the "founding" of deterrence theory. In fact, early in his own *Essay*, Beccaria (1985: 8) gives what we today will call a "shout out" to Bentham.

2  You have to love Gibbs' (1975: 130) candor with respect to the celerity of punishment, calling it "the most debatable variable in the deterrence doctrine." Beccaria, on the other hand, deeply embedded in the Enlightenment associationist psychology of Locke, Hume and others put celerity on equal deterrence footing with the certainty and severity of punishment.

3  As argued earlier in this chapter, in traditional Beccarian deterrence theory the predicted sign would be negative – the swifter punishment is the stronger the deterrent effect should be. As Loewenstein (1987) noted, this prediction ignores the fact that delayed punishment is frequently thought to be more severe because of the emotional impact of dread (a point raised by Gibbs 1975: 131). In other words, having to wait for punishment, and not getting it over with quickly, adds to the pain. Anyone who doubts this can just recall the oft-repeated phrase from their youth spoken by mothers – "wait until your father gets home!"

4  See Paternoster (1987, 2010); Nagin (1998, 2013); Paternoster & Bachman (2012); Apel & Nagin (2011); Piquero *et al.* (2011).

5  For another review which more considers deterrence studies in the economic literature, see Chalfin & McCrary (2014).

6 One key argument which has undermined the deterrence hypothesis and simultaneously provided a plausible potential explanation for the wealth of observed criminogenic effects of imprisonment is the hypothesis that facilities can encourage offending by serving as 'schools of crime' which facilitate the transition of criminal capital. For instance, Bayer, Hjalmarsson, & Pozen (2009) argue that this increase in offending is through exposure to deviant peers, though Nguyen *et al.* (2014) find important placement effects on future illegal income generation on top of controlling for peer exposure, which they argue is due to some individuals using placement as a "signal" of their criminal commitment.

7 Nagin *et al.* also considered a small, fourth group of studies which fell into a miscellaneous category.

8 Interestingly, dealing with age as a confounder in the context of sanctioning and length-of-stay effects could potentially be thought of as what Angrist & Pischke (2008) refer to as a 'fundamentally unidentified question' (or FUQ), that is, one that cannot be answered by any experiment. Specially, given the strong relationship between age and crime, two individuals given sanctions of different lengths (say one year and two years) can either be the same age at the beginning of the sanction or at the end, but it is mathematically impossible for them to be the same age at both, thus eliminating age as a confounder. This issue is conceptually identical to the issue of studying the effect of delayed school entry that Angrist & Pischke use as an example. Though not directly addressed by Nagin *et al.* (2009) this is a key point the implications of which deterrence researchers need to consider further.

9 It is also important to note that in the case where there are unobserved confounders, propensity-score methods are ineffective at solving the selection problem, and their effectiveness should be judged accordingly. The strength of propensity-score methods rests in applications of data for which there are a large number of pretreatment confounders. For example, Loughran *et al.* (2009) were able to rule out 66 covariates, over a broad range of categories, as confounders before identifying an essentially null effect of placement on recidivism among a sample of serious juvenile offenders.

10 Like any other method used to deal with selection bias, an IV approach relies on specific identifying assumptions, not all of which are directly testable (see Bushway & Apel, 2010). Therefore the usefulness of this methodology rests on the ability of the researcher to convince readers of the validity of these assumptions. Also, an IV approach can cause unintended issues in estimation, of which users and consumers should be aware (see Bound, Jaeger, & Baker, 1995).

11 Though the studies we consider above are attempts to study the specific deterrent effects of adult waiver, several other studies have considered the general deterrent effect of changing from juvenile to adult status. Levitt (1997) argues in favor of a deterrent effect to more serious sanctioning of juveniles, based on the decline in state-level crime associated with respective state differences in the age of majority. Conversely, two other studies find no real evidence of general deterrence. Lee & McCrary (2009) use data from Florida where the expected sentence length is quite different for individuals on either side of the age of majority (18 years). The authors find little evidence of a deterrent effect on the elasticity of crime. Similarly, Hjalmarrson (2009), using data from the National Longitudinal Survey of Youth shows that perceptions of punishment regarding changes around juvenile and adult sanctioning are not accurate, and the direction of the bias is such that it understates the changes in expected severity.

12   For instance, in many jurisdictions an older juvenile with multiple priors charged with a serious offense will likely be transferred with high probability, and it is unlikely that there will exist a comparable individual who would be retained in the juvenile system to serve as a counterfactual. In such an instance, matching estimators such as ones using a propensity score will be of no help.

13   Nagin *et al.* (2009: 181) articulate a similar sentiment, when posing the following question: "If the experience of imprisonment is criminogenic at least for some sizable segment of those imprisoned, the natural question from a public policy perspective is: what would be the impact on crime rates of incrementally cutting back on the use of the prison sanction?"

# References

Abrams, D.S. (2011). Building criminal capital vs. specific deterrence: The effect of incarceration length on recidivism. Working Paper.

Andenaes, J. (1974). *Punishment and Deterrence*. Ann Arbor: University of Michigan Press.

Andrews, D.A., Zinger, I., Hoge, R.D., Bonta, J.A., Gendreau, P., & Cullen, F.T. (1990). Does correctional treatment work? A clinically relevant and psychologically informed meta-analysis. *Criminology, 28*, 369–404.

Angrist, J.D., & Pischke, J.-S. (2008). *Mostly Harmless Econometrics*. Princeton, NJ: Princeton University Press.

Apel, R., & Nagin, D.S. (2011). General deterrence: A review of recent evidence. In M. Tonry (Ed.), *The Oxford Handbook of Crime and Criminal Justice* (pp. 179–206). New York: Oxford University Press.

Bales, W.D., & Piquero, A.R. (2011). Assessing the impact of imprisonment on recidivism. *Journal of Experimental Criminology, 8*, 71–101.

Bayer, P., Hjalmarsson, R., & Pozen, D. (2009). Building criminal capital behind bars: Peer effects in juvenile corrections. *The Quarterly Journal of Economics, 124*(1), 105–147.

Bayley, D.H. (1994). *Police for the Future*. Oxford: Oxford University Press.

Beccaria, C. (1985). *On Crimes and Punishments*. New York: Macmillan.

Becker, G.S. (1968). Crime and punishment: An economic approach. *Journal of Political Economy, 76*, 169–217.

Bentham, J. (1988[1789]). *An Introduction to the Principles of Moral and Legislation*. Amherst, NY: Prometheus Books.

Berube, D., & Green, D.P. (2007). The effects of sentencing on recidivism: Results from a natural experiment. Unpublished manuscript. New Haven, CT: Yale University.

Bishop, D., & Frazier, C.E. (2000). Consequences of transfer. In J. Fagan & F. Zimring (Eds.), *The Changing Borders of Juvenile Justice: Transfer of Adolescents to the Criminal Court* (pp. 13–43). Chicago, IL: University of Chicago Press.

Bishop, D.M., Frazier, C.M., Lanza-Kaduce, L., & Winner, L. (1996). The transfer of juveniles to criminal court: Does it make a difference? *Crime & Delinquency, 42*, 171–191.

Bound, J., Jaeger, D.A., & Baker, R.M. (1995). Problems with instrumental variables estimation when the correlation between the instruments and the endogenous explanatory variable is weak. *Journal of the American Statistical Association, 90*(430), 443–450.

Braga, A., Papachristos, A., & Hureau, D. (2012). Hot spots policing effects on crime. *Campbell Systematic Reviews, 8*.

Braga, A.A., & Weisburd, D.L. (2012). The effects of focused deterrence strategies on crime: A systematic review and meta-analysis of the empirical evidence. *Journal of Research in Crime and Delinquency, 49*, 323–358.

Bushway, S.D., & Apel, R.J. (2010). Instrumental variables in criminology and criminal justice. In A.R. Piquero & D. Weisburd (Eds.), *The Handbook of Quantitative Criminology*. New York: Springer.

Chalfin, A., & McCrary, J. (2014). Criminal deterrence: A review of the research. *Journal of Economic Literature*, forthcoming; preprint available at http://eml.berkeley.edu/~jmccrary/ chalfin_mccrary2014.pdf (accessed April 21, 2015).

Cook, P. (1980). Research in criminal deterrence: Laying the groundwork for the second decade. In N. Morris & M. Tonry (Eds.), *Crime and Justice: An Annual Review of Research* (pp. 211–268). Chicago, IL: University of Chicago Press.

Di Tella, R., & Schargrodsky, E. (2004). Do police reduce crime? Estimates using the allocation of police forces after a terrorist attack. *American Economic Review, 94*, 115–133.

Donohue, J., & Ho, D.E. (2005). Does terrorism increase crime? A cautionary tale. Working paper.

Durlauf, S.N., & Nagin, D.S. (2011). Imprisonment and crime: Can both be reduced. *Crime and Public Policy, 10*, 13–54.

Eck, J.E., & Maguire, E.R. (2005). Have changes in policing reduced violent crime? In A. Blumstein & J. Wallman (Eds.), *The Crime Drop in America*. Cambridge: Cambridge University Press.

Evans, W.N., & Owens, E.G. (2007). COPS and crime. *Journal of Public Economics, 91*, 181–201.

Fagan, J. (1995). Separating the men from the boys: The comparative advantage of juvenile versus criminal court sanctions on recidivism among adolescent felony offenders. In J. Howell, B. Krisbert, J.D. Hawkins, & J. Wilson (Eds.), *In a Sourcebook: Serious, Violent, and Chronic Juvenile Offenders*. Thousand Oaks, CA: Sage.

Fagan, J. (2008). Juvenile crime and criminal justice: Resolving border disputes. *Future of Children, 18*, 81–118.

Fagan, J., Kupchick, A., & Liberman, A. (2003). Be careful what you wish for: The comparative impacts of juvenile versus criminal court sanctions on recidivism among adolescent felony offenders. Columbia Law School: Public Law and Legal Theory Working Paper Group, #03–61.

Fagan, J., & Zimring, F.E. (Eds.) (2000). *The Changing Borders of Juvenile Justice: Transfer of Adolescents to the Criminal Court*. Chicago, IL: University of Chicago Press.

Feld, B. (1999). *Bad Kids. Race and the Transformation of the Juvenile Court*. New York: Oxford University Press.

Gendreau, P., Goggin, C., & Cullen, F.T. (1999). The effects of prison sentences on recidivism. A report to the Corrections Research and Development and Aboriginal Policy Branch, Solicitor General of Canada, Ottawa.

Gendreau, P., Goggin, C., Cullen, F.T., & Andrews, D.A. (2001). The effects of community sanctions and incarceration on recidivism. In *Compendium of Effective Correctional Programs*, vol. IV. Ottawa, Ontario: Correctional Service of Canada, Solicitor General of Canada.

Gendreau, P., Goggin, C., Fulton, B. (2000). Intensive probation in probation and parole settings. In C.R. Hollin (Ed.), *Handbook of Offender Assessment and Treatment*. Chichester: Wiley.

Gibbs, J.P. (1975). *Crime, Punishment, and Deterrence*. New York: Elsevier.

Green, D.P., & Winik, D. (2010). Using random judge assignments to estimate the effects of incarceration and probation on recidivism among drug offenders. *Criminology, 48*(2), 357–387.

Griffin, P. (2003). *National Overviews. State Juvenile Justice State Profiles*. Pittsburgh, PA: National Centre for Juvenile Justice (Online).

Hjalmarsson, R. (2009). Crime and expected punishment: Changes in perceptions at the age of criminal majority. *American Law and Economics Review, 11*(1), 209–248.

Kansas City Police Department. (1977). *Response Time Analysis*. Kansas City, MO: Kansas City Police Department.

Kelling, G., Pate, A.M., Dieckman, D., & Brown, C.E. (1974). *The Kansas City Preventive Patrol Experiment: A Summary Report*. Washington, DC: The Police Foundation.

Kennedy, D.M., Braga, A.A., Piehl, A.M., & Waring, E.J. (2001). *Reducing Gun Violence: The Boston Gun Project's Operation Ceasefire*. Washington, DC: US National Institute of Justice.

Kleck, G., & Barnes, J.C. (2010). Do more police lead to more crime deterrence? *Crime and Delinquency*. DOI: 10.1177/0011128710382263.

Klick, J., & Tabarrok, A. (2005). Using terror alert levels to estimate the effect of police on crime. *Journal of Law and Economics, 46*, 267–279.

Lee, D., & McCrary, J. (2009). The deterrent effect of prison: Dynamic theory and evidence. University of California Working Paper.

Levitt, S.D. (1997). Using electoral cycles in police hiring to estimate the effect of police on crime. *American Economic Review, 87*, 270–290.

Levitt, S.D. (2002). Using electoral cycles in police hiring to estimate the effect of police on crime: Reply. *American Economic Review, 92*, 1244–1250.

Lipsey, M.W., & Cullen, F.T. (2007). The effectiveness of correctional rehabilitation: A review of systematic reviews. *Annual Review of Law and Social Science, 3*, 297–320.

Lochner, L. (2007). Individual perceptions of the criminal justice system. *American Economic Review, 97*, 444–460.

Loewenstein, G. (1987). Anticipation and the valuation of delayed consumption. *Economic Journal, 97*, 666–684.

Loughran, T., Paternoster, R., & Thomas, K. (2014). Incentivizing responses to self-report questions in perceptual deterrence studies: An investigation of the validity of deterrence theory using Bayesian truth serum. *Journal of Quantitative Criminology, 30*(4), 677–707.

Loughran, T.A., Pogarsky, G., Piquero, A.R., & Paternoster, R. (2012). Reassessing the functional form of the certainty effect in deterrence theory. *Justice Quarterly, 29*, 712–741.

Loughran, T.A., Mulvey, E.P., Schubert, C.A., Chassin, L., Steinberg, L., Piquero, A.R., *et al.* (2010). Differential effects of adult court transfer on juvenile offender recidivism. *Law and Human Behavior, 34*(6), 476–488.

Loughran, T.A., Mulvey, E.P., Schubert, C.A., Fagan, J., Piquero, A.R., & Losoya, S.H. (2009). Estimating a dose–response relationship between length of stay and future recidivism in serious juvenile offenders. *Criminology, 47*, 699–740.

Marvell, T.B., & Moody Jr., C. (1996). Specification problems, police levels, and crime rates. *Criminology, 34*, 609–646.

Matsueda, R.L., Kreager, D.A., & Huizinga, D. (2006). Deterring delinquents: A rational choice model of theft and violence. *American Sociological Review, 71*, 95–122.

McCrary, J. (2002). Using electoral cycles in police hiring to estimate the effect of police on crime: Comment. *American Economic Review, 92*, 1236–1243.

Meade, B., Steiner, B., Makarios, M., & Travis, L. (2013). Estimating a dose-response relationship between time served in prison and recidivism. *Journal of Research in Crime and Delinquency, 50*, 525–550.

Mulvey, E.P., & Leistico, A.M. (2008). Structuring professional judgments of risk and amenability in juvenile justice. *Future of Children, 2*, 35–57.

Myers, D.L. (2003). The recidivism of violent youths in juvenile and adult court: A consideration of selection bias. *Youth Violence and Juvenile Justice, 1*(1), 79–101.

Nagin, D.S. (1998). Criminal deterrence research at the outset of the twenty-first century. In M.H. Tonry (Ed.), *Crime and Justice: A Review of Research*, vol. 23. Chicago, IL: University of Chicago Press.

Nagin, D.S. (2013). Deterrence: A review of the evidence by a criminologist for economists. *Annual Review of Economics, 5*, 83–105.

Nagin, D.S., Cullen, F.T., & Lero-Jonson, C. (2009). Imprisonment and reoffending. In M.H. Tonry (Ed.), *Crime and Justice: An Annual Review of Research*, vol. 38. Chicago, IL: University of Chicago Press.

Nagin, D.S., & Pogarsky, G. (2001). Integrating celerity, impulsivity, and extralegal sanction threats into a model of general deterrence: Theory and evidence. *Criminology, 39*, 865–982.

Nagin, D.S., & Pogarsky, G. (2003). An experimental investigation of deterrence: Cheating, self-serving bias, and impulsivity. *Criminology, 41*, 167–194.

Nagin, D.S., & Snodgrass, M.G. (2013). The effect of incarceration on reoffending: Evidence from a natural experiment in Pennsylvania. *Journal of Quantitative Criminology, 29*, 601–642.

Nguyen, H., Loughran, T.A., Paternoster, R., Fagan, J., & Piquero, A.R. (2014). (Crime) School is in session: Mapping illegal earnings to juvenile institutional placement. University of Maryland Working Paper.

Papachristos, A.V., Meares, T.L., & Fagan, J. (2007). Attention felons: Evaluating project safe neighborhoods in Chicago. *Journal of Empirical Legal Studies, 4*, 223–272.

Paternoster, R. (1987). The deterrent effect of the perceived certainty and severity of punishment: A review of the evidence and issues. *Justice Quarterly, 4*, 173–218.

Paternoster, R. (2010). How much do we really know about criminal deterrence? *Journal of Criminal Law and Criminology, 10*(3), 765–823.

Paternoster, R., & Bachman, R. (2012). Perceptual Deterrence Theory. In F. Cullen & P. Wilcox (Eds.), *The Oxford Handbook of Criminological Theory*, 649–671. New York: Oxford University Press.

Piliavin, I., Gartner, R., Thornton, C., & Matsueda, R. (1986). Crime, deterrence, and rational choice. *American Sociological Review, 51*, 101–119.

Piquero, A. R., Paternoster, R., Pogarsky, G., & Loughran, T. (2011). Elaborating the individual difference component in deterrence theory. *Annual Review of Law and Social Science 7*, 335–360.

Pogarsky, G. (2002). Identifying deterrable offenders: Implications for deterrence research. *Justice Quarterly, 19*, 431–452.

Sherman, L.W. (1990). Police crackdowns: Initial and residual deterrence. In M. Tonry & N. Morris (Eds.), *Crime and Justice: A Review of Research*, vol. 12. Chicago, IL: University of Chicago Press.

Sherman, L.W. (1992). *Policing Domestic Violence: Experiments and Dilemmas*. New York: Free Press.

Schubert, C.A., Mulvey, E.P., Loughran, T.A., Fagan, J., Chassin, L., Piquero, A.R., *et al.* (2010). Predicting outcomes for transferred youth: Findings and policy implications. *Law and Human Behavior, 34*(6), 460–475.

Sherman, L.W., & Berk, R. (1984). The specific deterrent effects of arrest for domestic assault. *American Sociological Review, 49*, 261–272.

Sherman, L.W., & Eck, J.E. (2002). Policing for prevention. In L.W. Sherman, D. Farrington, & B. Welsh (Eds.), *Evidence Based Crime Prevention*. New York: Routledge.

Sherman, L.W., Gartin, P., & Buerger, M. (1989). Hot spots of predatory crime: Routine activities and the criminology of place. *Criminology, 27,* 27–55.

Sherman, L.W., & Weisburd, D. (1995). General deterrent effects of police patrol in crime "hot spots": A randomized controlled trial. *Justice Quarterly, 12,* 625–648.

Snodgrass, M.G., Blokland, A.A.J., Haviland, A., Nieuwbeerta, P., & Nagin, D.S. (2011). Does the time cause the crime? An examination of the relationship between time served and reoffending in the Netherlands. *Criminology, 49*(4), 1149–1194.

Spelman, W., & Brown, D.K. (1981). Calling the police: A replication of the citizen reporting component of the Kansas City response time analysis. Washington, DC: Police Executive Research Forum.

Stafford, M.C., & Warr, M. (1993). A reconceptualization of general and specific deterrence. *The Journal of Research in Crime and Delinquency, 30,* 123–135.

Steinberg, L., & Scott, E. (2003). Less guilty by reason of adolescence: Developmental immaturity, diminished responsibility, and the juvenile death penalty. *American Psychologist, 58,* 1009–1018.

Turner, E. (2009). Using random case assignment and heterogeneity in attorney ability to examine the relationship between sentence length and recidivism. Unpublished Dissertation, University of Pennsylvania.

Villettaz, P., Killias, M., & Zoder, I. (2006). *The Effects of Custodial vs. Non-Custodial Sentences on Re-Offending: A Systematic Review of the State of Knowledge.* Philadelphia: Campbell Collaboration Crime and Justice Group.

Weisburd, D., & Eck, J. (2004). What can police do to reduce crime, disorder, and fear? *Annals of the American Academy of Political and Social Science, 593,* 42–65.

Williams, K.R., & Hawkins, R. (1986). Perceptual research on general deterrence: A critical review. *Law and Society Review, 20,* 545–572.

Winner, L., Lanza-Kaduce, L., Bishop, D.M., & Frazier, C.E. (1997). The transfer of juveniles to criminal court: Re-examining recidivism over the long term. *Crime and Delinquency, 43,* 548–563.

Wright, B.R., Caspi, A., Moffitt, T.E., & Paternoster, R. (2004). Does the perceived risk of punishment deter criminally-prone individuals? Rational choice, self-control, and crime. *Journal of Research in Crime and Delinquency, 41,* 180–213.

Zimring, F.E. (1998). *American Youth Violence.* New York: Oxford University Press.

# 5

# Contemporary Biosocial Criminology: A Systematic Review of the Literature, 2000–2012

J.C. Barnes, Brian B. Boutwell, and Kevin M. Beaver

With few exceptions, sociological thinking dominates the field of criminology (Walsh & Ellis, 2004). Peering through the walls of the discipline's framework, one can sometimes see traces of psychology, political science, and economics staring blankly back, yet the foundation of the field is clearly built on sociological theorizing. The vague specter of other disciplines (psychology, economics, etc.) is enough to provide the criminological student with the impression that the field is inherently interdisciplinary. But students are often surprised to hear that biological research is not interwoven more into the fabric of criminological discourse.

The more that one becomes acquainted with the state of the field the more it becomes apparent that criminology is bereft of many important advances uncovered in the hard sciences (Wright *et al.*, 2008). Specifically, the hegemony of sociological viewpoints has steered the field away from developments in biology, genetics, and evolutionary psychology (Udry, 1995). Despite criminology's insulation, a strand of biologically oriented scholarship has recently gained momentum. Referred to broadly as "biosocial criminology," this nascent body of literature has revealed a genetic link to criminal behavior (Raine, 1993; Rowe, 2001), that our evolutionary past is important to understand if we wish to know the origins of aggression and risky behavior (Ellis *et al.*, 2011), and that many of the "classic" studies in the criminological literature may have been misspecified due to the omission of biological/genetic variables (Wright & Beaver, 2005).

Bringing these points to bear is the primary concern of the emerging paradigm of biosocial criminology. This body of knowledge differs from the standard sociological viewpoint in many ways. For example, genetic influences on behavior are expected by biosocial criminology and their interaction with environmental factors

*The Handbook of Criminological Theory*, First Edition. Edited by Alex R. Piquero.
© 2016 John Wiley & Sons, Inc. Published 2016 by John Wiley & Sons, Inc.

has become one of the hallmark findings of the 20th and 21st centuries. Moreover, biosocial criminology proffers many new questions about the origins of criminality and it offers insight into some of the least understood associations known to criminologists (Udry, 1995). Though biosocial criminology is often linked with "Lombrosian" criminology, contemporary scholars have, in just a few years, amassed an important base of information about the biological and genetic influences on criminality and criminal behavior. Meta-analyses and literature reviews concerning certain aspects of the biosocial paradigm have emerged in recent years (e.g., Burt, 2009; Ferguson, 2010; Moffitt, 2005; Moffitt *et al.*, 2011; Rhee & Waldman, 2002) but a review tailored to biosocial research appearing in criminology journals has not yet been presented. The current study will fill this gap in the literature by offering a systematic review of the contemporary biosocial criminology literature. Before doing so, however, it is important to gain a conceptual understanding of biosocial criminology and its research domains.

## What is Biosocial Criminology?

Biosocial criminology is best understood as a general paradigm of research that analyzes biological, environmental, and sociological factors related to criminal behavior. Biosocial criminology highlights the importance of genetic effects, biological factors such as hormone levels, neurological events, societal influences, and even family influences in the etiology of antisocial behavior. In this way, *biosocial criminology* is a blanket concept that includes at least five major domains: evolutionary criminology, biological criminology, behavior genetics, molecular genetics, and neurocriminology. Each of the five domains will be described, and the literature bearing on these domains will be discussed below. It is important to note that none of the domains are mutually exclusive. To be sure, each domain must be blended with the others to attain a full picture of the origins of antisocial behavior, but separating them in this manner will facilitate an understanding of their interrelatedness and offers an avenue by which we can summarize the extant literature.

### Evolutionary criminology

As outlined by Quinsey (2002), evolutionary explanations of criminal behavior seek the "ultimate" causes in contrast to the standard focus on "proximal" causes. Ultimate causes of behavior are those that have been shaped by evolutionary forces over the deep time of evolution while proximal causes are the specific developmental, genetic, and environmental variables that criminologists typically seek out. For these reasons, evolutionary criminology may be able to offer insight into some of the most elusive questions faced by criminologists such as "Why are males overinvolved in violence?" and "Why does risky behavior peak during adolescence?" In order to answer these questions, evolutionary criminologists apply the principles of evolution by natural selection (Darwin, 1859) to human behavior (Tooby & Cosmides, 2005).

Other prominent scholars in the area of evolutionary psychology have provided thorough and thoughtful overviews of the field (Buss, 2009). We direct the reader to these additional volumes; however, a brief conceptualization of basic ideas is offered here. Evolutionary psychology – and by extension evolutionary criminology – views humans as being the product of millions of years of selection pressures (just like every other organism on the planet). Just as selection forces "designed" complex devices like the eye and the heart, these same forces (either directly or indirectly) would have also designed the mind along with everything that the mind does (Pinker, 2002). Evolution favored aspects of the mind that were adept at solving ancestral problems, most notably survival and reproduction.

In this regard, evolutionary psychology offers an explanation for the etiology of a wide range of human phenotypes, including some of the most heinous acts committed in the natural world. Daly & Wilson (1988), for instance, argued that evolutionary criminology offered an explanation and unique understanding of most types of homicides (e.g., infanticide, patricide, etc.). The key to understanding these abhorrent acts is to know something about the motivations of human behavior by linking them with our ancient ancestor's environment and the problems faced there. In short, evolutionary criminologists seek to understand contemporary humans' behavior by looking for the origins of that behavior in our remote environmental past, the African Savannah.

Another benefit of evolutionary criminology is that it offers an explanation of why certain characteristics appear to be universal across virtually all human cultures. Research has revealed that, while cultures differ in their tolerance of violence and aggression, all human cultures recognize certain acts, like intra-group homicide, to be antisocial (Brown 1991; Pinker, 2011). Another human universal is the sex gap in violence (as well as aggression), a finding that is so consistent that it may not be entirely inappropriate to canonize it as a "law" of criminology. The sex gap has proven invariant across cultures and across time (Campbell, 2009), suggesting evolutionary criminology may have insight on the issue. The sex gap, for instance, may reflect the unique evolutionary pressures placed on both males and females, a claim bolstered all the more by the uniformity of human behavior across cultural boundaries. In short, the sex bearing the largest parental investment (females)[1] should be expected to display fewer "risky" behaviors as a way to maximize their reproductive potential – which is precisely what the evidence bears out. In summary, evolutionary criminology seeks an understanding of the "ultimate" causes of criminal behavior by referring to universal patterns of human behavior that date back to our ancestors' time on the African Savannah.

## Biological criminology

One stream of biosocial criminological research focuses on the physiological factors, not just genetic factors that may be related to antisocial behavior. Though many of the genetic effects identified by behavioral and molecular genetics research is likely to work through physiological factors, it remains important to understand these mediating mechanisms. Three primary types of biological criminology research can be identified in the extant literature. First is research into hormonal linkages to antisocial behavior. Testosterone is one hormone that has received much attention and it is hypothesized to explain a portion of the sex gap in violent behavior. In general, research has shown testosterone levels to be correlated with aggressive and dominant behavior, but the temporal/causal ordering remains unclear. Testosterone levels can vary throughout the day, and baseline averages in testosterone levels fluctuate across the life-course. As a result, it is difficult to disentangle the exact mechanisms underlying the testosterone–aggression correlation (Archer, 2006; Mazur, 2009).

A second line of biological research in criminology has focused on resting heart-rate levels (Armstrong & Boutwell, 2012; Ortiz & Raine, 2004; Raine *et al.*, 1997). Resting heart-rate levels are thought to influence autonomic arousal levels that, in turn, influence sensation-seeking behaviors. Ortiz & Raine (2004) performed a meta-analysis on the available literature and reported a robust correlation between resting heart-rate and antisocial behavior. More directly, these authors revealed a consistent correlation between resting heart-rate and sensation-seeking behaviors, suggesting it is an important correlate of antisocial, aggressive, and perhaps even criminal involvement.

Finally, the third type of biological criminology research analyzes the role of pubertal onset/development in the etiology of antisocial behavior in adolescence (e.g., Barnes & Beaver, 2010; Haynie, 2003). These studies have consistently linked biological development with behavior, indicating the importance of such variables in criminological models and theories (Moffitt, 1993). Most studies have reported that early onset of puberty is associated with a relative increase in the risk of antisocial behavior, drug use, and general problem behaviors (e.g., Haynie, 2003).

## Behavior genetics

Behavior genetic research offers scientists a way to analyze both genetic and environmental influences on human behaviors and personality traits. To do so, behavioral geneticists rely on a key piece of information; different types of sibling pairs vary in the amount of genetic material that they share. Usually, the focus is on twins, wherein monozygotic twins (MZ twins, or, better known as identical twins) share 100 percent of their DNA while dizygotic twins (DZ twins, or, better known as fraternal twins) share only 50 percent of their distinguishing DNA on average. Capitalizing on this fact of nature allows behavior geneticists to estimate the relative contribution of heritability ($h^2$), shared environmental ($c^2$) effects, and nonshared environmental ($e^2$) effects in the etiology of behavioral outcomes. The heritability component ($h^2$) measures the amount of variance in a phenotype that can be attributed to genetic differences in the sample. A heritability estimate of .75, for example, would mean that three-fourths (75%) of the variance in the measure of interest is attributable to differences in genetic material between the respondents in the sample. The environmental components (i.e., $c^2$ and $e^2$) estimate the amount of variance in the phenotype that can be attributed to environmental factors. It is important to point out the shared ($c^2$) environment captures environmental influences that make two siblings more alike. For this reason, the shared environment is often believed to tap into parenting influences. Nonshared environmental influences ($e^2$) capture environmental effects that make siblings different from one another. Nonshared environments may capture, for instance, stochastic environmental effects or events where siblings have differing subjective interpretations or perceptions of the incident (Turkheimer & Waldron, 2000). Measurement error is also captured by the nonshared environmental component.

As mentioned above, behavior geneticists often rely on sets of twin pairs to estimate the relative contribution of heritability, the shared environment, and the nonshared environment in the variance of a trait. To be sure, behavior geneticists often utilize samples of twins (Plomin *et al.*, 2012), but it is possible to include other types of respondent pairs as long as the researcher indexes the individuals' level of genetic relatedness. For instance, some scholars have analyzed samples of adoptees to determine the relative contribution of genetic and environmental influences to behavior (Raine, 1993). One classic study revealed a correlation between adoptees' criminal records and their biological parents' criminal record (Mednick *et al.*, 1984). Specifically, Mednick and colleagues (1984) found that adoptees whose biological parents had a criminal record were more likely to have a criminal record as compared to adoptees whose parents did not have a criminal record.

In general, behavior genetic studies have emerged as one of the most popular methods among biosocial criminologists and, as a result, much is now known concerning the link between genetics and criminality. Recent meta-analyses have summarized the role of genetic and environmental influences in the etiology of aggression, delinquency, criminality, and other related phenotypes (Burt, 2009; Ferguson, 2010; Rhee & Waldman, 2002). These meta-analyses suggested that antisocial behavior is around 50 percent heritable, with the remaining variance being attributable primarily to nonshared environmental factors.

## Molecular genetics

Around the turn of the 21st century, genomic sciences took a huge leap forward when the human genome was successfully mapped. The mapping of the human genome was a harbinger for significant scientific advances on the horizon. Criminologists who are interested in unpacking the genetic influences on antisocial behavior have begun to rely on molecular genetics research methods to inform their studies (Beaver, 2009; Carey, 2003). To be brief, molecular genetics research involves identifying specific genes that may be associated with antisocial behavior. In order to comprehend how this might be possible, it is important to understand exactly what a gene is. Inside the nucleus of every cell in the human body (with the exception of red blood cells) is a set of 23 chromosomes (two each, 46 total). Wound around each chromosome is deoxyribonucleic acid, otherwise known as DNA. (Note that this is an oversimplification. See Snustad & Simmons (2012) for more detail.) DNA has a helical structure (think of a ladder that has been twisted in opposite directions on each end) and is made up of a sugar phosphate backbone (the sides of the ladder) and four nucleic acid base pairs (the rungs of the ladder). The base pairs are referred to as A, T, C, and G – the genetic alphabet – and can be written like so:

AATCGTTTC<u>GTGACGTAAGAT</u>TACGCCTCCT

The string of letters above might represent a portion of DNA. Imagine that the underlined set of contiguous letters worked together to perform a function in the human body. If this were the case, we could call this string of letters (GTGACGTAAGAT) a gene. Scientists estimate that humans carry around 23,000 genes. Interestingly, however, most humans carry the exact same genetic sequence for the large majority of genes. Indeed, only a fraction of the human genome is believed to differ from person to person – referred to as "distinguishing DNA" or "genetic polymorphisms." In large part, it is this portion of the human genome that molecular geneticists focus on when they are interested in explaining differences from one person to the next.

Recognizing these points, a body of criminological evidence has begun to accumulate showing a link between certain genetic polymorphisms and antisocial behaviors. Genetic polymorphisms have been linked to well-known predictors of antisocial behaviors such as ADHD (Faraone *et al.*, 2001) and gang membership (Beaver, DeLisi, Vaughn, & Barnes, 2010). Perhaps more important, molecular genetics research has demonstrated the importance of understanding the synergistic relationship between environmental stimuli and genetic influences on behavior. Referred to as gene-by-environment interaction (G×E), research has shown that certain genetic effects are more likely to manifest when combined with environmental risk factors like growing up in an adverse rearing environment (Caspi *et al.*, 2002). In other words, changes in the environment can alter the effects of genetic factors.

## Neurocriminology

Criminologists are beginning to recognize the importance of neurological mechanisms in the etiology of human behavior (Moffitt *et al.*, 2011). Of particular importance is that many of the influences discussed in this review (i.e., genes, hormones) must impact behavior *via* their impact on the brain (Raine, 2008). The brain is the epicenter for all human behavior and emotions. Neuroscience research has clearly demonstrated that certain regions of the brain appear to be critically important for understanding the etiology of antisocial behavior (Raine *et al.*, 2003; Yang *et al.*, 2005). As Raine (2008) explained, it is likely that most of the evolutionary, genetic, and biological risk factors that have been linked to antisocial behavior are mediated by the brain such that a gene that impacts antisocial behavior must manifest its impact on either the structure or the functioning of the brain.

Though neurocriminology provides important insight into the etiology of human behavior, most of the relevant literature appears in journals outside the boundaries of the criminological discipline and, therefore, were not captured by our literature search (see below). It is worth noting, however, an important line of criminological research has examined the link between direct measures of neurological functioning and criminality (Gilligan & Lennings, 2011; Mednick *et al.*, 1981). Many scholars have analyzed the role of indicators of neuropsychological deficits (Piquero, 2001; Moffitt, 1990) such as levels of self-control (Muraven *et al.*, 2006; Pratt & Cullen, 2000), birth complications (Beaver, Vaughn, DeLisi, & Higgins, 2010c), history of traumatic brain injury (Farrer *et al.*, 2012), and serious mental illness (Swartz & Lurigio, 2007) in the prediction of antisocial behaviors. We omit these studies from the current review for one primary reason: the degree to which criminological measures of neuropsychological deficits overlap with neurocriminological concepts is unclear at this point (but see Martens (2002) and Walsh & Bolen (2012) for a cogent review and conceptual discussion). Including neurocriminology in the present review would have forced many arbitrary decisions concerning which studies to include and which studies to exclude. Rather than risk potential bias in the review findings, we opted to omit this domain from the analysis presented below.

## The current focus

Contemporary biosocial criminology appreciates the complex etiology of antisocial behavior and, as a result, recognizes that such behavioral outcomes are unlikely to be the result of one influential factor. Instead, it is likely that a combination of genetic effects, biological influences, neurological events, and even environmental triggers are implicated in the origins of antisocial behavior. Further, evolutionary criminology suggests that these influences are likely to be rooted in our deep evolutionary history, probably dating back to at least our early human ancestors. Though biosocial criminology has been around for decades – perhaps dating back to the 1800s with Lombroso – it has only recently begun to emerge as a viable strand of criminological thought. As such, the purpose of this paper is to review recent biosocial criminology research appearing in criminology journal outlets. As will be described below, we performed a systematic literature search for any paper bearing on the biosocial criminology paradigm that has been published in a criminology journal since the turn of the 21st century. The work retrieved by this literature search touched on four of the five biosocial criminology domains: biological criminology, evolutionary criminology, behavior genetics, and molecular genetics. Recall that neurocriminology was omitted from the analysis due to the small number of articles that have been published in criminology journals.

# Literature Search Process and Inclusion Criteria

The literature search was conducted using the Web of Science (WOS) search engine on December 19, 2012. The WOS search engine was accessed and the following search criteria were entered into an "Advanced Search": "TI = (biosocial OR gene* OR evolution* OR biolog*) AND SU = Criminology & Penology." Specifically, we searched WOS for any article published in a journal included in the "Criminology & Penology" subject category that was written in English and used the term "biosocial," "gene*," "evolution*," or "biolog*" in its title. Note that several of the search terms included a wild card character (i.e., *). This allowed for the inclusion of any article that included the root term (e.g., "gene") but also included a suffix on that term. For instance, by including the wild card on the search term, gene, the search engine gathered any study that used the word "gene" as well as any study that included the word "genetic". The WOS search was restricted to papers published between January 1, 2000 and 12/1/2012. As noted above, our focus was on contemporary biosocial criminology research. We recognize that biosocial research appeared in criminology journals prior to the year 2000 and we have made reference to many of these studies in the introduction to this analysis. Note, however, that the goal of the present study was to "take stock" of recent biosocial criminology analyses. As such, we limited the search to papers published since 2000.

The WOS search netted a total of 314 articles. Because of the use of the wild cards, however, not all 314 papers were expected to meet our inclusion criteria. Specifically, each of the 314 articles was manually inspected to identify those that were appropriate for the analysis. Two primary inclusion criteria were implemented. First, it was necessary to determine which of the 314 articles presented a biosocial analysis. Due to the inclusion of the wild card (*) on the term "gene," a large number of studies were identified because they used the term "general" in the title. This was expected, but meant that we ended up with a large number of studies that were inappropriate for the analysis. For instance, a significant portion of the article pool included studies testing Agnew's (1992) general strain theory or those testing Gottfredson & Hirschi's (1990) *General Theory of Crime*. Thus, it was necessary to identify these articles and remove them from the pool of eligible papers. The second inclusion criterion was that only articles presenting a new empirical investigation were included. Although none of the 314 papers were qualitative studies (but see generally, Halsey & Deegan, 2012), a significant number were review papers, discussion pieces, or purely theoretical considerations of a biosocial concept or the integration of biosocial criminology with sociological criminology. These types of articles were removed from the analytic frame, though many have been cited in the introduction to this chapter. Implementation of the inclusion criteria trimmed the usable number of studies to a total of 41.

Before moving to the findings of the review, it is worth noting that a few papers were loosely related to the biosocial paradigm but were not included in the analysis because they did not directly test a biosocial hypothesis. For instance, several studies were gleaned that analyzed the intergenerational transmission of crime/ delinquency in families (Bijleveld & Wijkman, 2009; Kim *et al.*, 2009; Novero *et al.*,

2011; Ramakers *et al.*, 2011; Smith *et al.*, 2011). These studies are acknowledged here because the intergenerational transmission of crime is an important issue and the predictions made by biosocial criminology are clear: genetic inheritance explains a portion of the intergenerational transmission of behavior. Each study reported evidence to support the notion that crime "runs in families" but it is unclear from the available information whether the cross-generation correlation in criminal status is the result of inherited genetic factors, socialization factors, or some combination of both (though see Bijleveld & Wijkman, 2009 for a consideration of these points).

# Findings

Presented below is a summary of the biosocial criminology research that has been published in a criminology journal outlet since 2000. All relevant research studies are summarized according to the biosocial criminology domain to which they correspond. Recall that neurocriminology was omitted from the analysis due to the small number of articles that have been published in criminology journals.

## Evolutionary criminology findings

Several evolutionary criminological studies were identified ($n = 11$), but only two offered an empirical test of evolutionary hypotheses (Michalski *et al.*, 2007; Zwirs *et al.*, 2012).[2] Michalski and colleagues, working from an evolutionary perspective, analyzed siblicides (the killing of one's sibling[s]) in Chicago between 1870 and 1930. Based on evolutionary theory, the authors developed two hypotheses. First, they hypothesized that siblicides where the victim was a sibling-in-law would be more likely to be perpetrated by beating as compared to siblicides where the victim was a full sibling. The second hypothesis was that siblicides where the victim was a full sibling would be more likely to result from accidental circumstances than siblicides where the victim was a sibling-in-law. The authors found evidence to support both hypotheses by showing that beatings were more prevalent when the victim was a sibling-in-law and that accidental homicide was more prevalent when the victim was a full sibling. Statistical tests indicated that only the latter (full siblings more likely to die as the result of an accident) was statistically significant.

Zwirs and colleagues (2012) analyzed the phenotypic correlation between males and females in a marital, cohabiting, or dating relationship; a phenomenon referred to as "assortative mating" by evolutionary criminologists. To be brief, evolutionary criminology suggests individuals will prefer to mate with others who are like themselves, but of the opposite sex. Zwirs *et al.* (2012) reported evidence to support this notion by showing that couples correlated positively for many measures of antisocial behavior such as property crime, violence, and arrest records. Evidence for sorting based on shared environments rather than on behavior did emerge, however. Specifically, partner similarity for violent behavior was reduced when demographic factors were controlled.

## Biological criminology findings

As noted in the introduction, a body of research has explored the role of biological functioning (broadly defined) in the etiology of antisocial behavior. The analytic review uncovered several studies that can be classified as informing the biological criminology domain. Maletzky & Field (2003) reviewed the literature on hormonal treatment and sexual offending recidivism and performed an analysis on a pilot study that used hormonal treatment on sex offenders. The findings reported by these authors were promising in terms of the efficacy of hormonal treatment programs. Another study identified in the analysis had bearing on the correlation between resting heart-rate and criminality (Armstrong & Boutwell, 2012). Armstrong & Boutwell (2012) reported that college students who had a low resting heart-rate were less likely to be deterred from antisocial behavior as compared to those without a low resting heart-rate. In short, individuals with low resting heart-rate may be less deterrable from offending.

Other biological criminology studies analyzed the impact of environmental pathogens such as exposure to cigarette smoke (post-natal) and verbal IQ. Beaver and colleagues (2010c) reported a negative association between exposure to cigarette smoke and verbal IQ such that respondents exposed to cigarette smoke scored lower on the verbal IQ task. Beaver *et al.* (2010c) also reported a correlation between length of breastfeeding and verbal IQ. Respondents who were breastfeed longer performed better on the verbal IQ test. In a related analysis, Ratchford & Beaver (2009) reported that respondents who experienced birth complications and those of lower birth weight had reduced verbal IQ scores as compared to respondents who did not experience birth complications or those of higher birth weight.

Three studies integrated a biological focus into Agnew's (1992) general strain theory. First, Jackson (2012) reported that the effect of strain on delinquency may be contingent upon pubertal development such that youth who experience early puberty may be more affected by strain than youth who have not yet experienced puberty. The second study, conducted by Stogner & Gibson (2010), reported a link between physical health strains and non-violent offending frequency. Specifically, respondents who experienced greater physical strains reported a greater frequency of non-violent offending. Third, Schroeder *et al.* (2011) similarly found that respondents who reported poor physical health (or who experienced reductions in physical health) were more likely to onset in offending (or continue offending) as compared to those who did not experience poor health (or reductions in health).

## Behavior genetic findings

As can be seen in Table 5.1, the total number of behavior genetic studies is greater than any other type of biosocial criminology research domain. Indeed, 19 of the 41 studies included in the analysis were behavior genetic analyses. Rather than identify studies one-by-one, a general summary of the overall findings is offered here.

**Table 5.1**  Summary of Biosocial Criminology Research, 2000–2012

| Author(s) | Year | Data | Analysis Type | Primary Finding(s) |
|---|---|---|---|---|
| Michalski et al. | 2007 | Chicago | Evolutionary Criminology | Cause of siblicide varies according to sibling relatedness. Victims who are sibling-in-law are more likely to be beaten. Victims who are full siblings are more likely to die from an accident. |
| Zwirs et al. | 2012 | Gen. R | Evolutionary Criminology | Romantic partners correlate for many types of antisocial behavior. For most behaviors, the correlation was unaffected by controlling for demographic factors, suggesting partners select others who display similar levels of antisocial behavior. |
| Armstrong & Boutwell | 2012 | Students | Biological Criminology | Students with low resting heart-rate were less likely to be deterred from antisocial behavior. |
| Beaver et al. | 2010(c) | Add Health | Biological Criminology | Postnatal exposure to smoke and duration of breastfeeding predict verbal IQ in adolescence. |
| Jackson | 2012 | Add Health | Biological Criminology | The effect of strain on delinquency is moderated by the respondent's level of pubertal development. Those who experience early puberty are more sensitive to strains. |
| Maletzky & Field | 2003 | Oregon | Biological Criminology | Pilot study on hormonal treatment for sex offenders indicates promising outlook for reducing recidivism. |
| Ratchford & Beaver | 2009 | Add Health | Biological Criminology | Birth complications and low birth-weight predict verbal IQ in adolescence and may indirectly influence self-control and delinquency via verbal IQ. |
| Schroeder et al. | 2011 | WCF | Biological Criminology | Poor physical health predicts offending onset or escalations in offending patterns and is mediated by depression and anxiety. |
| Stogner & Gibson | 2010 | Add Health | Biological Criminology | Health strains increase involvement in nonviolent delinquency. |

*(Continued)*

**Table 5.1** *(Continued)*

| Author(s) | Year | Data | Analysis Type | Primary Finding(s) |
|---|---|---|---|---|
| Barnes & Beaver | 2012 | Add Health | Behavior Genetic | Moderate-to-large genetic influence on the overlap between victimization experiences and delinquency involvement. |
| Barnes et al. | 2012 | Add Health | Behavior Genetic | Small-to-moderate genetic influence on gang membership and victimization experiences from adolescence to adulthood. |
| Barnes et al. | 2011 | Add Health | Behavior Genetic | Moderate-to-large genetic influence on *life-course-persistent* (LCP) offending. Moderate genetic influence on abstaining. Small-to-moderate genetic influence on adolescence-limited (AL) offending. |
| Barnes & Boutwell | 2012 | Add Health | Behavior Genetic | Moderate genetic influence on delinquency in adolescence and criminality in adulthood. Large genetic influence on stability of criminal behavior over time. Environmental factors accounted for change. |
| Beaver | 2011 | Add Health | Behavior Genetic | Small-to-large genetic influences on perceptions of parenting (attachment, involvement, disengagement, and negativity). |
| Beaver et al. | 2008 | Add Health | Behavior Genetic | Moderate-to-large genetic influence on measures of self-control across two waves. Genetic influences accounted for large portion of stability in self-control over time. |
| Beaver et al. | 2009(a) | Add Health | Behavior Genetic | Moderate-to-large genetic influences on victimization experiences across two time periods. Genetic factors explained much of the stability in victimization over time. |
| Beaver et al. | 2009(c) | Add Health | Behavior Genetic | Moderate-to-large genetic influences on levels of self-control and delinquent peer affiliation. Few parenting factors operated as nonshared environmental influences on self-control or delinquent peer affiliation. |

| Author | Year | Data | Type | Findings |
|---|---|---|---|---|
| Beaver et al. | 2010(b) | Add Health | Behavior Genetic | Moderate-to-large portions of the covariance between self-control and parenting was due to shared genetic influences. The remaining covariance was due to nonshared environmental factors, suggesting child-driven effects are important. |
| Beaver et al. | 2011(a) | Add Health | Behavior Genetic | Moderate genetic influences on psychopathy score. Genetic risk for psychopathy predicts parental responses to individual. |
| Beaver et al. | 2011(b) | Add Health | Behavior Genetic | Large portion of the variance in delinquent peer association attributed to genetic factors. More than half of the stability in delinquent peer affiliation over time attributed to genetic influences. |
| Beaver et al. | 2011(d) | Add Health | Behavior Genetic | Male adoptees who had a biological father who was criminal scored high on a measure of psychopathy compared to other males. |
| Boisvert et al. | 2012 | Add Health | Behavior Genetic | Moderate-to-large genetic influences on self-control and delinquency/criminality individually. Genetic overlap explained much of the correlation between self-control and delinquency/criminality. |
| Larsson et al. | 2008 | TEDS | Behavior Genetic | Substantial genetic influence on callous-unemotional traits. Substantial genetic influence on antisocial behavior. Nonshared environment (and error) also important. |
| McCartan | 2007 | NLSY | Behavior Genetic | Moderate genetic influence on delinquency. Genetic factors interact with environment. |
| Rodgers et al. | 2001 | NLSY | Behavior Genetic | Moderate genetic influence on delinquency. Nonshared environment (and error) also important. |

(Continued)

**Table 5.1** (Continued)

| Author(s) | Year | Data | Analysis Type | Primary Finding(s) |
|---|---|---|---|---|
| Vaske et al. | 2012 | Add Health | Behavior Genetic | Moderate genetic influence on criminal behavior and violent victimization individually. Small-to-moderate genetic influence on correlation between criminal behavior and violent victimization. |
| Westerlund et al. | 2010 | Finland | Behavior Genetic | Moderate genetic influences on sociosexual behavior, sociosexual attitudes, and sexual coercion. Genetic factors common to each measure explained a portion of their correlation. |
| Wright & Beaver | 2005 | ECLS-K | Behavior Genetic | After accounting for genetic influences on self-control, parenting effects had weak and inconsistent effects. |
| Beaver | 2008 | Add Health | Molecular Genetic | A genetic risk index (including *DRD2*, *DRD4*, and *DAT1*) interacts with childhood exposure to abuse to predict violent delinquency for males. |
| Beaver et al. | 2007 | Add Health | Molecular Genetic | Variants of the *DRD2* gene interact with delinquent peers to predict victimization for White males. |
| Beaver et al. | 2010(a) | Add Health | Molecular Genetic | Variants of the *MAOA* gene interact with neuropsychological deficits to predict delinquency and self-control for White males. |
| Beaver et al. | 2009(b) | Add Health | Molecular Genetic | Variants of the *5HTT* gene interact with delinquent peers to predict self-control in adolescence and adulthood. |
| Beaver et al. | 2011(c) | Add Health | Molecular Genetic | Variants of the *DRD2* gene, the *DAT1* gene, and the *5HTT* gene predict victimization experiences (resiliency to victimization). |
| Beaver et al. | 2012 | Add Health | Molecular Genetic | Variants of the *DRD2* gene and the *DRD4* gene interact with neighborhood disadvantage to predict victimization (*DRD4*), association with delinquent peers (*DRD2*), and violent delinquency (*DRD2* & *DRD4*) for males. |

| | Year | | | |
|---|---|---|---|---|
| DeLisi et al. | 2009 | Add Health | Molecular Genetic | Variants of the *DRD2* gene interact with criminal father to predict serious delinquency, violent delinquency, and number of police contacts. |
| Schwartz & Beaver | 2011 | Add Health | Molecular Genetic | Variants of the *MAOA* gene interact with perceived prejudice to predict arrest for males. |
| Simons et al. | 2012 | FACHS | Molecular Genetic | Variants of the *5HTT* gene, the *DRD4* gene, and the *MAOA* gene, interact with hostile/demoralizing environment to predict aggression and adoption of street code. |
| Vaske et al. | 2011a | Add Health | Molecular Genetic | Variants of the *DRD2* gene predict victimization among self-reported offenders. |
| Vaughn et al. | 2009 | Add Health | Molecular Genetic | Variants of the *DAT1* gene predict neurocognitive skills and delinquent peers. Variants of the *DRD2* gene predict neurocognitive skills and maternal withdrawal. |
| Wright et al. | 2012 | Add Health | Molecular Genetic | Variants of the *DRD4* gene and the *DAT1* gene interact with maternal negativity to predict levels of self-control. |
| Yun et al. | 2011 | Add Health | Molecular Genetic | Variants of the *DAT1* gene predict a direct measure of peer delinquency (i.e., social network measure) for White males from high-risk families. |

In general, four key findings emerged from the extant behavior genetic research in criminology. First, measures of crime, criminality, and delinquency evince moderate-to-large genetic influences (e.g., Rodgers *et al.*, 2001). In other words, genetic factors appear to have a significant influence on variance in delinquency, criminal behavior, and measures of self-control. The environment also emerged as a salient predictor of variance. It is important to point out, however, that nonshared environmental influences were the predominant environmental factor. The second key finding to emerge was that a small-to-moderate portion of the variance in victimization experiences is due to genetic influences (e.g., Vaske *et al.*, 2012). The third key finding from behavior genetic research is that much of the overlap between key concepts in criminology (e.g., victim–offender overlap, self-control and delinquency overlap, psychopathy and negative parenting, etc.) is the result of genetic factors operating on both outcomes (e.g., Barnes & Beaver, 2012; Boisvert *et al.*, 2012). Finally, the fourth key finding to emerge from the behavior genetic research is that, after including controls for genetic influences, parenting measures tend to exhibit a null or weakened effect on levels of self-control and other similar constructs (Wright & Beaver, 2005). It is worth pointing out that all but one study (Beaver *et al.*, 2011d) used the twin method (or a variant of the twin study). Beaver and colleagues (2011d) analyzed a sample of adoptees and reported a correlation between biological father's arrest record and the child's score on a measure of psychopathy in adulthood.

## Molecular genetic findings

The final set of findings presented in Table 5.1 summarizes the biosocial criminological literature that has utilized a molecular genetic analysis strategy. A total of 13 studies were identified and the key findings from each are presented in the table. To summarize briefly, each of the studies identified a correlation between a particular genetic polymorphism and some form of antisocial behavior or a correlate of offending, such as self-control. All but one study utilized molecular genetic data available in the Add Health data. The lone exception was Simons and colleagues who drew on data from the Family and Community Health Study (FACHS). A total of five genes were analyzed across the 12 studies. The genes analyzed were three dopamine receptor or transporter genes (*DRD2, DRD4,* and *DAT1*), a serotonin transporter gene (*5HTT*), and the monoamine oxidase a gene (*MAOA*). Each study provides a unique outlook on the relationship between certain genetic polymorphisms and antisocial behavior. Two points, however, offer a concise summary of the available literature. First, though these five genes make up only a fraction of the human genome, each has been shown to correlate with antisocial outcomes, indicating the importance of genotype in the etiology of human antisocial behavior. Second, many of the studies reviewed (e.g., Simons *et al.*, 2012; Wright *et al.*, 2012) revealed the complex nature of human behavior by indicating that genetic effects alone were not enough to predict antisocial outcomes. Instead, several studies reported an interaction between genotype and environmental factors. In other words, *both* genetic risk *and* environmental risk were necessary to understand the etiology of antisocial behavior (e.g., Beaver, 2008).

## Discussion

Biosocial criminology is an emerging paradigm that has much to offer to the criminological discipline (Wright & Boisvert, 2009). Some of the most exciting offerings brought by biosocial criminology are the opportunities to investigate new ideas, incorporate new research methodologies, and increase theoretical potency (Wright & Boisvert, 2009). The goal of the current study was to summarize the recent biosocial criminological literature. In doing so, we suggest that contemporary biosocial criminology includes five domains of research: evolutionary criminology, biological criminology, behavior genetics, molecular genetics, and neurocriminology. Research bearing on the first four domains was included in the review. We did not assess the neurocriminological research because these studies have almost exclusively been published in journals outside of the criminological discipline. This is not to suggest that neurocriminology is inferior to the other domains, that it is less developed, or that it is in anyway less important. To be sure, some of the most fascinating findings of the 21st century have come out of neuroscience laboratories (Moffitt *et al.*, 2011). Unfortunately, the parameters of our literature search did not capture any of these studies.

Although biosocial criminology has begun to "come of age" over the past decade, it was somewhat surprising that so few studies were capture by our literature search. Indeed, barely more than 300 articles were captured by the initial search criteria. Once a manual inclusion process was carried out, this number was whittled down to less than 50. Though this is an improvement over previous decades, where the modal value for biosocial criminology research likely hovered in the single digits, 41 studies is far fewer than the number of studies testing mainstream criminological theories (i.e., the majority of studies captured by our initial search). It should be noted that the constraints placed on our literature search undoubtedly led to certain papers being overlooked (e.g., Cauffman *et al.*, 2005). This limitation, however, is unlikely to have led to the omission of a large body of research. Because we remain optimistic about the future of biosocial criminological research, we take this opportunity to highlight the need for much more attention and research into the different domains of the paradigm.

As for current efforts, five broad findings (with a few sub-points) emerged from the systematic review:

1    Genetic influences are important to consider when analyzing the etiology of antisocial behavior.

1.a   Behavior genetic research has shown that a moderate-to-large amount of the variance in antisocial behaviors (and its antecedents) is attributable to genetic factors.

1.b       Molecular genetics research has begun to identify specific genetic polymorphisms linked to antisocial behavior (and its antecedents).

2         Though biosocial criminology has repeatedly shown genetic factors to be important in the etiology of antisocial behavior, these research studies have also highlighted the importance of the environment.

2.a       Behavior genetic research has shown the environment to explain a substantial portion of the variance in antisocial behavior. But, it is important to distinguish between shared and nonshared environments.

2.a.i     Shared environments tend to have a negligible impact on variance in antisocial behaviors.

2.a.ii    Nonshared environments appear to explain the largest portion of environmental variance in antisocial behaviors.

3         Biosocial research reveals the synergistic relationship between genes and environments. It is not nature *vs.* nurture, it is both. Genes and environments *interact* to create behavioral outcomes.

4         The brain mediates the genetic effect (or much of it) identified by behavior genetics and molecular genetics research.

4.a       In other words, criminologists must begin to familiarize themselves with biological and neuroscience research. The absence of neurocriminological research in criminology journals is telling and must be addressed by today's scholars.

5         Evolutionary forces have shaped human development over eons. Evolutionary criminology recognizes this point and proposes answers to some of the "hard questions" such as why males are over-involved in violence.

5.a       Evolution can also raise new questions that have, heretofore, been ignored/unconsidered such as "why do siblicide perpetrators use violence when killing a sibling-in-law more often than when killing a full sibling?" (Michalski *et al.*, 2007).

In light of these observations, we conclude by drawing attention to two final points. The first point concerns the current state of criminological theory. Given the momentum of the biosocial paradigm, it may seem natural for scholars to ask whether there is a "biosocial theory" or whether we need a biosocial theory. As noted in this review, several scholars have begun to integrate biosocial tenets into extant criminological theories. Agnew's (1992) general strain theory appears to be one of the most popular for this type of integration (Schroeder *et al.*, 2011; Stogner & Gibson, 2010; Walsh, 2000). Other theories ripe for integration or adoption by the biosocial paradigm are Moffitt's (1993) developmental taxonomy (Barnes *et al.*, 2011), Gottfredson & Hirschi's (1990) self-control theory (Wright & Beaver, 2005), and Akers' social learning theory (Beaver *et al.*, 2011b). Given the wealth of criminological theories available to researchers, it is our position that the biosocial paradigm does not need a "new" theory. Instead, the biosocial paradigm is likely to continue gaining momentum by integrating new insights and ideas into existing theories.

The second point that must be considered by criminologists and biosocial criminologists alike is whether biosocial criminology has any insight into treatment or policy. Some scholars have argued very persuasively that biosocial criminology can and should inform public policy and intervention efforts (Maletzky & Field, 2003; Solomon & Heide, 2005; Vaske *et al.*, 2011). Nonetheless, criminologists remain skeptical about the value of adding a biosocial component to treatment, whether it will be harmful, and whether we have enough information to implement such a policy (Barnes, 2014). While we agree that there is still much to be learned from biosocial research before any holistic biosocial policy/intervention would be possible, the current knowledge base is very clear that the integration of biosocial criminological findings into policy discussions and intervention strategies is possible, it is promising, and it is no more dangerous than standard criminological policy/intervention.

In the years to come, scholars of crime will be forced to contemplate a handful of related, and very important, questions. Specifically, will we join the ranks of scientists who dispassionately examine evidence, formulate hypotheses free of ideological constraints, and test scientific questions without fear of what the results might say? We have no answer for this question now, only the hope that moving forward, all questions – regardless of their political correctness (or lack thereof) – will be fully on the table.

## Notes

1   To say that females invest more heavily does not negate the role of fathers in a modern society. Certainly, human fathers often invest quite heavily in their children, both emotionally and via the contribution of resources (i.e., protection, food, shelter, etc.). Even so, male investment cannot fully approach that of female investment for the simple fact that females gestate the fetus for nine months, all the while expending calories to the developing embryo. Moreover, females are limited in the number of eggs they can produce in a lifetime, whereas male production of sperm remains considerable for long stretches of the life-course.

2   Again, we recognize that there is a host of evolutionary psychological research bearing on the subject of aggression and violence. For the sake of brevity in this review, we opted to focus on those studies conducted by scholars with a criminological focus.

## References

**(\*study included in analysis)**

Agnew, R. (1992). Foundation for a general strain theory of crime and delinquency. *Criminology, 30*, 47–87.

Archer, J. (2006). Testosterone and human behavior. *Neuroscience and Biobehavioral Reviews, 30*, 319–345.

*Armstrong, T.A., & Boutwell, B.B. (2012). Low resting heart rate and rational choice: Integrating biological correlates of crime in criminological theories. *Journal of Criminal Justice, 40*, 31–39.

Barnes, J.C. (2014). The impact of biosocial criminology on public policy: Where should we go from here? In M. DeLisi & K.M. Beaver (Eds.), *Criminological Theory: A Life-Course Approach*, 2nd edition (pp. 83–98). Burlington, MA: Jones and Bartlett.

Barnes, J.C., & Beaver, K.M. (2010). An empirical examination of adolescence-limited offending: A direct test of Moffitt's maturity gap thesis. *Journal of Criminal Justice, 38*(6), 1176–1185.

*Barnes, J.C., & Beaver, K.M. (2012). Extending research on the victim–offender overlap: Evidence from a genetically informative analysis. *Journal of Interpersonal Violence, 27,* 3299–3321.

*Barnes, J.C., Beaver, K.M., & Boutwell, B.B. (2011). Examining the genetic underpinnings to Moffitt's developmental taxonomy: A behavioral genetic analysis. *Criminology, 49,* 923–954.

*Barnes, J.C., & Boutwell, B.B. (2012). On the relationship of past to future involvement in crime and delinquency: A behavior genetic analysis. *Journal of Criminal Justice, 40,* 94–102.

*Barnes, J.C., Boutwell, B.B., & Fox, K.A. (2012). The effect of gang membership on victimization: A behavioral genetic explanation. *Youth Violence and Juvenile Justice, 10,* 227–244.

*Beaver, K.M. (2008). The interaction between genetic risk and childhood sexual abuse in the prediction of adolescent violent behavior. *Sexual Abuse: A Journal of Research and Treatment, 20,* 426–443.

Beaver, K.M. (2009). *Biosocial Criminology: A Primer*. Dubuque, IA: Kendall/Hunt.

*Beaver, K.M. (2011). The effects of genetics, the environment, and low self-control on perceived maternal and paternal socialization: Results from a longitudinal sample of twins. *Journal of Quantitative Criminology, 27,* 85–105.

*Beaver, K.M., Barnes, J.C., May, J.S., & Schwartz, J.A. (2011a). Psychopathic personality traits, genetic risk, and gene-environment correlations. *Criminal Justice and Behavior, 38,* 896–912.

*Beaver, K.M., Boutwell, B.B., Barnes, J.C., & Cooper, J.A. (2009a). The biosocial underpinnings to adolescent victimization: Results from a longitudinal sample of twins. *Youth Violence and Juvenile Justice, 7,* 223–238.

Beaver, K.M., DeLisi, M., Vaughn, M.G., & Barnes, J.C. (2010). Monoamine oxidase A genotype is associated with gang membership and weapon use. *Comprehensive Psychiatry, 51,* 130–134.

*Beaver, K.M., DeLisi, M., Vaughn, M.G., and Wright, J.P. (2010a). The intersection of genes and neuropsychological deficits in the prediction of adolescent delinquency and low self-control. *International Journal of Offender Therapy and Comparative Criminology, 54,* 22–42.

*Beaver, K.M., Ferguson, C.J., & Lynn-Whaley, J. (2010b). The association between parenting and levels of self-control: A genetically informative analysis. *Criminal Justice and Behavior, 37,* 1045–1065.

*Beaver, K.M., Gibson, C.L., DeLisi, M., Vaughn, M.G., & Wright, J.P. (2012). The interaction between neighborhood disadvantage and genetic factors in the prediction of antisocial outcomes. *Youth Violence and Juvenile Justice, 10,* 25–40.

*Beaver, K.M., Gibson, C.L., Turner, M.G., DeLisi, M., Vaughn, M.G., & Holand, A. (2011b). Stability of delinquent peer associations: A biosocial test of Warr's sticky-friends hypothesis. *Crime & Delinquency, 57,* 907–927.

*Beaver, K.M., Mancini, C., DeLisi, M., & Vaughn, M.G. (2011c). Resiliency to victimization: The role of genetic factors. *Journal of Interpersonal Violence, 26,* 874–898.

*Beaver, K.M., Ratchford, M., & Ferguson, C.J. (2009b). Evidence of genetic and environmental effects on the development of low self-control. *Criminal Justice and Behavior, 36,* 1158–1172.

*Beaver, K.M., Rowland, M.W., Schwartz, J.A., & Nedelec, J.L. (2011d). The genetic origins of psychopathic personality traits in adult males and females: Results from an adoption-based study. *Journal of Criminal Justice, 39,* 426–432.

*Beaver, K.M., Shutt, J.E., Boutwell, B.B., Ratchford, M., Roberts, K., & Barnes, J.C. (2009c). Genetic and environmental influences on levels of self-control and delinquent peer affiliation: Results from a longitudinal sample of adolescent twins. *Criminal Justice and Behavior, 36,* 41–60.

*Beaver, K.M., Vaughn, M.G., DeLisi, M., & Higgins, G.E. (2010c). The biosocial correlates of neuropsychological deficits: Results from the National Longitudinal Study of Adolescent Health. *International Journal of Offender Therapy and Comparative Criminology, 54,* 878–894.

*Beaver, K.M., Wright, J.P., DeLisi, M., Daigle, L.E., Swatt, M.L., & Gibson, C.L. (2007). Evidence of a gene X environment interaction in the creation of victimization: Results from a longitudinal sample of adolescents. *International Journal of Offender Therapy and Comparative Criminology, 51,* 620–645.

*Beaver, K.M., Wright, J.P., DeLisi, M., & Vaughn, M.G. (2008). Genetic influences on the stability of low self-control: Results from a longitudinal sample of twins. *Journal of Criminal Justice, 36,* 478–485.

Bijleveld, C.C.J.H., & Wijkman, M. (2009). Intergenerational continuity in convictions: A five-generation study. *Criminal Behavior and Mental Health, 19,* 142–155.

*Boisvert, D., Wright, J.P., Knopik, V., & Vaske, J. (2012). Genetic and environmental overlap between low self-control and delinquency. *Journal of Quantitative Criminology, 28,* 477–507.

Brown, D.E. (1991). *Human Universals.* New York: McGraw Hill.

Burt, S.A. (2009). Are there meaningful etiological differences within antisocial behavior: Results of a meta-analysis. *Clinical Psychology Review, 29,* 163–178.

Buss, D.M. (2009). How can evolutionary psychology successfully explain personality and individual differences? *Perspectives on Psychological Science, 4,* 359–366.

Campbell, A. (2009). Gender and crime: An evolutionary perspective. In A. Walsh & K.M. Beaver (Eds.), *Biosocial Criminology: New Directions in Theory and Research.* New York: Routledge.

Carey, G. (2003). *Human Genetics for the Social Sciences.* Thousand Oaks, CA: Sage.

Caspi, A., McClay, J., Moffitt, T.E., Mill, J., Martin, J., Craig, I.W., *et al.* (2002). Role of genotype in the cycle of violence in maltreated children. *Science, 297,* 851–854.

Cauffman, E., Steinberg, L., & Piquero, A.R. (2005). Psychological, neuropsychological, and physiological correlates of serious antisocial behavior in adolescence. *Criminology, 43,* 133–176.

Daly, M., & Wilson, M. (1988). *Homicide.* New York: Aldine.

Darwin, C. (1859). *On the Origins of Species.* London: John Murray.

*DeLisi, M., Beaver, K.M., Vaughn, M.G., & Wright, J.P. (2009). All in the family: Gene X environment interaction between *DRD2* and criminal father is associated with five antisocial phenotypes. *Criminal Justice and Behavior, 36,* 1187–1197.

Ellis, B.J., Del Giudice, M., Dishion, T.J., Figueredo, A.J., Gray, P., Griskevicius, V., *et al.* (2011). The evolutionary basis of risky adolescent behavior: Implications for science, policy, and practice. *Developmental Psychology, 48,* 598–623.

Faraone, S.V., Doyle, A.E., Mick, E., & Biederman, J. (2001). Meta-analysis of the association between the 7-repeat allele of the dopamine D4 receptor gene and attention deficit hyperactivity disorder. *American Journal of Psychiatry, 158,* 1052–1057.

Farrer, T.J., Frost, R.B., & Hedges, D.W. (2012). Prevalence of traumatic brain injury in intimate partner violence offenders compared to the general population: A meta-analysis. *Trauma, Violence, & Abuse, 13,* 77–82.

Ferguson, C.J. (2010). Genetic contributions to antisocial personality and behavior: A meta-analytic review from an evolutionary perspective. *The Journal of Social Psychology, 150,* 1–21.

Gilligan, D.G., & Lennings, C.J. (2011). An examination of the divergent general, specific, and other criminogenic risk/needs across neuropathic and psychopathic pathways to homicide. *International Journal of Offender Therapy and Comparative Criminology, 55,* 693–715.

Gottfredson, M.R., & Hirschi, T. (1990). *A General Theory of Crime.* Stanford, CA: Stanford University Press.

Halsey, M., & Deegan, S. (2012). Father and son: Two generations through prison. *Punishment & Society, 14,* 338–367.

Haynie, D.L. (2003). Contexts of risk? Explaining the link between girls' pubertal development and their delinquency involvement. *Social Forces, 82,* 355–397.

*Jackson, D.B. (2012). The role of early pubertal development in the relationship between general strain and juvenile crime. *Youth Violence and Juvenile Justice, 10,* 292–310.

Kim, H.K., Capaldi, D.M., Pears, K.C., Kerr, D.C.R., & Owens, L.D. (2009). Intergenerational transmission of internalising and externalising behaviours across three generations: Gender-specific pathways. *Criminal Behaviour and Mental Health, 19,* 125–141.

*Larsson, H., Viding, E., & Plomin, R. (2008). Callous-unemotional traits and antisocial behavior: Genetic, environmental, and early parenting characteristics. *Criminal Justice and Behavior, 35,* 197–211.

*McCartan, L.M. (2007). Inevitable, influential, or unnecessary? Exploring the utility of genetic explanation for delinquent behavior. *Journal of Criminal Justice, 35,* 219–233.

*Maletzky, B.M., & Field, G. (2003). The biological treatment of dangerous sexual offenders, a review and preliminary report of the Oregon pilot *depo-Provera* program. *Aggression and Violent Behavior, 8,* 391–412.

Martens, W.H.J. (2002). Criminality and moral dysfunctions: Neurological, biochemical, and genetic dimensions. *International Journal of Offender Therapy and Comparative Criminology, 46,* 170–182.

Mazur, A. (2009). Testosterone and violence among young men. In A. Walsh & K.M. Beaver (Eds.), *Biosocial Criminology: New Directions in Theory and Research.* New York: Routledge.

Mednick, S.A., Gabrielle, W.F., & Hutchings, B. (1984). Genetic influences in criminal convictions: Evidence from an adoption cohort. *Science, 224,* 891–894.

Mednick, S.A., Volavka, J., Gabrielli, W.F., and Itil, T.M. (1981). EEG as a predictor of antisocial behavior. *Criminology, 19,* 219–229.

*Michalski, R.L., Russell, D.P., Shackelford, T.K., & Weekes-Shackelford, V.A. (2007). Siblicide and genetic relatedness in Chicago, 1870–1930. *Homicide Studies, 11,* 231–237.

Moffitt, T.E. (1990). The neuropsychology of juvenile delinquency: A critical review. *Crime and Justice: An Annual Review of Research, 12*, 99–169.

Moffitt, T.E. (1993). Adolescence-limited and life-course persistent antisocial behavior: A developmental taxonomy. *Psychological Review, 100*, 674–701.

Moffitt, T.E. (2005). The new look of behavioral genetics in developmental psychopathology: Gene-environment interplay in antisocial behaviors. *Psychological Bulletin, 131*, 533–554.

Moffitt, T.E., Ross, S., & Raine, A. (2011). Crime and biology. In J.Q. Wilson & J. Petersilia (Eds.), *Crime and Public Policy*. New York: Oxford University Press.

Muraven, M., Pogarsky, G., & Shmueli, D. (2006). Self-control depletion and *The General Theory of Crime. Journal of Quantitative Criminology, 22*, 263–277.

Novero, C.M., Loper, A.B., & Warren, J.I. (2011). Second-generation prisoners: Adjustment patterns for inmates with a history of parental incarceration. *Criminal Justice and Behavior, 38*, 761–778.

Ortiz, J., & Raine, A. (2004). Heart rate level and antisocial behavior in children and adolescents: A meta-analysis. *Journal of the American Academy of Child and Adolescent Psychiatry, 43*, 154–162.

Pinker, S. (2002). *The Blank Slate: The Modern Denial of Human Nature*. New York: Viking.

Pinker, S. (2011). *The Better Angels of Our Nature: Why Violence has Declined*. New York: Viking.

Piquero, A.R. (2001). Testing Moffitt's neuropsychological variation hypothesis for the prediction of life-course persistent offending. *Psychology, Crime & Law, 7*, 193–215.

Plomin, R., DeFries, J.C., Knopik, V.S., & Neiderhiser, J.M. (2012). *Behavioral Genetics*, 6th edition. New York: Worth.

Pratt, T.C., & Cullen, F.T. (2000). The empirical status of Gottfredson and Hirschi's *General Theory of Crime*: A meta-analysis. *Criminology, 38*, 931–964.

Quinsey, V.L. (2002). Evolutionary theory and criminal behavior. *Legal and Criminological Psychology, 7*, 1–13.

Raine, A. (1993). *The Psychopathology of Crime: Criminal Behavior as a Clinical Disorder*. San Diego, CA: Academic Press.

Raine, A. (2008). From genes to brain to antisocial behavior. *Current Directions in Psychological Science, 17*, 323–328.

Raine, A., Lencz, T., Taylor, K., Hellige, J.B., Bihrle, S., Lacasse, L., *et al.* (2003). Corpus callosum abnormalities in psychopathic antisocial individuals. *Archives of General Psychiatry, 60*, 1134–1142.

Raine, A., Venables, P.H., & Mednick, S.A. (1997). Low resting heart rate at age 3 years predisposes to aggression at age 11 years: Evidence from the Mauritius Child Health Project. *Journal of the American Academy of Child and Adolescent Psychiatry, 36*, 1457–1464.

Ramakers, A.A.T., Bijleveld, C., & Ruiter, S. (2011). Escaping the family tradition. *British Journal of Criminology, 51*, 856–874.

*Ratchford, M., & Beaver, K.M. (2009). Neuropsychological deficits, low self-control, and delinquent involvement: Toward a biosocial explanation of delinquency. *Criminal Justice and Behavior, 36*, 147–162.

Rhee, S.H., & Waldman, I.D. (2002). Genetic and environmental influences on antisocial behavior: A meta-analysis of twin and adoption studies. *Psychological Bulletin, 128*, 490–529.

*Rodgers, J.L., Buster, M., & Rowe, D.C. (2001). Genetic and environmental influences on delinquency: DF analysis of NLSY kinship data. *Journal of Quantitative Criminology, 17,* 145–168.

Rowe, D.C. (2001). *Biology and Crime.* Los Angeles, CA: Roxbury.

*Schroeder, R.D., Hill, T.D., Haynes, S.H., & Bradley, C. (2011). Physical health and crime among low-income urban women: An application of general strain theory. *Journal of Criminal Justice, 39,* 21–29.

*Schwartz, J.A., & Beaver, K.M. (2011). Evidence of a gene X environment interaction between perceived prejudice and MAOA genotype in the prediction of criminal arrests. *Journal of Criminal Justice, 39,* 378–384.

*Simons, R.L., Lei, M.K., Stewart, E.A., Beach, S.R.H., Brody, G.H., Philibert, R.A., *et al.* (2012). Social adversity, genetic variation, street code, and aggression: A genetically informed model of violent behavior. *Youth Violence and Juvenile Justice, 10,* 3–24.

Smith, C.A., Ireland, T.O., Park, A., Elwyn, L., & Thornberry, T.P. (2011). Intergenerational continuities and discontinuities in intimate partner violence: A two-generational prospective study. *Journal of Interpersonal Violence, 26,* 3720–3752.

Snustad, P.D., & Simmons, M.J. (2012). Principles of Genetics (6th Ed.). Hoboken, NJ: Wiley.

Solomon, E.P., & Heide, K.M. (2005). The biology of trauma: Implications for treatment. *Journal of Interpersonal Violence, 20,* 51–60.

*Stogner, J., & Gibson, C.L. (2010). Healthy, wealthy, and wise: Incorporating health issues as a source of strain in Agnew's general strain theory. *Journal of Criminal Justice, 38,* 1150–1159.

Swartz, J.A., & Lurigio, A.J. (2007). Serious mental illness and arrest: The generalized mediating effect of substance use. *Crime & Delinquency, 53,* 581–604.

Tooby, J., & Cosmides, L. (2005). Conceptual foundations of evolutionary psychology. In D.M. Buss (Ed.), *The Handbook of Evolutionary Psychology.* Hoboken, NJ: Wiley.

Turkheimer, E., & Waldron, M. (2000). Nonshared environment: A theoretical, methodological, and quantitative review. *Psychological Bulletin, 126,* 78–108.

Udry, J.R. (1995). Sociology and biology: What biology do sociologists need to know? *Social Forces, 73,* 1267–1278.

*Vaske, J., Boisvert, D., & Wright, J.P. (2012). Genetic and environmental contributions to the relationship between violent victimization and criminal behavior. *Journal of Interpersonal Violence, 27,* 3213–3235.

Vaske, J., Galyean, K., & Cullen, F.T. (2011). Toward a biosocial theory of offender rehabilitation: Why does cognitive-behavioral therapy work? *Journal of Criminal Justice, 39,* 90–102.

*Vaske, J., Wright, J.P., & Beaver, K.M. (2011a). A dopamine gene (*DRD2*) distinguishes between offenders who have and have not been violently victimized. *International Journal of Offender Therapy and Comparative Criminology, 55,* 251–267.

*Vaughn, M.G., Beaver, K.M., & DeLisi, M. (2009). A general biosocial paradigm of antisocial behavior: A preliminary test in a sample of adolescents. *Youth Violence and Juvenile Justice, 7,* 279–298.

Walsh, A. (2000). Behavior genetics and anomie/strain theory. *Criminology, 38,* 1075–1108.

Walsh, A., & Bolen, J. (2012). *The Neurobiology of Criminal Behavior: Gene–Brain–Culture Interaction.* Burlington, VT: Ashgate.

Walsh, A., & Ellis, L. (2004). Ideology: Criminology's Achilles' heel? *Quarterly Journal of Ideology: A Critique of Conventional Wisdom, 27,* 1–25.

*Westerlund, M., Santtila, P., Johansson, A., Varjonen, M., Witting, K., Jern, P., *et al.* (2010). Does unrestricted sociosexual behavior have a shared genetic basis with sexual coercion? *Psychology, Crime & Law, 16*, 5–23.

*Wright, J.P., & Beaver, K.M. (2005). Do parents matter in creating self-control in their children? A genetically informed test of Gottfredson and Hirschi's theory of low self-control. *Criminology, 43*, 1169–1202.

Wright, J.P., Beaver, K.M., DeLisi, M., Vaughn, M.G., Boisvert, D., & Vaske, J. (2008). Lombroso's legacy: The miseducation of criminologists. *Journal of Criminal Justice Education, 19*, 325–338.

Wright, J.P., & Boisvert, D. (2009). What biosocial criminology offers criminology. *Criminal Justice and Behavior, 36*, 1228–1240.

*Wright, J.P., Schnupp, R., Beaver, K.M., DeLisi, M., & Vaughn, M. (2012). Genes, maternal negativity, and self-control: Evidence of a gene X environment interaction. *Youth Violence and Juvenile Justice, 10*, 245–260.

Yang, Y., Raine, A., Lencz, T., Bihrle, S., Lacasse, L., & Colletti, P. (2005). Volume reduction in prefrontal gray matter in unsuccessful criminal psychopaths. *Biological Psychiatry, 57*, 1103–1108.

*Yun, I., Cheong, J., & Walsh, A. (2011). Genetic and environmental influences on delinquent peer affiliation: From the peer network approach. *Youth Violence and Juvenile Justice, 9*, 241–258.

*Zwirs, B., Verhulst, F., Jaddoe, V., Hofman, A., Mackenbach, J., & Tiemeier, H. (2012). Partner similarity for self-reported antisocial behaviour among married, cohabiting and dating couples: The Generation R Study. *Psychology, Crime & Law, 18*, 335–349.

# 6

# A Developmental Perspective on Adolescent Risk-Taking and Criminal Behavior

Elizabeth Cauffman,* Caitlin Cavanagh, Sachiko Donley, and April Gile Thomas

## Introduction

Adolescence is a time of significant developmental change. In addition to being a period of profound biological and cognitive transformations, adolescence is also a time of numerous psychosocial and emotional changes. Recent research on adolescent development suggests that, despite their improvements in cognitive abilities, deficits in psychosocial maturity explain a great deal of the increased risk-taking and criminal behavior observed in the second decade of life. In fact, numerous advances have been made with respect to understanding the causes, correlates, and consequences of adolescent risk-taking and criminal behavior. Considering the large number of youth arrested and processed in juvenile courts each year, it is important to identify the underlying mechanisms that may account for this behavior. Sociologists, criminologists, anthropologists, economists, and others have all grappled with understanding adolescent crime and proposed various theories to explain it. While the findings from these literatures are extremely important, the focus of this chapter will be on the psychological explanations of adolescent risk-taking in general, and adolescent crime in particular.

In the sections that follow, we review three main areas. First, we explore what is known about normative adolescent development and whether criminal behavior is an abnormal event during the adolescent years or whether engagement in this type of behavior may be considered a normal manifestation of adolescence. The second section of this review focuses on the psychological mechanisms that may explain adolescent risk-taking and crime. Specifically, we review the advances in the

---

*Authors are listed alphabetically as all authors contributed equally.

*The Handbook of Criminological Theory*, First Edition. Edited by Alex R. Piquero.
© 2016 John Wiley & Sons, Inc. Published 2016 by John Wiley & Sons, Inc.

socioemotional system (making adolescents more sensitive to rewarding stimuli, particularly those of a social nature) and the cognitive control system (critical in self-regulation and impulse control) that may account for this type of behavior. Finally, we conclude our review by considering how the relations between developmental changes and criminal behavior may inform our treatment of youth in the justice system.

## Is Adolescent Crime Normal?

Criminal behavior among adolescents is common. Approximately 1.5 million adolescents are arrested each year, and between 10 and 15% of arrests nationwide are minors under the age of 18 (United States Department of Justice, 2009; 2012). According to Moffitt's developmental theory of crime (1993), most youth both begin and end their criminal careers during adolescence. These "adolescent limited" offenders are distinguished from "life course persistent" offenders, a smaller, high-risk group for whom antisocial behavior begins at a young age and persists into adulthood. Theoretical and empirical research has framed adolescent limited antisocial behavior as ephemeral and developmentally normative. Other research, however, finds that an elevated level of antisocial behavior during adolescence (even when limited to that life stage) is not normal, but instead indicative of risk (Roisman, Monahan, Campbell, Steinberg, & Cauffman, 2010). This, then, raises the question, is crime during the adolescent years normal? What are the mechanisms responsible for adolescent crime? The focus of this section is to discuss how and why elevated risk-taking (which may result in crime) takes place during adolescence.

### The age–crime curve

One of the most stable patterns in crime over the past century is the relation between age and criminal behavior. The "age–crime curve" describes an inverted U-shaped pattern in which criminal behavior increases during adolescence, peaks around age 17 or 18, and declines into adulthood (Farrington, 1986; Tremblay & Nagin, 2005) before plateauing at very low levels after the third decade of life (Farrington, Loeber, & Howell, 2012). This relation between age and crime appears to be distinct from period and cohort effects (Farrington, 1986; Farrington, Loeber, & Howell, 2012), and has been documented since the early nineteenth century (Quetelet, 1833).

Although the age–crime curve is observed across cultures, cohorts, and eras, this is certainly not to say that every individual follows the same offending trajectory. For example, early neighborhood disadvantage is associated with higher peak levels of offending, sustained for longer periods of time, relative to individuals from advantaged neighborhoods (Fabio, Tu, Loeber, & Cohen, 2011). The timing of attainment of adult milestones classically associated with crime desistence (e.g., marriage, gainful employment) may also affect the shape of an individual's age–crime curve

(Loeber & Farrington, 2014). There is evidence that the age–crime curve looks similar among girls and boys when measuring self-reported engagement in criminal activity, although girls may peak earlier when considering arrests (Liu, 2014). Despite natural individual differences, the pattern is clear: crime increases during adolescence, peaking in late adolescence and declining into early adulthood.

In order to understand this pattern, it is important to delineate, and draw parallels between crime and general risk-taking. The psychological study of adolescent crime frames criminal behavior as a specific type of general risk-taking (Steinberg, 2013). Indeed, it is well established in the psychological literature that adolescents are more likely than children or adults to take risks (Steinberg, 2008a, b), even when such risks are noncriminal in nature. In fact, the same inverted U-shaped curve is seen for a number of risk-taking behaviors, including accidental drowning, self-inflicted injury (Center for Disease Control and Prevention, 2014) and driver deaths (Naumann, Dellinger, Zaloshnja, Lawrence & Miller, 2010). Both adolescent risk-taking and adolescent crime are characterized by impulsive acts committed without thought to their consequences. Thus, the age–crime curve may be considered a specific instance of a more general age–risk curve that characterizes adolescent behavior.

Non-psychological criminogenic risk factors do not fully explain the relation between age and crime. For example, the presence of co-offenders (Stolzenberg & D'Alessio, 2008) and economic status (Shulman, Steinberg, & Piquero, 2013) have been rejected as explanations for the direct effect of age on crime. Critically, psycho-social factors (e.g., cognitive development, impulse control) may shape the age–crime curve. For example, Loeber and colleagues (2012) find that youth higher in impulsivity (particularly in the presence of low IQ) may have a higher peak in offending behavior (Loeber *et al.*, 2012). This research highlights the importance of considering normative patterns of adolescent psychosocial development when studying the relationship between age and crime.

## Why do adolescents engage in crime?

A great deal of research has focused on general risk factors for adolescent crime, such as socioeconomic factors, familial factors, and social factors (see review by Murray & Farrington, 2010); however, the present chapter is more concerned with the developmental processes that underlie adolescents' engagement in criminal behavior. What normative developmental changes can help explain why criminal behavior peaks during the adolescent years? Adolescence marks a period of dramatic growth in capacities that are relevant to engagement in crime, such as impulse control (Littlefield, Sher, & Steinley, 2010), cognitive abilities (Kuhn, 2009), and psychosocial maturity (Cauffman & Steinberg, 2000). Because these abilities are not fully developed during adolescence, adolescents are increasingly vulnerable to general risk-taking and, in the extreme, crime. Recent work suggests that maturity of these capacities may be prompted by biological changes, as the surge in pubertal hormones during adolescence is thought to initiate reorganization and development of the brain (Nelson, Leibenluft, McClure, & Pine, 2005; Blakemore, Burnett, & Dahl, 2010). In fact, modern technologies have allowed researchers to examine how the biological processes of adolescence may be responsible for some of the functional changes that are observed during this same time (Asato, Terwilliger, Woo, & Luna, 2010).

## Activation of the socio-emotional system

Pubertal hormones are thought to influence neuronal processes, leading to a reorganization of the brain during adolescence (Nelson *et al.*, 2005). Reward-related brain regions, including the ventral striatum and anterior insula, demonstrate increased activation during adolescence, resulting in a period of increased responsivity to rewards during adolescence (Van Leijenhorst *et al.*, 2010). Indeed, this is shown behaviorally, as Cauffman and colleagues (2010) found that reward-seeking behaviors during a gambling task tended to follow an inverted U-shaped trajectory across development that peaked in mid to late adolescence, leading adolescents to be more sensitive to positive or rewarding feedback than children or adults. Likewise, sensation-seeking, the seeking of novel or rewarding stimuli, has been shown to follow a curvilinear trajectory across development, increasing between the ages of 10 and 15 and declining thereafter (Steinberg *et al.*, 2008). Subsequently, adolescents are not only more sensitive to rewards, but actively seek out rewarding experiences.

Adolescents tend to find experiences involving peers to be especially rewarding (Csikszentmihalyi, Larson, & Prescott, 1977). This sensitivity to specifically social rewards, such as peer acceptance, during adolescence is consistently seen across many studies using various methodological approaches (see review by Sebastian, Viding, Williams, & Blakemore, 2010). During puberty, it is thought that gonadal hormones affect the activity of oxcytocin in socioemotional brain regions, specifically the amygdala and the nucleus accumbens (Nelson, Leibenluft, McClure, & Pine, 2005). Oxcytocin plays a crucial role in social bonding and regulates the recognition of social stimuli (Insel & Fernald, 2004). This change in the activity of oxcytocin in the socioemotional system of the brain is thought to make adolescents respond differently to social stimuli, affecting their subsequent emotional and behavioral responses.

Peers may have a particularly strong effect on adolescents' reward sensitivity. When in the presence of peers, adolescents appear to value more immediate rewards over long-term benefits (O'Brien, Albert, Chein, & Steinberg, 2011). This bias toward short-term gains while in the presence of peers may lead adolescents to discount the potential consequences of risky decisions and may explain, to some degree, adolescents' tendency to engage in risk-taking in the presence of peers. There is substantial psychological research illustrating this. For example, during a computerized driving task, adolescents who were randomly assigned to a condition of peer observation were found to take more risks than those adolescents who were assigned to perform the task alone (Gardner & Steinberg, 2005). Adult participants' risk-taking during the driving task did not significantly vary by condition however (Gardner & Steinberg, 2005). A follow-up study was conducted using fMRI to measure participants' brain activity during the same driving task under a solo condition and peer-observation condition (Chein *et al.*, 2011). The presence of peers was again found to increase risk taking among adolescents but not adults. Notably, when adolescents performed the task under peer conditions they demonstrated greater activation of brain regions related to reward during the decision-making component of the task than was seen in the solo trials; in contrast, adults' activation in these brain regions did not vary by social context (Chein *et al.*, 2011). This is in line with research that suggests that resistance to peer influence increases linearly between the ages of 14 and 18 and plateaus thereafter (Steinberg & Monahan, 2007).

We not only see the effect of peers on adolescent risk-taking in controlled laboratory and fMRI studies, but we also see it in the characteristics of adolescent-perpetrated crime. It is well established that juveniles are more likely than adult offenders to commit crimes in groups (McCord & Conway, 2005; Reiss, 1986; Reiss & Farrington, 1991). Evidence for juvenile co-offending has been consistent since soon after the founding of the juvenile justice system (e.g. Shaw & Moore, 1931). In 2008, 37.5% of the homicides committed by offenders age 14 to 17 involved multiple offenders. That same year, 27.5% of the homicides committed by 18- to 24-year-olds and only 13.7% of homicides committed by offenders over age 25 involved multiple offenders (Cooper & Smith, 2011). This relation between age and likelihood of offending in groups is also seen in studies that use self-reported measures of offending. Goldweber and colleagues (2011) asked 14- to 17-year-old, serious, male juvenile offenders to report on their offending behaviors over the course of a prospective, 3-year study. Juveniles were also asked to report if these offenses were committed alone or with others. Of the 937-participant sample 83% was categorized as "increasingly solo offenders" illustrating that with age, offenders were less likely to offend in groups and more frequently offending alone (Reiss & Farrington, 1991). As mentioned previously, from a psychological perspective, adolescent crime is considered to be a specific type of general risk-taking (Steinberg, 2013). And as such, crime statistics (from both official reports and self-reports) offer an example of how adolescents' increased risk-taking, especially in the context of peers, manifest in criminal and offending behaviors.

## Activation of the cognitive control system

Dual systems theory (Steinberg, Albert, Cauffman, Banich, Graham, & Woolard, 2008) points to a temporal gap in the development of the aforementioned socioemotional system (making adolescents more sensitive to rewarding stimuli, particularly that of a social nature) and the cognitive-control system (critical in self-regulation and impulse control). As discussed in the previous section, the affective neural system develops more rapidly, and activation of this reward system is heightened during adolescence. Meanwhile, the cognitive-control system develops more gradually (Steinberg *et al.*, 2008). Cognitive-control functions (also known as executive functions) can be broken down into three core components: inhibition (involving selectivity attention, impulse control, and behavioral inhibition), set-shifting (mental flexibility), and working memory (the ability to hold and manipulate information in one's mind) (Miyake *et al.*, 2000). Because development of the cognitive-control system and affective system occurs asynchronously, adolescents' affective system may override their still-developing cognitive-control system. As the cognitive-control system matures, however, it becomes more capable of blocking impulses from the affective system (Knoch & Fehr, 2007), leaving individuals better equipped for making good decisions in the face of emotionally distracting stimuli, such as peers. This capacity for self-regulation continues to develop beyond adolescence (Steinberg, 2010); thus, much of adolescents' engagement in crime has been attributed to their heightened proclivity for rewards during a time in which self-regulation is still immature (Steinberg, 2010).

Cognitive-control functions emerge during childhood but grow more sophisticated during adolescence and early adulthood as a result of continued brain maturation; this is particularly true for inhibitory control (Ordaz, Foran, Velanova, & Luna, 2013). Although the majority of brain growth occurs prior to adolescence, considerable refinement within the brain occurs during adolescence – particularly among regions involved in cognitive control, such as the prefrontal cortex, which are among the last to develop (Giorgio *et al.*, 2010). This refinement is evidenced by brain-imaging studies that reveal increases in white matter volume (Giedd, 2004) and density (Paus *et al.*, 1999) across adolescence, as well as decreases in grey matter (Sowell, 2001). White matter contains neural pathways connecting different regions of the brain; these paths allow for the transmission of neural impulses that are essential for cognitive, motor, and sensory functions (Paus, 2010). Increases in white matter volume that take place across adolescence are reflective of increased axonal diameter and greater thickness of the myelin sheath surrounding the axon, both of which improve transmission velocity of neural impulses and lead to faster processing (Paus, 2010). Decreases in grey matter volume are thought to reflect synaptic pruning (the systematic elimination of synapses that are not used or are less efficient; Luciana, 2013), as well as increased myelination (Paus *et al.*, 2008). Grey matter loss due to synaptic pruning may result in improved accuracy on cognitive tasks, whereas loss due to myelination may increase efficiency and reduce reaction times (Sowell, 2001). Recent research finds synaptic pruning is not complete during early adolescence, as was once thought, but rather continues well into the third decade of life (Petanjek *et al.*, 2011). Together, the changes in brain structure that occur across adolescence may facilitate improvements in many aspects of cognition, particularly executive control (Kuhn, 2006).

Adolescents' cognitive abilities largely match those of adults in situations that are nonemotional (reflective of "cold" cognitive processes; Kuhn, 2009) and they are capable of mature decision-making in such contexts (Figner, Mackinlay, Wilkening, & Weber, 2009). However, in situations that elicit "hot" cognition (contexts that evoke an affective response, such as those involving the presence of others or the potential for reward), adolescents perform more poorly than adults (Figner *et al.*, 2009). For instance, in an impulse-control task (the Go/No Go) using rewarding social cues (happy faces) and neutral cues (calm faces), adolescents showed reduced performance, compared with children and adults, in their ability to control their impulses in the presence of socially rewarding cues (Somerville, Hare, & Casey, 2011). Adolescents, relative to adults or children, demonstrated increased activation in brain regions related to reward, such as the ventral striatum, during trials requiring inhibition of responses to rewarding cues (Somerville *et al.*, 2011). This evidence is consistent with the dual systems explanation of adolescent risk-taking. Thus, while adolescents may be developmentally capable of enacting mature cognitive control, the brain systems responsible for such control may become hijacked by the presence of emotional stimuli and lead to poor cognitive control. This can become problematic in real-world situations, which tend to take place under conditions of greater arousal.

The combination of a limited cognitive-control system and an activated socioemotional system offers an explanation for heightened risk-taking during adolescence. As mentioned previously, support for an activated socioemotional system is seen in adolescents' tendency to take risks and commit crimes with their peers. Considering adolescents' heightened sensitivity to social rewards, we expect to see, and do see, that they are more likely than adults to commit crimes in groups. But what characteristics of adolescent criminal behavior support the notion of a still-developing cognitive-control system? If adolescents have more difficulty regulating their impulsivity, we should expect to see adolescents committing crimes in more impulsive ways. In other words, there should be evidence that adolescent crime is less planned and less premeditated compared to adult crime. Indeed, data support these conclusions. First, we present information about the types of crimes adolescents commit and second, we present statistics about when adolescents commit crimes.

Although juvenile arrests represent a small proportion of all arrests, adolescents represent a disproportionately large percentage of arrests for property crimes. Property crimes can generally be defined as the unlawful taking of property without the use of violence, including burglary, larceny-theft, motor vehicle theft, and arson. While juveniles represented only 11% of all arrests in 2012, they accounted for 18% of all property arrests (Snyder & Sickmund, 2006). In fact, the most common reason for arrest among juveniles was larceny-theft (a property crime that involves taking another's possessions). Whereas for adults, the most common reason for arrest was drug abuse violations. This trend in disproportionately high percentages of juvenile arrests for property crimes is not limited to most recent crime statistics data. Rather it has been consistent since the 1980s (Snyder, 1999).

Although arrested juveniles are just as likely as arrested adults to be accused of a violent crime, the time of day at which these violent crimes are committed tends to differ between adult and juvenile offenders. Violent crimes involving adult offenders increase hourly from 6 a.m. until 10 p.m. – the time when most adult-offended violence crimes take place, and then decrease until 6 a.m. About a quarter of all violent crime involving an adult offender takes place between 8 p.m. and 12 p.m. in the evening (Snyder & Sickmund, 2006). Unlike adult-perpetrated violent crimes, violent crimes involving a juvenile offender peak in the afternoon between 3 p.m. and 4 p.m., the hour that marks the end of school for many students. Interestingly, on non-school days (Saturday, Sunday, vacation days and holidays), the time pattern of juvenile-perpetrated violent crime is more similar to that of adult-perpetrated violent crimes, peaking in the evening at 8 p.m.

Both the timing and the types of crimes juveniles are involved in support the notion of juveniles' engagement in more impulsive criminal acts. When criminal opportunity presents itself, individuals with low impulse-control are more likely to be delinquent (Gottfredson & Hirschi, 1990). As evidenced by the timing of juvenile crimes, adolescents are more likely to engage in low-level property crimes when an opportunity to do so presents itself. During after-school hours, when adult supervision is largely absent, juvenile property crimes peak. If these juvenile crimes are indeed crimes of impulse and opportunity, we would then expect to see a drop in delinquency when adolescents are engaged in structured and supervised activities after school. Indeed, there is good evidence that adolescents involved in certain after-school activities are less likely to commit delinquent acts during this time (Mahoney, 2000).

In summary, adolescents' heightened proclivity toward rewarding and thrilling sensations (Van Leijenhorst *et al.*, 2010) during a time in which self-regulation and impulse control are not fully developed (Steinberg *et al.*, 2008) leave them vulnerable to engaging in risky or criminal behavior – particularly in contexts that are emotional or socially rewarding (Figner *et al.*, 2009). These functional changes are thought to be the result of structural changes in brain physiology brought about by the influx of pubertal hormones that occur within adolescence (Sisk & Zehr, 2005). The developmental changes described herein leave adolescents more likely to commit crimes that are impulsive and occur in the heat of the moment, rather than crimes that are premeditated (White *et al.*, 1994). Similarly, the social reorientation of the brain that occurs during adolescence may explain the trend seen in criminological research that indicates adolescents commit crimes more commonly in groups, whereas adults more often commit solo acts of illegal behavior.

## Adolescent desistance from crime

As adolescents transition to adulthood and their cognitive- and emotional-control systems become fully mature, we would expect to see improvements in self-regulation and a gradual ceasing of engagement in criminal behavior. Thus, one way to consider the impact of psychosocial development on crime is through a study of why and when adolescents desist from criminal behavior. The Pathways to Desistance Study was designed for the express purpose of examining the second half of the age–crime curve: the desistance tail. Pathways, a prospective longitudinal study of over 1,300 felony-level adolescent offenders, tracked desistance from crime across adolescence and into adulthood. Participant youth, serious felony-level offenders, were interviewed over 7 years (see Schubert *et al.*, 2004 for details on the study's methodology).

The Pathways study found that most youth, despite being serious offenders, do indeed desist from crime; less than 10% of the participating youth persisted in high-level offending after 7 years (Mulvey *et al.*, 2010). Indeed, the major factor that distinguished the youth who persisted from those who desisted was normative psychosocial development. Specifically, youth who persisted in offending displayed less psychosocial maturity (particularly impulse control, suppression of aggression, and future orientation), while youth who desisted displayed developmentally normative increases in these domains (Monahan, Steinberg, Cauffman, & Mulvey, 2009). In fact, the direct effects of age on crime among Pathways participant youth were eliminated when statistical models include psychological constructs, which account for nearly three-quarters of crime desistance between ages 15 and 25 (Sweeten, Piquero, & Steinberg, 2013). In sum, the desistance tail of the age–crime curve may be largely (though certainly not wholly) explained by normative developmental changes that occur across adolescence and into adulthood.

## Should Adolescents be Treated Differently for Their Crimes?

It is clear that adolescents differ from adults, both in the nature of the crimes they commit and in the mechanisms driving their criminal behavior. Yet, fundamental to our justice system is the belief that individuals who break the law warrant punishment. Should adolescents' youthful characteristics and developmental stage mitigate their culpability for their criminal behavior? Where is the line drawn between fair treatment and a just system? This section discusses how criminological and legal best practices for juvenile offenders are informed by developmental psychology. Specifically, we discuss the notion that juvenile offenders are not as culpable for their crimes as are adult offenders. We also examine differences in justice system treatment between youth and adults, and the consequences of justice system involvement (particularly when youth are held to adult standards) for youth development.

### Are juvenile offenders as culpable as adult offenders?

The juvenile justice system was developed a century ago with rehabilitation and protection as its central tenets. The adult criminal justice system, on the other hand, is designed to mete out punishment for crimes, with retribution and incapacitation as central objectives. The goals of the two systems are different by design, a clear acknowledgement that youth crime is fundamentally different from adult crime.

At the end of the twentieth century, however, the juvenile justice system began to change course. "Get tough" crime policies shifted the dialogue surrounding juvenile offending from rehabilitation to public safety and punishment (Feld, 2003; Pickett & Chiricos, 2012). Public opinion matched this sentiment, registering an interest in *both* punitive measures for youth offenders and rehabilitative programs (Bishop, 2006; Nagin, Piquero, Scott, & Steinberg, 2006; Piquero, Cullen, Unnever, Piquero, & Gordon, 2010). This resulted in a parallel shift in the court's treatment of juvenile offenders; the number of detained youth increased (Sickmund, 2004), as did the number of youth transferred to adult court (Bishop, 2000) or housed in adult facilities (Austin, Johnson, and Gregoriou, 2000), despite a clear trend of reduced youth offending overall (United States Department of Justice, 2009).

Following this shift, the issue of adolescent culpability became ambiguous. The founding wisdom of the juvenile justice system is that if youth are not as capable of mature judgment as adults, it stands to reason that they are also less culpable for their crimes. However, because "mature judgment" is not a unidimensional construct, it can be difficult to define in ways that can easily inform legal policy.

On one hand, as described above, there is a wealth of research that adolescents are able to make mature, reasoned decisions when the context is non-emotional, and when given time to ponder the decision (Steinberg, Cauffman, Woolard, Graham, & Banich, 2009). Adolescents reach this type of "cognitive maturity" in their mid-teens. Indeed, there is no evidence of a difference in the ability to understand facts about court proceedings between adults and adolescents over 16 years old, implying that competency to stand trial is attained around age 15 (Grisso *et al.*, 2003). In fact, the body of developmental research on youth's cognitive maturity was used to inform the United States Supreme Court decision in *Hodgson v. Minnesota* (1990). This decision upheld adolescents' right to terminate a pregnancy without permission from a parent, with the understanding that adolescent decision-making skills in thoughtful, reasoned situations are equal to those of adults.

However, "cognitive maturity" must be distinguished from "psychosocial maturity." Characteristics associated with psychosocial maturity (e.g., impulsivity, sensation-seeking, future orientation, susceptibility to peer influence) continue to develop into adulthood (Cauffman & Steinberg, 2000). As a result, adolescents are subject to poor judgment in the presence of peers, when decisions are highly emotional, when rewards are salient, and when the decision is rushed (Steinberg *et al.*, 2009). This knowledge formed the basis of three recent US Supreme Court decisions. *Roper v. Simmons* (2005) abolished the juvenile death penalty; regardless of the heinousness of the crime, youth under the age of majority (18 years) are not eligible for the death penalty. Similarly, in the case of *Graham v. Florida* (2010), the Supreme Court found that sentencing adolescents to life without parole for a non-homicide crime constituted cruel and unusual punishment, in violation of the 8th Amendment. In 2012, *Miller v. Alabama* extended the Graham decision by abolishing life without parole for juvenile offenders regardless of offense. Importantly, the majority arguments in *Roper*, *Graham* and *Miller* included a discussion of youth culpability: because adolescents are developmentally immature relative to adults, the court found that they are inherently less blameworthy for their crimes. Developmental psychological research indicates that juvenile and adult decision-making is fundamentally different, and the crimes that result from such decisions should be studied differently by criminologists, and treated differently by the law.

## How does the system treat juvenile offenders?

It has been established that youth warrant differential treatment by the legal system. But how are youth treated in today's justice system? The goal of the current juvenile justice system is to aid in a youth's reform through rehabilitative care and *parens patriae* (acting as a protective parent). Once in the system, the expectation is that juveniles will be treated in a developmentally appropriate manner, to aid in their rehabilitation and meet their unique needs.

*Treatment amenability*    Generally, juvenile justice officials consider youth offenders to be more amenable to treatment than adult offenders (Scott & Grisso, 1997). Within the juvenile court, the age of the offender may play a role in the court's perception that the juvenile can be rehabilitated. For example, in a survey over 70,000 juvenile court referrals, the youngest offenders were more likely to be informally processed (i.e., diverted or receive informal probation), while middle adolescents – whom the researchers argue might be perceived by justice system actors as "true" adolescents – were most likely to receive traditional juvenile court sentences, such as formal probation (Mears *et al.*, 2014).

*Adult vs. juvenile processing and waiver*    Another foundational aspect of the juvenile justice system, however, is the option to transfer a youth offender to the adult court system. Waiver to adult court may happen in cases where a juvenile's offense warrants more substantial punishment, or when juvenile court resources are no longer adequate for repeat offenders (Schubert *et al.*, 2010). Older youth with a greater history of prior offenses are more likely to be transferred than younger, less experienced youth who commit the same crime (Poulos & Orchowsky, 1994). However, waiver to adult court has psychological and criminological implications for the transferred youth. Some researchers have found that transferring youth may be counter-productive to the goal of rehabilitation. For example, a study matching youth processed in the juvenile court and the adult court found that youth who remained in juvenile court displayed a relatively lower rate of recidivism, regardless of the severity of their sentence (Fagan, 1996). Although the length of sentence received was comparable across the two courts, youth waived to criminal court had higher incarceration rates (Fagan, 1996). A similar study found that youth transferred to criminal court were not only more likely to reoffend than their juvenile court counterparts, but also more likely to reoffend sooner and more seriously (Bishop, Frazier, Lanza-Kaduce, & Winner, 1996). Other research reports no overall effect of transfer to criminal court on recidivism, but instead notes differential effects for youth with different needs and histories, implying that "one size fits all" waiver policies may not be effective (Loughran *et al.*, 2010).

Theoretically, one may assume that juveniles who are transferred to the adult court system will be treated with leniency due to their age. The research comparing the treatment of (transferred) youth and adults by the criminal justice system tells a different story, however, Kurlychek & Johnson (2010) find that those juveniles who are waived to adult court receive, on average, additional sentencing penalties (termed the "juvenile penalty") relative to matched young adult offenders. Specifically, transferred youth received sentences that are up to 75% more severe than those given to similarly situated young adult offenders. This "juvenile penalty" may be particularly marked among youth who were transferred as a result of a discretionary judicial waiver, implying that greater discretion on the part of the courts is associated with greater disparity in treatment faced by transferred youth (Kurlychek & Johnson, 2010). Perhaps the act of transferring a juvenile to the adult court system attaches a stigma to that youth that he is "unsalvageable," sending the message that punishment should be severe (Kurlychek & Johnson, 2010) – a far cry from the rehabilitative nature of treatment intended for juvenile offenders.

This stigma is also manifest in concern that youth tried as adults, but incarcerated in juvenile facilities will be a danger to the other youth in the facility who were not processed by the juvenile court. In other words, according to this logic if a youth commits an offense serious enough to be waived, the youth must be qualitatively worse than a youth who was not waived, and will be more likely to instigate victimization and institutional offending. This notion was tested directly, using a sample of youth incarcerated in a juvenile facility who had either been processed in juvenile court or adult court (Bechtold & Cauffman, 2014). Youth processed through adult court actually committed *fewer* institutional offenses than juvenile court youth, and there was no difference in victimization among the two groups (Bechtold & Cauffman, 2014). This research underscores the fact that adolescent offenders, regardless of their treatment by the juvenile justice system, are still youth. On the basis of both theoretical and applied psychological research, it is clear that the youthful status of juvenile offenders both merits and necessitates developmentally appropriate treatment by the law.

*Implications of status offenses*    One manner in which the courts treat youths differently from adults is through the enforcement of so-called status offenses. Status offenses are those in which a given behavior is considered illegal for the simple fact that the offender is a minor and for which the same offense would not be considered a crime if committed by an adult (Steinhart, 1996). As a result of the institution of status offenses, juveniles can be prosecuted for relatively minor offenses such as breaking curfew, truancy, or running away from home. Following the 1974 Juvenile Justice and Delinquency Prevention Act, courts were prohibited from placing youth in secure confinement for status offenses. However, an amendment to this act (termed the valid court order [VCO] exception) in 1980 allowed for the detention of status offenders for violations of a valid court order. Following this amendment, many states put forth new legislation that allowed for the secure detention of adjudicated status offenders (see review by Steinhart, 1996).

More than 400,000 youth were arrested in United States in 2004 for a status offense (Sickmund, 2004). In 2011, 1687 youth were committed and 499 were detained for committing a status offense (Sickmund, Sladky, Kang, & Puzzanchera,

2013). Yet, prosecuting youth for minor or status offenses may have serious long-term implications on youth development.

Status offenses that may be particularly devastating to youths' successful development involve those offenses that carry more serious consequences. For example, sexting, the "sending or posting sexually suggestive text messages and images, including nude or semi-nude photographs, via cellular telephones or over the Internet" (*Miller v. Skumanick*, 2009, p. 1), in a sense, represents a unique case of a status offense that may be more destructive than others. Sexting qualifies as a status offense in that the behavior is deemed legal when engaged in by two consenting adults, but considered a crime when engaged in by two minors (Barry, 2010). Sexting by minors is considered a violation of child pornography laws federally (although this may vary according to state laws); youths who are convicted of child pornography for their sexting behaviors face serious consequences, including potential registration as a sex offender (depending on which state the act occurred in), incarceration for a minimum of 5 years (as per 18 U.S.C. § 2252A), and a felony criminal record. These legal consequences may have far-reaching effects on other areas of an adolescent's life, as they have the potential to impact a youth's employment and earning potential (Western, 2002), educational opportunities (Sweeten, 2006), future orientation (Trommsdorff & Lamm, 1980), and psychological wellbeing (Forest *et al.*, 2000). In fact, some have argued that sexting behavior should be considered separate from child pornography, and that specific legislation be designed to address the unique situations in which sexting behavior occurs (Thomas & Cauffman, 2014). In fact, based on developmental science, it has been suggested that juveniles should be considered less culpable for sexting behavior than adults, and recommended that the punishment for minors be more developmentally appropriate (Thomas & Cauffman, 2014).

According to Moffitt's taxonomy of antisocial behavior (1993), youth who come into contact with the justice system may become "ensnared," resulting in them veering off-course from a normative developmental trajectory of desistance from antisocial behavior during the transition to adulthood. Youths who would have otherwise desisted from crime post-adolescence may become entrenched in crime and persist in antisocial behavior as adults as a result of such snares. Snares are considered to be particularly problematic due to their ability to compromise a youth's successful transition to adulthood.

One way in which system involvement can interfere with youth development is through providing exposure to negative peer influence. Youth who are committed or detained within facilities are often housed with or placed in treatment services with other delinquent youth. These situations may provide opportunities to befriend and learn from fellow inmates. This type of "peer deviancy training" has been found to lead to increased problem behavior among adolescents (Dishion, McCord, & Poulin, 1999). Remember, adolescents are particularly vulnerable to the influence of their peers (Chein *et al.*, 2011) as a result of the social orientation that develops during this time (Nelson *et al.*, 2005).

Another way in which juvenile arrest may influence youth development is through labeling the youth as a deviant, which can have severe implications for behavior. Stigma associated with status as a criminal may lead delinquent youths to increase their involvement with deviant peers, thereby leading to increased subsequent criminal behavior. Bernburg, Krohn, & Rivera (2006) empirically tested the concepts of this theory in their longitudinal study of urban adolescents. Following formal contact with the juvenile justice system, youth were found to have greater association with deviant peer networks and greater likelihood of subsequently joining a gang. Justice system involvement was associated with subsequent delinquency and this effect was mediated by involvement in delinquent peer groups (Bernburg *et al.*, 2006).

Finally, juvenile justice system involvement may negatively affect youths' academic performance and lead to an increased rate of school drop-out (Sweeten, 2006; Bernburg & Krohn, 2003). Stage–environment fit theories posit that a mismatch between an adolescent's needs and the opportunities provided in their social context may result in detriment to their development (Eccles *et al.*, 1993). In many ways, schools offer a developmentally normative experience for adolescents. When taken out of a school context and incarcerated or detained, juvenile offenders' developmental needs may not be met, resulting in long-term negative effects. Sweeten (2006) conducted a longitudinal study to examine the effects of first-time arrest and court involvement among adolescents. Justice-system contact increased the likelihood of high school dropout, independent of adolescents' delinquency.

Involvement with the justice system may interfere with the accomplishment of normative developmental milestones and indirectly lead to a continued life of crime. Enacting a domino effect of sorts, the consequences of justice-system involvement (e.g., arrest, labeling, incarceration) leave youth more likely to drop out of school (Sweeten, 2006), which is then associated with a reduced earning potential (Western, 2002), and a greater likelihood of future incarceration (Lochner & Moretti, 2004). In a sense, involvement with the justice system during adolescence disrupts the completion of normative tasks necessary for successful psychosocial development (Steinberg, Chung, & Little, 2004).

## Conclusion

It is easy to lose sight of the fact that adolescents who commit crime, like other adolescents, exhibit capabilities and developmental challenges that change considerably with time. Overlooking the underlying changes that are occurring as an offender progresses through adolescence, when considering trajectories of delinquent behavior, is analogous to overlooking the slope of the green when considering the path of a golf ball. Particularly relevant to delinquent behavior is the development of decision-making skills and maturity of judgment. While cognitive abilities develop early in adolescence, such psychosocial factors as responsibility (e.g., self-reliance, sense of identity), perspective (e.g., consideration of long-term consequences and the views of others), and temperance (e.g., avoidance of risk-taking, and impulse control) continue to develop into late adolescence and early adulthood, and have been found to be more predictive of socially responsible decision-making than age (Steinberg & Cauffman, 1996; Cauffman & Steinberg, under review). These psycho-social elements of mature judgment are likely to be affected by life experiences and are, in turn, expected to affect how youth respond to the legal system, and how they approach criminal opportunities.

As highlighted throughout this review, there is incontrovertible evidence that psychological development continues throughout adolescence and into young adulthood. Furthermore, the biological underpinnings of the behavioral studies on which these conclusions are based have yielded new insights into adolescent behavior in general, and adolescent crime in particular. Recent brain-imaging research does not change the portrait of adolescent risk taking painted by behavioral research; however, it does make the story more compelling. It is one thing to say that adolescents do not control their impulses, stand up to peer pressure, or think through the consequences of their actions as well as adults, and to cite performance on behavioral tests as evidence; it is quite another to say that they do not do these things because their brains are not yet wired to support such mature decision-making. Yet, that is what recent studies linking anatomical and functional markers of brain development indicate (Casey, Getz, & Galvan, 2008; Giedd, 2008). It is important that justice system responses take such developmental considerations into account. Although offenders should unquestionably face consequences for their offenses, the sanctions applied should be appropriate to the offender's developmental status, amenability to future change, and degree of culpability (which may be lowered because of the diminished reasoning capacity implied by a lack of fully developed impulse control, resistance to peer pressure, or ability to recognize long-term negative consequences of risky behavior). Punitive sentencing of juveniles in adult facilities leads to increased rates of reoffending, compared with treatment within the juvenile justice system. Developmentally appropriate sanctions tailored to adolescents' developmental status, rather than sentences aimed solely at retribution, would improve public safety and lead to better individual outcomes as well.

## References

Asato, M.R., Terwilliger, R., Woo, J., & Luna, B. (2010). White matter development in adolescence: A DTI study. *Cerbral Cortex, 20*, 2122–2131. doi: 10.1093/cercor/bhp292.

Austin, J., Johnson, K.D., & Gregoriou, M. (2000). *Juveniles in Adult Prisons and Jails: A National Assessment.* Washington, DC: U.S. Department of Justice, Office of Justice Programs, Bureau of Justice Assistance.

Barry, J.L. (2010). The child as victim and perpetrator: Laws punishing juvenile "sexting." *Vanderbilt Journal of Entertainment and Technology Law, 13*, 129–153.

Bechtold, J., & Cauffman, E. (2014). Tried as an adult, housed as a juvenile: A tale of youth from two courts incarcerated together. *Law and Human Behavior, 38*(2), 126–138.

Bernburg, J.G., & Krohn, M.D. (2003). Labeling, life chances, and adult crime: The direct and indirect effects of official intervention in adolescence on crime in early adulthood. *Criminology, 41*, 1287–1318.

Bernburg, J.G., Krohn, M.D., & Rivera, C.J. (2006). Official labeling, criminal embeddedness, and subsequent delinquency: A longitudinal test of labeling theory. *Journal of Research in Crime and Delinquency, 43*(1), 67–88. doi: 10.1177/0022427805280068.

Bishop, D.M. (2000). Juvenile offenders in the adult criminal justice system. *Crime and Justice, 27*, 81–167.

Bishop, D.M. (2006). Public opinion and juvenile justice policy: Myths and misconceptions. *Criminology & Public Policy, 5*(4), 653–664.

Bishop, D.M., Frazier, C.E., Lanza-Kaduce, L., & Winner, L. (1996). The transfer of juveniles to criminal court: Does it make a difference? *Crime & Delinquency, 42*, 171–191.

Blakemore, S., Burnett, S., & Dahl, R. (2010). The role of puberty in the developing adolescent brain. *Human Brain Mapping, 31*, 926–933. doi: 10.1002/hbm.21052.

Casey B.J., Getz, S., Galvan, A. (2008) The adolescent brain. Developmental Review, *28*(1), 62–77. doi: 10.1016/j.dr.2007.08.003

Cauffman, E., & Steinberg, L. (2000). (Im)maturity of judgment in adolescence: Why adolescents may be less culpable than adults. *Behavioral Sciences & the Law, 18*, 741–760.

Cauffman, E., Shulman, E.P., Steinberg, L., Claus, E., Banich, M., Graham, S., *et al.* (2010). Age differences in affective decision making as indexed by performance on the Iowa Gambling Task. *Developmental Psychology, 46*(1), 193–207. doi: 10.1037/a0016128.

Center for Disease Control and Prevention (2014). *Injury Prevention & Control: Data & Statistics.* http://www.cdc.gov/injury/wisqars/ (accessed April 21, 2015).

Chein, J., Albert, D., O'Brien, L., Uckert, K., & Steinberg, L. (2011). Peers increase adolescent risk taking by enhancing activity in the brain's reward circuitry. *Developmental Science, 14*(2), F1–F10. doi: 10.1111/j.1467-7687.2010.01035.x.

Cooper, A., & Smith, E.L. (2011). Homicide trends in the United States, 1980–2008. Washington, DC: U.S. Department of Justice, Bureau of Justice Statistics.

Csikszentmihalyi, M., Larson, R., & Prescott, S. (1977). The ecology of adolescent activity and experience. *Journal of Youth and Adolescence, 6*, 281–294.

Dishion, T.J., McCord, J., & Poulin, F. (1999). When interventions harm: Peer groups and problem behavior. *American Psychologist, 54*(9), 755–764. doi: 10.1037/0003-066X.54.9.755.

Eccles, J.S., Midgley, C., Wigfield, A., Buchanan, C.M., Reuman, D., Flanagan, C., *et al.* (1993). Development during adolescence: The impact of stage-environment fit on young adolescents' experiences in schools and in families. *American Psychologist, 48*(2), 90–101.

Fabio, A., Tu, L.C., Loeber, R., & Cohen, J. (2011). Neighborhood socioeconomic disadvantage and the shape of the age–crime curve. *American Journal of Public Health, 101*, S325–S332.

Fagan, J. (1996). The comparative advantage of juvenile versus criminal court sanctions on recidivism among adolescent felony offenders. *Law & Policy, 18*, 77–114.

Farrington, D.P. (1986). Age and crime. *Crime and Justice, 7*, 189–250.

Farrington, D.P., Loeber, R., & Howell, J.C. (2012). Young adult offenders. *Criminology & Public Policy, 11*, 729–750.

Feld, B.C. (2003). The politics of race and juvenile justice: The "due process revolution" and the conservative reaction. *Justice Quarterly, 20*, 765–800.

Figner, B., Mackinlay, R.J., Wilkening, F., & Weber, E.U. (2009). Affective and deliberative processes in risky choice: Age differences in risk taking in the Columbia Card Task. *Journal of Experimental Psychology: Learning, Memory, and Cognition, 35*(3), 709–730. doi: 10.1037/a0014983.

Forest, C.B., Tambor, E., Riley, A.W., Ensminger, M.E., & Starfield, B. (2000). The health profile of incarcerated male youths. *Pediatrics, 105*(2), 286–291.

Gardner, M., & Steinberg, L. (2005). Peer influence on risk taking, risk preference, and risky decision making in adolescence and adulthood: An experimental study. *Developmental Psychology, 41*(4), 625–635.

Giedd, J.N. (2004). Structural magnetic resonance imaging of the adolescent brain. *Annals of the New York Academy of Sciences, 1021*, 77–85.

Giedd, J.N. (2008). The teen brain: Insights from neuroimaging. *Journal of Adolescent Health, 42*(4), 335-343. doi: 10.1016/j.jadohealth.2008.01.007.

Giorgio, A., Watkins, K.E., Chadwick, M., James, S., Winmill, L., Douaud, G., *et al.* (2010). Longitudinal changes in grey and white matter during adolescence. *NeuroImage, 49*(1), 94–103.

Goldweber, A., Dmitrieva, J., Cauffman, E., Piquero, A.R., & Steinberg, L. (2011). The development of criminal style in adolescence and young adulthood: Separating the lemmings from the loners. *Journal of Youth and Adolescence, 40*(3), 332–346.

Gottfredson, M.R., & Hirschi, T. (1990). *A General Theory of Crime.* Stanford, CA: Stanford University Press.

*Graham v. Florida,* 130 S. Ct. (2010).

Grisso, T., Steinberg, L., Woolard, J., Cauffman, E., Scott, E., Graham, S., *et al.* (2003). Juveniles' competence to stand trial: A comparison of adolescents' and adults' capacities as trial defendants. *Law and Human Behavior, 27*, 333–363.

*Hodgson v. Minnesota,* 497 U.S. 417 (1990).

Insel, T., & Fernald, R. (2004). How the brain processes social information: Searching for the social brain. *Annual Review of Neuroscience, 27*, 697–722.

Knoch, D., & Fehr, E. (2007). Resisting the power of temptations: The right prefrontal cortex and self-control. *Annals of the New York Academy of Sciences, 1104*, 123–134.

Kuhn, D. (2006). Do cognitive changes accompany developments in the adolescent brain? *Perspectives on Psychological Science, 1*(1), 59–67.

Kuhn, D. (2009). Adolescent thinking. In R.M. Lerner & L. Steinberg (Eds.), *Handbook of Adolescent Psychology.* Hoboken, NJ: Wiley & Sons.

Kurlychek, M.C., & Johnson, B.D. (2010). Juvenility and punishment: Sentencing juveniles in adult criminal court. *Criminology, 48*, 725–758.

Littlefield, A.K., Sher, K.J., & Steinley, D. (2010). Developmental trajectories of impulsivity and their association with alcohol use and related outcomes during emerging and young adulthood. *Alcoholism: Clinical and Experimental Research, 34*(4), 1409–1416. doi: 10.1111/j.1530-0277.2010.01224.x.

Liu, S. (2014). Is the shape of the age-crime curve invariant by sex? Evidence from a national sample with flexible non-parametric modeling. *Journal of Quantitative Criminology, 1–31.*

Lochner, L., & Moretti, E. (2004). The effect of education on crime: Evidence from prison inmates, arrests, and self-reports. *American Economic Review, 94*(1), 155–189.

Loeber, R., & Farrington, D.P. (2014). Age–crime curve. In G. Bruinsma & D. Weisburd (Eds.), *Encyclopedia of Criminology and Criminal Justice* (pp. 12–18). New York: Springer.

Loeber, R., Menting, B., Lynam, D.R., Moffitt, T.E., Stouthamer-Loeber, M., Stallings, R., *et al.* (2012). Findings from the Pittsburgh Youth Study: Cognitive impulsivity and intelligence as predictors of the age–crime curve. *Journal of the American Academy of Child & Adolescent Psychiatry, 51*, 1136–1149.

Loughran, T.A., Mulvey, E.P., Schubert, C.A., Chassin, L.A., Steinberg, L., Piquero, A.R., *et al.* (2010). Differential effects of adult court transfer on juvenile offender recidivism. *Law and Human Behavior, 34*(6), 476–488.

Luciana, M. (2013). Adolescent brain development in normality and psychopathology. *Developmental Psychopathology, 25*(4 pt2), 1325–1345. doi: 10.1017/S0954579413000643.

Mahoney, J.L. (2000). School extracurricular activity participation as a moderator in the development of antisocial patterns. *Child Development, 71*, 502–516.

McCord, J., & Conway, K. (2005). *Co-Offending and Patterns of Juvenile Crime: Research in Brief.* Washington, DC: U.S. Department of Justice, Office of Justice Programs, National Institute of Justice (NCJ 210360).

Mears, D.P., Cochran, J.C., Stults, B.J., Greenman, S.J., Bhati, A.S., & Greenwald, M.A. (2014). The "true" juvenile offender: Age effects and juvenile court sanctioning. *Criminology, 52*, 169–194.

*Miller v. Alabama, 567 U.S., 132 S. Ct. 2455, 183 L. Ed. 2d 407 (2012).*

*Miller v. Skumanick,* No. 3:09CV540, 605 F. Supp. 2d 634, 640 (M.D. Pa. 2009).

Miyake, A., Friedman, N.P., Emerson, M.J., Witzki, A.H., Howerter, A., & Wager, T.D. (2000). The unity and diversity of executive functions and their contributions to complex "frontal lobe" tasks: A latent analysis. *Cognitive Psychology, 41*, 49–100.

Moffitt, T.E. (1993). Adolescence-limited and life-course-persistent antisocial behavior: A developmental taxonomy. *Psychological Review, 100*, 674–701.

Monahan, K., Steinberg, L., Cauffman, E., & Mulvey, E.P. (2009). Trajectories of antisocial behavior and psychosocial maturity from adolescence to young adulthood. *Developmental Psychology, 45*(6), 1654–1668. doi: 10.1037/a0015862.

Mulvey, E.P., Steinberg, L., Piquero, A.R., Besana, M., Fagan, J., Schubert, C., *et al.* (2010). Trajectories of desistance and continuity in antisocial behavior following court adjudication among serious adolescent offenders. *Development and Psychopathology, 22*, 453–475.

Murray, J., & Farrington, D.P. (2010). Risk factors for conduct disorder and delinquency: Key findings from longitudinal studies. *The Canadian Journal of Psychiatry, 55*(10), 633–642.

Nagin, D.S., Piquero, A.R., Scott, E.S., & Steinberg, L. (2006). Public preferences for rehabilitation versus incarceration of juvenile offenders: Evidence from a contingent valuation survey. *Criminology & Public Policy, 5*, 627–651.

Naumann, R.B., Dellinger, A.M., Zaloshnja, E., Lawrence, B.A., & Miller, T.R. (2010). Incidence and total lifetime costs of motor vehicle-related fatal and nonfatal injury by road user type, United States, 2005. *Traffic Injury Prevention, 11*(4), 353–360.

Nelson, E.E., Leibenluft, E., McClure, E.B., & Pine, D.S. (2005). The social re-orientation of adolescence: A neuroscience perspective on the process and its relation to psychopathology. *Psychological Medicine, 35*, 163–174. doi: 10.1017/S0033291704003915.

O'Brien, L., Albert, D., Chein, J., & Steinberg, L. (2011). Adolescents prefer more immediate rewards when in the presence of their peers. *Journal of Research on Adolescence, 21*(4), 747–753. doi: 10.1111/j.1532-7795.2011.00738.

Ordaz, S.J., Foran, W., Velanova, K., & Luna, B. (2013). Longitudinal growth curves of brain function underlying inhibitory control through adolescence. *The Journal of Neuroscience, 33*(46), 18109–18124. doi: 10.1523/JNEUROSCI.1741-13.2013.

Paus, T. (2010). Growth of white matter in the adolescent brain: Myelin or axon? *Brain and Cognition, 72*, 26–35.

Paus, T., Keshavan, M., & Giedd, J.N. (2008). Why do many psychiatric disorders emerge during adolescence? *National Review of Neuroscience, 9*, 947–957.

Paus, T., Zijedenbos, A., Worsley, K., Collins, D.L., Blumenthal, J., Giedd, J.N., *et al.* (1999). Structural maturation of neural pathways in children and adolescents: In vivo study. *Science, 283*, 1908–1911.

Petanjek, Z., Judas, M., Simic, G., Rasin, M.R., Uylings, H.B., Rakic, P., *et al.* (2011). Extraordinary neoteny of synaptic spines in the human prefrontal cortex. *Proceedings of the National Academy of Science of the United States of America, 108*(32), 13281–13286.

Pickett, J.T., & Chiricos, T. (2012). Controlling other people's children: Racialized views of delinquency and whites' punitive attitudes toward juvenile offenders. *Criminology, 50*, 673–710.

Piquero, A.R., Cullen, F.T., Unnever, J.D., Piquero, N.L., & Gordon, J.A. (2010). Never too late: Public optimism about juvenile rehabilitation. *Punishment & Society, 12*(2), 187–207.

Poulos, T.M., & Orchowsky, S. (1994). Serious juvenile offenders: Predicting the probability of transfer to criminal court. *Crime & Delinquency, 40*, 3–17.

Quetelet, A. (1833). La precision des résultats croit comme la racine carree du nombre des observations. *Annales d'Hygiene Publique et de Medecine Légalé, 9*, 308–336.

Reiss, A.J. (1986). Co-offender influences on criminal careers. *Criminal Careers and Career Criminals, 2*, 121–160.

Reiss, A.J., & Farrington, D.P. (1991). Advancing knowledge about co-offending: Results from a prospective longitudinal survey of London males. *Journal of Criminal Law and Criminology, 82*, 360–395.

Roisman, G.I., Monahan, K.C., Campbell, S.B., Steinberg, L., & Cauffman, E. (2010). Is adolescence-onset antisocial behavior developmentally normative? *Development and Psychopathology, 22*, 295–311.

*Roper v. Simmons*, 543 U.S. 551 (2005).

Schubert, C.A., Mulvey, E.P., Steinberg, L., Cauffman, E., Losoya, S.H., Hecker, T., *et al.* (2004). Operational lessons from the Pathways to Desistance project. *Youth Violence and Juvenile Justice, 2*, 237–255.

Schubert, C.A., Mulvey, E.P., Loughran, T.A., Fagan, J., Chassin, L.A., Piquero, A.R., *et al.* (2010). Predicting outcomes for youth transferred to adult court. *Law and Human Behavior, 34*(6), 460–475.

Scott, E.S., & Grisso, T. (1997). The evolution of adolescence: A developmental perspective on juvenile justice reform. *Journal of Criminal Law and Criminology, 88*, 137–189.

Shaw, C.R., & Moore, M.E. (1931). *The Natural History of a Delinquent*. Chicago, Chicago University Press.

Sebastian, C., Viding, E. Williams, K.D., & Blakemore, S.-J. (2010). Social brain development and the affective consequences of ostracism in adolescence. *Brain and Cognition, 72*, 134–145.

Shulman, E.P., Steinberg, L.D., & Piquero, A.R. (2013). The age–crime curve in adolescence and early adulthood is not due to age differences in economic status. *Journal of Youth and Adolescence, 42*, 848–860.

Sickmund, M. (2004). *Juveniles in Corrections* (p. 18). Washington, DC: U.S. Department of Justice, Office of Justice Programs, Office of Juvenile Justice and Delinquency Prevention.

Sickmund, M., Sladky, T.J., Kang, W., & Puzzanchera, C. (2013) Easy access to the Census of Juveniles in Residential Placement. Online. Available at http://www.ojjdp.gov/ojstatbb/ezacjrp/ (accessed April 21, 2015).

Sisk, C.L., & Zehr, J.L. (2005). Pubertal hormones organize the adolescent brain and behavior. *Frontiers in Neuroendocrinology, 26,* 163–174.

Snyder, H.N. (1999). The overrepresentation of juvenile crime proportions in robbery clearance statistics. *Journal of Quantitative Criminology, 15,* 151–161.

Snyder, H.N., & Sickmund, M. (2006). *Juvenile Offenders and Victims: 2006 National Report.* Washington, DC: U.S. Department of Justice, Office of Justice Programs, Office of Juvenile Justice and Delinquency Prevention.

Somerville, L.H., Hare, T., & Casey, B.J. (2011). Frontostriatal maturation predicts cognitive control failure to appetitive cues in adolescents. *Journal of Cognitive Neuroscience, 23*(9), 2123–2134. doi: 10.1162/jocn.2010.21572.

Sowell, E.R., Thompson, P.M., Tessner, K.D., & Toga, A.W. (2001). Mapping continued brain growth and gray matter density reduction in dorsal frontal cortex: Inverse relationships during post-adolescent brain maturation. *The Journal of Neuroscience, 21,* 8819–8829.

Steinberg, L. (2008a). Adolescent development and juvenile justice. *Annual Review of Clinical Psychology, 16*(3), 47–73.

Steinberg, L. (2008b). A social neuroscience perspective on adolescent risk taking. *Developmental Review, 28*(1), 78–106.

Steinberg, L. (2010). Commentary: A behavioral scientist looks at the science of adolescent brain development. *Brain Cognition, 72*(1), 160–164.

Steinberg, L. (2013). The influence of neuroscience on U.S. Supreme Court decisions about adolescents' criminal culpability. *Nature Reviews Neuroscience, 14,* 513–518.

Steinberg, L., & Cauffman, E. (1996). Maturity of judgment in adolescence: Psychosocial factors in adolescent decision making. *Law and Human Behavior, 20*(3), 249–272.

Steinberg, L., Albert, D., Cauffman, E., Banich, M., Graham, S., & Woolard, J. (2008). Age differences in sensation seeking and impulsivity as indexed by behavior and self-report: Evidence for a dual systems model. *Developmental Psychology, 44*(6), 1764–1778.

Steinberg, L., Cauffman, E., Woolard, J., Graham, S., & Banich, M. (2009). Are adolescents less mature than adults? Minors' access to abortion, the juvenile death penalty, and the alleged APA "flip-flop." *American Psychologist, 64,* 583–594.

Steinberg, L., Chung, H.L., & Little, M. (2004). Reentry of young offenders from the justice system: A developmental perspective. *Youth Violence and Juvenile Justice, 2*(1), 21–38. doi: 10.1177/1541204003260045.

Steinberg, L., & Monahan, K.C. (2007). Age differences in resistance to peer influence. *Developmental Psychology, 43*(6), 1531–1543. doi: 10.1037/0012-1649.43.6.1531.

Steinhart, D.J. (1996). Status offenses. *The Future of Children, 6*(3), 86–99.

Stolzenberg, L., & D'Alessio, S.J. (2008). Co-offending and the age-crime curve. *Journal of Research in Crime and Delinquency, 45,* 65–86.

Sweeten, G. (2006). Who will graduate? Disruption of high school education by arrest and court involvement. *Justice Quarterly, 23*(4), 462–480.

Sweeten, G., Piquero, A.R., & Steinberg, L. (2013). Age and the explanation of crime, revisited. *Journal of Youth and Adolescence, 42,* 921–938.

Thomas, A., & Cauffman, E. (2014). Youth sexting as child pornography: Developmental science supports less harsh sanctions for juvenile sexters. *New Criminal Law Review, 17*(4), 631–651.

Tremblay, R.E., & Nagin, D.S. (2005). The developmental origins of physical aggression in humans. In R.E. Tremblay, W.H. Hartup, & J. Archer (Eds.), *Developmental Origins of Aggression* (pp. 83–106). New York: Guilford Press.

Trommsdorff, G., & Lamm, H. (1980). Future orientation of institutionalized and noninstitutionalized delinquents and nondelinquents. *European Journal of Social Psychology, 10*(3), 247–278.

United States Department of Justice (2009). Uniform Crime Report. Crime in the United States. Available at http://www2.fbi.gov/ucr/cius2009/data/table_38.html (accessed April 21, 2015).

United States Department of Justice (2012). Uniform Crime Report. Ten Year Arrest Trends. Available at http://www.fbi.gov/about-us/cjis/ucr/crime-in-the-u.s/2012/crime-in-the-u.s.-2012/tables/32tabledatadecoverviewpdf (accessed April 21, 2015).

Van Leijenhorst, L., Zanolie, K., Van Meel, C.S., Westenberg, P.M., Rombouts, S.A.R.B., & Crone, E.A. (2010). What motivates the adolescent? Brain regions mediating reward sensitivity across adolescence. *Cerebral Cortex, 20*, 61–69. doi: 10.1093/cercor/bhp078.

Western, B. (2002). The impact of incarceration on wage mobility and inequality. *American Sociological Review, 526–546.*

White, J.L., Moffitt, T.E., Caspi, A., Bartusch, D.J., Needles, D.J., & Stouthamer-Loeber, M. (1994). Measuring impulsivity and examining its relationship to delinquency. *Journal of Abnormal Psychology, 103*(2), 192–205.

# 7

# Social Disorganization Theory's Greatest Challenge: Linking Structural Characteristics to Crime in Socially Disorganized Communities

Charis E. Kubrin and James C. Wo

Why do some neighborhoods have higher crime rates than others? What is it about certain communities that consistently generate high crime rates? These are the central questions of interest for social disorganization theory, a macro-level perspective concerned with explaining the spatial distribution of crime across areas. Social disorganization theory has emerged as the critical framework for understanding the relationship between community characteristics and crime in urban areas. According to the theory, certain neighborhood characteristics – most notably poverty, residential instability, and racial heterogeneity – can lead to social disorganization. Social disorganization, in turn, can cause crime. In this chapter, we first describe social disorganization theory, laying out the theory's key principles and propositions. We then discuss one of the most serious and enduring challenges confronting the theory – identifying and empirically verifying the social interactional mechanisms that link structural characteristics of communities, such as poverty and residential instability, to heightened crime rates in socially disorganized communities. And finally, we present some promising new directions for the theory by discussing several theoretical concepts that may be useful for scholars interested in identifying and measuring the theory's interactional mechanisms; these include social capital, collective efficacy, and social networks. We conclude the chapter with some remarks about one additional important theoretical direction for social disorganization theory: incorporating the role of neighborhood subculture in explanations of crime and delinquency.

*The Handbook of Criminological Theory*, First Edition. Edited by Alex R. Piquero.
© 2016 John Wiley & Sons, Inc. Published 2016 by John Wiley & Sons, Inc.

## Social Disorganization Theory

The origins of social disorganization theory date back to the early 1900s. In 1929, two researchers from the University of Chicago, Clifford Shaw and Henry McKay, began a series of studies using official records which showed that in the city of Chicago, rates of delinquency, criminality, and commitment to correctional institutions varied markedly by area. In particular, rates were highest in slums near the city center and diminished as distance from the center of the city increased, except in areas of industry and commerce just outside of the central district, which had some of the highest rates. Shaw and McKay also found that rates of crime and delinquency exhibited a remarkable consistent patterning over many decades; in particular, the spatial pattern of rates revealed significant long-term stability even though the nationality structure of the population in the inner-city areas changed greatly over time. Shaw and McKay thus determined that crime and delinquency were not the result of personal characteristics of the residents who lived in the neighborhoods but were tied to the neighborhoods themselves. Since areas of high and low crime and delinquency maintained their relative positions over many years, a key theoretical task became to explain the existence and stability of these area differentials over time.

A fundamental part of their explanation involved the concept of social disorganization. Social disorganization refers to the inability of a community to realize the common values of its members and maintain effective social controls. As Kornhauser describes, "Social disorganization exists in the first instance when the structure and culture of a community are incapable of implementing and expressing the values of its own residents." (Kornhauser, 1978:63) According to the theory, a common value among neighborhood residents is the desire for a crime-free community. In essence, then, socially disorganized neighborhoods are ineffective in combating crime.

A socially organized community is characterized by (1) solidarity, or an internal consensus on essential norms and values (e.g., residents want and value the same things, such as a crime-free neighborhood); (2) cohesion, or a strong bond among neighbors (e.g., residents know and like one another); and (3) integration, with social interaction occurring on a regular basis (e.g., residents spend time with one another). Conversely, a disorganized community has little solidarity among residents and lacks social cohesion or integration. Perhaps the greatest difference between socially organized and disorganized neighborhoods is the levels of informal social control in those neighborhoods. Informal social control is defined as the scope of collective intervention that the community directs toward local problems, including crime (Kornhauser, 1978; Shaw & McKay, 1969). It is the informal, nonofficial actions taken by residents to combat crime in their communities, such as, for example, when residents question persons about suspicious activity or admonish misbehaving youth and inform parents of their children's misconduct. In essence, residents act as the "eyes and ears" of the community and their informal surveillance, and even simple presence, deters others from engaging in crime. According to the theory, socially disorganized neighborhoods have lower levels of informal social control, and thus experience higher crime rates when compared to more socially organized neighborhoods.

Ecological characteristics of neighborhoods influence the degree of social disorganization in the community. This is because certain characteristics can impede the development of social ties that promote the ability to solve common problems, including crime. Ecological characteristics of greatest interest to social disorganization researchers include poverty, joblessness, population mobility or turnover, racial composition, and family disruption, among others. Although community characteristics such as poverty or residential instability are related to crime, these factors themselves do not directly cause crime, according to the theory. That is, ecological characteristics are related to crime only indirectly through various neighborhood processes such as informal social control. As such, poverty, residential instability, and other ecological characteristics are important in as much as they affect the mediating processes of social disorganization.

In light of the above discussion, the basic social disorganization causal model can be expressed as: neighborhood characteristics → social ties → informal social control → crime. Sampson describes the processes by which neighborhood characteristics and crime are associated:

> Neighborhood characteristics such as family disorganization, residential mobility, and structural density weaken informal social control networks; informal social controls are impeded by weak local social bonds, lowered community attachment, anonymity, and reduced capacity for surveillance and guardianship; other factors such as poverty and racial composition also probably affect informal control, although their influence is in all likelihood indirect; residents in areas characterized by family disorganization, mobility, and building density are less able to perform guardianship activities, less likely to report general deviance to authorities, to intervene in public disturbances, and to assume responsibility for supervision of youth activities; the result is that deviance is tolerated and public norms of social control are not effective (Sampson, 1987: 109).

## Social Disorganization Theory's Greatest Challenge

Like all other theories discussed in this volume, there are ongoing challenges facing social disorganization theory, some of which have been resolved more fully than others. These challenges have been discussed at length in two important assessments of the theory at different points in time: Bursik (1988) and Kubrin & Weitzer (2003). Although these scholars identify several challenges, perhaps the greatest involves identifying and measuring the social mechanisms that account for heightened crime rates in socially disorganized neighborhoods. Stated alternatively, a major conceptual limitation of social disorganization research is the relative lack of attention paid to the processes that mediate the effect of community characteristics (see also Byrne & Sampson, 1986).

Given the primitive nature of data analysis during the early 1900s, it is not surprising that scholars were unable to conduct sophisticated analyses that would allow them to fully test social disorganization theory's arguments. Early Chicago school theorists "tested" the theory by plotting the spatial distribution of crime in the city to determine whether it was consistent with the theory's predictions, and then correlated characteristics of neighborhoods with crime rates. Studies were able to document, for example, that poor, mobile, and racially heterogeneous neighborhoods had the highest crime rates but they could not specify the mechanisms (e.g., social ties, informal social control) accounting for this relationship. This was problematic, in part, because it did not allow researchers to rule out competing theoretical explanations such as strain, which also theorize a poverty–crime association.

Even decades after the early work of Chicago School researchers, little progress had been made in this area. Studies included the "front end" of social disorganization models, that is, attributes of the community, as well as the "back end" or crime and delinquency outcomes, but continued to leave out the crucial middle, or indicators reflecting how much social disorganization is occurring in a neighborhood (Kubrin, Stucky, & Krohn, 2009: 91). Significant progress was finally achieved with the publication of Robert Sampson and Byron Groves' 1989 study, which used data from a large national survey of Great Britain to formally test social disorganization theory. Sampson & Groves (1989) constructed community-level measures of neighborhoods (e.g., low socio-economic status, ethnic heterogeneity, residential mobility, family disruption, and urbanization) as well as the mediating dimensions of social disorganization (e.g., sparse local friendship networks, unsupervised teenage peer groups, and low organizational participation) and determined how both sets of measures impacted neighborhood crime rates. The findings were largely supportive of social disorganization theory: communities characterized by strong social ties and informal control had lower rates of crime and delinquency. Moreover, these dimensions of social disorganization were found to explain, in large part, the effects of community structural characteristics on crime rates. This latter finding was important because it verified for the first time that the structural conditions themselves do not influence crime; rather, they are important only inasmuch as they produce social disorganization.

Despite this progress, only a handful of studies (e.g., Elliott *et al.*, 1996; Sampson & Groves, 1989; Warner & Rountree, 1997) have fully documented the theoretical processes laid out by social disorganization theory. Perhaps more importantly, the findings we do have from this small but critical literature suggest these processes may not be so straightforward. An increasing finding emerging from the literature is that social ties may not play the expected role (see Kubrin & Weitzer, 2003: 375–379). As such, researchers are only beginning to fully identify, understand, and empirically verify the social-interactional mechanisms that link structural characteristics to crime in neighborhoods. In an attempt to address this shortcoming, in part, in the remainder of the chapter we discuss some promising theoretical developments for social disorganization theory.

## Promising Theoretical Developments

For decades following the early Chicago School studies, research testing social disorganization theory, by and large, emphasized the critical role of two theoretical constructs: social ties and informal social control, as discussed earlier. In more recent years, however, scholars have begun to introduce additional theoretical concepts that borrow from – but go well beyond – social ties and informal social control. These include collective efficacy, social capital, and social networks. For the remainder of this chapter, we discuss these promising new theoretical directions in social disorganization theory.

### Collective efficacy

As noted earlier, Sampson and Groves (1989) incited renewed interest in social disorganization theory and its ability to explain variations in community crime rates. Recall their argument emphasized the formation and utility of social ties in terms of providing effective social action (i.e., informal social control) to fight crime. In recent years, scholars have begun to suggest that perhaps dense social networks of strong ties might not be sufficient, in and of themselves, to fulfill social control functions (Browning *et al.*, 2004; Kubrin & Weitzer, 2003; Pattillo, 1998; Sampson, 2006, Sampson *et al.*, 1997, Venkatesh, 2000, 2006). According to some, what appears to be missing is the key factor of purposive action, that is, just how ties are activated and resources mobilized to enhance informal social control (Sampson et al., 1997).

Sampson, Raudenbush, & Earls (1997) address this deficiency in their formulation of the concept of collective efficacy, which they define as, "the linkage of mutual trust and the willingness to intervene for the common good" (921). As is evident from the definition, collective efficacy integrates cohesion and mutual trust among residents with a culturally-derived neighborhood dynamic (i.e., shared expectations for control). The concept advances previous theorizing by taking into account mechanisms of social action that may be facilitated by, but do not necessarily require, an interconnected network of strong ties (Sampson, 2006: 152). Since "efficacy" refers to the ability to achieve a desired effect or outcome, in the context of the theory, collective efficacy is best conceptualized as a task-specific concept that captures the perceived ability of a neighborhood to solve crime problems.

Importantly, there are two components of collective efficacy. The first component is the willingness of residents to intervene for the common good of the neighborhood. Such willingness, according to Sampson and colleagues (1997), is a necessary precursor for establishing informal social control, or the degree to which actual behaviors are undertaken by residents as a means to address and prevent crime. To measure this component of collective efficacy, or the willingness to intervene, in a survey (The Project on Human Development in Chicago Neighborhoods, or PHDCN Survey), Sampson and colleagues asked 8,782 residents of 343 neighborhoods in Chicago the likelihood that their neighbors would intervene in the following (hypothetical) scenarios: (1) if children were skipping school and hanging out on a street corner; (2) if children were spray-painting graffiti on a local building; (3) if children were showing disrespect to an adult; (4) if a fight broke out in the front of their house; and (5) if the fire station closest to their home was threatened with budget cuts. Respondents answered using a five-item Likert-type scale. The assumption is that those neighborhoods that score high on the collective willingness to intervene scale are more likely to actually intervene when faced with these and similar situations, thereby reducing the likelihood for crime in those communities.

The second component of collective efficacy is the combination of cohesion and mutual trust. The importance of common values and similar goals among residents dates back to the earliest social disorganization research (Park & Burgess, 1925; Shaw & McKay, 1942). When residents are mostly self-interested and care little about the community at large, it is inherently difficult for the neighborhood to procure resources and to activate social ties to prevent crime. However, when there is cohesion and mutual trust among residents, there is a greater likelihood that residents will acknowledge problems in the community, will achieve consensus on how to address them, and will solve the problems in a more collective fashion. In this sense, cohesion and mutual trust are precursors to problem solving. Sampson and colleagues measure this component of collective efficacy by asking respondents in their survey the extent to which they agree with the following statements: (1) people around here are willing to help their neighbors; (2) this is a close-knit neighborhood; (3) people in this neighborhood can be trusted; (4) people in this neighborhood generally don't get along with each other; and (5) people in this neighborhood do not share the same values. Not surprisingly, measures of social cohesion and shared expectations for control were highly correlated across neighborhoods in Chicago. The two components were combined to create a summary measure of collective efficacy.

Sampson and colleagues (1997) contribute to social disorganization theory in two fundamental ways; first, they empirically demonstrate that collective efficacy has a significant negative effect on violent crime, in line with what social disorganization theory would predict, and second, they show that associations of concentrated disadvantage and residential instability with violent crime are largely mediated by collective efficacy. The second contribution is arguably the most significant as it implies that neighborhood characteristics are relevant to crime insofar as they produce (or fail to produce) collective efficacy.

In the years since Sampson and colleagues (1997) introduced the concept, studies examining collective efficacy in Chicago and beyond have proliferated. In general, findings from this literature echo what Sampson and colleagues documented – communities with greater levels of collective efficacy have lower rates of crime and violence, controlling for other factors, and that collective efficacy mediates the effects of ecological characteristics on crime and violence (Browning 2009; Browning, Feinberg, & Dietz, 2004; Mazerolle, Wickes, & Mc Broom, 2010; Sampson & Raudenbush, 1999). Moreover, given an emphasis on purposive action, the prevailing assumption has become that the explanatory power of collective efficacy is not limited to just certain types of crime or violence. For example, Browning (2002) examines the impact of collective efficacy on partner violence. Using Sampson *et al.'s* survey data, as well as other data sources, he demonstrates that collective efficacy has a crime-reducing impact on partner violence, independent of individual and relationship characteristics that heighten domestic violence risk. Another study by Dekeseredy, Alvi, & Tomaszewski (2003), which examines women's victimization in Ontario public housing, also documents support for collective efficacy's impact. In essence, it is becoming clearer that collective efficacy likely impacts a range of crimes and delinquent behaviors, as well as other related outcomes such as social disorder (see, e.g., Sampson & Raudenbush, 1999).

In recent years, collective efficacy scholars have turned their attention to the role of peers and the extent to which parental supervision of teenage peer groups may matter for crime. Maimon & Browning (2010) once again utilize PHDCN survey data to identify whether collective efficacy modifies the effect that unstructured peer socialization has on violent behavior. Their multilevel models, involving 842 Chicago residents in 78 neighborhoods, confirm that collective efficacy has a negative (independent) influence on violence. More importantly, they find that an "individual's unstructured socializing with peers is less likely to result in violence within high collective efficacy neighborhoods" (466). Their results provide evidence that collective efficacy can attenuate the deleterious effects of other social pressures on crime.

Of course in assessing collective efficacy's usefulness for social disorganization theory, and impact in the field more generally, one should consider the concept's predictive validity in relation to other correlates of crime – a task that Pratt & Cullen (2005) undertake in their meta-analysis of macro-level crime predictors. Pratt and Cullen identify over 200 studies from 1960 to 1999 that have examined the ecological correlates of crime, and perform a meta-analysis to determine which predictors have strong and stable effects on crime rates. Their findings reveal that relative to the other predictors, collective efficacy ranks fourth (out of 23) in weighted effect size. Sampson (2006) argues this finding supports the notion that collective efficacy is a robust predictor of crime rates, and is fundamental to social disorganization theory.

In his presidential address at the 2012 annual meeting of the American Society of Criminology, Robert J. Sampson suggested that collective efficacy, in effect, helps neighborhoods mitigate several problems – most notably, crime and violence. Findings from the small but growing literature indicate he might be right. Yet there remain only a limited number of studies that have empirically assessed just how collective efficacy affects crime and related outcomes (for a more detailed discussion on this point, see Pratt & Cullen, 2005). For this reason, researchers must continue to explore how collective efficacy impacts crime at varying points of time and in varying social contexts. This will entail applying sophisticated and innovative methodological approaches. Currently, we know very little about, for example, the longitudinal or reciprocal relationship between collective efficacy and crime.

## Social capital

One source in which scholars have recognized immense potential for understanding variation in community crime rates is the impact of local organizations. Social disorganization theory presumes that local organizations conducive to pro-social interaction such as churches, youth groups, charities, civic associations, and political groups, can enhance neighborhood informal social control. This is because civic and social organizations facilitate the sharing of common values and goals among residents, thereby increasing the collective ability to disseminate information, mobilize resources, and utilize social networks towards combating crime (Peterson, Krivo, & Harris, 2000; Triplett, Gainey, & Sun, 2003; Wilson, 1987).

Recently, criminologists have adopted the concept of social capital, defined as "the investment in social relations with expected returns" (Lin, 1999:30), in order to argue that civically engaged communities yield crime-control benefits. Scholars posit that the investment in communal social relations (i.e., civic engagement) is reflected by residents' participation in civic and social organizations. Prosocial interaction that originates within organizational settings extends to other settings in the greater community, ultimately providing the expected return: the emergence or enhancement of informal social control. In this sense, social capital refers to the potential for effective social action, as it does not directly encapsulate purposive action.

In criminology, social capital's operationalization most frequently reflects Lin's (1999) higher-order conceptualization, specifically, with respect to the investment in communal social relations. Previous studies have measured social capital using at least one of the following types of indicators: (1) a simple count of the number of civic and social organizations in the neighborhood; (2) residents' participation in these types of organizations; and (3) the level of trust among residents. The simple count reflects investment in terms of the availability and opportunity for residents to participate in pro-social organizational settings. Residents' organizational participation signifies the actual investment made in these organizations. Finally, residents' trust levels reveal the emotional investment that underlies interpersonal relationships. Studies typically combine these indicators into a summary measure of social capital or alternatively use one of them as a single-measure construct (Beyerlein & Hipp, 2005; Lee, 2008; Peterson, Krivo, & Harris, 2000; Putnam, 2000; Rosenfeld, Messner, & Baumer, 2001).

The seminal work of Putnam (1995, 2000) is arguably considered the standard research on social capital to date. For Putnam, social capital is conceived as a multidimensional concept reflected by two general forms: trust and social participation. The concept primarily features indices of political participation, civic participation, religious participation, workplace connections, informal social ties, philanthropy, altruism, and volunteering. According to Putnam (1995), levels of social capital in the United States have declined significantly since the 1960s. Putnam's evidence in support of this claim includes declining participation rates in bowling leagues, church attendance, The Boy Scouts, labor unions, and parent–teacher associations. Putnam maintains this decline is problematic to the extent that "successful outcomes are more likely in civically engaged communities" (Putnam 1995: 65). In support of this contention, state-level analyses of archival and survey data reveal both trust and social participation to be negatively associated with crime (Putnam, 2000). Thus, consistent with social disorganization theory, civically active communities have a greater ability to solve and prevent crime, all else equal.

Recent research has built on Putnam by incorporating diverse measures of social capital into analyses. Beyerlein & Hipp (2005), for example, investigate the religious component of civic engagement on crime in US counties. Acknowledging differences in social networks among religious traditions, their models specify the number of congregations per 100,000 for several denominations of Christianity, including mainline Protestantism, evangelical Protestantism, and Catholicism. Beyerlein and Hipp find that greater numbers of congregations per capita – regardless of the denomination – are associated with lower crime rates across counties. In another study, Lee (2008) develops a civic engagement index that not only includes the number of religious congregations, but also the number of civic associations, sport leagues, and hobby and special interest groups in his analysis of rural US counties. Lee (2008) finds that areas with higher levels of civic engagement have lower crime rates. And in a third study, Peterson, Krivo, & Harris (2000) examine whether the presence of recreation centers and libraries impact crime rates in neighborhoods in Columbus, Ohio. Peterson and colleagues discover that while libraries have little impact on crime, the presence of recreation centers appears to mitigate violent crime in the most disadvantaged Columbus neighborhoods.

Two key challenges for researchers have been assessing the reciprocal influence that crime has on social capital and determining social capital's spatial effects. One study by Rosenfeld, Messner, & Baumer (2001) examines the reciprocal nature of the social capital–crime relationship. Rosenfeld and colleagues perform a series of structural equation models (SEM), which reveal that their latent variable of social capital (which includes a dimension for both organizational participation and trust) is negatively associated with homicide rates across a sample of metropolitan and nonmetropolitan counties. This protective effect is unaffected by standard correlates of crime as well as the reciprocal influence that homicide has on social capital. Hipp, Petersilia, & Turner (2010) address the spatial effects of social capital in their investigation of how the availability of social capital (oriented) organizations affects the likelihood of recidivism for California parolees. Examining the number of such organizations within two miles of the parolee's current address, Hipp and colleagues find that a one standard deviation increase in the availability of social capital oriented organizations decreases the likelihood of recidivating by more than 40%. Although the analysis estimates an individual-level outcome (recidivism of individual parolees), it is not unreasonable to suggest that this protective effect applies at the community level as well.

As previously alluded, social capital can be theorized along several dimensions as well as using a variety of methodological approaches. Yet, there is a pressing need to identify the general effect that social capital has on crime rates across aggregate units of analysis. Pratt & Cullen (2005) begin to address this need by providing a (quasi) quantitative synthesis of studies associated with social capital. They focus explicitly on the impact of noneconomic institutions, which capture those studies that examine the level of religious and political participation within communities – two indicators frequently applied in the operationalization of social capital. They find that the strength of noneconomic institutions ranks first (out of 23) in weighted effect size and, in line with predictions, such institutions are negatively associated with crime. Although their measure is only a proxy for social capital, the strength of the effect size suggests that social capital is potentially a robust predictor of lower crime rates, and therefore crucial to understanding the establishment of social control.

The studies building upon Putnam's seminal work are generally supportive of an inverse relationship between social capital and crime. However, we suggest it would be premature to conclude that social capital is a robust predictor of lower crime rates, mainly because current studies differ so drastically with respect to units of analysis, research settings, time-periods, and estimated outcomes. Moreover, there is a developing concern regarding the extent to which social capital is theoretically distinct from collective efficacy and social networks (Kubrin & Weitzer, 2003). Scholars have identified mutual trust as a dimension of both social capital and collective efficacy. Similarly, mutual trust may condition the relationship between social networks and crime. In summary, although social capital presents the opportunity to better understand the emergence of social control in communities, more research must be done before it is fully incorporated into social disorganization theory.

## Social ties and neighborhood networks

From the earliest formulations of social disorganization theory, the concept of social ties has occupied a central place in the theory. An enduring assumption is that socially disorganized neighborhoods lack the social ties that activate mechanisms of informal social control (Kornhauser, 1978; Kubrin & Weitzer, 2003; Park & Burgess, 1925; Sampson, 2006; Sampson & Groves, 1989; Shaw & McKay, 1942). So when crime problems emerge, the theory reasons, residents are unable to effectively respond via the dissemination of information, the implementation of guardianship behavior, the mobilization of resources, and the coordination of civic events. According to the theory, the formation and maintenance of informal social control thus requires the neighborhood to have an abundant supply of strong ties that connect residents to one another. Accordingly, criminologists have long examined how the presence of social ties as well as their utility and content are related to neighborhood crime rates.

Despite substantial work in this area, the measurement of social ties is generally limited to two types of indicators: (1) the quantity of social ties, and (2) the content of those ties. Such information is typically ascertained via survey questions which instruct respondents to provide information about their social exchanges and inter-actions with fellow neighbors. The first indicator reflects an assumption that there is a high correspondence between an abundance of social ties and the activation of informal social control mechanisms. In contrast, the second indicator suggests that the type of social ties among residents (e.g., family, friends, acquaintances, or strangers) will differentially impact the ability to prevent crime. According to the theory, those social ties that represent emotional investment and reflect frequent interaction are deemed to be "strong," while those ties that exhibit less familiarity and interaction are considered to be "weak." Accordingly, the strength of neighbor-hood ties is considered fundamental to the informal control of crime.

Despite the theory's predictions, the collective body of research suggests that the evidence in support of social ties' impact is mixed with respect to crime reduction. Some studies identify social ties as a catalyst for effective social action to fight crime (e.g., Sampson & Groves, 1989) while others demonstrate that social ties may actually facilitate crime (e.g., Pattillo, 1998). In regards to the former, the seminal article by Sampson and Groves, discussed earlier, lends considerable support to the notion that an interconnected network of strong ties characterizes lower-crime neighborhoods. Recall they used data from a large national survey of Great Britain. The survey included a question instructing respondents to indicate how many of their friends reside in their local community, from which Sampson and Groves constructed a community measure of local friendship networks defined as "the mean level of local friendships" (784). Their network measure captures the abundance of social ties char-acterized by frequent interaction and emotional investment. Also recall that Sampson and Groves show that the mediating dimension of local friendship networks has an independent effect on crime and delinquency outcomes, net of (exogenous) neigh-borhood characteristics. This finding suggests that neighborhood networks do appear to activate and maintain mechanisms of informal social control.

The promise of social ties for social disorganization theory is less apparent in Bellair's (1997) study, which explicitly assesses how the frequency of interaction among neighborhood residents influences crime. Using survey data from residents of 60 urban neighborhoods (spanning three states), Bellair finds that social inter-action, here defined as the percentage of community residents who get together once a year or more, reduces community rates of burglary, motor vehicle theft, and robbery. He also finds that social interaction largely mediates the effect of neighborhood characteristics on community crime, in support of social disorganization theory. Yet Bellair's findings ultimately raise questions regarding the value of social ties for the theory. Although social interaction is significantly associated with community crime rates in the direction the theory predicts, the fact that even infrequent interaction can reduce community crime rates challenges the theory's assumption that strong and dense ties are what matter most; Bellair's "once a year or more" definition reflects a level of interaction that is arguably less than what the perspective theorizes.

Other studies produce conflicting evidence regarding the impact of social ties. For example, using survey data from the city of Seattle, Warner & Rountree (1997) document mixed support for social ties' crime reducing impact. Their measure of social ties, or what they refer to as "local ties," reflects the extent to which respondents had done each of the following: (1) borrowed tools or food from neighbors; (2) had lunch or dinner with neighbors; and (3) had helped neighbors with problems. While Warner and Rountree find that local ties are associated with lower rates of assault in Seattle neighborhoods, they contrastingly find that these ties are associated with higher rates of burglary. As a result, Warner and Rountree question the assumption that social ties automatically translate into greater levels of informal social control, as the theory predicts.

Even more troubling are findings from studies which suggest that social ties may, in fact, serve as a source of social capital for offenders, thereby increasing the likelihood of offending. Browning, Feinberg, & Dietz (2004) arrive at this conclusion in their study of the impact of collective efficacy and social ties on violent crime rates in Chicago neighborhoods. Using Sampson's PHDCN survey data, they discover that while collective efficacy is associated with diminished rates of violence, social ties and exchange between residents appears to diminish neighborhood social control. Browning and colleagues also conclude that the "regulatory effects of collective efficacy on violence are substantially reduced in neighborhoods characterized by high levels of network interaction and reciprocated exchange" (503).

Questionable findings regarding social ties' impact are not limited to quantitative analyses. A study by Pattillo (1998) qualitatively documents the complex relationships among social ties, informal social control, and crime. Through participant observation and face-to-face interviews in a middle-class black neighborhood in Chicago, she finds that residents are highly connected to one another and that these strong ties are characterized by emotional investment and frequent interaction. As a result, and in support of social disorganization theory, the neighborhood is able to keep crime to a relatively acceptable level through the supervision of youth, the identification of strangers, and the mobilization of community organizations. However, the value of these ties comes with a trade-off; Pattillo also finds that the social ties frequently connect law abiding residents and criminals, thereby making it more challenging for the neighborhood to eradicate criminal activity. This occurs because residents are reluctant to publicly shame or legally sanction those with whom they are closely tied (even in the face of illegal behavior). Once again these findings, which reveal that social ties can simultaneously enhance and undermine informal social control, question the relevance of this concept for social disorganization theory.

Although the evidence in support of social ties is mixed, we do not mean to suggest that criminology should abandon studying the impact of neighborhood networks on crime. Instead, the present challenge is to pinpoint the specific characteristics of networks that precipitate and mitigate crime. Doing this will require scholars to recognize, as Sampson (2006: 164) points out, that "not all networks are created equal." In the context of social disorganization theory, this means acknowledging that while neighborhood networks may be capable of facilitating effective social action, they are likely not sufficient, in and of themselves, to fulfill social control functions. Sampson (2006) lists three reasons why neighborhood networks should not be equated with effective social control: (1) weak ties can be equally important in the activation of informal social control (see also Granovetter, 1973); (2) strong ties can undermine social control efforts; and, (3) social ties may connect law-abiding citizens with criminals and vice versa. In extending and refining the concepts of social ties and neighborhood networks for social disorganization theory, researchers must account for these "social facts."

## Conclusion

Social disorganization theory has long occupied an important place in criminological thought and continues to do so well into the 21st century. But as with all theories, in order to survive it must be continuously subjected to testing and then reevaluated in light of the empirical evidence. Despite the theory's predictive power, in this chapter, we have suggested there is room for improvement, particularly when it comes to specifying the social interactional mechanisms that link structural characteristics of communities, such as poverty and residential instability, to heightened crime rates in socially disorganized communities. We have also suggested that such improvement may occur by attending to more recent theoretical concepts that borrow from, but go beyond, social ties and informal social control. These include collective efficacy, social capital, and social networks. In this chapter, we have defined these concepts, explicated their usefulness for social disorganization theory, and reviewed the empirical literature on their effectiveness. We believe these concepts hold significant promise.

We conclude with one final suggestion regarding the fundamental challenge involved in linking structural characteristics to crime in socially disorganized communities. This final suggestion is related to the role that neighborhood culture/subculture likely occupies for social disorganization theory. Although often downplayed (and even ignored) by scholars today, neighborhood subculture was of key interest to Shaw and McKay and other early social disorganization theorists. A central question for these scholars centered on how neighborhood subcultures became entrenched and affected rates of delinquency. They posed the question: Under what economic and social conditions does crime develop as a social tradition and become embodied in a system of criminal values?

Shaw and McKay found evidence regarding the impact of neighborhood subculture on crime and delinquency. Of particular interest is their finding that areas of low economic status were characterized by diversity in norms and standards of behavior, rather than uniformity (recall that solidarity, or an internal consensus on norms and values, is critical for social organization). Shaw and McKay found that in poor communities, youth were exposed to a wide variety of contradictory (and sometimes unlawful) standards rather than to a relatively consistent and conventional pattern of norms. It was also determined that in these communities, children were exposed to adult criminals, from whom they could learn (illegal) behavior.

In essence then, alongside social ties and informal social control, neighborhood subculture constituted a critical component of social disorganization theory, and helped to account for why crime rates were higher in disorganized neighborhoods. Decades following Shaw and McKay, researchers continued to examine how neighborhood subculture impacted crime and delinquency, as well as how it was itself impacted by neighborhood conditions (e.g., Miller, 1958; Cloward & Ohlin, 1960; Kornhauser, 1978). Unfortunately, for reasons that have been explicated elsewhere (see Sampson & Bean, 2006), neighborhood subculture increasingly became irrelevant to the theory. Discussions regarding neighborhood subculture's impact became obsolete and empirical examinations of the theory did not include measures reflecting local subculture.

Most recently, however, cultural explanations have been resurrected in neighborhood research, which we argue is a positive development. Scholars are both theorizing culture's potential impact on community crime rates (Anderson, 1999; Fagan & Wilkinson, 1998; Kubrin & Weitzer, 2003; Sampson & Bean, 2006) as well as empirically examining just how culture and crime are associated in both organized and disorganized communities (Berg *et al.*, 2012; Kirk & Papachristos, 2011; Sampson & Bartusch, 1998; Stewart & Simons, 2006; Warner, 2003). Research on cultural effects is relatively new, so there is much to be worked out with respect to the precise role that subculture occupies in social disorganization theory. But scholars are beginning to sort out the issues and progress in occurring. Although we are unable to review the important findings from this nascent but growing literature, what we can say here is that it is becoming abundantly clear that, in the words of Kubrin & Weitzer (2003: 380), "cultural factors deserve greater attention" and can no longer be ignored. As Shaw and McKay and other early theorists believed, we cannot understand variations in crime rates across communities without also understanding the role that neighborhood subcultures occupy in the calculus. Along with greater attention to the concepts of collective efficacy, social capital, and social networks, future work must continue to specify subculture's critical role.

## References

Anderson, E. (1999). *Code of the Street*. New York: Norton.

Bellair, P.E. (1997). Social interaction and community crime: Examining the importance of neighbor networks. *Criminology, 35*, 677–703.

Berg, M.T., Stewart, E.A., Brunson, R.K., & Simons, R.L. (2012). Neighborhood cultural heterogeneity and adolescent violence. *Journal of Quantitative Criminology, 28*, 411–435.

Beyerlein, K., & Hipp, J.R. (2005). Social capital, too much of a good thing? American religious traditions and community crime. *Social Forces, 84*, 995–1013.

Browning, C.R. (2002). The span of collective efficacy: Extending social disorganization theory to partner violence. *Journal of Marriage and the Family, 64*, 833–850.

Browning, C.R. (2009). Illuminating the downside of social capital. *American Behavioral Scientist, 52*, 1556–1578.

Browning, C.R., Feinberg, S.L., & Dietz, R.D. (2004). The paradox of social organization: Networks, collective efficacy, and violent crime in urban neighborhoods. *Social Forces, 83,* 503–534.

Bursik, R.J. (1988). Social disorganization and theories of crime and delinquency – problems and prospects. *Criminology, 26,* 519–551.

Byrne, J. & Sampson, R.J. (1986). Key Issues in the social ecology of crime. In J. Byrne & R. Sampson (Eds.), *The Social Ecology of Crime.* New York: Springer-Verlag.

Cloward, R., & Ohlin, L. (1960). *Delinquency and Opportunity: A Theory of Delinquent Gangs.* New York: Free Press.

Dekeseredy, W.S., Alvi, S., & Tomaszewski, A.E. (2003). Perceived collective efficacy and women's victimization in public housing. *Criminology and Criminal Justice, 3,* 5–27.

Elliott, D.S., Wilson, W.J., Huizinga, D., Sampson, R.J., Elliott, A., & Rankin, B. (1996). The effects of neighborhood disadvantage on adolescent development. *Journal of Research in Crime and Delinquency, 33,* 389–426.

Fagan, J., & Wilkinson, D. (1998). Guns, youth violence, and social identity in inner cities. In M. Tonry & M. Moore (Eds.), *Crime and Justice, 24* (pp.105–188). Chicago: University of Chicago Press.

Granovetter, M.S. (1973). The strength of weak ties. *American Journal of Sociology, 78,* 1360–1380.

Hipp, J.R., Petersilia, J., & Turner, S. (2010). Parolee recidivism in California: The effect of neighborhood context and social service agency characteristics. *Criminology, 48,* 947–979.

Kirk, D.S., & Papachristos, A.V. (2011). Cultural mechanisms and the persistence of neighborhood violence. *American Journal of Sociology, 116,* 1190–1233.

Kornhauser, R. (1978). *Social Sources of Delinquency.* Chicago: University of Chicago Press.

Kubrin, C.E., & Weitzer, R. (2003). New directions in social disorganization theory. *Journal of Research in Crime and Delinquency, 40,* 374–402.

Kubrin, C.E., Stucky, T.D., & Krohn, M.D. (2009). *Researching Theories of Crime and Deviance.* New York: Oxford University Press.

Lee, M.R. (2008). Civic community in the hinterland: Toward a theory of rural social structure and violence. *Criminology, 46,* 447–478.

Lin, N. (1999). Building a network theory of social capital. *Connections, 1,* 28–51.

Maimon, D., & Browning, C.R. (2010). Unstructured socializing, collective efficacy, and violent behavior among urban youth. *Criminology, 48,* 443–474.

Mazerolle, L., Wickes, R., & McBroom, J. (2010). Community variations in violence: The role of social ties and collective efficacy in comparative context. *Journal of Research in Crime and Delinquency, 47,* 3–30.

Miller, W.B. (1958). Lower class culture as a generating milieu for gang delinquency. *Journal of Social Issues, 14,* 5–19.

Park, R.E., & Burgess, E.W. (1984[1925, 1967]). *The City: Suggestions for Investigation of Human Behavior in the Urban Environment.* Chicago: University of Chicago Press.

Pattillo, M.E. (1998). Managing crime in a black middle-class neighborhood. *Social Forces, 76,* 747–774.

Peterson, R.D., Krivo, L.J., & Harris, M.A. (2000). Disadvantage and neighborhood violent crime: Do local institutions matter? *Journal of Research in Crime and Delinquency, 37,* 31–63.

Pratt, T.C., & Cullen, F.T. (2005). Assessing macro-level predictors and theories of crime: A meta-analysis. In M. Tonry (Ed.), *Crime and Justice: A Review of Research,* Vol. *32* (pp. 373–450). Chicago: University of Chicago Press.

Putnam, R.D. (1995). Bowling alone: America's declining social capital. *Journal of Democracy*, 6, 65–78.

Putnam, R.D. (2000). *Bowling Alone: The Collapse and Revival of American Community.* New York: Simon & Shuster.

Rosenfeld, R., Messner, S.F., & Baumer, E.P. (2001). Social capital and homicide. *Social Forces*, 80, 283–309.

Sampson, R. J. (1987). Urban black violence: The effect of male joblessness and family disruption. *American Journal of Sociology*, 93:348–382.

Sampson, R.J. (2006). Collective efficacy theory: Lessons learned and directions for future inquiry. In F.T. Cullen, J.P. Wright, & K. Blevins (Eds.), *Taking Stock: The Status of Criminological Theory* (pp. 149–167). New Brunswick, NJ: Transaction.

Sampson, R.J., & Bartusch, D.J. (1998). Legal cynicism and (subcultural?) tolerance of deviance: The neighborhood context of racial differences. *Law and Society Review*, 32, 777–804.

Sampson, R.J., & Bean, L. (2006). Cultural mechanisms and killing fields: A revised theory of community-level racial inequality. Pp. 8–36 In R.D. Peterson, L.J. Krivo, & J. Hagan (Eds.), *The Many Colors of Crime: Inequalities of Race, Ethnicity, and Crime in America* (pp. 8–36). New York: New York University Press.

Sampson, R.J., & Groves, W.B. (1989). Community structure and crime: Testing social-disorganization theory. *American Journal of Sociology*, 94, 774–802.

Sampson, R.J., & Raudenbush, S. (1999). Systematic social observation of public spaces: A new look at disorder in urban neighborhoods. *American Journal of Sociology*, 105, 603–651.

Sampson, R.J., Raudenbush, S.W., & Earls, F. (1997). Neighborhoods and violent crime: A multilevel study of collective efficacy. *Science*, 277, 918–924.

Shaw, C.R., & McKay, H. (1969 [1942]). *Juvenile Delinquency and Urban Areas.* Chicago: University of Chicago Press.

Stewart, E.A., & Simons, R.L. (2006). Structure and culture in African-American adolescent violence: A partial test of the code of the street thesis. *Justice Quarterly*, 23, 1–33.

Triplett, R.A., Gainey, R.R., & Sun, I.Y. (2003). Institutional strength, social control, and neighborhood crime rates. *Theoretical Criminology*, 7, 439–467.

Venkatesh, S. (2000). *American Project: The Rise and Fall of a Modern Ghetto.* Massachusetts: Harvard University Press.

Venkatesh, S. (2006). *Off the Books: The Underground Economy of the Urban Poor.* Massachusetts: Harvard University Press.

Warner, B.D. (2003). The role of attenuated culture in social disorganization theory. *Criminology*, 41, 73–97.

Warner, B.D., & Rountree, P.W. (1997). Local social ties in a community and crime model: Questioning the systemic nature of informal social control. *Social Problems*, 44, 520–536.

Wilson, W.J. (1987). *The Truly Disadvantaged: The Inner City, the Underclass, and Public Policy.* Chicago, IL: The University of Chicago Press.

# 8

# Routine Activities, Delinquency, and Youth Convergences

## Jose R. Agustina and Marcus Felson

### Why is Important to Analyze Youth Convergences

Taken together, four basic and well-established empirical findings in criminology tell us to take a close look at youth hangouts:

- Crime participation peaks in adolescence (Hirschi & Gottfredson, 1983);
- Crime is often highly concentrated in space and time (Chainey & Ratcliffe, 2005; Weisburd, Grof, & Yang, 2012);
- At least half of all crime occurs through co-offending (Reiss, 1988); and
- Youths who spend more time in activities not structured by adults also tend to break more laws (Osgood *et al.*, 1996).

It is thus important to know where youths hang out together but in the absence of adults. Hanging out greatly enhances the volume of crime in nearby times and places, and also contributes noticeably to a larger crime rate.

The emphasis on youths together away from parents goes back at least to Felson and Gottfredson's (1984) effort to estimate generational change in adolescent activities. That research asked respondents to think back to when they were 17 years old, then to report the time at which they had to go to bed weekdays and weekends, whether parents noticed nocturnal tardiness, whether they spent the afternoons home or elsewhere, whether adults were present with them, and how many nights per week they had family dinner at home together. The paper found quite strong trends towards more adolescent activity away from parents. The survey questions in that paper influenced several subsequent studies by others. The sharpest results emerged from the sharpest questions – those that asked carefully where youths

*The Handbook of Criminological Theory*, First Edition. Edited by Alex R. Piquero.
© 2016 John Wiley & Sons, Inc. Published 2016 by John Wiley & Sons, Inc.

spend time and with whom. An emphasis upon tangibility proves very important for delinquency analysis.

The important point is that it makes good sense to focus on settings where youths spend unsupervised time with peers. Ideally one wants to know much more, namely exactly where, when, and how do youths meet, make plans and perhaps commit delinquent acts not far away. However, we should not presume that youths entering a given setting know in advance what will follow. "Delinquency and drift" is a phrase introduced by David Matza (1964), reminding us that the endpoint of a process is not necessarily known or planned at its outset. Nor do activities near peers without supervision produce crime every time. Youth hangouts will sometimes set the stage for crime and delinquency; most of the time nothing much happens. The hanging out without formal adult structure is largely a matter of situational drift that can lead to crime more readily than time spent under adult control or supervision.

Studying time spent is important for understanding how daily activities set the stage for crime outcomes. Cohen & Felson (1979) may have been the first to use time spent in the denominator to show that some routine activities and settings are many times riskier than time spent in other activities or settings. That point was especially pursued by Lemieux (2010; see also Lemieux & Felson, 2012). The greatest risks occur on the way to and from school, as well as in leisure settings. Crimes per thousand hours spent hanging out with other youths are many times greater than the same amount of time spent with parents.

In 1912 George E. Bevans conducted perhaps the first study of time use, asking working men in New York to estimate hours they spent doing a number of activities on each day of the week (Bevans, 1913). Included were studies of time in bars and other activity categories. Since that time many hundreds of time-use studies have been conducted around the world, including, since 2002, the annual American Time Use Survey with thousands of respondents annually. Some time-use surveys are conducted for youths, or at least have sufficient data to produce youth subsamples.

Time-use methodologies are increasingly applied to youths and especially to delinquent behavior,[1] and this strongly confirms the ideas suggested by Felson & Gottfredson, (1984), Felson (1995) and Osgood et al. (1996) – that time spent with peers but without parents is the most criminogenic. Strong support for the routine activity ideas is presented by Wikström and colleagues (2012), who conducted several waves of surveys with over 700 youths in Peterborough, UK. We calculated from data in tables 7.3 and 7.4 of that study that, hour for hour, self-reported youth crimes are 28 times more common in unstructured peer activities than in time spent with family. Hour for hour, unstructured peer activities are 2.75 times more criminogenic than other peer activities. The comparison to school-time is also noteworthy, with crimes committed per 10,000 hours in unstructured peer activities almost 20 times more numerous than in equivalent person-hours spent at school.

Research by Wim Bernasco and colleagues (2013) confirms this among Netherlands youths. Although the published sample is small, their larger sample finds that hour-for-hour, teen offending is 16 times more likely per 10,000 person-hours spent unsupervised, compared to time spent supervised by parents (Table 8.1).

**Table 8.1**   Teenage offending per 10,000 person-hours

| | |
|---|---|
| Supervised by parents | 2.4 |
| Supervised by other adults | 5.1 |
| Unsupervised | 39.3 |

This is highly consistent with the argument presented in Felson & Gottfredson (1984), and Felson (2003), which stressed that young offenders meet in informal, unsupervised, and recurrent settings that persist beyond the participation of any single list of persons, to the extent that the offender-convergence setting became a stable and predictable source of co-offenders. This argument was picked up by Osgood and associates (1996), and many papers have followed up on the idea. It is important not only to ask whether youths spend time together with adults absent, but also whether they have a stable hangout setting in which to do so.

## Are Youth Hangouts Stable?

Youth hangouts refer to a setting, not merely a place. Thus, a hangout may only be present after school on school days, or in a certain mall on Saturdays. The concept of hangout implies recurrence, but some room should be allowed for shifting hangouts. Nonetheless, meeting places that shift unpredictably are less likely destinations. We should distinguish meetings among people who know each other well and can email or text one another on where to meet today. But an adolescent convergence setting with a predictable time and place can serve those who are not necessarily invited or are not receiving up-to-date messages. Bichler, Malm, & Enriquez, (2014) refer to "magnetic facilities," such as malls or other destinations, which one can go to with near-certainty that someone will be around. By measuring and analyzing the "pull" of specific places, criminologists can better understand where crime and delinquency occur, learning what looking for in that settings. Absence of close adult supervision may be one of the requirements.

Yet, youths in Arlington, Texas, were somewhat more nuanced. They wanted toilets and did not mind unobtrusive police protection on the side, so long as they could circulate freely.

In Arlington, Texas, young people agreed with increasing police presence in their hangout area (Bell, 1989). The City of Arlington had exhausted most of the conventional means to control teenage cruising along Cooper Street. Adult concepts of what teenagers ought to do were not acceptable to the teenagers themselves, but so long as their own idea was accepted by the city, they did not mind police proximity. This raises an interesting substantive issue. Too little adult presence feeds delinquency. Too much adult presence and intrusion drives teenagers away, if they have a choice in the matter. A happy medium might reduce delinquency if it results in more time being spent in relatively safe settings.

The importance of time continues to emerge in routine activity research, including studies of teenagers. Soulé *et al.* (2008) have shown in a recent study that juvenile victimization and delinquency peak during the school day, while substance abuse peaks during the weekend. Disaggregating by offense, however, one learns that more serious violent offenses occur soon after school lets out on weekdays. Although simple assaults that are reported to police occur more during school hours, increasing evidence (Lemieux & Felson, 2012) shows that hour for hour the after-school period is the riskiest.

As an intermediate summary, youths spend time in both supervised and unsupervised environments. The latter allow them to relax without a rigid or fixed schedule. Some youth settings become regular hangouts, which produce more temptations under fewer controls and set the stage for crime and delinquency there or in nearby times and places. Youth activity settings can be compared and contrasted in terms of youth presences, adult absences, agendas and organization of activities, and problem outcomes there or in nearby settings.

In this paper we will emphasize Routine Activity Theory approach in analyzing youth convergent settings as a crime-place-oriented focus. The situational approach shifts attention away from the personal histories of offenders toward the dependence of crime on opportunities presented by the routine activities of everyday life. Birkbeck & LaFree (1993) noted that this shift corresponds to Sutherland's (1947) distinction between historical explanations, which account for crime by past events, and situational explanations, which account for crime by the circumstances in which it occurs.

For a deep and comprehensive analysis of the subject matter, we will review how criminological theory evolved from its origin and what the next steps are presumably going to be. Our starting point is that the emergence of theories of crime that emphasize the influence of routine activities (Cohen & Felson, 1979) or lifestyle (Hindelang, Gottfredson, & Garofalo, 1978) is one of the most significant developments in the study of deviance over the past decades (Osgood *et al.*, 1996: 635). Since the Cohen and Felson article in 1979, "Social Change and Crime Rate Trends: A Routine Activity Approach," more than three decades of fruitful research have shown the influential impact of Routine Activity Theory in criminological theory.

To properly understand Routine Activity Theory's novelty and fully benefit from its potential, we will look back to the origin and historical context in which Routine Activity Theory came out, and we will examine the subsequent evolution of such a groundbreaking theory. Moreover, beyond a review of its theoretical evolution, one could ask if, at present, some updates are needed to give a current account of Routine Activity Theory and, additionally, what new challenges Routine Activity Theory faces in continuously changing social circumstances.

Among the relevant social and criminological changes in the last decades, it is worth noting the increasing importance given in criminological theory to juvenile delinquency and its prevention.

This chapter shows a particular review of Routine Activity Theory by considering in historical and sociological perspective some of its core constructs – namely, the absence of handlers and managers – when applied to juvenile delinquency. In analyzing the evolution of the routine activity approach from its origin to the present day, one can also get a deeper understanding of some of the most relevant sociological and criminological changes. Routine Activity Theory's flexibility is a guarantee of its adaptation to social changes.

As we will discuss, by reviewing how Routine Activity Theory changed the way of looking at crime event in contrast with socialization theories, the accent is placed on crime dynamics and convergences in time and place. Such a new approach is particularly illuminating when it comes to youth crime. Adolescents' vulnerability to peer pressure and contextual particularities leads us to stress that an intensified situational approach is especially applicable to juvenile delinquency far beyond its application to adult crime. All this process should emphasize the importance of building up a middle-range theory of hangouts as a criminogenic setting.

The cornerstone of such a hangouts theory is that crime seeks times and places that are largely unsupervised. Thus, to understand delinquency, one always should ask whether somebody is watching at a particular place or nearby (Felson, 2006: 79). Consequently to the crime analysis triangle approach, crime prevention depends on three types of control agent – handlers, guardians, and place managers – although their importance varies by offense, setting, and offender age. In reference to offender age, Felson argues that at age 10, handlers are pivotal, and criminal action depends on a lack of parental supervision; while at age 16 such supervision is much more difficult to carry out. Hence, guardians of property and managers of places become more relevant for adolescents' crime prevention (Felson, 2006: 81).

Thus, we aim to focus on youth convergences in settings. As has been remarked (Bottoms & Wiles, 2002: 621):

> Environmental criminology is the study of crime, criminality, and victimization as they relate, first, to particular places and, secondly, to the way that individuals and organizations shape their activities spatially, and in so doing are in turn influenced by place-based or spatial factors.

## Looking Back: Routine Activity Theory's Novelty in Historical Context

Since at least the early 1900s, social science has examined the ways in which the social environment, by influencing youths, generates juvenile delinquency. The dominating idea in this field is that socialization of youths occurs over a considerable number of years, and that its impact persists over a substantial period of time. In fact, traditionally, criminology had predominantly focused on variations among individuals and their socialization, and neglected variations among situations (Felson, 1995: 19). Crime theorists, as Felson (2006: 97) argues, often focus on criminogenic information transmitted a considerable time before a crime occurs which, unfortunately, complicates greatly the task of verifying that A caused B.

The advent of Routine Activity Theory and Situational Crime Prevention strategies produced a contrary hypothesis, that potential offenders can be influenced very quickly to commit a deviant act or to avoid it. If this is true, social settings could produce deviant behavior without necessarily producing long-term changes in disposition, while such dispositions could be set aside by short-term temptations and illicit opportunities. From this understanding, it is much more practical to specify crime cues emitted just before the crime event, or leading to a crime later on that same day or quite soon.

This situational insight (Felson, 1995: 16–19), founded on the basic human frailty, explains how individuals, and especially adolescents, vary greatly in their behavior from one situation to another. Each individual varies in different situations on any given day. Almost everyone has ups and downs, ins and outs, anger and calm, conformity and defiance. Are youths as likely to get drunk with their parents present or absent? Are males no more rowdy among other males than they are in the presence of females? Do the same students who are quiet in a college class remain quiet at a college football game? Is juvenile delinquency no more likely to occur among a group of juveniles than it is when one juvenile is alone? Such an insight has been incorporated into a whole social science field known as situational social psychology. Although it is undeniable that individuals have personalities, situational social psychologists believe that the stability of personality is often exaggerated, that specific situations also have powerful effects on individuals.

Such an approach is not entirely incompatible with traditional socialization theory, but its emphasis is quite different. Moreover, this approach suggests that ordinary youths can commit delinquent acts without requiring a deviant peer culture. The purpose of this article is to review theories and research from this point of view. In so doing, we will not be very specific in our use of the words "crime," "delinquency," or "deviance," or in detailing particular types of infractions against societal rules. Rather, we consider broadly how particular settings influence whether or not juveniles produce such infractions.

## Evolution from a Strong Sociological Inquiry to a Focused-Situational Analysis

Students of adolescence have long been aware of tangible, situational elements of behavior. For example, early work referred to "hanging out in pool halls" as harmful to young people, and during the Progressive era many states introduced laws prohibiting youths from going there or punishing adults for allowing them in. Yet subsequent theoretical codification of these ideas by Sutherland clearly emphasized how youths internalized delinquent definitions; he mentioned the opportunity to carry out forbidden behaviors, but only in passing. Accordingly, the modern emphasis by some scholars upon immediacy of situational effects is a departure from the historical socialization literature. In his classic book on adolescent culture in high schools, James Coleman (1961) clearly took youth settings into account, yet emphasized once more a longer-term socialization over a short-term opportunity structure. Csikszentmihalyi, Larson, & Prescott (1977) developed the technology for measuring adolescent activities by using beepers, yet once more gave the greater weight to their subjective experience of those activities.

Earlier sociological consideration of the practical side of daily activities was found in Pitirim Sorokin's research on time use, a survey mostly of young adult women in the Boston area (Sorokin & Berger, 1939). Their data displayed major differences in the group sizes and circumstances of specific activities, some of which occurred in large groups, others in small groups, and other activities largely taking place alone. However, that work did not emphasize the independent impact of daily settings on behavior. Chicago school researchers were quite aware that settings influence deviant behavior, and that youths leave their own zone of residence to break rules (Shaw, McKay, & McDonald, 1938).

Despite the recognition that specific settings can influence immediate behavior, a broader environmentalism was more typical of Chicago School ideas.

The focus upon settings themselves as causal factors developed more in the psychological fieldwork by Roger Barker (see, e.g., Barker & Wright, 1954). Barker began this research tradition by dividing a small town in Kansas into several hundred behavior settings, tracing how the local people shifted their activities hour-by-hour among these settings. Thus, the same classroom might house a history-class setting one hour and an English-class setting the next hour. Barker also noted informal settings, such as "in front of the local gas station" where local boys "hang out" after school. Perhaps his most important contribution was to demonstrate that informal and apparently unstructured activities might actually have a degree of structure, recurring at the same time and place day in and day out. Barker also explained that certain behavior settings recurred even if the specific participants differed from one day to the next, at least to a certain degree. That indicated that structure is possible even when exact rosters of participation change. Barker clearly explained that the settings themselves had an impact on behavior beyond socialization of individuals. As he later explained (Barker, 1963), a person contributes to the setting, but is also constrained by it. A behavior setting secures the behavior appropriate to it. Although Barker did not talk about activities at nearby times and places, he nonetheless saw settings as ordered, self-regulated, composed of stable patterns, with nesting subsystems – implying that behavioral influence can carry over from one setting to another.

A much more physical approach than Barker's is taken by the routine activity approach. From the outset, Cohen & Felson (1979) named three types of social entity whose presences and absences affect a crime event. Such an event normally requires the convergence of a likely offender and a suitable target, in the absence of a capable guardian against crime. When these three diverge in time and space, a crime event is impossible or unlikely to occur. The routine activity approach recognizes crime possibilities in nearby times and places if daily life sets the stage for their occurrence. Thus, school locations and timing set the stage for crime victimizations on the way home from school. Further elaborations (Felson, 2006) noted that offenders needed to escape their own family and other interferences with delinquent behavior. Eck (1994) added the notion that some locations invite or discourage deviant behavior, and that the difference is often the presence or absence of a "place manager." These include apartment superintendents, storeowners, homeowners, long-time residents, or others who tend to discourage deviant behavior on the premises they supervise. Eck (1994; 2003) combined his and the elements of routine activities developed by Felson to produce the "problem analysis triangle." Its six elements can be summarized to understand how a youth can commit a delinquent act: He or she must evade handlers (such as parents); find a place with a place manager absent or incapacitated; then find an unguarded target. Unless these elements converge, a delinquent act is unlikely (except in the case of cybercrime, which poses a different set of routine requirements).

Although juvenile and adult deviances overlap, they have two frequent (but not necessary) differences. First, acts of deviance by the young more likely occur with other offenders present at the time of the incident; in contrast, many adult offenders carry out criminal acts alone, even if others assist them. Albert Reiss (1988) compiled extensive evidence that co-offending exceeds lone offending during adolescence, while lone offending predominates during adult ages. Andresen & Felson (2010a, 2010b, 2012) provided detailed evidence that co-offending declines dramatically as youths approach age 20, and continues to decline afterwards. Second, acts of deviance by the young are often incidental to social life. Thus, young offending is often an extension of social life, with the proceeds of crime often somewhat incidental. We do not wish to push this point too far, or to deny acquisitive purposes for juvenile thefts. But the immediate social aspect of crime is often noted in studies of juvenile delinquency. On the other hand, adult offending also involves direct socializing before or after, even if offenders tend to carry out many acts on their own.

To incorporate the social aspect of deviant behavior, Felson (2003) developed the concept of "convergence settings," namely, places and times where likely offenders converge and socialize. In such settings they sometimes cook up crimes, or they may wander into crime at nearby times and places. This concept has been applied to juveniles by Bichler *et al.* (2014), who discovered that youths in greater Los Angeles often converged on particular movie theaters, malls, or other juvenile hangouts. Although the same idea has been applied to organized adult offenders (see Kleemans, Melvin, & Weenink, 2012), our current emphasis is on the juvenile manifestation. Here, Barker's concept of behavior setting is especially useful because it helps us understand that joint activities may have a structure, even if such activities are informal and even if the specific participant changes from day to day or hour to hour.

One of the most widely studied applications of routine activities to juveniles is that by Wayne Osgood *et al.* (1996), linking juvenile delinquency to "unstructured socializing." The main idea (broadly consistent with routine activity theory) is that settings that are structured – particularly by adults – tend to produce relatively fewer infractions against societal laws and rules. Unstructured settings produce more infractions. It is interesting to contrast Osgood's interpretations with those of Coleman (1961). First, Coleman saw high schools as largely under the control of youths, not teachers. Second, Coleman did not view youth settings as unstructured, but rather as their own subculture with a set of rules and expected behaviors. Osgood's ideas also contrast with the notion that informal settings where youths "hang out" are recurrent in time and space, and structured in the sense that individuals are constrained by those settings. These quibbles do not disprove Osgood's basic point that adult dominance makes settings less suitable for delinquent behavior, while youth dominance does just the opposite. As a result, adolescent hangouts are expected to generate crime and delinquency, then and there as well as in nearby times and places.[2]

## Looking Through: Completing the Crime Analysis Triangle

In "Those Who Discourage Crime" (Felson, 1995), Felson gives account of the updates and the subsequent improved explanatory capability of the three core elements of his approach. Just as a guardian supervises the suitable target, a handler supervises the likely offender. Thus, social control in society requires keeping suitable targets near capable guardians and likely offenders near intimate handlers. But, what was the role of places?

Based on Eck's (1994) study of the spatial structure of illegal drug markets, which credited important roles in discouraging crime to those who control or monitor places, Routine Activity Theory takes an extraordinary step forward. Integrating Felson's (1986) work with his own, Eck notes three objects of supervision: the suitable target of crime; the likely offender; and the amenable place for crime to occur. Whichever way it is put, an offender has to get loose from his handlers, then find a target unprotected by guardians in a place free from intrusive managers. "Place manager" is the broad term Eck uses to describe this general role. Thus, handler, guardian, and manager can all interfere with criminal behavior, however inadvertently (Felson, 1995).

By integrating Eck's (1994) contribution, Routine Activity Theory focused more intensively on settings. As a matter of fact, from then on a growing body of research and experience shed light on local offender convergence settings. Much can be learned from "crime prevention through environmental design" (Crowe & Zahm, 1994; Felson *et al.*, 1996); "environmental criminology" (Brantingham & Brantingham, 1999; Rengert, 1996); "situational prevention" (Clarke, 1997; Smith & Clarke, 2000); "problem-oriented policing" (Goldstein, 1997); and "broken windows policing" (Kelling, 1999). All these situations pay close attention to settings and situations that feed crime.

Just a little later, the concept of "offender convergence settings" (Felson, 2003), based on this new emphasis, set the stage for a better understanding of how and why youths converge at some settings. Such concept, built on earlier work that explains how human behavior can be better understood by using "behavioral settings" as a unit of analysis (Barker, 1968), showed how some facilities and places have the capacity to host an array of crime opportunities while fostering a large, regenerating pool of potential accomplices. A facility can promote co-offending, as potential accomplices are able to gather with sufficient time for informal unstructured activity while remaining insulated from others who would interfere (Felson, 2003, 2006). Most important, offender convergence settings provide "structure and continuity in the face of individual, group, or network instabilities" (Felson, 2003: 158). According to Barker, even if the roster of participants changes entirely, the "behavior setting" itself persists, these settings being stable, irrespective of the specific individuals present.

Additionally, an individual's activities are carried out in a variety of physical and social settings. Settings may diverge depending on particular factors that make particular types of offending easier. In this regard, Clarke and Eck (2005: 66) described "crime facilitators" as situational characteristics that "help offenders commit crimes or acts of disorder." Facilitators may influence the risks, efforts, rewards, provocations, or excuses associated with crime (Clarke, 2009; Clarke & Eck, 2005). They include physical, social, and chemical facilitators. "Physical facilitators" include tools or aspects of the physical environment that enhance an offender's capabilities or serve to overcome prevention measures. "Social facilitators" increase rewards from crime, or provide encouragement and legitimization. And "chemical facilitators" increase the ability of offenders to ignore risks or moral constraints.

Subsumable within the categories of facilitators referred by Clarke & Eck (2005), Wortley (2008) has also described "situational precipitators," which include "prompts" that trigger criminal behavior by surfacing criminally motivating thoughts, feelings or desires; social "pressures" that promote inappropriate behavior; "permissions" that permit normally forbidden behavior; and "provocations" that create stress and provoke antisocial—often aggressive—responses.

## Looking Forward: Sociological Trends from the 1980s on and Beyond

Cohen & Felson (1979) described some micro-level assumptions of Routine Activity Theory approach looking back to the crime rate trends in the post-World War II United States. If routine activities, as they argued, may occur (1) at home, (2) in jobs away from home, and (3) in other activities away from home, the increased probability, based on dramatic sociological changes, of non-household activities involving a non-member of the household triggered a bulk of new opportunities for crime.

However, Routine Activity Theory is not a historical explanation for a shift in crime rates upon an unprecedented sociological transformation in terms of, among others, mobility, family structure, urban design, and social relationships. Routine Activity Theory approach has a flexible nature that makes it adaptable to changing social circumstances. Such flexibility, however, requires Routine Activity Theory researchers to keep updated to social changes in order to properly analyze the immediate environments in which crimes occur.

Social trends in recent decades continue to showng more people living alone, and a growth in family instability. As a consequence, youths are increasingly unsupervised. Moreover, in a digital era, teens are permanently connected and exposed to peer pressure. For a grown up digital generation, tech habits undoubtedly make life riskier. Opportunities are increasing – e.g., anonymity, lack of self-control, and awareness (of risks). Relationships are more fragile and impulsive. Getting into trouble seems easier.

Given changing environments, from physical to virtual ones, the old problems associated with a street corner where youths hang out may somehow be different. At least, we have to admit that there are now new meeting points and new forms of circumventing parental or any sort of supervision thanks to permanent virtual communications. Such virtual offender convergence settings should change the way we approach crime analysis and crime prevention.[3]

As Soudijn & Zegers (2012) have put it, carding is a good example of offender convergence settings in virtual space. Carding is a term used in the world of cybercrime that involves the fraudulent use of personal data taken from bank cards and credit cards (Peretti, 2008). Research has shown that people involved in carding can find each other through specialized online carding forums (Holt & Lampke, 2009; Peretti, 2008). Some of these carding forums are open to anyone who is interested in this type of illegal activity, whilst other forums have protected entry. These carding forums have a number of different functions; they provide a meeting place where carders can exchange information, start new illicit processes or deal in stolen data, goods, services, and software. In this way, the forums display strong similarities to what Felson calls "offender convergence settings" (Felson, 2003).

As Jaishankar's (2008) "space transition theory" has shown, people behave differently when they move from one space to another. The postulates of the theory are as follows:

1. Persons with repressed criminal behavior in physical space have a propensity to commit crimes in cyberspace that they otherwise would not commit due to their status and position.
2. Identity flexibility, dissociative anonymity, and lack of deterrence factors in cyberspace may provide the offenders with the means to commit cybercrimes.
3. Offenders' criminal behavior in cyberspace is likely to be imported to physical space; and criminal behavior in physical space may be exported to cyberspace.
4. Intermittent ventures of offenders to cyberspace and the dynamic spatiotemporal nature of cyberspace give offenders an escape.
5. Strangers are likely to join together in cyberspace to commit crimes in physical space; and associates in physical space are likely to join to commit crimes in cyberspace.
6. Individuals from closed societies are more likely to commit crimes in cyberspace than individuals from open societies.
7. The conflict between the norms and values of physical space and the norms and values of cyberspace may lead to cybercrimes.

# Identifying Unsupervised Settings as a Priority for Policymakers

As stated earlier, unstructured settings produce more infractions (Osgood *et al.*, 1996). However, there are many different sorts of unsupervised or unstructured settings.

Interestingly, as Miller's (2012) research has recently shown, different settings, because they may encompass different situational factors, tend to support different types of offending. His research proves and applies to specifics the insight of Cornish & Clarke (2008: 26): "the factors weighed by offenders, and the variables influencing their decision-making, will… differ greatly with the nature of the offence." Such a crime-specific character of settings is supported by empirical evidence. For example, as quoted by Miller, individual hotspots show a notable degree of crime specialization (Weisburd, Maher, & Sherman, 1992). Moreover, studies of youth delinquency show that patterns of variation through the day, or between school days and non-school days (and by implication settings), are very different according to the offense type considered (Gottfredson & Soulé, 2005; Jacob & Lefgren, 2003).

Youth hangouts often lead to a variety of problems nearby. These problems do not necessarily occur exactly at the hangout, and are not necessarily criminal in the extreme sense; they include annoyances such as noise and litter. But nearby thefts and violence can also be associated, at least according to the studies that are beginning to be published.

As Felson (2003) has put it, it would be a serious mistake to think of an entire "tough neighborhood" as a uniform and unified criminogenic setting. That is why the focus has to address a specific setting occurring only at particular hours. For example, a street corner might serve as an offender convergence setting only after 9:00 pm.

At this point, the difference between space, place, and setting becomes extremely useful (Felson, 2006: 102–3), setting being "a location for recurrent use, for a particular activity, at known times." There are many different types of spaces and places that may or may not become settings (see also Kayden, 2000). The degree of organization varies from spaces where people don't go, go by, or go through, to places where people stop briefly, remain for a while, or small and large destinations.

Yet only a few scholars have studied youth hangouts as a specific type of setting, generally finding that some adult influence in an area tends to improve the situation. Thus, it would be very useful to undertake research in this area.

## The "If we can't beat 'em, join 'em" approach.

- In Stockholm, Sweden, a series of police crackdowns on drug activity produced a notable increase in the average age of the drug-abusing population in the area, interfering in the accomplice-regeneration process (Knutsson, 1997).
- In Mississauga, Canada, Crime Prevention Services of the Peel Regional Police were asked to assist with a security review of a problem plaguing a child care center, located in the heart of a residential community. The design of the building and slope of the land necessitated the development of a large, concrete,

retaining wall in the northeast corner of the property. Unfortunately, the wall was used for cover by trespassers, loiterers, and other abnormal individuals, who were attracted to the dry and sunken nature of the space defined by the wall. This, along with a variety of other factors, had made this a favored hangout for area teens who used it as sort of a staging area prior to engaging in a range of illegal or undesired activities that included graffiti, access to the roof and damage to the vents, break-ins, drug and alcohol use, and sexual activity. However, by implementing "Crime Prevention Through Environmental Design" techniques, crime was weeded out with the help of an urban garden and a CCTV system.

- In Austin, Texas, the enactment of the ordinance, No Sit, No Lie.

## Hangouts as Gateways for Delinquency and Transitional Spaces

Many criminogenic settings have fully legitimate purposes. Often, youths go to bars or other public places just to be social. Yet, as we have seen, socializing sometimes fosters delinquency (Felson, 2006: 97). Looking at the spatial and functional relation between crime settings and convergence settings, the typology of settings provided by Eck *et al.* (2011) is striking. Apart from crime site, they refer to three types of crime-related settings:

1. They refer to Felson's (2003) convergent setting by describing it as a proprietary or proximal place that facilitates the meeting of potential offenders who might not know each other. Unlike meeting comfort spaces, offenders usually have little or no control over these places, and the situation often provides limited privacy to offenders. Importantly, convergent settings have important legitimate uses and typically serve mostly non-offenders. Offenders make use of the legitimate functions of these places for their own ends.
2. Interestingly, comfort spaces (Hammer, 2011) are usually proprietary places offenders use to help carry out their criminal activity. They can serve as locations for meeting (provides a comfortable private place for offenders to meet and socialize), supplying (a stash location for goods stolen from crime sites or for supplying black-market sites, often in close proximity to crime sites, or staging (provide safe haven in close proximity to customers and targets, giving an offender a space in which to observe neighborhood activities without great risk of apprehension by police). Unlike convergent settings, offenders exercise some control over the functioning of the place.
3. Finally, corrupting spots are proprietary places that support transactions that stimulate offenders to commit crimes at other places. The most obvious corrupting spots are places used by criminal receivers and others who purchase stolen goods. Some drug dealing spots can be considered corrupting.

However, Lemieux & Felson (2012) have recently examined the high risk associated with transit between activities – and, hence, between places. They looked to several broad types of daily activity that expose people to the risk of violence. A very strong general pattern is observed, with very high relative risk in transit and leisure activities and low risk in home and work activities. The observation that transit activities are more risky than leisure activities is especially surprising. The essential point they made is that people usually spend much less time in transit than at destinations themselves. All in all, their study was concerned about violent crime, and focused not only on youth crime.

Ethnographic studies have shown how unsupervised settings are crucially influential on juveniles. Youths look for unsupervised spaces and shape their own setting. People remake environments, but thereafter environments reshape us (Felson, 2006: 70).

As Robinson has put it, space is a good starting point for ethnographic study into youth, as it sets the stage in which dramas unfold. He argues that space should be considered as a character itself – a member of the group whose actions should form part of data collection. "For space acts as initiator: in space other issues can evolve and occur. In space, risk-taking behaviors transpire. Space bears witness to crime and conceals drug use. In it, embodiment is progressed –it endorses transition. It also portrays and signifies the social exclusion and marginalization of youth." (Robinson, 2009: 501).

> Willis (1990) conducted a study of young people on the streets and found that the street acted as a conveyor of their activities. The street not only functioned as a physical meeting place but also embodied meanings and metaphors relevant to the young people's lives. It was a container of escape and diversion but also represented home. The street yielded opportunity – a place to be seen and to view others. In this respect the street becomes a place of sharing, a confrontational challenging space, but one that promises ownership for those who put the time and effort into claiming it – especially after dark." (Robinson, 2009, p. 508).

"Space is a social product, or a complex social construction, that shapes perceptions and spatial practices, based on values and the social production of meanings" (Lefebvre, 1991). Lefebvre proposes that geographical space needs to be understood as fundamentally social and he highlights the importance of lived experience. Harvey argues that the question "What is space?" must be replaced by the question "How is it that distinctive human practices create and make use of distinctive spaces?" (1973: 14). He contends that social practices generate space, and in turn these spaces enable, modify and constrain those practices (Robinson, 2009: 505).

MacDonald & Marsh (2005) highlight the fact that relatively few studies consider criminal and drug-use careers alongside an exploration of youth leisure to chronicle youth transitions (Robinson, 2009: 509).

Humans affect crime by shaping landscapes. Criminologists have long recognized that construction affects crime opportunity in serious ways (Crowe & Zahm, 1994). For example, a garden with picket fences allows youths to be seen after entry and before departing; in contrast, solid walls hide the presence of delinquents, except for the short time entering and leaving the perimeter (Felson, 2006: 70).

## Proposing Ten principles for Routine Activities of Youths and an Eight Supervision-degree Scale

Drawing on the above-mentioned research we can assert: when youths are together with no adults around, they are more likely to get into trouble. Thus, youth crime cannot be properly understood without analyzing youth convergence settings and the contradictory forces that lead youths to one setting or another. From the research on youth convergences and crime, by analyzing what youths and adults want, the following ten principles emerge. They do not describe youth crime itself but, rather, pre-criminal situations conducive to crime.

1. Many youths wish to escape from adult proximity.
2. Yet many youths wish to maintain at least some adult proximity.
3. Many adults wish to escape from youth proximity.
4. Yet many adults want at least some other adults to remain proximate to youths.
5. Some adults lose money when youths are near.
6. Yet some adults make money off youths.
7. Youth proximity is essential for mass education to occur.
8. Youth proximity is normal and essential for basic social imperatives.
9. People are social, especially when young.
10. Adult sponsorship of an agenda does not guarantee adult control of all activities.

In accordance with the types of spaces and settings where youths hang out, we propose a supervision-degree scale that measures the intensity of youths being supervised.

1. Long-term runaways.
2. Regular truants.
3. Occasional truants.
4. Youths who leave school and return.
5. Youths who leave school and do not return.
6. Youths who evade teachers on school grounds.
7. Youths who find afternoon youth hangouts.
8. Youths who do not hang out with other youths.

## Final Considerations for Future Research

To improve policy on juvenile crime, every local agency needs to list and classify the offender convergence settings in its area, carefully noting exact locations and timing. It seems much simpler and more practical to regulate settings than offenders. By modifying or removing settings, youth offenders may have trouble finding one another or arranging subsequent crimes (Felson, 2003).

Despite the fact that established digital generations are permanently connected, and adolescents may virtually converge, real-space convergence settings remain crucial, especially if we consider that youth offenders need to screen each other informally during periods of what others may see as inaction (Sullivan, 1989a, b).

A variety of crime-prevention strategies might be useful case by case – redesign, shut down, divert, mix with other activities, or whatever assists the crime-depletion process. Efforts should be focused on increasing the level of supervision tolerated by youth hanging out in any spot. Much research is needed to explore what would be most effective in this regard.

## Notes

1  For more on the space–time budget method, see Hoeben, Bernasco, Weerman, Pauwels, & van Halem (2014).
2  Hoeben and Weerman show that unstructured socializing has even more impact when taking its location into account. *See* Hoeben & Weerman (2014).
3  Modern hand-held electronics have led to additional research opportunities for measuring adolescent activities. See Van Gelder & Van Daele (2014).

## References

Andresen, M.A. & Felson, M. (2010a). The Impact of co-offending. *British Journal of Criminology, 50*, 66–81.

Andresen, M.A., & Felson, M. (2010b). Situational crime prevention and co-offending. *Crime Patterns and Analysis, 3*(1), 3–13.

Andresen, M.A., & Felson, M. (2012). Co-offending and the diversification of crime types. *International Journal of Offender Therapy and Comparative Criminology, 56*(5), 811–829.

Barker, R.G. (1963). On the nature of the environment. *Journal of Social Issues, 19*(4), 17–38.

Barker, R.G. (1968). *Ecological Psychology: Concepts and Methods for Studying the Environment of Human Behavior*. Stanford, CA: Stanford University Press.

Barker, R.G., & Wright, H.F. (1954). *Midwest and its Children: The Psychological Ecology of an American Town* (pp. 1–19). New York: Row, Peterson.

Bell, J. (1989). Cruising Cooper Street. *The Police Chief* (January), 26–29.

Bernasco, W., Ruiter, S., Bruinsma, G., Pauwels, L., & Weerman, F. (2013). Situational causes of offending: A fixed-effects analysis of space-time budget data. *Criminology, 51*, 895–926.

Bevans, G.E. (1913). *How Working Men Spend Their Spare Time*. New York: Columbia University Press.

Bichler, G., Malm, A., & Enriquez, J. (2014). Magnetic facilities: Identifying the convergence settings of juvenile delinquents. *Crime & Delinquency, 60*(7), 971–998. doi:10.1177/0011128710382349.

Birkbeck, C., & LaFree, G. (1993). The situational analysis of crime and deviance. *Annual Review of Sociology, 19*, 113–137 doi: 10.1146/annurev.so.19.080193.000553.

Bottoms, A.E., & Wiles, W. (2002). Environmental criminology. In M. Maguire, R. Morgan, & R. Reiner (Eds.), *Oxford Handbook of Criminology* (pp. 620–656). Oxford: Oxford University Press.

Brantingham, P. & Brantingham, P. (1999). A theoretical model of crime hot spot generation. *Studies on Crime and Crime Prevention, 8*(1), 7–26.

Chainey, S., & Ratcliffe, J. (2005). *GIS and Crime Mapping.* London: Wiley.

Clarke, R.V. (1997). Introduction. In: R. Clarke (Ed.), *Situational Crime Prevention: Successful Case Studies* (2nd edition). Guilderland, NY: Harrow and Heston.

Clarke, R.V. (2009). Situational crime prevention: Theoretical background and current practice. In M.D. Krohn, A.J. Lizotte & G. Penly Hall (Eds.), *Handbook of Crime and Deviance* (pp. 259–276). New York: Springer.

Clarke, R.V., & Eck, J.E. (2005). *Crime Analysis for Problem Solvers in 60 Small Steps.* US Department of Justice Office of Community Oriented Policing Services.

Cohen, L.E., & Felson, M. (1979). Social change and crime rate trends: A routine activity approach. *American Sociological Review, 44,* 588–608.

Coleman, J.S. (1961). *The Adolescent Society.* New York: Free Press of Glencoe.

Cornish, D.B., & Clarke, R. (2008). *The Rational Choice Perspective: Environmental Criminology and Crime Analysis.* Portland: Willan Publishing.

Crowe, T.D., & Zahm, D. (1994). Crime prevention through environmental design. *Land Management, 7,* 22–27.

Csikszentmihalyi, M., Larson, R., & Prescott, S. (1977). The ecology of adolescent activity and experience. *Journal of Youth and Adolescence, 6,* 281–294.

Eck, J.E. (1994). Drug markets and drug places: A case-control study of the spatial structure of illicit drug dealing. Doctoral dissertation, University of Maryland, College Park.

Eck, J.E. (2003). Police problems: The complexity of problem theory, research and evaluation. In J. Knutsson (Ed.), *Problem-Oriented Policing: From Innovation to Mainstream* (pp. 67–102). Monsey, NY: Criminal Justice Press.

Eck, J.E., Madensen, T.D., & Hammer, M. (2011). Peek-a-boo: Responses to hidden crime places. 22nd Annual Problem-Oriented Policing Conference, October 10–12, 2011, Miami, FL.

Felson, M. (1986). Routine activities, social controls, rational decisions, and criminal outcomes. In D. Cornish & R.V.G. Clarke (Eds.), *The Reasoning Criminal.* New York: Springer-Verlag.

Felson, M. (1995). Those who discourage crime. In J.E. Eck & D. Weisburd (Eds.), *Crime and Place* (pp. 53–66). Monsey, NY: Criminal Justice Press.

Felson, M. (2003). The process of co-offending. In M.J. Smith and D.B. Cornish (Eds.), Theory for Practice in Situational Crime Prevention (pp. 149–168). Monsey, NY: Criminal Justice Press.

Felson, M. (2006). *Crime and Nature.* Thousand Oaks, CA: Sage.

Felson, M., Belanger, M.E., Bichler, G.M., Bruzinski, C.D. *et al.* (1996). Redesigning Hell: Preventing crime and disorder at the Port Authority Bus Terminal. In R.V. Clarke (Ed.) *Preventing Mass Transit Crime* (pp. 5–92). Monsey, NY: Criminal Justice Press.

Felson, M., & Gottfredson, M. (1984). Adolescent activities near peers and parents. *Journal of Marriage and the Family, 46,* 709–714.

Goldstein, A.P. (1997) Controlling vandalism: the person–environment duet. In A. Goldstein & J. Conoley (Eds.), *School Violence Intervention: A Practical Handbook.* New York: Guilford Press.

Gottfredson, D., & Soulé, D. (2005). The timing of property crime, violent crime and substance abuse among juveniles. *Journal of Research in Crime and Delinquency, 42*(2), 110–120.

Hammer, M. (2011). Crime places of comfort. Unpublished Masters Demonstration Project paper. Cincinnati, OH: University of Cincinnati, School of Criminal Justice.

Harvey, D. (1973). *Social Justice and the City*. Baltimore, MD: Johns Hopkins University Press.

Haynie, D.L., & Osgood, D.W. (2005). Reconsidering peers and delinquency: How do peers matter? *Social Forces, 84*(2), 1109–1130.

Hindelang, M.J., Gottfredson, M.R., & Garofalo, J. (1978). Victims of personal crime: An empirical foundation for a theory of personal victimization. Cambridge, MA: Ballinger.

Hirschi, T., & Gottfredson, M. (1983). Age and the explanation of crime. *American Journal of Sociology, 89*, 552–584.

Hoeben, E., & Weerman, F. (2014). Situational conditions and adolescent offending: Does the impact of unstructured socializing depend on its location? *European Journal of Criminology, 11*: 481–499.

Hoeben, E.M., Bernasco, B., Weerman, F.M., Pauwels, L., & Van Halem, S. (2014). The space–time budget method in criminological research. *Crime Science, 3*, 12.

Holt J.T., & Lampke, E. (2009). Exploring stolen data markets online: Products and market forces. *Criminal Justice Studies, 23*(1), 33–50.

Jacob, B.A., & Lefgren, L. (2003). Are idle hands the Devil's workshop? Incapacitation, concentration, and juvenile crime. *American Economic Review, 93*(5), 1560-1577.

Jaishankar, K. (2008). Space transition theory of cyber crimes. In F. Schmalleger & M. Pittaro (Eds.), *Crimes of the Internet* (pp. 283–301). Upper Saddle River, NJ: Prentice Hall.

Kayden, J.S. (2000). *Privately Owned Public Space: The New York City Experience*. New York: Wiley.

Kelling, G.L., & National Institute of Justice (US). (1999). Broken windows and police discretion. Washington, DC: US Dept. of Justice, Office of Justice Programs, National Institute of Justice.

Kleemans, E.R., Melvin, R.J., & Weenink, A.W. (2012). Organized crime, situational crime prevention and routine activity theory. *Trends in Organized Crime, 15*, 87–92.

Knutsson, J. (1997). Restoring public order in a park. In: R. Homel (Ed.), *Crime Prevention Studies*, vol. 4. Monsey, NY: Criminal Justice Press.

Lefebvre, H. (1991). *The Production of Space* (Trans. N. S. Donald). Oxford: Blackwell.

Lemieux, A.M. (2010). Risks of violence in major daily activities: United States, 2003–2005. Unpublished doctoral dissertation. Rutgers University, Newark, NJ.

Lemieux, A.M., & Felson, M. (2012). Risk of violent crime victimization during major daily activities. *Violence and Victims, 27*(5), 635–655.

MacDonald, R., & Marsh, J. (2005) *Disconnected Youth? Growing up in Poor Britain*. Basingstoke: Palgrave.

Matza, D. (1964). *Delinquency and Drift*. New York: Wiley.

Miller, H.V. (2012). Correlates of delinquency and victimization in a sample of Hispanic youth. *International Criminal Justice Review, 22*, 153–170.

Osgood, D.W., & Anderson, A.L. (2004). Unstructured socializing and rates of delinquency. *Criminology, 42*(3), 519–549.

Osgood, D.W., Wilson, J.K., Bachman, J.G., O'Malley, P.M., & Johnston, L.D. (1996). Routine activities and individual deviant behavior. *American Sociological Review, 61*, 635–655.

Peretti, K.K. (2008). Data breaches: What the underground world of "carding" reveals. *Santa Clara Computer and High Technology Law Journal, 25*, 345–414.

Reiss, A.J. (1988) Co-offending and criminal careers. In M. Tonry & N. Morris (Eds.), *Crime and Justice: A Review of Research*, vol. *10*, 117–170. Chicago: University of Chicago Press.

Rengert, G. (1996). *The Geography of Illegal Drugs*. Boulder, CO: Westview Press.

Robinson, C. (2009). "Nightscapes and leisure spaces": An ethnographic study of young people's use of free space. *Journal of Youth Studies*, *12*(5), 501–514.

Shaw, C.R., McKay, H.D., & McDonald, J.F. (1938). *Brothers in Crime: A Study in Juvenile Delinquency, with Special Reference to the Five Brothers*. Chicago: University of Chicago Press.

Smith, M.J., & Clarke, R.V. (2000). Crime and Public Transport. In M. Tonry (Ed.) *Crime and Justice: A Review of Research*, vol. *27*. Chicago: University of Chicago Press.

Soudijn, M.R.J., & Zegers, B.C.H.T. (2012). Cybercrime and virtual offender convergence settings. *Trends in Organized Crime*, *15*, 111–129. doi: 10.1007/s12117-012-9159-z.

Soulé, D., Gottfredson, D.C., & Bauer, E. (2008). It's 3 p.m. Do you know where your child is? A study on the timing of juvenile victimization and delinquency. *Justice Quarterly*, *25*, 623–646.

Sorokin, P.A., & Berger, C.Q. (1939). *Time-Budgets of Human Behavior*. Cambridge, MA: Harvard University Press.

Sullivan, M.L. (1989a). Absent fathers in the inner city. *Annals of the American Academy of Political and Social Science*, *501*, 48–58.

Sullivan, M.L. (1989b). *Getting Paid: Youth Crime and Employment in the Inner City*. Ithaca, NY: Cornell University Press.

Sutherland, E.H. (1947). *Principles of Criminology*. 4th edition. Philadelphia: Lippincott.

Van Gelder, J.-L. & Van Daele, S. (2014). Innovative data collection methods in criminological research. *Crime Science*, *3*, 1–4.

Weisburd, D., Maher, L., & Sherman, L. (1992). Contrasting crime general and crime specific theory: The case of hot spots of crime. In F. Adler & W. Laufer (Eds.), New Directions in Criminological Theory, *Advances in Criminological Theory*, vol. *4* (pp. 45–69). New Brunswick, NJ: Transaction Press.

Weisburd, D., Grof, E.R., & Yang, S.M. (2012). *The Criminology of Place: Street Segments and our Understanding of the Crime Problem*. Oxford: Oxford University Press.

Wikström, P.-O., Oberwittler, D., Treiber, K., & Hardie, B. (2012). *Breaking Rules: The Social and Situational Dynamics of Young People's Urban Crime*. Oxford: Oxford University Press.

Willis, P. (1990). *Common Culture*. Milton Keynes: Open University Press.

Wortley, R. (2008). Situational precipitators of crime. In R. Wortley & L. Mazerolle (Eds.) *Environmental Criminology and Crime Analysis* (pp. 48–69). Cullompton: Willan Publishing.

# 9

# Environmental Criminology

## Aiden Sidebottom and Richard Wortley

## Overview

Criminology is a diverse field of study comprising many subdisciplines, which differ in their assumptions, methods and aims. Reflecting this diversity, the usual definition of criminology is broadly framed as the *scientific study of crime and criminals* (e.g., *Oxford English Dictionary*, 2013). One might expect from this definition that the study of crime and the study of criminals has attracted similar levels of theoretical and research attention. Yet traditionally most criminological research has focused on the latter, exploring the developmental and macro-social conditions – family dynamics, schooling, social organization, and the like – presumed to produce the criminal offender. Many attempts to reduce crime reflect this focus, and are best thought of as efforts to alter offender criminality through, say, enriching childhood experiences or reducing social inequalities.

This chapter provides an overview of environmental criminology. Our aim is to demonstrate what is distinctive about this approach and the role it plays in understanding and preventing crime. The chapter is structured as follows. We begin by charting the criminological and psychological foundations of environmental criminology. This is followed by a description of the key theories of environmental criminology. Next we discuss how environmental criminology is applied in the service of policing and crime prevention. In the final section we discuss some of the criticisms of and controversies within environmental criminology, and speculate on future research directions.

*The Handbook of Criminological Theory*, First Edition. Edited by Alex R. Piquero.
© 2016 John Wiley & Sons, Inc. Published 2016 by John Wiley & Sons, Inc.

## Historical and Conceptual Foundations of Environmental Criminology

The first exposition of "environmental criminology" as a distinct field of study was Paul and Patricia Brantingham's (1981) book of that name (although the term itself was coined some ten years earlier by Jeffery, 1971). The Brantinghams defined environmental criminology as the study of the 'discrete location in time and space... in which a criminal event occurs" (Brantingham & Brantingham, 1981: 7). Environmental criminologists, therefore, ask:

> questions about where and when crimes occur. They ask about the physical and social characteristics of crime sites. They ask about the movements that bring the offender and target together at the crime site. They ask about the perceptual processes that lead to the selection of crime sites and the social processes of ecological labelling. Environmental criminologists also ask about the spatial patterning in laws and the ways in which legal rules create crime sites. They ask about the spatial distribution of targets and offenders in urban, suburban, and rural settings. (Brantingham & Brantingham, 1981: 7)

The intention of the Brantinghams was to set out a criminological approach that was distinct from the usual focus on explaining offending behavior from a biological, developmental and/or sociological perspective. Common to these traditional theories was a preoccupation with identifying *distal* risk factors judged to be causally related to criminal behavior. It followed that reductions in crime are best achieved through altering offender motivation, either in advance of criminal involvement for individuals exhibiting known risk factors or as part of rehabilitation efforts to reduce reoffending. The propensity to commit crime was assumed to be relatively stable across different situations and to reliably distinguish offenders from non-offenders. Environmental criminology, on the other hand, is concerned with *crime* rather than *criminality*. It is the study of crime events and crime patterns in terms of *proximal* environmental risk factors. It is an applied branch of criminology, concerned with explaining, predicting, and preventing crime.

However, environmental criminology should not be thought of as a unitary theory, and nor were the Brantinghams the first to focus on immediate environmental contributions to crime. Environmental criminology is best conceptualized as an overarching framework that comprises several approaches linked by a common interest in crime events. In this section we examine the historical and conceptual foundations of environmental criminology. We begin by tracing the interest in criminology in crime and place. We then examine the model of human behavior that provides the conceptual foundation for the role of immediate environments in crime.

### Criminological roots

Despite the relative neglect of the immediate environment in modern criminology, some of the earliest recognizable criminological research explained crime in terms of contributing environmental features. Notably, in the early nineteenth century

André-Michel Guerry (1833) and Lambert Adolphe Quetelet (2013) independently analyzed French crime data to produce what would today be called crime maps. They showed that crime was unevenly distributed across space, that the distribution varied by crime type and that the patterns appeared to reflect the availability of crime opportunities as opposed to area-level poverty, then assumed to be the main cause of crime. They found, for example, that property crime was higher in wealthy, industrialized areas than in poorer rural areas. To borrow the apocryphal response of notorious bank robber William Sutton when asked why he robbed banks, more theft occurred in the city because "that's where the money is." Crime mapping subsequently became popular in Victorian England and later in the US, and has become a mainstay analytic technique in environmental criminology (see Chainey & Ratcliffe, 2005).

The Chicago School of the first half of the twentieth century offered the first formal criminological theory in which the spatial distribution of crime occupied center-stage. A branch of the human ecology movement, the Chicago School was concerned with the distribution of social groups as a function of the structural qualities and physical geography of the urban environment. The city was characterized as a superorganism comprising subcommunities bound together in symbiotic relationships. One of the dominant concepts, developed by Shaw & McKay (1942) in particular, was that of the city as a series of concentric zones. Each zone has distinctive land uses that determine the socioeconomic characteristics of the population. Crime rates are highest for residential areas closest to the center of the city, where the population is under greatest economic and social pressure and where crime opportunities abound. Crime rates decrease the further the zone is from the center. Moreover, the population of the city is in a state of flux. Ecosystems in the natural world are characterized by a process of invasion, domination and succession as plants and animals compete for habitat. Likewise, immigrants into the city typically begin in the central residential zones where rents are cheap, but they gradually move to the outer zones as they become more affluent and move up the social ladder.

The Chicago School was very influential in the development of traditional sociological criminology after World War II, paving the way for social disorganization theory and other subcultural approaches. But its ecological underpinnings and the finding that delinquency persists in certain geographic regions despite repeated ethnic turnover also has important lessons for environmental criminology (Brantingham & Brantingham, 1981).

The period 1971–1986 saw what we can, in hindsight, rightly call the golden age of environmental criminology. In the space of 15 years most of the foundational theories and approaches in the field were published. Kicking off this boom were two books with remarkably similar titles published within a year of each other. The first was C. Ray Jeffery's (1971) *Crime Prevention Through Environmental Design*: the second was Oscar Newman's (1972) *Defensible Space: Crime Prevention Through Urban Design*. As the titles indicate, both books had an applied focus, setting out respective agendas for preventing crime based around altering criminogenic environmental conditions. Jeffery presented a wide-ranging analysis of the role of the immediate environment in crime, covering not just urban design but also the importance of effective behavioral therapies, swift legal deterrence and evidence-based crime policies. While the title of Jeffery's book – usually shortened to CPTED – is now typically used as a generic label to describe both of their approaches, in fact it has been the more narrowly focused ideas of Newman that have had greater lasting impact. Newman was an architect and he was interested in the role of building design and town planning in promoting and preventing crimes. The key to prevention, argued Newman, was urban design that encouraged residents to develop a sense of ownership (territoriality) over their immediate neighborhood, and through their increased sense of responsibility and heightened vigilance, deter potential intruders. Through this process, public and semi-public areas that might otherwise generate crime become defensible spaces. Today, CPTED is largely understood in terms of these architectural and town planning principles.

The works of Jeffery and Newman were the catalyst for a flurry of activity examining the role of immediate environments in crime, and they laid the groundwork for the development of the key theories and approaches that now underpin environmental criminology. We take up the story of these remaining theories a little later in this chapter. Before that, next we examine a similar shift of focus onto the immediate environment that occurred in psychology around the same time and that has important implications for environmental criminology.

## Psychological roots

While environmental criminology is primarily concerned with crime and place rather than with the psychological antecedents of the offender, the approach only makes sense if we have a model of human behavior that incorporates a significant causal role for the immediate environment. That is, we need to show that immediate environments have a nontrivial effect on the way individuals act in particular situations.

Thinking in this way is notoriously difficult. Giving full recognition to the role that immediate environments play in behavior is deeply counterintuitive. Human beings, it seems, are hard-wired to see the world from the perspective of actors. There is a term for this phenomenon – fundamental attribution error (Ross, 1977). We typically interpret the causes of other people's negative behavior in dispositional terms and downplay extenuating environmental factors. When someone else is angry, it is because he/she has a hostile personality. Of course, we don't apply the same rule to our own behavior. When we are angry it is because we have had a bad day, we are tired, or we have been provoked. It is thought that the fundamental attribution error has evolved as an adaptive information-processing strategy designed to help us make efficient (if not entirely accurate) judgments about our complex social world (Andrews, 2001). At any rate, despite identifying the phenomenon, it seems that psychologists are as liable to commit the fundamental attribution error as everyone else: like criminology, psychology has been traditionally concerned with developing theories that explain behavior in terms of dispositional constructs such as personality, attitude, and psychological disorder.

The dispositional bias in psychology was most famously challenged by Walter Mischel (1968). Mischel argued that internal traits were poor predictors of behavior. Instead, individuals were found to behave very differently across different settings such that an extrovert in one situation can be shy and sheepish in another (think Michael Jackson on stage versus being interviewed). Mischel's conclusions are supported by extensive psychometric research showing that the correlation between personality traits and their supposed behavioral expression is typically of the order of 0.4, a moderate level of association that explains just 16% of the variance (e.g., Nisbett, 1980). Mischel proposed an alternative, behavioral-specificity model. While individuals do possess traits, those traits are expressed under certain prescribed conditions. It has become a central tenet of psychology that all behavior occurs as the result of a person–situation interaction (see Wortley, 2012).

Several classic experiments provide dramatic demonstrations of the power of the immediate environment on human behavior. Perhaps most notable is Philip Zimbardo's (1970) Stanford prison experiment. Zimbardo and colleagues were interested in the behavioral effects of institutional settings. They sought to explore, amongst other things, whether the violence often observed in prisons can be wholly attributed to dispositional factors and "bad" people or whether the environment itself might provoke such behavior. To investigate this, 24 psychologically normal, male college students (selected from over 70 applicants) were randomly assigned to be either a prisoner or a prison guard in a simulated prison in a basement at Stanford University. Those individuals assigned to act as guards received no formal training but were asked to instill a "sense of powerlessness" on the part of the prisoners and subject them to the commands and conditions characteristic of life in prison, such as referring to them by their ID numbers rather than their names. Revolt and rioting by the prisoners soon followed. What was striking about the Stanford Prison Experiment was the reaction of the guards, who acted with increasing aggression and hostility towards the prisoners, oftentimes deliberately humiliating and punishing them, to the extent that the experiment had to be cancelled after only six days.

Another noteworthy (and notorious) experiment was Stanley Milgram's (1974) electric shock study. Milgram sought to investigate whether the "blind obedience" witnessed in Nazi Germany and the large-scale killing of Jews was specific to particular individuals in that particular time and place or whether such behavior was, in theory, generalizable. In his study, participants were recruited in the belief that they were taking part in research on memory and the effects of punishment. Participants were informed that the experiment consisted of a teacher and a learner. The learner was required to memorize a series of word couplets and, when presented with one word by the teacher, respond by stating the corresponding word. Success was rewarded and failure punished by the teacher flicking a switch that administered an electric shock. Thirty switches were present, each increasing in voltage from a minor 15V to a fatal 450V. From the perspective of the participant, assignment to the role of teacher or learner appeared random – straws were drawn – but in reality the learner was a stooge and the electric shock machine phony. Critically, Milgram was present during the word association task to remind participants of the purpose of the study should they show unease at what they were being asked to do – which many did. The results are now infamous: despite halting concerns and at times clear distress, nearly two-thirds of participants administered all thirty electric shocks, tantamount to electrocuting the "learner." Consistent with Hannah Arendt's (1963) observations from watching the trail of Adolf Eichmann, a leading architect of the holocaust, evil displayed much banality.

The experiments of Milgram and Zimbardo are but two well-known examples attesting to the power of situations. There are many others. Moreover, similar effects can be observed outside of the laboratory, most recently with the abuse committed against prisoners at Abu Ghraib in 2003–4 during the Iraq war (see Zimbardo, 2007). Taken together, they patently demonstrate how the behavior of everyday people can be shaped by the immediate environment. The implications hold particular relevance for criminology: criminal behavior is not solely the province of "bad" people, but is a potential outcome for "normal" people under conducive conditions.

## Key Perspectives in Environmental Criminology

As alluded to previously, environmental criminology is best thought of as a family of theories that share a common interest in crime events and the causal influence of the immediate environment. Three perspectives, considered to form the bedrock of environmental criminology are examined: the routine activity approach, crime pattern theory, and the rational choice perspective. These perspectives vary, among other things, in the level of aggregation at which environmental influences are examined, running from macro-, through meso-, to micro-analysis.

### Routine activity approach

The routine activity approach (RAA) seeks to explain how macro-level social factors affect the daily routines of citizens, and how these routines in turn are responsible for variations in crime rates over space and time. RAA was first developed by Cohen & Felson (1979) in order to make sense of the rise in direct contact predatory crime experienced in the US following World War II. As with the era in which Guerry and Quetelet's research was undertaken, conventional wisdom at the time advanced a rather simple notion that poverty was a key driver of crime: lessening the former should produce falls in the latter. Yet the evidence showed the reverse to be true; crime rates in the US *increased* in the decades following 1945 despite improvements in aspects of social welfare commonly implicated in crime. Many theories of criminality failed to adequately explain this trend: there was no observable decline in the quality of parenting, the importance of the family unit, the extent of social inequalities, etc. Contrariwise, Cohen & Felson (1979) demonstrated that the crime patterns could be attributed to large-scale and somewhat prosaic societal changes that increased the likelihood of potential victims and offenders coming into contact with one another. For example, they found that there were particular increases in daytime domestic burglary, compared with nighttime domestic burglary and commercial burglary. They concluded that this increase was driven by (1) higher levels of household wealth, accompanied by the ownership of relatively expensive and portable consumer goods (e.g., small electrical appliances), that made domestic burglaries more lucrative; and (2) the increase in the number of females entering the workforce, and therefore, the increased number of houses left unguarded during the day.

The key insight of Cohen & Felson (1979) was the recognition that crime is dependent on more than simply criminals; rather, it requires a convergence in space and time of a likely offender (someone motivated to commit crime), and a suitable target (someone or something that the likely offender is attracted to offend against), without the presence of suitable guardians (someone who is able and empowered to protect the target). Moreover, this convergence is not haphazard but is explicable in terms of the natural rhythms of everyday life. This shift in thinking held important implications for the study and prevention of crime: (1) it suggested that crime will concentrate where the routine movements of victims and offenders overlap; (2) that the source of these movements can be legitimate activities unrelated to crime; (3) that fluctuations in the supply and movement of offenders, victims, and guardians as a function of their everyday routine activities can explain variations in crime rates; and (4) that disrupting the convergence of these elements can lead to crime reductions.

Examples of crimes patterned by routine activity abound. There has not only been a general increase in daytime burglary as Cohen & Felson (1979) report, but burglaries tend to increase in pleasant weather when home owners are more likely to be away (Hipp *et al.*, 2004). Likewise, sexual assaults increase in warm weather when potential offenders and victims are more likely to be out socializing, often with one another (McLean, 2007). Rates of assaults involving juveniles (as both victims and perpetrators) peak in mid-afternoon on weekdays (but not weekends), coinciding with the release of students from school (Snyder *et al.*, 1996). And young males have the highest rates of physical victimization because they are more likely than other sociodemographic groups to lead risky lifestyles that place them in harm's way (Jensen & Brownfield, 1986).

## Crime pattern theory

The RAA sets out the "chemistry of crime" (Felson, 2002): those elements that must be present for crime to occur. Yet it says little about how these elements converge in time and space. This is the subject of crime pattern theory (CPT) (Brantingham & Brantingham, 1995; 2008), which considers how offenders locate or encounter crime opportunities as part of their routine activities. Where RAA focused on the effects of broad societal trends, CPT is chiefly interested in the spatial patterns of crime in the urban landscape, providing an account of the clustering of crime events in time and space at a meso-level of analysis. It is well known that human mobility patterns are non-random. Our everyday movements are dominated by the need to travel to and from work or school and our regular visits to certain community or recreational locations. In CPT, these key locations that we frequent are referred to as nodes, and the regular routes that connect them are referred to as paths. Skewed spatial activity gives rise to skewed spatial awareness, so that we become familiar with the areas that we visit frequently, while our knowledge of areas that we seldom visit remains hazy. CPT uses the term "awareness spaces" to refer to the areas around the nodes and paths that we are familiar with as a consequence of our daily routines. According to CPT, offenders prefer to commit crime within their awareness spaces since it is in these areas that they are likely to possess superior knowledge about available crime targets and other factors that may affect crime commission (such as the street layout, the likelihood of encountering capable guardians, etc.). Considered a different way, crime is expected to cluster in areas that are familiar to population groups liable to commit crime which contain plentiful crime opportunities but where the perceived risks of detection are judged to be low.

There are four kinds of location at which crime is more likely to occur (Brantingham & Brantingham, 1995; 2008). First, a *crime generator* is a location that attracts large numbers of people for legitimate purposes, such as a sports stadium, shopping mall, bus station, or nightclub. The volume of people provides a large pool of potential victims for pickpockets and muggers, and may generate jostling and stresses that lead to assaults. Second, a *crime attractor* is a location that draws potential offenders for the specific purpose of committing crime. Crime attractors include seedy bars, drug markets, and red-light districts where offenders come to fence stolen goods, sell or obtain drugs, or pimp for prostitutes. Third, a *crime enabler* is a location at which there is little regulation of behavior, or, in RAA terms, there is an absence of capable guardians. Crime enablers include unattended car parks and playgrounds, where crimes can occur unobserved. The final location is known as an *edge*. An edge is the boundary between neighborhoods or districts that individuals encounter at the fringe of their nodes or paths. Edges can take many forms, ranging from physical barriers (such as roads or rivers) that clearly delineate two areas, to perceptual barriers that signal a change in land use or demographic profile, such as two neighborhoods that differ markedly in affluence and ethnic composition. Edges are locations where territorial conflicts can arise between those from either side of the edge or where offenders may commit crime just outside their neighborhood with little fear that they will be recognized. Moreover, edges often comprise an assortment of land uses (such as residential, commercial, and retail) which can give rise to crime opportunities.

A prediction that follows from crime pattern theory is that offenders generally will not travel far from their nodes in order to commit crime. So-called journey-to-crime research confirms this prediction. Snook (2004), for example, examining data from 41 serial burglars, found that the median distance travelled to commit a burglary was 1.7 kilometers. The rate of decay for crime trip distance was rapid, following an inverted J-curve; 33% of burglary sites were within one kilometer of offenders' homes, 25% between one and two kilometers, and 15% between two and three kilometers. Further, burglaries do not just offend close to home but typically do so along the path between home and another significant node (Rengert & Wasilchick, 1985). Similar distance–decay patterns have been found for numerous other crime types (see Townsley & Sidebottom, 2010; Wiles & Costello, 2000).

The RAA and CPT make for good bedfellows. The former describes the necessary conditions for crime to occur and the latter describes where and when these conditions are most likely to overlap as a function of peoples' routine activities (be they prospective offenders, victims and/or guardians). It should be stressed, however, that neither approach advances a deterministic model of crime causation. Put differently, unlike the immutable laws that govern much chemistry, it is not assumed that when the elements of the chemistry of crime meet in space and time that they *inevitably* produce crime – a highly motivated bike thief might ignore a poorly locked cycle if it is parked outside a police station. This is because environmental criminology depicts offenders as purposive decision-makers. It assumes that individuals who find themselves in criminogenic environments make situated decisions as to whether to exploit the crime opportunities on offer. This decision making process is encapsulated in the rational choice perspective (RCP) (Clarke & Cornish, 1985; Cornish & Clarke, 1986), described below.

## Rational choice perspective

The RCP is a micro-level account of the role of immediate environments in specific crime locations. The first detailed description of the RCP explanation of crime was by Clarke & Cornish (1985), but the approach had its genesis in research on absconding from residential institutions for delinquents conducted by Clarke (1967) nearly 20 years beforehand. Seeking to identify characteristics of residents that reliably identified absconders, Clarke found instead that the best predictors of absconding were aspects of the environment, such as hours of daylight, features of the school's regime, and the distance to the absconder's home. These and similar findings led Clarke to put forward opportunity as a fundamental but neglected cause of crime (Mayhew, Clarke, Sturman, & Hough, 1976). Offender decision-making was ultimately proposed as the mechanism through which opportunity leads to deviant behavior (Clarke, 1980), and it is this idea that became refined as the RCP.

The RCP examines immediate environments from the subjective perspective of potential offenders. According to the RCP, crime is a choice, and offenders choose to commit crime in much the same way that we choose to execute any type of behavior. The decision-making process is understood in terms of the perceived risks, efforts and rewards associated with a particular behavior in a given setting. Crime is considered more likely to occur if the perceived gains outweigh the perceived losses (broadly defined). It is rational only insofar as the decision-making process assumed to precede criminal behavior is deliberative and informed by information in the immediate environment. Clearly in many cases rational does not equal successful – offenders may earn very little, get caught, condemned or even killed. Decisions may also be misdirected as a consequence of limited knowledge, drugs, or conformity, as well as the many cognitive biases that characterize human decision making (see Kahneman, 2012). The rational in the RCP is hence a "bounded" one, aware of the fallibility of human decision making and the shifting conditions under which criminal choices are often made.

A key feature of the RCP is that the decision to participate in crime is *crime-specific*. A prolific shoplifter might not countenance the theft of a motor vehicle, let alone committing robbery or sexual assault. This is because the risk–effort–reward calculus presumed to precede crime is considered to be a function of a person–situation interaction: specific crimes are committed for different reasons, require different conditions and demand different resources: an expert burglar adept at picking locks may possess inadequate techniques, tools, and temperament to commit armed robbery. Of course many offenders display much versatility and participate in various crime types over their criminal career (for a recent discussion see McGloin, Sullivan, & Piquero, 2009); however it is nevertheless argued by proponents of the RCP that different crimes located at different points along offender trajectories serve different purposes and require different methods for commission that are consistent with a crime-by-crime rational decision-making process. The RCP has been used to explain a wide variety of crimes, including burglary (Bennett & Wright, 1984; Homel, Macintyre & Wortley, 2013; Nee & Meenaghan, 2006), car theft (Copes & Cherbonneau, 2013; Webb & Laycock, 1992), shoplifting (Carroll & Weaver, 1986), armed robbery (Petrosino & Brensilber, 2003; Wright & Decker, 1997), drug selling (Jacobs, 1996), computer crimes (Newman & Clarke, 2003), sexual offending (Beauregard & Leclerc, 2007), stalking (Thompson & Leclerc, 2013) and terrorism (Clarke & Newman, 2006).

Clarke & Cornish (1985) recognized at the outset that crimes seldom occur at a single point in time and space, and nor do they involve a single decision. Rather, crime events have a beginning, middle and end, and across the crime-commission process many separate decisions are required. Cornish (1994) developed this insight into the concept of crime scripts. Borrowed from the concept of event schema in cognitive psychology (Schank & Abelson, 1977), a crime script sets out the sequence of actions adopted prior to, during and following the commission of a particular crime. As the crime event unfolds, the offender needs to make rational choices in order to move from one step to the next. With practice, the decision-making becomes automatic, and eventually offenders are able to complete the complex sequence of actions instinctively, without the need for laborious deliberation. Crime scripts have proved a popular method of deconstructing crime events and have been applied to a wide range of offences, such as check forgery (Lacoste & Tremblay, 2003), organized crime (Hancock & Laycock, 2010) and international child sex trafficking (Brayley, Cockbain, & Laycock, 2011).

## Theory for Practice

In shifting the focus from the criminal to the crime event, environmental criminology placed a greater emphasis on the causal role of opportunities in crime. This gained traction with prevention-minded scholars and practitioners, and the concepts and methods of environmental criminology have since made significant contributions to policing and crime prevention. Here, we discuss five such examples: crime mapping, predictive policing, problem-oriented policing, situational crime prevention, and design against crime. As we move through these topics, you will see that the contributions of environmental criminology to crime control are of two main sorts: environmental criminology can assist with the identification of the places in which crime occurs; and it can help with the formulation of strategies to respond to crime at those places.

### Crime mapping

The roots of crime mapping go back to the national crime maps of Guerry and Quetelet in the nineteenth century, and later to the mapping of intracity crime patterns by the Chicago School. Until the mid-twentieth century, however, mapping crime was a laborious, manual process. Developments in computer technology in the second half of the twentieth century have revolutionized the production of crime maps as well as greatly expanding their functionality. From the 1960s, mainframe-based geographic software became available (Canada Geographic Information System: CGIS) and by the mid-1980s desktop versions of GIS were developed. Crime mapping has become an indispensable research tool for environmental criminologists, and professional tool for the crime analysts who provide tactical, operational, and strategic advice to police.

A key concept in crime mapping is that of the crime hotspot. A hotspot is an area that contains a higher concentration of crime or disorder compared with surrounding areas (see Eck *et al.*, 2005). Hotspots can vary in size depending upon the interest of the investigator. Thus, a suburb can be a hotspot within a city, a street can be a hotspot within a suburb, and an address can be a hotspot within a street. Hotspots are an example of the Pareto principle – the so-called 80/20 rule – that holds that a small number of contributors to a phenomenon typically account for a disproportionately large amount of that phenomenon. One of the first studies on crime hotspots was by Sherman, Gartin, & Bueger (1989). They found that a small number of Minneapolis addresses (3.3%) were responsible for more than half (50.4%) of all dispatched police calls for service. Hotspots have since been mapped for a wide range of crime and disorder, including burglary (Johnson & Bowers, 2004), street robbery (Ratcliffe, 2010), cash-in-transit robbery (Hepenstal & Johnson, 2010), alcohol-related violence (Block & Block, 1995), terrorist insurgency (Braithwaite & Johnson, 2012), and maritime piracy (Marchione & Johnson, 2013).

Hotspots are the obvious targets for the deployment of police resources. Random police patrols have a long history in policing and are commonly assumed to play a crucial role in community safety by increasing police visibility. In fact, research has shown that simply increasing patrols in a general way has little effect on local crime rates (Kelling *et al.*, 1974; Pate, 1986). Against this background, a number of studies have shown modest though worthwhile reductions in crime following the targeted policing of hotspots (Braga & Bond, 2008; Jones & Tilley, 2004; Ratcliffe *et al.*, 2011; Sherman & Weisburd, 1995; Weisburd & Braga, 2006; Weisburd & Green, 1995; see Braga, 2007 for a systematic review). In one of the earliest studies, Sherman & Weisburd (1995) examined the effects of hotspot policing, comprising a mix of foot and vehicle patrols, in Minneapolis. One hundred and ten crime hotspots were identified and randomly allocated to control and treatment conditions (55 in each condition). The control hotspots received normal levels of police patrolling; the treatment condition received an additional three hours of police patrolling during peak crime times for a year. Sherman & Weisburd reported a 13% reduction in crime in the treatment areas over the year of the experiment. More recently, Ratcliffe *et al.* (2011) examined hotspot foot patrol policing in Philadelphia. One-hundred-and-twenty violent crime hotspots were identified and randomly allocated to control and treatment conditions (sixty per condition). In the treatment areas, patrols comprising two officers ran from 10.00a.m. to 2.00a.m. Tuesday morning through to Saturday night for a period of three months. The researchers estimated that the foot patrols resulted in the prevention of 90 violent crimes in the treatment areas, with a displacement of 37 to nearby areas, leaving a net reduction of 53 crimes, representing a 23% fall.

## Predictive policing

Traditional crime-mapping techniques present information about where and when crime *has* occurred. A more recent application of environmental criminology is the much-storied prospect of predictive policing, which is rooted in research on repeat and near-repeat victimization. Predicting when and where crime is most likely to occur is the holy grail of crime analysis. Knowledge on "tomorrow's" high-risk locations can better inform the allocation of preventive resources. Though numerous factors have been identified as robust correlates of victimization, the consensus in the literature is that prior victimization is one of the most significant predictors of future victimization. Repeat victimization is thus a common occurrence and has been identified across several units of analysis (people, products, places, properties) and for various crime types (Grove *et al.*, 2012; Pease, 1998). It follows that falling victim to crime is typically associated with a heightened chance of future victimization, which gradually decays over time.

But what of the risk of victimization to comparable targets located nearby? In the past ten years research has shown that elevations in crime risk are not limited to the initial victim but are found to be communicable in space and time, so-called near-repeat victimization (Bowers & Johnson, 2004; Townsley *et al.*, 2000). To use burglary as an example, properties located close to a burgled home display an elevated risk of being burgled for a short period of time. In this sense the offender is characterized as an "optimal forager," looking to exploit available opportunities in a given area before moving elsewhere, all the time attempting to increase gains whilst minimizing the risk of capture or detection.

Like repeat victimization, near-repeat patterns have been observed for a wide range of crime types, including burglary (Johnson *et al.*, 2007), shootings (Ratcliffe & Rengert, 2008), insurgent activity (Townsley, Johnson, & Ratcliffe, 2008) and maritime piracy attacks (Marchione & Johnson, 2013). The regularity with which repeats and near-repeats are observed, and the extent to which they make up a significant proportion of an area's victimizations, has led to several efforts to produce software which translate the theory into a practical crime-fighting tool. The first was known as ProMap (prospective mapping) which works by computing constantly shifting risk estimates based on previous crimes. For example, following a burglary event households located nearby will be considered to be at a greater risk of burglary compared to other households for a period of about a month. Closer homes are considered to be more at risk than homes which are further away. In producing risk estimates ProMap provides an evidence-based means of deploying resources in a bid to prevent repeats, such as through the police speaking with households located nearby a burgled property soon after the initial crime event to ensure they take necessary precautions and be mindful of burglars operating in the area (an intervention known as cocooning). Early trails of ProMap were encouraging and performed better at identifying risky areas than other hotspotting techniques and the predictions of local police officers (see Johnson, Bowers, Birks, & Pease, 2008). Several other predictive software packages have since been established (see Mohler *et al.*, 2011). Presently we are aware of several experiments in both the US and UK using different predictive methods to deploy police resources.

## Problem-oriented policing

Problem-oriented policing (POP) is an approach for improving police effectiveness. It was first mooted in 1979 by Herman Goldstein in response to what he saw as a largely reactive and underperforming model of policing which typically dealt with crime on a case-by-case basis, chasing the observable symptoms of crime and paying little attention to the underlying causes. Goldstein called for a reorientation towards the main substance of policing, which he suggested was the identification of persistent police-relevant problems of concern to the local community. POP encouraged a shift away from default police tactics (such as enforcement) in favor of formulating preventive strategies attuned to the local context and justified by comprehensive analysis of relevant data, often working in collaboration with other (nonpolice) groups.

POP remains a popular model of policing. Many law-enforcement agencies in the US and UK have sought to incorporate Goldstein's ideas, to varying degrees of success (Knutsson & Clarke, 2006; Scott, 2000). When done well, evidence from several case studies and experiments has shown the approach to be effective (see Weisburd *et al.*, 2010). Part of the popularity of POP is likely attributable to Eck & Spelman's (1987) SARA model (Scanning, Analysis, Response, Assessment), which has become the dominant method by which problem-oriented work is delivered.

POP is often discussed in the same breath as environmental criminology. It is commonly thought of as a vehicle through which concepts from environmental criminology are applied in practice. Yet this is a function more of experience than by design. At root, POP holds no allegiances with any criminological theories: it is interested in improving police effectiveness, and to this end would, in principle, embrace any theoretical perspective. Yet in practice, from the very beginning, once police forces began to experiment with POP it became clear that the analysis of problems was improved when supported by theory, and as Scott *et al.* (2008: 234) observe, "while most criminological theories were of little practical value to the police, a small but growing movement called environmental criminology was developing a set of theories that were useful." For example, the requisite elements of crime set out in the RAA provided a useful template to structure the analysis of presenting problems – later organized into the problem triangle (see Eck, 2003) – prompting analysts to collect data on the offender, victim, and location components of a problem.

## Situational crime prevention

If opportunities cause crime, then blocking opportunities should reduce it, without the need to alter criminal disposition. This is the mission of situational crime prevention, which is concerned with opportunity-reduction measures that "(1) are directed at highly specific forms of crime, (2) involve the management, design and manipulation of the immediate environment in as systematic and permanent a way as possible, (3) make crime more difficult and risky, or less rewarding and excusable as judged by a wide range of offenders" (Clarke, 1997: 4).

Situational crime prevention does not refer to a single type of situational measure. Instead it comprises a catalogue of techniques (currently 25) that focus on the proximal causes of crime (Cornish & Clarke, 2003). These techniques are organized around five broad strategies which reflect the mechanism(s) through which measures are expected to reduce crime: by increasing the perceived effort, increasing the perceived risks, reducing the perceived rewards, reducing provocations, and removing excuses. Situational crime prevention is based (largely) upon a rational-choice model of the offender, one whose behavioral choices are open to and influenced by changes in the immediate environment. It maintains that, all things being equal, an individual will be less likely commit crime if the perceived risks and efforts in doing so increase, rewards are reduced, provocations are blunted and salient rules are emphasized. Intuition suggests that while this situated decision-making might well be true for carefully considered acquisitive crimes, it should not be expected of highly emotional and expressive crimes. But even here individuals contemplating such behaviors have been found to be highly susceptible to situational changes. Take suicide. Clarke & Mayhew (1988) report how the changeover from toxic to non-toxic gas in British households from the 1960s produced a dramatic drop in incidences of the then-popular suicide method of carbon monoxide poisoning through gas inhalation. The stemming of a cheap, widely available, and painless suicide method, thus affording opportunities to change one's mind, appeared to reduce a presumably highly motivated problem behavior, with little evidence that thwarted suicide-attempters adopted one of the many other suicide methods available.

Situational crime prevention remains a popular method of cutting crime. Over time its scope has widened from being applied mainly to high-volume property crimes to cybercrimes (Newman & Clarke, 2003), terrorism (Clarke & Newman, 2006) and sex offenses against children (Wortley & Smallbone, 2006). It is a practical method which appeals to agencies responsible for crime reduction, often producing rapid results. To some industries it is simply standard business practice, as with retailers who put their most desirable items in the most secure locations and keep their cash in electronic tills. Though expectedly there are examples of poorly developed and poorly implemented situational interventions, there is now a very large number of studies attesting to the effectiveness of situational measures designed to reduce specific types of crime (see Clarke, 1997).

## Design against crime

Design against crime (DAC) is a subfield of situational crime prevention. It is a multi-disciplinary field that uses design knowledge, tools and techniques to reduce crime and promote community safety (Ekblom, 2008). For convenience, it can be divided into two broad categories: the design of the built environment (crime prevention through environmental design, otherwise known as CPTED) and the design of products. The former can be traced directly to the pioneering work of Jeffery (1971) and Newman (1972) discussed earlier in this chapter, and refers to ways in which buildings and the wider environment (such as the street network) are constructed and configured so as to reduce opportunities for crime, and reduce the fear of victimization. A classic example is the housing estate that clearly delineates public from private space, is organized to maximize opportunities for natural surveillance, and contains houses which are secure and difficult to access for would-be offenders. The latter shares the same objectives albeit in reference to "design products," be they objects, places or systems. Classic examples here are cars and laptops designed with inbuilt security measures to thwart thieves, or glassware designed to shatter on impact to reduce the harms caused by "glassings" (e.g., Shepherd, 1994).

Designing against crime is not new: moats have long been dug around castles to protect against sieges; coins have long contained milled edges to guard against the precious metals being clipped and profited from. What is new is the growing recognition that design plays a central role in the prevalence and patterns of crime, and how, armed with this knowledge, designers and crime-preventers can look to reduce crime and lessen the harms it causes. To this aim, the past two decades have witnessed a mounting effort to collect evidence of effective design-based interventions and document the many challenges encountered. Ekblom (2008) describes how effective DAC must balance the "troublesome trade-off" of creating something which is secure but which also satisfies the many other consumer and societal expectations, such as cost, aesthetics, and safety; it must look to anticipate risk and not just react to spikes in crime at which point retrofitting is often more costly and constrained; and it must be adaptive, to avoid obsolescence, mindful that offenders invariably look to counter anticrime measures (Ekblom, 1999).

## Criticisms, Controversies and Future Directions

Interest in the immediate environment in which crime occurs has existed since the very beginnings of criminology, and environmental criminology as a distinct field of study has been around for more than 40 years. Nevertheless, environmental criminology has generally struggled for acceptance within mainstream criminology, though arguably its popularity and influence is growing. In this section we evaluate the contributions and future of environmental criminology as seen both from outside and within the field.

### Immediate environments as a cause of crime

Perhaps the most common criticism levelled at environmental criminology is that, by not focusing on social and dispositional factors, it ignores the root causes of crime. At one level this criticism is entirely accurate; environmental criminology does, by and large, ignore the causative role in crime of social and dispositional factors. But, for that matter, as we have observed, traditional criminology pays scant attention to the causative role of the immediate environment. It is simply the nature of academic enquiry that researchers tend to focus on fairly narrow areas of interest rather than on grand unified theory. As we discuss in more detail later, the lack of attention to distal causes does not mean that environmental criminologists believe that crime can be explained entirely by immediate environmental factors.

But, of course, the real bite in this criticism is the implication that the immediate environment does not play a meaningful role in causing crime, and hence it is not worthy of deep theoretical consideration. At best, it is argued, the environment helps account for the distribution of a set amount of crime that would have occurred in any case. This criticism is most often raised in connection with the crime-prevention strategies associated with environmental criminology. If offenders are thwarted in their criminal endeavors through policing strategies or situational prevention initiatives, then surely, the argument goes, they will simply try their luck elsewhere.

Crime will not be prevented; it will simply be pushed around – displaced – to other locations, targets or times.

At a theoretical level, we can clearly recognize this criticism as an expression of the fundamental attribution error. It fails to acknowledge that all human behavior, even crime, is a product of an interaction between an individual and his/her immediate environment. Tilley & Laycock (2002) exposed the fallacy of this line of reasoning through a clever thought experiment. They invite you to imagine the outcome if all measures to deter offenders were suddenly abandoned: people did not lock their houses when they went out; they left their keys in their unlocked cars; they simply left their money on an unattended counter when they purchased goods; they were subject to no ticket inspections on trains or customs checks as they arrived at an airport. Would crime, in these circumstances, increase? If you answered yes – and surely this is the only rational conclusion – then you believe that displacement is not the inevitable consequence of situational prevention. If it is not clear why this is so, let us continue the experiment. Imagine now that we were to reintroduce all the security measures that we had previously done away with. Logically we would now expect to see crime fall to previous levels. Thus, we can conclude that changes to the immediate environment can produce real drops in crime.

Moreover, there is good empirical evidence to refute the displacement argument. Guerette & Bowers (2009) conducted a meta-analysis on 574 situational crime prevention interventions. They found that displacement occurred in just 26% of cases, and where displacement did occur it was typically less than the amount prevented. Further, in 27% of cases there was a diffusion of benefit. That is to say, there was a spillover effect, with crime drops in areas and at times not targeted by the interventions (see Clarke & Weisburd, 1994). In short, environmental criminology does not ignore the root causes of crime; the immediate environment *is* a root cause of crime.

## The motivations of the offender

As has been acknowledged, environmental criminology is noticeably thin on the nature of the offender. Criminal motivation is simply taken for granted. All three of the key underpinning perspectives (RAA, CPT and RCP) are based on a model of the offender as predator. As Cornish & Clarke (2008: 39) put it:

> In accordance with good-enough theorizing the original depiction of the offender was of an individual bereft of moral scruples – and without any defects such as lack of self-control that might get in the way of rational action. He (or she) was assumed to arrive at the crime setting already motivated and somewhat experienced in committing the crime in question, and to evaluate criminal opportunities on the basis of the likely rewards they offered, the effort they required, and the risks that were likely to involve. Although this picture has been modified over the years (Cornish & Clarke, 2003) the offender as antisocial predator has remained the perspective's default view.

As noted in the previous section, this view of the offender has been criticized from outside of the field on the grounds that it does not acknowledge the developmental and sociological (distal) roots of criminal motivations. However, for very different reasons this view of the already-motivated offender has also been challenged from within environmental criminology. Wortley (2001; 2008) has argued that the default position of the antisocial predator undervalues the role of the immediate environment in creating or intensifying criminal motivations. Individuals do not necessarily enter the crime scene ready to offend. As Zimbardo's (1970) simulated prison study and Milgram's (1974) obedience to authority study show, good people are capable of evil acts given the right circumstances. Most "ordinary" people will commit crimes from time to time (Gabor, 1994) while even otherwise predatory offenders may be induced to commit crimes that they were not originally intending to commit. The static offender-as-predator model does not fully capture the reciprocal nature of the person–situation interaction (Wortley, 2012). Individuals do not just act on the immediate environment; the immediate environment has the capacity to change individuals.

Drawing on research from social, behavioral and cognitive psychology, Wortley (2001; 2008) proposed four ways that immediate environments can actively precipitate crime. First, immediate environments can present cues that prompt the individual to perform criminal acts. For example, exposure to weapons and other symbols of violence can increase access to aggression-related thoughts and feelings and thus prime the individual for violence. Second, immediate environments can exert social pressures to offend. Social influences include the tendency for individuals to conform to group norms, to obey authority figures, and to engage in herd behavior. Third, immediate environments can interfere with moral judgments and permit the performance of normally proscribed acts. Individuals may blame alcohol, rule ambiguity, depersonalizing social systems, or other environmental circumstances for their actions. Finally, immediate environments can create aversive emotional arousal that provokes a criminal response. Being thwarted, constrained, insulted, threatened, annoyed, overwhelmed, or discomforted may be accompanied by emotional responses such as irritability and frustration, and behavioral responses that include aggression.

As Cornish & Clarke (2008) indicate in the quote above, recent reformulations of the RCP have taken some account of situational precipitators. Cornish & Clarke (2003) proposed three basic types of offender. The first is the antisocial predator, a criminally motivated individual who actively seeks out or creates crime opportunities. The second is the mundane offender, an individual characterized by poor self-control who opportunistically responds to easy criminal temptations. The third is the provoked offender, an individual who reacts to situational stresses and frustrations to commit a crime they would not have otherwise committed. Cornish & Clarke also added a set of new situational crime prevention strategies under the heading of "reducing provocations" to address the crimes of the provoked offender.

## Environmental criminology in non-western settings

Like most branches of criminology, environmental criminology is fundamentally a product of Western concepts and research, and is also largely concerned with urban crime. This begs the question: how well do the principles of environmental criminology transfer to non-Western (often rural) settings? Examples of environmental criminological research conducted in such settings are scarce. This is likely attributed to a shortage of relevant crime data, the interests of research funding bodies, and the infant status of criminology as a discipline in many parts of the world. Encouragingly, in recent years there has been a slow trickle of studies applying the concepts of environmental criminology in developing countries. Analyzing data collected as part of a large household survey, Sidebottom (2012) showed how residential burglary in Malawi displayed broadly similar repeat victimization patterns to those commonly observed in Anglo-American research. In Mexico, Pires & Clarke (2012) reported how a model designed to identify the features that make mass-produced consumer goods prone to theft – those that are concealable, removable, available, valuable, enjoyable, and disposable, or CRAVED (Clarke, 1999) – can yield useful insight into the problem of parrot poaching, suggesting that a considerable number of parrot thefts can be described as opportunist thefts as opposed to the work of highly motivated professional poachers.

Expanding the scope of environmental criminology to investigate novel contexts and crime types is an important avenue for further research. From a theoretical perspective, it promises to enrich and refine prevailing crime-event theories through systematically applying them across diverse settings. Perhaps more importantly, such research could also usefully inform crime-prevention policy and practice in settings often characterized by high crime rates and limited preventive resources. Yet it is also an avenue of research likely to encounter several challenges, of which we highlight only three. First is the lack of reliable crime data, be it official crime statistics or victimization surveys. Consequently, determining innovative ways to collect adequate primary data or discovering extant datasets (perhaps collected for non-criminological purposes) that can be re-analyzed from a crime-event perspective is important. The second concerns generalizability and whether well-established theoretical concepts such as opportunity and guardianship, or analytical frameworks such as CRAVED, require adaptation and modification when applied in different contexts. The final challenge relates to the process of deriving crime-prevention interventions from crime analysis in settings where the police, so often the agents of crime prevention in Western settings, invariably have scarce resources and are often mainly limited to urban centers. It is to this point that research is noticeably lacking. What is now needed are studies undertaken in non-Western settings that translate analysis into prevention, and provide practical demonstrations of interventions informed by analysis and report the process of evaluating their impact and implementation.

## Integrating environmental criminology and criminology

We began this chapter by describing how environmental criminology emerged in response to criminology's neglect of the immediate environment as a casual factor in crime. A focus on crime events and the proximal causes of crime marked environmental criminology out from most other criminological theories, and to some extent it still does. But is it true to say that environmental criminology still occupies the margins of mainstream criminology? At risk of being noncommittal: yes and no. No, because most of the top-tier criminology journals now regularly publish research in the environmental criminology tradition. This was not always the case, and book series such as *Crime Prevention Studies* originated in part to provide a scholarly outlet for this type of research. Environmental criminology also takes its place in the many compendiums and textbooks on criminological theory and research (such as this handbook). Despite this, to the best of our knowledge there are still only four books (including one in two editions) dedicated to the subject of environmental criminology (Andresen, Brantingham, & Kinney, 2010; Brantingham & Brantingham, 1981; and Wortley & Mazerolle, 2008), it does not have a dedicated scholarly journal, and theories of criminality continue to outnumber theories on crime.

In recent years there have been growing calls to better integrate theories of criminality with theories of crime. Frank Cullen (2011), in his 2010 Sutherland Address to the American Society of Criminology, laments at what he sees as a failure of contemporary criminology to produce sufficient policy-relevant research. This is attributed, in part, to the peripheral status still accorded to many crime event theories. As Cullen summarizes, "most criminologists know a lot about criminality or propensity and almost nothing about crime or crime events" (2011: 314).

But the lack of dialogue has not just been in one direction. Cullen went on to say that the mistake of environmental approaches was "to give only marginal attention to the way in which criminal decision making is bounded by factors that offenders import into the crime situation" (2011: 315). Addressing this issue, Wortley (2012) has pointed out that the person–situation interaction, argued to provide the conceptual foundations of environmental criminology, has two distinct meanings. The first meaning – the sense in which the term is typically used by environmental criminologists – is of a reciprocal relationship between the individual and his/her immediate surroundings. The central concept here is bidirectional causation; the environment acts on the individual and the individual responds by acting on the environment (and so on). The second meaning – the sense in which the term is more usually used in the social sciences – is of an interdependent relationship between person and situation. Here the effect of the immediate environment is seen to vary according to the nature of person. Different individuals will react differently to the same environmental stimuli such that some will be dispositionally more susceptible to criminogenic situations than will others. In other words, even in environmental criminology the propensity of the offender matters.

Cullen concluded his Sutherland Address by setting out a research agenda to bring environmental criminology into the mainstream, declaring that "the future of criminology will be advanced by exploring systematically the nexus between propensity and opportunity – between offender and situation" (2011: 315). We can only agree with these sentiments.

# References

Andresen, M.A., Brantingham, P.J., & Kinney, J.B. (Eds.) (2010). *Classics in Environmental Criminology*. Boca Raton, FL: Taylor & Francis.

Andrews, P.W. (2001). The psychology of social chess and the evolution of attribution mechanisms: Explaining the fundamental attribution error. *Evolution and Human Behavior, 22*, 11–29.

Arendt, H. (1963). *Eichmann in Jerusalem: A Report on the Banality of Evil*. New York: Penguin.

Beauregard, E., & Leclerc, B. (2007). An application of the rational choice approach to the offending process of sex offenders: A closer look at the decision-making. *Sexual Abuse: A Journal of Research and Treatment, 19*, 115–133.

Bennett, T., & Wright, R. (1984). *Burglars on Burglary*. Aldershot: Gower.

Block, R.L., & Block, C.R. (1995). Space, place and crime: Hot spot areas and hot places of liquor-related crime. *Crime and Place, 4*, 145–184.

Bowers, K., & Johnson, S.D. (2004). The burglary as a clue to the future: The beginnings of prospective hot-spotting. *European Journal of Criminology, 1*, 237–255.

Braithwaite, A., & Johnson, S.D. (2012). Space-time modeling of insurgency and counterinsurgency in Iraq. *Journal of Quantitative Criminology, 28*, 31–48.

Braga, A.A. (2007). Policing crime hot spots. In B.C. Welsh & D.P. Farrington (Eds.), *Preventing Crime* (pp. 179–192). New York: Springer.

Braga, A.A., & Bond, B.J. (2008). Policing crime and disorder hot spots: A randomized controlled trial. *Criminology, 46*, 577–608.

Brantingham, P.J., & Brantingham, P.L. (Eds.) (1981). *Environmental Criminology*. Beverly Hills: Sage.

Brantingham, P.L., & Brantingham, P.J. (1995). Criminality of place: Crime generators and crime attractors. *European Journal on Criminal Policy and Research, 3*, 1–26.

Brantingham, P.J., & Brantingham, P.L. (2008). Crime pattern theory. In R. Wortley & L. Mazerolle (Eds.), *Environmental Criminology and Crime Analysis* (pp. 79–93). Cullompton: Willan.

Brayley, H., Cockbain, E., & Laycock, G. (2011). The value of crime scripting: Deconstructing internal child sex trafficking. *Policing, 5*, 132–143.

Carroll, J., & Weaver, F. (1986). Shoplifters perceptions of crime opportunities: A process-tracing study. In D.B. Cornish & R.V.G Clarke (Eds.), *The Reasoning Criminal: Rational Choice Perspectives on Offending*. New York: Springer-Verlag.

Chainey, S., & Ratcliffe, J. (2005). *GIS and Crime Mapping*. Chichester: Wiley.

Clarke, R.V.G. (1967). Seasonal and other environmental aspects of abscondings by approved school boys. *British Journal of Criminology, 7*, 195–206.

Clarke, R.V. (1980). Situational crime prevention: Theory and practice. *British Journal of Criminology, 20*, 136–147.

Clarke, R. (Ed.) (1997). *Situational Crime Prevention: Successful Case Studies*, 2nd edition. New York: Harrow and Heston.

Clarke, R.V. (1999). *Hot Products: Understanding, Anticipating, and Reducing Demand for Stolen Goods*. Police Research Series Paper 112. London: Home Office Policing and Reducing Crime Unit.

Clarke, R.V., & Cornish, D.B. (1985). Modeling offenders' decisions: A framework for research and policy. In M. Tonry & N. Morris (Eds.), *Crime and Justice: An Annual Review of Research* (pp. 147–185). Vol. 6. Chicago: University of Chicago Press.

Clarke, R., & Mayhew, P. (1988). The British gas suicide story and its criminological implications. In M. Tonry & N. Morris (Eds.), *Crime and Justice: An Annual Review of Research*. Vol. 10. Chicago: University of Chicago Press.

Clarke, R.V., & Newman, G.R. (2006). *Outsmarting the Terrorists*. Westport: Praeger Security International.

Clarke, R.V., & Weisburd, D. (1994). Diffusion of crime control benefits: Observations on the reverse of displacement. In R.V. Clarke (Ed.), *Crime Prevention Studies*. Monsey, NY: Criminal Justice Press.

Cohen, L., & Felson, M. (1979). Social change and crime rate changes: A routine activity approach. *American Sociological Review, 44*, 588–608.

Copes, H., & Cherbonneau, M. (2013). The risks and rewards of motor vehicle theft: Implications for criminal persistence. In B. Leclerc & R. Wortley (Eds.), *Cognition and Crime: Offender Decision-Making and Script Analyses*. London: Routledge.

Cornish, D. (1994). The procedural analysis of offending and its relevance for situational prevention. In R.V. Clarke (Ed.), *Crime Prevention Studies*. Monsey, NY: Criminal Justice Press.

Cornish, D., & Clarke, R. (1986). Introduction. In D. Cornish & R. Clarke (Eds.), *The Reasoning Criminal: Rational Choice Perspectives on Offending*. New York: Springer.

Cornish, D.B., & Clarke, R. (2003). Opportunities, precipitators and criminal decisions: A reply to Wortley's critique of situational crime prevention. In M. Smith & D.B. Cornish (Eds.), *Theory for Situational Crime Prevention*. Monsey, NY: Criminal Justice Press.

Cornish, D.B., & Clarke, R.V. (2008). The rational choice approach. In R. Wortley & L. Mazerolle (Eds.), *Environmental Criminology and Crime Analysis* (pp. 21–47). Cullompton: Willan.

Cullen, F. (2011). Beyond adolescence-limited criminology: Choosing our future. The American Society of Criminology 2010 Sutherland Address. *Criminology, 49*, 287–330.

Eck, J.E. (2003). Police problems: The complexity of problem theory, research and evaluation. In J. Knutsson (Ed.), *Problem-Oriented Policing: From Innovation to Mainstream* (pp. 79–113). Monsey, NY: Criminal Justice Press.

Eck, J.E., & Spelman, W. (1987). *Problem-Solving: Problem-Oriented Policing in Newport News*. Washington, DC: Police Executive Research Forum.

Eck, J.E., Chainey, S., Cameron, J., Leitner, M., & Wilson, R. (2005). *Mapping Crime: Understanding Hot Spots*. USA: National Institute of Justice.

Ekblom, P. (1999). Can we make crime prevention adaptive by learning from other evolutionary struggles? *Studies on Crime and Crime Prevention, 8*, 27–51.

Ekblom, P. (2008). Designing products against crime. In R. Wortley & L. Mazerolle (Eds.), *Environmental Criminology and Crime Analysis* (pp. 195–220). Cullompton: Willan.

Felson, M. (2002). *Crime and Everyday Life*, 2nd edition. Thousand Oaks, CA: Sage.

Gabor, T. (1994). *Everybody Does It: Crime by the Public*. Toronto: University of Toronto Press.

Goldstein, H. (1979). Improving policing: A problem-oriented approach. *Crime and Delinquency, 25,* 236–258.

Grove, L., Farrell, G., Farrington, D.P., & Johnson, S.D. (2012). *Preventing Repeat Victimization: A Systematic Review.* Stockholm: Swedish National Council for Crime Prevention.

Guerette, R.T., & Bowers, K. (2009). Assessing the extent of crime displacement and diffusion of benefit: A systematic review of situational crime prevention evaluations. *Criminology, 47,* 1331–1368.

Guerry, A.M. (1833). *Essay on the Moral Statistics of France: A Sociological Report to the French Academy of Science.* Reprinted 2002, Edwin Mellen Press.

Hancock, G., & Laycock, G. (2010). Organised crime and crime scripts: Prospects for disruption. In K. Bullock, R.V. Clarke, & N. Tilley (Eds.), *Situational Prevention of Organised Crimes.* Cullompton: Willan.

Hepenstal, S., & Johnson, S.D. (2010). The concentration of cash-in-transit robbery. *Crime Prevention and Community Safety, 12,* 263–282.

Hipp, J.R., Bauer, D.J., Curran, P.J., & Bollen, K.A. (2004). Crimes of opportunity or crimes of emotion: Testing two explanations of seasonal change in crime. *Social Forces, 82,* 1333–1372.

Homel, R., Macintyre, S., & Wortley, R. (2013). How burglars decide on targets: A computer-based scenario approach. In B. Leclerc & R. Wortley (Eds.), *Cognition and Crime: Offender Decision-Making and Script Analyses.* London: Routledge.

Jacobs, B. (1996). Crack dealers' apprehension avoidance techniques: A case of restrictive deterrence. *Justice Quarterly, 13,* 359–382.

Jeffery, C.R. (1971). *Crime Prevention Through Environmental Design.* Beverly Hills, CA: Sage.

Jensen, J.F., & Brownfield, D. (1986). Gender, lifestyles, and victimization: Beyond routine activity. *Violence and Victims, 1,* 85–99.

Johnson, S.D., & Bowers, K. (2004). The stability of space-time clusters of burglary. *British Journal of Criminology, 44,* 55–65.

Johnson, S.D., Bernasco, W., Bowers, K.J., Elffers, H., Ratcliffe, J., Rengert, G., *et al.* (2007). Space-time patterns of risk: A cross national assessment of residential burglary. *Journal of Quantitative Criminology, 23,* 201–219.

Johnson, S.D., Bowers, K.J., Birks, D., & Pease, K. (2008). Predictive mapping of crime by ProMap: Accuracy, units of analysis and the environmental backcloth. In D. Weisburd, W. Bernasco, & G. Bruinsma (Eds.), *Putting Crime in its Place: Units of Analysis in Spatial Crime Research.* New York: Springer.

Jones, B., & Tilley, N. (2004). *The Impact of High-Visibility Patrols on Personal Robbery.* Research Findings No. 201. London: Home Office.

Kahneman, D. (2012). *Thinking Fast and Slow.* New York: Macmillan.

Kelling, G., Pate, A., Dieckman, D., & Brown, C. (1974). *The Kansas City Preventive Patrol Experiment: Technical Report.* Washington, DC: Police Foundation.

Knutsson, J., & Clarke, R.V. (Eds.) (2006). *Putting Theory to Work: Implementing Situational Prevention and Problem-Oriented Policing.* Crime Prevention Studies, Vol. *20.* Monsey, NY: Criminal Justice Press.

Lacoste, J., & Tremblay, P. (2003). Crime innovation: A script analysis of patterns in cheque forgery. In M. Smith & D.B. Cornish (Eds.), *Theory for Practice in Situational Crime Prevention*, Vol. *16.* Monsey, NY: Criminal Justice Press.

Marchione, E., & Johnson, S.D. (2013). Spatial, temporal and spatio-temporal patterns of maritime piracy. *Journal of Research in Crime and Delinquency, 50,* 504–524.

Mayhew, P.M., Clarke, R.V., Sturman, A., & Hough, J.M. (1976). *Crime as Opportunity*. Home Office Research Study, No. 34. London: Her Majesty's Stationary Office.

McLean, I. (2007). Climatic effects on incidence of sexual assault. *Journal of Forensic and Legal Medicine, 14*, 16–19.

McGloin, J.M., Sullivan, C.J., & Piquero, A.R. (2009). Aggregating to versatility? Transitions among offender types in the short term. *British Journal of Criminology, 49*, 243–264.

Milgram, S. (1974). *Obedience to Authority: An Experimental View*. New York: Harper and Row.

Mischel, W. (1968). *Personality and Assessment*. New York: Wiley.

Mohler, G.O., Short, M.B., Brantingham, P.J., Schoenberg, F.P., & Tita, G.E. (2011). Self-exciting point process modeling of crime. *Journal of the American Statistical Association, 106*(493), 100–108.

Nee, C., & Meenaghan, A. (2006). Expert decision making in burglars. *British Journal of Criminology, 46*, 935–949.

Newman, O. (1972). *Defensible Space: Crime Prevention Though Urban Design*. New York: Macmillan.

Newman, G.R., & Clarke, R.V. (2003). *Superhighway Robbery: Preventing e-Commerce Crime*. Cullompton: Willan.

Nisbett, R.E. (1980). The trait construct in lay and professional psychology. In L. Festinger (Ed.), *Retrospections on Social Psychology*. New York: Oxford University Press.

Oxford English Dictionary (2013). http://www.oed.com/ (accessed April 23, 2015).

Pate, A.M. (1986). Experimenting with foot patrol: The Newark experience. In D.P. Rosenbaum (Ed.), *Community Crime Prevention: Does it Work* (pp. 137–156). Newbury Park, CA: Sage.

Pease, K. (1998). *Repeat Victimisation: Taking Stock*. Crime Detection and Prevention Paper Series Paper 90. London: Home Office.

Petrosino, A.J., & Brensilber, D. (2003). The motives, methods and decision making of convenience store robbers: Interviews with 28 incarcerated offenders in Massachusetts. *Crime Prevention Studies, 16*, 237–264.

Pires, S., & Clarke, R.V. (2012). Are parrots CRAVED? An analysis of parrot poaching in Mexico. *Journal of Research in Crime and Delinquency, 49*, 122–146.

Quetelet, L.A.J. (2013[1842]). *A Treatise on Man and the Development of his Faculties*. Cambridge: Cambridge University Press.

Ratcliffe, J. (2010). Crime mapping: Spatial and temporal challenges. In A. Piquero & D. Weisburd (Eds.), *Handbook of Quantitative Criminology* (pp. 5–24). New York: Springer.

Ratcliffe, J., & Rengert, G. (2008). Near-repeat patterns in Philadelphia shootings. *Security Journal, 21*, 58–76.

Ratcliffe, J.H., Taniguchi, T., Groff, E., & Wood, J. (2011). The Philadelphia Foot Patrol Experiment: A randomized controlled trial of police patrol effectiveness in violent crime hotspots. *Criminology, 49*, 795–831.

Rengert, G., & Wasilchick, J. (1985). *Suburban Burglary: A Time and Place for Everything*. Springfield, IL: C.C. Thomas.

Ross, L. (1977). The intuitive psychologist and his shortcomings: Distortions in the attribution process. In L. Berkowitz (Ed.), *Advances in Experimental Social Psychology* (pp. 173–220). New York: Academic Press.

Schank, R.C., & Abelson, R. (1977). *Scripts, Plans, Goals, and Understanding*. Hillsdale, NJ: Earlbaum.

Scott, M. (2000). *Problem-Oriented Policing: Reflections of the First Twenty Years*. Washington, DC: Department of Justice Office of Community-Oriented Policing Services.

Scott, M., Eck, J., Knutsson, J., & Goldstein, H. (2008). Problem-oriented policing and environmental criminology. In R. Wortley & L. Mazerolle (Eds.), *Environmental Criminology and Crime Analysis* (pp. 221–246). Cullompton: Willan.

Shaw, C.R., & McKay, H.D. (1942). *Juvenile Delinquency and Urban Areas: A Study of Rates of Delinquents in Relation to Differential Characteristics of Local Communities in American cities*. Chicago: The University of Chicago Press.

Shepherd, J. (1994). Preventing injuries from bar glasses. *British Medical Journal, 308*, 932–933.

Sherman, L.W., Gartin, P.R., & Buerger, M.E. (1989). Hot spots of predatory crime: Routine activities and the criminology of place. *Criminology, 27*, 27–56.

Sherman, L., & Weisburd, D. (1995). General deterrent effects of police patrol in crime hotspots: A randomized controlled trial. *Justice Quarterly, 12*, 625–648.

Sidebottom, A. (2012). Repeat burglary victimization in Malawi and the influence of housing type and area-level affluence. *Security Journal, 25*, 265–281.

Snook, B. (2004). Individual differences in distance traveled by serial burglars. *Journal of Investigative Psychology and Offender Profiling, 1*, 53–66.

Snyder, H.N., Sickmund, M., & Poe-Yamagata, E. (1996). *Juvenile Offenders and Victims: 1996 Update on Violence*. Washington, DC: U.S. Department of Justice.

Thompson, C., & Leclerc, B. (2013). The rational choice perspective and the phenomenon of stalking: An examination of sex differences in behaviours, rationales, situational precipitators and feelings. In B. Leclerc & R. Wortley (Eds.), *Cognition and Crime: Offender Decision-Making and Script Analyses*. London: Routledge.

Tilley, N., & Laycock, G. (2002). *Working Out What to Do: Evidence-Based Crime Reduction*. Crime Reduction Research Series Paper 11. London: Home Office.

Townsley, M., & Sidebottom, A. (2010). All offenders are equal, but some are more equal than others: Variation in journeys to crime between offenders. *Criminology, 48*, 897–917.

Townsley, M., Homel, R., & Chaseling, J. (2000). Repeat burglary victimisation: Spatial and temporal patterns. *Australian and New Zealand Journal of Criminology, 33*, 37–63.

Townsley, M., Johnson, S.D., & Ratcliffe, J. (2008). Space time dynamics of insurgent activity in Iraq. *Security Journal, 21*, 139–146.

Webb, B., & Laycock, G. (1992). *Tackling Car Crime: The Nature and Extent of the Problem*. Crime Prevention Unit Paper 32. London: Home Office.

Weisburd, D.L., & Braga, A.A. (Eds.) (2006). *Police Innovation: Contrasting Perspectives*. New York: Cambridge University Press.

Weisburd, D.L., & Green, L. (1995). Policing drug hot spots: The Jersey City DMA Experiment. *Justice Quarterly, 12*, 711–736.

Weisburd, D., Telep, C.W., Hinkle, J.C., & Eck, J.E. (2010). Is problem-oriented policing effective in reducing crime and disorder? Findings from a Campbell systematic review. *Criminology & Public Policy, 9*, 139–172.

Wiles, P., & Costello, A. (2000). *The "Road to Nowhere": The Evidence for Traveling Criminals*. Home Office Research Study 207. London: Research, Development and Statistics Directorate.

Wortley, R. (2001). A classification of techniques for controlling situational precipitators of crime. *Security Journal, 14*, 63–82.

Wortley, R. (2008). Situational precipitators of crime. In R. Wortley & L. Mazerolle (Eds.), *Environmental Criminology and Crime Analysis*. Cullompton: Willan.

Wortley, R. (2012). Exploring the person–situation interaction in situational crime prevention. In N. Tilley & G. Farrell (Eds.), *The Reasoning Criminologist: Essays in Honour of Ronald V. Clarke*. London: Routledge.

Wortley, R., & Mazerolle, L. (Eds.) (2008). *Environmental Criminology and Crime Analysis*. Cullompton: Willan.

Wortley, R., & Smallbone, S. (Eds.) (2006). *Situational Prevention of Child Sexual Abuse. Crime Prevention Studies*. Monsey, NY: Criminal Justice Press.

Wright, R., & Decker, S. (1997). *Armed Robbers in Action: Stickups and Street Culture*. Boston, MA: Northeastern University Press.

Zimbardo, P.G. (1970). The human choice: Individuation, reason, and order, vs deindividuation, impulse, and chaos. In W.J. Arnold & D. Levine (Eds.), *Nebraska Symposium on Motivation 1969*. Lincoln, NE: University of Nebraska Press.

Zimbardo, P. (2007). *The Lucifer Effect*. New York: Random House.

# 10

# Control as an Explanation of Crime and Delinquency

## Chester L. Britt and Michael Rocque

## Introduction and Overview

Our chapter is focused on what are referred to as control theories of crime and delinquency. We begin by describing the key elements of any control theory: What assumptions go into the theory? What is its domain of explanation? Are there different levels of explanation? What kinds of variations in control theory have been proposed? In what ways has control theory evolved? What does it explain well? Not so well? Is it possible for control theory to accommodate new findings? In particular, how do findings on the biological influences of behavior and the operation of social networks affect our understanding of crime and control theory's relevance? The following discussion attempts to address these questions in a way that offers a fair assessment of the strengths and weaknesses of control theories of crime.

## What is a Control Theory of Crime?

In its most general form, a control theory of crime is simply a theory of behavior that is rooted in the classical school of thought (Britt & Gottfredson, 2003; Roshier, 1989). In other words, the theory assumes that people generally act in ways that are to their benefit. We could just as easily present a control theory of general behavior, since the mechanisms that are claimed to explain behavioral choices are the same. A control theory of crime asserts that the primary cause of an individual engaging in a criminal act results from too few controls on their behavior. Put another way, when individuals feel that they are, in some sense, free to commit criminal acts, such acts are more likely to occur. What differentiates a control theory of crime from virtually

*The Handbook of Criminological Theory*, First Edition. Edited by Alex R. Piquero.
© 2016 John Wiley & Sons, Inc. Published 2016 by John Wiley & Sons, Inc.

all other theories of crime is that no special motivation is required that would push or pull individuals into committing criminal acts.

We also note that there are many different types of control theory, which vary by the specific source of control the theory sees as most important. The key mechanism is fundamentally the same throughout all control theories, but how the theory explains the weakening of controls and the subsequent likelihood of criminal behavior varies. The following discussion begins to connect the various elements that are important to understanding the components of control theories.

## Building Blocks: Assumptions of Control Theory

There are two core assumptions – one individual, one societal – that provide the foundation from which many different versions of control theory have been proposed. At the individual level, the key assumption in control theory is that individuals will generally act in their own self-interest. As pointed out by Bob Roshier (1989), this has been a central element of many behavioral theories that have their roots in the classical school of thought (e.g., Hobbes, 1962 [1651]). To say that individuals are self-interested does not imply that they are rational, as assumed in much economic theory. Rather, the expectation is that most individuals, when confronted with making a behavioral choice, will decide on an action that is perceived to be in their self-interest. The benefit could be economic, psychological, or social – the type of benefit is less important than the perception of some benefit resulting from the choice. It is also likely the behavioral choice will be made out of habit, or with faulty consideration of the full range of options (Kahneman & Tversky, 1979).

More recently, this kind of assumption has been characterized as "agency" in various criminological works (e.g., Farrall & Bowling, 1999; Laub & Sampson, 2003; Paternoster & Pogarsky 2009; Paternoster, Pogarsky, & Zimmerman, 2011). While less explicitly focused on the self-interest of the individual making a choice, these works have highlighted the expectation that individuals choose both criminal and non-criminal acts. This helps to distinguish control theories from other theories of crime that emphasize offenders being pushed or pulled into criminal acts, with little attention to any choices individuals may make – akin to Dennis Wrong's (1961) classic statement about the oversocialized person acting without thinking. Thus, crime is not necessarily required when constraints or controls are lifted, it is only expected to be more likely to occur.

To say that individuals will choose crime if it is perceived to be in their self-interest implies that no special motivation is required to commit criminal acts. In contrast to cultural deviance or strain theories of crime, which focus on the changing of individuals' motivations as an explanation for crime, control theory assumes that any individual at any time could commit a crime. A new system of values is not required to steal or to harm another person. For example, there is no special motivation that would explain why a person chooses to take things from open garages, rob a convenience store clerk at gun point, or encourage clients to make fraudulent investments. The benefits of these acts are viewed as obvious.

One of the implications of control theory's views about self-interest and dismissal of any special motivation needed to explain crime is that crime is viewed as just one form of behavior that the theory can account for. Clearly, the consequences of crime may be very harmful for individuals and society, and there are variations in the severity of the consequences of crimes for individuals and society, but the consequences are not viewed as helpful for explaining why the acts were committed in the first place. Put another way, this conception of crime suggests that offenders will generally be versatile – individuals who commit crimes will tend not to concentrate on a single type, but engage in a wide variety of different types of crime.

At the societal level, the key assumption made in control theory is the idea that society can introduce a variety of mechanisms that will prevent or reduce the chances of individuals perceiving crime as being in their self-interest. As we explain below, these mechanisms may take a variety of different forms and are all focused on enhancing the negative consequences of a criminal act. Relatedly, control theory assumes this kind of societal intervention is possible due to the operation of a social order that reflects a common set of norms and values (Kornhauser, 1978). Social order is sustained by a wide range of social institutions – some formal, some informal – that reflect these norms and values.

The combination of assumptions about individual self-interest and social control leads control theory to place the primary cause of crime in weak controls over individuals' behavior. Without any consideration of the source or type of controls, control theory expects that individuals who are under a high level of control will be unlikely to commit crime, since the personal and social costs of crime will not be perceived to be in their self-interest. Alternatively, individuals who are under weak controls will be much more likely to commit crimes – they have, in some sense, been "freed" to commit criminal acts, since the personal and social costs of crime are viewed as low relative to the perceived benefits of crime. It is also important to emphasize, in this very general sketch of control theory, that it is not deterministic. The individual is always assumed to have agency – behavioral choices are made, for better or worse, that may run counter to expectations based on degree of control individuals are exposed to.

## Sources of Control

Given that control theories of crime claim the cause of criminal behavior is the weak control of individuals, we might ask what are the sources of control? The two key dimensions that need to be considered in thinking about the sources of control on individual behavior are: (1) internal v. external and (2) formal v. informal.

## Internal v. External

We start by considering the location of control – whether internal or external to the individual. By internal control, we are referring to mechanisms that function within the individual and include such characteristics as self-control (Gottfredson & Hirschi, 1990; Hirschi, 2004), morality (Wikström *et al.*, 2012), and impulsiveness (Wilson & Herrnstein, 1985). Alternatively, these kinds of characteristics have been referred to as ways of thinking about an individual's propensity to crime – they are expected to influence individual behavioral choices in ways that may decrease or increase the chances of crime commission, but should not be viewed as motivations for crime. Important to control theory is the idea that internal sources of control have the potential to prevent crimes from occurring by operating in ways that make it difficult for an individual to see the value in committing a crime, and make it easy to see the costs of crime. For example, according to Michael Gottfredson and Travis Hirschi (1990), individuals with low levels of self-control will have short-term orientations and make behavioral choices without thinking through the long-term consequences. An implication of this perspective is that criminal acts – something that involves the use of force or fraud to meet one's needs, according to Gottfredson & Hirschi – will be more attractive because of the immediate benefits provided to the offender. Per-Olof Wikström and colleagues (e.g., 2012) explain, in a similar way, that an individual's level of morality – how strongly the person holds common values of right and wrong – will influence behavioral choices. To the extent an individual has a high level of morality, criminal and delinquent acts will be avoided, because they would conflict with the individual's personal morality. In both of these cases, the individual characteristic – self-control or morality – is viewed as the mechanism (i.e., the internal control) that inhibits criminal acts from being committed.

External controls refer to the influence of legal, political, cultural, and social institutions. These institutions may provide a strictly external source of control through direct supervision or surveillance. Most individuals will avoid committing criminal acts when they know they are being watched – by a parent, by a supervisor at work, or by a police officer with a radar gun alongside a highway. It is not necessary for there to be an emotional or social tie to the party performing the supervision. Rather, the individual is inhibited from committing some acts out of a concern for being observed and caught and the personal, social, and/or legal consequences that would likely follow.

External controls may also be represented in the ties that individuals have to a wide range of social institutions. In much of the research literature, these are commonly assumed to be family, peers, school, and workplace. Each type of social tie is expected to function as a source of virtual supervision – the parent, the teacher, or the colleague at work may not be physically present, but they are psychologically present in the individual, so that they have the power to affect behavioral choices. How does this happen? For control theory, the key theoretical mechanism is found in the "social bond" (Hirschi, 1969) that represents how well connected an individual is to any number of these conventional social institutions. The stronger the social bond, the stronger the ties of the individual to conventional society, and consequently a reduced likelihood of crime, because the social costs of crime outweigh whatever immediate benefits may be provided by the crime. It is important to note that this does not mean individuals are engaged in some kind of rational calculus about how or whether some act would have social costs and how to quantify these costs. Rather, it is the idea that engaging in some criminal act, should it be found out about by one's parents, peers, spouse, or colleagues, would create difficult interpersonal situations that inhibits a great many acts.

Internal controls may also overlap with external controls, and could be thought of as reflecting a continuum of control. For example, Hirschi's (2004) reconceptualization of the social bond and linking it to self-control provides one example, while Wikström's (Wikström *et al.*, 2012) situational action theory and its emphasis on morality provides another example. In both of these approaches, an individual-level characteristic is conceptualized through that individual's ties to conventional society. In reconceptualizing self-control, Hirschi (2004; see also Gottfredson, 2011) suggests that self-control can be measured, in part, by the level of attachment to a parent, which has traditionally been viewed as a measure of the social bond (Hirschi, 1969). This assertion reflects the notion that internal controls condition external controls – the ability of a spouse or a parent to influence behavioral choices will be contingent on the degree of internal control an individual has, and whether the social consequences of an action are given any consideration. Distilling this notion further: Does the social tie matter for the individual? If so, to what degree? In a similar way, Wikström and colleagues' (Wikström *et al.*, 2012) conceptualization of individual morality also combines notions of internal and external control. Morality is a characteristic of individuals and provides an indicator of propensity to commit crimes, yet it is measured by assessing how well the individual has internalized conventional society's norms and values – an external control. It might also be noted that Wikström's notion of morality parallels Hirschi's (1969) discussion of the "belief" element of the social bond, which we discuss in more detail below.


## Formal v. Informal


The second key dimension is formal versus informal sources of control. Formal sources of social control are typically represented by the criminal justice system and the role that legal sanctions – both threat and application – may play in affecting behavioral choices. This form of control is represented most commonly in the "deterrence theory" literature, where the key idea being assessed is the expectation that individuals will consider the costs and benefits of potential criminal acts (see Nagin, 2013). To the extent the potential costs outweigh the potential benefits of a criminal act, deterrence theory suggests that individuals will refrain from committing crimes. For our purposes here, it is enough to note that it is the expected role of the state through the application of laws by the criminal justice system that is the primary source of control over the behavior of individuals.

In contrast to the emphasis on formal institutions of social control, informal controls refer to a wide range of social institutions, such as the family, the school, the workplace, as well as friends and peers of individuals. The mechanism that links any informal social institution to behavioral choices is comparable to that linking a formal institution of social control to crime: behavioral choices have consequences for the individual and their social ties. To the extent a criminal act would make an important social relationship vulnerable, individuals are expected to be less likely to engage in the behavior. Hirschi's (1969) description of the social bond and its poten-tial to affect behavioral choices helped to clarify the role that family, school and peers play as sources of control. Specifically, the stronger the emotional attachment and commitment to any conventional social institution, the less likely criminal choices become, due to the restrictive influence of the social institution on the indi-vidual's behavior. For example, youth with close relationships with at least one par-ent are less likely to commit criminal acts out of concern for maintaining that relationship and not wanting to disappoint that parent. This is the "virtual supervi-sion" noted above that helps to regulate behavioral choices, as the youth thinks about how a parent might react if present to see what was going on (Hirschi, 1969).

## Levels of Explanation: Macro-, Micro-, and Multilevel Control Theories

Ruth Kornhauser's *Social Sources of Delinquency* (1978) noted that control theory is premised on a conception of social order independent of cultural values – the idea that there are nearly universal norms that prohibit such behaviors as murder, assault, and theft (1978:40). What this view of social order implies is that control theory is fundamentally a macro-level theory of crime, even when it narrows its attention to individuals and their behaviors. In other words, the explanation for individual criminal behavior necessarily relies on the same social order described by Kornhauser as key to the macro-level versions of the theory. Her use of the control theory label for both macro and micro versions has helped to highlight the commonalities across various strands of control theory and argues against a common misconception that control theory is a strictly micro-level theory of crime.

Up to this point, our discussion has focused on the components and mecha-nisms of control theory in very general terms. We have made brief references to some specific examples of control theory to illustrate the various sources of control. Our focus will now turn to describing some of the major theoretical efforts aimed at explaining how the weak control of individuals leads to an increased likelihood of crime. Although there are a variety of ways that we could present this material, we have focused on the level of explanation, since it seems to us a more intuitive way of addressing each specific theory (see Kornhauser, 1978; Paternoster & Bachman, 2010). In the discussion that follows, we start with macro-level control theories, then discuss micro-level control theories, followed by attempts to link the macro and micro versions of control theory. Our discussion is by necessity brief, and we limit it to a small number of exemplar theories, but hope to point interested readers to other sources they may find useful for further understanding of control theories of crime.

## Macro-level control theory

If we follow Kornhauser's (1978) analysis, the earliest control theories were macro-level theories aimed at explaining patterns of crime and delinquency across larger social (geospatial) units, such as neighborhoods, cities, states, and nations. The work emanating from the "Chicago School" provided a strong foundation for what Clifford Shaw and Henry McKay (1942) would later assemble into an explanation linking numerous indicators of social disorganization, such as unemployment, poverty, population density, immigration, as well as crime. Their social disorganization theory described how the economic characteristics of a community were related to population turnover and population heterogeneity, which in turn helped to elevate all of the other indicators of social disorganization. Robert Park and Ernest Burgess (1925) had sketched out a notion of social control that described how the same processes made it difficult for communities to self-regulate the behaviors of residents. Put another way, social control and social disorganization were essentially the same thing: they reflected how well or how poorly communities were able to self-regulate and achieve common goals (Kornhauser, 1978). Descriptions of social disorganization theory focused on the links among these various indicators of social problems, explaining how there was no requirement for individuals to be motivated to commit crime – or any other form of behavior – they were not pushed or pulled into crime, but it was a natural consequence of individual self-interest being allowed to manifest itself where there was limited ability of the community to monitor the behavior of individuals within the community.

Robert Bursik's (1988) paper on linking social disorganization theory to crime and delinquency is often credited with having resurrected the theory as an explanation for crime, since it had fallen out of favor in the 1960s and 1970s, when much of the field turned to explanations that emphasized social and political power. Bursik's exegesis of the disorganization perspective helped to lay the groundwork for renewed testing of the disorganization theoretical framework. He accomplished this by illustrating where the Shaw and McKay (1942) approach was inadequate, but not inherently problematic, in using core ideas in their theory to study crime. In discussing the primary criticisms of disorganization theory – its focus on trying to explain individual behavior, the notion that ecological structures were stable, ways to measure disorganization, ways to measure crime, and normative assumptions in the theory – Bursik laid out a research agenda that he and others have tested in many different ways over the past two decades.

Following Bursik's (1988) redefinition of disorganization theory, Sampson & Groves (1989) published one of the first comprehensive and systematic tests of social disorganization theory. One of the key theoretical distinctions that they helped to clarify was the use of the systemic model (see, e.g., Kasarda & Janowitz, 1974; Sampson, 1988) that characterized a community as a web of formal and informal ties based in family life and ongoing socialization in the community (Sampson & Groves, 1989:777). They went on to discuss how social organization and social disorganization were simply ends of a continuum that could be used to describe community self-regulation, which could then be used to explain behaviors such as crime. More directly, they explained how community-level indicators of disorganization – urbanization, family disruption, low economic status, ethnic heterogeneity, and residential mobility – would affect the number of unsupervised teens, participation in informal and voluntary community groups, and friendship networks that would, in turn, influence levels of crime. For Sampson and Groves, the key source of social control resided in organizational participation and friendship networks – to the extent these were weak or became weak over time, the likelihood of crime increased, due to the weak control of individuals within a community.

Other research in the social disorganization tradition also started to pay attention to feedback loops, where increased disorganization leads to increased crime, which in turn increases disorganization later. Robert Bursik and Harold Grasmick (1993) proposed an expanded systemic model that included multiple sources of control – some individual, some neighborhood – and explained how each was related to neighborhood crime levels. Dina Rose and Todd Clear (1998) expanded on Bursik & Grasmick's model to incorporate feedback loops that were linked to the exercise of formal social control (what Bursik and Grasmick had called "public control"). They argued that in neighborhoods where there was more intervention by the police, resulting in higher levels of incarceration of individuals from those neighborhoods, there would be increasingly negative consequences for social organization. Todd Clear and Natasha Frost's (2013) analysis of incarceration and its effects in a mix of both rural and urban areas illustrates just how damaging the overuse of formal social control can be for communities.

More recently, there has been relatively little theoretical development on a strictly macro-level disorganization theory of crime. Rather, the theoretical attention has moved to explaining individual-level behavior in the context of community-level characteristics. We discuss these multilevel theories of crime that emerge from this work below.

### Micro-level control theory

*Early individual-level control theories*  The use of control theory to explain individual behavior emerged in the early 1950s, where the emphasis was primarily on trying to understand conformity as a way of learning about the causes of juvenile delinquency. The rise of individual level control theory is tied to the increase in the usage of the self-report survey, which provided a direct way to test the theory. Some of the exemplars of this work include, but are not restricted to, Albert Reiss, Walter Reckless, Jackson Toby, F. Ivan Nye, and David Matza.

One of the first empirical studies to utilize the control perspective was conducted by Albert Reiss (1951). Reiss argued that personal control and social control – what we have labeled internal and external controls – were both important to explaining delinquency. Reiss defined personal control as "the ability of the individual to refrain from meeting needs in ways which conflict with the norms and rules of the community" and social control as "the ability of social groups or institutions to make norms or rules effective" (1951:196). Thus, this is a classic control perspective, ignoring motives as not necessary to be explained and positing delinquency as being the result of unrestrained behavior. Reiss analyzed a sample of over 1,000 juvenile probationers in Chicago, finding measures of both types of control in the juveniles' case files. Reiss demonstrated relationships between failure on probation (e.g., recidivism) and marital status and economic income of parents, delinquency of the juvenile's neighborhood, and psychosocial characteristics such as "mature ego and superego." The latter, personal controls, were derived from psychiatric examinations and are therefore somewhat subjective. While this was an important study to introduce the use of data to test a theoretical position, the results have been criticized for being "quite weak" (Bernard, Snipes, & Gerould, 2010). Nonetheless, this study did foreshadow the delineation of "control" into social and self components.

A related theory was offered by Walter C. Reckless (1961). Relying on similar ideas, but different labels than Reiss, Reckless argued that delinquency is the result of weak inner and outer containment. The genesis of Reckless's ideas stemmed from a 1956 paper with Simon Dinitz and Ellen Murray (1956), where they argued that "good boys" internalized prosocial values and cared about what others thought of them. This "good self-concept" became a primary factor for what they call "inner containment." Reckless's "Containment theory" was more fully explicated in his 1961 book, *The Crime Problem*. The primary assertion of containment theory is that crime would be committed without the presence of controls (or containments). Reckless identified typical external or outer containments, such as supervision, that previous theories had pointed to. Similar to Reiss's work, he argued that a strong superego or conscience also helped prevent delinquency.

In an attempt to move beyond general claims that more control meant less delinquency, Jackson Toby (1957) focused on trying to explain the mechanisms by which control works. Consistent with the individual level assumptions of most control theories, Toby stated "[c]linical study reveals that the impulses to steal and murder and rape are universal" (1957:16). Toby then suggested that the cause of criminal and delinquent behavior is a lack of controls in certain areas, and a focus on traditional social controls as an explanation was insufficient. It is not just the absence of controls that is relevant; it is how those controls are internalized. In other words, there must be something about controls that can differentiate delinquents from nondelinquents. He proposed the term "stake in conformity" to suggest that those for whom there is a future, delinquency is seen as simply not worth the risk. Using education as the basis for the theory, Toby posits that those whose parents encourage their learning, take schooling seriously, and build up stakes in conformity and the possibility of a bright future will be prevented from risking and losing it all by breaking the law.

Nye's (1958) research not only proposed a variation of control theory that focused on the family, but was one of the first tests of control theory to be illustrated through the relatively new method of the self-report survey that was becoming increasingly common after World War II. Nye relied on three surveys of youth in the State of Washington, and argued that parental control within familial relationships was the primary factor in preventing juvenile delinquency. Like Reiss and Reckless, Nye described control as having both internal and external forms. Direct control was represented by the use of supervision by parents, indirect control referred to the desire to avoid crime because of familial and other relationships, and internal control was the inner restraint of the conscience. Nye's use of self-reports of relatively minor delinquency was pathbreaking and helped to set the stage for theory testing and development in coming decades. He found relationships between delinquency and a variety of familial factors, including too-strict and too-lenient supervision, familial cohesiveness, and familial stability.

David Matza's (1964) *Delinquency and Drift* began with the proposition that traditional theories of delinquency produced an "embarrassment of riches" by predicting too much crime. If juveniles were really driven to commit crime by biological or personality imperatives, they would be much more delinquent than reality suggests. Matza then introduced the term "drift" to illustrate the notion that most juvenile delinquents are not committed to delinquency but drift in and out of a state of deviance. While some interpret drift theory as a type of learning theory (see, e.g., Akers & Sellers, 2012), it fits perfectly within the control tradition. For example, Matza argues that drift occurs when social controls are "loosened" (1964:29). The image Matza produced was of a juvenile who was "free" of societal constraints (or controls) and who therefore was more free to commit delinquency than at other times. One such constraint included guilt or responsibility – committing crimes is easier when it is "not my fault." This idea stemmed from Matza's earlier work with Greshem Sykes in delineating so-called "techniques of neutralization" (Sykes & Matza, 1957). Matza, consistent with control theories, argued that agency is important in the explanation of crime. He also suggested that the simple freedom of a lack of control may in fact not be enough, and that juveniles must feel a desire to take control of their lives and do something about their situation. Delinquency is thus somewhat of an agentic statement of personal control.

*The social bond and crime*   Travis Hirschi's (1969) *Causes of Delinquency* has perhaps had the greatest impact on notions of control theory, relative to any other work that has been published. In part, the impact of Hirschi's effort was due to a combination of his delineating key hypotheses from three different theories of crime: control, cultural deviance, and strain. He then set about testing these hypotheses using individual self-report delinquency data. At the time of its publication, only Nye's work (1958; Nye & Short, 1957) had attempted to test whether delinquent behavior could be measured by asking adolescents to respond to questions about their behavior. Hirschi (1969) connected the self-report method with a systematic comparison of the three different theories, more often than not showing the patterns in the data to be more consistent with control theory than either cultural deviance or strain theory.

The control theory model proposed by Hirschi (1969) linked what he called the social bond to delinquency. In his formulation, the social bond consisted of four key elements: attachment to conventional others; commitment to conventional goals; involvement in conventional activities; and beliefs consistent with society's norms and values. In general, the greater the level of all four of these elements, the stronger the social bond to conventional society and the less likely a person was to commit criminal or delinquent acts.

What does each of the elements refer to? Attachment is the emotional, psychological, and social connections an individual has with others, such as, family, friends, and teachers. If the behavior is expected to harm the individual's social ties, it should be less likely to occur. These are the social ties and relationships that are key to social disorganization theory noted above. Commitment is the degree to which an individual is focused on achieving conventional goals (e.g., high school or college graduation, employment, etc.). Commitment represents more of a self-reflective aspect of the social bond, where individuals are expected to assess – however crudely and inaccurately – the consequences of different types of behavior for achieving their goals. Involvement is simply the amount of time or relative share of time that is spent in conventional activities. Individuals who are more involved in conventional activities, such as, amount of time spent on completing homework for school and spending time with family, should have less time to engage in criminal or delinquent activities. Belief is the degree to which an individual has the same beliefs about right and wrong as the common value system. The more in line the individual's belief system is with the common value system, then the less likely the person is to commit a criminal or delinquent act.

Although it is conceptually useful to distinguish each of these four elements of the social bond, they are not independent of each other. As Hirschi (1969) explained, in detail, each element has the effect of reinforcing every other element. For example, individuals who have greater levels of attachment to others, will also tend to have greater levels of commitment to achievement and stronger beliefs in the common value system. The social bond, then, may be conceptualized as running along a continuum. At one end of the continuum would be individuals with high levels of all four elements, while at the other end, would be individuals with low levels of all four elements. Individuals with a mix – higher on some elements and lower on other elements – would fall somewhere in between. Based on Hirschi's (1969) cumulative set of findings, as well as other research published in the decades after his work, belief may be the most important of the elements (see also Costello & Vowell, 1997; Matsueda, 1982), followed by attachment and commitment. Although intuitively appealing for control theory, Hirschi (1969) found relatively weak effects of involvement on crime – most crime does not require much time to commit, so even a person who spends nearly every waking hour in conventional activities could commit a crime in a matter of minutes, much as Matza (1964) predicted.

*Individual propensity and crime: self-control and morality*    Micro-level control theories of crime have continued to evolve, but always with the focus on how weak controls of the individual result in opportunities for crime. Some of these developments focus much more heavily on internal controls, rather than external or social controls. For example, Wilson & Herrnstein (1985) focused on impulsiveness as an individual characteristic that resulted in a greater likelihood for crime among some individuals. Other works have focused on self-control (Gottfredson & Hirschi, 1990) and morality (Wikström *et al.*, 2012) as indicators of an individual propensity to commit crime. In propensity-based theories, the primary source of control is internal – a reflection of an individual's ability to monitor and regulate their own behavior. Controls external to the individual are still important – two individuals with similar propensities to commit crime will still differ in their criminal behavior based on differences in social (external) controls. Regardless of how individual propensity to crime is characterized, the key mechanism for any of these approaches is again that weak control of the individual – internal and external – is likely to result in a greater likelihood of crime.

Michael Gottfredson and Travis Hirschi's (1990) general theory of crime linked individual self-control – the ability to monitor and regulate one's behavior – to criminal behavior and has had a profound impact on the field in the 25 years following its publication. They built their theory on the basis of a wide range of disparate findings about the causes of crime, and pulled them together in a way that allowed for a seemingly simple, but actually very complex, theory of criminal behavior. In their conceptualization, low self-control has six components:

- A tendency to choose actions that offer immediate gratification
- A preference for simple tasks
- A preference for thrilling or risk-seeking activities
- A preference for physical as opposed to mental acts
- A minimal tolerance for frustration
- An insensitive and self-centered orientation (1990:90)

Each of these six characteristics is expected to contribute to an individual's overall level of self-control. The lower an individual's level of self-control, the greater the probability of a criminal act.

Their theory has periodically been misrepresented as relying only on self-control to explain criminal behavior. The other component to their theory is opportunity – that for two individuals with identical low levels of self-control, the one who is placed in a setting with greater opportunities for crime will have a greater likelihood of committing the act. Alternatively, individuals with high levels of self-control are not expected to commit crimes, regardless of the potential opportunities. An important aspect of the interaction of self-control and opportunity for Gottfredson & Hirschi (1990) is that opportunities are better thought of as perceived opportunities. For example, it is common to find cars with their engines running outside of a convenience store – the driver has run into the store to pick up some item and left the car running in the lot. Most people, when walking by such a car would pay little attention to it, other than perhaps notice the driver was not inside the car. A few others – those with low levels of self-control, according to Gottfredson & Hirschi – may perceive an opportunity to steal a car. Clearly, an opportunity to steal a car is not perceived every time such a vehicle is spotted – just that individuals with low self-control would be most likely to perceive such a situation as an opportunity for a crime.

Although there has been extensive research aimed at measuring self-control, there is still considerable disagreement about how best to measure such a complex trait. Among the alternatives are attitudinal items that try to gauge measure some aspect of each of the six elements and behavioral indicators of each of the six elements – both have their strengths and weaknesses and some researchers have taken to including some of each. Another unresolved issue is the lack of clarity in Gottfredson & Hirschi's (1990) discussion about whether the contribution of each of the six elements is equal or if some subset of items is relatively more important. Research aimed at measuring self-control has yet to resolve this issue.

A more recent theoretical contribution that has spurred a growth in research on individual propensity to crime in combination with opportunities for crime appears in Wikström and colleagues' (2012) situational action theory (SAT). Wikström's work has not set out to challenge directly any of the key elements of control theory, but its main proponents have tried to characterize it as something other than a control theory, even though its foundation comes from decades of findings supportive of control theory. Similarly, Wikström and colleagues have also tried to distance the theory from differential association, social learning, and cultural deviance theories of crime. We view SAT as a somewhat more specified version of Gottfredson & Hirschi's (1990) general theory of crime, in that it links an indicator of individual propensity (morality rather than self-control) to crime and to an interaction with situational opportunities for crime.

The key individual characteristic in SAT is an individual's morality, which leads some individuals to be more or less likely to commit crimes. What is morality in SAT? Morality is made up of beliefs in the law – whether it's wrong, or the degree to which it is wrong to violate the law. Wikström *et al.*'s (2012) description of the meaning and measurement of morality is nearly indistinguishable from Hirschi's (1969) description of the belief element of the social bond. Hirschi's (2004) more recent explication of the link between self-control and the social bond as he described it in *Causes of Delinquency* (1969) further complicates separating Wikström's notion of morality from Gottfredson & Hirschi's notion of self-control (see also, Gottfredson, 2011). This is not to say they are the same thing, just that there is a great deal of similarity.

The mechanism that links morality to criminal behavior is found in the interaction of the social settings individuals find themselves in with the person's morality to condition the likelihood of crime (Wikström *et al.*, 2012). In those social settings where individuals are freer to violate the laws (i.e., there are weaker controls), the person's morality takes on a more important and primary role – much like self-control and/or the social bond. Even in those settings where there may be ample opportunities for crime, if the person's morality is strong enough, it will more likely override perceived opportunities, with the person still being unlikely to commit a criminal act.

Another similarity between SAT and Gottfredson & Hirschi's (1990) self-control theory is the link between morality and self-control with the kinds of social settings individuals pursue. Both theories describe how individuals with higher propensities to crime (i.e., lower morality or self-control) are more likely to seek out situations and opportunities that are more crime-prone: those settings where there will be fewer sources of control/regulation/supervision. Wikström and colleagues' development of SAT has been more precise than Gottfredson & Hirschi (1990) in explaining how an individual's morality (propensity) creates situational opportunities, but the key mechanism is fundamentally the same.

## Multilevel control theory

Consistent with much of control theory's history, attention has focused exclusively on either the macro-level or the micro-level – attempts to explain variation in crime rates across geospatial units or in criminal behavior across individuals, respectively. The renewed interest in social disorganization theory in the late 1980s and early 1990s, combined with a growing body of agreed-upon correlates of individual criminal behavior, led some scholars to start trying to link the macro- and micro-levels of explanation. Funding from both the US National Institute of Justice and the Macarthur Foundation in the early 1990s for the Project on Human Development in Chicago Neighborhoods (PHDCN) kicked off this effort and has had profound impact in criminology, demography, sociology, and public health in the two decades following the start of data collection (see Sampson (2012) for a detailed history of the project). The accumulation of findings that link a wide range of neighborhood characteristics with individual outcomes has facilitated the development of what we may call multilevel control theories of crime. Key to these theories are explanations of why macro-level characteristics interact with individual characteristics to affect individual behavior.

Robert Sampson's work in this area has been extensive. His *Great American City* (2012) is an attempt to summarize roughly 25 years of his research that cuts across numerous fields. His collective efficacy theory presented in this volume, as well as numerous other publications (e.g., Sampson, 2006; Sampson, Raudenbush, and Earls, 1997), takes the core notion from social disorganization theory – that crime is higher in areas with weak social controls – and extends it with his notion of collective efficacy, which can then be linked to individual behavior. Collective efficacy has two primary components: shared expectations about social control, and social cohesion or trust. Shared expectations about social control refers to the perception that individuals have regarding the likelihood their neighbors will take action if confronted with an issue, such as children skipping school or breaking up a fight in front of their home. Social cohesion or trust refers to the quality of the relationships individuals have with their neighbors. It does not require that individuals be particularly close to their neighbors emotionally, psychologically, or socially. Rather, it is a perception that their neighbors are generally good and trustworthy people. The two components of collective efficacy are highly correlated with each other and often combined into a single indicator.

Neighborhood levels of collective efficacy are influenced by many other factors viewed as important in social disorganization theory: residential turnover, economic inequality, and residential segregation by race or economic position. Sampson (2012) notes, though, that the key factor to influence collective efficacy is what he calls concentrated disadvantage, which is the combination of people receiving public assistance funds (i.e., welfare), poverty, unemployment, female-headed households, racial composition, and population density of children. Areas that score high on concentrated disadvantage will be neighborhoods where these six elements make it difficult for residents to develop and/or sustain both shared expectations about social control and social cohesion. In large part, concentrated disadvantage leads to weak organization and voluntary associations in these neighborhoods, which then negatively affects collective efficacy.

How is collective efficacy linked to crime at the macro-level? Communities with high levels of collective efficacy will have a high degree of shared expectations for social control and a high level of trust in their neighbors – an indicator of the strength of social controls. Consequently, neighborhoods with high levels of collective efficacy should have lower rates of crime, because social controls are higher and opportunities for crime should be reduced. Those communities with low levels of collective efficacy should then have much higher rates of crime, because the social controls are weak, freeing many more individuals to engage in criminal activity. Consistent with the expectations of social disorganization theory, concentrated disadvantage also directly affects crime rates – greater levels of disadvantage are correlated with higher rates of crime – but Sampson and colleagues have shown that collective efficacy mediates some of the relationship with crime (see, e.g., Kirk & Papachristos, 2011; Sampson, 2012).

Linking a neighborhood's collective efficacy to individual criminal behavior is straightforward: Areas with low collective efficacy have weak social controls, so individuals will be freer to engage in criminal acts. Interestingly, an individual's criminal behavior is not directly linked to their own residential neighborhood level of collective efficacy (Sampson, Morenoff, & Raudenbush, 2005). Rather, an individual's criminal behavior appears to be due more to the level of collectively efficacy where the crime occurs (Sampson, 2012). What this implies is that individuals committing crimes will seek opportunities in areas with low levels of collective efficacy – those places where there are few controls on individuals' behavior and others are least likely to intervene to prevent a crime, which is consistent with propensity-based versions of control theory (e.g., Gottfredson & Hirschi, 1990; Wikström *et al.*, 2012).

Building on notions of opportunity, another multilevel control theory includes the work of Pamela Wilcox and colleagues. In "Criminal Circumstance" they develop an "opportunity" or routine activities theory of crime (Wilcox, Land, & Hunt, 2003). Their theoretical approach elaborates on the classic statement of routine activities by

Cohen & Felson (1979; Felson & Cohen, 1980, 1981). Routine activities theory notes that there are three elements required for a crime to occur: a motivated offender, lack of a capable guardian to intervene, and an opportunity to commit a crime. Similar to other control theories, motivation of the offender is largely taken as unproductive and generally assumed rather than needing to be explained (see, e.g., Wilcox, Gialopsos, & Land, 2012). Wilcox *et al.* (2003) argue that opportunity is not something that exists only on the individual or the macro-level, but both. And these opportunities – which are represented by absence of social control and presence of capable guardians – can interact across levels. How can opportunity be multilevel? On the individual level, a person may be seen as vulnerable – for example, a college student walking alone at night listening to her iPod. At the same time, on the macro-level, neighborhoods will be seen as differentially attractive, much as Sampson (2012) described low collective efficacy neighborhoods as attractive for crime because of low levels of social control. Alternatively, other neighborhoods may be seen as attractive because of a large concentration of wealth with relatively low levels of security (unlocked doors, easily accessible and portable devices, etc.).

Although many of the attempts at multilevel control theory have started with a macro-level approach to explaining crime, by extending social disorganization theory, a number of more recent attempts have started with a micro-level control theory (e.g., Gottfredson & Hirschi, 1990) and tried to link higher-level characteristics to explain individual variation. For example, recent work has shown that community factors influence the distribution of self-control in individuals (Pratt, Turner, & Piquero, 2004; Turner, Piquero, & Pratt, 2005). Turner and colleagues (2005) showed that neighborhood and school factors played a role in individual youth levels of self-control. Similarly, Zimmerman (2010) analyzed the interaction between neighborhood factors and impulsivity, finding that impulsivity was differentially related to likelihood of offending across neighborhood characteristics, such as collective efficacy and legal cynicism. Impulsivity was more strongly related to crime in lower criminogenic areas. In other variations on linking multilevel characteristics to crime, some researchers have examined individual level factors at the macro level. Eisner (2001) and Pinker (2011) both argue, for example, that violent crime has declined across the centuries due to an increase in macro-level self-control. Note, though, that each of these alternatives comes back to the same theoretical mechanism: crime is a result of weak controls on individuals. Regardless of whether we start at the macro-level and work down to individual behavior, or at the micro-level and work up to social conditions, the source of crime is the same.

## Considering Time: Life-course and Developmental Theories

Much of the more recent theoretical development in criminology has focused on the incorporation of time into a theory of crime. Many of the more traditional control theories have been static – the focus has been on a snapshot at a particular point in time. Dynamic theories attempt to incorporate notions of time into the theory and to explain change in behavior over time, rather than patterns of behavior at a single point in time.

While early control theories were (sometimes erroneously) thought to apply solely to adolescence, in recent years, criminologists have directly applied it to crime over the life-course. Terrence Thornberry's (1987) "interactional theory" was one of the first systematic attempts at explaining change in individuals over time. Interactional theory uses the insights from both control and social learning theories to explain delinquency and crime over the life-course. Thornberry (1987) restricted his theory to delinquency, intent on trying to explain crime from the ages of 11 to 20. There are three parts of the theory, with each part reinforcing and feeding into the others. In the first stage, early development of delinquency is caused by a lack of social controls, particularly bonds to parents, which leads to lack of commitment to school and weak conventional beliefs – these are the key elements of the social bond proposed in Hirschi's (1969) work, discussed above. When the social bond is weak – or weakens over time – youth are then expected to associate with delinquent peers, which then leads to delinquent behavior. Thornberry (1987) argued that the association with delinquent peers will result in youth learning delinquent values that increase the chances of delinquency. However, he also noted "the premise of interactional theory is that the fundamental cause of delinquency is the attenuation of social controls over a person's conduct" (Thornberry, 1987:873). If the fundamental cause is weak controls, then it is not clear why delinquent values need to be learned to facilitate delinquency. Interactional theory is therefore an extension of Hirschi's (1969) description of social control theory by demonstrating how controls may change in form and vary in their effect on delinquency over time. For example, "attachment to parents, commitment to school, and belief in conventional values are not static attributes of the person, invariant over time" (Thornberry, 1987:875). To Thornberry argues that attachment to parents is not likely to be the most salient predictor of crime in middle adolescents, when youth are trying to exert their independence and forge an identity. Here peers – delinquent and non-delinquent – may take on an increased role. Finally, in late adolescence, other social institutions, such as the military and employment come to the fore, as well as attachments to newly developed families (spouse, children). Thus, Thornberry shows how attachments and commitments to social institutions change over time in the life-course.

On the heels of this work, Robert Sampson and John Laub developed their age-graded theory of informal social controls. Reconstructing data from the classic Glueck Unraveling Juvenile Delinquency study, Sampson and Laub were able to create a window into the lives of boys from childhood into mid-adulthood. Their initial theoretical specification, published in *Crime in the Making* (1993) offered distinct causal processes for different stages of the life-course, similar to Thornberry. In early life, parental relationships and relationships with teachers provide the control necessary to reduce delinquency. Importantly, these bonds explain the relationship between structural factors (e.g., poverty and family disruption) and crime. In middle adolescence, the theme of continuity is stressed, whereby those who were delinquent in childhood are likely to remain so in adolescence. Finally, in adulthood, bonds to work, military, and spouses explain crime regardless of the individual's past. Sampson and Laub argued that it was not just the timing or existence of bonds that mattered for the individual, but it was the quality of the bond. Thus, meaningful work and strong marriages were seen as integral to turning around one's deviant pathway – what they called "turning points." Following in the tradition that Hirschi started, Sampson & Laub (1993) not only specified a theory but went on to test it extensively, finding much support for their propositions.

In 2003, Laub & Sampson published a follow-up to their original work, examining the lives of the Glueck men to age 70. This was, according to the authors, "arguably the longest study of crime and delinquency in the world" (Laub & Sampson, 2003: 8). Utilizing a mix of qualitative and quantitative methods, Laub and Sampson again found that adult social bonds are salient for desistance from crime. However, this follow-up paid particular attention to the notion of agency, finding that many of the men stopped offending because they made a decision to do so, and those who did not stop, chose not to. Much of the more recent scholarly attention to Sampson and Laub's theoretical perspective has been focused on the effects of adult social bonds on crime. Research has tended to support their propositions, showing that attachments to spouses and employment are negatively related to crime in adulthood (Horney, Osgood, & Marshall, 1995; Sampson, Laub, & Wimer, 2006; Siennick & Osgood, 2008).

Another life-course or developmental theory of crime that is control oriented has been offered by Marc Le Blanc (1997, 2006). Le Blanc proposed a developmental theory that integrates environmental and individual factors to explain crime over the life-course. The theory includes four main types of control: (1) bonding, (2) unfolding, (3) modeling, and (4) constraining. Bonding represents relationships within a community or between individuals. Unfolding is the process of development with respect to community or individuals. Modeling represents the factors that influence prosocial behavior. Finally, constraining is the traditional application of control (e.g., supervision). So long as these factors are consistent, prosocial behavior will persist over time. For Le Blanc, criminal offending is most likely to emerge when the social bond weakens, meaning that controls on individuals are weak and insufficient to prevent crime from occurring. Thus, like Thornberry, this theory includes elements of social learning theory to try and explain how or why the social bond weakens over time. The seeming integration of control and social learning theory is not problematic for control theories, since these theories would typically see these elements as either irrelevant or redundant to the key control mechanisms (see debate between Costello, 1997, 1998 and Matsueda, 1997). More recently, Le Blanc (2006) has expanded on this theory, by illustrating how self-control and social control interact over time.

## Challenges and Opportunities for Control Theory

Throughout its history, control theory has evolved in numerous ways to accommodate new facts about the nature and distribution of crime, as well as the changing interests of different academic fields. These changes have pushed the theory to emphasize different levels of analysis and explanation, as well as to incorporate the notion of how behavior develops over time. As we look to the continued evolution of control theory, it seems to us that there are at least four areas that are likely to continue to move or start to move control theory in new and interesting ways: (1) general v. specific theory; (2) biological explanations for human behavior; (3) peer influences; and (4) network science. To the extent that control theory is able to adapt to these four sets of issues, it will continue to be one of the most relevant and prominent theories of crime in the field. Should control theory prove unable to address the findings or concerns that emerge from these areas, its relevance will no doubt decline.

First, control theory represents an eclectic set of general theories of crime rather than crime-specific theories. The assumption of many a control theorist is that the explanation can be applied to all types of crime – indeed all types of antisocial behavior. While this may seem an overreach for any theory of crime, its justification is twofold. First, control theory is a flexible theory – recall that the key cause of crime is viewed as weak control of the individual. Controls may take on a variety of different forms – internal or external, formal or informal, and also be age-specific. Second, one of the more historically recent and convincing set of findings in criminology shows that criminal offenders are versatile in their offending patterns (see, e.g., Britt, 1996; Farrington, Snyder, & Finnegan, 1988). Put another way, offenders do not focus all of their attention and effort on a specific type of crime – what has been referred to as specialization. In fact, individuals who commit crimes also tend to experience more accidents, injuries, failure in personal relationships, and poor employment histories (see, e.g., Laub & Sampson, 2003; Piquero, Farrington, & Blumstein, 2007), which argues against the need for a crime-specific explanation. Researchers have applied control theory to crimes as diverse as white-collar offenses (Hirschi & Gottfredson, 1987; Lasley, 1988) and genocide (Brannigan & Hardwick, 2003).

Control theorists also claim that the theoretical perspective may be applied equally well to different cultures and societies or historical periods. Although comparative criminology is still a relatively new subfield, there is growing evidence that the key elements of control theory apply well across different societies. Research in Africa (Marenin & Reisig, 1995), Asia (Zhang & Messner, 1996), Europe (Vazsonyi, Pickering, Junger, & Hessing, 2001), and Middle East (Özbay & Özcan, 2006) all point to the likelihood that control theory applications are not be limited to the United States. It is more difficult to assess the historical claims of control theory, because the data are more limited. However, we note that data finding support for control theory spans much of the twentieth and early twenty-first centuries in the United States, ranging from Sampson & Laub's (1993) analysis of the Glueck data, whose participants were born in the early part of the twentieth century, while more recent analyses of the PHDCN data touch on youth born in the 1990s and reflects their experiences in the early twenty-first century (e.g., Zimmerman, 2010). Digging further into history, one finds—somewhat anecdotal—evidence that marriage may have reduced crime in frontier America. Pinker (2011) argues that when men traveled West, lawlessness and crime ruled; yet when women followed them, violence declined.

Second, research on the biological bases of human behavior has become increasingly prevalent in the study of crime. Of note, this work does not take a deterministic approach to linking biology and criminal behavior. Rather, the goal is more along the lines of trying to understand how biological characteristics interact with psychological, social, and other "environmental" characteristics to affect the likelihood of criminal behavior. This research generally falls under the rubric of "biosocial" work. Research on brain development has shown that development is not complete for most adults until they are in their mid-20s, which is also broadly consistent with age-graded patterns of all forms of risky and criminal behavior (see, e.g., Raine, 2013; Rocque, 2014). This growing body of research helps to highlight the importance of trying to understand how something like brain development conditions the likelihood of criminal behavior (Vaske, Galyean, & Cullen, 2011), perhaps through altering an individual's propensity to crime.

Another area of biological research relevant to control theory has claimed that a wide range of biological indicators and characteristics explain the apparent links between those variables traditionally thought of as control variables (e.g., self-control, and attachment) and crime. Blonigen (2010), for example, argues that biological characteristics are more proximal to behavioral choices, so that if a biological trait predicts crime, it comes between any other social or psychological indicator and crime. Beaver's (e.g., 2008, 2011) research claims that individual propensity to crime is biologically based, implying that the observed relationship between self-control and crime is spurious and largely a consequence of the biological characteristics of individuals.

Control theory's continued development and relevance as an explanation of crime will require the incorporation of many biologically based findings as they emerge from ongoing research. Fundamentally, there is nothing inherently problematic for control theory with accommodating key findings in biological research on human behavior, especially since the biological research on crime has shied away from a deterministic approach. Crimes are a relatively infrequent form of human behavior, suggesting it is difficult to see how any biological research could take a strong position on determinism and continue to be supported by the data. Short of that, much of this work seems more focused on trying to understand either those factors that affect propensity to crime and/or other social and psychological characteristics and their effects on crime. We have seen little in the biological research that takes issue with the fundamental premise of control theory – that criminal behavior is more likely when controls (individual and social) are weak. Biological research should help control theory to further explicate the mechanisms that link weak controls on behavior to crime. For example, research has found that genetics play a role in individual levels of self-control (Beaver, Wright, & De Lisi, 2008; Wright & Beaver, 2005), which is entirely consistent with the premises of general control theory.

Third, decades of research on the self-reported delinquency of adolescents has shown a relatively large and positive correlation between the respondent's level of delinquency and that of his or her friends (see, e.g., Warr, 2002). Much of this research has also concluded that control theory is either irrelevant or invalid, because it is viewed as unable to explain peer effects. Regardless of the orientation of the research, however, there has been relatively little attention focused on the mechanism that links the delinquency level of two or more individuals (Warr, 2002). Why is there a high degree of similarity of delinquency among friends? Attempts to answer this question have focused on such features as density of social networks (Haynie, 2001), both density of social network and length of time together (Sarnecki, 2001), and instigation to crime (McGloin & Nguyen, 2012). Haynie (2001) finds that networks with more social ties – those that are denser – show greater similarity of delinquency levels, while Sarnecki (2001) finds that co-offending groups have loose ties and tend to be short-lived. McGloin & Nguyen (2012) suggest that instigation could come in the form of providing motivation for crime, identifying opportunities for crime, or even peer pressure and coercion, yet they are unable to test directly any of these possible links. Other research has focused on gangs (Fleisher, 2006; Roman, Cahill, Lachman, Lowry, Orosco, & McCarty, 2012) and dating relationships (Haynie, Giordano, Manning, & Longmore, 2005; Lonardo, Giordano, Longmore, & Manning, 2009) to show relatively high levels of peer similarity, but has not done much to explain the similarity.

Much of the extant work in control theory as opposed to research in social learning theory has also failed to specify the mechanism responsible for similarity of delinquency level among friends (see, e.g., Costello, 2010; Laub & Sampson, 2003; and, Sampson & Laub, 1993). This research has examined the positive effects of peers and often found evidence that leads to conformity, but similar to the research noted above, there is little evidence that speaks to the mechanism that leads to conformity between two or more peers. In much control theory research, it is typical for the similarity of crime and delinquency or conformity among peers to be written off as a matter of self-selection – the "birds of a feather, flock together" maxim (Hirschi, 1969). In light of the extensive research that unequivocally establishes a link between peers, control theory will need to deal with the social processes at work in small groups – how does socialization occur within a small group? What are the social dynamics at work in the small group that form, strengthen and possibly weaken social ties over time (see, e.g., Britt, 2003; Sánchez-Jankowski, 1991; Young, 2011)? Are individuals with weak ties more likely to be influenced by delinquent peers (see Thornberry, 1987)? These are questions that remain for control theorists.

Fourth, network science refers to what is popularly known as "Big Data" – the meta-data that results from our many electronic signatures and other activities of daily living that leave a trace of our activities throughout the day (and night). In 2013, there was extensive media attention to the US National Security Agency's (NSA's) electronic surveillance activities that illustrate for the general public the many ways that the US government can follow individuals without their knowledge or consent. Although the justification for the NSA's efforts is the prevention of terrorist activities, it is interesting to note that the techniques used by the NSA are no different than those used researchers to track the behavior of large numbers of individuals over time and space (see, e.g., González, Hidalgo, & Barabási, 2008). How might these meta-data help us to understand criminal behavior? In the simplest of ways, the ability to track a very large population minute-by-minute, say, based on the location of a cell phone and/or electronic communication, will help us to understand how and where people congregate that does not require them to recall and self-report locations. The researcher already knows. It is already possible to track not just the volume, but also the content, of text messages, emails, and other forms of electronic social media that again hold the potential for understanding the dynamics of human behavior (Barabási, 2010), some of which will be criminal. Other online applications, such as Google Now, record the content of a person's email conversations, syncing it with that person's calendar and other applications, perhaps even on their smart phone. The application may then provide tips on driving routes, suggest a time to leave for a dinner reservation, what to pack for an upcoming trip, and much more – it is a level of surveillance many users fail to contemplate when using different applications and services, but which will continue to shed light on how people spend their time. For control theory, there is nothing inherently special about criminal behavior compared to noncriminal behavior, aside from the consequences. Thus, a more general understanding of how, when, and where people interact will no doubt shed light on the routine activities of people and the social dynamics underlying many forms of both criminal and noncriminal behavior.

## Conclusion

Control theory is a general and flexible explanation for the causes of all types of criminal and antisocial behavior. In its simplest form, control theory posits the primary cause of crime in the weak control of individuals. The theory may be applied to explain the criminal behavior of individuals, the variations in crime rates across geospatial units, and the behavior of individuals by using neighborhood or community-level characteristics to create a multilevel explanation. The source of control may be internal or external to the individual, it may be from a formal or informal institution, and it may change over time to reflect age-specific variations in the sources of control.

## References

Akers, R.L., & Sellers, C.S. (2012). Criminological theories: introduction. *Evaluation and Application, 6th* edition, Los Angeles: Roxbury.

Barabási, A.-L. (2010). *Bursts: The Hidden Pattern Behind Everything We Do*. New York: Dutton.

Beaver, K.M. (2008). Nonshared environmental influences on adolescent delinquent involvement and adult criminal behavior. *Criminology, 46*, 341–370.

Beaver, K.M. (2011). The effects of genetics, the environment, and low self-control on perceptions of maternal and paternal socialization: Results from a longitudinal sample of twins. *Journal of Quantitative Criminology, 27*, 85–105.

Beaver, K.M., Wright, J.P., & DeLisi, M. (2008). Delinquent peer group formation: Evidence of a gene X environment correlation. *Journal of Genetic Psychology, 169,* 227–244.

Bernard, T.J., Snipes, J.B., & Gerold, A.L. (2010). *Vold's Theoretical Criminology.* New York: Oxford University Press.

Blonigen, D.M. (2010). Examining the relationship between age and crime: Contributions from the developmental literature on personality. *Clinical Psychology Review, 30,* 89–100.

Brannigan, A., & Hardwick, K.H. (2003). Genocide and general theory. In C.L. Britt & M. Gottfredson (Eds.), *Control Theories of Crime and Delinquency: Advances in Criminological Theory,* Vol. *12* (pp. 109–131). New Burnswick, NJ: Transaction.

Britt, C.L. (1996). The measurement of specialization and escalation in the criminal career: An alternative modeling strategy. *Journal of Quantitative Criminology, 12,* 193–222.

Britt, C.L. (2003). Self-control, group solidarity, and crime: An integrated control theory. In C.L. Britt & M. Gottfredson (Eds.), *Control Theories of Crime and Delinquency: Advances in Criminological Theory,* Vol. *12* (pp. 161–178). New Burnswick, NJ: Transaction.

Britt, C.L., & Gottfredson, M.R. (2003). Editors' introduction. In C.L. Britt & M. Gottfredson (Eds.), *Control Theories of Crime and Delinquency: Advances in Criminological Theory,* Vol. *12* (pp. 1–4). New Burnswick, NJ: Transaction.

Bursik, R.J., Jr. (1988). Social disorganization and theories of crime and delinquency: Problems and prospects. *Criminology, 26,* 519–552.

Bursik, R.J., Jr., & Grasmick, H.G. (1993). *Neighborhoods and Crime: The Dimensions of Effective Community Control.* New York: Lexington Books.

Clear, T., & Frost, N.A. (2013). *The Punishment Imperative: The Rise and Failure of Mass Incarceration in America.* New York: New York University Press.

Cohen, L.E., & Felson, M. (1979). Social change and crime rate trends: A routine activity approach. *American Sociological Review, 44,* 588–608.

Costello, B.J. (1997). On the logical adequacy of cultural deviance theories. *Theoretical Criminology, 1,* 403–428.

Costello, B.J. (1998). The remarkable persistence of a flawed term: A rejoinder to Matsueda. *Theoretical Criminology, 2,* 85–92.

Costello, B.J. (2010). Peer influence toward conformity. *Journal of Criminal Justice, 33,* 97–116.

Costello, B.J., & Vowell, P.R. (1997). Testing control theory and differential association: A reanalysis of the Richmond Youth Project data. *Criminology, 37,* 815–842.

Eisner, M. (2001). Modernization, self-control and lethal violence. The long-term dynamics of European homicide rates in theoretical perspective. *British Journal of Criminology, 41,* 618–638.

Farrall, S., & Bowling, B. (1999). Structuration, human development and desistance from crime. *British Journal of Criminology, 39,* 253–268.

Farrington, D.P., Snyder, H.N., & Finnegan, T.A. (1988). Specialization in juvenile court careers. *Criminology, 26,* 461–488.

Felson, M., & Cohen, L.E. (1980). Human ecology and crime: A routine activity approach. *Human Ecology, 8,* 389–406.

Felson, M., & Cohen, L.E. (1981). Modeling crime rate trends – A criminal opportunity perspective. *Journal of Research in Crime and Delinquency, 18,* 138–164.

Fleisher, M.S. (2006). Degree centrality and youth gangs as an ecological adaptation. In J. Short & L. Hughes (Eds.), *Studying Youth Gangs* (pp. 85–98). Walnut Creek, CA: AltaMira Press.

González, M.C., Hidalgo, C.A., & Barabási, A.-L. (2008). Understanding human mobility patterns. *Nature, 453,* 779–782.

Gottfredson, M.R. (2011). Sanctions, situations, and agency in control theories of crime. *European Journal of Criminology, 8*, 128–143.

Gottfredson, M.R., & Hirschi, T. (1990). *A General Theory of Crime.* Palo Alto, CA: Stanford University Press.

Haynie, D.L. (2001). Delinquent peers revisited: Does network structure matter? *American Journal of Sociology, 106*, 1013–1057.

Haynie, D., Giordano, P.C., Manning, W.D., & Longmore, M.A. (2005). Adolescent romantic relationships and delinquency involvement. *Criminology, 43*, 177–210.

Hirschi, T. (1969). *Causes of Delinquency.* Berkeley, CA: University of California Press.

Hirschi, T. (2004). Self-control and crime. In R.F. Baumeister & K.D. Vohs (Eds.), *Handbook of Self-Regulation: Research, Theory, and Applications* (pp. 537–552). New York: Guilford Press.

Hirschi, T., & Gottfredson, M.R. (1987). Causes of white collar crime. *Criminology, 25*, 949–974.

Hobbes, T. (1962 [1651]). *Leviathan.* London: Collier Books.

Horney, J., Osgood, D.W., & Marshall, I.H. (1995). Criminal careers in the short-term: Intra-individual variability in crime and its relation to local life circumstances. *American Sociological Review, 60*, 655–673.

Kahneman, D., & Tversky, A. (1979). Prospect theory: An analysis of decision under risk. *Econometrica, 47*, 263–291.

Kasarda, J.D., & Janowitz, M. (1974). Community attachment in mass society. *American Sociological Review, 39*, 328–339.

Kirk, D.S., & Papachristos, A.V. (2011). Cultural mechanisms and the persistence of neighborhood violence. *American Journal of Sociology, 116*, 1190–1233.

Kornhauser, R.R. (1978). *Social Sources of Delinquency: An Appraisal of Analytic Models.* Chicago: University of Chicago Press.

Lasley, J.R. (1988). Toward a control theory of white collar offending. *Journal of Quantitative Criminology, 4*, 347–362.

Laub, J.H., & Sampson, R.J. (2003). *Shared Beginnings, Divergent Lives: Delinquent Boys to Age 70.* Cambridge, MA: Harvard University Press.

Le Blanc, M. (1997). A generic control theory of the criminal phenomenon: The structural and the dynamical statements of an integrative multilayered control theory. In T.P. Thornberry (Ed.), *Developmental Theories of Crime and Delinquency* (pp. 215–287). New Brunswick, NJ: Transaction.

Le Blanc, M. (2006). Self-control and social control of deviant behavior in context: Development and interactions along the life-course. In R.J. Sampson & P.O. Wikström (Eds.), *The Explanation of Crime: Context, Mechanisms, and Development* (pp. 195–242). Cambridge: Cambridge University Press.

Lonardo, R.A., Giordano, P.C., Longmore, M.A., & Manning, W.D. (2009). Parents, friends, and romantic partners: Enmeshment in deviant networks and adolescent delinquency involvement. *Journal of Youth and Adolescence, 38*, 367–383.

Marenin, O., & Reisig, M. (1995). A general theory of crime and patterns of crime in Nigeria: An exploration of methodological assumptions. *Journal of Criminal Justice, 23*, 501–518.

Matsueda, R.L. (1982). Testing control theory and differential association: A causal modeling approach. *American Sociological Review, 47*, 489–504.

Matsueda, R.L. (1997). "Cultural deviance theory": The remarkable persistence of a flawed term. *Theoretical Criminology, 1*, 429–452.

Matza, D. (1964). *Delinquency and Drift*. New York: Wiley.

McGloin, J.M., & Nguyen, H. (2012). It was my idea: Considering the instigation of co-offending. *Criminology, 50,* 463–494.

Nagin, D. (2013). Deterrence: A review of the evidence by a criminologist for economists. *Annual Review of Economics, 5,* 83–105.

Nye, F.I. (1958). *Family Relationships and Delinquent Behavior*. Westport, CT: Greenwood Press.

Nye, F.I., & Short, J.F., Jr. (1957). Scaling delinquent behavior. *American Sociological Review, 22,* 326–331.

Özbay, Ö., & Özcan, Y.Z. (2006). A test of Hirschi's social bonding theory: Juvenile delinquency in the high schools of Ankara, Turkey. *International Journal of Offender Therapy and Comparative Criminology, 50,* 711–726.

Park, R.E., & Burgess, E. (1925). *The City: Suggestions for the Investigation of Human Behavior in the Urban Environment*. Chicago: University of Chicago Press.

Paternoster, R., & Bachman, R. (2010). Control theories. In E. McLaughlin & T. Newburn (Eds.), *The Sage Handbook of Criminological Theory* (pp. 114–138). London: Sage.

Paternoster, R., & Pogarsky, G. (2009). Rational choice, agency and thoughtfully reflective decision making: The short and long-term consequences of making good choices. *Journal of Quantitative Criminology, 25,* 103–127.

Paternoster, R., Pogarsky, G., & Zimmerman, G. (2011). Thoughtfully reflective decision making and the accumulation of capital: Bringing choice back in. *Journal of Quantitative Criminology, 27,* 1–26.

Pinker, S. (2011). *The Better Angels of our Nature: The Decline of Violence in History and its Causes*. New York: Viking Press.

Piquero, A.R., Farrington, D.P., & Blumstein, A. (2007). *Key Issues in Criminal Career Research: New Analyses of the Cambridge Study in Delinquent Development*. New York: Cambridge University Press.

Pratt, T.C., Turner, M.G., & Piquero, A.R. (2004). Parental socialization and community context: A longitudinal analysis of the structural sources of low self-control. *Journal of Research in Crime and Delinquency, 41,* 219–243.

Raine, A. (2013). *Anatomy of Violence: The Biological Roots of Crime*. New York: Pantheon.

Reckless, W.C. (1961). *The Crime Problem*. 3rd edition. New York: Appleton-Century Crofts.

Reckless, W.C., Dinitz, S., & Murray, E. (1956). Self concept as an insulator against delinquency. *American Sociological Review, 21,* 744–746.

Reiss, A.J., Jr. (1951). Delinquency as the failure of personal and social controls. *American Sociological Review, 16,* 196–207.

Rocque, M. (2014). The lost concept. The (re)emerging link between maturation and desistance from crime. *Criminology and Criminal Justice*. Online publication before print. doi: 10.1177/1748895814547710.

Roman, C.G., Cahill, M., Lachman, P., Lowry, S., Orosco, C., & McCarty, C. (2012). *Social Networks, Delinquency, and Gang Membership: Using a Neighborhood Framework to Examine the Influence of Network Composition and Structure in a Latino Community*. Washington, D.C.: Urban Institute.

Rose, D.R., & Clear, T.R. (1998). Incarceration, social capital, and crime: Implications for social disorganization theory. *Criminology, 36,* 441–479.

Roshier, B. (1989). *Controlling Crime: The Classical Perspective in Criminology*. Chicago: Lyceum Books.

Sampson, R.J. (1988). Local friendship ties and community attachment in mass society: A multilevel systemic model. *American Sociological Review, 53,* 766–779.

Sampson, R.J. (2006). Collective efficacy theory: Lessons learned and directions for future inquiry. In F.T. Cullen, J.P. Wright, & K. Blevins (Eds.), *Taking Stock: The Status of Criminological Theory* (pp. 149–167). New Brunswick, NJ: Transaction.

Sampson, R.J. (2012). *Great American City: Chicago and the Enduring Neighborhood Effect.* Chicago: University of Chicago Press.

Sampson, R.J., & Groves, W.B. (1989). Community structure and crime: Testing social-disorganization theory. *American Journal of Sociology, 94,* 774–802.

Sampson, R.J., & Laub, J.H. (1993). *Crime in the Making: Pathways and Turning Points Through Life.* Cambridge, MA: Harvard University Press.

Sampson, R.J., Laub, J.H., & Wimer, C. (2006). Does marriage reduce crime?: A counter-factual approach to within-individual causal effects. *Criminology, 44,* 465–508.

Sampson, R.J., Morenoff, J.D., & Raudenbush, S.W. (2005). Social anatomy of racial and ethnic disparities in violence. *American Journal of Public Health, 95,* 224–232.

Sampson, R.J., Raudenbush, S.W., & Earls, F. (1997). Neighborhood and violent crime: A multilevel study of collective efficacy. *Science, 277,* 918–924.

Sánchez-Jankowski, M. (1991). *Islands in the Street: Gangs and American Urban Society.* Berkeley, CA: University of California Press.

Sarnecki, J. (2001). *Delinquent Networks.* Cambridge: Cambridge University Press.

Siennick, S.E., & Osgood, D.W. (2008). A review of research on the impact on crime of transitions into adult roles. In A. Liberman (Ed.), *The Long View of Crime: A Synthesis of Longitudinal Research* (pp. 161–187). New York: Springer.

Shaw, C.R., & McKay, H.D. (1942). *Juvenile Delinquency and Urban Areas.* Chicago: University of Chicago Press.

Sykes, G., & Matza, D. (1957). Techniques of neutralization: A theory of delinquency. *American Sociological Review, 22,* 664–670.

Thornberry, T.P. (1987). Toward an interactional theory of delinquency. *Criminology, 25,* 863–892.

Toby, J. (1957). Social disorganization and stake in conformity: Complementary factors in the predatory behavior of hoodlums. *Journal of Criminal Law and Criminology, 48,* 12–17.

Turner, M.G., Piquero, A.R., & Pratt, T.C. (2005). The school context as a source of self-control. *Journal of Criminal Justice, 33,* 327–339.

Vaske, J., Galyean, K., & Cullen, F.T. (2011). Toward a biosocial theory of offender rehabilitation: Why does cognitive-behavioral therapy work? *Journal of Criminal Justice, 39,* 90–102.

Vazsonyi, A.T., Pickering, L.E., Junger, M., & Hessing, D. (2001). An empirical test of a general theory of crime: A four-nation comparative study of self-control and the prediction of deviance. *Journal of Research in Crime and Delinquency, 38,* 91–131.

Warr, M. (2002). *Companions in Crime: The Social Aspects of Criminal Conduct.* New York: Cambridge University Press.

Wikström, P.-O.H., Oberwittler, D., Treiber, K., & Hardie, B. (2012). *Breaking Rules: The Social and Situational Dynamics of Young People's Urban Crime.* Oxford: Oxford University Press.

Wilcox, P., Gialopsos, B.M., & Land, K.C. (2012). Multilevel criminal opportunity. In F.T. Cullen & P. Wilcox (Eds.), *The Oxford Handbook of Criminological Theory* (pp. 579–601). New York: Oxford University Press.

Wilcox, P., Land, K.C., & Hunt, S.A. (2003). *Criminal Circumstance: A Dynamic Multi-Contextual Criminal Opportunity Theory*. New Brunswick, NJ: Transaction.

Wilson, J.Q., & Herrnstein, R.J. (1985). *Crime and Human Nature*. New York: Simon and Schuster.

Wright, J.P., & Beaver, K.M. (2005). Do parents matter in creating self-control in their children? A genetically informed test of Gottfredson and Hirschi's theory of low self-control. *Criminology, 43*, 1169–1202.

Wrong, D.H. (1961). The oversocialized conception of man in modern sociology. *American Sociological Review, 26*, 183–193.

Young, J.T.N. (2011). How do they "end up together"? A social network analysis of self-control, homophily, and adolescent relationships. *Journal of Quantitative Criminology, 27*, 251–273.

Zhang, L., & Messner, S.F. (1996). School attachment and official delinquency status in the People's Republic of China. *Sociological Forum, 11*, 285–303.

Zimmerman, G.M. (2010). Impulsivity, offending, and the neighborhood: Investigating the person–context nexus. *Journal of Quantitative Criminology, 26*, 301–332.

# 11

# Strain, Economic Status, and Crime

## Robert Agnew

This chapter provides an overview of classic and general strain theory, the leading versions of strain theory. It then draws on these theories to discuss the relationship between economic status and crime. Economic status is a core variable in criminology: classic strain theory was developed to explain its presumed effect on crime, and general strain theory devotes much attention to it. Both classic and general strain theory argue that poorer individuals are more likely to experience certain strains or stressors. Classic strain theory focuses on the blockage of economic goals and relative deprivation; while general strain theory focuses on a range of strains, including family, school, peer, work, and neighborhood problems. These strains lead to negative emotions, such as frustration and anger, creating pressure for corrective action. Individuals sometimes cope through crime. They may engage in income-generating crime to achieve their economic goals, strike out at others to vent their frustration, and use illicit drugs to feel better. Poorer individuals are said to be more likely to cope in this manner because they are lower in social control and more often associate with criminal peers, among other things (Agnew, 2007; Baron, 2014; Merton, 1968).

Despite these arguments, studies of the relationship between economic status and crime have produced mixed results. In fact, most studies suggest that economic status is unrelated or weakly related to individual offending (Tittle & Meier, 1990). And certain prominent criminologists have challenged the validity of strain theory as a result (e.g., Hirschi, 1969; Kornhauser, 1978). Motivated by such challenges, this chapter reexamines the relationship between strain, economic status, and crime. The chapter begins by describing the research on economic status and crime. Overviews of classic and general strain theory are then provided. Next, the effects of economic status on strains and the likelihood of criminal coping are examined. Based on

*The Handbook of Criminological Theory*, First Edition. Edited by Alex R. Piquero.
© 2016 John Wiley & Sons, Inc. Published 2016 by John Wiley & Sons, Inc.

these examinations, it is argued that economic status generally has a modest relationship to strains and the likelihood of criminal coping over much of its range. But *very poor* individuals are substantially more likely to experience most strains and to engage in criminal coping. Also, *rich* individuals are more likely to experience certain strains conducive to corporate and state crimes. The relationship between economic status and strain, however, varies somewhat across groups and over time – with such variation a function of several factors that influence the perception of and reaction to economic status. These arguments allow strain theory to better explain the mixed data on economic status and crime.

## Economic Status and Crime

Economic status refers to the individual's net income from work; income from other sources (e.g., family, unemployment compensation, welfare); net wealth, including debts and the value of material possessions; and the monetary value of the goods and services produced for personal use and received from others. These goods and services include food, housing, and medical care; and others include family, friends, charities, and government organizations. *Very poor* individuals can be defined in absolute and relative terms. In absolute terms, the very poor lack the economic resources to obtain those items and services commonly viewed as necessities in their societies (Brady, 2003). In relative terms, their economic resources are a small percentage of those possessed by others. There is currently no well justified cutoff point for "small," but a somewhat arbitrary cutoff used by certain researchers is 50% of the median economic resources in a community or nation – although researchers have explored cutoffs as low as 5% (Brady, 2003). Those who are very poor in absolute or relative terms should be more likely to experience most of the strains listed below, although the absolute measure is more relevant to certain strains (e.g., the inability to obtain necessities) and the relative to others (e.g., relative deprivation).

Most individual-level studies find that economic status has a weak effect on self-reported crime (for overviews, see Agnew & Brezina, 2011; Braithwaite, 1981; Costelloe & Michalowski, 2009; Dunaway, Cullen, Burton, & Evans, 2000; Hagan, 1992; Tittle & Meier, 1990). Poorer individuals are more likely to be arrested and sanctioned, although this relationship is often viewed as suspect given evidence of bias against the poor (Braithwaite, 1981). Macro-level studies generally find that poorer areas have more crime, but there are prominent exceptions (Chiricos, 1987; Parker, 2008; Pratt & Cullen, 2005). This is the case with many poor communities occupied by first-generation immigrants, for example (e.g., Lee, Martinez, & Rosenfeld, 2001). Further, studies of crime trends sometimes find that poor economic conditions do not increase crime (for overviews, see Rosenfeld & Fornango, 2007; Rosenfeld, 2009; Yearwood & Koinis, 2011). For example, crime increased dramatically during the 1960s, despite the fact that all major sociodemographic groups experienced major improvements in their economic status (LaFree, 1998; Wilson, 1983). And crime decreased from 2008 to 2011, despite the massive economic recession that began in 2008.

It is important to note that most of above research measures economic status in terms of income from work and, to a lesser extent, poverty status and unemployment during the past year. These measures are problematic, ignoring many of the components of economic status just listed. For example, the US poverty measure, developed in the early 1960s, does not take account of taxes, transfers, cash gifts, near-income, and in-kind services (e.g., housing assistance, food stamps, and Medicaid) (see Brady, 2003, for an overview). Further, these measures do not consider the duration of low economic status, even though poverty and unemployment are usually short-lived for a large percentage of people. As a consequence, these measures do not do a good job of identifying the very poor. Further, the above research often employs samples that underrepresent the very poor, such as school and telephone samples (Hagan, 1992; Hagan & McCarthy, 1997).

Studies which correct for these problems tend to find that the very poor are substantially more likely to engage in crimes involving interpersonal acts of violence and theft (Agnew & Brezina, 2011; Bjerk, 2007; Elliott & Ageton, 1980). For example, several studies find that *persistent* poverty and unemployment are strongly related to such crimes (Aaltonen, Kivivuori, & Martikainen , 2011; Farnworth, Thornberry, Krohn, & Lizotte, 1994; Jarjoura, Triplett, & Brinker, 2002; Thornberry & Christenson, 1984). At the macro-level, there is evidence that very poor communities are especially likely to be high in these crimes (Krivo & Peterson, 1996). And studies tend to find a relationship between economic conditions and trends for these crimes when they examine such things as chronic unemployment and wages among the unskilled, which better index severe economic hardship (e.g., Bushway, 2011; Carlson & Michalowski, 1997; Colvin, 2000; Gould *et al.*, 2002; Michalowski & Carlson, 1999; Rosenfeld & Messner, 2009; Yearwood & Koinis, 2011). At the same time, there is good reason to believe that richer individuals are substantially more likely to engage in corporate and state crimes (Agnew, Piquero, & Cullen 2009; Agnew *et al.*, 2011). Corporate crimes refer to crimes committed by corporate officials at least in part for the benefit of their corporation; crimes committed by states include a range of human rights violations, such as genocide and the suppression of peaceful assembly.

In sum, it appears that the *very poor* are generally more likely to engage in street crime and the *rich* in corporate and state crime. But over much of its range, the relationship between economic status and crime is weak. There are, however, certain exceptions – such as the low crime rates of many very poor first-generation immigrants to the US. These are the facts about economic status and crime that strain theory must explain.

## Overview of Classic Strain Theory

The classic strain theories of Merton (1938), Cohen (1955), and Cloward & Ohlin (1960) state that all individuals in the United States are encouraged to pursue the cultural goal of economic success (or the somewhat broader goal of middle-class status). While not the only goal in the US, it is said that special emphasis is placed on it – with success judged largely in terms of one's economic status. As a consequence, a substantial percentage of people at all economic levels are said to place a *high absolute and relative value on economic success*. Classic strain theorists are somewhat unclear about the nature of economic success, but they most often convey the impression that success is a limited and achievable goal (see Agnew, 1997; Cullen & Messner, 2007).

While people at all economic levels are encouraged to pursue economic success, poorer individuals are said to have more trouble achieving it through legitimate channels – such as getting a good education and a well-paid job. Among other things, they are less well-prepared for school, attend inferior schools, cannot afford college, and lack the connections to secure good jobs. As a result, poorer individuals are more likely to experience goal-blockage and the negative emotions that result from it. Some may then cope through crime.

More recently, researchers in the classic strain tradition have argued that individuals evaluate their economic circumstances not only in terms of some cultural goal or standard, but also by comparing themselves to others in their reference group (e.g., Agnew, 1997; Baron, 2014; Bernburg, Thorlindsson, & Sigfusdottir, 2009; Blau & Blau, 1982; Burton & Dunaway, 1994; Cohen, 1965; LaFree & Drass, 1996; Merton, 1968; Messner, Raffalovich, & McMillan, 2001; Parker, 2008; Passas, 1997; Stiles Liu, & Kaplan, 2000). There is some disagreement over whom individuals select as reference others, but it is often assumed that people compare themselves to proximate others, such as friends, neighbors, and classmates; and/or to similar others, such as those in the same racial group. Relative deprivation is said to exist if individuals believe that they have fewer economic resources than these others *and* they both want and feel entitled to these resources. This sense of entitlement partly derives from the fact that *others like themselves* possess these resources. Like goal blockage, relative deprivation results in negative emotions such as frustration and anger. And we would expect poorer individuals to be higher in relative deprivation, so long as individuals select reference others as just described.

Classic strain theorists emphasize that not all strained individuals cope through crime. Criminal coping is said to be more likely when strained individuals (a) have a weak commitment to legitimate norms; (b) blame their strain on others; (c) associate with criminal peers – especially gang members; and (d) have the skills and opportunities to engage in crime (see Agnew, 1997; Baron, 2014). Poorer individuals are said to be more likely to possess these characteristics, partly because the strain they experience contributes to them. For example, their inability to achieve economic success by following legitimate norms weakens their commitment to such norms (Merton, 1968). And strained individuals who regularly interact with one another sometimes form gangs as a method of coping with their strain (Cloward & Ohlin, 1960; Cohen, 1955). A major exception, however, is that poorer individuals lack the skills and opportunities to engage in most corporate and state crimes.

In sum, classic strain theory states that poorer individuals are more likely to experience the strains of goal blockage and relative deprivation and to cope with these strains through crime. The mixed data on the relationship between economic status and crime therefore pose a challenge to the theory.

## Overview of General Strain Theory

General strain theory (GST) incorporates and extends classic strain theory (Agnew, 1992, 2007). Most notably, GST focuses on a much broader array of strains, with strains being defined as events or conditions that are disliked. Strains fall into three groups. Individuals may be unable to achieve their goals, including economic, status, autonomy, and other goals. They may lose things they value, including material possessions, friends, and family members. And they may be treated in a negative or aversive manner by others; for example, they may be verbally and physically abused by family members, peers, and employers.

GST makes a distinction between "objective" and "subjective" strains. Objective strains refer to events and conditions disliked by most people in a given group. Subjective strains refer to events and conditions disliked by the people who are experiencing them. This distinction is important because people often differ in their subjective reaction to the same objective strain. In fact, this is one of the key points made below. Low economic status is an objective strain in the United States, but a range of factors influence the extent to which people subjectively dislike their low status. For example, people are more likely to dislike their low economic status when they place great emphasis on economic goals and compare themselves to more privileged others.

Strains, especially subjective strains, lead to negative emotions, such as anger and frustration. These emotions create pressure for corrective action, and crime is one possible response. Not surprisingly, research suggests that economic strains – which involve not having enough money – are most strongly related to income-generating crimes (e.g., Felson *et al.*, 2012; Rosenfeld, 2009). Individuals who cannot get money through legal channels may attempt to get it through crimes such as theft, drug selling, and prostitution. But economic strains may also result in violent crime and drug use, as people vent their negative emotions or seek relief from them.

GST states that some strains are more likely to lead to crime than others, largely because they generate strong negative emotions, overwhelm legal coping resources, and are conducive to criminal coping. Among other things, such strains are high in magnitude. That is, they are high in degree (e.g., a large versus small monetary loss), are of long duration, and are expected to continue into the future. Also, they involve the core goals, values, needs, identities, and/or activities of individuals. Criminogenic strains are also seen as unjust, which helps generate strong anger. And they are easily resolved through crime. This is the case with economic strains, which are readily resolved through income-generating crimes, but is not the case with a strain such as the death of a family member.

Finally, GST states that some people are more likely to cope with strains through crime than others. Criminal coping is more likely among those with poor coping skills and resources (e.g., poor social skills and inadequate problem-solving skills). It is more likely among those with few conventional social supports; that is, family, friends, and others who can provide assistance. It is more likely among those who are low in social control or have little to lose by engaging in crime (e.g., are unemployed, doing poorly in school, do not get along with parents). It is more likely among those who are disposed to criminal coping, including those who associate with other criminals, hold beliefs favorable to crime, and possess traits such as low constraint and negative emotionality (are easily upset, tend to act without thinking). Finally, it is more likely when individuals are in situations where the costs of crime are seen as low and the benefits as high.

Unlike classic strain theory, GST was not developed to explain the presumed link between low economic status and crime. But GST states that low economic status is associated with, or increases exposure to, many strains conducive to crime, including the inability to achieve economic goals; family problems, such as parental rejection, child abuse, and the use of harsh and erratic discipline; school problems, such as low grades and poor relations with teachers; work at "bad" jobs, such as those with unpleasant working conditions and few benefits; marital problems; criminal victimization; and residence in deprived communities plagued by a host of problems. Further, GST states that low economic status increases the likelihood of criminal coping. For example, poorer individuals are less likely to possess the skills and resources that facilitate legal coping, including money, a good education, social skills and problem-solving skills, and connections to influential others. So, like classic strain theory, GST predicts that the poor should be more likely to engage in crime and it, too, is challenged by the mixed data on economic status and crime.

## The Impact of Economic Status on Strains

Research from several areas suggests that the arguments of classic and general strain theory regarding economic status and strain are in need of revision. It is not simply the case that the poor experience more strains. Economic status tends to have a modest effect on most strains across much of its range, although the very poor and the rich are substantially more likely to experience certain strains. Further, the relationship between economic status and strains is influenced by several factors. Several major strains are considered below, with a focus on those economic strains that involve not having enough money.

### Goal blockage and relative deprivation

Recent research has examined those strains that are the focus of classic strain theory: the blockage of economic goals and relative deprivation. Goal blockage is typically measured by asking respondents about their chances for achieving goals such as "a good paying job" (see Burton & Cullen, 1992, for an overview). Relative deprivation is usually measured by asking respondents whether they have as much money as others, such as friends, neighbors, classmates, and, occasionally, people in the country as a whole (e.g., Agnew *et al.*, 1996; Baron, 2007, 2014; Bernburg *et al.*, 2009; Burton & Cullen, 1992; Burton, Cullen, Evans, & Dunaway, 1994; Burton & Dunaway, 1994; Stiles *et al.*, 2000). Such studies usually find that goal blockage and relative deprivation have a moderately strong effect on crime compared to other causes. A few studies have also examined dissatisfaction with one's economic status, which tends to have a relatively strong effect on crime and to at least partly mediate the effects of goal blockage and relative deprivation on crime (Agnew *et al.*, 1996; Baron, 2007, 2008, 2014; Cernkovich, Giordano, & Rudolph, 2000; Felson *et al.*, 2012; Hagan & McCarthy, 1997; Wright *et al.*, 1999). These findings have their parallel at the macro-level, with research finding that consumer perceptions of their economic situation and opportunities influence trends in the rate of certain crimes (Rosenfeld, 2009; Rosenfeld & Fornango, 2007). It should be noted, however, that studies rarely measure the magnitude and perceived injustice of goal blockage and relative deprivation, nor do they take account of the conditioning variables described by classic and general strain theory. When these issues are corrected, researchers may find that these types of strain have even larger effects on crime (see Agnew *et al.*, 1996, Baron, 2007, 2008; Rebellon, Piquero, Piquero, & Thaxton, 2009).

Contrary to strain theory, the effect of economic status on goal blockage, relative deprivation, and monetary dissatisfaction is generally modest in size (e.g., Agnew *et al.*, 1996; Stiles *et al.*, 2000; Wright *et al.*, 1999). For example, Agnew *et al.* (1996) found that family income explains less than 2% of the variation in these factors. This modest effect helps explain the generally weak relationship between economic status and crime. There are several possible reasons for the modest effect of economic status:

*Richer individuals may pursue economic goals beyond their reach*    Richer individuals tend to pursue higher economic goals than poorer individuals (see especially Agnew, 1980, 1983; Della Fave & Klobus, 1976; Easterlin, 2003). Also, there is some evidence that economic goals are *ever-escalating*, such that individuals who achieve a particular economic goal then turn to the pursuit of a higher goal (Easterlin, 2003; Wolbring, Keuschnigg, & Negele, 2013). These arguments were advanced by Merton (1968:190) at one point, when he stated that "in the American Dream there is no final stopping point… at each income level Americans want about twenty-five percent more (but of course this 'just a bit more' continues to operate once it is obtained)." Similarly, Messner & Rosenfeld (2001:63–64) state that "the American Dream offers 'no final stopping point'… [and] requires 'never-ending achievement'" (also see Agnew, 1997). So, richer as well as poorer individuals are often unable to achieve their economic goals, although goal blockage is still somewhat more common among the poor (e.g., Agnew, 1986; Della Fave & Klobus, 1976).

*Richer individuals may compare themselves to more advantaged others*    While some criminologists assume that individuals compare themselves to similar or proximate others, others assume that they compare themselves to more advantaged others – with rich individuals comparing themselves to still richer individuals. This being the case, relative deprivation should also be common among rich individuals. This focus on upward comparisons is said to be a function of an egalitarian ideology that encourages everyone to aim high; to historically high rates of mobility, which also encourage everyone to aim high; and to the mass media – which regularly features and encourages comparisons with more privileged others (see Passas, 1997). While there is some anecdotal evidence for this argument, the larger literature on social comparison suggests that there is no simple answer to the question of who people select as comparison others (Suls, Martin, & Wheeler, 2002; Suls & Wheeler, 2000). Individuals tend to compare themselves to proximate and similar others, but sometimes compare themselves to dissimilar others – including more or less advantaged others.

*Poorer individuals may lower their economic goals, compare themselves to less advantaged or similar others, or avoid social comparison*    Poorer individuals *sometimes* adapt to their deprived situation by lowering their economic goals or by "stretching" their goals, making a distinction between "preferred" and "minimally acceptable" goals (Agnew, 1983, 2000). There is no good data on the extent to which poorer individuals make downward or lateral social comparisons. That said, the social comparison literature indicates that individuals have a strong need to maintain or enhance their self-evaluation and, when threatened, they *sometimes* respond by comparing themselves to those who are worse off or at least similar to themselves – including real, imagined, and prototypical others (Suls *et al.*, 2002; Suls & Wheeler, 2000). They may also avoid social comparison and instead make internal comparisons, perhaps focusing on the fact that their current economic circumstances are an improvement over the past. More research is needed on the relationship between economic status and the types of social comparisons that are made.

*Individuals often exaggerate their current and expected economic situation*    Individuals may not only avoid economic strain by lowering their goals or making downward/ lateral comparisons, but also by exaggerating their current and expected economic status. There is much evidence that people tend to overestimate their positive attributes and underestimate their negative ones, both in absolute terms and relative to others. Among other things, people often overestimate their academic and job performance, popularity, and economic success (Agnew, 1986; Gouveia & Clarke, 2001). With respect to economic success, many objectively poor individuals view themselves as "middle class" (Jackman & Jackman, 1973). People also tend to underestimate their chances of experiencing many negative events and overestimate their chances of experiencing many positive ones – including economic success (Agnew & Jones, 1988; Gouveia & Clarke, 2001). It is not clear whether poorer individuals are more likely than richer to exaggerate their economic success, but one can argue that there is more room and motivation for exaggeration among the poor.

*Individuals pursue several goals, ranking those they are better able to achieve as more important*   Classic strain theorists argue that most people in the US place a high absolute and relative emphasis on the goal of economic success, so that the failure to achieve this goal produces much frustration. Data, however, suggest that most people play greater absolute and relative emphasis on other goals, including those involving family, friends, religion, health, and self actualization (Agnew, 1983, 1986). And even among job-related goals, things such as a steady income and important work are ranked as higher in absolute and relative importance than a high income (lower-income respondents focus more on a steady income, higher-income on important work) (Agnew, 1983). Relatedly, data suggest that individuals tend to place more emphasis on those goals they are better able to achieve (Agnew, 1983, 1986; Kohn, 1977). Further, the overwhelming majority of individuals are able to at least partly achieve some of their important goals, thereby alleviating their strain (Agnew, 1986). So, poorer individuals may also avoid strain by assigning less relative and absolute importance to economic success. The happiness literature provides limited support for this argument: income only has a modest effect on happiness and one's level of happiness is more strongly influenced by things such as having a spouse or partner, good health, and the quality of one's job (Ball & Chernova, 2008; Easterlin, 2003).

In sum, there are several reasons why economic status has only a modest effect on goal blockage and relative deprivation over most of its range. Richer individuals may pursue higher or ever-escalating economic goals and/or compare themselves to more advantaged others. Poorer individuals may pursue lower goals, make downward or lateral comparisons, avoid social comparison, exaggerate their current and expected economic status, and/or place less emphasis on the goal of economic success. There is some evidence that each of these processes is operative, although we do not yet have a good idea of how common they are and to what extent they help account for the modest relationship between economic status and crime.

At the same time, there is reason to believe that these processes may be less common among the *very poor*. Again, the "very poor" are unable to obtain those goods and services viewed as necessities and/or their economic status is *much lower* than most others. Consequently, they may have trouble lowering their economic goals to a point where they are achievable, comparing themselves to less advantaged others, exaggerating their current level of economic success, and de-emphasizing the importance of money. We lack good data in this area, however, since studies usually fail to distinguish the very poor from others and/or employ samples that underrepresent the very poor.

It is also important to note that these processes likely vary over time and across groups. For example, a central theme in the anomie literature is that individuals are more likely to pursue higher goals and make upward comparisons during times of economic prosperity – when those around them are doing well (Agnew, 1997; Passas, 1997). It has also been argued that certain groups place much more emphasis on material success than others. This is said to be true of certain inner-city youth, where displays of material possessions are a key source of status (Anderson, 1999; Currie, 1997).

## The experience of economic problems

Economic problems are the direct result of not having enough money and involve (a) the inability to obtain valued objects, services, or activities; (b) the loss or threatened loss of these things; and (c) the need to engage in undesired activities. Examples include not having enough money to pay bills or buy the things you want; having to sell possessions or cut back on certain activities, such as eating out; moving to cheaper living quarters; and working a second job. Individuals experiencing such problems usually want more money and what others have, so this strain overlaps with both goal blockage and relative deprivation. But this strain is distinct in that it manifests itself in a range of concrete problems, certain of which may create much pressure for corrective action in the near term. For example, individuals may be regularly harassed by bill collectors or exhausted from working multiple jobs. We might therefore expect this strain to have a stronger relationship to crime.

The limited research in this area finds that economic problems have a relatively strong relationship with crime (for reviews see Agnew *et al.*, 2008; Bernburg *et al.*, 2009). Certain research suggests that the relationship is nonlinear, with crime increasing only after a few economic problems are experienced (Agnew *et al.*, 2008). The relationship between economic status and economic problems is only modest in size, however. In particular, a substantial percentage of poorer people report no or only a few economic problems, while many richer people report several problems. Agnew *et al.* (2008) report that family income explains only about 1% of the variation in economic problems. They find that 60% of individuals with 2002 family incomes of less than $10,000 report zero or one of 16 economic problems, while 18% of individuals with family incomes above $70,000 report three or more economic problems (versus 27% of those with incomes less than $10,000). This modest relationship likely reflects the fact that many poor individuals have learned to live within their means; while many richer individuals spend beyond their means. There is much encouragement to do so in market societies such as the US, which place great emphasis on consumerism.

Again, however, we might expect that those who are very poor to be substantially more likely to report economic problems. Testing this proposition requires that we better measure economic status; for example, we measure the duration of poverty and give more consideration to the varied components of economic status listed above. Research should also measure the perceived injustice and magnitude of these problems (e.g., their perceived severity, duration).

## Inability to obtain necessities through legal means

An especially important subcategory of economic problems involves the inability to obtain necessities through legal means. Necessities include those things needed for physical survival and wellbeing, particularly food, shelter, adequate clothing, security, and necessary medical care. They also include those things perceived as necessities, with such perceptions varying across groups and over time (Brady, 2003).

Many in the US, for example, view automobiles, air conditioning, and cell phones as necessities. This type of strain should have a strong effect on crime, given that it is high in magnitude. But it has not received much attention from criminologists, despite the fact that substantial numbers of people in the US experience homelessness, hunger, inadequate medical care, and ongoing threats to their physical security (e.g., Hagan & McCarthy, 1997; National Alliance to End Homelessness, 2012; World Hunger Education Services, 2012).

Nevertheless, a few studies indicate that crime is more likely among those living on the street, those who report they are hungry and lack adequate clothing, and – in one study – those who report they lack adequate food, furniture, and medical care (Baron, 2007; Hagan & McCarthy, 1997; Stiles *et al.*, 2000). Beyond that, much data indicate that crime is substantially higher among those whose physical security has been threatened, including those who have been victimized, have had close others victimized, and have witnessed violence in their homes and communities (e.g., Hagan & McCarthy, 1997; Harrell, 2010).

Very low economic status is strongly related to this type of strain, by definition. And data indicate that that hunger and homelessness are much more common in poor households, but become quite uncommon once a certain minimal income level is reached (National Alliance to End Homelessness, 2012; World Hunger Education Services, 2012).

## Inability to satisfy addictions, including for drugs, gambling, and shopping, through legal means

Some individuals are addicted to behaviors such as drug use, gambling, and shopping. That is, they are preoccupied with the behaviors and have much difficulty restraining themselves from engaging in them, even when doing so might cause harm. Some have a genetic predisposition for these addictions, although social factors also contribute to them. In fact, strain or stress is said to be a contributing factor (Bahr, 2011). Once developed, there appears to be some biological basis for the addictions, with individuals experiencing a change in the "reward circuitry" of their brains (Bahr, 2011). There is good reason to believe that the inability to satisfy *certain* addictions through legal channels has a strong effect on crime, particularly addictions to drugs, gambling, and – to a lesser extent – shopping.

The inability to satisfy these addictions constitutes a strain of great magnitude, given the overwhelming compulsion to engage in the addictive behaviors. Also, addictions to drugs and gambling put individuals in contact with criminals, which may increase their disposition for criminal coping. There has been some research here, most focusing on drugs. Data suggest that individuals more often engage in crime when using drugs, partly because of the need to secure money (Bahr, 2011; Slocum, Simpson, & Smith, 2005). Further, qualitative research suggests that many hardcore criminals engage in crime partly because of their very strong desire to maintain the "party lifestyle," which involves frequent drug and alcohol use, gambling, and lavish expenditures on certain consumer products (e.g., Shover, 1996).

We would expect this strain to be much more common among the very poor, since by definition they lack the money to finance their addictions through legal channels. Those with somewhat more money may also turn to crime in order to finance their addictions, but it is likely that they will soon fall into the ranks of the very poor as they exhaust their financial resources.

## The effect of economic status on other strains

The above strains involve *not having enough money* to meet economic goals, prevent relative deprivation, avoid economic problems, obtain necessities, and feed addictions. But economic status may affect other strains as well. There is a large literature suggesting the low economic status contributes to most of the criminogenic strains identified in GST, including parental rejection, child abuse, harsh and erratic disciple, negative school experiences, work at "bad" job, marital problems, victimization, and residence in deprived communities plagued by a host of problems (e.g., Agnew, 2007; Bradley & Corwyn, 2002; Brooks-Gunn & Duncan, 1997; Currie, 1997).

The effect of economic status on these strains is largely indirect. For example, poor parents experience certain of the economic strains listed above, such as economic problems; these strains contribute to depression and anger; these negative emotions contribute to poor parenting practices, such as parental rejection and harsh and erratic disciplinary techniques; and these practices in turn function as criminogenic strains for the children in such families (Agnew, 2007). To give another example, poor parents provide less cognitive stimulation to their children (e.g., have fewer books in the home, less often read to their children), this limits the children's intellectual development, and this limited development increases the likelihood that the children will later experience school- and work-related strains (Guo & Harris, 2000).

The fact that economic status is the first link in an often long causal chain helps explain its modest association with the final link in the chain, crime. Also, while low economic status increases exposure to the above strains, the effect is strongest for those of very low economic status – such as those who have been poor for several years (see Brooks-Gunn & Duncan, 1997). This, too, helps explains the weak effect of economic status on crime in most studies, since these studies fail to identify the very poor and/or undersample them.

## Strains that more often impact richer individuals

Most of the strains listed above are more common among poorer individuals, with some largely limited to the poor. But there are certain strains that are more often experienced by richer individuals, including:

- Personal economic problems that presuppose some level of financial wellbeing, such as losses in the stock market and the various financial problems encountered by business owners (see Agnew *et al.*, 2009).

- Strains associated with the corporate and political roles more often occupied by richer individuals. Corporate executives, for example, have some responsibility for the performance of their companies and may experience much strain when that performance is threatened, with such threats including low and declining profits, government regulations, and increased competition (see Agnew *et al.*, 2009)
- Threats to the privileged position of richer individuals, a strain emphasized by conflict theorists. These threats may stem from the government (e.g., higher taxes, burdensome regulations), the larger community (e.g., higher crime, riots), and other rich individuals (Agnew, 2011).

These strains are most relevant to the explanation of corporate and states' crimes, since these crimes are designed to alleviate the strains (e.g., increase corporate profits, evade government regulations, exercise greater control over disruptive groups) of richer individuals.

## Economic status and criminal coping

As noted, classic and general strain theory state that poorer individuals are not only more likely to experience most strains, but are also more likely to cope with them in a criminal manner. Recent research, however, suggests a more complex relationship between economic status and criminal coping. As Wright *et al.* (1999) point out, while poorer individuals possess certain characteristics conducive to crime (and criminal coping), richer individuals possess others. In particular, richer individuals are more often socialized to have a desire for risk-taking and they possess more social power – which enables them to better resist sanctions (also see Kohn, 1977). Chambliss (1973) makes a similar point in his discussion of the "Saints" and the "Roughnecks," describing how the richer Saints use their positive reputations, social skills, and access to cars and money to hide their delinquent acts and to escape sanction if detected. Brezina & Aragones (2004) elaborate on this point in their discussion of how "positive labeling" facilitates crime. Individuals who are labeled in a positive manner, for example, may be subject to less supervision – making it easier to commit criminal acts without sanction. Further, certain research describes how the resources more often possessed by richer individuals, including money, creativity, power, and autonomy, can facilitate criminal coping (Agnew, 1990; Cullen, Larson, & Mathers, 1985; Wright *et al.*, 2001; also see Hagan, 1992; Tittle, 1995). Among other things, such resources undermine efforts at social control and increase opportunities for crime (e.g., it is easier to cope through illicit drug use if you have the money to buy drugs).

Recent research in psychology has extended these arguments, suggesting that richer individuals are more likely to be self-interested, greedy, and low in compassion (e.g., Piff *et al.*, 2012; Stellar *et al.*, 2012). Among other things, this is said to stem from the fact that their self-interest and greed are more often reinforced. Also, their less stressful environments are said to reduce compassion for others. As a consequence, richer individuals are more likely to engage in selfish/unethical behavior in certain laboratory and naturalistic experiments. It should be noted that these findings are compatible with the arguments of many conflict theorists, who state that richer individuals are interested in protecting their privileged position, care little about the plight of the poor, and will harm others if threatened (Agnew, 2011). Further, recent research suggests that while poorer individuals may lack certain skills and resources that facilitate legal coping, their previous exposure to stress may increase their tolerance for and ability to cope with current stressors (Seery, Holman, & Silver, 2010).

Taken as a whole, there is, therefore, some uncertainly about how economic status influences the likelihood of criminal coping. Wright *et al.* (1999) argue that the forces promoting crime (and criminal coping) among poorer and richer individuals tend to balance out. Their argument, however, may not apply to the very poor, who are especially high in those factors that promote criminal coping and who may lack many of the factors that hinder such coping. For example, while the experience of *moderate* stress in the past increases the ability to cope with current stressors, past experiences with *severe* stress reduce the ability to effectively cope (Seery *et al.*, 2010). And, as suggested above, the very poor are substantially more likely to have experienced severe stress.

## Conclusion

Classic and general strain theory state that low economic status increases both strain and the likelihood of criminal coping, thereby contributing to what should be a strong relationship between low economic status and crime. Data on the relationship between economic status and crime, however, are mixed. Most studies find a weak relationship, but some a strong relationship. This chapter suggested certain revisions in strain theory to better explain these mixed results and guide future research. In particular, it was argued that economic status generally has a modest effect on strains and the likelihood of criminal coping over much of its range. Poorer individuals are often able to avoid strains through a variety of strategies, such as pursuing more limited economic goals, making downward or lateral social comparisons, avoiding social comparison, exaggerating their current and expected economic status, and limiting consumption. And richer individuals often experience strains because they pursue lofty or ever-escalating economic goals, make upward comparisons, and consume beyond their means. Likewise, while poorer individuals are more inclined to criminal coping for certain reasons, richer individuals are more inclined for other reasons. These arguments help explain the weak relationship between economic status and crime in most research.

At the same time, it was argued that *very poor* individuals are much more likely to experience most strains and to engage in criminal coping. This helps explain why certain studies show a strong relationship between economic status and crime. Such studies tend to employ measures that better identify the very poor and/or samples that better represent them. For example, such studies measure the duration of poverty. Community-level studies generally find that poor communities have higher crime rates partly because they pick up the offending of the very poor individuals who tend live in these communities. (Also, individual-level poverty *in combination* with residence in poor communities is especially conducive to crime (Agnew & Brezina, 2011).) Likewise, studies on crime trends are more likely to find an effect for economic status when they employ measures more likely to pick up severe deprivation. So *very low* economic status is strongly related to offending, but the relationship weakens among the less poor. It should be noted that the research on happiness provides indirect support for this argument. The very poor are less happy, but the relationship between income and happiness weakens once a minimal income level is passed (Drakopoulos, 2008; Wolbring *et al.*, 2013).

It was further argued that the rich are more likely to experience certain strains, particularly those conducive to corporate and state crimes. Also, richer individuals, of course, have more opportunities to engage in such crimes. Finally, it was argued that the relationship between economic status and crime may vary across groups and over time. That is because a range of factors influence whether one's economic status is viewed as a strain, including the goals that individuals pursue, the types of social comparisons they make, the extent to which they exaggerate their current and expected economic status, their level of consumption, and what they view as necessities. We lack anything close to a full theory here, although the important role that individual, group, and historical factors can have on the relationship between economic status and crime can be illustrated by considering three cases that might at first glance be taken as evidence against strain theory.

*The relatively low crime rate of very poor first-generation immigrants*   Immigrants usually migrate with the hope of improving their economic status, but they often experience much poverty after first arriving in the US. Their generally low crime rates might be explained in several ways. They have low economic goals, reflecting the more limited goals in their country of origin. They compare their current economic circumstances to the even worse circumstances that they experienced and others still experience in their country of origin. They exaggerate their current and expected economic status, partly because of their often optimistic orientation (associated with migration). They have a more limited view of what constitutes a "necessity," reflecting their experiences in their country of origin. While they desire economic success, they also place great emphasis on other goals, such as family and religion. And they are less inclined to engage in criminal coping: they have elected to cope through migration rather than crime. They are better able to tolerate their deprivation, given their prior experience coping with stressors. And they possess characteristics that reduce the likelihood of criminal coping: among other things, they are often strongly tied to family and community, morally opposed to crime, heavily involved in work, and high in self-control. All of the above factors, however, are less characteristic of second- and subsequent-generation immigrants – helping to account for the increased crime in these groups.

*The increase in crime during the 1960s, despite increasing prosperity*   While prosperity increased during the 1960s, structural and cultural changes may have led to an increase in economic goals as well. Many of the structural barriers to economic progress were crumbling as a result of the civil rights movement, the War on Poverty, and a robust economy. There was a strong cultural emphasis on economic success, reflected in the increased mass marketing of consumer products and the political/media coverage devoted to the eradication of poverty. People may have become more likely to compare themselves to more advantaged others; both those regularly depicted in the media and to their socially mobile friends and neighbors. Relatedly, the increase in prosperity at the local level may have made it harder to exaggerate one's economic status, since people were surrounded by visible symbols of economic success. But while most people were doing well, some were not, particularly teen-agers and young adults in poor, inner-city communities (LaFree, 1998; Wilson, 1983). Among other things, manufacturing jobs that paid a decent wage began to move out of such communities in the 1960s (Carlson & Michalowski, 1997; Colvin, 2000; LaFree, 1998). As a result, there was a widening gap between the rich and poor (LaFree, 1998; LaFree & Drass, 1996). The goal blockage and sense of relative deprivation experienced by those not sharing in the increased prosperity was probably quite strong. Further, this strain occurred in a context that was conducive to criminal coping. Among other things, moral values were being questioned, inner-city communities were becoming more disorganized as the working and middle-classes fled to the suburbs, there was an increase in family disruption, and the certainty and severity of punishment were low (LaFree, 1998; Wilson, 1983).

*The decline in crime since 2008, despite the severe economic recession*   The crime drop occurred despite a sharp increase in unemployment, a drop in real wages, a dramatic drop in household wealth, and an increase in poverty. This drop was surprising given that the crime drop in the 1990s appears to be partly due to the economic expansion during that time, especially the increase in entry-level jobs and wages (e.g., Barker, 2010; Baumer, 2008; Parker, 2008; Rosenfeld & Fornango, 2007; Yearwood & Koinis, 2011). The post-2008 crime drop might be explained by arguing that cultural and structural conditions led many individuals to lower their economic goals and make downward or lateral comparisons. The economic decline was wide-spread, frequently affecting family, friends, and neighbors; the decline was the main topic of political conversation; and stories of economic hardship were regularly featured in the media. While inequality increased, the increase was concentrated in the top 1% or, more accurately, fraction of 1%. Social comparisons with this very privileged group seem unlikely. Further, the conservative political movement had some success in diverting attention from economic issues (Frank, 2004). In addition, the recession was quickly followed by a major increase in government spending, a significant portion of which was devoted to food, housing, and unemployment compensation – allowing many to obtain necessities. Related to this, a large percentage of the young males who might otherwise be living in poverty were in prison or the military. Beyond that, the larger cultural and political context in which the decline occurred was quite different from that of the 1960s. Among other things, there was an increased emphasis on moral values and the certainty and severity of punishment were high.

Most of these arguments are speculative, but many can be tested. This chapter, in fact, contains numerous suggestions for further research. The most basic involve better measuring economic status, in an effort to distinguish the very poor from others; collecting samples that contain sufficient numbers of the very poor; examining the strains described above, certain of which have been neglected by criminologists; and better measuring these strains, including their magnitude and perceived injustice. Researchers should also devote more attention to those factors that may influence the subjective reaction to one's economic status, including the relative and absolute emphasis placed on economic success, the types of social comparison that are made, the extent to which current and future economic status is exaggerated, views about what constitutes a necessity, and the emphasis placed on consumerism. Finally, researchers should devote more attention to those factors that condition the relationship between the above strains and crime. Engaging in these efforts will of course involve much work, but it will help make better sense of perhaps the most perplexing relationship in criminology – that between economic status and crime.

# References

Aaltonen, M., Kivivuori, J., & Martikainen, P. (2011). Social determinants of crime in a welfare state. *Acta Sociologica, 54*(2), 161–181.

Agnew, R. (1980). Success and anomie. *The Sociological Quarterly, 21*, 53–64.

Agnew, R. (1983). Social class and success goals. *The Sociological Quarterly, 24*, 435–452.

Agnew, R. (1986). Challenging strain theory. Paper presented at the American Society of Criminology meetings, Atlanta.

Agnew, R. (1990). Adolescent resources and delinquency. *Criminology, 28*(4), 535–565.

Agnew, R. (1992). Foundation for a general strain theory of crime and delinquency. *Criminology, 39*(1), 47–87.

Agnew, R. (1997). The nature and determinants of strain: Another look at Durkheim and Merton. In N. Passas & R. Agnew (Eds.), *The Future of Anomie Theory* (pp. 27–51). Boston, MA: Northeastern University Press.

Agnew, R. (2000). Sources of criminality: Strain and subcultural theories. In J.F. Sheley (Ed.), *Criminology* (pp. 349–371). Belmont, CA: Wadsworth.

Agnew, R. (2007). *Pressured Into Crime: An Overview of General Strain Theory*. New York: Oxford University Press.

Agnew, R. (2011). *Toward a Unified Criminology*. New York: New York University Press.

Agnew, R., & Brezina, T. (2011). *Juvenile Delinquency: Causes and Control*. New York: Oxford University Press.

Agnew, R., Cullen, F.T., Burton, V.S., Jr., Evans, T.D., & Dunaway, R.G. (1996). A new test of classic strain theory. *Justice Quarterly, 13*(4), 681–704.

Agnew, R., & Jones, D.H. (1988). Adapting to deprivation: An examination of inflated educational expectations. *Sociological Quarterly, 29*(2), 315–337.

Agnew, R., Matthews, S.K., Bucher, J., Welcher, A.N., & Keyes, C. (2008). Socioeconomic status, economic problems, and delinquency. *Youth & Society*, 40(2), 159–181.

Agnew, R., Piquero, N.L., & Cullen, F.T. (2009). General strain theory and white-collar crime. In S.S. Simpson & D. Weisburd (Eds.), *The Criminology of White-Collar Crime* (pp. 35–60). New York: Springer.

Anderson, E. (1999). *Code of the Street*. New York: W.W. Norton.

Apel, R. (2009). Employment and crime. In J.M. Miller (Ed.), *21st Century Criminology* (pp. 118–124). Los Angeles: Sage.

Bahr, S.J. (2011). Drug use, abuse, and addiction. In C.D. Bryant (Ed.), *The Routledge Handbook of Deviant Behavior* (pp. 290–297). London: Routledge.

Ball, R., & Chernova, K. (2008). Absolute income, relative income, and happiness. *Social Indicators Research*, 88, 497–529.

Barker, V. (2010). Explaining the great American crime decline. *Law & Social Inquiry*, 35(2), 489–516.

Baron, S.W. (2007). Street youth, gender, financial strain, and crime. *Deviant Behavior*, 28, 273–302.

Baron, S.W. (2008). Street youth, unemployment, and crime. *Canadian Journal of Criminology and Criminal Justice*, 50(4), 399–434.

Baron, S.W. (2014). Monetary strain and individual offending. In G. Bruinsma & D. Weisburd (Eds.), *Encyclopedia of Criminology and Criminal Justice* (pp. 3127–3137). New York: Springer.

Baumer, E.P. (2008). An empirical assessment of the contemporary crime trends puzzle. In National Academy of Sciences, *Understanding Crime Trends: Workshop Reports* (pp. 127–176). Washington, DC: National Academies Press.

Bernburg, J.G., Thorlindsson, T., & Sigfusdottir, I.D. (2009). Relative deprivation and adolescent outcomes in Iceland. *Social Forces*, 87(3), 1223–1250.

Bjerk, D. (2007). Measuring the relationship between youth criminal participation and household economic resources. *Journal of Quantitative Criminology*, 23, 23–39.

Blau, J.R., & Blau, P.M. (1982). The cost of inequality. *American Sociological Review*, 47, 114–129.

Brady, D. (2003). Rethinking the sociological measurement of poverty. *Social Forces*, 81(3), 715–752.

Bradley, R.H., & Corwyn, R.F. (2002). Socioeconomic status and child development. *Annual Review of Psychology*, 53, 371–399.

Braithwaite, J. (1981). The myth of social class and criminality reconsidered. *American Sociological Review*, 46, 36–57.

Brezina, T., & Aragones, A.A. (2004). Devils in disguise: The contribution of positive labeling to "sneaky thrills" delinquency. *Deviant Behavior*, 25, 513–535.

Brooks-Gunn, J., & Duncan, G.J. (1997). The effects of poverty on children. *The Future of Children*, 7(2), 55–71.

Burton, V.S., Jr., & Cullen, F.T. (1992). The empirical status of strain theory. *Journal of Crime and Justice*, 15(2), 1–30.

Burton, V.S., Jr., Cullen, F.T., Evans, T.D., & Dunaway, R.G. (1994). Reconsidering strain theory. *Journal of Quantitative Criminology*, 10(3), 213–239.

Burton, V.S., Jr., & Dunaway, R.G. (1994). Strain, relative deprivation, and middle-class delinquency. In G. Barak (Ed.), *Varieties of Criminology* (pp. 79–95). Westport, CT: Praeger.

Bushway, S. (2011). Labor markets and crime. In J.Q. Wilson & J. Petersilia (Eds.), *Crime and Public Policy* (pp. 183–209). Oxford: Oxford University Press.

Carlson, S.M., & Michalowski, R.J. (1997). Crime, unemployment, and social structures of accumulation. *Justice Quarterly, 14*(2), 209–241.

Cernkovich, S.A., Giordano, P.C., & Rudolph, J.L. (2000). Race, crime, and the American dream. *Journal of Research in Crime and Delinquency, 37*(2), 131–170.

Chambliss, W.J. (1973). The Saints and the Roughnecks. *Society, 11*(1), 24–31.

Chiricos, T.G. (1987). Rates of crime and unemployment: Analysis of aggregate research evidence. *Social Problems, 34*(2), 187–212.

Cloward, R., & Ohlin, L. (1960). *Delinquency and Opportunity.* Glencoe, IL: Free Press.

Cohen, A.K. (1955). *Delinquent Boys.* Glencoe, IL: Free Press.

Cohen, A.K. (1965). The sociology of the deviant act: Anomie theory and beyond. *American Sociological Review, 30*(1), 5–14.

Colvin, M. (2000). *Crime and Coercion.* New York: St. Martin's Press.

Costelloe, M.T., & Michalowski, R.J. (2009). Social class and crime. In J.M. Miller (Ed.), *21st Century Criminology* (pp. 153–161). Los Angeles: Sage.

Cullen, F.T., Larson, M.T., & Mathers, R.A. (1985). Having money and delinquent involvement. *Criminal Justice and Behavior, 12*(2), 171–192.

Cullen, F.T., & Messner, S.F. (2007). The making of criminology revisited. *Theoretical Criminology, 11*(1), 5–37.

Currie, E. (1997). Market, crime and community. *Theoretical Criminology, 1*, 147–172.

Della Fave, L.R., & Klobus, P.A. (1976). Success values and the value stretch. *The Sociological Quarterly, 17*, 491–502.

Drakopoulos, S.A. (2008). The paradox of happiness. *Journal of Happiness Studies, 9*, 303–315.

Dunaway, R.G., Cullen, F.T., Burton, V.S., Jr., & Evans, T.D. (2000). The myth of social class and crime revisited. *Criminology, 38*(2), 589–632.

Easterlin, R.A. (2003). Explaining happiness. *Proceedings of the National Academy of Sciences, 100*(19), 11176–11183.

Elliott, D.S., & Ageton, S.E. (1980). Reconciling race and class differences in self-reported and official estimates of delinquency. *American Sociological Review, 45*, 95–110.

Farnworth, M., Thornberry, T., Krohn, M., & Lizotte, A. (1994). Measurement in the study of class and delinquency. *Journal of Research in Crime and Delinquency, 31*(1), 32–61.

Felson, R.B., Osgood, D.W., Horney, J., & Wiernik, C. (2012). Having a bad month: General versus specific effects of stress on crime. *Journal of Quantitative Criminology, 28*(2), 347–363.

Frank, T. (2004). *What's the Matter with Kansas.* New York: Owl Books.

Gould, E.D., Weinberg, B.A., & Mustard, D.B. (2002). Crime rates and local labor market opportunities in the United States: 1977–1997. *The Review of Economics and Statistics, 84*(1), 45–61.

Gouveia, S.O., & Clarke, V. (2001). Optimistic bias for negative and positive events. *Health Education, 101*(5), 228–234.

Guo, G., & Harris, K.M. (2000). The mechanisms mediating the effects of poverty on children's intellectual development. *Demography, 37*(4), 431–447.

Hagan, J. (1992). The poverty of a classless criminology. *Criminology, 30*(1), 1–20.

Hagan, J., & McCarthy, B. (1997). *Mean Streets.* Cambridge: Cambridge University Press.

Harrell, E. (2010). *Adolescent Victimization and Delinquent Behavior.* El Paso: LBF Scholarly.

Hirschi, T. (1969). *Causes of Delinquency.* Berkeley, CA: University of California Press.

Jackman, M.R., & Jackman, R.W. (1973). An interpretation of the relation between objective and subjective social status. *American Sociological Review, 38*, 569–582.

Jarjoura, G.R., Triplett, R.A., & Brinker, G.P. (2002). Growing up poor: Examining the link between persistent childhood poverty and delinquency. *Journal of Quantitative Criminology, 18*(2), 159–187.

Kohn, M. (1977). *Class and Conformity.* Chicago: University of Chicago Press.

Kornhauser, R.R. (1978). *Social Sources of Delinquency.* Chicago: University of Chicago Press.

Krivo, L.J., & Peterson, R.D. (1996). Extremely disadvantaged neighborhoods and urban crime. *Social Forces, 57*(2), 619–650.

LaFree, G. (1998). *Losing Legitimacy.* Boulder, CO: Westview.

LaFree, G., & Drass, K.A. (1996). The effect of changes in intraracial income inequality and educational attainment on changes in arrest rates for African Americans and whites, 1957 to 1990. *American Sociological Review, 61*, 614–634.

Lee, M.T., Martinez, R., Jr., & Rosenfeld, R. (2001). Does immigration increase homicide? Negative evidence from three border cities. *The Sociological Quarterly, 42*(4), 559–580.

Merton, R.K. (1938). Social structure and anomie. *American Sociological Review, 3*(5), 672–682.

Merton, R.K. (1968). *Social Theory and Social Structure.* New York: Free Press.

Messner, S.F., Raffalovich, L.E., & McMillan, R. (2001). Economic deprivation and changes in homicide arrest rates for white and black youths, 1967–1998. *Criminology, 39*(3), 591–614.

Messner, S.F., & Rosenfeld, R. (2001). *Crime and the American Dream.* Belmont, CA: Wadsworth.

National Alliance to End Homelessness (2012). *The State of Homelessness in America 2012.* National Alliance to End Homelessness. http://shnny.org/research/the-state-of-homelessness-in-america-2012, accessed April 24, 2015.

Parker, K.F. (2008). *Unequal Crime Decline.* New York: New York University Press.

Passas, N. (1997). Anomie, reference groups, and relative deprivation. In N. Passas & R. Agnew (Eds.), *The Future of Anomie Theory* (pp. 62–94). Boston, MA: Northeastern University Press.

Piff, P.K., Stancato, D.M., Cote, S., Mendoza-Denton, R., & Keltner, D. (2012). Higher social class predicts increased unethical behavior. *Proceedings of the National Academy of Sciences, 109*, 4086–4091.

Pratt, T.C., & Cullen, F.T. (2005). Assessing macro-level predictors and theories of crime: A meta-analysis. *Crime and Justice: A Review of Research, 32*, 373–450.

Rebellon, C.J., Piquero, N.L., Piquero, A.R., & Thaxton, S. (2009). Do frustrated economic expectations and objective economic inequity promote crime? *European Journal of Criminology, 6*(1), 47–71.

Rosenfeld, R., & Fornango, R. (2007). The impact of economic conditions on robbery and property crime: The role of consumer sentiment. *Criminology, 45*(4), 735–769.

Rosenfeld, R. (2009). Crime is the problem: Homicide, acquisitive crime, and economic conditions. *Journal of Quantitative Criminology, 25*(3), 287–306.

Rosenfeld, R., & Messner, S.F. (2009). The crime drop in comparative perspective: The impact of the economy and imprisonment on American and European burglary rates. *British Journal of Sociology, 60*(3), 445–471.

Seery, M.D., Holman, E.A., & Silver, R.C. (2010). What does not kill us: Cumulative lifetime adversity, vulnerability, and resilience. *Journal of Personality and Social Psychology, 96*(6), 1025–1041.

Shover, N. (1996). *Great Pretenders: Pursuits and Careers of Persistent Thieves.* Boulder, CO: Westview.

Slocum, L.A., Simpson, S.S., & Smith, D.A. (2005). Strained lives and crime. *Criminology*, *34*(4), 1067–1110.

Stellar, J.E., Manzo, V.M., Kraus, M.W., & Keltner, D. (2012). Class and compassion. *Emotion*, *12*(3), 449–459.

Stiles, B.L., Liu, X., & Kaplan, H.B. (2000). Relative deprivation and deviant adaptations. *Journal of Research in Crime and Delinquency*, *37*(1), 64–90.

Suls, J., Martin, R., & Wheeler, L. (2002). Social comparison: Why, with whom, and with what effect? *Current Directions in Psychological Science*, *11*(5), 159–162.

Suls, J., & Wheeler, L. (Eds.) (2000). *Handbook of Social Comparison Theory and Research.* New York: Kluwer.

Thornberry, T.P., & Christenson, R.L. (1984). Unemployment and criminal Involvement. *American Sociological Review*, *49*, 398–411.

Tittle, C.R. (1995). *Control Balance: Toward a General Theory of Deviance.* Boulder, CO: Westview.

Tittle, C.R., & Meier, R.F. (1990). Specifying the ses/delinquency relationship. *Criminology*, *28*(2), 271–299.

Wilson, J.Q. (1983). *Thinking About Crime.* New York: Basic Books.

Wolbring, T., Keuschnigg, M., & Negele, E. (2013). Needs, comparisons, and adaptation: The importance of relative income for life satisfaction. *European Sociological Review*, *29*, 86–104.

World Hunger Education Services (2012). *Hunger in America.* Available at http://www.worldhunger.org/articles/Learn/us_hunger_facts.htm (accessed April 24, 2015).

Wright, B.R., Caspi, A., Moffitt, T.E., Miech, R.A., & Silva, P.A. (1999). Reconsidering the relationship between sex and delinquency. *Criminology*, *37*(1), 175–194.

Wright, J.P., Cullen, F.T., Agnew, R.S., & Brezina, T. (2001). "The root of all evil?" An exploratory study of money and delinquent involvement. *Justice Quarterly*, *18*(2), 239–268.

Yearwood, D.L., & Koinis, G. (2011). Revisiting property crime and economic conditions. *The Social Science Journal*, *48*(1), 145–158.

# 12

# Social Learning Theory

## Ronald L. Akers and Wesley G. Jennings

## Introduction

This chapter provides a theoretical overview of Akers' social learning theory and his more recent social structure social learning extension. Specifically, it begins with a brief overview of the theoretical origins of social learning theory and a description of the four core theoretical elements. The following section reviews the relevant empirical evidence that has tested social learning theory as an explanation for crime and deviance, with particular attention to the results from a recent meta-analysis. A separate section detailing the findings from recent cross-cultural empirical tests of social learning theory is also provided. Next, Akers' social structure social learning extension is discussed with attention to the research that has assessed this theoretical extension. The chapter concludes by offering a series of suggestions for future social learning research.

## Theoretical Origin

The origin of social learning theory is rooted in an effort to link elements of Sutherland's differential association theory with more general principles of behavioral psychology. Accordingly, Sutherland originally proposed the following nine propositions that he considered to illustrate his theory of differential association (Sutherland, 1947:6–7):

1. Criminal behavior is learned.
2. Criminal behavior is learned in interaction with other persons in a process of communication.

*The Handbook of Criminological Theory*, First Edition. Edited by Alex R. Piquero.
© 2016 John Wiley & Sons, Inc. Published 2016 by John Wiley & Sons, Inc.

3. The principal part of the learning of criminal behavior occurs within intimate personal groups.

4. When criminal behavior is learned, the learning includes (a) techniques of committing the crime, which are sometimes very complicated, sometimes very simple; and (b) the specific direction of motives, drives, rationalizations, and attitudes.

5. The specific direction of motives and drives is learned from definitions of the legal codes as favorable or unfavorable.

6. A person becomes delinquent because of an excess of definitions favorable to violation of law over definitions unfavorable to violation of the law.

7. Differential associations may vary in frequency, duration, priority, and intensity.

8. The process of learning criminal behavior by association with criminal and anti-criminal patterns involves all of the mechanisms that are involved in any other learning.

9. Although criminal behavior is an expression of general needs and values, it is not explained by those general needs and values, because noncriminal behavior is an expression of the same needs and values.

Drawing from this original serial list, Burgess & Akers (1966) later latched on to the sixth principle: the principle of differential association. In essence, for Sutherland, this principle is not complex. Specifically, individuals learn two types of definitions for a particular behavior, either a favorable definition of the behavior or an unfavorable definition of the behavior. According to this principle, and applied to explain crime and deviance, the probability that a person will perform a criminal or deviant act increases when they learn definitions favorable to violating the law in excess of definitions that are learned that are unfavorable toward violating the law. This key principle influenced Burgess and Akers to modify Sutherland's original serial list in an effort to further elucidate the process wherein the learning occurs. Burgess & Akers' (1966:132–145) revised serial list is as follows:

1. Criminal behavior is learned according to the principles of operant conditioning (reformulation of Sutherland's principles 1 and 8).

2. Criminal behavior is learned both in nonsocial situations that are reinforcing or discriminative and through that social interaction in which the behavior of other persons is reinforcing or discriminative for criminal behavior (reformulation of Sutherland's principle 2).

3. The principal part of the learning of criminal behavior occurs in those groups which comprise the individual's major source of reinforcements (reformulation of Sutherland's principle 3).

4. The learning of criminal behavior, including specific techniques, attitudes, and avoidance procedures, is a function of the effective and available reinforcers, and the existing reinforcement contingencies (reformulation of Sutherland's principle 4).

5. The specific class of behaviors which are learned and their frequency of occurrence are a function of the reinforcers which are effective and available, and the rules or norms by which these reinforcers are applied (reformulation of Sutherland's principle 5).
6. Criminal behavior is a function of norms which are discriminative for criminal behavior, the learning of which takes place when such behavior is more highly reinforced than noncriminal behavior (reformulation of Sutherland's principle 6).
7. The strength of criminal behavior is a direct function of the amount, frequency, and probability of its reinforcement (reformulation of Sutherland's principle 7).

The efforts of Burgess & Akers to infuse principles of behavioral psychology, most notably operant conditioning, into Sutherland's differential association theory was met was some theoretical criticisms at the time of its first iteration. In light of these criticisms, Akers later made theoretical modifications, refinements, and moved away from the serial list of revised Sutherland principles. In this regard, he opted to state social learning theory as it is known and understood today according to its four core theoretical elements: differential association, definitions, differential reinforcement, and imitation (Akers & Sellers, 2013). In its most basic sense, social learning theory as originally postulated by Burgess and Akers and later polished and refined by Akers refers to:

> The probability that persons will engage in criminal and deviant behavior is increased and the probability of their conforming to the norm is decreased when they differentially associate with others who commit criminal behavior and espouse definitions favorable to it, are relatively more exposed in-person or symbolically to salient criminal/deviant models, define it as desirable or justified in a situation discriminative for the behavior, and have received in the past and anticipate in the current or future situation relatively greater reward than punishment for the behavior (Akers, 1998, p. 50).

## Core Theoretical Elements

The concept of differential association as it is expressed in Akers' social learning theory primarily focuses on the importance of the interactions that persons have with others in their peer group such as neighbors, churches, school teachers, the law, and authority figures, as well as "virtual groups" such as those established through the mass media, the internet, cell phones, etc. (Warr, 2002). These interactions are believed to provide the context wherein the process of social learning occurs. Specifically, should an individual differentially associate with peers or other groups that hold attitudes favorable toward violations of the law and evince pro-criminal or pro-deviant attitudes and values, then it is expected that the probability that the individual would engage in crime or deviance would be increased. Following this logic, Akers not only discusses the importance of the interaction with criminal or deviant peer groups, he also argues that the amount of time spent in this interaction/association will hold prominence in affecting the ratio of criminal to noncriminal associations.

The definitions component of social learning theory refers to the attitudes, values, and orientations that individuals hold toward crime and deviance as well as conforming behavior. In essence, the attitudes, values, and orientations that a person considers more right or wrong, good or bad, desirable or undesirable, justified or unjustified, appropriate or inappropriate, excusable or inexcusable, affect their own likelihood for participating in non-conforming or conforming behavior. These personal definitions favorable or unfavorable to crime and deviance can be expressed as general definitions (e.g., covering a wide range of behaviors) or specific to a particular behavior or to a particular situation. Furthermore, definitions may be positive definitions ("It is fun to steal beer from the store I work at") or neutralizing definitions ("I am not stealing beer from the store; I work there and am underpaid; thus, I am just taking what is owed to me"). Akers also considers these personal definitions as operating on a continuum as described and illustrated as follows:

> Definitions favorable to deviance include weakly held general beliefs and more strongly held deviant justifications and definitions of the situation; those unfavorable to deviance include more strongly held conventional beliefs and deviant definitions that are weakly subscribed to. ... Think of two parallel continua running in opposite directions:

1. General and Specific Conforming Beliefs/Definitions:

| | |
|---|---|
| Strongly held | Absent or weakly held |
| Unfavorable to Deviance | Favorable to Deviance |

2. General and Specific Non-Conforming Beliefs/Definitions

| | |
|---|---|
| Strongly held | Absent or weakly held |
| Favorable to Deviance | Unfavorable to Deviance |

(Akers, 1998, p. 83).

Differential reinforcement concerns the balance of perceived, experienced, or anticipated reward/s and punishment/s that may accompany or follow the performance of a particular behavior. For instance, Akers argues that value is attributed to a behavior that is rewarded, and the more frequently the behavior is rewarded (rather than punished) the higher the value becomes for the behavior. Thus, behaviors that are performed frequently and are rewarded frequently (and are thus highly reinforced) are those behaviors that an individual is likely to continue to choose to perform. Differential reinforcement can occur in a variety of ways including via positive reinforcement, negative reinforcement, positive punishment, and/or negative punishment.

The fourth and final element of Akers' social learning theory is imitation. This element is likened to the concept of vicarious reinforcement (Bandura, 1979) wherein individuals directly observe the behaviors performed/modeled by others including the consequences of others' behaviors. Or in other words, should an individual observe another person commit a criminal or deviant act and also observe its related rewards (and absence of punishment), then an individual may in turn engage in the same behavior as a result of imitation. The effect that imitation exerts in the social learning process is considered to be contingent on a variety of factors and circumstances such as the characteristics of the model themselves, the actual behavior itself being modeled, and any directly observed consequences for the model.

## Empirical Support from a Meta-Analytic Perspective

Social learning theory has been subjected to a considerable amount of empirical testing in the literature across a variety of samples, places, time periods, and types of crime and deviance. Generally, the bulk of the evidence has identified and supported social learning theory as an explanation for crime and deviance (for reviews, see Akers & Jensen, 2006; Akers & Jennings, 2009; Akers & Sellers, 2013; Jennings & Akers, 2011; Jennings *et al.*, 2010). In lieu of the vast amount of published studies and recent reviews on social learning theory, we focus on a recent meta-analysis published by Pratt and colleagues (2010) as a source for illustrating the robustness of the support that has been empirically revealed for social learning theory as an explanation for crime and deviance.

Pratt *et al.*'s (2010) meta-analysis involved systematically searching the literature for all of the studies measuring social learning variables in the leading criminal justice/criminology journals between 1974 and 2003. After having performed an exhaustive search of the available literature, their search identified 133 studies that had measured social learning variables. Furthermore, these 133 studies generated 246 statistical models which reported 704 effect-size estimates and represented 118,403 cases. Following a detailed coding protocol, Pratt *et al.* reported the percentage of effect sizes that were statistically significant, the mean effect sizes (and corresponding confidence intervals), as well as a series of moderator analyses to assess the 'stability' of the effect sizes across a host of dimensions such as sampling frame, race of sample, gender of sample, and age of sample.

Regarding the effect sizes, Pratt *et al.* (2010) estimated independent mean effect sizes for each of the four core elements of Akers' social learning theory. Their results indicated that each of the four core elements had a significant and independent mean effect size as a predictor of crime and deviance, with the largest mean effect size being found for differential association, followed by definitions, differential reinforcement, and imitation. Pratt *et al.* also provided independent mean effect sizes for different measurement sources for each of the four core elements with the following measurement sources yielding independent mean effect sizes: differential association (peers' behaviors, parents' behaviors, others' behaviors, peers' attitudes, and a differential association index); definitions (antisocial attitudes/definitions and a definitions index); differential reinforcement (peer reactions, parental reactions, rewards minus costs, and a differential reinforcement index); and imitation (witnessing and a differential imitation index). Concerning the moderator analyses, Pratt *et al.* reported that only 10 of the 55 moderator analyses that were estimated were statistically significant, which provided relatively robust evidence that social learning theory and its four central components, by and large, showed evidence of stability or 'general effects' across samples with different characteristics (e.g., sampling frame, race of sample, gender of sample, and age of sample).

## Cross-Cultural Tests

Although the recent reviews of Akers' social learning theory (Akers & Jensen, 2006; Akers & Jennings, 2009; Jennings & Akers, 2011; Jennings *et al.*, 2010) and Pratt *et al.*'s (2010) more recent meta-analysis have revealed considerable evidence in support of the robustness of social learning theory as an explanation for crime and deviance, it is also important to recognize and review the empirical evidence concerning the cross-cultural applicability of social learning theory (as any general theory of crime and deviance should be able to explain crime and deviance across geographical/cultural contexts). In this vein, there have been several recent cross-cultural studies that we review in detail (for examples of older cross-cultural studies see, Bruinsma, 1992, Wang & Jensen, 2003, Zhang & Messner, 1995).

Miller, Jennings, Alvarez-Rivera, & Miller (2008) recently examined the cross-cultural efficacy of social learning theory for predicting substance use among Puerto Rican adolescents attending public and private schools in San Juan, Puerto Rico. Using a series of regression models where they estimated the effects of definitions and differential association on cigarette, alcohol, and marijuana use, Miller *et al.* demonstrated that both aspects of social learning theory were generally predictive of substance use and these findings largely held across schools (e.g., public or private) and biological sex. Relying on the same data (although only using the public school Puerto Rican youth), Miller, Jennings, Alvarez-Rivera, & Lanza-Kaduce (2009) explored the mediating role of low self-control on the relationship between maternal attachment and deviance. Their results indicated that maternal attachment and low self-control both predicted deviance, although social learning (specifically the element of differential association) was still an independent predictor of deviance as well.

More recently, Jennings, Park, Tomsich, Gover, & Akers (2011) investigated the relationship between self-control and social learning and the overlap in dating violence perpetration and victimization among a large sample of South Korean college students. Utilizing a series of bivariate probit models that model the joint relationship/overlap between two dependent variables, Jennings *et al.* reported that both self-control and social learning emerged as significant predictors of dating violence perpetration and victimization. Furthermore, the effect of childhood physical abuse on both outcomes was generally more robust compared with witnessing father-perpetrated violence against the mother or mother-perpetrated violence against the father.

Finally, Meneses & Akers (2011) provided one of the first empirical studies to directly compare the applicability of several general theories of crime and deviance (general strain theory, social bonding, self-control, and social learning) for explaining Bolivian college students' marijuana use. After estimating a series of step-by-step models, Meneses & Akers (2011) demonstrated that although there were considerable differences between Bolivian and American college students regarding their use of marijuana (with American students being more likely to and to frequently use marijuana), all of the general theories had varying levels of magnitude as predictors of marijuana use. Having said this, the results also suggested that the effects of social learning theory were generally larger in magnitude compared to the other general theories of crime.

## Social Structure Social Learning: A Cross-Level Theoretical Model

From the beginning of the development of social learning theory, Akers made specific and frequent reference throughout the years to the compatible relationship between social learning as a social psychological theory at the micro-level and social structural theories of crime at the macro-level, building on even earlier assertions by Sutherland (1947) and Cressey (1960) with regard to differential association theory. He made and reiterated the general point that social learning is the main process, or set of cognitive/behavioral mechanisms, by which the structural conditions and variables defined and conceptualized in structural theories (e.g., social disorganization, anomie, conflict, control) produce deviant or conforming behavior, and often stated that there are good prospects for cross-level integration of social learning and structural theories (see Akers, 1968, 1973, 1985, 1998; Burgess & Akers, 1966). However, it was not until later that he went beyond these general statements to propose explicitly a cross-level (micro, meso, macro) theoretical model. A preliminary model was outlined for drug and alcohol abstinence, use, and abuse (Akers, 1992). Akers (1998), then went on to present a fuller discussion and presentation of the social structure social learning (SSSL) model as a general theory of crime and deviance and has continued to present discussions, further specification, and empirical research on this theoretical extension (see Akers, 2009; Akers & Jensen, 2003; Akers & Sellers, 2009; 2013).

Social structure social learning (SSSL) retains the central proposition earlier articulated by Akers that the social learning variables of differential association, definitions, differential reinforcement, and imitation are hypothesized to be the principal variables in the process by which social structural causes have an impact on individual behavior, that is, the social learning variables will substantially (although not necessarily fully) mediate the effect of structural variables on criminal and deviant behavior. Consider the following quotations as explicit statements on how this process may operate:

> SSSL links the main distal (macro- and meso-level) structural causes of crime found in the social structure and context to the behavior of individuals through the main proximate cognitive/behavioral causes of behavior (i.e. as found in social learning processes and mechanisms) at the micro-level. Crime rates across groups, sociodemographic categories, neighborhoods, communities, and societies are said to reflect their respective crime-inducing and crime-inhibiting characteristics, and they do so because the operation of the social learning variables are said to reflect those same structural characteristics. Not all structural variables are correlated (positively or negatively) with crime rates, but SSSL proposes that the main effects of whatever social structural factors are found empirically to be related to crime rates will be substantially mediated by the social learning variables (Akers, 2009:xxviii).

> The general culture and structure of society and the particular communities, groups, and other contexts of social interaction provide learning environments in which the norms define what is approved and disapproved, behavioral models are present, and the reactions of others (for example, in applying social sanctions) and other stimuli attach different reinforcing or punishing consequences to individuals' behavior. ... Differences in the societal or group rates of criminal behavior are a function of the extent to which cultural traditions, norms, social organization, and social control systems provide socialization, learning environments, reinforcement schedules, opportunities, and immediate situations conducive to conformity or deviance (Akers, 1998:322–323).

Although the concept of "social structure" (and references to groups, societies, and social systems when discussing social structure as in the quotations above) is commonly found in sociology and criminology, its meaning and the way it is used varies considerably. To specify more clearly the meaning of social structure in SSSL Akers identified and defined four main dimensions or vectors of social structure. These dimensions of social structure affect the probabilities that individuals will be exposed to deviant and conforming associations, models, definitions, and reinforcement.

*Differential social organization*   Akers takes this term from, and uses it in a similar manner to, Sutherland (1947), but Akers disagrees with Sutherland that it is a preferred alternative label for the concept of social disorganization. That is, it refers to the overall macro-level, integral characteristics such as culture, history, population density, age composition, racial make-up and others that distinguishes one community, region, society, or social system from another and which may be correlated with, or form the basis for, differences across these social entities in rates of crime and delinquency.

*Differential location in the social structure*   This dimension refers to the well-known sociodemographic variables of class, gender, age, race, ethnicity, and others that are commonly found in research as control variables or sometimes as indirect indicators of causal variables. These are, of course, social characteristics of individuals, but in SSSL they are conceptualized as social structural variables in the sense that persons' race, gender, class, and so on indicate their relative location in society by placing them in social categories, groups, statuses, and roles within the larger, overall social structure of society (hence the term location in the social structure). That location entails variations in power, lifestyles, and life chances vis-a-vis others' locations which could have effects on variations in learning experiences and in criminal and deviant behavior.

*Theoretically defined structural variables*  Structural theories of crime and delinquency include social disorganization, anomie, institutional anomie, conflict, feminist, and Marxist/critical, and each specifies one or more abstract categories of causes or criminogenic conditions of groups, communities, or societies such as structural malintegration, lack of social cohesion, class and other inequalities, social disorganization, group conflict, patriarchy, and other concepts. These have been measured in various ways, including using some of the structural correlates mentioned above. Some are very difficult to measure for empirical research and not all are supported by empirical research as major causes of crime. But to the extent that the structural conditions or variables proposed by the theories produce variations in rates of crime and deviance they should also have an impact on variations in (and have their effects on crime mediated by) the social learning variables.

*Differential social location in groups*  This dimension is a meso-level or more immediate social context of individuals' membership in and relation to primary, secondary, and tertiary reference groups such as the family, friendship and peer groups, leisure groups, colleagues, and work groups. It includes the same set of groups as the concept of differential association. But, it does not refer directly to the deviant/nondeviant behavior and attitudes of those groups; rather it refers to the size, organization, and structure of those groups (for example, two-parent or one-parent family) that may be related to deviant behavior.

To summarize, SSSL hypothesizes that the social learning variables are the principal cognitive/behavioral variables linking the structural factors in rates of crime and delinquency to individual behavior. To the extent that similarities and differences in the macro or meso-level social structure (virtually every aspect of which can be categorized under one or more of the dimension identified in SSSL) empirically affect the differences and similarities in rates of crime and deviance, they do so by empirically affecting the content, value, and direction of the social learning variables which increases or decreases the probability of individuals' deviant behavior.

## Conclusions and Directions for Future Research

Considering the current state of the voluminous literature that reports tests of Akers' social learning theory, it is readily apparent and often argued to be one of the most consistent and relevant explanations of crime and deviance (Akers & Jennings, 2009). Furthermore, the cross-cultural and international efficacy of social learning theory has also become evident, particularly through more recent and large scale empirical tests. Social learning theory and its application to prevention and prevention programs is also well known in criminology and the sociology of deviance, as well as it being a standard entry in criminology and criminal justice textbooks.

In comparison, the SSSL model is much less known and has thus far been tested in a limited, but growing, number of research projects, many of which test only partial models (for reviews, see Jennings & Akers, 2011). That research generally has found supportive evidence for the major proposition of the theory, i.e. the mediating role of social learning on the effects of structural conditions on various deviant behaviors. However, nonsupportive evidence has also been reported, and suggestions have been made to further develop SSSL by incorporating both the mediating effects of the social learning variables on structural correlates and moderating effects of social structure on the operation of the social learning variables (for reviews of this research see Akers, 2009; Akers & Sellers, 2013).

Going forward, future research examining social learning theory generally and the more recent SSSL extension should continue to focus on the cross-cultural and international generalizability of social learning as an explanation for crime and deviance. Second, social learning research should make an effort to further unpack the mediating and moderating effects of SSSL. Third, future studies should not concentrate so much on competing social learning theory with other general theories of crime as it is well established that social learning theory is a robust and independent predictor of crime and deviance relative to and alongside other 'competing' general theories of crime. Rather, there may be theoretical room for integration of social learning principles into other general theories of crime in an effort to build a theoretical model with an even greater ability to explain the variation in crime and deviance above and beyond the variance explained by any one specific "general theory of crime." In the end, social learning theory has rightfully earned its place as one of the core general theories of crime, and continued commitment to replicate its effects globally, further test the more recent SSSL extension, and to engage in theoretical integration discussions are likely areas where social learning research should be directed toward in the 21st century.

## References

Akers, R.L. (1968). Problems in the sociology of deviance: Social definitions and behavior. *Social Forces, 46*, 455–465.

Akers, R.L. (1973). *Deviant Behavior: A Social Learning Approach*. Belmont, CA: Wadsworth.

Akers, R.L. (1985). *Deviant Behavior: A Social Learning Approach*. 3rd edition. Belmont, CA: Wadsworth.

Akers, R.L. (1992). *Drugs, Alcohol, and Society*. Belmont, CA: Wadsworth.

Akers, R.L. (1998). *Social Learning and Social Structure: A General Theory of Crime and Deviance*. Boston, MA: Northeastern University Press.

Akers, R.L. (2009). *Social Learning and Social Structure: A General Theory of Crime and Deviance*. New Brunswick, NJ: Transaction.

Akers, R.L., & Jennings, W.G. (2009). The social learning theory of crime and deviance. In M. Krohn, A. Lizotte, & G. Hall (Eds.), *Handbook on Criminology and Deviance* (pp. 103–120). New York: Springer.

Akers, R.L., & Jensen, G.F. (2003). *Social Learning Theory and the Explanation of Crime: A Guide for the New Century. Advances in Criminological Theory. Vol. 11.* New Brunswick, NJ: Transaction Publishers

Akers, R.L., & Jensen, G.F. (2006). The empirical status of social learning theory of crime and deviance: The past, present, and future. In. F.T. Cullen, J.P. Wright, & K.R. Blevins (Eds.), *Taking Stock: The Status of Criminological Theory.* New Brunswick, NJ: Transaction.

Akers, R.L., & Sellers, C.S. (2009). *Criminological Theories: Introduction, Evaluation, and Application.* 5th edition. New York: Oxford University Press.

Akers, R.L., & Sellers, C.S. (2013). *Criminological Theories: Introduction, Evaluation, and Application.* 6th edition. New York: Oxford University Press.

Bandura, A. (1979). *Social Learning Theory.* Englewood Cliffs, NJ: Prentice Hall.

Bruinsma, G.J. (1992). Differential association theory reconsidered: An extension and its empirical test. *Journal of Quantitative Criminology, 8,* 29–49.

Burgess, R.L., & Akers, R.L. (1966). A differential association-reinforcement theory of criminal behavior. *Social Problems, 14,* 128–147.

Cressey, D.R. (1960). Epidemiology and individual conduct: A case from criminology. *Pacific Sociological Review, 3,* 47–58.

Jennings, W.G., & Akers, R.L. (2011). Social learning theory. In C.D. Bryant (Ed.), *The Handbook of Deviant Behavior* (pp. 106–113). New York: Routledge.

Jennings, W.G., Maldonado-Molina, M., & Komro, K.A. (2010). Sex similarities/differences in trajectories of delinquency among urban Chicago youth: The role of delinquent peers. *American Journal of Criminal Justice, 35,* 56–75.

Jennings, W.G., Park, M., Tomsich, E., Gover, A., & Akers, R.L. (2011). Assessing the overlap in dating violence perpetration and victimization among South Korean college students: The influence of social learning and self-control. *American Journal of Criminal Justice, 36,* 188–206.

Meneses, R.A., & Akers, R. (2011). A comparison of four general theories of crime and deviance: Marijuana use among American and Bolivian university students. *International Criminal Justice Review, 21,* 333–352.

Miller, H.V., Jennings, W.G., Alvarez-Rivera, L.L., & Miller, J.M. (2008). Explaining substance use among Puerto Rican adolescents: A partial test of social learning theory. *Journal of Drug Issues, 38,* 261–284.

Miller, H.V., Jennings, W.G., Alvarez-Rivera, L.L., & Lanza-Kaduce, L. (2009). Self-control, maternal attachment, and deviance among Hispanic adolescents. *Journal of Criminal Justice, 37,* 77–84.

Pratt, T., Cullen, F.T., Sellers, C.S., Winfree, T.L., Jr., Madensen, T.D., Daigle, L.E., *et al.* (2010). The empirical status of social learning theory: A meta-analysis. *Justice Quarterly, 27,* 765–802.

Sutherland, E.H. (1947). *Principles of Criminology.* 4th edition. Philadelphia: J.B. Lippincott.

Wang, S., & Jensen, G.F. (2003). Explaining delinquency in Taiwan: A test of social learning theory. In R.L. Akers & G.F. Jensen (Eds.), *Social Learning Theory and the Explanation of Crime: A Guide for the New Century. Advances in Criminological Theory,* Vol. 11 (pp. 65–84). New Brunswick, NJ: Transaction.

Warr, M. (2002). *Companions in Crime: The Social Aspects of Criminal Conduct.* Cambridge: Cambridge University Press.

Zhang, L., & Messner, S.F. (1995). Family deviance and delinquency in China. *Criminology, 33,* 359–387.

# 13

# Cultural Processes, Social Order, and Criminology

Mark T. Berg, Eric A. Sevell, and Eric A. Stewart

## Introduction

### Classical theorists and culture

Social scientists have long sought to explain patterns of deviant and illegal behavior using the related conceptual devices of culture and structure. Industrialization and urbanization around the beginning of the 20th century introduced tremendous changes to social interaction and the organization of social life. Many classical social theorists were concerned with the changes brought about by these transitions, and the social and psychological life of the city. Whether described in terms of solidarity (Durkheim), the metropolis (Simmel), or the emerging bureaucracy (Weber), early theorists were intent on mapping the consequences, for better or worse, of the changing social order. Broadly, they were concerned with the onset of urban social problems and individual disorders such as crime, delinquency, and mental illness.

The struggle of individuals to maintain a sense of autonomy and individuality in the face of rapid social change became a primary substantive concern during the turn of the 20th century. Whereas rural life is characterized by sensory mental imagery that flows slowly, habitually, and evenly, the psychological basis of the metropolitan type of individuality consists of the intensification of stimulation. As a result of this, Simmel (1971) argued that overstimulation resulted in the mental adaptation of a "blasé" attitude, which fundamentally affected societal culture and the way individuals would relate to one another. Although perhaps less critical of these consequences than his contemporaries, Simmel was nonetheless interested in the sort of interactional changes the emerging period of modernity brought about for individuals and communities.

*The Handbook of Criminological Theory*, First Edition. Edited by Alex R. Piquero.
© 2016 John Wiley & Sons, Inc. Published 2016 by John Wiley & Sons, Inc.

However, other scholars, recognizing the vast societal changes taking place, engaged in subsequent speculation about the ways such social and cultural transformations could erode foundations of morality and solidarity among individuals and society. Durkheim (1984, 1995) argued that a state of normlessness for some individuals could arise (i.e., anomie) as a result of the drastic changes in living conditions. Because individual acts are conditioned by the degree to which the individual is integrated into society, the potential breakdown of this integration was of primary concern. Weber (1922, 1930) was concerned with bureaucracy and the impersonal order that an increasing adherence to rational-legal authority brought with it. These transitions brought with them important cultural changes that were largely embedded in ideas. Drawing an analogy to a switchman on a train track, Weber argues that culture can determine the tracks along which action has been pushed by some motivational dynamic. The emergence of capitalism, fueled by the protestant ethic, shifted the cultural ideal of wealth accumulation from one that was historically immoral, to more recently moral, and contemporarily, amoral. As wealth accumulation became an end in and of itself towards which action was directed, a concern of Weber's was the orientation by which individuals approached this goal. With an all-encompassing focus on wealth accumulation, actions that were once enacted for the sake of their value were increasingly seen as merely instrumental in the attainment of this goal.

Despite the fact that many of these classical theorists and their ideas are often forgotten or ignored, their presence still looms large in contemporary literature. Durkheim and Simmel's work is commonly echoed in modern discussions of non-conventional behavior. While teaching in Europe, one of Simmel's students was Robert Park, who has been credited as a founder of the Chicago School. In addition to Park's (1925) own research on urbanization, he personally invited W.I. Thomas to the University of Chicago, where together their influential ideas would spawn decades of subsequent research. The work by these authors was in large part incorporated into Shaw & McKay's (1942) early theorizing about community, crime, and culture. Furthermore, whether recognized or not, Durkheim's notion of societal integration and social control remains the linchpin of many contemporary theoretical explanations (e.g., Bursik & Grasmick, 1993; Sampson & Wilson, 1995). Weber also contributed to theorizing on anomie and strain by arguing that culture organizes economic activity, which, thus, can bring about deviance and rule breaking in order to achieve an ideal.

## Waxing and waning of cultural explanations

From its historically intellectual roots, the concept of culture has played an important, and at times contentious, role in explanations of deviant behavior and community and crime. Although disregarded for some time, culture has reemerged into a period of theoretical and empirical expansion. An extensive inventory of criminological research places emphasis on cultural mechanisms – the symbolic, relational aspect of social organization – to account for the uneven representation of crime within society. While dimensions of social structure are also critically important in this literature, what distinguishes it from other criminological research is the explanatory power granted to culture to explain the genesis and scope of socially disapproved behaviors.

Yet, despite their scientific potential, cultural explanations of behavior have been the subject of sharp criticism both within and outside of academia. Part of this treatment is related to the fact that culture itself is a highly abstract conceptual notion, making the assumptions of existing research especially vulnerable to misinterpretation. At minimum, a profitable theory is one that is testable, falsifiable, and simple. Many theories that specify culture as an organizing principle often articulate a disparate mélange of assumptions, and do not approximate a sufficient theoretical perspective. These matters have diminished the appeal of cultural explanations, causing some analysts to reject them outright (e.g., Kornhauser, 1978). As a consequence, for many years criminological research neglected any serious attempts to explain deviant behavior as a product of cultural mechanisms. Now, the discipline appears to be open once more to the potential for treating non-conventional culture as an influential variable in the explanation of deviant behavior.

Because it is a ubiquitous property of social life, culture has been invoked to account for differences in human behavior across multiple units of analyses (e.g., nations, states, neighborhoods, and individuals). Likewise, theories in this domain often vary in their analytical objectives; for example, some specify cultural variables to explain the spatial or temporal distribution of crime rates, while others model such differentiation among individuals or small groups. However, the resurgence of cultural explanations has made much more progress in some areas than others. For example, Merton's (1938) understanding of culture as a macro-structure has received limited treatment in contemporary criminological research on crime and variation in cultural processes. Despite its potential theoretical utility, contemporary researchers have largely ignored the *culture structure*, a critically important component of system-level anomie and individual-level strain. Although possibly the lingering result of past criticisms and dismissals (see Kornhauser, 1978), the neglect of the conceptualization of culture as a macro-level structure is an odd oversight by researchers.

Despite these shortcomings, culture has made great strides in other areas of contemporary theory, such as those focusing on individual-level explanations. Criminological research that applies a cultural explanation to individual-level behaviors often explicitly or implicitly integrates a consideration of contextual processes. In fact, neighborhood context has long been salient to research on the normative dimension of criminal behavior because it is a social setting where network-based ideas and justifications are inhered and enacted. As Matza (1964:25) has remarked, "the ideas and practices that are transmitted within groups and neighborhoods occupy a strategic position in the sociological view" of crime and delinquency. Any scholarly discussion of culture and criminal behavior must consider the social context in which individuals are embedded in order to fully understand the nature of these effects.

## The task at hand

This chapter examines the broad criminological research which specifies deviant, criminal, and violent behavior as a product of the interaction between individuals, local context, and cultural systems. Specifically, the discussion of existing material is organized within a multilevel interpretation and delineates the linkage between individual and ecologically situated processes. Just as in the mid 20th century, cultural explanations still permeate studies of criminal behavior in the urban metropolis. In the first section, "Culture and Deviant Behavior: Early Perspectives" we discuss early contributions to the study of a changing social order and its consequences for culture and behavior. Additionally, we discuss assumptions contained in several early theoretical treatments of culture and deviant behavior, and why interest in cultural theories waned for a period of several years. This section proceeds with a discussion of perspectives from the early Chicago school, Shaw and McKay, and anomie and strain theorists, finally concluding with criticism of these perspectives, notably by systemic theorists and cultural attenuation perspectives. The shortcomings of these latter perspectives are also discussed. The second section, "Cultural Processes and Deviant Behavior: Recent Developments" focuses on the propositions derived from urban sociology and recent cognitive-based accounts. This section traces the revival of cultural perspectives on deviant behavior, and carefully articulates the way culture is understood conceptually in more recent and refined perspectives. It discusses the work of scholars such as William Julius Wilson (1987), Elijah Anderson (1999), and those invoking Goffman's (1974) notion of frames (e.g., Berg *et al.*, 2012; Stewart & Simons, 2006), while additionally focusing on more abstract notions of culture, including Swidler's (1986) "toolkit," Bourdieu's (1990) habitus, and Vaisey's (2009) dual-process model. The chapter's conclusions are re-emphasized in the Conclusion.

## Culture and Deviant Behavior: Early Perspectives

### Cultural change and social order: the early Chicago school

In addition to expanding theoretical potential, many early scholars from the Chicago School added a flavor of empiricism to theorizing on culture and social order. In-depth, ethnographic work allowed for a more nuanced understanding of the way broad societal transitions affected individuals at the ground level. For example, the work of W.I. Thomas and Florian Znaniecki (1920) on *The Polish Peasant in Europe and America* was a major inspiration in the early Chicago School of Criminology and spawned decades of further investigation. Their work highlighted the difficulties associated with immigration, and the disorientations of life caused by the rapid movement of rural people with different cultural traditions into the midst of an industrializing US cities. Thomas and Znaniecki's work was a prototype for what would later be termed social disorganization theory, and elaborated the connection between culture and poverty. Work by Frederic Thrasher also addressed these issues, albeit in a slightly different fashion. Thrasher (1927) was among the first to thoroughly investigate and develop propositions about gangs and gang activity in the inner city. Among other important findings, he documented that (1) gang boys have similar rates of delinquency as non-gang boys; that (2) gang boys have very similar values to non-gang boys; and that (3) delinquents in or out of the slums are more disabled in interpersonal relationships. Because of the conclusions he draws in regard to the concepts of "gang" and "subculture," Thrasher's (1927) work played an important role in social theorizing that would take place many decades later (see Bursik & Grasmick, 1993; Kornhauser, 1978).

Robert Park, along with Ernest W. Burgess, developed the concentric zone theory of the city, which was published in Park's (1925) monumental work, *The City*. Continuing the organismic analogy developed by Durkheim, and borrowing the ecological concept of succession, the authors predicted (and subsequently observed) that cities would take the form of concentric rings moving outward, with a zone of deterioration immediately surrounding the city center, succeeding to increasingly prosperous residential zones moving outward toward the city's edge. This is an observation that would inspire, and be subsequently confirmed by, later work by Shaw and McKay (1942), which was fundamental in shaping their conclusions. Work by Wirth (1938) was also instrumental in shaping subsequent work done by Shaw & McKay, particularly in regard to the structural components of social disorganization. Namely, Wirth focused on the ways in which population size, density, and racial/ethnic heterogeneity affected social organization. In addition to citing structural variables, Wirth also noted the "schizoid" psychology of the urban city, analogous to Simmel's notion of the blasé attitude.

Taken together, the above authors and their ideas created a conceptual foundation for the subsequent study of social order, culture, and behavior that would heavily influence later works, particularly that of Shaw and McKay and other pioneering criminologists and social scientists. Many of the original questions posed by these early scholars are still without answers, and remain as relevant today as they were almost a century ago.

## Shaw and McKay and cultural theorizing

As noted, scholars in the Chicago school were deeply concerned with investigating the behavioral consequences of normative change among people undergoing the social transition from traditional settings to modern urban life (e.g., Park, 1925; Thomas & Znaniecki, 1920; Thrasher, 1927; Wirth, 1938). Working in this intellectual climate, Shaw and McKay fashioned a pioneering model centered on the concept of "social disorganization" that implicated *both* the cultural and the network-related aspects of neighborhoods as sources of delinquency. It is important to begin with the foundational work developed by these Chicago School scholars in order to make sense of the differences and similarities between traditional and contemporary explanations. By and large, scholarly treatments of Shaw and McKay gloss over the micro-level cultural component of their work; however, their ideas are critically important to understanding subsequent research in this domain, and continue to be relevant in contemporary thinking.

The Shaw & McKay (1942, 1969) model conceived of the local neighborhood as an important context for delinquency because it represents a place where personal and primary group relations are formed; these ensuing relations are integral to mechanisms of social control (i.e., social regulation) and socialization (i.e., culture). As for the latter aspect of their model pertaining to the nature of cultural processes, Shaw & McKay (1942) theorized that the normative rationale for criminal behavior is transmitted through face-to-face interactions, eventually becoming embedded as a delinquent tradition within certain neighborhoods. Oral history or biographical data revealed that "these traditions of delinquency [were] preserved and transmitted" not only by peer contacts, but also through the family network (Shaw & McKay, 1971:260). Furthermore, Shaw and McKay formulated two key assumptions relating to the *content* of culture in poor, high-crime neighborhoods (see Kobrin, 1971). First, they argued that delinquent norms coexist with mainstream norms. Stated in their words, the typical delinquent community is "often distinguished by a confusion and wide diversification of its norms or standards," ranging from orientations that are strictly conventional to those that are delinquent in character, rather than displaying a relative consistent and conventional pattern (Shaw, McKay, & MacDonald, 1938:101). Second, Shaw and McKay stressed that the "dominant cultural tradition in every community is conventional, even in those having the highest rates of delinquents" (1969:320). Put differently, they believed that while delinquent conduct norms exist within high-delinquency neighborhoods, they are less socially significant than mainstream norms (see Whyte, 1943). Taken together, Shaw and McKay understood the culture of impoverished neighborhoods to be characteristically (1) heterogeneous or conflicting, while (2) largely conventional in nature.

Shaw & McKay (1969) offered an explanation that had a dual explanatory focus, one that both emphasized the macro-social or community distribution of crime, and elaborated the micro-social processes, particularly those occurring in primary groups, which facilitated the transmission of criminal traditions in high-crime areas. Their emphasis on neighborhood-based social networks as carriers of cultural resources effectively merged these macro and micro explanations. Social change or urban growth dynamics became a less salient premise for their model as it developed. Indeed, analytical and theoretical focus shifted from the linkage between urban growth dynamics and crime to that of social status and crime. Shaw and McKay slowly recast their explanatory framework to account for the link between neighborhood inequality and stratification and patterns of criminal behavior. As a result, their model attributed theoretical power not only to intergroup processes but also to the role of structural position in shaping criminal conduct norms in poor urban neighborhoods.

Subsequent theoretical treatments of cultural processes integrated conceptual developments from Shaw and McKay's earlier model (see Short, 1971). Kobrin (1951:656), for instance, theorized that a duality of conduct norms, rather than hegemony of either criminal or conventional norms, was "the fundamental sociological fact in the culture" of high-crime communities. Also within the theoretical vein of social process, Sutherland's (1947) model identifies a dynamic, ongoing course of interaction among individuals and groups that produces criminal acts (Matsueda, 1988). His model assumes that differential social organization – or the relative exposure of groups and actors to ratios favorable and unfavorable to crime – is a feature of collectivities, including communities. Certain groups, such as youths from poor urban areas, theoretically are at risk for involvement in crime because their "social organizational context" exposes them to an excess of definitions favoring crime (Matsueda, 1988:282). Finally, the strain-based theory of Cloward & Ohlin (1960) modified the cultural aspects of Shaw and McKay's thesis to suggest that the alignment between conventional and criminal networks was necessary to explain neighborhood variation in the nature of criminal activity.

## The social system and anomie

*Socioeconomic position and culture* Characteristics of social structure, including inequality and stratification, became particularly important in later variants of Shaw and McKay's model in order to account for the relative stability of high rates of crime in impoverished areas. To be sure, Sutherland and others did not explicitly theorize the relevance of these characteristics for cultural processes or crime. Nonetheless, the linkage between social status and involvement in deviant behavior permeated subsequent developments in cultural theorizing. Although loosely specified (a point which Kornhauser (1978) strongly critiques), Shaw and McKay increasingly incorporated elements of Merton's (1938) structural anomie theory and what would later be called strain theories of deviance into their model. Focusing on the various disjunctures present between the culture and social structures, Shaw & McKay (1942:187) argued that "it is understandable, then, that the economic position of persons living in the areas of least opportunity should be translated at times into unconventional conduct, in an effort to reconcile the idealized status and their practical prospects for attaining this status." Importantly, they emphasized that such efforts to achieve an advantageous position in the economic and social life of the city may be "seriously thwarted" by many structural restrictions.

*The social structure and culture structure* In many Western cultures, and particularly in the United States, the social system can be thought of as consisting of two components: a social structure and a culture structure. The social structure refers to the "organized set of relationships in which members of the society or group are variously implicated" (Messner, 1988). The structural aspect of anomie highlights the opportunity structure that is present in a given society. The culture structure refers to an "organized set of normative values governing behavior which is common to members of a group or society" (Messner, 1988). There are two main components of the culture structure. First, goals, purposes, interests, etc., are held out as legitimate objects attainable by all or for diversely located members of society. Merton (1938) and later scholars (Messner & Rosenfeld, 1997) argue, analogously to Weber's protestant ethic, that the "American Dream" is an abstract cultural idea towards which action is directed. Additionally, this concept recognizes that while individuals are bounded to some relative position in the social structure, the goals they strive toward are free to migrate across structural constraints. Second, the culture structure defines, regulates, and controls the acceptable or "normative" means of achieving the culturally prescribed goals. This concept refers broadly to the socially approved procedures for realizing the cultural goals noted above. Implicit in this component of the culture structure is recognition that the means to achieve various goals, just like individuals themselves, are also distributed throughout and constrained by social structural arrangements. As Messner (1988:37) notes, Merton's conception of the culture structure derives from his "firm belief that human action can only be understood within the context of the concrete, socio-cultural environment."

*System level disjunctures*    Put most simply, anomie refers to the structural mismatch between cultural goals and structural means. This disjuncture occurs primarily at the system level when the culture structure promotes success goals common to all while the social structure restricts access to normative means. Merton (1938:681) places an important emphasis on the notion that it requires the full configuration of poverty, limited opportunity, and a commonly shared system of success symbols to explain the higher associations of deviant behavior and poverty in American society than in others "where rigidified class structure is coupled with differential class symbols of achievement." Moreover, a further disjuncture can occur between the two components of the culture structure whereby a disproportionate emphasis can be placed on cultural success goals while the institutional means are largely ignored or viewed as ancillary. The broad success goal that Merton (1938) and later anomie and strain theorists (Bernard, 1987; Messner, 1988) have in mind when they speak of such goals is that of monetary success, i.e., the embodiment of the "American Dream" (Messner & Rosenfeld, 1997). They do not invoke monetary success in a Marxian sense of material dominance, but in a Weberian sense of symbolic ideology. Success is, as Merton (1938) originally noted, largely about the *symbolic* value that it carries. This fundamental point should not be ignored. As Rosenfeld (1989) notes, promoting meritocracy results in a paradox whereby individuals actually run the risk of self degradation by competing in a system that is idealistically egalitarian and open in opportunity to everyone. Because this level of equality is a romantic ideal, and not an empirical reality, the rigid and often immobile social structure in the United States creates an atmosphere ready to engender feelings of failure and loss in individuals. After all, if one is competing in a race one perceives to be fair, the only one to blame in the event of failure is oneself.

*Theoretical complications*    anomie is a property of social systems, not individuals. As Messner (1988:45) notes, "the utility of developing an individual-level analogue is by no means self-evident." Anomie does not deterministically or mechanically result in strain or deviant behavior. Rather, anomie at the system level can create certain pressures that make deviant behavior more probabilistic than it would be otherwise (Rosenfeld, 1989). Social structure sets constraints at the micro-level that individuals must deal with when contending with disjunctures at the macro-level. There can be no direct link between anomie and individual deviant motivations because motivations are simply not a property of social systems, and taking such a view would lead one into the trap of teleology. Recognizing that motivation can only lie within individuals, Merton's (1938) original argument alludes, although rather vaguely, to processes of relative deprivation and feelings of frustration. As noted, anomie is a structural argument and thus Merton's (1938) focus was not necessarily developed for an individual-level analogue, which is perhaps why it has often been ignored or dismissed in subsequent research.

Amongst other criticisms discussed below, Kornhauser's (1978) dismissal of strain also contributed to its subsequent disappearance from the literature. Kornhauser (1978:148) argues that by introducing class differences into his theory, "Merton has vitiated most of the force of strain theory." She goes on further to argue that strain is "superfluous" in explaining deviant behavior because weak internal controls resulting from lower-class socialization patterns would result in deviance all by themselves. For example, Kornhauser (1978) argues that in the case of Shaw and McKay, strain is present in their model only so far as it affects social controls. Because anomie is a relative constant and produces no additional or novel explanatory power, Kornhauser (1978) dismisses strain not only in the context of the social disorganization model, but as an explanation for more general patterns of deviant behavior.

*Strain and group-level processes*    However, such dismissal of strain may have been successful only as a result of obscuring Merton's (1938) original argument and discarding its important nuances. Anomie may indeed be a constant of a given social system, but it is not relevant to explanations of variation in motivation or behavior; this was never an argument Merton intended to draw (Messner, 1988). As noted above, Merton's arguments pertaining to motivation and behavior are somewhat vague and allude to social psychological processes of relative deprivation and feelings of frustration. Although vague, this is an incredibly important point that many past and present scholars have identified in attempts to elaborate this component of Merton's theory more clearly.

For example, Cohen (1955) developed a theory from these earlier theoretical strands – in addition to Mertonian strain theory – in which aspects of social status and cultural mechanisms were logically united. His perspective maintains that "structural deficits" experienced by working-class youths translate into "cultural deficits" when viewed against middle-class standards. Groups of working-class youths collectively reject middle-class values and devise an oppositional status system where respect is conferred to those who excel at criminal behaviors. Members of the so-called "delinquent subculture" develop dependence to their system for identity, which gives it a strong degree of salience. To account for the distribution of delinquency (including violence), Cohen's (1955) theory grants causal power to group-based subcultural processes; moreover, it stipulates that these processes are disproportionately located among working-class youths.

Further evidence of a link between social status and culture comes from Miller's (1958) perspective; he delineates the unique cultural conditions motivating lower-class adolescents to engage in delinquency. Miller posits that the lower-class cultural system is distinctive in its symbolic content, or what is referred to as "focal concerns." Personal rank is earned by exhibiting behavioral hallmarks sanctioned by the lower-class cultural system; for example, displaying physical prowess in the face of a rival incurs a reputation for toughness – a core focal concern. Wolfgang (1958:329–330) also tethered class and culture together to account for the social origins of serious offending. He reasoned that a "subculture of violence" exists among a portion of the lower class "where toleration – if not encouragement – of violence is part of the normative structure." Building on these assumptions, Wolfgang & Ferracuti (1967:153) later proposed that among groups who display the highest rates of homicide "we should find in the most intense degree a subculture of violence."

More broadly, social psychology offers the analytical and conceptual tools to make sense of a strain argument. As Agnew & Passas (1997:68) note, "the concept of relative deprivation forges micro–macro links by connecting subjective feelings of individuals with culturally and socially patterned comparisons made through the selection of reference groups." Again, arguing that anomie is a constant does not invalidate the very separate argument made by strain perspectives. Even if anomie is a culturally persistent state, this ignores the important recognition that anomie produces socially patterned and subjective consequences for different individuals based largely on their position within the social structure. Individuals perceive relative deprivation, whether it is in regard to social status or economic means, through various social psychological processes that all individuals in society experience. Important here (and what Kornhauser's critique may have missed) is that the reference group one can draw from to make comparisons is socially and culturally unlimited, whereas the social positions one makes such comparisons from are potentially limited.

*A future for examining culture through the lens of anomie and strain?*   Despite the areas of potentially novel research noted above and a slight resurgence in anomie and strain research in past decades (Bernard, 1987; Messner, 1988; Rosenfeld, 1989; Messner & Rosenfeld, 1997), current research on these issues remains largely absent in the literature. This is unfortunate given the theoretical utility these ideas offer. In a period when cultural explanations of nonconventional behavior are making a great resurgence in the literature, it is surprising that current research ignores the cultural propositions offered by anomie and strain theorists. Although a constant at the macro-level, the indirect effects of anomie at the individual level may be of primary importance. The process of socialization necessarily assumes some sort of content to which an individual is socialized toward. Merton's conception of anomie reminds us that individuals are socialized toward both means and goals. As he originally argued, one must consider all components of the social system in order to subsequently understand the responses made by individuals. Additionally, the cultural components of Merton's theory are important for understanding variation in individual behavior. As Weber argued long ago, ideas motivate action. Thus, explanations that seek to avoid reinventing the wheel must consider the cultural dimensions of strain as they relate to variation in motivation and action.

## Criticisms and controversy

By the late 1970s, a wave of criticism greatly diminished the intellectual standing of theoretical perspectives that granted power to cultural mechanisms. For example, Suttles (1968:3, 6) argued that residents of slum neighborhoods do not necessarily reject conventional norms but suspend them to negotiate a practical, rather than ideal, "personalistic order" because the standards of wider society are inapplicable within their environment. Later, Kornhauser (1978:76–79) argued in that culture is "attenuated" or "disused" in poor neighborhoods, and challenged the importance of unconventional values for explaining criminal conduct (see Warner, 2003). Furthermore, she reasoned that "slum life" – her reference to a distinctive culture among residents of lower-class neighborhoods – "lacks complete definition and manifests considerable inauthenticity" (Kornhauser, 1978:134). Kornhauser thus interpreted Shaw & McKay's (1969) theory as purely a control model, while accusing Sutherland (1947) of assuming a theoretical position of "boundless cultural relativism" and envisioning a society "without a center" (Kornhauser, 1978:192). From Kornhauser's perspective, Sutherland's theory "contains a hidden but simple variety of structural determinism" (1978:190); moreover, it denies humans a distinct nature and assumes that all behavior is valued.

In a similar line of analysis, Kornhauser (1978:208) accused Miller (1958) of theorizing cultural processes that exist "only in his imagination." As for Wolfgang & Ferracuti (1967), their model is allegedly "restricted to the empty search for a subculture to account for the roots of violence" (Kornhauser, 1978:188). More broadly, Kornhauser questioned whether a modern society could sustain a culture that genuinely sanctions predatory behavior, for it would have no value in societies whose existence depends on lawful interactions.

Despite her critique, there was not a uniform scholarly opinion about the impotence of non-conventional culture as a causal mechanism. For example, an empirical study by Hindelang (1974) challenged prevailing notions about value-consensus, suggesting that youths do not universally subscribe to a common value-system irrespective of their delinquent involvement (e.g., Sykes & Matza, 1957).

Nonetheless, as time has revealed, the devastating consequences of Kornhauser's critique for the theoretical vitality of cultural perspectives cannot be ignored (see Matsueda, 1988, 2007). But beyond this, the politically charged controversy involving the "culture of poverty" thesis further marginalized any discussion of culture in social science research. For these reasons, subsequent developments in criminological theory placed very little emphasis on cultural variation as an explanation of crime. Instead they held a consensus view of the social order and thereby sought to explain law violation only as a product of a breakdown in regulation (e.g., Bursik & Grasmick, 1993).

## Systemic interpretations of cultural effects

*Reviving social disorganization perspectives*   Systemic theory (Bursik & Grasmick, 1993) was largely an attempt to revive Shaw & McKay's (1942) social disorganization perspective, which, as noted, had long fallen out of favor and was considered little more than historically interesting by many scholars. In the wake of intellectual and moral critique, more contemporary accounts of culture held a consensus view of cultural variability, but drew on interpretations suggesting that culture is weak or "attenuated" (Kornhauser, 1978; Warner, 2003), and this affects the ability of communities to enact social control, or collective responses to crime. Systemic theory (Bursik & Grasmick, 1993:4) posits that the "capacity for community regulation is determined by the extensiveness and density of the formal and informal networks within the neighborhood that bind residents together as a social community." Borrowing heavily from Hunter (1985), Bursik & Grasmick (1993) highlighted three levels of social control. Private control refers to intimate formal primary groups, parochial control refers to the effects of broader local interpersonal networks and interlocking of local institutions, and, finally, public control refers to the ability of a community to secure public goods and services that originate outside the neighborhood.

*The public level of control*   This last level of control is of particular importance when one considers that evidence has been presented of the existence of relatively stable neighborhoods characterized by strong interpersonal ties, which nonetheless experience high rates of crime. As Bursik (2002:75) notes, by recognizing the public level of control, systemic theory was able to account for "dynamics of gang formation and maintenance that could not be anticipated by the Shaw and McKay model." While some scholars had invoked subcultural explanations to account for this discrepancy, Bursik & Grasmick (1993:38) argue that this approach is incorrect, and rather, such findings "emphasize the need to expand the focus of control beyond the internal dynamics of the community." Citing a wide body of evidence, Busik & Grasmick (1993) argued that it is difficult to affect the nature of a neighborhood environment through the internal efforts of the neighborhood alone. Despite their best efforts, peer groups, the family, and local institutions (e.g., schools) may be powerless to regulate the behavior of neighborhood residents. Areas undergoing rapid residential turnover are often characterized by fleeting and ineffective affectual relations at the private level. At the parochial level, residential turnover, in addition to factors such as racial/ethnic heterogeneity, impedes residents' ability to perform informal surveillance, dictate movement governing rules, and engage in direct interventions (Bursik & Grasmick, 1993:35). Thus, these groups must also be able to marshal resources from external agencies that control the funding and investment that would increase the sorts of social control noted above.

Additionally, Busik & Grasmick (1993:50) argued that "the dynamics that give rise to ecological changes underscore the need to consider the systemic implications of the public sphere of control." As noted, one of the longstanding patterns in research in crime and delinquency during the era of Shaw & McKay (1942) was the existence of stability among change; that is, rates of delinquency in Chicago areas remained persistent over time despite rapid residential mobility and racial/ethnic turnover. However, Busik & Webb (1982) discovered that the patterns Shaw & McKay observed (1942) only hold until about 1950, at which point neighborhoods undergoing compositional change began to be characterized by changing rates of delinquency. Although unclear as to exactly why, Bursik & Webb (1982) posited that such findings might be due to macro-level issues of racism and discrimination, primarily in the form of housing and neighborhood development.

*Obviating the subcultural explanation*    Systemic theory, a purely control perspective, focused the intellectual spotlight on the public level of control, rather than acknowledging the possibility that social ties could transmit distinctly antisocial capital, to explain social disorganization. This is particularly true of the stable, densely tied, high-crime areas noted above. Conforming to the theoretical assumption of cultural attenuation, Bursik & Grasmick (1993) ultimately concluded that the considerations noted above once again underscore the need to elaborate how external economic and political decision making can affect the ability of neighborhood residents to internally regulate themselves. Residents of stable, high-crime neighborhoods may have every desire to regulate themselves by conventional standards, but public-level agencies and institutions that are at best apathetic and at worst overtly hostile toward residents' needs may hinder them. Thus, residents in some neighborhoods may be unable to activate the public level of control that has been hypothesized to be so important to subsequent levels of control. The possibility that such residents may be unwilling is not acknowledged since culture, according to systemic theory, can only vary in degree and not content.

*Evidence for the public level of control*    Citing work by Wilson (1987, 1991), Bursik & Grasmick (1993) note that changes in the political economy of urban areas may reflect a neighborhood's ability to lobby industry and government in an effort to bring jobs and other resources into the area. This is an important contrast to previous work, which describes the evolution of the city as a process of "natural" areas of market and housing demand (Park, 1925; Shaw & McKay, 1942). As Sampson (2012:41) concludes, "with the purposeful segregation of low-income public housing, withdrawal of needed services, government subsidized development by the private sector, zoning, red-lining, blockbusting ... it is no longer possible to think of neighborhoods as purely natural areas." Some neighborhoods may be powerless when faced with the overwhelming influence of public bureaucracies and private money.

For example, Bursik & Grasmick (1993) note that residents of Harlem and other particular areas of New York have raised great concern over the concentration of services for the homeless, the mentally ill, and drug abusers in their localities while other areas of the city evince a relative paucity of these services. While the city notes economic considerations for their decisions, residents argue it is because they are simply powerless to stop it. Research into public housing reveals similar processes, where the distribution of such housing is tied much more closely to power relations than it is to any legitimate economic or market dynamics (Bursik & Grasmick, 1993:55).

Additionally, abuse by police, and a growing sense of perceived injustices has led many to feel like they must rely on their own resources for solving problems. Sampson (2012:102) notes that incarceration in the US is now so common, "that is has become a normal stage in the life course for many disadvantaged young men." Recognizing this increasing and ongoing process, many scholars have turned their focus to the potential consequence of cynicism. For example, Carr, Napolitano, & Keating (2007) launched an investigation to explore the consequences of legal cynicism among youths in a high-crime area. Specifically, they examined whether negative experiences with, and dispositions toward, police and legal officials led to an outright rejection of public legitimacy, or if they led to feelings that were more ambivalent. The authors found that although youths held overwhelmingly negative views toward police, they often continued to cite them as a potentially fruitful source of future crime prevention. They thus conclude that such an inconsistency seems to support an argument for cultural attenuation rather than an antisocial subculture. It is not that residents and youth in high-crime neighborhoods are unwilling to marshal support from police, but they may feel that they are simply unable to do so, as the above research suggests.

*The public level of control and gangs*     As noted, gangs in the context of stable, well-organized and high crime areas present a challenge for the assumptions of traditional social disorganization perspectives. While such perspectives can account for the emergence of gangs in unstable, institutionally weak areas (i.e., those marked by weak social controls), the context noted above presents a direct challenge. Bursik & Grasmick (1993) note that typically subcultural or class-based explanations have been posited to account for such situations. However, they dismiss such a notion, once again invoking the criticisms of Kornhauser (1978) to argue that while distinct groups may exists in society, the content of their culture is always more or less some degree of conventional culture. Moreover, Bursik & Grasmick (1993) argue that the definitional aspect of gangs (i.e., their variance across place and time) makes any conclusions about them unrepresentative and without prospect for generalizability. This leads the authors to conclude that although some contradictory evidence may exist in the literature, they do not "feel" that the bulk of contemporary research "presents convincing case for the existence of a unique crime-based subculture ... that can explain ... an ongoing criminal traditional within neighborhoods" (1993:139). As noted, Bursik & Grasmick (1993:146) also argued that the existence of stable, densely tied, high-crime areas does not contradict the systemic theory, but "with a consideration of the private, parochial, and the public orders of control, [systemic theory] can account for the processes described … in a logically consistent manner." They simply note that attenuation of parochial and public levels of control would make gang and gang related activity more "likely to arise" (1993:141).

*Theoretical complications and problematic assumptions*    Despite the cogency of Bursik & Grasmick's (1993) original arguments, other recent evidence suggests that residents in neighborhoods characterized by dense networks but high crime rates may be overtly *unwilling* to marshal the support and resources of the public realm. Work by Sampson & Bartusch (1998), and Kirk & Papachristos (2011) shows that the inability to turn to public sources, and the hostile stance the public level of control often takes toward inner-city residents, have led to ecological patterns of social cynicism that lead some residents to hold contempt for the wider scheme of things. These two studies do not operationalize cynicism consistently though they employ the same data. Both studies find a paradox whereby individuals may simultaneously believe in the substance of the law, while holding contempt toward and mistrust of the agents of the law. However, as opposed to a "temporary disenchantment" with the law that Carr *et al.* (2007) argue more accurately portrays cynicism, other work illustrates the presence of distinctly nonconventional culture. For example, Anderson (1999) argues that beyond factors such as structural adversity and a history of racial oppression, a prevailing climate of legal hostility sustains a code of honor, making residents reluctant to enlist the state to intervene in conflicts (see Cooney, 1998). Many come to perceive the criminal justice system as unfair, unresponsive, and discriminatory against minorities. As a result, residents are unlikely to invoke the police or courts to resolve interpersonal disputes, making violence a more probable mode of conflict management. Consistent with Anderson's assertions, other studies in this literature find that a deep distrust in agents of the criminal justice system contributes to the development of a retaliatory ethic in poor urban neighborhoods. A common belief among offenders is that regardless of the circumstances, any interaction with police is likely to invite undeserved legal trouble; therefore, many strive to "avoid the police whenever possible" (Rosenfeld, Jacobs, & Wright, 2003:298). As a response, a mode of aggressive "personal justice" receives strong social sanction, while conventional models of conflict resolution that invoke the legal system are far less salient. A recent study by Topalli (2005) demonstrates that "hardcore" offenders who inhabit poor urban landscapes are chastised and ostracized for cooperating with contacting legal authorities to report a transgression committed against them. Local cultural standards placed an intense emphasis on retaliation and personal justice. As a result, offenders felt compelled to employ neutralization techniques in order to justify instances in which they *failed* to uphold an image of toughness.

Additionally, Bursik & Grasmick (1993) may have been far too dismissive of nonconventional culture in their explanation of gangs (and the ecological stability of violence) via the public level of control. The authors expended most of their attention on gangs in parsing components of definitions rather than approaching the theoretical challenges underpinning the broader discussion. Bursik & Grasmick (1993) never directly address the potential that gangs transmit non-conventional culture through dense network ties because, as noted, their perspective allows that culture can only vary in degree, but not content. Thus, the authors invoke the public level of control as a deus ex machina to account for the presence of gangs and their potential relation to stable, high-crime neighborhoods. Both potential problems are explained away by the same vague invocation of a public level of control. Indeed, as noted above, Bursik & Grasmick (1993) do present compelling evidence of the complications to social organization that the public level of control can present; however, the amount of variance in behavior it can truly account for is questionable.

In addition to some of the older literature that the authors admittedly dismiss, more recent research presents evidence to contradict the notion that densely tied networks can only transmit conventional and pro-social conduct norms (Anderson, 1999; Browning, Feinberg, & Dietz, 2004). For example, Browning *et al.* (2004) argue based on the results of their analysis that although social networks may contribute to neighborhood collective efficacy (i.e., a perceived dimension of social control), they also may provide a source of social capital for offenders, which could diminish the impact of collective efficacy. The authors found that the regulatory effects of collective efficacy were substantially reduced in communities where high levels of network interaction and reciprocated exchange were present. Thus, the paradox of densely tied, high-crime neighborhoods may be explained by this negotiated coexistence model, leading Browning *et al.* (2004:527) to suggest that the "tendency to view social capital as unproblematically positive should be tempered in favor of a more realistic assessment."

*Integrating the code of the street*   Bursik (2002), acknowledging the possible shortcomings of systemic and pure control perspectives, notes that while Bursik & Grasmick (1993) made the assumption of cultural attenuation a priori, it is now clear that an alternative "code of the street" (Anderson, 1999) may be especially relevant to an explanation of densely tied, high-crime areas. Such research has shown that many of the systemic theory's assumptions are naïve or incomplete; Bursik & Grasmick (1993) failed to recognize that extensive ties could simultaneously tie individuals to law abiding citizens and gang members (Kobrin, 1951), and that such capital could be distinctly antisocial (Warner & Wilcox-Rountree, 1997; Anderson, 1999). Further analyses have also shown that conceptually, informal social control and networks are not interchangeable (Bellair & Browning, 2010). In light of such overwhelming evidence, Bursik (2002:80) concludes that there may be an "undeveloped appreciation for the complicated nature of network dynamics." Thus, the existence of stable, densely tied, high-crime areas may be explained by an active unwillingness to marshal public support, as opposed to simply being unable to, as traditional systemic theory and cultural attenuation perspectives would assume. Furthermore, this recognition reinvigorates cultural accounts of deviant behavior that specify some dimension or degree of nonconventional or antisocial capital as a causal variable.

# Cultural Processes and Deviant Behavior: Recent Developments

## Theoretical revival of cultural processes

*Social isolation and culture as adaptation*   For many years, the controversy surrounding cultural models dissuaded young scholars from making a strong effort to examine unlawful or deviant conduct through a cultural lens (see Small, Harding, & LaMont, 2010). Wilson's (1987) research on the implications of urban poverty reignited scholarly interest in cultural explanations of unconventional behavior, particularly within predominantly African-American neighborhoods. According to his thesis, large-scale processes of deindustrialization – a loss of manufacturing jobs, coupled with a decline in real wages among low-skilled workers – engendered an outmigration of middle-class residents and increased the proportion of impoverished families, all of which fueled an erosion of neighborhood social institutions. Wilson believed these transformations deprived residents of not only important institutional resources but also conventional role models engaged in legitimate adult behaviors. According to Wilson (1996), even though poor neighborhoods exhibit high levels of social integration, they are socially isolated from elements representative of mainstream society. Their social interactions are often "confined to those whose skills, styles, orientations and habits are not as conducive to promoting positive social outcomes" (Wilson, 1996:64). Wilson believed that such social isolation contributes to the formation of "ghetto-related" cultural models. While these models may prove useful in the local milieu, they are inadequate to the attainment of success in wider society.

Expanding on these ideas, Sampson & Wilson (1995) proposed that the concentration of socioeconomic deprivation, together with social isolation, fosters cultural istinctiveness and gives rise to "cognitive landscapes" or "ecologically structured norms" that are less apt to assign negative sanctions to violent and illegal conduct. Moreover, the sheer visibility of ghetto-related behaviors in public spaces, brought about by residents' collective inability to contain them, gives the appearance to residents that these behaviors are acceptable. Sampson & Wilson (1995) *suggest* that residents of poor communities often behave in ways consistent with ghetto-related norms for two reasons: as an adaptation to structural constraints, and because they are modeling conduct that is common in their neighborhood milieu – this conduct proves to be useful in local social interactions. Moreover, the authors imply that residents do not internalize or espouse ghetto-related norms, despite their behaviors (see Sampson & Bean, 2006:16). Hence, deviant or illicit behaviors are not genuinely reflective of their actual normative orientation towards nonconventional models. Combined, Wilson and Sampson & Wilson invoke culture to account for the disproportionate concentration of serious violence among residents of poor neighborhoods. Early theoretical models of culture and crime tended to exaggerate group-based differences in violent conduct norms by suggesting a strong and ubiquitous status–culture linkage, which seemed to invite sharp criticism. Sampson and Wilson's framework implicitly adopts a notion of cultural effects conceived as *practical devices* – rather than oppositional values – that coexist alongside mainstream models and emerge as an adaptation to socioeconomic exigencies. Stated differently, residents of impoverished urban environments engage in illicit conduct because it theoretically serves various symbolic (e.g., status) or material (i.e., financial) needs in their local milieu. Nowhere do these models explicitly assume that members of these communities often act in accordance to *internalized* oppositional norms. By Sampson and Wilson's account, most ghetto residents harbor mainstream beliefs; structural constraints cause a disjuncture between these beliefs and the nature of their actual behaviors. Neighborhood context is therefore granted a strong causal role in the genesis of illicit behavior.

*Mixed social milieus and the code of the street*    Explanations derived from urban sociology do not specify a *distinctive* oppositional culture as did earlier theoretical statements in which culture is an organizing principle (e.g., Cohen (1955)). By contrast, Anderson's work (1999) recasts discussions of cultural processes in a way that appears to assign a unique cultural orientation to some residents of poor urban neighborhoods. More specifically, Anderson (1999) describes the existence of a "street-code" embedded in the social fabric of an impoverished Philadelphia area. The street code he observes is a collection of informal rules that direct interpersonal public behavior, which provides a rationale "allowing those who are inclined to aggression to precipitate violent encounters in an approved way" (Anderson, 1999:33).

At the heart of the street code is an emphasis on respect. Residents of poor neighborhoods, particularly young males, develop a social identity that is consistent with the street culture in order to manage the demands of a social context maintained by violence. In fact, Anderson (1999:131) observed adolescents who precipitated altercations with the primary focus of building respect on the streets; some appeared to crave respect to the point they would endanger their physical wellbeing. Within this context, it is imperative for an individual not to yield to challengers because doing so conveys weakness, which ultimately enhances the probability of future victimization.

Anderson (1999:82) also describes how the urban landscape he observes is occupied by two coexisting groups of people: those who hold a "decent" orientation and those whose lives conform more closely to standards of the code – a group he refers to as "street." All residents have a strong incentive to be familiar with the behavioral imperatives of the street code, irrespective of whether they adhere more closely to the normative expectations of a conventional or oppositional orientation. Such knowledge is necessary for operating in public (Anderson, 1999:33). Those cognizant of the street code recognize how to properly comport themselves, how to circumvent serious confrontations without losing respect, and the appropriate strategies to manage interpersonal conflicts, including incidents in which they were victimized. Residents who are ignorant to the rules of the code may inadvertently act in a manner that jeopardizes their own safety.

As Matsueda and colleagues (2006:339) note, the honor culture is an institutional feature of street life and it produces a "strong incentive to acquire knowledge of its expectations." In this way, the street code represents an ecologically situated property that governs interpersonal action, independent of actors' own cultural inclinations. As more people in a neighborhood engage in ways that conform to the street culture, the level of violence escalates and the number of people who rely on violence for defensive purposes increases.

Overall, Anderson's perspective explicitly defines the existence of an oppositional culture that is derived from socioeconomic deprivation and that promotes violent behavior (e.g., Wolfgang & Ferracuti, 1967); moreover, his perspective implies that in the presence of an oppositional culture, certain residents (i.e., decent) will commit socially disapproved behaviors at odds with their own orientation for reasons which are functional in their social environment.

## Empirical evaluation of cultural processes

*Quantitative evaluation*   A small but growing body of research involving survey-based indicators of oppositional conduct norms has examined propositions from contemporary cultural frameworks about the multilevel consequences of oppositional norms for violent behavior. These investigations focus on recent formulations; however, they also speak to the validity of earlier theoretical frameworks. Stewart & Simons (2006) found that neighborhoods with high levels of structural disadvantage and violence led adolescents to adopt a street code orientation, where they believed that the use of interpersonal violence is justified to gain respect. Additionally, adoption of street code beliefs was predictive of violence, even after controlling for neighborhood disadvantage and experiences with racial discrimination. With the same data as before, Stewart, Schreck, & Simons (2006) observed that adolescents who lived in violent neighborhoods and embraced street code values were at heightened risk of being victimized.

A small number of multilevel studies have examined the role of cultural context in shaping violence, net of individual-level measures of cultural processes. Insofar as an oppositional culture is a socially embedded property, it should exert an effect on behavior apart from an actor's own orientation. A number of these studies focus on school culture, which is important because these environments represent one of the staging areas (besides the neighborhood) in which alternative cultural models are manifested and socially transmitted. However, the results of these studies are mixed with regard to contextualized school culture and violent beliefs as predictors of violence. For example, Ousey & Wilcox (2005) found that individual-level violence values were predictive of violence while school culture of violence was not. By contrast, Felson *et al.* (1994) found a school-level cultural climate favoring violence, as well as similar individual-level attitudes, were predictive of violent offending (and property offending) among high school males.

More recently, Stewart & Simons (2010) discovered that a neighborhood-level indicator of the street-code predicted violent conduct among urban males, apart from an individual-level measure of the street-code. Their findings thus suggest that the extent to which espousal of the street code is related to violence is not simply a product of individual cultural beliefs.

Other quantitative work relies on a measure of neighborhood socioeconomic conditions as a proxy for neighborhood-level oppositional culture. Generally, this research conforms to theoretical predictions about the way culture operates to affect violent behavior (see Simcha-Fagan & Schwartz, 1986). For example, Baumer and colleagues (2003) discovered that victims of violence were more apt to resist an attacker in highly disadvantaged neighborhoods, which supports Anderson's as well as Wolfgang and Ferracuti's prediction about the importance of defending one's reputation within an honor culture. Kubrin & Weitzer (2003:178) found that "cultural retaliatory homicides" in St. Louis were concentrated in impoverished neighborhoods where, far from being isolated events, they were "collectively tolerated, endorsed and rewarded by other residents." More recently, Berg & Loeber's (2011) analysis showed that the oft-cited positive effect of violent offending on violent victimization was magnified in the most disadvantaged Pittsburgh neighborhoods, whereas it was nonexistent in more affluent environments. Because other social processes are also correlated with neighborhood socioeconomic conditions, the possibility exists that the foregoing research is not sufficiently capturing the consequences of cultural mechanisms using measures that tap aspects of structural disadvantage. But as Sampson & Bean (2006:32–33) remark, unconventional conduct norms appear to "find continued expression in concentrated disadvantage."

*Qualitative evaluation*    Key empirical insights about the way culture operates to influence criminal behavior, especially serious crime, are found in recent qualitative studies. Much of this research subsumes non-conventional or oppositional norms and street code under the broad concept of "street culture." For example, and as noted above, studies have found that deep distrust in agents of the criminal justice system may result in a disenchanted and retaliatory ethic in poor urban neighborhoods (Anderson, 1999; Rosenfeld *et al.*, 2003). Moreover, such studies reveal that among very serious offenders, cooperation with legal authorities is grounds for being ostracized if not worse (Topalli, 2005). We should add that contemporary studies that find that oppositional conduct norms are socially enforced reach conclusions similar to those from earlier criminological studies on cultural effects. Shaw & McKay (1971:275) found, for example, that the "delinquent group seeks... to regulate the behavior of its members... [and] inflicts punishment upon those who violate its rules." In fact, there are clear parallels between the findings of early ethnographies and those of present day, with the main exception that current studies often focus on the cultural context of violence using samples of serious offenders.

## State of current research and alternative perspectives

*Issues in recent cultural theorizing*   Overall, there is a theoretically informed body of evidence that provides good reasons to believe that involvement in deviant behavior such as serious crime is partially a function of oppositional cultural processes, and these processes are often concentrated and transmitted within resource-deprived environments. Not only are these findings useful to evaluating the merits of a culture-based theoretical perspective, but they also have the potential to redefine assumptions from alternative theoretical models. As noted above, urban ethnographies and other statistical analyses describe a social landscape that is at odds with systemic and other cultural-attenuation perspectives. As we see it, an adequate theory of community effects must move beyond a pure control model and accommodate a broader understanding of cultural dynamics if the goal is to accurately predict individual variation in criminal behavior.

Still, important nuances in research on the cultural context of crime must be reconciled in order to develop a complete understanding of how culture actually influences serious offending. First, if values propel actors to criminal behavior, then we should not expect actors who espouse criminal values to frequently depart from their beliefs, nor should we observe people who harbor conventional values to frequently engage in serious offenses. But research contains myriad examples of these circumstances (e.g., Edin & Kefalas, 2005; Valentine, 1978). Therefore, cultural frameworks that specify a values–behavior linkage are perhaps too deterministic or without agency and may *overpredict* the amount of offending that should theoretically occur. Insofar as people commonly behave in a manner inconsistent with the values they articulate, particularly with regard to the appropriateness of law violation, this perspective deserves logical clarification. In fact, analysts have criticized assumptions of cultural frameworks more broadly, for suggesting that individuals are oversocialized into a social system, and enact cultural rules "unproblematically" (DiMaggio, 1997:265; see also Wrong, 1961).

Second, following Wilson's (1996) work, when culture *is* invoked by researchers to explain the impact of neighborhood disadvantage on delinquency, "emphasis is often placed on the isolation of residents from mainstream social networks and mainstream culture" (Harding, 2007:342). As Small & Newman (2001:35–38) note, in the wake of the social isolation thesis, the culture of poor neighborhoods is often conceptualized as oppositional, internally homogenous, and devoid of conventional elements (e.g., Peterson & Harrell, 1992; Massey & Denton, 1993; Tigges, Browne, & Green, 1998). Yet, critics contend that the assumptions that have evolved from the social isolation thesis do not coincide with the nuanced nature of cultural effects described in some urban ethnographic work. By these accounts, poor neighborhoods manifest a variety of competing cultural orientations, some of which are conventional and some of which are illicit (see Patillo-McCoy, 1999; Rainwater, 1970; Young, 2004). Not all residents – or even a majority of them – sell drugs or routinely engage in violence (Small, 2004:7–11). In fact, Hannerz (1969:12) made the case that the cultural fabric of poor communities is not monolithic and distinct; he finds these environments to "consist of a web of intertwining but different individual and group lifestyles." He introduces the concept of "cultural repertoire" to describe the litany of competing orientations and meanings selectively adopted by individuals in poor neighborhoods (1969:186). These repertoires allegedly enable individuals to negotiate the contradictions between the culture of wider society and their own structural location. In short, there is a shortage of valid evidence to suggest that cultural isolation is an accurate description of the cultural context of poor neighborhoods.

*Moving forward: the "toolkit" perspective*   Perspectives from sociology and cultural anthropology may offer a solution to the foregoing two issues that challenge the logic of cultural explanations. Based partially on Hannerz's insights, sociologists have recently developed a cognitive perspective of neighborhood culture where it is defined as fragmented and composed of skills or habits (DiMaggio, 1997:293; Small & Newman, 2001:34–36). For example, Swidler's (1986) theory of culture as a "toolkit" has steered intellectual attention away from the oft-cited notion that culture shapes human action by defining values. Her perspective posits, instead, that culture is more of a style or a set of skills than a collection of values that cause behavior to unfold in a particular pattern (Swidler, 1986:275). In theory, culture directs behavior by providing the kit from which actors select different tools to construct a "strategy of action." For example, young men may sell drugs instead of holding a legitimate job not because they disavow the cultural status equated with maintaining a job, but because the repertoire (i.e., skills, meanings) required for "playing that game" would necessitate fundamental cultural retooling (Swidler, 1986:277; see Quinn & Holland, 1987). In this way, the toolkit perspective assumes that people are "skilled users" of the heterogeneous or fragmented culture to which they are exposed. More importantly, it focuses on the sources of stability in a person's beliefs, including the implicit cues embedded in neighborhood context (DiMaggio, 1997).

Similarly, cultural *frames* are part of an individual's toolkit, serving as filters through which they understand the way the world works (Goffman, 1974). Benford & Snow (2000) posit that frames "simplify and condense the 'world out there' by selectively punctuating or encoding" various aspects within one's present and past environment. Frames do not cause behavior, as much as make it more likely to occur (Lamont, 1999; Lamont & Small, 2008:81). Moreover, they structure how we interpret events and react to them. Frames thus define expectations about the *practical* consequences of various behaviors, and influence one's decision-making irrespective of their own normative orientations. For example, a person may strongly believe that violent retaliation is not appropriate, but do so anyway because it protects them from falling victim to future exploitation in their neighborhood. Such radical departures from one's values are more readily understood under a cognitive framework of culture.

*Moving forward: the "habitus" and the dual-process model of culture*   However, research has also shown that a holistic interpretation of culture must account for culture being operative at multiple levels of consciousness (Vaisey, 2009). Thus, in contrast to the more agentically based toolkit perspective of culture, a more habitual, and structuring interpretation of culture can be found in the notion of the habitus (Bourdieu, 1990). These are not conflicting theories of culture, but complementary parts of a more comprehensive theory of action and behavior. Bourdieu (1990:52, 55) describes the habitus as a "structuring structure," the product of history and past experiences organized as a set of dispositions that makes possible "the production of all the thoughts, perceptions, and actions." The habitus acts as a system of cognitive and motivating structures in a "world of already realized ends"; action is perceived as "spontaneity without consciousness or will" (1990:53, 56). This allows for an explanation of patterned action that does not presuppose conscious aiming or a teleological nature. The habitus framework helps to avoid the scholastic fallacy, which refers to the overly agentic view of action whereby individuals are attributed a higher degree of cognition and consciousness than actually occurs (e.g., traditional rational choice models) (Desmond, 2006).

Thus, the most comprehensive conceptualization of culture is one that recognizes it in the context of a dual-process model. Swidler's (1986) toolkit perspective helps to avoid the problems of determinism that stem from structuralist perspectives, while Bourdieu's (1990) habitus helps to avoid characterizing individuals as having the logic of the logician. Vaisey (2009) offers a particularly illustrative metaphor of the dual-process model of culture as an individual riding an elephant. At one level, the individual consciously tries to guide the elephant, steering it toward a particular direction (i.e., the "toolkit" perspective of culture). However, at the other level, the elephant is much more powerful than the individual trying to guide it, and so inevitably one's best attempt to direct it will always be limited; sometimes the elephant will take the individual in a certain direction without their recognition or consent (i.e., the more habitual, or habitus-driven perspective of culture). Critics of this perspective may complain that an empirically testable analog to this complex conception of culture is not readily achievable. However, sacrificing validity for the sake of parsimony is a price research in this area can no longer afford; the amount of time it took to reconcile structural and subcultural explanations of behavior as potentially complementary should stand as evidence toward this point.

Taken together, cognitive perspectives of culture presuppose that norms, preferences, and standards are invoked both habitually and strategically, instead of following in a deterministic, lock-step fashion. Cognitive perspectives are more theoretically sensitive than traditional interpretations of cultural effects, which imply a tight cause and effect relationship between values and behavior (e.g., Cohen, 1955; Miller, 1958). More importantly, these viewpoints are distinct from the conception of culture in poor neighborhoods as a configuration of coherent oppositional values. To be sure, there are elements of a cognitive perspective in Wilson's (1996) description of *how* culture is used and why oppositional behavior is *enacted*. However, his research relies on the notion of "social isolation" as a basic premise to define the content of culture in poor neighborhoods.

*Cultural heterogeneity and culture as cognition*   More recently, Harding (2010) modifies current thinking about culture, neighborhood effects, and unconventional behaviors in several ways: First, he interprets the implications of cultural heterogeneity for adolescent behavior using the notions of culture as a toolkit and frame and, second, he develops his assumptions from Shaw & McKay's (1969) theoretical formulation. According to Harding (2010), adolescents in disadvantaged neighborhoods are exposed to a diversity of contradictory cultural models, meaning that their cultural repertoire is constructed from a broader range of frames from which they can select styles of behavior. It is more probable that youths from these neighborhoods will come into contact with a wider array of lifestyles. Within such contexts, illicit models of behavior will be encountered frequently, increasing the likelihood they will be "transmitted by precept" (Hannerz, 1969).

Because neither conventional nor illicit orientations dominate the social landscape of disadvantaged neighborhoods, youths theoretically have a wider range of legitimate, socially supported alternatives from which to *choose* when deciding upon an appropriate course of action (e.g., whether or not to engage in violent retaliation). According to Harding, adolescents who are reared in these settings can readily observe examples of people who have achieved status and local success through conflicting means. Consequently, the drawbacks versus advantages of engaging in a particular behavior versus another may be poorly defined, providing a weaker signal about which option is the best course of action. On occasions when a particular option "doesn't seem to be working out it is easier to shift course because another option is available – with local approval" (Harding, 2007:349). As a result, youths are able to find sufficient normative justification to make an unobstructed transition from involvement in conventional behaviors to unconventional alternatives when conventional behavior becomes personally unfulfilling, ineffective, or encumbered by obstacles.

Similar to Shaw & McKay (1969), Harding (2010) assumes that neighborhoods marked by cultural heterogeneity supply a wider range of normatively reinforced options regarding conventional and illicit courses of action. However, by integrating a cognitive conception of culture into neighborhood-effects research, he extends this line of thinking beyond the problematic value–behavior formulation, and thus clarifies the cultural mechanisms underlying the effects of neighborhood conditions on adolescent behavior.

Empirical research in criminology is only beginning to examine the validity of cognitive-based theories of cultural effects. Berg and colleagues (2012) recently discovered in a multilevel study of urban youths that neighborhood disadvantage increased collective disagreement regarding the inappropriateness of pro-social conduct norms (i.e., cultural heterogeneity). The authors found that youths exposed to such a cultural milieu had a higher probability of committing violence. Furthermore, those who held a pro-social orientation were less likely to behave in ways consistent with that orientation if they resided in culturally heterogeneous neighborhoods. Combined, the findings of Berg and colleagues thus suggest that cultural heterogeneity is tied to structural conditions and has negative consequences for youth behaviors.

# Conclusion

## Early perspectives

Cultural processes and their subsequent consequences on human behavior have been a concern of social scientists for well over a century. Classical scholars such as Durkheim, Simmel, and Weber were all in one way or the other interested in the fundamental changes in culture and human interaction that were brought about by the industrial revolution and increasing urbanization. The lasting impression of these scholars can clearly been seen in work that emerged from the Chicago School in the first half of the 20th century. Influential figures such as W.I. Thomas, Frederic Thrasher, Robert Park, and Ernest W. Burgess largely set the stage for what was to become burgeoning fields of criminology and urban sociology. These scholars, continuing in the footsteps of those before them, were primarily interested with understanding the social dynamics that governed city life, and the potential breakdown of the social and moral fabrics of society under such conditions.

Some of the most influential work to emerge out of the Chicago School is that of Shaw and McKay, which articulated an argument for the role of culture in a neighborhood context. Shaw and McKay argued that culture was transmitted through face-to-face interaction, and handed down to subsequent generations in the community. Moreover, they noted that the social milieu of most youths in inner-city areas is a mix of delinquents and nondelinquents, and that even in the most disorganized areas the dominant tradition is still conventional. As noted above, these two latter points would continue to prove their importance to theorizing well after their creation.

In addition to work by Shaw & McKay, other important scholars such as Robert Merton and those who followed in the anomie and strain traditions also posited accounts for human behavior that had a distinctly cultural element. At the macro level, Merton (1938) outlined the culture structure as part of his system level theory of anomie. Other scholars, such as Cohen (1955) and Miller (1958), invoked the notion of distinct subcultures in order to account for the existence of gangs and the subsequent consequence of deviant behavior and criminal offending. As noted, because of criticisms in the literature and misinterpretations by researchers, anomie and strain perspectives were largely discounted and ignored for some time. Although experiencing a slight resurgence, because they have been vaguely articulated such perspectives rarely grace the literature, although they might provide fruitful avenues for future research.

## Theoretical dissolution and reemergence of cultural explanations

Despite the appeal cultural explanations played in the first half of the 20th century, by the middle of the second half they had come under intense criticism, and were largely discarded. The damaging critiques of scholars such as Ruth Kornhauser (1978) relegated the role of culture to a process of attenuation. In this view, culture could only vary by degree, but not by content. Thus, any notion that individuals could truly transmit or abide by nonconventional values and culture was discarded. Such views were largely popularized by more contemporary scholars such as Bursik & Grasmick (1993), who articulated a vague version of the cultural attenuation perspective within the framework of systemic theory. Despite its appeal, and despite some validation by empirical evidence, ethnographic data continued to display evidence that was contradictory to the assumptions noted above. Eventually, even Bursik (2002) himself admitted that he and fellow researchers might have under appreciated the dynamic role that social ties may have in facilitating a "code of the street."

After a period of neglect by researchers and overshadowing by alternative theoretical frameworks, cultural explanations are again reentering theoretical discussions about the etiology of socially disapproved behaviors. The contributions of Anderson (1999) and Wilson (1987, 1996) set in motion current efforts to understand the interplay between neighborhood socioeconomic conditions, race, cultural organization, and patterns of socially disproved behavior, including violence and illicit marketplace activities. Unlike many earlier perspectives, culture is often viewed as a concept inherently entangled with structural properties of places, drawing attention to both aspects simultaneously instead of isolating one from the other. When contemporary scholars invoke culture to explain urban violence, discussions have often focused on the behavioral consequences of "social isolation" (Wilson, 1996); however, alternative formulations derived from a cognitive interpretation of culture challenge the logic of this perspective. Complementary concepts such as Goffman's (1974) "frameworks," Swidler's (1986) "toolkit," and Bourdieu's (1990) "habitus" allow for a more comprehensive, yet less deterministic view of culture that avoids an overly agentic or structural interpretation of individuals and action.

If there is one distinct takeaway point that our review of the literature should emphasize, it is that explanations of deviant behavior and crime that intend to sufficiently account for variation in human action might necessarily be complex. If the cost of parsimony is an obscuration of empirical reality, then the benefits are simply not worth it. Although many authors have overcome this reification by integrating elements of cultural deviance and control models (Berg *et al.*, 2012; Harding, 2010), others insist that crime must be the result of either a pure control model (underpinned by cultural attenuation assumptions) model or a subcultural deviance model. Based on past evidence, researchers should be more than willing to assume that some communities exhibit what has been characterized as cultural attenuation (Suttles, 1968), while others exhibit what has been characterized as the "code of the streets" (Anderson, 1999). Indeed, some explanations may be better suited for some situations than for others, and this should not mean that such theories are unsound or should be disused if they fail to explain everything. Culture is a complex concept, and we caution against any interpretation that posits a totalizing explanation.

# References

Agnew, R., & Passas, N. (1997). *The Future of Anomie Theory*. Boston, MA: Northeastern University Press.

Anderson, E. (1999). *Code of the Street: Decency, Violence and the Moral Life of the Inner City*. New York: W.W. Norton.

Baumer, E.P., Horney, J., Felson, R.B., & Lauritsen, J.L. (2003). Neighborhood disadvantage and the nature of violence. *Criminology, 41*, 39–72.

Bellair, P., & Browning, C. (2010). Contemporary disorganization research: An assessment and further test of the systemic model of neighborhood crime. *Journal of Research in Crime and Delinquency, 47*, 496–521.

Benford, R.D., & Snow, D.A. (2000). Framing processes and social movements: An overview and assessment. *Annual Review of Sociology, 26*, 611–639.

Berg, M.T., & Loeber, R. (2011). Examining the neighborhood context of the violent-offending–victimization relationship: A prospective investigation. *Journal of Quantitative Criminology, 27*, 427–451.

Berg, M.T., Stewart, E.A., Brunson, R.K., & Simons, R.L. (2012). Neighborhood cultural heterogeneity and adolescent violence. *Journal of Quantitative Criminology, 28*, 411–435.

Bernard, T.J. (1987). Testing structural strain theories. *Journal of Research in Crime and Delinquency, 24*, 262–280.

Bourdieu, P. (1990). *The Logic of Practice*. Stanford, CA: Stanford University Press.

Browning, C.R., Feinberg, S.L., & Dietz, R.D. (2004). The paradox of social organization: Networks, collective efficacy, and violent crime in urban neighborhoods. *Social Forces, 83*, 503–534.

Bursik, R.J. (2002). The systemic model of gang behavior: A reconsideration. In C.R. Huff (Ed.), *Gangs in America*, 3rd edition. Thousand Oaks, CA: Sage.

Bursik, R.J., & Grasmick, H.G. (1993). *Neighborhoods and Crime*. New York: Lexington.

Bursik, R.J., & Webb, V. (1982). Community change and patterns of delinquency. *American Journal of Sociology, 88*, 24–42.

Carr, P.J., Napolitano, L., & Keating, J. (2007). We never call the cops and here is why: a qualitative examination of legal cynicism in three Philadelphia neighborhoods. *Criminology, 45*, 445–480.

Cloward, R.A., & Ohlin, L.E. (1960). *Delinquency and Opportunity Structure: A Theory of Delinquent Gangs*. New York: Free Press.

Cohen, A.K. (1955). *Delinquent Boys: The Culture of the Gang*. New York: Free Press.

Cooney, M. (1998). *Warriors and Peacemakers: How Third Parties Shape Violence*. New York: New York University Press.

Desmond, M. (2006). Becoming a firefighter. *Ethnography, 7*, 387–421.

DiMaggio, P.J. (1997). Culture and cognition. *Annual Review of Sociology, 23*, 263–287.

Durkheim, E. (1984 [1893]). *The Division of Labor in Society*. New York: Free Press.

Durkheim, E. (1995 [1912]). *The Elementary Forms of Religious Life*. New York: Free Press.

Edin, K., & Kefalas, M. (2005). *Promises I Can Keep: Why Poor Women Put Motherhood Ahead Of Marriage*. Berkeley, CA: University of California Press.

Felson, R.B., Liska, A.E., South, S.J., & McNulty, T.L. (1994). The subculture of violence and delinquency: individual vs. school context effects. *Social Forces, 73*, 155–173.

Goffman, E. (1974). *Frame Analysis: An Essay on the Organization of Experience*. Cambridge, MA: Harvard University Press.

Hannerz, U. (1969). *Soulside: Inquiries into Ghetto Culture and Community.* New York: Columbia University Press.

Harding, D.J. (2007). Cultural context, sexual behavior, and romantic relationships in disadvantaged neighborhoods. *American Sociological Review, 72,* 341–364.

Harding, D. (2010). *Living the Drama: Community, Conflict, and Culture among Inner-City Boys.* Cambridge, MA: Harvard University Press.

Hindelang, M.J. (1974). Moral evaluations of illegal behaviors. *Social Problems, 21,* 370–385.

Hunter, A.J. (1985). Private, parochial, and public school orders: The problem of crime and incivility in urban communities. In G.D. Suttles & M.N. Zald (Eds.), *The Challenge of Social Control: Citizenship and Institution Building in Modern Society* (pp. 230–242). Norwood, NJ: Ablex.

Kirk, D.S., & Papachristos, A.V. (2011). Cultural mechanisms and the persistence of neighborhood violence. *American Journal of Sociology, 116,* 190–233.

Kobrin, S. (1951). The conflict of values in delinquency areas. *American Sociological Review, 16,* 653–661.

Kobrin, S. (1971). The formal logical properties of Shaw and McKay's delinquency theory. In H.L. Voss & D.M. Peterson (Eds.), *Ecology, Crime, and Delinquency.* New York: Applebury-Century-Croft.

Kornhauser, R.R. (1978). *The Social Sources of Delinquency: An Appraisal of Analytical Methods.* Chicago, IL: University of Chicago Press.

Kubrin, C.E., & Weitzer, R. (2003). Retaliatory homicide: Concentrated disadvantage and neighborhood culture. *Social Problems, 50,* 157–180.

Lamont, M. (1999). *The Cultural Territories of Race: Black and White Boundaries.* Chicago, IL: University of Chicago Press.

Lamont, M., & Small, M.L. (2008). How culture matters: Enriching our understanding of poverty. In A.C. Lin & D.R. Harris (Eds.), *The Colors of Poverty: Why Racial and Ethnic Disparities Persist.* New York: Russell Sage.

Massey, D.S., & Denton, N.A. (1993). *American Apartheid: Segregation and the Making of the Underclass.* Cambridge, MA: Harvard University Press.

Matsueda, R.L. (1988). The current state of differential association theory. *Crime and Delinquency, 34,* 277–306.

Matsueda, R.L. (2007). On the compatibility of social disorganization and self-control. In E. Goode (Ed.), *Out of Control: Assessing the General Theory of Crime.* Stanford, CA: Stanford California Press.

Matsueda, R.L., Drakulich, K., & Kubrin, C.E. (2006). Race and neighborhood codes of the street. In R.D. Peterson, L.J. Krivo, & J. Hagan (Eds.), *The Many Colors of Crime: Inequalities of Race, Ethnicity and Crime in America.* New York: New York University Press.

Matza, D. (1964). *Delinquency and Drift.* New York: Wiley.

Merton, R. (1938). Social structure and anomie. *American Sociological Review, 3,* 672–682.

Messner, S.F. (1988). Merton's "Social Structure and Anomie": The road not taken. *Deviant Behavior, 9*(1), 33–53.

Messner, S.F., & Rosenfeld, R. (1997). *Crime and the American Dream,* 2nd edition. Belmont, CA: Wadsworth.

Miller, W.B. (1958). Lower-class culture as a generating milieu of gang delinquency. *Journal of Social Issues, 14,* 5–19.

Ousey, G.C., & Wilcox, P. (2005). Subcultural values and violent delinquency: A multilevel analysis in middle schools. *Youth Violence and Juvenile Justice, 3,* 1–20.

Park, R.E. (1925). Community organization and juvenile delinquency. In R.E. Park, E.W. Burgess, & R.D. McKenzie (Eds.), *The City: Suggestions for Investigation of Human Behavior in the Urban Environment.* Chicago, IL: University of Chicago Press.

Patillo-McCoy, M. (1999). *Black Picket Fences: Privilege and Peril Among the Black Middle Class.* Chicago: University of Chicago Press.

Peterson, G.E., & Harrell, A.V. (1992). Introduction: Inner-city isolation and opportunity. In A.V. Harrell & G.E. Peterson (Eds.), *Drugs, Crime, and Social Isolation: Barriers to Urban Opportunity.* New York: Urban Institute.

Quinn, N., & Holland, D. (1987). Culture and cognition. In D. Holland & N. Quinn (Eds.), *Cultural Models in Language and Thought.* Cambridge: Cambridge University Press.

Rainwater, L. (1970). *Behind Ghetto Walls: Black Families in a Federal Slum.* Chicago, IL: Aldine Transaction.

Rosenfeld, R. (1989). Robert Merton's contributions to the sociology of deviance. *Sociological Inquiry, 59,* 453–466.

Rosenfeld, R., Jacobs, B.A., & Wright, R. (2003). Snitching and the code of the street. *British Journal of Criminology, 43,* 291–309.

Sampson, R.J. (2012). *Great American City.* Chicago, IL: University of Chicago Press.

Sampson, R., & Bartusch, D. (1998). Legal cynicism and (subcultural?) tolerance of deviance: The neighborhood context of racial differences. *Law and Society Review, 32,* 777–804.

Sampson, R.J., & Bean, L. (2006). Cultural mechanisms and killing fields: A revised theory of community-level racial inequality. In R.D. Peterson, L.J. Krivo, & J. Hagan (Eds.), *The Many Colors of Crime: Inequalities of Race, Ethnicity, and Crime in America.* New York: New York University Press.

Sampson, R.J., & Wilson, W.J. (1995). Toward a theory of race, crime and urban inequality. In J. Hagan & R.D. Peterson (Eds.), *Crime and Inequality.* Palo Alto, CA: Stanford University Press.

Shaw, C.R., & McKay, H.D. (1942). *Juvenile Delinquency and Urban Areas.* Chicago, IL: University of Chicago Press.

Shaw, C.R., & McKay, H.D. (1969). *Juvenile Delinquency and Urban Areas,* revised edition. Chicago, IL: University of Chicago Press.

Shaw, C.R., & McKay, H.D. (1971). Male juvenile delinquency as group behavior. In J.F. Short Jr. (Ed.), *The Social Fabric of the Metropolis: Contributions of the Chicago School of Urban Sociology.* Chicago, IL: University of Chicago Press.

Shaw, C.R., McKay, H.D., & MacDonald, J.F. (1938). *Brothers in Crime.* Chicago, IL: University of Chicago Press.

Short, J.F., Jr. (1971). Introduction. In J.F. Short Jr. (Ed.), *The Social Fabric of the Metropolis: Contributions of the Chicago School of Urban Sociology.* Chicago, IL: University of Chicago Press.

Simcha-Fagan, O., & Schwartz, J.E. (1986). Neighborhood and delinquency: An assessment of contextual effects. *Criminology, 24,* 667–699.

Simmel, G. (1971). *On Individuality and Social Forms.* Chicago, IL: University of Chicago Press.

Small, M.L. (2004). *Villa Victoria: The Transformation of Social Capital in a Boston Barrio.* Chicago, IL: University of Chicago Press.

Small, M.L., Harding, D., & Lamont, M. (2010). Reconsidering culture and poverty. *Annals of the American Academy of Political and Social Sciences, 629,* 6–27.

Small, M.L., & Newman, K. (2001). Urban poverty after the truly disadvantaged: The rediscovery of the family, neighborhood and culture. *Annual Review of Sociology, 27,* 23–45.

Stewart, E.A., Schreck, C.J., & Simons, R.L. (2006). "I ain't gonna let no one disrespect me": Does the code of the street reduce or increase violent victimization among African-American adolescents. *Journal of Research in Crime and Delinquency*, 43, 427–458.

Stewart, E.A., & Simons, R.L. (2006). Structure and culture in African-American adolescent violence. A partial test of the code of the street thesis. *Justice Quarterly*, 23, 1–33.

Stewart, E.A., & Simons, R.L. (2010). Race, code of the street and violent delinquency. A multilevel investigation of neighborhood street culture and individual norms of violence. *Criminology*, 48, 569–605.

Sutherland, E.H. (1947). *Criminology*, 4th edition. Philadelphia, PA: Lippincott.

Suttles, G.D. (1968). *The Social Order of the Slum: Ethnicity and Territory in the Inner City*. Chicago, IL: University of Chicago Press.

Swidler, A. (1986). Culture in action: Symbols and strategies. *American Sociological Review*, 51, 273–286.

Sykes, G.M., & Matza, D. (1957). Techniques of neutralization: A theory of delinquency. *American Sociological Review*, 22, 664–670.

Thomas, W.I., & Znaniecki, F. (1920[1996]). *The Polish Peasant in Europe and America: A Classic Work in Immigration History*. Champaign, IL: University of Illinois Press.

Thrasher, F.M. (1927). *The Gang*. Chicago, IL: University of Chicago Press.

Tigges, L.M., Browne, I., & Green, G.P. (1998). Social isolation of the urban poor: Race, class, and neighborhood effects on social resources. *Sociological Quarterly*, 39, 53–77.

Topalli, V. (2005). When being good is bad: An expansion of neutralization theory. *Criminology*, 43, 797–836.

Vaisey, S. (2009). Motivation and justification: A dual-process model of culture in action. *American Journal of Sociology*, 114, 1675–1715.

Valentine, B. (1978). *Hustling and Other Hard Work: Lifestyles in the Ghetto*. New York: Free Press.

Warner, B.D. (2003). The role of attenuated culture in social disorganization theory. *Criminology*, 41, 73–99.

Warner, B.D., & Wilcox-Rountree, P. (1997). Local ties in a community and crime model: Questioning the systemic nature of informal social control. *Social Problems*, 44, 523–539.

Weber, M. (1922 [1978]). *Economy and Society: An Outline of Interpretive Sociology*. Berkeley, CA: University of California Press.

Weber, M. (1930). *The Protestant Ethic and the Spirit of Capitalism*. New York: Routledge.

Whyte, W.F. (1943). *Street Corner Society: The Social Structure of an Italian Slum*, 4th edition. Chicago, IL: University of Chicago Press.

Wilson, W.J. (1987). *The Truly Disadvantaged: The Inner-City, and the Underclass, and Public Policy*. Chicago, IL: University of Chicago Press.

Wilson, W.J. (1991). Studying inner-city social dislocations: The challenge of public agenda research. *American Sociological Review*, 56, 1–15.

Wilson, W.J. (1996). *When Work Disappears: The World of the New Urban Poor*. New York: Knopf.

Wirth, L. (1938). Urbanism as a way of life. *American Journal of Sociology*, 44, 1–24.

Wolfgang, M.E. (1958). *Patterns in Criminal Homicide*. Philadelphia, PA: University of Pennsylvania Press.

Wolfgang, M.E., & Ferracuti, F. (1967). *The Subculture of Violence*. London: Tavistock.

Wrong, D.H. (1961). The oversocialized conception of man in modern sociology. *American Sociological Review*, 26, 183–193.

Young, A.A., Jr. (2004). *The Minds of Marginalized Black Men: Making Sense of Mobility, Opportunity and Life Chances*. Princeton, NJ: Princeton University Press.

# 14

# Labeling Theory: Past, Present, and Future

## Ruth Triplett and Lindsey Upton

## Introduction

In the 1960s, labeling, whether called theory, perspective, or sensitizing framework, turned the attention of criminologists to the importance of social reactions to behavior, both their effects and their causes. Drawing strongly on symbolic interactionism (see Matza, 1969; Schur, 1971), theorists working in this area asked criminologists to think of deviance and deviants as social constructions that result from a process of interaction. This way of thinking led to the development of two related but separate areas of theory and analysis. The first area explored the importance of social reactions in shaping the behavior of those who are reacted to, or labeled, as deviant. Along with this focus came an emphasis on analytic methods that called for the discovery of meaning through exploration and inspection using qualitative methods (Blumer, 1969). The second area, though not the focus here, addressed questions regarding the development of definitions of behaviors as deviant or criminal, as well as the mechanisms through which formal social control agencies such as the police decide who to process as criminal, and thus label.

The ideas expressed in labeling rose to popularity in the 1960s, as counterpoints to the focus of anomie, social learning, and subcultural theories dominant at the time. Becker's edited volume, *The Other Side* (1964), filled with pieces that would become classics by scholars such as Erikson, Kitsuse, Lemert, Reiss, and Schur, and Becker's own book, *Outsiders* (1963), won the attention of the field. What followed was a period of influence that went beyond even academia to affect criminal justice policies across the US. Labeling's dominance was not long-lasting though. The decline in the second half of the 1970s and into the 1980s came as its ideas about the effects of social reactions were subjected to critique and empirical testing.

*The Handbook of Criminological Theory*, First Edition. Edited by Alex R. Piquero.
© 2016 John Wiley & Sons, Inc. Published 2016 by John Wiley & Sons, Inc.

In addition, reaction to the rebellion of the 1960s set the mood for theories with an individual focus.

The history of labeling theory is not over, however. Despite a decline in the attention criminologists would give it, works that expanded labeling in important ways continued throughout the 1980s and 1990s. Many of these works promoted the integration of labeling ideas with theories of the cause of individual offending, or strengthened its symbolic interactionist roots. In addition, since the turn of the century, the changing social context and various trends in current criminological theory and research suggest a door is opening for renewed attention to a theory that many, perhaps, thought or hoped was long dead.

## Emergence of Labeling

Labeling first rose to the attention of criminologists in the 1960s, a decade of questioning and radical differences in visions for the future of the country. John F. Kennedy was assassinated in 1961, ending "Camelot," though Lyndon Johnson would continue with the War on Poverty. The Civil Rights Movement and Women's Rights Movement were calling attention to disparities by race and gender, and demanding change. For example, the civil rights movement's call for change led to passage of the landmark Civil Rights Act of 1964, which banned segregation in public places and employment discrimination on the basis of race, religion, and sex, as well as the Voting Rights Act of 1965, which outlawed discriminatory practices in voting. In 1965, however, Malcolm X was assassinated followed by Martin Luther King, Jr. in 1968. Protest extended to treatment of prisoners a well as the Vietnam War. In protest over overcrowding and living conditions, prisoners in Attica rioted in 1971. The riot led to the death and injury of 43 hostages and inmates. In addition, protests against the Vietnam War were building during the 1960s. One indication of the radically different stances in the country on the war was the Kent State shootings of students by National Guard officers in 1970. These events were indicative of a time of unrest and questioning. They set the mood for a new set of questions for the field of criminology.

Pfohl (1994, 2009) argues that it is not just the time period, however, that is important to understanding the emergence of labeling. He argues place is important as well, in particular the University of Chicago and the west coast. The University of Chicago was where many early labeling theorists were educated. There they learned about symbolic interactionism – the importance of meaning and its development from interaction with others – and associated methods for exploring meaning. A number of individuals trained at the university found jobs in California as the state university system expanded in the 1960s to provide educational opportunities for a growing state population. Pfohl (1994, 2009) argues that since public education was relatively affordable, the student population at the state universities was fairly diverse. That put the young criminologists from the elite University of Chicago in contact with students from a variety of different ethnic and class backgrounds, some of whom were active in the civil rights or feminist movements and antiwar protests. In addition, he argues, at the same time that the campuses were getting more liberal, politics in California was getting more conservative. Ronald Reagan became governor and, in conjunction with a conservative board of regents, worked to stem radicalism in California's universities. Their attempts to do so merely highlighted the need for a new perspective in criminology which included consideration of the role of social reactions in crime.

Though the 1960s saw labeling rise to popularity, three earlier works laid the groundwork for much that was to come. Perhaps, the earliest work identified with labeling is a 1918 article entitled "The Psychology of Punitive Justice" by George Herbert Mead. In this piece, Mead writes of the hostile attitude that is found in punitive justice. This attitude helps to draw the community together and to define boundaries regarding criminal behavior. At the same time, it makes offenders outcasts, creating consequences for their future behavior. Importantly, it is Mead (1934), and later Blumer (1969), whose work in symbolic interactionism creates a framework on which later labeling theorists would build.

The next scholar whose work is important to the development of labeling is Tannenbaum (1938). His focus is on the definition of the situation and the process through which labels are initiated, as well as their effect. Tannenbaum begins with the argument that people view youths who break the law as somehow different, or worse, than those who do not break the law. This view of juvenile delinquents as different affects, in turn, both the way society reacts to the youths that it defines as delinquent and the ways in which youths who are defined as delinquent will respond to society's reaction.

The process of defining a youth as delinquent, which he calls the "dramatization of evil," begins with a conflict between the youth and the community over how to define particular activities. He argues that what the youth might define as just a fun activity, members of the community define as bad. Examples of this can be found in the contemporary contradiction between the opinions of adults and juveniles on behaviors such as texting while driving, sexting, downloading music through sources other than iTunes and paid download managers, and accessing TV shows and movies online for free through various non-producer or non-network websites. Adults might view sexting as heinous, simply from its assumed construction of extreme sexual images and verbiage. A similar contradiction in opinion can be found in accessing TV shows, movies, and music for free. Many adults, and the law, favor upholding copyright laws and payment by consumers for the production of the work of the artist. However, youths are increasingly in a world where finding ways to access such media in free ways is possible, shared, and consumed. Many who violate these laws do not view their actions as evil, but rather a normal part of everyday youth life.

The process does not stop, however, with conflict over the definition of an act but moves on to a change in attitude about the youth. As the conflict persists, Tannenbaum argues that the community's attitude toward the youth hardens. Now it is not merely the act that is defined as bad, but the youth as well. Once community members define the youth as bad, changes begin in the way they interact with him or her. Parents begin to exclude the youth from activities with their children and the youth begins to feel isolated from others. These changes in the way people respond make the youth conscious of the fact that the community views him or her as bad. Over time the youth comes to define him- or herself as bad as well. It is this process of "defining, identifying, segregating, describing, emphasizing, making conscious and self-conscious" (1938:20) which Tannenbaum refers to as *tagging*. According to Tannenbaum the changes caused by the dramatization of evil and tagging lead the youth to further delinquent acts.

The most notable of the early works central to labeling is Edwin Lemert's *Social Pathology* published in 1951. The importance of this work for labeling starts with the distinction it makes between primary and secondary deviance. Primary deviance is the name given to the initial acts of deviance that an individual commits that are "rationalized or otherwise dealt with as functions of a socially acceptable role" (75). The reasons that an individual might commit an act of primary deviance include all of those covered by the major criminological theories focused on explaining individual criminal behavior. Strain, support of a peer group, or lack of social control are some of those reasons. Since acts of primary deviance are committed by almost everyone, are temporary, and are not very serious, Lemert did not focus on their causes. The second type of deviance, however, was his focus, and social reactions play a role in its development. Secondary deviance is deviance that occurs "when a person begins to employ his deviant behavior or a role based upon it as a means of defense, attack, or adjustment to the overt and covert problems created by the consequent societal reaction to him" (76). A good example of secondary deviance is that which occurs after an offender adopts a criminal identity as a result of the change in the way people react to him or her.

Beyond the distinction between primary and secondary deviance, the importance of Lemert's work comes from the emphasis he placed on the fact that that the movement from primary deviance to secondary deviance is the result of a process. For example, he outlined a sequence of interactions that begins with an act of primary deviance. This act causes a social reaction. Further acts of deviance may then occur, resulting in stronger reactions. If this cycle continues, an individual may embrace a deviant role, thus leading to secondary deviance. The emphasis on process and its contingent nature is central to understanding how social reactions affect behavior. Despite the importance that Lemert's ideas will take on in later years, they did not initially receive much attention. It is Becker's work that sparks the interest of the field (See Pfohl, 1994, 2009 and Gibbons, 1979).

A large part of Becker's (1963) contribution to labeling theory comes from his discussion of the development of deviant careers in *Outsiders*. In this book he outlines three phases to the development of a criminal or deviant career. The first phase is the initial act of rule-breaking which may or may not be intentional. Like Lemert, Becker's focus is not on the factors that lead to the initial act. The second phase of the deviant career begins when the rule breaker is caught and labeled deviant. The label has important consequences for how people will view the individual (an individual's public identity), how they will interact with the individual, and how the individual will see him or herself (self-identity). The label of "criminal" shapes how others interact with the offender because, according to Becker, this label is so stigmatizing in our society that it becomes a master status, overriding any other role or position an individual may hold. In short, a master status as "criminal" becomes the defining characteristic of individuals so labeled, regardless of any other characteristic they may have. The final phase in development of a criminal career comes when the labeled person moves into a deviant group. Becker argues that movement into a deviant group further affects the individual's social identity, social interaction and self-image. Movement into a deviant group also provides the individual with rationalizations, motives and attitudes that support deviant behavior.

Much of the focus of discussion of labeling is on the ideas of the importance of social reactions in shaping criminal careers, and that is the focus here. It is important to recognize, however, that another important part of Becker's work centers around two related questions. The first is how do some acts come to be defined as deviant or criminal? The second is how do some people come to be defined as deviant or criminal? Becker points to the development of moral crusades which involves two types of moral entrepreneurs: rule-creators and rule-enforcers. Rule-creators are those who feel that there is some evil in the world which necessitates the development of a rule to prevent it. Focused on the content of the rule, rule-creators campaign to win support for their view and the creation of a rule. Rule-enforcers are those who, though they may not be interested in the development of a new rule or its contents, are interested in enforcing the rule once it is made. They are also interested in justifying their work. Becker argues that since the content of the rules is not their focus, they may develop their own views of which rules are important to enforce and which offenders, among all of those who break the rules, are those they should focus on. It is this part of Becker's work that gives us the labeling perspective on the creation of rules and law as well as the idea of the differential enforcement of the law.

Becker's ideas helped turn the attention of many in criminology to labeling through the 1960s and into the 1970s. Wellford & Triplett (1993) argue that support for labeling theory came from those who valued the theory for turning attention to the way attempts at social control can lead to more crime. Support for the theory led to calls for radical changes in criminal justice and juvenile justice policy, including the deinstitutionalization of juvenile offenders, decriminalization of status offenses, and the diversion of juvenile offenders from the juvenile justice system.

Critics, however, registered a number of important concerns regarding labeling (see for example Ball, 1983; Wellford, 1975). Wellford & Triplett (1993) argue that three criticisms were key to the decline in interest in labeling that was soon to come. The first criticism was the idea that not everyone who is labeled goes on to commit more crimes. In fact, critics, drawing on work in deterrence, argued that punishment often reduces the likelihood that an offender will reoffend. Labeling, thus far, had paid little attention to this possibility. A second key criticism was that labeling theory ignores the response of the individual to the label. The idea that everyone responds in the same way, even to the same social reaction, ignored the importance of individual differences. Finally, some critics were also concerned about how society was to respond to crime if every response led to labels and more crime. These individuals found the call of some labeling theorists for a different approach to dealing with crime, especially radical non-intervention (see Schur, 1973) unsatisfactory. In addition, others (see Plummer, 1979) have argued that labeling drifted away from the symbolic interactionist ideas it was founded on, creating the misunderstanding of labels as being deterministic of behavior.

In addition to criticism of the theory, by the late 1970s the social context was changing; it became significantly different throughout the 1980s and 1990s. The War on Poverty had become the War on Drugs and the War on Crime. Rehabilitation as a framework for sentencing would give way to calls for punishment. The idea that the field of criminology did not know what caused crime and that the state could best spend its energies on punishment (see Wilson, 1975) led to calls for increases in sentencing and the development of sentencing guidelines. In this context, the number of people placed under some kind of supervision by the criminal justice system began to climb to what is now seen as mass incarceration. The social context was not supportive of a theory that may seem to place the blame for crime on those reacting to it.

## Interest Remains

Despite the decline in interest, ideas important to labeling are found in key works published throughout the 1980s and 1990s. These later works tempered the original statements by the labeling theorists of the 1960s, addressing some of the most important criticisms. Many of them integrated labeling ideas with other theories or drew from labeling's symbolic interactionist roots to develop a more complete theory of the self. These ideas are found in the works of Link and his colleagues on a modified labeling theory, Braithwaite's _Crime, Shame and Reintegration_ (1989), Sherman's defiance theory (1993), Heimer & Matsueda's differential social control (1994) and Sampson & Laub's life course theory of cumulative disadvantage (1997).

### Link (1983, 1987, 1989): modified labeling theory of mental illness

In a series of papers in the 1980s, Bruce Link and his colleagues (Link 1987; Link & Cullen, 1983; Link, Cullen, & Wozniak, 1987; Link, Struening, Shrout, & Dohrenwend, 1989) outlined and tested a modified labeling theory of mental illness. Their work provides some answer to the criticisms that not everyone who gets labeled goes on to continue their deviance and that there are differences in individual responses to labels. In addition, Link and his colleagues' work is important for the attention it focuses on the power of social conceptions and our socialization into them, as well as the emphasis on how employment and social networks, as well as identity, are shaped by labels.

Link and his colleagues begin by arguing that as part of socialization into American society, people come to internalize particular societal conceptions of the mentally ill: who the mentally ill are, what it is to be mentally ill, and how the mentally ill will be treated in our society. Overall, they argue that our socialization teaches us that those who are labeled mentally ill will be devalued – they will suffer a loss of status – and discriminated against – people will distance themselves from them. Knowledge of how our society treats the mentally ill leads those who need psychiatric treatment to expect that they will be devalued and discriminated against, and thus rejected. It is the expectation of rejection that Link and his colleagues argue leads to possible negative consequences for those who are labeled mentally ill.

What is central to their contribution is the idea that not everyone labeled mentally ill responds in the same way. In fact, they argue that the expectation of rejection leads to one of three possible responses – secrecy, withdrawal, or education. Secrecy refers the strategy of hiding psychiatric treatment from friends, family, and co-workers. In withdrawal the individual stops socializing with friends, family, and others who they expect will reject them. Finally, individuals who choose education as a response disclose their label and actively try to change the attitudes of those around them. Link and his colleagues argue that each of these responses has different negative consequences for the individual's social ties, earning-power and self-esteem. Of the three, though, they predict that withdrawal is the most harmful. Withdrawal means that ties to others will be reduced, which can open the individual to decreases in earning power and to lower self-esteem. The reduction in ties to others, earning power, and self-esteem leaves the individual vulnerable to a new mental disorder or a repeated episode of an existing disorder.

Though focused on the mentally ill, Link's work has much to suggest about the labeling that occurs when someone is caught and processed for breaking the law. It suggests the need to consider social conceptions of offenders, how all are socialized into them, and how those conceptions can shape not only the reactions of individual to those labeled as offenders but the reactions of the offenders themselves. It also asks us to think about the negative consequences, beyond changes in identity, and how they are related to the possibility of further offending.

## Braithwaite (1989): *Crime, shame and reintegration*

Perhaps the most influential work in the 1980s to include labeling appeared in 1989 – Braithwaite's *Crime, Shame and Reintegration*. Braithwaite integrates social control, opportunity, subcultural, and labeling theories to understand variation in crime rates across societies. The theory starts with an idea drawn from social control theory. Societies which are high in communitarianism, where individuals are "densely enmeshed in interdependencies which have the special qualities of mutual help and trust" (100), will have lower crimes rates than societies that are low in communitarianism and interdependence. The central explanation for this is differences in how these societies respond to, or shame, those who deviate from the laws.

Braithwaite defines shaming as "all process of expressing disapproval which have the intention or effect of invoking remorse in the person being shamed and/or condemnation by others who become aware of the shaming" (100). He argues that communitarian societies, of which Japan is an example, use one type of shaming – reintegrative shaming. This type of shaming uses disapproval "which is followed by efforts to reintegrate the offender back into the community of law-abiding or respectable citizens through words or gestures of forgiveness or ceremonies to decertify the offender as deviant" (101). Braithwaite argues that reintegrative shaming leads to lower crime rates because it allows individuals to maintain bonds to conventional others. In addition, reintegrative shaming is effective in conscience-building. Societies low in communitarianism, such as the US, however, are likely to use disintegrative shaming, where few efforts are made to bring the offender back into the community of non-offenders. Disintegrative shaming leads to a blockage in legitimate opportunities for success, the formation of criminal subcultures, and the development of illegitimate opportunities to fulfill needs, all of which lead to higher rates of crime.

Braithwaite's work illustrates the power of social reactions, but by integrating labeling with other theories he was able to strengthen its explanatory capacity. At the same time, he showed how there might well be truth in both the labeling prediction that punishment lead to more crime and the prediction of deterrence theories that it reduces crime. Continuing this conversation at the level of the individual is the next theorist, Sherman (1993).

## Sherman (1993): defiance theory

Sherman, interested in furthering the conversation about when punishment leads to more crime and when it leads to less, integrates ideas from a variety of sources to argue that the effects of punishment depend on characteristics of the punishment as well as the person being punished. He draws on Braithwaite (1989) to argue that some forms of punishment stigmatize the person, and from Tyler (1990) to argue that the effect of a punishment depends on whether it is perceived as legitimate or just. Individual characteristics, found in the level of the social bond, will also affect the individual's response to punishment.

Sherman predicts that punishment can lead to one of three results – defiance, deterrence, or none. Defiance, which is "the net increase in the prevalence, incidence, or seriousness of future offending against a sanctioning community" (459), occurs when four conditions are met. The offender perceives the punishment as unfair, the offender feels stigmatized by the punishment, the offender does not feel shame at what has been done, and the offender is not well bonded to society. When the four conditions are absent, behavior is deterred. When some of the conditions are present and some are absent the punishment is likely to have little effect on future behavior.

Sherman's work continues the conversation regarding the differential impact that reactions to rule-breaking can have. While Braithwaite's work emphasized the characteristics of the reaction itself and linked this to crime rates, Sherman points to the importance of understanding how those who are labeled perceive the punishment.

## Heimer & Matsueda (1994) – differential social control

So far, these key works of the 1980s and 1990s have dealt with questions regarding the differential response to labels, giving various explanations for why reactions do not automatically lead to more criminal behavior. There are three reasons why Heimer & Matsueda's (1994) theory of differential social control is important for labeling: first, it returns to the symbolic interactionist roots of labeling; second, it uses this framework to expand on the role of the "self" and links it to social control; finally, it focuses our attention on the power of labels given by informal others to shape identity.

In the theory of differential social control, Heimer and Matsueda are interested in the mechanisms through which social control occurs. Role-taking is central to their theory. It involves reflected appraisals, attitudes towards delinquent behavior, expectations regarding the reactions of significant others to delinquent behavior, having delinquent friends, and habit. All five of these are important individual-level characteristics explaining involvement in crime. It is in the idea of reflected appraisals that the ideas of labeling about self identity are seen. Reflected appraisals indicate that how an individual thinks of him or herself depends on what he or she perceives others, such as parents and friends, think of him or her.

As they argue, though, role taking occurs with social organizational contexts which vary both in terms of the content of the roles they stress and their ability to regulate behavior. Some groups stress roles for their members that are largely law-abiding while others support delinquent roles. Heimer and Matsueda suggest that people participate in a wide variety of groups, so it is thus the ability of a group to regulate its members' behavior, through the development of commitment to the group and its roles, which determines the likelihood of delinquency. This is the idea of "differential organizational control."

Heimer and Matsueda's work encourages a focus on the self, locating it within a society consisting of various groups with both a differential ability to control behavior and a differential willingness to control behavior according to conventional standards.

As the 1990s drew to a close, a final work was published that focused not on identity but other important changes that result from response to crime.

## Sampson & Laub (1997): a life-course theory of cumulative disadvantage

Sampson & Laub draw on their own age-graded theory of informal social control (1993), and the work by Link and colleagues described above, to explain the stability of criminal behavior among some individuals. Drawing on Link's work they suggest "a developmental model where delinquent behavior has a systematic attenuating effect on the social and institutional bonds linking adults to society (e.g., labor force attachment, marital cohesion)." They posit, for example, that length of incarceration as a juvenile has effects on the ability to maintain stable employment as an adult. They argue that these disadvantages accumulate over the life-course, making change increasingly difficult, and explaining the persistence of criminal behavior.

By placing labeling ideas within a life-course perspective, Sampson & Laub (1997) returned the focus to an idea central to the work of early labeling theorists such as Lemert and Becker. Social reactions and their consequences occur as part of a process. The success of their work in calling attention to the importance of process comes from their access to data across a long period of time which allows them to explore the mechanisms through which the consequences of punishment affect behavior.

## Current and Future Prospects

Since the 1990s, changes in the social context suggest a door is opening for renewed attention to labeling. With the highest incarceration rate per capita, and a large percentage of inmates serving time for drug-related offenses, increasing concerns in the US over mass incarceration have raised questions about both its efficacy and fairness. In addition, Cullen & Agnew (2011) point out that interest in labeling may be connected to the increased attention to the effect of our high incarceration rates. The fact that almost everyone we send to prison will eventually return to the community – "they all come back" as Travis (2005) writes – has raised the question of collateral and unintended consequences of punishment. The constructed image and rhetoric dating back even before that of the Reagan era has helped construct the label of "offender" to a point which affects prospects for rehabilitation and community reentry far beyond serving actual prison time. The label that comes with a criminal record extends the consequences of the punishment process. It thus may affect the ability of others to see an ex-convict as something other than an offender, as well as the ability of the individual to see his or her self as something other than an offender.

September 11th, 2001 is among many symbolic events which inspired increased securitization in an increasingly globalized and technologically advanced world. In response to this act of terrorism, homeland security and issues of control were brought to the forefront of American politics. The War on Terror quickly raised questions over the label "terrorist" and the net-widening effects witnessed by large groups of people experiencing alienation and oppression because they belong to a group to which the word "terrorist" has become attached.

Today's social context is filled with elements of exclusion and inclusion, using labels and categorization of individuals to perpetuate the construction of "the other." While this is not new, the current social climate is one in which media and technology increasingly, and quickly, influence and interact with constructions and definitions of crime, criminality, and ways to control. For example, Occupy

Wall Street signifies a larger global movement to acknowledge corporate greed and protesting civil intolerance for corporate corruption and neglect of humanity. Occupy is a label which has come to represent many forms of unity, particularly unity through protest. Examples include Occupy Wall Street, Occupy various cities such as Occupy Oakland, Occupy Sandy (informally coined events which use Occupy label to indicate coming together in times of crisis and devastation such as Superstorm Sandy).

Today, crises are quickly broadcast nationally and indeed across the globe. Often, the crisis at hand calls for swift social reaction. The debate and polarization around gun laws and ownership after the 2012 school shootings of 20 children and 6 adults in Sandy Hook Elementary in Connecticut is one very recent example. Discussion of securing our nation through crime-control tactics may well pique the interest of scholars in labeling and other interactionist perspectives.

Social context alone will not lead to increased attention of the field of criminology to labeling. It needs the impetus of scholars who address questions central to labeling. There are works since the 1990s that tackles issues raised by early labeling theorists and wrestle with past problems. A few such notable works are discussed below.

## Bernburg and colleagues (2003, 2006) – testing for factors mediating the effects of labels

One indication of renewed interest in labeling is found in the work of Bernburg and his colleagues as they examine factors which may mediate the effect of social reactions on offending. Drawing on the work of Sampson & Laub (1997), Bernburg & Krohn (2003) used data from the Rochester Youth Development Study (RYDS) to examine how intervention by the police and the juvenile justice system affects youths' chances of offending as adults. The RYDS is a multi-wave panel study which allowed Bernburg and Krohn to follow a sample of 605 males for a nine-year period. They posited that educational attainment and employment would both be detrimentally affected by official intervention and that this in turn would increase the risk of offending as an adult. Their results supported their predictions and, thus, labeling. Official intervention, by the police or the juvenile justice system, decreased the chance of graduating high school. Having not advanced to graduation, in turn, decreased the chance of employment. These factors mediated some of the effect of official intervention on criminal behavior as an adult. They also drew on labeling to predict that the effects of these labels would be more severe on individuals in disadvantaged groups which have fewer resources for overcoming the labels. Their findings supported this prediction as well, affects were stronger for lower-class males and African Americans. Interestingly, Bernburg & Krohn (2003) note that police and juvenile justice contact as a youth had direct effects on adult offending even after controlling for educational attainment and employment. They conclude by suggesting that there must be factors other than these that are important in explaining the connection between intervention and future offending.

Bernburg, Krohn, & Rivera (2006) draw on the work of Becker (1963) to explore another factor which may explain the connection between punishment and offending – movement into deviant peer groups. Deviant peer groups may facilitate offending in a number of ways, including supporting deviant identity, and providing rewards, as well as norms and values, supportive of delinquent behavior. Using data from the Rochester Youth Development Study (RYDS) once again, they found that youths who had contact with the juvenile justice system were more likely to become members of a gang in a later period, and to be involved in groups with higher levels of delinquency. They also found that contact increased the seriousness of later offending. Once again, however, they found that there remained a direct effect of intervention on offending. They call for further exploration of factors that explain the relationship between intervention and offending, including changes in identity.

The research of Bernburg and his colleagues, and supportive findings, may lead others to explore the process through which labels affect the probability of future offending. In addition, their support for Sampson and Laub's view of labels as part of a process occurring across the life-course may encourage continued exploration of ways to integrate labeling into life-course theories. The integration of labeling into other theories will broaden its appeal as well, perhaps, as strengthening its ability to explain criminal behavior.

## Steffensmeier & Ulmer (2005) – confessions of a dying thief

Bernburg and his colleagues exemplify the way that quantitative methods can be used to explore the long-term effects of labels. The work of Steffensmeier & Ulmer (2005) illustrates the importance of using ethnographic analysis to inform our understanding. In this case, the analysis was of the life of one man, Sam Goodman. Building on Ulmer's (1994, 2000) own work on commitment and labeling, they use concepts from differential association/social learning and opportunity theory as well to explore criminal careers. In terms of labeling, they find that formal and informal reactions did work in important ways to increase Sam's commitment to crime as a way of life. For example, they discuss how prison, though not a place he wanted to return to, acted as a "school of crime," increasing Sam's knowledge and contacts, and reinforcing norms supportive of criminal life. Also, having been in prison meant that Sam faced blocked opportunities for employment and did not fear the possibility of future punishment by the courts. Interestingly, in terms of identity, a key focus of labeling theory, Steffensmeier & Ulmer report that while his identity was one of a criminal, Sam also held contradictory and ambivalent feelings about it. At points he indicated a desire to be viewed as more legitimate, and used techniques of neutralization to protect his view of himself.

Continuing the focus on the role that labeling theory can have in helping explain crime over the life course, Steffensmeier & Ulmer's work also shows how success-fully its ideas can be integrated with other theories. They purposely connect labeling with theories based in symbolic interactionism, and which view crime and criminality as the result of both a process and situational contingencies.

## Hirschfield (2008) – the declining significance of delinquent labels

Not all the work in the 2000s designed to test labeling finds supportive for its contentions. In his work, Hirschfield (2008) returns the focus to key labeling contentions about the effects on identity on the likelihood of future offending. By focusing sharply on a group of youths who live in severely disadvantaged neighborhoods he is able to point out limitations of labeling as it currently stands, and possibilities for future development.

In his research, Hirschfield conducted interviews with 20 youths who had been participants in the Comer's School Development Program Evaluation. This study included 800 juvenile arrestees and was intended to examine the effects that contact with the juvenile justice system had on a number of attitudinal and behavioral outcomes of minority youths. The youths Hirschfield interviewed had been arrested an average of 5.7 times.

Intending to test some of labeling's most basic contentions, Hirschfield asked first if these youths saw arrest as stigmatizing. Hirschfield learned from the interviews that the answer to this question was "no," for two basic reasons: first, the youths in the sample suggested that arrest was just too common an occurrence to cause much damage to their reputations; second, for many of the youths, an arrest was just another indicator of stigmatization that had already occurred. Teachers did not need knowledge of an arrest, or another arrest, to tell them that a particular person was a troublemaker. Hirschfield next addressed the question of whether arrest resulted in rejection by significant others. Again, the answer to this question was largely "no" for this sample of youths. Even family members who were disappointed in the youth supported them. Peers either had been arrested before themselves, and thus were sympathetic, or were not aware of the arrest. Finally Hirschfield asked, was arrest harmful to self-perceptions? Once again the answer was "no." He found that youths' perceptions of themselves were highly resistant to the effects of being labeled through arrest. The context in which these youths grew up and lived was simply not one that viewed arrest as stigmatizing.

Hirschfield's findings are clearly not supportive of labeling contentions, but he does not suggest a wholesale rejection of labeling. Hirschfield argues that labeling theory is too narrow in its current state. It focuses too much on how members of mainstream society think about arrest and imprisonment. He writes that the work of those examining labeling's ideas tends to show too little awareness of the context from which many who are arrested come. In addition, he warns that we should not take his findings and "reduce" them to a contingency. Hirschfield calls, instead, for a multilevel labeling framework. He writes, "The normalization and de-legitimation of official labels are entrenched conditions for poor African-American neighborhoods across the United States, wrought by decades of mass arrests and imprisonment. These emergent realities, rooted in social policy and social structure, call for theories, which, like labeling theory but on a much wider scale, implicate the justice system in helping perpetuate delinquency, crime, and imprisonment"(597).

## Cultural criminology – cultural enterprise and contested meaning

In the 1970s and 1980s a connection between labeling and conflict criminology grew out of the interest of labeling theorists, like Becker, in how definitions of deviance and deviants came to be. This connection led to hypotheses about the enforcement of the law based on individual characteristics such as class and race that came to be identified as labeling's differential enforcement hypothesis. Lemert (1967/1972) and others (Wellford & Triplett, 1993) have argued this connection to conflict theory was not a necessary, nor a particularly, helpful connection for labeling. Today there is an interesting connection between labeling theory and critical criminology in the form of cultural criminology. Only the future will show whether this connection is helpful for labeling, but there is potential.

Cultural criminology, as expressed in the works of scholars such as Keith Hayward, Jeff Ferrell, and Mike Presdee (see for example, Ferrell, Hayward, & Young, 2008; Ferrell & Sanders, 1995; Hayward & Presdee, 2010; Hayward & Young, 2004; Presdee, 2000), is an alternative to mainstream approaches to understanding crime, criminality, and control which incorporates multiple theories, methods, and disciplines. It has a number of obvious connections with labeling. Like many early labeling theorists, its proponents firmly rejects positivism (Ferrell, Hayward, & Young, 2008; Spencer, 2011). In addition, like labeling theory, cultural criminology is rooted in the symbolic interactionist perspective. This common root means that cultural criminology, like labeling, is interested in interaction and the construction of meaning. Cultural criminology aims to provide a deconstructed understanding of social interactions, interpretations, and constructions occurring at all levels (micro, meso, and macro) and the effects on an individual's identity. It views crime, criminality and control as *cultural enterprises* and sees them as products of ongoing social interaction and power relations, filled with *contested meaning*. While this is not the place to review all of cultural criminology, a couple of areas illustrate the work that cultural criminologists are doing in key areas of labeling theory.

In their view of crime and control as part of a cultural enterprise, one way in which cultural criminologists advance labeling is by providing an understanding of how labels, and the processes of applying them and reacting to them, are produced by a culture at large and enacted in reality (Law & Urry, 2004; Spencer, 2011). Cultural criminologists examine how the processes of applying and reacting to labels affect the lived, day-to-day experience of individuals situated within a culture, how the day-to-day productions further perpetuate meanings and definitions at the macro level, and lastly how the macro, meso, and micro interact in a dynamic process of constructing, producing, and enacting meaning. A key element to this strand of cultural criminology is the importance of understanding the individual and groups, particularly deviant and criminal, situated within the social context of a given culture.

Cultural criminology, then, situates crime, criminality, and social control within the context of a particular culture (Ferrell, Hayward, & Young 2008; Ferrell & Sanders 1995; Presdee 2000). A major part of our culture today stems from technological advancements made over the past few decades. In the current social context, knowledge is increasingly produced by the media, including TV, music, and movies. Online media and immediate access to information via iPhones, iPads, laptops, mean that the individual is situated within a context in which he or she continually consumes information. This information includes images that shape the construction and production of reality and individual identity. Cultural criminologists examine how these mediated images shape the construction and production of reality and identity.

In terms of crime and the media, a concept often used in cultural criminology is the "spectacle of crime and punishment" (see work by Michelle Brown, Michel Foucault). The "spectacle of crime and punishment" refers to the image of crime experienced and consumed by people on a daily basis. In many ways, the power of an image shapes what individuals in society come to know and define as crime and criminality, and how they behave in relation to crime, criminality, and mechanisms of formal and informal control. From the many advertisements for how to protect oneself from potential victimization on TV to images depicting criminal conviction and interaction with the justice system (i.e. mug shots, crime shows, police blotters, etc.), individuals no longer need to experience crime themselves in order to understand its various elements nor to understand the label's meaning.

Cultural criminology acknowledges the changed nature of culture in which the image is just as influential in communication, language and rhetoric today as the word. Much like the way words shape popular understandings of crime, criminality, and control, the image and consumerism is used to further media and cultural studies. In an increasingly technologized world, images play an important part in the construction of identity, space, and consumption (Ferrell & Sanders, 1995). Cultural criminologists suggest individuals are both products of and producers of culture, that being individuals construct definitions and give meaning to the world as it is constructed, and also consume and enact such definitions and meanings constructed. In this case, deviants and criminals are created, mediated, and constructed through language and images produced by mass media (Hayward & Young, 2004).

Another area that cultural criminology is expanding beyond earlier labeling is in the idea of crime and control as products of ongoing social interaction and power relations, filled with *contested meaning*. Cultural criminologists acknowledge power shapes contested definitions in reality, particularly the intersection of symbolic and material world, and the ways in which economic and political power cannot be disconnected from its understanding (Ferrell & Sanders, 1995). For instance, power and politics as expressed in relation to race, class, and gender relations situated within a culture (Ferrell, Hayward, & Young, 2008; Spencer, 2011). The poor and marginalized are often the least powerful within the class structure in the shaping of formal controls of the justice system and informal controls in society (Spencer, 2011). Cultural criminology has long noted this lack of power and oppression in its scholarly work.

An example of understanding each sentiment from a cultural criminology perspective includes considering the impact of geography, space, place, and its relation to the identity-making process and subsequent controls. This includes who a person is and who is controlled. The labeling process, particularly societal reactions to deviance, may differ greatly from urban to rural settings, each is shaped by culture and politics at micro and macro levels. A contemporary example can be witnessed among moonshiners. *Moonshiner* is a label filled with stereotype, stigma, often relegated to a specific place within the US, perhaps the Appalachian mountains and similar mid- to southeast rural settings. Today, mass produced media allows society access to imagery of a *moonshiner* as well as see its deviant and illegal activities; mass media allows individuals to consume TV shows and thus produce their own reality and subsequent behaviors toward moonshiners (see the Discovery Documentary, *Moonshiners*, for this dramatized enactment of moonshining). A cultural criminologist might deconstruct the image of a *moonshiner*, not only through qualitative methods such as interviewing moonshiners to better understand the identity process and day-to-day lived experiences, but also to incorporate media and political content analyses on social reactions to moonshining, including potential effects of control by law enforcement on such activities. The perspective aims to provide understanding of social reactions, stigma, and stereotype given such national broadcasting and the effects of dramatized imagery of moonshining as criminal.

Hayward (2010:4) also adds this orientation, examining phenomena at a place where "moral entrepreneurship, political innovation and experiential resistance intersect." In essence, cultural criminology attempts to orient its readers and consumers with a historical, social, and culturally charged understanding of crime, criminality, and control within late-modern culture (Hayward, 2010). Its research and theory focus on unveiling understanding of the conflict between self-expression, identity and exertion of informal and formal control over groups. Cultural criminologists acknowledge the "continuous generation of meaning around interaction; rules created, rules broken, a constant interplay of moral entrepreneurship, moral innovation and transgression" (Hayward & Young, 2004) and how this observation of the nature of reality is important in consideration of scholarly work.

The current social and cultural climate lends a context ripe for tools used by cultural criminologists. Ours is a world in which

> the street scripts the screen and the screen scripts the street; [where] there is no clearly linear sequence, but rather a shifting interplay between the real and the virtual, the factual and the fictional. Late modern society is saturated with collective meaning and suffused with symbolic uncertainty as media messages and cultural traces swirl, circulate, and vacillate... Ferrell, Hayward, & Young (2008:123–124).

Cultural criminology acknowledges society today is situated within "a place of irony," giving this perspective many new doors, great prospects for scholars, and a potential rise in popularity. Cultural criminologists refer to this time as late modernity, one "which is characterised by the rise of a more individualistic, expressive society, where vocabularies of motives, identities and human action begin to lose their rigid moorings in social structure" (Hayward & Young, 2004).

# Conclusion

Labeling rose to attention in the tumultuous 1960s, when deep divides in society were apparent and many were questioning the practices and structures that supported the divide. It fell out of favor before it could develop into a more complete framework for explaining crime. Twenty years ago, Wellford & Triplett (1993) argued that labeling had not lived up to the potential expressed in the work of theorists like Lemert. They suggested there were three reasons for this. First, they argued, is the tendency of labeling, like most theories of criminology, to try and explain a broad range of criminal behavior with a narrowly focused model. Certainly the idea that labels and reactions to them are the only, or even most important, reason that people re-offend is incomplete. Second, is the connection with conflict theory that developed in the 1970s and 1980s. Wellford & Triplett argue that this connection meant that labeling became associated with the same criticisms of these early conflict theories and to the same end. Finally, is the tendency to drift away from the symbolic interactionist foundation upon which the writing of early labeling theorists was grounded (see also the discussion with Lemert in Laub, 1983). Importantly, this means paying attention to the meaning of the label for those it is applied to and not simply focusing on the application of the label. They argued that the future of labeling, should there be one, "seems quite clear." Such research, they wrote, must be longitudinal and have a developmental component. It should focus on the labeling process both informal and formal and emphasize labeling that happens early in life. Finally, they argued, it must avoid the problem of treating labels as objects rather than symbols of objects and be part of a larger theoretical model.

The field has not seen again the interest in labeling that the works of Lemert & Becker sparked in the 1960s, and it may never. There has been some important work done in the intervening decades, however, much of it taking the path that Wellford & Triplett suggested was necessary. Many of these works have integrated labeling's ideas with other theories for a broader explanation of crime. The theory integrations that seem most promising are those with theories from the life-course perspective and those which share labeling's roots in symbolic interactionism. It is notable as well that some are calling for more attention to the role of culture and the development of societal conceptions of crime and criminality. Finally, the ability to more accurately test some of labeling's key contentions has been aided by the existence of data sets which follow individuals over long periods of time. Whether these works will spark interest among a wide range of criminologists in the current social context only time will tell. But the door remains open.

# References

Ball, R.A. (1983). Development of basic norm violation: Neutralization and self-concept within a male cohort. *Criminology, 21*, 75–94.

Becker, H. (1963). *Outsiders: Studies in the Sociology of Deviance*. New York: Free Press.

Becker, H. (1964). *The Other Side*. New York: Free Press.

Bernburg, J.G., & Krohn, M. (2003). Labeling, life chances, and adult crime: The direct and indirect effects of official intervention in adolescence on crime in early adulthood. *Criminology, 41,* 1287–1318.

Bernburg, J.G., Krohn, M., & Rivera, C.J. (2006). Official labeling, criminal embeddedness, and subsequent delinquency: A longitudinal test of labeling theory. *Journal of Research in Crime and Delinquency, 43,* 67–88.

Blumer, H. (1969). *Symbolic Interactionism: Perspective and Method*. Berkeley, CA: University of California Press.

Braithwaite, J. (1989). *Crime, Shame and Reintegration*. Cambridge: Cambridge University Press.

Cullen, F., & Agnew, R. (2011). *Criminological Theory: Past to Present*, 4th edition. New York: Oxford University Press.

Ferrell, J., Hayward, K.J., & Young, J. (2008). *Cultural Criminology*. London: Sage.

Ferrell, J., & Sanders, C.R. (1995). *Cultural Criminology*. Boston, MA: Northeastern University Press.

Gibbons, D.C. (1979). *Criminological Enterprise*. Englewood Cliffs, NJ: Prentice-Hall.

Hayward, K.J. (2010). Opening the lens: cultural criminology and the image. In K. Hayward & M. Presdee (Eds.), *Framing Crime: Cultural Criminology and the Image* (pp. 1–16). New York: Routledge.

Hayward, K.J., & Presdee, M. (2010). *Framing Crime: Cultural Criminology and the Image*. London: Routledge.

Hayward, K.J., & Young, J. (2004). Cultural criminology: Some notes on the script. *Theoretical Criminology, 8*(3), 259–273.

Heimer, K., & Matsueda, R. (1994). Role-taking, role commitment, and delinquency: A theory of differential social control. *American Sociological Review, 59,* 365–390.

Hirschfield, P.J. (2008). The declining significance of delinquent labels in disadvantaged urban communities. *Sociological Forum, 23*(3), 575–601.

Laub, J. (1983). *Criminology in the Making: An Oral History*. Boston, MA: Northeastern University Press.

Law, J., & Urry, J. (2004). Enacting the social. *Economy and Society, 33*(3), 390–410.

Lemert, E. (1951). *Social Pathology: A Systematic Approach to the Theory of Sociopathic Behavior*. New York: McGraw-Hill.

Lemert, E. (1967/1972). *Human Deviance, Social Problems and Social Control*, 2nd edition. Englewood Cliffs, NJ: Prentice-Hall.

Link, B. (1987). Understanding labeling effects in the area of mental disorders: An assessment of the effects of expectations of rejection. *American Sociological Review, 52,* 96–112.

Link, B., & Cullen, F. (1983). Reconsidering the social rejection of ex-mental patients: Levels of attitudinal response. *American Journal of Community Psychology, 11,* 261–273.

Link, B., Cullen, F., Struening, E., Shrout, P., & Dohrenwend, B. (1989). A modified labeling theory approach to mental disorders: An empirical assessment. *American Sociological Review, 54,* 400–423.

Link, B., Cullen, F., & Wozniak, J. (1987). The social reaction of former mental patients: Understanding why labels work. *American Journal of Sociology, 92,* 1461–1500.

Matza, D. (1969). *Becoming Deviant*. Englewood Cliffs, NJ: Prentice-Hall.

Mead, G.H. (1918). The psychology of punitive justice. *American Journal of Sociology, 23,* 577–602.

Mead, G.H. (1934). *Mind, Self and Society*. Chicago, IL: University of Chicago Press.

Pfhol, S. (1994). *Images of Deviance and Social Control: A Sociological History*, 2nd edition. New York: McGraw-Hill.

Pfhol, S. (2009). *Images of Deviance and Social Control: A Sociological History*, 2nd edition, reissued in paperback. Longrove, IL: Waveland Press.

Plummer, K. (1979). Misunderstanding labeling perspectives. In D. Downes & P. Rock (Eds.), *Deviant Interpretations* (pp. 85–121). Oxford: Martin Robertson.

Presdee, M. (2000). *Cultural Criminology and the Carnival of Crime*. London: Routledge.

Sampson, R., & Laub, J. (1993). *Crime in the Making: Pathways and Turning Points through Life*. Cambridge, MA: Harvard University Press.

Sampson, R., & Laub, J. (1997). A life-course theory of cumulative disadvantage and the stability of delinquency. In T. Thornberry (Ed.), *Developmental Theories of Crime and Delinquency*. New Brunswick, NJ: Transaction.

Schur, E. (1971). *Labeling Deviant Behavior: Its Sociological Implications*. New York: Harper and Row.

Schur, E. (1973). *Radical Non-Intervention: Rethinking the Delinquency Problem*. Englewood Cliffs, NJ: Prentice-Hall.

Sherman, L.W. (1993) Defiance, deterrence, and irrelevance: a theory of the criminal sanction. *Journal of Research in Crime and Delinquency, 30*(4) 445–473.

Spencer, D. (2011). Cultural criminology: An invitation … to what? *Critical Criminology, 19*(3), 197–212.

Steffensmeier, D., & Ulmer, J. (2005). *Confessions of a Dying Thief*. New Brunswick, NJ: Aldine Transaction.

Tannenbaum, F. (1938). *Crime and the Community*. Boston, MA: Ginn.

Travis, J. (2005). *But They All Come Back: Facing the Challenges of Prisoner Reentry*. Washington, DC: Urban Institute Press.

Tyler, T. (1990). *Why People Obey the Law*. New Haven, CT: Yale University Press.

Ulmer, J. (1994). Revisiting Stebbins: Labeling and commitment to deviance. *Sociological Quarterly, 35*, 135–157.

Ulmer, J. (2000). Commitment, deviance and social control. *Sociological Quarterly, 41*, 315–336.

Wellford, C. (1975). Labeling theory and criminology: An assessment. *Social Problems, 22*, 332–345.

Wellford, C., & Triplett, R. (1993). The future of labeling theory: Foundations and promises. In F. Adler & W.S. Laufer (Eds.), *New Directions in Criminological Theory*, Vol. 4 (pp. 1–22). New Brunswick, NJ: Transaction.

Wilson, J.Q. (1975). *Thinking About Crime*. New York: Basic Books.

## Further Readings

Brown, M. (2009). *The Culture of Punishment: Prison, Society Spectacle*. New York: New York University Press.

Ferrell, J. (1999). Cultural criminology. *Annual Review of Sociology, 25*, 395–418.

Ferrell, J. (2006). *Empire of Scrounge*. New York: New York University Press.

Hamm, M. (2007). *Terrorism as Crime: From Oklahoma City to Al-Qaeda and Beyond*. New York: New York University Press.

Hayward, K. (2004). *City Limits*. London: Glass House Press.

Lovell, J. (2009). *Crimes of Dissent*. New York: New York University Press.

# 15

# Feminist Theory

## Joanne Belknap

## Introduction: The Identification, Application, and Advancement of Feminist Theory to Studying Crime

Criminology as an academic discipline and a set of theories has focused most consistently on why some people offend, but has also addressed victimization risks and experiences, decision-making by criminal legal system[1] officials (e.g., police, judges, parole officers), how individuals experience incarceration, and some other crime-related topics. The implications for all of these topics are profound, particularly for translating the theories into policies. Moreover, theorizing about crime is additionally complicated by the overlap among these phenomena and how they vary across individuals' personal factors, such as their demographic characteristics. For example, how is offending addressed when routine activities are provided different official surveillance, such as racial-profiling, and women of color are more likely than white women to be stopped and charged? What happens when an individual's victimization is processed as her/his offending, such as when a woman abused by her partner who calls the police is arrested instead of, or with, the abuser, because the abuser lies to the police and tells them that she abused him? And what about official criminal legal system decision-makers who are consciously or unconsciously biased, believing women are more responsible than men when they harm their own children? And is there any appeal when judges and other criminal legal system personnel adhere to laws that enact institutionalized oppression that disproportionately impacts poor women of color (e.g., a requirement for a parolee to live with non-felons)? Feminist theory, as it has been applied to criminology, has attempted to address these and other intersections of oppression (e.g., gender, race, class, and sexuality) and of victim and offender (e.g., the criminalization of victims).

*The Handbook of Criminological Theory*, First Edition. Edited by Alex R. Piquero.
© 2016 John Wiley & Sons, Inc. Published 2016 by John Wiley & Sons, Inc.

There is not one feminist theory, but rather numerous strains of feminist theory, including Marxist, socialist, liberal, radical, and postmodern. The strains are united in their attempts to use feminist theory as "a woman-centered description and explanation of human experience and the social world," recognizing "that gender governs every aspect of personal and social life" (Danner 1989:51). Just as feminist theory has expanded in depth, nuances, and applications over the decades, so have feminist criminologists' use and discussion of feminist theory grown. This chapter briefly summarizes some of the contributions and challenges of feminist theory as it has been applied to studying crime and advocating for justice. In addition to the inclusion of women and girls in criminology research, the main contributions of feminist theory applications for crime and justice are: (1) incorporation of the intersections of oppression (i.e., sexism cannot be adequately studied without a lens that allows for other forms of oppression); (2) feminist pathways theory; and (3) masculinity studies. These three contributions are the focus of this chapter.

Feminist theory, with a focus on patriarchy and gender differences, is ideal for understanding crime due to the long-standing fact that "being male" is one of the best predictors for most crime and delinquency (Church, Wharton, & Taylor, 2009). Feminist criminology scholars differ markedly from most of the more biological or sociobiological criminology scholars on the etiology of crime. The biological and sociobiological criminologists are more loyal to the perspective that the gender differences in offending, particularly for violent offenses, are a result of different testosterone levels and boys/men being "wired" differently than girls/women. The sociobiological criminologists frequently view men's violence against women as men's and women's distinct adaptations to biological needs (see Belknap, 2015). In contrast, feminist criminologists are more likely to examine criminal offending and victimization in terms of learned behaviors that can often vary across gender, and the gendered power differentials in patriarchal societies (see Belknap, 2015).

How children are raised, gendered media representations, and gendered criminal legal responses to victims and offenders can and do distort views of who "counts" in victimization and offending (see Belknap, 2015). One of the most basic manners that childrearing is gendered is that girls are typically monitored far more than boys by their parents, thus having less access to delinquency at the same time that relative to boys, they are expected to help more with younger siblings and around the home (see Bottcher, 2001). But restricting daughters' relative to sons' freedom to roam the neighborhood and be unsupervised is also motivated by parents' (and other guardians') goals of protecting girls from sexual abuse, *and* restricting girls from consensual sex that will "ruin their reputations." These gendered childrearing and monitoring differences strongly influence girls' and boys' abilities to commit crimes, but also how their offending and victimizations are perceived. For example, boys' consensual activities do not mar their reputations; in fact, sexual prowess typically adds to boys' masculinity status, which in turn, buttresses their reputations. Sadly, even in today's world, girls' reputations are often tarnished by being sexually active, particularly becoming pregnant, and this is often regardless of whether the sex is consensual or abuse (coerced or forced). Such judgments, and even abuse, can come from some officials in the criminal legal system in addition to the general public (e.g., Richie, 2012). In fact, it could be argued that girls' reputations are more damaged for being raped than boys' reputations are for raping.

Compared to the research on both offending and victimized boys and men, studies on offending and victimized girls and women were incredibly sparse until the 1970s, with the second wave of the women's/feminist movement. After centuries of ignoring girls and women in criminology studies, or including them but doing so in sexist theories designed to study boys and men, feminist criminological scholarship kick-started at an almost unprecedented level in the late 1970s. Furthermore, there were no journals specifically for gender or feminist scholarship in the context of crime until the journal *Women & Criminal Justice* started in 1989, and then, specifically addressing victimization, the feminist and criminology journal *Violence Against Women*, which debuted in 1995. Since then, only one other feminist journal specifically about feminist criminology has appeared; indeed, it is called *Feminist Criminology,* and it began publishing in 2006. Prior to the 1990s, feminist criminological scholars typically faced weighty challenges in trying to publish their feminist work in mainstream journals, and were often told by colleagues that their focus was "too narrow" if they "only" studied women and/or girls. Then, in some cases, even publishing in a feminist journal was, and sometimes still is, considered less important scholarship than the "malestream" journals.

However, as more and more women have attended graduate school and become criminology scholars, feminist criminology has advanced in leaps and bounds. (Of course, not all women criminologists are feminist scholars, nor are all feminist scholars women.) Additionally, the implementation of the Violence Against Women Act in 1994 (and reauthorized three times since) allowed unprecedented funding for research on rape (and other sexual abuses), intimate partner abuse (domestic violence), and stalking. This act and the funding has not necessarily resulted in solely "feminist" assessments of violence against women (and girls), but given the huge commitment of federal funding, it has certainly legitimized studying violence against women and girls. At the same time it is important to understand that Violence Against Women Act funding and feminist criminology have also significantly advanced the research and understanding of boys' and men's sexual abuse, stalking, and intimate partner abuse victimizations, and particularly boys' sexual abuse victimizations. Due to these many factors, there has been a huge surge in the inclusion of women and girls in research samples and feminist criminological publications since the 1990s.

## Feminist Theory Contribution 1: Recognizing the Intersections of Oppression

The most notable advancement for both "feminist theory" in general and "feminist theory" as it has been applied to crime, is the recognition that sexism as one form of oppression, that while substantial, cannot be viewed in a vacuum. More specifically, studying sexism must include a wide lens that does not essentialize women/girls (or boys/men), but rather allows for the varied intersections of oppressions and privileges that individuals hold. At the same time as examining individual experiences, victimization, offending, and processing by the criminal legal system, it is also vital to research and respond to the more aggregate societal and criminal legal system structures and decision-making. *Institutionalized bias* occurs and impacts offending, victimization, and labeling individuals "offenders" (including racial-profiling) when laws and policies restrict access to education, employment, attorneys, and so on. For example, institutionalized sexism – often intersecting with classism, racism and other forms of oppression – results when employers do not want to hire women to work at night, restricting women's access to legitimate employment. Another example of institutionalized sexism that frequently intersects with classism and racism is when parole boards require inmates leaving prison not to live with another felon. This rule impacts incarcerated women more than incarcerated men because the women are more likely to have men mates who are felons than men are to have women mates who are felons. Similarly, when women go to prison their children are more likely to be raised by a non-parent, including foster care, than when men who are parents are incarcerated, because the men can more often rely on the mothers of their children to be out of prison and able to take care of their children.

Over the decades since the 1970s, feminism has increasingly advocated the need to view patriarchy and sexism through a wider lens that accounts for other forms of oppression, most commonly racism and classism, but also heterosexism, religious identity, citizenship, and so on. Hillary Potter's (2013) exemplary article on "intersectional criminology" traces the extensive and lengthy history of Black women's activism *and* development of feminist criminological theory. Thus, feminist theory has not only advanced to endorse the intersections of oppression, including racism, classism, homophobia, nationalism, and so on, but feminist criminologists have pushed criminological theory to address the significance of oppressions other than sexism. To this end, Hillary Potter, drawing on Black feminist and critical race feminist theories identified *black feminist criminology*:

> Black feminist criminology necessarily places the Black woman and her intersecting identities at the center of any analysis, as opposed to considering her identity as nonessential. Black feminist criminology specifically considers issues of crime, deviance, violence, and the workings of the criminal justice system in the lives of people of color (2008:7).

Vernetta D. Young (1980, 1986), publishing in the leading criminology journals, was one of the original criminologists grappling with feminist criminology and the profound intersections of race and gender. In 1980, using national victimization data to compare comparing crime patterns across race by gender and across gender by race, she debunked assumptions of the time. In 1986 she confronted feminist criminology for failing to recognize that gender expectations vary for Black and

White women, which in turn, have negative repercussions for Black women and girls who are victimized and/or offend. Thus, Young (1980, 1986) was critical in addressing the lack of intersectionality in feminist criminology.

Beth E. Richie's excellent book, *Arrested Justice: Black Women, Violence and America's Prison Nation* (2012), is a powerful account of the intersections of sexism, racism, classism, and heterosexism/homophobia. Richie intertwines feminist theory with individual cases, and structural/aggregate-level data (statistics) on incarceration and arrest rates. Regarding institutional bias, Richie explains "institutional regulations designed to intimidate people without power into conforming with dominant cultural expectations," including legislated decisions to use English-only laws and ideologically conservative values (2012:3). The individual-level data are from three cases of victimizations of African American women and girls that resulted in horrific injustices whereby they were processed by the criminal legal system as offenders.

## Feminist Theory Contribution 2: Feminist Pathways Theory

Most criminological theories attempt to address why people (and most typically, youth) offend (although some focus more on victimization risks). Moreover, although "being male is the strongest predictor of delinquency" (Church *et al.*, 2009:11), gender was rarely addressed in criminological theories until the 1970s. A classic article by Kathleen Daly and Meda Chesney-Lind, "Feminism and Criminology," published in 1988, criticized most criminological research that either routinely excluded girls/women/gender, or if they did include girls (or women), simply added them to the existing theories developed to understand boys' and men's offending. More specifically, Daly & Chesney-Lind (1988) referred to this practice as "add-women-and-stir," or simply trying to fit women/girls into theories and statistical models designed to study boys/men and crime.

A major contribution of the second wave of the feminist movement in the 1970s (and following into the 1980s and 1990s) was the recognition of the epidemic levels of violent and other (nonviolent) abuse victimizations reported by girls and women, largely at the hands of men (and, and to a lesser extent, boys). In recent years, gender-based abuses (those with higher prevalence of women/girl victims and men/boy perpetrators) have most typically included sexual abuse, physical abuse by a current or former intimate or dating partner, and stalking victimizations. Significantly, gender-based abuse also includes forced marriages (forcing girls as young as 11 to marry older men), female-genital mutilation, and human sex trafficking (Belknap, 2015).

Although today more scholars identify child sexual and nonsexual physical abuses and child neglect as strains and stresses (consistent with Agnew's general strain theory reported in Chapter 11 of this book), and/or as life events that can derail a youth from law-abiding to offending (consistent with developmental/life-course theories presented in Chapter 18 of this book), historically and sometimes even currently, childhood victimization traumas have been ignored in the general strain theory and developmental/life-course theories (see Belknap, 2015).

Therefore, attempts to conduct feminist theorizing about girls' and women's offending, should address how society (e.g., parents, peers, teachers, neighbors), the criminal legal system (the police, courts, and detention facilities), and even the media, portray and reinforce sexist perceptions around girls' and boys' behaviors. Additionally, when studying these portrayals it is necessary to examine the intersections of sexism with racism, classism, nationalism, heterosexism, and other types of oppression. For example, do news reports, fictional movies, society, the criminal legal system, and/or others view White women and girls who are victims of rape or intimate partner abuse more sympathetically and credibly than women and girls of color with the same victimizations? Furthermore, serious attempts to develop feminist theory in its application to criminological studies such as general strain theory, life-course theory, and pathways theory must examine not only the rates, timing, and extensiveness of childhood maltreatment and other traumas (e.g., the death of a parent), but also whether youths' responses to trauma are gendered in such a way that Hay's (2003) work indicates: that boys are more likely to externalize (offend) and girls are more likely 8 to internalize (feel guilty and become depressed).

Scholarship on the abusive, chaotic, and traumatic lives that incarcerated girls and women experienced prior to incarceration, largely at the hands of abusive parents, guardians, and boyfriends/husbands, dates back at least to 1917 (see Belknap, 2015). This research seems to have gone unnoticed despite being published in reputable journals and by women with medical degrees and doctorates of philosophy (Belknap, 2015). In the late 1970s, some research started being published in scholarly journals on the high rates of victimization, particularly sexual abuse by fathers and step-fathers, among girls working in prostitution/sex work and not in prison or jail (see Belknap, 2015, for a review). Since the 1980s more and more research documents the extraordinarily high rates of victimization among incarcerated women and girls, particularly sexual abuse and intimate partner abuse victimizations (see Belknap, 2015).

In the late 1980s, Cathy Spatz Widom (1989) began publishing her expansive data reconstructing the lives of women and men, including their criminal histories, by matching these now adults who had official (court-substantiated) records of childhood physical abuse, sexual abuse, and/or neglect, with a cohort of their peers who had no official records of these childhood victimizations. Widom's *cycle of violence* research found that although most childhood maltreatment survivors do not go on to become offenders, these victimizations still proved to be significant risk factors for subsequent offending. Widom's cycle of violence is certainly highly consistent with the feminist pathways research, and her inclusion of both men and women in the sample indicates that the feminist pathways theory is also appropriate to understand boys' and men's offending.

One of the earliest studies to detail the profound intersections of sexism and racism in what is now referred to as feminist pathways theory is Regina Arnold's (1990) classic article entitled "Processes of Victimization and Criminalization of

Black Women." Arnold identifies *dimensions of victimization* (e.g., racism, patriarchy, family violence, economic marginalization, and "mis-education"), and *dimensions of criminalization* (e.g., structural dislocation, the processing and labeling of status offenders, and associations with other criminals). She argues "that for young Black girls from lower socioeconomic classes, involvement in 'precriminal' behavior may be viewed as active resistance to victimization" (1990:153). These precriminal, victim-resistant behaviors include running away, truancy, and stealing. "Once this process of criminalization is set in motion, sustained criminal involvement becomes the norm as well as a rational coping strategy" (1990:153).

Beth E. Richie's (1996) book, *Compelled to Crime: The Gender Entrapment of Battered, Black Women*, is another significant contribution to feminist pathways theory. Richie's intensive life-history interviews with incarcerated women led to her identification of "gender entrapment" in the complications and contradictions endemic in incarcerated Black, battered women's lives. Hillary Potter (2008) expanded Richie's work to Black women survivors of intimate partner abuse in the community (who were not incarcerated) in her book *Battle Cries: Black Women and Intimate Partner Abuse*. This research, although not specifically about pathways, expanded not only Richie's (1996) work on pathways, but the existing feminist work on intimate partner abuse. More specifically, Potter (2008) identified *dynamic resistance* and some Black women intimate partner abuse survivors' "fighting back," where she not only dissected gender and race, but how they intersected with religion and class.

A large, recent, multisite study on women in US jails confirms not only the strong impact of adverse life-events (also called traumas), including abuse, on women's and girls' offending, but also how these traumas are often related to serious mental illness (DeHart *et al.*, 2014; Lynch *et al.*, 2014). Incarcerated women not only have significantly more adverse life-events and serious mental illness compared to non-incarcerated women, but compared to incarcerated men. This multisite study found that only 9% of the women did not meet any of the criteria for any lifetime serious mental illness, post-traumatic stress disorder (PTSD), or substance use disorder (Lynch *et al.*, 2014). Moreover, women with serious mental illness were more likely to report prior violent victimization, repeat offenses/offending, and to be charged with violent crimes (Lynch *et al.*, 2014). Women who had serious mental illness were more likely to be survivors of child physical abuse, child sexual abuse, childhood caregiver incarceration, childhood caregiver alcohol/drug addiction, witnessing violence, being attacked nonsexually as an adult, adult intimate partner abuse (domestic violence), and adult sexual violence (usually, rape) (Lynch *et al.*, 2014). Moreover, when the onset of the women's offending was in adulthood (instead of youthful onset of offending), it was significantly related to being a survivor of intimate partner abuse (DeHart *et al.*, 2014). For example, among this multisite study of women in US jails, compared to women with no violent partners, women with violent partners were twice as likely to deal drugs and/or have drug charges and they were four times as likely to do sex work (DeHart *et al.*, 2014).

Over time, the feminist-based theory suggesting victimization/trauma is a risk factor for offending has been referred to as pathways theory or feminist pathways theory. Feminist pathways, life-course, and cycle of violence perspectives/theories all confirm the significance of life trajectories and events correlated with offending. Although this research has been applied almost exclusively to incarcerated women and girls, when it has been applied to boys it indicates that their traumas, including childhood sexual abuse, while less prevalent, are also risk factors for subsequent offending (for a review see Belknap, 2015). The pathways theory is a distinctively feminist criminological theory that has important implications for general strain and life-course developmental theories, and also for boys' trajectories to offending.

## Feminist Theory Contribution 3: The Role of Masculinities

Given the lives and neighborhoods often fraught with disrespect, violence and other traumas documented in many offenders' lives, it is useful to identify basic human reactions to these experiences and how they might be gendered. Moreover, how responding to challenging lives, including micro-aggressions and violence, can in turn, result in reactions that are often criminalized. Wilkinson-Ryan & Hoffman (2010) discuss the significance of "breach," and how people often feel angry, offended, and may want to retaliate, even when retaliation is costly, when they feel duped and/or betrayed. Elijah Anderson's (1999) classic book, *Code of the Street: Decency, Violence and the Moral Life of the Inner City*, is a powerful ethnography of predominantly African-American Philadelphia neighborhoods. Anderson describes "the code of the street" as the means by which aggressive and even violent retaliation against interpersonal attacks and insults are necessary to insure one's safety and maintain or gain respect, particularly for young Black men. The code of the street has been found in numerous studies since, including Victor Rios's (2011) ethnography of Latino and Black boys/young men in Oakland, and Nikki Jones's (2010) ethnography on young Black women in inner-city Philadelphia. Similarly, Wilkinson's (2009) analysis of life-history interviews with 416 young, violent, male offenders in New York City reported the most common trigger or "spark" of violent events was challenges to their masculinity or status.

Most of the research addressing the retaliation motive of offenders has been qualitative. For example, Reid-Quiñones and her colleagues (2011) conducted a study using audio-recorded interviews of 263 inner-city girls and boys about their recent experiences of violent victimization. As might be expected, victimized youth "were angry; expressed concerns about being negatively evaluated by self and others; expressed revenge goals; and coped by using primary engagement, social support, and aggressive strategies" (2011:51). The youth who witnessed violence were afraid for themselves and others (and losing relationships) and focused on survival and avoidant behaviors. Notably, the responses to victimization and witnessing violence did not vary across gender. Calvete & Orue (2011) used three waves of data on 650 youth in Spain to study how both violent victimization and witnessing violence at Time 1 were related to both reactive aggression and proactive aggression at Time 3. Their findings support the importance of including both victimization and witnessing violence as impacting subsequent aggression, and how this varies by gender, whether the victimization was direct or witnessed, and the potential mediating roles of social-cognitive mechanisms. The found that compared to girls, boys reported more exposure to all types of violence, except violence in the family. Boys were also more likely to use proactive and reactive aggression in response to violence.

Garot (2009:66) points out that "criminologists have mostly overlooked the emotional dynamics of disputes," and identified "emotive dissonance" as a means by which "young people must restrict their desire to retaliate due to structural constraints." He conducted life-history interviews of boys/young men in a small inner-city school for dropouts in a poverty-stricken area of a large Western city to examine their drug use, gang affiliation, fights, school experiences, and intimate and family relationships, and focused on ways the youth resisted using retaliation. The first, similar to Jones (2010), was to present themselves as strong, tough, independent, and as capable as any male of defending themselves. The second was to remain silent about their victimizations, to reject the notion that they needed special protection. Yet, all of these ethnographies remind us that youth of color living in primarily poor neighborhoods usually refrain from using violence or retaliating. At the same time it is reasonable to expect that failure to protect our citizenry from violence and abuse in their everyday lives and by the criminal legal system, inevitably increases victimization and offending.

Finally, in addition to the historic invisibility of childhood maltreatment in strain-theory studies, and evidence that girls are more likely than boys to experience such maltreatments, a fair amount of research also indicates that girls and boys respond to strain and trauma differently (e.g., Broidy & Agnew, 1997). For example, one study found there were no gender differences in girls' and boys' self-reported anger levels from experiencing family-perpetrated abuse, but that boys are more likely to externalize their anger and turn it into delinquency, whereas girls are more likely to internalize their anger and transform it into guilt (self-blame) (Hay, 2003).

In sum, the role of masculinity has proven to be vital to understand offending and responses to marginalization caused by race, gender, class, sexuality, and so on. The code of the street is complicated, but significant, and is often related to the retaliation and self-protection aspects of offending. Although it has been used almost exclusively to examine boys' and men's offending, Nikki Jones (2010) has documented its use in how inner-city girls/young women in Philadelphia have to walk a fine line in staying safe in their everyday lives, including going to and from school. Feminist theory as applied to criminology needs to more adeptly engage with the ways in which masculinity and femininity are related to offending, retaliation, and survival, particularly among the most impoverished living in neighborhoods with the least resources.

## Conclusions

In addition to simply including women/girls in research samples, the most significant contributions of feminist theory to criminological theory have been: (1) recognition of the intersectional approach to oppression when studying offending, victimization, and criminal legal system responses; (2) the identification of feminist pathways theory (the link between trauma and offending); and (3) the potential role of masculinity and femininity in explaining gender differences in offending. This chapter addressed each of these.

Feminist criminology has widened the lens not only to include girls/women in studies on offending and victimization, but also to document ways that victimization is related to offending (and offending is related to victimization). Feminist scholarship has advocated the defining and measuring of gender-based abuse, at the same time that it has recognized the victimizations of boys/men in ways that had never been documented, including how pathways theory is relevant for boys' and men's offending, as well as girls' and women's offending. Future feminist scholarship on crime must continue to attempt to be rigorous and comprehensive in addressing the many ways that sexism intersects with other forms of oppression including racism, classism, homophobia/heterosexism, immigrant-status, and so on. At the same time that large quantitative studies are useful to determine the rates of phenomena, relationships between variables, and criminal legal system decision-making, smaller qualitative samples and ethnographic studies are necessary for collecting richer, deeper data that allow for more nuanced understandings of what Richie (1996) identifies as the contradictions and complications in many offending and abused women's and girls' lives. Clearly, such data are also necessary for understanding offending men's and boys' lives, and feminist criminology is paving the way for these advances in criminology theory.

## Note

1 The author uses the term "criminal legal system" rather than "criminal justice system" given that so much of what we observe and study is of the injustices in our official system.

## References

Anderson, E. (1999). *Code of the Street: Decency, Violence, and the Moral Life of the Inner City.* New York: W.W. Norton.

Arnold, R.A. (1990). Processes of victimization and criminalization of black women. *Social Justice, 17*(3), 153–166.

Belknap, J. (2015). *The Invisible Woman: Gender, Crime, and Justice,* 4th edition. Belmont, CA: Cengage.

Bottcher, J. (2001). Social practices of gender: How gender relates to delinquency in the everyday lives of high-risk youths. *Criminology, 39*(4), 893–931.

Broidy, L., & Agnew, R. (1997). Gender and crime: A general strain theory perspective. *Journal of Research in Crime and Delinquency, 34*(3), 275–306.

Calvete, E., & Orue, I. (2011). The impact of violence exposure on aggressive behavior through social information processing in adolescents. *American Journal of Orthopsychiatry, 81*(1), 38–50.

Church, W.T., II, Wharton, T., & Taylor, J.K. (2009). An examination of differential association and social control theory family systems and delinquency. *Youth Violence and Juvenile Justice, 7*(1), 3–15. doi: 10.1177/1541204008324910.

Daly, K., & Chesney-Lind, M. (1988). Feminism and criminology. *Justice Quarterly, 5*(4), 497–538.

Danner, M.J.E. (1989). Socialist feminism. In B.D. MacLean & D. Milovanovic (Eds.), *New Decisions in Critical Criminology* (pp. 551–554). Vancouver: Collective Press.

DeHart, D., Lynch, S., Belknap, J., Dass-Brailsford, P., & Green, B. (2014). Life history models of female offending: The roles of serious mental illness and trauma in women's pathways to jail. *Psychology of Women Quarterly, 38*(1), 138–151. doi: 10.1177/0361684313494357.

Garot, R. (2009). Reconsidering retaliation: Structural inhibitions, emotive dissonance, and the acceptance of ambivalence among inner-city young men. *Ethnography, 10*(1), 63–90.

Hay, C. (2003). Family strain, gender, and delinquency. *Sociological Perspectives, 46*(1), 107–135. doi: 10.1525/sop.2003.46.1.107.

Jones, N. (2010). Between good and ghetto: African American girls and inner-city violence. New Brunswick, NJ: Rutgers University Press.

Lynch, S.M., DeHart, D.D., Belknap, J.E., Green, B.L., Dass-Brailsford, P., Johnson, K.A., *et al.* (2014). A multisite study of the prevalence of serious mental illness, PTSD, and substance use disorders of women in jail. *Psychiatric Services, 65*(5), 670–674. doi: 10.1176/appi. ps.201300172.

Potter, H. (2008). *Battle Cries: Black Women and Intimate Partner Abuse.* New York: New York University Press.

Potter, H. (2013). Intersectional criminology: Interrogating identity and power in criminological research and theory. *Critical Criminology, 21*(3), 305–318. doi: 10.1007/s10612-013-9203-6.

Reid-Quiñones, K., Kliewer, W., Shields, B.J., Goodman, K., Ray, M.H., & Wheat, E. (2011). Cognitive, affective, and behavioral responses to witnessed versus experienced violence. *American Journal of Orthopsychiatry, 81*(1), 51–60.

Richie, B.E. (1996). *Compelled to Crime: The Gender Entrapment of Battered Black Women.* New York: Routledge.

Richie, B.E. (2012). *Arrested Justice: Black Women, Violence, and America's Prison Nation.* New York: New York University Press.

Rios, V.M. (2011). *Punished: Policing the Lives of Black and Latino Boys.* New York: New York University Press.

Widom, C.S. (1989). The cycle of violence. *Science, 244*(4901), 160–166.

Wilkinson, D. (2009). Events Dynamics and the Role of Third Parties in Urban Youth Violence. Final Report Submitted to the U.S. Department of Justice. Grant 2006-IJ-CX-0004. https://www.ncjrs.gov/pdffiles1/nij/grants/227781.pdf. Accessed July 23, 2015.

Wilkinson-Ryan, T., & Hoffman, D.A. (2010). Breach is for suckers. *Vanderbilt Law Review, 63*(4), 1002–1045.

Young, V.D. (1980). Women, race, and crime. *Criminology, 18*(1), 26–34.

Young, V.D. (1986). Gender expectations and their impact on black female offenders and victims. *Justice Quarterly, 3*, 305–327.

# 16

# Critical Criminology

## Martin D. Schwartz and Henry H. Brownstein

## Introduction

Critical criminological theory, the subject of this essay, is a descriptive term that covers a broad range of theoretical positions. To be included under the same umbrella any group of theories must share certain suppositions and viewpoints, but in this case they typically don't speak with a single voice: there are also differences between them. Some of these differences may seem to those outside the tradition to be fairly major. Some seem that way even to other people huddling under that same umbrella. What brings them all together as critical criminological work is that to some degree the variants of critical criminology locate one of the prime "causes" or origins of criminal behavior in the economic structure of society and the inequalities of the class system that this structure generates. Critical theories focus on the various systems that both divide power unequally and also distribute power and material resources inequitably by race, ethnicity, and gender (Friedrichs, 2009). In solving societal problems, they "regard major structural and cultural changes within society as essential steps to reduce crime and promote social justice" (DeKeseredy, 2011:7). Still, many are unwilling to wait patiently for that major change, and call in the short run for incremental changes to unpack the trend in recent years toward more punitive and harsh sentences, the militarization of the police, and the move toward privatizing the criminal justice system that makes it profitable to cause pain.

One of the other things that bring together critical criminology theorists is a self-reflection that sees themselves in opposition to mainstream criminology. For example, many critical criminologists reject the positivist notion that a researcher can be completely objective and divorced from her own personal politics. Although some critical criminologists use traditional scientific and statistical modes of

*The Handbook of Criminological Theory*, First Edition. Edited by Alex R. Piquero.
© 2016 John Wiley & Sons, Inc. Published 2016 by John Wiley & Sons, Inc.

analysis, many others insist that only qualitative and ethnographic methodologies that give voice to the feelings of the various dispossessed in society are valid tools. Thus, it is relatively common that some of the discussion of how to draw the boundaries of critical criminology includes an explanation of what critical criminology is *not*. For this reason, some of the examination below will draw upon this tradition and make these distinctions.

While there is a point of agreement that pulls all critical theories together, outside the tradition and within the broader circles of criminology there remains some confusion about what to call these theories. Mainstream criminologists commonly call the field "conflict theory," an older name that is now rarely used by people who actually work within the tradition. Some of the confusion comes from the fact that conflict theories were popular through much of the twentieth century. They were indeed rooted in an analysis of economic struggles between groups in society, quite literally an analysis of the conflicts and struggles between groups in a society. While some of these theories were critical, indeed radical or Marxist, others engaged in this analysis in a way that could and often did easily fit into a conservative, noncritical approach. Conflict theories were only a part of the broad landscape of theories that emerged in the later part of the twentieth century, and only a few theorists continue to self-define in this way.

Some other mainstream criminologists also refer to the field as "radical criminology," a term used by a few radical conflict criminologists many years ago. Properly, however, the field is critical criminology, a term that has been used since the 1970s to tie together theorists from a broad variety of theoretical frameworks that base their analysis on unequal power relationships that play out in class, race, ethnicity, and gender terms. Today, the Division on Critical Criminology of the American Society of Criminology, and the Section on Critical Criminal Justice of the Academy of Criminal Justice Sciences are large organizations that bring together these diverse theorists.

## The Role of Theory

In essence, a theory is an explanation that helps people to understand that which is otherwise incomprehensible. A criminological theory explains how and why some people at some times and in some circumstances deviate or not from some social norm or norms; how and why some or all other people around them, each with varying degrees of socially legitimate authority, respond or not to real or imagined transgressions or antisocial actions or behavior; and how and why that response does make a difference, or not. In social science, theory contributes to a better understanding of a social phenomenon by serving as a link between established knowledge and new knowledge that is grounded in a compelling analytic framework to achieve a richer and more comprehensive explanation of the phenomenon.

Of course it is not so simple. First, not all theories are useful or even compelling. Thomas Kuhn suggests that for a theory to be a good theory it needs to have the following characteristics: accuracy, consistency, scope, simplicity, and fruitfulness

(1970:321). A second difficulty arises when an analytic framework is proposed that by scientific standards is not logical or defensible. This typically occurs when we try to fill in gaps in our knowledge with assumptions derived from an ideology that cannot be substantiated or verified by scientific evidence. Rather, such assumptions may be based on beliefs, values, attitudes, and the like. This has been common throughout the history of science, when moralistic values are used to attack scientific judgments. For example, in 2003 the US House Committee on Energy and Commerce required the National Institutes of Health (NIH), the primary federal agency funding medical and scientific research, to justify awards made to over 200 grantees because their research related to the subject of sexual behavior (Kaiser, 2003:758). In response Alan Leshner, a former director of an NIH Institute, wrote, "Whenever science is attacked on ideological grounds, its integrity and usefulness are threatened. Society cannot afford for moralistic dogma to replace scientific judgment when the public's welfare is at stake" (2003:1479).

Criminological theory is a good example of how theory can guide research in a particular direction, though not always the most productive or defensible direction. But this is the way science works, and it is not necessarily a bad thing. When the analytic framework of a theory with its concepts, ideas, and assumptions are integrated and blended in a meaningful and compelling way they form the basis of a general orientation toward or way of thinking about a phenomenon (Kuhn, 1970). As George Ritzer wrote, such a paradigm "serves to define what should be studied, what questions should be asked, how they should be asked, what rules should be followed in interpreting the answers obtained" (1975:7). In the advancement of science and knowledge over time, paradigms compete and replace each other. As one paradigm replaces another the way of thinking about a phenomenon, such as crime or criminal behavior or crime control, changes and theories from the new paradigm guide science and research. Naturally, what happens is more complex than that, but the idea holds that criminological theories of the late twentieth century led research and science in directions that may not be appropriate for what we know and how we view the world in the twenty-first century.

## Mainstream and Critical Criminological Theory

Early in the nineteenth century, living in the afterglow of the Enlightenment, social thinkers who considered phenomena like criminal behavior, crime, or justice viewed them through a lens of philosophical values. Specifically, these values favored reason over tradition and faith, and skepticism over superstition. In this classical or neoclassical tradition, criminological theory was based on the assumption that human beings have free will. Therefore they are responsible for their actions and will act to minimize discomfort and maximize gratification (cf., Beccaria, 1963; Bentham, 1843). There is no way to test whether or not human beings have free will so it is not surprising that other social thinkers later based theories of criminal behavior, crime, and justice on the belief that humans do not act freely. Rather, human behavior is a consequence of independent biological, cultural, or social factors (cf., Goddard, 1914; Lombroso, 1876; Lombroso-Ferrero & Savitz, 1972; also, see Fishbein, 1990). In the twentieth century a number of mainstream criminological theories developed out of these traditions and flourished.

Meanwhile, critical criminological theories were growing from another tradition that believed it was possible to tie together and assimilate various assumptions supporting the possibility that human beings are able to create themselves, with assumptions that support the possibility that human beings are products of their social, cultural, and physical world (see Bohm & Vogel, 2011; Lynch & Groves, 1989).

Thus, at their core mainstream and critical criminological theories are clearly distinguished by the different paradigms and assumptions: mainstream theories emanating from classical, neoclassical, and positivist thought, and critical theories from Marxist thought in its various expressions (see Eisenstadter & Henry, 2006; Gibbs, 1987; Taylor, Walton, & Young, 1973). Contemporary mainstream theories propose explanations of criminal behavior, crime, and justice in the context of, for example, social disorganization, social control or bonding, socialization or, specifically, differential association, and anomie or strain (Akers & Sellers, 2008; Curran & Renzetti, 2001; Jacoby, 2004; Lilly, Cullen, & Ball, 2011). Contemporary critical theories propose explanations that emphasize understanding how criminal or deviant behavior and crime as social phenomena are constructed, and how and why people come to be labeled by others as criminal or deviant. All of this is understood in the context of inherent faults and flaws in the structure of modern society, and results in an unequal distribution of social resources, including not only material goods or wealth but also power, status, and even personal and community wellbeing (DeKeseredy, 2011; DeKeseredy & Dragiewicz, 2012; Schwartz & Hatty, 2003).

Like research in many other fields, criminology theory has been heavily influenced by government policy and government funding. Late in his career, Donald Cressey reminisced about the speech he gave when awarded the American Society of Criminology's Sutherland Award. At that time, he spoke of a growing awareness that criminality is not inherent in certain people, coming out in a measurable form. He predicted major shifts in criminology theory. Later, he wrote:

> In 1967, of course, no one knew that the Law Enforcement Assistance Administration was going to throw billions into a war on crime or that the so-called "research arm" of LEAA, the National Institute of Law Enforcement and Administration of Justice, was going to be more interested in financing studies about what to do about "the crime problem" than in financing studies about why there is a "crime problem" to worry about (1978:171).

Mainstream criminological theories at the time were well served by, and served well, the direction for research embedded in the LEAA funding bonanza. Mainstream theory has moved the field to studies that address questions about things like control, management, and regulation of crime and criminals. The importance here is that critical criminological theory has the potential to move the field toward studies that address underlying questions about crime, criminal behavior, and justice in the context of socially constructed differences in race, class, gender, and age as they relate to the social significance of power, influence, and authority (Brownstein, 2013). Cressey concluded that, given the attraction of LEAA funding, criminologists in the late twentieth century in the United States became "technical assistant[s] to politicians bent on repressing crime, rather than a scientist[s] seeking valid propositions stated in a causal framework" (1978:173). Going a step further, looking particularly at criminal justice responses to drugs, Elliott Currie concluded that not only had criminology during the period supported more repressive policies and practices but consequently our response to crime and criminal behavior has done "everything but improving lives" (Currie, 1993:332).

It was noted earlier that not all theories are of equal value, and critical criminological theories are not one set of ideas or concepts comprising a single theory. Below we consider different expressions of contemporary critical criminology: how, within the context of critical criminology, each forms an analytic framework for explaining criminal behavior, crime, and justice; and how each might inform research going forward in a scientific process toward enhancing our knowledge of criminal behavior, crime, and justice.

## Critical Criminology

A problem in discussing our topic is that while there may be some shared roots, shared perspectives, and shared methods, "critical criminology," as we have emphasized already, is an umbrella term for a variety of perspectives that challenge mainstream criminology assumptions. Although it may be an inconvenience for textbook writers, there is no single or unitary theory or set of shared ideas that can be called critical criminology or even the now-disused (except by textbook writers) conflict criminology. Below, we consider different expressions of contemporary critical criminology and how each of these theoretical positions forms an analytic framework for explaining criminal behavior, crime, and justice, and how each might inform research going forward in a scientific process toward enhancing our knowledge.

Overall, each of these criminologies sees itself in opposition to mainstream criminology, which might be termed by their practitioners as establishment, administrative, managerial, correctional, or positivistic criminology. Critical criminologists see mainstream criminology as narrowly focused on individual and street offenders, and aimed at providing social engineering on behalf of the state (Friedrichs, 2009). Methodologically many critical criminologists reject limiting the study of crime completely to the "scientific method," which suggests the ability to objectively generate and study data in order to confirm or reject research hypotheses grounded in the research tradition. This is not to suggest that some critical criminologists do not use quantitative methodologies and statistical methods to test research hypotheses. Left realists and feminists in particular have engaged in extensive and national level research with large data sets. However, broadly and generally, critical criminologists are more likely to adopt a qualitative and interpretive approach.

## Feminist criminology

Although strands of feminism have been strong and popular for many years, the major move into crime and critical criminology came from the recognition that most mainstream criminology, and in fact most critical criminology, simply ignored the problem of women and girls in conflict with the law. Sometimes, starting in the 1960s, when mainstream criminologists did decide to include women they simply added sex or gender as a variable in statistical analysis. At a minimum, feminist criminologists argue that gender is an essential lens through which to examine crime and society. One of the first things that feminists saw with this lens is that society is most often based on a patriarchal hierarchy that provides benefits to many men. Meda Chesney-Lind, for example, one of the pioneers of feminist analysis of delinquency, has long argued that delinquency theory has ignored girls and their unique forms of victimization (1989). Worse, she found that a lack of a gendered lens blinded theorists to the role that the juvenile justice system played in sexualizing girls' delinquency, and criminalizing their survival strategies. At the time when much of the criminological theory we read today was originally written, ascribing large and complex motivations to men and boys engaged in crime, the literature still mainly attributed female delinquency to sexual wants and needs, such as attracting boys. Girls were seemingly immune to complex motivation, in the minds of criminologists.

In recent years, Jody Miller has been active in expanding feminist criminology's reach, arguing that a gendered lens is essential to the study of men's and boy's situations and, further, to the intersection of race and class with gender (2008). For example, after about 150 years of studying crime and its causation, the one factor most associated with criminal acts is the one that is least discussed: that the overwhelming majority of criminal acts are committed by men (Schwartz & Hatty, 2003). How does the operation of male roles and behavior, along with male privilege, affect their dominance in property, violent, and white collar crimes? A gendered lens requires looking at gender and its role in influencing behavior.

Early feminist criminology was heavily concerned with the lack of attention generally paid in criminology to the victimization experiences of women; sexual assault, battering, and child abuse, and the reaction (or lack of reaction) of the state to these crimes were important topics. More recently, however, feminists have broadened their scope dramatically, taking on such topics as the relationship between women's surviving of victimization experiences and women's offending, and a substantially more nuanced understanding of female criminality. For example, Jody Miller's work centers on the gendered nature of violence in the community, especially African-American communities marked by extreme inequality. Thus, the sociology of place is added as a concern to race, class and gender. Of course, feminist critical criminologists share a belief that modern capitalist society is patriarchal, hierarchical, and stratified, teaching many in society what has been termed hegemony – that systems of male superiority and privilege are not only fully acceptable, but have become a part of nature and everyday common sense. Miller (2008), for example, showed the ways in which society blamed girls for their own sexual victimization, shaping and forming gender stereotypes that not only affected the girls' self-perceptions and behavior, but also allowed boys and men to control public space.

## Left realist theory

The origins of left realism lie in the 1970s in Great Britain, where some radical criminologists strongly proclaimed that concern about street crime was a racist media scare designed to justify massive repressive measures against members of the working class, something that at the time was sometimes called "right realism" by those who opposed such policies. Certainly, criminologists to the left of center had not devoted much attention to the plight of victims of street crime, ceding that concern to conservatives in favor of a concern with white collar and corporate crime. In an attempt to reclaim that field for progressive analysis, left realists argued that the primary targets of street crime were themselves members of the working class. They used crime victimization surveys to show that the primary victims of robbery, burglary, and rape were working-class people. Worse, these people were also the primary victims of white collar, corporate, and state crime. Elliott Currie (2010) has argued that much of the left has engaged in what he terms "progressive retreatism," ceding the issue of street crime to right, while doing little on the left but complain.

Another difference from other left-leaning theories was that left realists such as Jock Young did not feel any need to be constrained by other leftist or Marxist theories (Hayward, 2010). In a period when many criminologists on the left rejected anything mainstream, left realists borrowed any ideas that seemed to have explanatory value. For example, Lea & Young (1984) borrowed extensively from Robert K. Merton (strain) and Albert K. Cohen (subculture) to develop the notion of relative deprivation – that absolute poverty does not cause crime; some of the very poorest people on Earth are relatively crime-free. Rather, it is extreme income differences (the gap between the rich and the poor in any specific society) that leads to discontent with the political structure. Like Cohen, they argued that disenfranchised people may come together in subcultural formations that may legitimate criminal behavior (1984).

More recently, DeKeseredy & Schwartz (2010) have argued that conservative economic policies have led to deindustrialization, the decline of family farms, and other attacks on the ability of young men to act out masculinity norms in a socially approved manner. Many economically marginalized men, they argue, engage in violence as a form of compensatory masculinity, attempting to gain through posturing a masculinist image that, before deindustrialization, was available through employment as a member of the working class. Gibbs (2010) has argued that left realist theory is useful in attempts to explain terrorist acts, in that economically marginalized men are the pool from which terrorists draw. Dragiewicz (2010) has used left realism to analyze how many ostensibly middle-class men feel marginalized by newer laws on child support and violence against women, seeking out similar men to reassert patriarchal masculinity.

Finally, in a field where it is not uncommon that recommendations for massive societal overhaul are the only changes theorists have to recommend, left realists separated themselves by engaging in extensive recommendations for short-term, progressive anticrime measures. While in the early days this heavily involved a concern for the democratic control of the police, more recently Roger Matthews (2009) has developed a newer left realism that calls for the linking of theory, method, and intervention, with an emphasis on recognizing the state as a central organizing concept "that provide(s) the conceptual frameworks through which we make sense of the social world" (2009:346). This notion of supporting change and intervention to relieve the suffering of crime victims has been attacked by some elements of the left, which views it as tinkering that will only delay larger change by reinforcing the existing power structure (e.g., Jamieson & Yates, 2009). Left realists, however, always stood for improving the position of the working class where possible, which would include lowering the street crime rate, at the same time that steps are being taken to reduce corporate and white collar crime.

## Convict criminology

Correctional institutions, prisoners and ex-convicts have long been the subject of criminological inquiry, whether the focus is psychological, sociological, philosophical, or biological. Authors across the political spectrum have written at extraordinary length to explain what prisoners think, and why they act as they do. It seems that the only voices missing from this discussion are those of prisoners or ex-convicts themselves (Ross & Richards, 2003). In an attempt to fill that gap, American ex-convicts who had gone on to earn advanced degrees and enter higher education as faculty members founded the school of convict criminology, along with some nonconvict academics. Part of the goal of the movement is to show that the authentic voice of those who have experienced prisons has been missing from academic discourse on the subject. However, another goal of the movement is to show that people with direct experience of imprisonment have a point of view about the entire nature of prisons and correctional reform.

The goal of these theorists is not automatically to end prisons and imprisonment, but rather to use prior experience as inmates along with the tools learned as academics to engage in ethnographic research to give a more realistic picture of the prison experience. Still, based on both experience and new research, it is not surprising that the members of this school of thought have found the prison experience to be something short of uplifting. Rather, they have found it destructive and incapable of meeting any goals of providing change, reducing crime, or promoting social justice (DeKeseredy, 2011). Certainly the American grand experiment of incarcerating tremendous numbers of low-level offenders in conditions of humiliation and degradation has been a major point of attack. As Friedrichs (2009) has pointed out, such criminologists have found critical criminology a welcome home for arguments that a proper understanding of crime must include viewpoints from the bottom up, along with a realization of the poverty of such extreme measures taken by a society against some of its most disadvantaged citizens. At this point, convict criminology has shown a great deal of energy, and provided important and interesting ethnographies, but the next step is to rise above description into a unique school of thought (Lilly, Cullen, & Ball, 2011).

## Cultural criminology

One of the newer variants of critical criminology, cultural criminology had its origins in the 1990s. The original focus is not new, of course: critical criminologists have long been interested in the influence of culture, the media, and popular culture. What marks this school of thought is the sustained focus of a group of theorists on how representations in the media and mass culture shape our understanding of human behavior. In turn, as people begin to accept media-generated images as an accurate picture of behavior, these images then proceed to shape public policy in such areas as drug policy and criminal punishment (Ferrell, Hayward, & Young, 2008).

This field has its roots in a number of areas, but labeling theory of the 1960s, and the work of British theorists such as Stanley Cohen, were important. In particular, the notions of *moral panics* and *folk devils* is essential (Cohen, 1980). Media representations, even without any facts to support them, can result in media and moral panics about such things as increased violence among juvenile girls, new (at least to the media) drugs that almost invariantly are portrayed as sponsored by minority groups but infiltrating and destroying good middle-class kids, and rave parties. Any of these, and many others, can provoke a panic that leads to ill-conceived new laws, police crackdowns, massive imprisonment, and social exclusion. Of course, the nature of moral panics is that they are massive overreactions to minor threats. To sustain them, the media must create *folk devils*, or some group to blame for the crisis.

Jock Young (2009:1–2) has said that cultural criminology "zooms in on phenomenal experience of crime, victimization and punishment, stressing anger, humiliation, exuberance, excitement, and fear. It reveals the energy of everyday life, whether in the transgressive breaking of rules or in the repressive nature of conformity and boredom." Jeff Ferrell, a founder of the field, argues (2003:71) that the field examines the role of "image, style and symbolic meaning among criminals and their subcultures, in the mass media's representation of crime and criminal justice, and in public conflicts over crime and crime control."

Cultural criminologists, led by theorists such as Ferrell, have undertaken to provide a rich or "thick" description of people who live at the margins of the social order, such as graffiti artists, drug users, street people, and skydivers, using not only ethnographic approaches but also direct participant observation to provide colorful observations of the socially marginalized. This has led to attacks from mainstream criminologists and deviance theorists, who claim that the field is sensationalizing the exotic but lacks substance. As Muzzatti (2006) points out, however, these critiques can only exist by equating style with substance, or in this case, a lack of substance. There is no question, however, that cultural criminology depends for its energy on a rejection of, and intellectual resistance to, mainstream constructions and policies.

## Crimes of the powerful

Critical criminologists have also been leaders in the fields of crimes of the privileged, and crimes of the state, arguing that the main focus of mainstream criminology has been on the behavior of the poorest and weakest members of any society. David Friedrichs has led the way for the study of crimes of the elites with his comprehensive and powerful *Trusted Criminals* (2010), dealing not only with crime by people in positions of trust, but also by corporations themselves in the furtherance of corporate goals. A number of important critical criminologists have been active in this area, with many tracing their roots as colleagues or students of Ronald Kramer or Ray Michaelowski, such as Dawn Rothe, Rick Matthews, and David Kauzlarich.

As the field has progressed, it has become obvious that there are four more or less distinct areas of inquiry currently: crimes of the state, corporate crime, state-corporate crime, and crimes of globalization.

*Crimes of the state* perhaps start in modern times with the Holocaust, but have been regularly committed throughout the world, killing tens of millions and injuring or making homeless just as many (Rothe & Kauzlarich, 2014).

*Corporate crime* investigates the damage done by corporate entitles, whether in stock fraud, banking or environmental destruction, which has also been extraordinary in the recent past (Friedrichs, 2010).

When the state and corporate interests work together in mutual but illegal interest, some theorists have found, the result can be termed *state-corporate crime*. Unfortunately, we tend to find out about these crimes when a disaster occurs, whether it is a space shuttle blowing up, or an environmental disaster (Michaelowski & Kramer, 2006).

An example of the call for the expansion of definitions of social harm within criminology beyond the borders of what is currently criminalized in law is the field of *crimes of globalization*, a term invented by David Friedrichs (Friedrichs & Friedrichs, 2002). The most commonly cited of these are the acts of various international and world bodies such as the World Bank to promote and encourage the expansion of capitalist interests into less developed parts of the world, which has not only led to massive political corruption, but also to increasing prices which has increased misery, food shortages, environmental disaster and increased health problems among much of the poor.

## Postmodern criminology

Although postmodern thought, a mostly European phenomenon, had important influences on humanities scholars much earlier, it was not until the 1980s that postmodernism began to influence critical criminologists in North America. Even then, among all of the various strains of critical criminology, postmodern criminology remained the least developed and the least understood (Schwartz & Friedrichs, 1994). Of course, as David Friedrichs points out (2009), there is no reason to assume that postmodern thought is automatically progressive or critical. Some segments of it are avowedly apolitical, and others are "inherently conservative and reactionary." At best it can only be described as "a loose collection of themes and tendencies" (2009:213).

However, some critical criminologists, such as Stuart Henry and Dragan Milovanovic (2005), have adapted the postmodern claims that truth is not only unknowable, but also that claims to knowledge of what is correct and true are a form of tyranny imposed by those in a position of power on everyone else. This is a place where postmodern theorists diverge from most other critical criminologists. While it is not only usual but just about mandatory for critical criminologists to champion the voice and the interests of the weaker and less-possessed members of society, postmodernists reject any ability to speak on behalf of others (Schwartz & Friedrichs, 1994).

*Constitutive criminology* Although postmodernists reject the use of broader definitions and concepts such as the "state," Henry & Milovanovic have developed an attempt to bring together some of the themes of the postmodern project with some of the main concerns of critical criminology. This new field of "constitutive criminology" is devoted to locating and describing how meaning is produced around crime. People who commit acts that are termed criminal, people involved in the formal system of control of such criminals, and the people who study these actors, all come together to jointly produce the meaning of crime. To study this constitutive criminologists bring in many of the tools of postmodern inquiry to discuss discursive practices, the role of symbols and symbolic meaning, and the role of ideology in shaping these practices and symbols (Henry & Milovanovic, 2005).

## Peacemaking criminology

Hal Pepinsky and Richard Quinney (1991) published *Criminology as Peacemaking*, a book of essays by criminologists where each wrote about crime and crime control from a critical and commonsense perspective in a religious or humanist or feminist tradition while thinking about things like human rights and conflict resolution. The collection introduced what has since become the basis of what is known as peacemaking criminology. Given that at the time the world, and particularly the United States, was "at war" with crime, and indeed remains so, the idea of making peace had a certain symmetrical appeal.

In the same year Pepinsky published another book in which he described peacemaking criminology in simple and straightforward terms: "Rather than doing things to offenders, peacemaking requires us to do things with offenders and others" (1991:96). More broadly, the idea assumes a belief that in a democratic society each participant in a social interaction or experience has a unique perspective of that interaction. If one believes that each perspective is equally valid and worthy of consideration, it then follows that decisions should be made about how to respond to actions or behaviors considered inappropriate or antisocial through means that are developed by a group of participants who maintain control through some synthetically legitimated source of power and authority (see Pepinsky, 1991; Pepinsky & Jesilow, 1984; Pepinsky & Quinney, 1991).

The idea for a criminological theory based on making peace has its roots in a European tradition of peace research stemming from organizations like the International Peace Research Institute in Oslo (see Galtung, 1984). Relating the notion of peace directly to crime and crime control, Nils Christie has argued that peace in social relationships can be viewed as an alternative to war in that "imposing punishment within the institution of law means the inflicting of pain, intended as pain. This is an activity which often comes into dissonance to esteemed values such as kindness and forgiveness" (1981:5). By its nature, the current criminal justice system is based on tearing people and societies apart. Arguably then, peacemaking criminological theory is about finding the interconnectedness between and among people rather than focusing on their differences and using those differences to diminish the status of others for whatever reason.

In more recent years criminologists have tried to develop peacemaking criminology as a variant of critical theory, explaining crime and crime control in terms of the need to overcome the inherent faults and flaws of the social institutions of justice that make power and authority the dominant forces in decisions about how people should treat each other. John Fuller, for example, argues that changes in the criminal justice system need to promote rehabilitation and change in the offender, which a system of inflicting pain does not do: "Peacemaking criminology attempts to bridge the gap between individual responsibility for his/her actions and requires that the offender take responsibility for his/her actions and rehabilitation while challenging the state to provide a system of justice that is fair to all and does not simply reinforce the power arrangement in society" (2003:85). John Wozniak has suggested, similarly, that a change in how we all behave can affect the behavior of those who harm others: "At its core, peacemaking criminology reveals that, instead of waging a war on crime, we can create social arrangements in which the needs of all are taken into account. In particular, peacemaking criminology calls upon us to refuse to invest in a social ethic that separates us from one another and instead to visualize all people – including those responsible for serious harms – as being connected" (2000:283). This kind of new system was particularly attractive to people who were concerned about illicit drugs and the long-term and loud language proclaiming that America was engaged in a war on drugs. A number of criminologists tried to use peacemaking to propose an alternative to this war

(Alexander, 1990; Brownstein, 1992; Reinarman & Levine, 1990), though not necessarily as a theory of crime or justice or drug policy.

While there are criminologists who today treat peacemaking as a theory, it is not clear that it is one. A criminological theory has to explain a social phenomenon such as crime or crime control in a way that offers a compelling analytic framework made up of ideas and concepts that guide researchers and other analysts to a richer and more complete explanation of the phenomenon. Looking at its origin in peace research and in early writings on peacemaking in criminology, rather than serving as an explanation it appears to be more of a program to try to change the way or ways people relate to each other in the face of personal and social transgressions. Even a prominent advocate for peacemaking criminology like John Fuller writes that it "has a long way to go before it can reach the status and acceptance of the more established and traditional criminology theories. At present, it represents more of a philosophy or perspective than it does a well-developed theory" (2003:95).

## Other critical criminologies

The opening premise of this chapter was that there are a number of criminologies that gather together under the umbrella of critical criminology; that the field is enormously broader than a notion of "conflict theory" or "Marxist theory," neither of which describe even a fraction of the field. It is no longer possible to write one essay that represents all of critical criminology. Thus, the areas quickly introduced here do not exhaust the field. There are many other criminologies still trying to gain a foothold and adherents, which very well may be an important part of a future review of this sort. Of course, it would be impossible to cover all of these nascent critical criminologies, but the two most likely to expand in the future are *green criminology* and *queer criminology*.

As environmental concerns began to permeate social sciences generally, some criminologists have been particularly interested in the study of certain social practices that are harmful to the environment. Certainly, finding examples to study of illegal behavior that has led to massive mercury or lead poisoning of waterways, corporate waste that has destroyed groundwater supplies, illegal destruction of forests and catchbasins, and many similar highly destructive actions have not been hard to find, and green criminologists have devoted attention to the criminological study of these practices. Pioneered by Rob Whyte of Tasmania and Michael Lynch of South Florida, this field has grown to include a truly international membership in the International Green Criminology Working Group.

But what is this field? As of yet there is not so much as a working agreement on the definition of "green criminology." Obviously, the narrowest definition would be crimes against the environment as defined by legal statutes; violations of existing environmental law. Others, however, argue for broader definitions, to include any harms to the environment or animals, regardless of the legal status of this behavior. There are many exceptionally destructive acts that are still not criminalized in national or international law. A still broader definition would take into account the fact that many states and corporations have the power to shape our perceptions and definitions of environmental harm, and would argue that studies should include harms covered up in this fashion (White, 2014). Obviously, this fledgling field has a great deal of potential for development and expansion, and given the number of people in academia generally interested in environmental issues, some expansion within criminology seems assured.

Within green criminology there has been a growing understanding of the human-centered nature of today's more common environmental concerns. Even within such fields as conservation, legal concern has been driven by a desire to hoard, manage, husband, or maintain resources for humans to use or exploit at a later time. To the extent that this is changing, it is no doubt due to a growing understanding of the extent to which human exploitation of the environment is changing the very nature of the ecological system, and the extent to which it may be permanently damaged (e.g., global warming).

A related subfield of green criminology is *non-speciesist criminology*, which reminds us that among the natural resources that have been ravaged by humans are non-human animals. Of course, many have been shot or fished just about out of existence, such as the buffalo and the passenger pigeon. But today animals continue to be victimized in many ways by the criminal behavior of social institutions, business enterprises, and individual humans. The leading proponent of this field is Piers Beirne (2009), who has long argued against animal cruelty and human speciesism. He points out that although animals appear in criminology most often in discussions of companion animals abused as part of studies of domestic violence, there is a great need for a solid core of criminologists to develop the wider field of animal abuse and violence. Unfortunately, "at the moment, these building blocks are more hoped for than actual" (Beirne, 2002:384).

Another newer field with great potential but as yet still struggles to locate a uniform definition and place is *queer criminology*. Obviously, the field examines the relationship of LBGTQ people to criminal behavior, and their treatment by the justice system. Just as obvious to anyone who has engaged with queer theory generally, part of the project is to identify and critique heteronormative behaviors and binary presumptions that stand in the way of justice. However, as Ball (2014) points out, there are many ways for a queer criminology to engage with queer theory generally, some of which may not involve engagements with the concept of "queer" in exactly the same way. Ball suggests that there is substantial work ahead to develop this field.

There are several other important critical criminologies. *Critical Race Criminology* is an exceptionally important field – just look at the historical record of racism in the development of criminal justice system policies and practices and our criminological theories. For example, Biko Agozino (2003), in what he terms *counter-colonial criminology*, criticizes criminologists for allowing colonial imperialist powers and slaveholders to oppress, rule, and kill large numbers of people without being blamed, analyzed, or even named as criminals. Other race theorists look at how racist ideologies still today form the cultural images that we use in the West to develop the practices and policies of our criminal justice system. Still, while critical race theory is alive, active and important, most of its adherents do not consider themselves critical criminologists.

# References

Agozino, B. (2003). *Counter-Colonial Criminology: A Critique of Imperialist Reason*. London: Pluto.

Akers, R.L., & Sellers, C.S. (2008). *Criminological Theories – Introduction, Evaluation, and Application*, 5th edition. New York: Oxford University Press.

Alexander, B.K. (1990). *Peaceful Measures: Canada's Way Out of the War on Drugs*. Toronto: University of Toronto Press.

Ball, M. (2014). What's queer about queer criminology? In D. Peterson & V.R. Panfil (Eds.), *Handbook of LGBT Communities, Crime, and Justice (pp. 531–555)*. New York: Springer.

Beccaria, C. (1963). *On Crimes and Punishments*. Indianapolis, IN: Bobbs-Merrill.

Beirne, P. (2002). Criminology and animal studies: A sociological view. *Animals & Society*, 10(4), 381–386.

Beirne, P. (2009). *Confronting Animal Abuse: Law, Criminology, and Human–Animal Relationships*. Lanham, MD: Rowman & Littlefield.

Bentham, J. (1843). *The Works of Jeremy Bentham. Vol. I. An Introduction to the Principles of Morals and Legislation*. Edinburgh: William Tait.

Bohm, R.M., & Vogel, B.L. (2011). *A Primer on Crime and Delinquency Theory*. Belmont, CA: Wadsworth.

Brownstein, H.H. (1992). Making peace in the war on drugs. *Humanity and Society*, 16, 217–235.

Brownstein, H.H. (2013). *Contemporary Drug Policy*. New York: Routledge.

Chesney-Lind, M. (1989). Girls, crime, and women's place: Toward a feminist model of female delinquency. *Crime & Delinquency*, 35, 5–29.

Christie, N. (1981). *The Limits of Pain*. Irvington-on-Hudson, NY: Columbia University Press.

Cohen, S. (1980). *Folk Devils and Moral Panics*. Oxford: Basil Blackwell.

Cressey, D.R. (1978). Criminological theory, social science, and the repression of crime. *Criminology*, 16, 171–191.

Curran, D.J., & Renzetti, C.M. (2001). *Theories of Crime*. Boston: Allyn and Bacon.

Currie, E. (1993). *Reckoning – Drugs, the Cities, and the American Future*. New York: Hill and Wang.

Currie, E. (2010). Plain left realism: An appreciation and some thoughts on the future. *Crime, Law, and Social Change*, 54(2), 111–124.

DeKeseredy, W.S. (2011). *Contemporary Critical Criminology*. New York: Routledge.

DeKeseredy, W.S., & Dragiewicz, M. (Eds.) (2012). *Routledge Handbook of Critical Criminology*. New York: Routledge.

DeKeseredy, W.S., & Schwartz, M.D. (2010). Friedman economic policies, social exclusion, and crime: Toward a gendered left realist subcultural theory. *Crime, Law, and Social Change*, 54(2), 159–170.

Dragiewicz, M. (2010). A left-realist approach to anti-feminist fathers' rights groups. *Crime, Law, and Social Change*, 54(2), 197–212.

Einstadter, W.J., & Henry, S. (2006). *Criminological Theory: An Analysis of its Underlying Assumptions*. Lanham, MD: Rowman & Littlefield.

Ferrell, J. (2003). Cultural criminology. In M.D. Schwartz & S.F. Hatty (Eds.), *Controversies in Critical Criminology* (pp. 71–84). Cincinnati: Anderson.

Ferrell, J., Hayward, K., & Young, J. (2008). *Cultural Criminology: An Invitation*. London: Sage.

Fishbein, D.H. (1990). Biological perspectives in criminology. *Criminology*, 28, 27–72.

Friedrichs, D.O. (2009). Critical criminology. In J.M. Miller (Ed.), *21st Century Criminology: A Reference Work*. Thousand Oak, CA: Sage.

Friedrichs, D.O. (2010). *Trusted Criminals: White Collar Crime in Contemporary Society*. Belmont, CA: Cengage.

Friedrichs, D.O., & Friedrichs, J. (2002). The World Bank and crimes of globalization: A case study. *Social Justice*, 29(1–2), 1–12.

Fuller, J. (2003). Peacemaking criminology. In M.D. Schwartz & S.E. Hatty (Eds.), *Controversies in Critical Criminology* (pp. 85–95). Cincinnati: Anderson.

Galtung, J. (1984). *Twenty-Five Years of Peace Research – Ten Challenges and Some Responses*. Berlin: Berghoff Stifung.

Gibbs, J.C. (2010). Looking at terrorism through left realist lenses. *Crime, Law, and Social Change*, 54(2), 171–185.

Gibbs, J.P. (1987). The state of criminological theory. *Criminology*, 25, 821–840.

Goddard, H.H. (1914). *Feeblemindedness: Its Causes and Consequences*. New York: MacMillan.

Hayward, K.J. (2010). Jock Young. In K.J. Hayward, S. Maruna, & J. Mooney (Eds.), *Fifty Key Thinkers in Criminology* (pp. 260–267). London: Routledge.

Henry, S., & Milovanovic, D. (2005). Postmodernism and constitutive theories of criminal behavior. In R.A. Wright & J.M. Miller (Eds.), *Encyclopedia of Criminology*, Vol. 2 (pp. 1245–1249). New York: Routledge.

Jacoby, J.E. (Ed.) (2004). *Classics of Criminology*. Prospect Heights, IL: Waveland Press.

Jamieson, J., & Yates, J. (2009). Young people, youth justice and the state. In R. Coleman, J. Sim, S. Tombs, & D. Whyte (Eds.), *State, Power, Crime*. London: Sage.

Kaiser, J. (2003). Biomedical politics. NIH roiled by inquiries over grants hit list. *Science*, 302, 758.

Kuhn, T. (1970). *The Structure of Scientific Revolutions*. Chicago, IL: Chicago University Press.

Lea, J., & Young, J. (1984). *What Is To Be Done About Law and Order?* New York: Penguin.

Leshner, A.I. (2003). Editorial: Don't let ideology trump science. *Science*, 302, 1479.

Lilly, J.R., Cullen, F.T., & Ball, R.A. (2011). *Criminological Theory*, 5th edition. Thousand Oaks, CA: Sage.

Lombroso, C. (1876). *The Criminal Man*. Milan: Hoepli.

Lombroso-Ferrero, G., & Savitz, L. (1972). *Criminal Man, According To The Classification Of Cesare Lombroso*. Original by G. Lombroso-Ferrerro, 1911. Montclair, NJ: Patterson Smith.

Lynch, M.J., & Groves, W.B. (1989). *A Primer in Radical Criminology*. New York: Harrow and Heston.

Matthews, R. (2009). Beyond "so what" criminology. *Theoretical Criminology*, 13, 341–362.

Michalowski, R.J., & Kramer, R. (Eds.) (2006). *State-Corporate Crime: Wrongdoing at the Intersection of Business and Government*. Piscataway, NY: Rutgers University Press.

Miller, J. (2008). *Getting Played: African-American Girls, Urban Inequality, and Gendered Violence*. New York: New York University Press.

Muzzatti, S.L. (2006). Cultural criminology. In W.S. DeKeseredy & B. Perry (Eds.), *Advancing Critical Criminology* (pp.63–82). Lanham, MD: Lexington Books.

Pepinsky, H.E. (1991). *The Geometry of Violence and Democracy*. Bloomington: Indiana University Press.

Pepinsky, H.E., & Jesilow, P. (1984). *Myths That Cause Crime*. Cabin John, MD: Seven Locks Press.

Pepinsky, H.E., & Quinney, R. (Eds.) (1991). *Criminology as Peacemaking*. Bloomington, IN: Indiana University Press.

Reinarman, C., & Levine, H.G. (1990). A peace movement has emerged against the war on drugs. *ASA Footnotes,* February 3, 9.

Ross, J.I., & Richards, S.C. (2003). Introduction: What is the new school of convict criminology? In J.I. Ross & S.C. Richards (Eds.), *Convict Criminology* (pp. 1–14). Belmont, CA: Wadsworth.

Rothe, D.L., & Kauzlarich, D. (2014). Crimes of the powerful. In G. Bruinsma & D. Weisburd (Eds.), *Encyclopedia of Criminology and Criminal Justice*. New York: Springer.

Ritzer, G. (1975). *Sociology: A Multiple Paradigm Science*. Boston, MA: Allyn and Bacon.

Schwartz, M.D., & Friedrichs, D.O. (1994). Postmodern thought and criminological discontent: New metaphors for understanding violence. *Criminology*, 32, 221–246.

Schwartz, M.D., & Hatty, S.E. (Eds.) (2003). *Controversies in Critical Criminology*. Cincinnati, OH: Anderson.

Taylor, I.R., Walton, P., & Young, J. (1973). *The New Criminology: For a Social Theory of Deviance*. London: Routledge & Kegan Paul.

White, R. (2014). Green criminology. In G. Bruinsma & D. Weisburd (Eds.), *Encyclopedia of Criminology and Criminal Justice*. New York: Springer.

Wozniak, J.F. (2000). The voices of peacemaking criminology: Insights into a perspective with an eye toward teaching. *Contemporary Justice Review*, 3, 267–289.

Young, J. (2009). Mike Presdee. *Guardian*, August 20.

## Suggested Readings

DeKeseredy, W.S. (2011). *Contemporary Critical Criminology*. New York: Routledge.

DeKeseredy, W.S., & Dragiewicz, M. (Eds.) (2012). *Handbook of Critical Criminology*. London: Routledge.

Ferrell, J., Harward, K., & Young, J. (2008). *Cultural Criminology: An Invitation*. London: Sage.

Friedrichs, D.O. (2009). *Trusted Criminals: White Collar Crime in Contemporary Society*, 4th edition. Belmont, CA: Cengage.

Renzetti, C.M. (2013). *Feminist Criminology*. London: Routledge.

Schwartz, M.D., & Hatty, S.E. (2003). *Controversies in Critical Criminology*. Cincinnati: Anderson.

# 17

# Integrating Criminological Theories

## Marv Krohn and Jeffrey T. Ward

## Integrating Criminological Theories

The purpose of theory within any discipline including criminology is to explain phenomena. George Homans (1967) distinguished two functions of a science: to discover and to explain. Discovery is finding that two or more phenomena are related to one another. For example, we find that school achievement is inversely related to delinquent behavior. We are then left with the need to explain that relationship. That is, we need to place it within a context, one that helps us understand what might be behind the observed relationship. For example, school achievement might accord the youth more status with classmates and, thus, reduce the need to acquire that status by misbehaving. Or it might indicate that the student might have a deeper interest or commitment to achieving and delinquent behavior would be incompatible with it. The purpose of theory is to provide an account of why the observed relationship(s) exists and, in doing so, to suggest other hypotheses that might provide further support for the explanation.

Most times we are not dealing with a single discovery or observed relationship. Rather we are dealing with multiple observed relationships that may be related to one another. In those cases, we rely on theory to integrate or unify those empirical findings (Hempel, 1966). So, in one sense, the goal of all theory is to be integrative. However, the development of theories to explain criminal behavior does not always reflect that integrative goal. Rather, a number of "middle range" theories (Merton, 1968) have been generated that include partial answers to the question of why people commit crime. Those theories serve the purpose of focusing our attention on a certain set of discrete facts while blinding us to other possibilities that might help account for crime (Cuzzort, 1989). Our understanding of criminal behavior should

*The Handbook of Criminological Theory*, First Edition. Edited by Alex R. Piquero.
© 2016 John Wiley & Sons, Inc. Published 2016 by John Wiley & Sons, Inc.

advance when these theories are placed in opposition or competition with one another. That is, theories that are better able to explain criminal behavior are entertained while theories that are less capable of explaining crime are abandoned (Hempel, 1966; Stinchcombe, 1968). This process seldom occurs (Elliott, Huizinga, & Ageton, 1985). The result is that we have an abundance of theories that, at best, explain a modest amount of the variance in criminal behavior (Liska, Krohn, & Messner, 1989). Bernard (1991) has argued that the prevalence of theories has actually impeded scientific progress.

Given the complexity of human behaviors and the contexts in which they occur, however, some theorists argue that we need to combine the good or effective ideas from different middle range theories into a more complete explanation that has the potential of integrating or unifying empirical findings (Agnew, 2011; Bernard, 1991; Elliott *et al.*, 1985; Pearson & Weiner, 1985). The goal then of theoretical integration is to combine "two or more pre-existing theories, selected on the basis of their perceived commonalities, into a single reformulated theoretical model with greater comprehensiveness and explanatory value than any one of its component theories" (Farnworth, 1989:95). If successful, theoretical integration should reduce the number of theoretical perspectives while increasing the ability of a single theory to explain criminal behavior (Elliott, 1985).

## Types of Theoretical Integration

Theoretical integration can be conceptualized along two dimensions: the *substance* or types of ideas that are incorporated into an integrated perspective and the *form* in which ideas are combined evidenced by the form or structure of a resulting theory. With regard to the substance of the theory, two considerations are prominently identified: level of aggregation and cross-discipline integration. First, level of aggregation refers to whether theoretical integration occurs within the same level or across levels of analysis. The more common variety is integration of theories at the same level of aggregation. For example, attempts to integrate social control theory and some form of social learning theory are perhaps the most prominent type of theoretical integration. Both address the issue of delinquent or criminal behavior primarily at the individual or social psychological (micro) level of aggregation. Alternatively, an integrated theory may borrow ideas from two macro-level theories. For example, aspects of conflict theory have been incorporated in social disorganization theory in order to account for the impact of political and economic decisions on the ecology of neighborhoods (Bursik, 1989).

Although theoretical work of the early Chicago school was moving in this direction (Kornhauser, 1979; Shaw & McKay, 1942), they did not formally attempt to provide an integrated theory. Recently, it has become popular to incorporate ideas from theories that were originally addressing crime from different levels of aggregation. These integrated theories typically begin by identifying the social context or the social structural characteristics of different groups of people. They then suggest that social processes will either mediate the relationship between the social structural characteristics and criminal behavior or that the social structural characteristics will serve to moderate the impact of the social processes (e.g., see Akers, 1998). Attempts at cross-level integration have become more popular with the introduction of data sets that have individual level data for people in different social contexts, and with the development of analytical models to examine such data (see Raudenbush & Bryk, 2002).

The other type of integration based upon the substantive ideas a theory presents is cross-discipline integration. This is a most challenging form because it requires knowledge of theories that have been generated in different disciplines and sufficient understanding of the concepts of both disciplines to incorporate ideas into a coherent, integrated theory. For the past 25 years or so, the need to explain crime and its impact on other aspects of the life-course has become of paramount interest to criminologists. This requires that the focus should not be limited to the juvenile years as was historically true, but rather, extended to both the adult years and childhood. The generation of these developmental theories involves learning from other disciplines about processes that affect people at different ages in their life course. For example, child developmentalists have much expertise to offer regarding the influence of trait-like characteristics such as hyperactivity, temperament, and aggression on other aspects of a child's life including parenting and interactions in school. In turn, these traits may be genetically linked. Many of the developmental or life course theories, then, have integrated theories from different disciplines to more fully account for the development of criminal behavior and its consequences (Farrington, 2005; Moffitt, 1993; Thornberry & Krohn, 2001).

The ways in which ideas from different theories can be integrated can take several different forms. On one level, it is necessary to distinguish between conceptual integration and propositional integration. Conceptual integration identifies similarities in the concepts that are employed by two different theories. For example, although there are important differences between social control theory's concept of belief and differential association theory's concepts of definitions favorable and unfavorable to the violation of the law (Sutherland & Cressey, 1978), there is also a basic similarity between the two in that they both refer to attitudes people hold regarding the law or the criminal justice system. Akers (1999) uses that basic similarity to absorb both concepts under a social learning theory umbrella in a process that he refers to as conceptual absorption.

This type of integration is of limited utility unless the absorption of concepts from one theory into another is the first step in truly integrating the ideas the theories contribute and not just limited to changing the vernacular. It must be recognized that even where there is conceptual consistency across theories, it is possible that the two theories use those concepts to make opposite predictions. For example, there is some conceptual overlap between Hirschi's concept of attachment to friends and Sutherland's notion of the intensity of differential association. Yet, Hirschi predicted that those who are strongly attached to friends are less likely to engage in delinquent behavior whereas Sutherland argued that the directional effect of intensity of associations is dependent on the patterns of definitions learned from those friends. Hence it would be quite possible that one who has an intense relationship with a friend (strongly attached to) would be more likely to commit delinquent behavior.

Some scholars argue that the only true type of theoretical integration is at the propositional, not the conceptual, level. Thornberry (1989:52) suggests that "theoretical integration is the act of combining two or more sets of logically interrelated propositions into one larger set of propositions in order to provide a more comprehensive explanation of a particular phenomenon." The implications of his definition include the notion that key theoretical propositions of the constituent theories need to be included to consider the theory to be truly integrated. It is not sufficient to incorporate a concept or even an isolated proposition from one theory into the other. Admittedly, this is a high bar to pass and integrated theories generally only approach meeting such criteria.

Travis Hirschi (1989) identified three different forms of propositional integration that are now commonly used. Parallel or side-by-side integration is used when attempting to explain different aspects or types of crime within a unified theoretical structure. The subject matter of interest is partitioned into distinct categories. Often much of the theoretical argument is comprised of justifying the distinct categories. Once the categories are justified, different causal processes are identified to account for each distinct type. For example, a popular developmental theory suggests that there are two types of offenders, adolescence limited and life-course persistent, with each having a distinct pathway to committing the type of crime characteristic of their category (Moffitt, 1993).

The degree to which this approach truly integrates propositionally different theoretical approaches is problematic. Parallel integration is integrative in the sense that most cases of the phenomenon of interest (i.e., crime) are accounted for by the theory. Yet the explanations that explain the different types are not necessarily propositionally linked. In fact, they are often very distinct as in the case of Moffitt's taxonomic theory.

A second form of theoretical integration is what Hirschi (1989) called the end-to-end or sequential approach. It is the most common type of theoretical integration. With this approach, propositions from one theory are linked sequentially with propositions from another theory. Another way of stating this is the independent variables in theory A explain variables in theory B making the latter dependent on the former. The result is a causal model that suggests that theory A's variables precede theory B's variables in time and therefore, theory B's variables are more proximal to what is ultimately trying to be explained (i.e., crime).

There are several examples of this type of theoretical integration but the one most often identified is Elliott *et al*'s (1979) integrated theory. Elliott and colleagues link elements of strain, social control, and differential association theory into a causal chain that suggests strain and social control lead adolescents to have more delinquent friends which, in turn, leads to delinquent behavior.

Hirschi (1989) is critical of this approach because it ignores the assumptive differences of the constituent theories and it gives causal prominence to variables from one set of theories over those of another (differential association over social control variables). Thornberry (1989) arrived at a theoretical outcome similar to that proposed by Elliott *et al.* (1989) through what he called theoretical elaboration. Thornberry starts with one theory (social control theory) instead of multiple theories. That theory is then modified, if necessary, based on the empirical evidence. With this approach, the theorist need not be concerned with the assumptive differences of the constituent theories. Additionally, the order of the variables in terms of their proximity to the dependent variable would also be determined by what prior research has demonstrated. By undergoing this process, Thornberry (1987) developed an approach that incorporates a similar set of variables and causal model as contained in Elliott *et al.'s* theory.

The third and most difficult type of theoretical integration to do is deductive integration, or in Hirschi's terminology, the up-and-down approach. Essentially, this type of theoretical integration attempts to identify a higher level of abstraction or generality under which the propositions from constituent theories can be incorporated (Kubrin *et al.*, 2009). There are two distinct ways of doing this. The first, theoretical reduction (Nagel, 1961), is to recognize that theory A contains more abstract or general propositions than theory B. The propositions of theory B then are integrated into theory A, resulting in a single new theory (Bernard & Snipes, 1996). Burgess & Akers (1966) differential association-reinforcement theory is often identified as exemplifying this type of approach. Burgess and Akers reinterpret and deduce the propositions of differential association from the more general principles of operant conditioning forming a new theory. A second type of deductive integration, known as theoretical synthesis, is to identify either a more abstract theory or set of principles that will accommodate the propositions from two or more constituent theories into a new theory containing parts of both these theories. For example, Krohn (1986) used the principles from the social network approach to synthesize the ideas from social control and differential association theory, forming what he labeled social network theory.

Although it might seem self-evident that combining the good ideas from different constituent theories into one that should have more explanatory power is a worthy goal, not everyone agrees. The next section takes a detailed look at the inherent controversy surrounding the integration of criminological theories.

## Controversy Over Theoretical Integration

Many deem theoretical integration as rather problematic. There are a number of reasons for objections to integrating theories including: (1) the appropriate way to advance science; (2) the potential incongruity between assumptions of some of the constituent theories; and (3) the resulting complexity of integrated theories.

## The development of science

The scientific explanation of phenomena advances through the generation of theory that spawns testable hypotheses or propositions that are tested using appropriate techniques. When two or more theories provide explanations for a phenomenon, the question arises as to what might be the best course of future action. Should we examine each theory and simply allow the results of the examinations to determine which theory we continue to pursue (theory competition)? Or should we seek to take parts of each theory that seem to be effective in predicting the outcome(s) and combine them into an integrated theory (theoretical integration)?

Travis Hirschi (1989) forcefully argued that the experience of the physical sciences demonstrates that theoretical competition is the more efficient way to increase our understanding of some phenomenon. Each theory should be examined, results replicated, and the theory that is most successful (hypotheses supported) should be the one we pursue, while the less successful theory should be discarded. Ideally, the choice between the theories should be based on a *critical test*. A critical test is research that serves to support one of the theories while refuting the other, thereby clearly demarcating the direction that future theorizing should pursue. For example, in physics, a substance filling the universe known as "luminiferous Ether" was believed to be the way in which electromagnetic waves, including light, propagated through space; that is, waves were thought to be unable to travel in empty space. The classic Michelson-Morley experiment conducted in 1887 disproved the existence of Ether, which redirected scientific thinking and paved the way for one of the greatest theoretical ideas ever advanced – the theory of special relativity.

The difficulty in developing scientific knowledge through theoretical competition in criminology is due to the object of study (i.e., criminal behavior); therefore, there are few studies that provide a critical test between theoretical perspectives. Human behavior is difficult to isolate from extraneous variables. If an attempt is made to isolate criminal behavior, the situation is typically an artificial one and could be partially explained by the special circumstances created. Moreover, there are ethical considerations in manipulating experimental conditions to induce criminal behavior that may not be a problem in critical tests done in the physical sciences. Hence, there is an inevitable degree of imprecision in examining criminal behavior that decreases the opportunity for a critical test between theoretical perspectives.

The difficulty of studying human behavior results in ambiguity over the definitiveness of empirical findings. This state, in turn, makes it difficult to give up on any theory since it is always possible that the next (imperfect) test of the perspective will generate findings more favorable to that theory. Hence, theoretical competition in the pursuit of an explanation of criminal behavior has resulted in a proliferation of theories instead of the intended elimination of them. This is also, perhaps in large part, due to the imprecise predictions that criminological theories make in the first place. Criminological theories, as well as most theories in the social sciences, yield predictions only with respect to the direction of an effect; the size of the effect is something that is empirically determined rather than theoretically predicted

(Taagepera, 2008). This imprecision is largely avoided in the hard sciences through the use of logical, quantitatively predictive models. Couple imprecise quantitative predictions with imperfect empirical tests and the result is painfully slow and somewhat uncertain scientific progress. It can be argued that far more attention needs be paid to making more detailed quantitative predictions and to conducting better empirical tests of those predictions if criminologists ever hope to subject any theory to a true critical test. If we cannot pare the theories through competition and elimination in this way, another avenue of advancing criminological science is through the integration of some of the ideas from potential constituent theories. At least this is the hope of those who pursue integration.

## Conflicting assumptions

Most theories either explicitly or implicitly contain assumptions on which their explanation and hypotheses are predicated. Many of these assumptions are either impossible or very difficult to subject to empirical verification. For that reason, they are often called meta-theoretical assumptions. If the goal is to truly integrate the ideas of one theory with those of another, then meta-theoretical assumptions need to be considered. In some instances these assumptions are not compatible, rendering integration that meshes the entirety of the constituent theories impossible.

The issue of conflicting meta-theoretical assumptions has been raised in regard to the most common integration of theoretical ideas – the integration of propositions from social control theory with those from a social learning perspective (either social learning theory or differential association theory). At the heart of the controversy is an epistemological assumption regarding the nature of humans. Social control theory assumes that humans are rational beings who simply try to maximize their pleasure and minimize their pain. Based on that assumption, social control theorists argue that there is no need to suggest a motivation that pushes or pulls an individual to commit criminal behavior. Rather, they argue that it is incumbent on the theorist to account for why people do not commit criminal behavior. Their explanations address the sources of social control or constraint. An important component of social learning theories is the influence of peers in the learning of definitions and the providing of reinforcements that make criminal behavior more likely. Social learning theories suggest that, at least in part, criminal behavior is caused by these influences.

The typical combination of these theories suggests that with the weakening of the elements of the social bond, people are no longer constrained from deviant behavior and gravitate toward peers who are engaged in deviant behavior. Those associations result in their own involvement in deviant behavior. By combining the two theories in this way, a motivation is provided for deviant behavior (the push or pull of associations). If you assume that humans are rational and what is needed is not the provision of a motivating force, as social control theorists argue, then by providing one you are not truly integrating the theories.

Yet, it seems intuitively correct to suggest that the weakening of the tie to one's parents increases the probability of associating with the type of peers that parents would not want their children to hang out with. This example is one of the reasons that Thornberry (1989) advocated theoretical elaboration rather than theoretical integration. Essentially, Thornberry suggests that true theoretical integration, which would include a merging of the assumptive base, is difficult at best. Therefore, he argues that we begin with a theoretical base, in his case social control theory, and then allow empirical evidence to determine how to expand or elaborate on the base. If research demonstrates that attenuation of the parent–child bond is related to an increased probability that youth will associate with delinquent others, then incorporate that fact into the theory. Ultimately, the elaborated theory will be judged on how well it accounts for the behavior and not on whether it represents a true integration.

## Complexity of integrated theories

One of the key criterion in evaluating theories is whether a theory is parsimonious; that is, whether a theory that is more succinct and employs fewer concepts and propositions can account for the phenomenon as well as another theory that is more complex. A parsimonious theory that does equally well in accounting for behavior is simply more efficient, easier to test, and, presumably, directs our attention to the truly important factors.

By its very nature, integrated theory, regardless of its form and content, adds complexity. Integrated theory may add variables, levels of analysis, and, in some cases, different types of deviance. For example, Elliott *et al.*'s integrated theory combines the constituent theories of strain, social control, and differential association theory into a single causal model. If we take social control theory by itself and assume that each element of the bond is measured within only one context (family, school, peers), and that each of those elements is related in some way to one another, there are at least ten hypothesized relationships. If we then add to that even a limited number of variables from strain and differential association theories and generate hypotheses suggesting relationships among the social control variables and the new variables added into the integrated theory, it is easy to see the complexity that the new theory introduces.

A complex model such as Elliott *et al.*'s integrated theory is difficult to examine in its entirety. What often happens with empirical investigations of these complex theories is that they are examined in sections (see, for example, Thornberry *et al.*, 1991, 1994). The question arises as to whether examining a theory in parts provides for an adequate test of the theory. If the theory is too complex, it may be difficult to falsify and if that is the case it violates one of the key criterion on which we evaluate theories. As Gibbons (1994:185) states, such theories may "muddy the empirical waters and make it more, rather than less, difficult to disentangle causal influences and to identify the differential contribution that each of them makes to the behavioral outcome."

Another issue that arises out of the increased complexity of integrated theories is the logical coherence of the resulting theory. There is a tendency to add variables without appropriate theoretical justification and explanation. Cao (2004:161) states that "integration can lead to sloppy theorizing in which scholars pick a variable they like from one theory and then a variable from another, but they do not reconcile the philosophic differences behind these variables." Such theorizing might result in "theoretical mush" (Gibbons, 1994; Hirschi, 1979).

The counter argument to the concern about theories becoming overly complex is the recognition that in many cases the reasons why humans behave in the way they do is complex. Therefore, to adequately explain why we behave as we do requires a certain level of complexity that may go beyond theories that concentrate on one or two main themes. If we think or perhaps know (from extant research) that certain variables are related either directly or indirectly to deviant behavior, do we not include it in our theory because it raises the level of complexity? What this means is the theorist must be cognizant of both whether the theory can be falsified through empirical investigation and the precision with which the added links in the theory are theoretically justified. However, theoretical integration should not be avoided simply on the basis of increased complexity.

## Examples of Integrated Theories of Criminal Behavior

There is no single formula for integrating theories of criminal behavior. In this section, we highlight several examples of integrated theories of criminal behavior, which enables a look into some of the ways in which theoretical ideas might be amalgamated to attempt to provide a better or more complete explanation of crime. We focus on Moffitt's (1993) and Elliott *et al*'s (1979, 1985) theories because they serve as prototypical examples of theoretical integration. In addition, we review Hirschi's (2004) intriguing merger of self- and social-control theories to illustrate some of the complexities that may arise when attempting to integrate longstanding criminological perspectives.

Taking a life-course perspective on the development of antisocial behavior, Moffitt (1993) advanced a dual taxonomy theory of offending which suggests that the general population is comprised of fundamentally different types of individuals. Moffitt argues that there are two offender types – life-course persistent (LCP) and adolescence limited (AL) – each with a distinct etiology of crime and delinquency. The more troubling of the two types of offenders are the LCPs because, as their name implies, these individuals begin offending early in life and continue offending throughout adulthood and their antisocial activity is more frequent and serious than that of AL offenders. Fortunately, LCPs comprise less than 10% of the population. The risk for LCP offending is set in motion when an individual with neuropsychological deficits is raised in an adverse environment.

Neuropsychological deficits refer to shortcomings in nervous system functioning and/or structure and can arise from biological and developmental difficulties as well as traumatic injuries. Neuropsychological deficits can result in difficult temperament, low cognitive ability, and/or problematic behavior. Importantly, Moffitt suggests that individuals with neuropsychological deficits are more likely to be reared in problematic home environments. For example, a child who develops neuropsychological deficits through exposure to high quantities of alcohol in the womb may also experience an adverse rearing context during the formative years. From this description of the LCPs, it is clear that the substance of integration is *cross-discipline*. An examination of the etiology of offending of AL offenders to follow will demonstrate that the form of the integration is *parallel*.

Most people dabble in some delinquency during their teenage years. Moffitt suggests that AL offending is the product of a maturity gap between biological and social ages as well as social mimicry. Specifically, the maturity gap arises because teenagers feel they are physically able to partake in adult activities, such as sex and drinking alcohol, but are discouraged from doing so due to social customs. As a response to this maturity gap, AL offenders mimic some behaviors of LCP offenders (who are seen as having a desired quality of autonomy) and engage in acts to assert their independence (e.g., get drunk, joyride). During adolescence, delinquency is seen as something which provides certain benefits to the AL offender. During the transition from adolescence to adulthood, AL offenders take note of the quickly eroding maturity gap and desist in their offending because the various benefits of conforming behavior in the adult social world become apparent.

It is worth noting that Moffitt also offers an explanation for nonoffenders or "abstainers." Put succinctly, individuals are likely to abstain from offending if they experience late puberty or are thrust into adult roles at a young age which reduces the occurrence or duration of a maturity gap, or they have personal characteristics or opportunity structures which inhibit the learning of delinquency. In sum, Moffitt ties together key ideas from various disciplines including biology, developmental psychology, and sociology to advance two different explanations for criminal behavior. Her taxonomy approach to integration highlights that criminologists need to consider multiple avenues to offending (parallel integration) and that explaining a given pathway to offending necessitates a multidisciplinary approach (cross-discipline integration).

In one of the better-known theoretical integrations, Elliott and colleagues (1979; see also Elliott *et al.*, 1985) link elements of strain, social control, and social learning to delinquent behavior in a causal chain. Specifically, their end-to-end theoretical model begins with familial and school strains, which are brought about by disconnect between an individual's aspirations and achievements in these arenas. Experiencing high levels of familial and school strains fosters weak social bonds including lowered commitment, involvement, and attachment to both parents and schools. In turn, people who are weakly bonded are likely to form relationships with delinquent peers, setting off the process of learning antisocial behavior as specified by social learning theory. The most proximate cause of crime and delinquency is, therefore, social learning; strain and social bonding are thought to influence these behaviors indirectly. As the unit of analysis is the individual, Elliott and colleagues theory is a same-level (micro) integrative effort.

It is important to note that in bringing these three theories together by way of proposition integration, Elliott and colleagues were forced to address some conflicting theoretical assumptions – particularly between social control and social learning theory. Control theory operates from the assumption that criminal motivation is innate and does not require explanation, whereas social learning theory suggests that motivation for criminal behavior is a product of learning definitions favorable to law violation and expecting or actually experiencing reinforcement for criminal behavior. The assumption of constant variation in motivation for offending was dropped when merging these theories, which appears to be a logical choice and is supported by the literature. In sum, Elliott *et al.*'s (1979) integrated model was one of criminology's earlier attempts to place key ideas within the discipline into a casual sequence in order to better explain individual variation in offending behavior. As such, the substance of Elliott *et al.*'s theory is best characterized as same-discipline and same-level and the form of the model is prototypical sequential proposition integration.

Sometimes, attempts to integrate theories are not quite as neat as the examples just discussed. To illustrate this point, we consider the difficulties of the theoretical integration known as "redefined self-control" (see Hirschi, 2004), which is an amalgamation of social- and self-control theories. Traditionally control theories come in two distinct varieties: social-control (Hirschi, 1969) and self-control (Gottfredson & Hirschi, 1990). While both perspectives begin with the assumption that humans are inherently self-interested and therefore criminologists need to explain why individuals refrain from engaging in criminal behavior, the precise meaning and sources of control are quite distinct. Social control theory holds that individuals who are strongly bonded to society will be controlled from engaging in criminal and delinquent behavior. There are four fundamental elements of the social bond: attachment, commitment, involvement, and belief. Individuals who have strong attachments to others, such as parents, will refrain from delinquency because the parent will be psychologically present when the temptation to commit deviance arises. Those who are committed and involved in conventional activities have more to lose from misbehavior and less time to misbehave, respectively. Belief in conventional order provides the moral barrier to delinquency.

While Hirschi started out emphasizing the social aspects of control in his original theory, he essentially abandoned this idea two decades later during his collaborations in favor of a trait theory of control. Gottfredson & Hirschi (1990) argue that those who "lack self-control will tend to be impulsive, insensitive, physical (as opposed to mental), risk-taking, short-sighted, and nonverbal, and … there is a considerable tendency for these traits to come together in the same people …" (90). An individual's level of self-control, which is argued to be stable once developed, is a direct function of parental socialization practices. Specifically, parents will instill self-control in their children when they successfully monitor their children, know appropriate from inappropriate behavior, and consistently correct misbehavior.

In 2004, Hirschi took on the daunting task of merging his theories. His revised theory is best summarized as follows:

> Redefined, self-control becomes *the tendency to consider the full range of potential costs of a particular act*. This moves the focus from the *long-term* implications of the act to its *broader* and often contemporaneous implications. With this new definition, we need not impute knowledge of distant outcomes to persons in no position to possess such information ... Put another way, self-control is the set of inhibitions one carries with one wherever one happens to go. Their character may be initially described by going to the elements of the bond identified by social control theory. (Hirschi, 2004:543, emphasis in original)

Hirschi goes on to claim that social-control and self-control are the "same thing" and that social bonds are therefore stable. Given these claims, redefined self-control might be seen as an attempt at deductive theoretical integration. That is, redefined self-control is boarder and encompasses a concern with both short-term and long-term costs of an act. Further, people have a tendency to consider consequences of behaviors as a direct function of their social bonds. But for those well versed in the two varieties of control, Hirschi's theoretical integration may feel a bit contrived, and his initial test of the theory only leads to additional confusion. In describing cost consideration, Hirschi (2004) argued that costs differ in both "number" and "salience." However, his measure of redefined self-control was nothing more than an index of various social bonding items. While Hirschi assumes that social bonding levels and the tendency to consider the full range of costs of a particular act (i.e., redefined self-control) are similar, the limited empirical evidence testing this claim suggests this is invalid (for a review and theoretical discussion, see Ward, Boman, & Jones, 2012). Therefore, Hirschi's integration may not be a deductive integration after all; instead, might be viewed as taking somewhat of an end-to-end form with social bonds influencing one's level of redefined self-control. While the form of the theoretical integration is murky, what is clear is that the substance of the theory is same-discipline and same-level.

## The Future of Theoretical Integration

We have examined the different types of theoretical integration and provided several examples of integrated theories to illustrate the differences in integrative efforts to explain crime. We have also identified the controversies surrounding attempts to integrate theories. Critics of integration have raised some valid concerns regarding whether the discipline of criminology is helped or harmed by such efforts. In spite of those concerns, it seems evident that the movement toward combining ideas from different theories with the hope of providing explanations that are more effective in explaining crime is proceeding at an accelerated rate. There are a number of reasons why theorists continue to pursue it. Among them, we identify four that are particularly germane to the future of theoretical integration. They include: (1) discoveries in the areas of sociogenetics and brain/cognitive development; (2) the developmental and life-course approach to the understanding of crime; (3) the increasing recognition that context is important, particularly neighborhood context; and (4) research designs and analytical methods combined with available data sets that allow for the examination of the complexities of integrative theories.

## Sociogenetic approach and other trait-like characteristics

One of the most significant scientific discoveries of the past 75 years was the double helix structure of DNA and subsequent research on the sequencing of chemical base pairs that make up DNA. The decoding of DNA reinvigorated the sociogenetic approach to the study of criminal behavior, providing hope that the identification of certain alleles that comprise DNA, could help explain the propensity for criminal behavior.

The research on discovering the genetic basis of criminal behavior is still in its relative infancy. However, most scholars suggest that if crime is partially explained by a person's genetic basis, that genetic basis represents either a predisposition for criminal behavior or a susceptibility to specific environments or environmental conditions generally. In either case, research is clear in suggesting that genes interact with social context to influence antisocial behavior (as opposed to having direct effects). So, for example, a genetic predisposition toward alcoholism may only be realized in an environment where alcoholic drinks are readily available. Hence, to account for the impact of a person's genes on criminal behavior requires the integration of ideas from both biogenetics and disciplines such as psychology and sociology. Other trait-based theories of criminal behavior have also seen a reemergence.

In most cases, trait-like variables have been incorporated in extant developmental theories, with variables from these disciplines predicted to moderate the effect of traits or vice versa. In some ways, it is evident that theoretical development in criminology, including integration of ideas, lags behind the discoveries that are being made regarding the role of genetics and neuropsychological functioning. We anticipate that as criminologists become more conversant with genetics and other areas like cognitive and brain functioning, integrative theoretical perspectives will catch up with the empirical discoveries being made.

## Developmental and life-course approaches

Most early theories of criminal behavior applied most directly to juveniles. There were a number of reasons for this, including the assumed age of onset, the age at which prevalence was the highest, and the implications for prevention programs. However, when we recognized that there was a relatively small group of offenders who disproportionally contributed to the overall crime problem, that these offenders tended to onset at earlier ages, and that they continued their criminal careers into adulthood, it became evident that the limited focus on the adolescent years was not adequate if we wanted to truly understand criminal behavior.

This recognition led to expanding the focus from adolescence to pre-adolescent years, as well as determining what happened to these chronic or career offenders in their adult years. The life-course approach to the explanation of criminal behavior is arguably the dominant theoretical approach in criminology today. Most life-course theories combine elements of constituent theories in one way or another. In part, this was necessitated by the inclusion of the childhood years in their purview of interest. In order to understand how both the manifestation of traits and early childhood experiences were important in explaining early onset, criminologists, who had been predominantly trained in sociology, looked to child developmentalists for help. Hence, in the integration of ideas from different theories, the resultant constructions were likely to be cross-discipline integrations.

Because life-course theories attempt to cover a broad age spectrum, they tend to be more complex than theories that focus primarily on the adolescent years. Further, when you consider onset and desistance and trace the duration of trajectories of offending over time, one may obtain a picture of different types of offenders which require unique explanations (Moffitt, 1993). As a result of these factors, life-course theories are often subject to the criticisms stated above concerning overcomplexity, a lack of internal logical coherence, and difficulty in examining the entire model as a whole. In spite of these criticisms, we do not anticipate that the discipline will backtrack on the importance it has placed on explaining crime, its antecedents, and its consequences across the life-course. Instead, we anticipate that theorists will work to develop the needed coherence among various parts of their theories and ever-more sophisticated methods will be developed to allow for more complete examinations of their ideas.

## Neighborhood as a context for development

Neighborhood characteristics have traditionally been seen as having either a direct or indirect effect on criminal behavior. Typically, structural characteristics have been seen as exogenous variables in models and, if included, the social dynamics that characterize neighborhoods (i.e. collective efficacy, social integration) have been seen as mediating variables. Whether one considers these models to be a true rendering of the social disorganization perspective (Kornhauser, 1979) or an attempt to integrate macro-level theories with more process-oriented theories, depends on one's interpretation of the Chicago tradition. The role of neighborhood and larger societal contexts has also been argued to provide the structure in which individual level processes unfold. For instance, Akers (1998) suggests that social structure does not have direct effects on criminal behavior; rather, the social structure sets the context for learning, and it is learning that ultimately is the proximate cause of delinquency.

Recent theorizing about neighborhoods has considered these contexts as moderating forces. That is, theoretically important variables at the individual level, such as genes or labeling, may be seen to have different effects depending on the neighborhood context in which people live and interact. An alternative way of looking at these interactions is to suggest that some individuals, such as those with a certain genetic makeup, are more susceptible to problematic environments. The range of theoretically important variables that have been or could be examined in these ways is wide. To account for these possibilities, theoretical ideas will have to be merged to incorporate reasons why different neighborhood contexts have moderating effects for some variables and perhaps not for others (and vice versa). We view this as an emerging area for integrating theories.

## Research designs and analytical tools

Much of what we discuss in this section is dependent on having the right kind of data and the ability to analyze it in a way that is consistent with the theoretical approach. The past 30 years has seen the accumulation of data sets that not only allow for an examination of individuals and their behaviors over the life-course, but also can be analyzed within neighborhood contexts. The symbiotic interplay between research and theory is evident. Theoretical developments stimulate the need for more expansive data sets while the availability of such data sets allow theorists to incorporate an expanding set of conceptual tools.

In addition to the increasing availability of data sets that lend themselves to examining integrated theories, the statistical tools used to analyze those data have become more sophisticated. Some important examples include the increased use of hierarchical linear models, structural equation modeling, and group-based trajectory analysis. Hierarchical linear modeling (HLM; see Raudenbush & Bryk, 2002) allows researchers to disentangle the proportion of variance in a construct that is attributable to two (or more) levels, such as individuals and neighborhood. Beyond this important descriptive information, HLM enables the researcher to predict variation at both levels and model cross-level interactions, thereby explaining what neighborhood factors predict variation in individual level effects of interest. With repeated measures data, HLM can also be employed to model trajectories of behavior and explain variation in both within- and between-individuals in an analogous manner to that just described.

When a researcher suspects that multiple trajectories best characterize development rather than a single trajectory around which people are essentially normally distributed, they can turn to the group-based trajectory method (see Nagin, 2005) or growth mixture modeling. While it has been recently argued that the group-based trajectory method should not be used as an attempt to "confirm" a given number of trajectory groups (Skardhamar, 2010), it is quite useful to examine if there are fundamentally distinct groups that emerge from a given data set. Researchers can also explore whether certain factors can predict trajectory group membership, determine whether life experiences have differential effects across trajectory groups, and examine if there are meaningful relationships between different behavioral trajectories either concurrently or sequentially.

As causal models become increasingly complex with the addition of feedback loops and numerous constructs in integrated theories, structural equation modeling offers a way to test models in a comprehensive rather than piecemeal fashion. Further, structural equation models can estimate structural path coefficients that are free from measurement error. A key benefit of employing comprehensive tests of models using structural equations is the ability to constrain various model parameters in accordance with theory and test for the decrement in model fit. These benefits enable a more straightforward and transparent test of complex theories. However, estimation difficulties can arise as measurement and/or structural model complexity increases. In sum, the statistical tools and data available to researchers are permitting increasingly more informative investigations into integrated theories and criminological theories more generally. As quantitative criminologists become more versed in the methodological literature and think deeply and carefully about appropriate implementation, we anticipate there will be important advances in integrated theory that result.

# References

Agnew, R. (2011). *Toward a Unified Criminology*. New York: New York University Press.

Akers, R.L. (1998). *Social Learning and Social Structure: A General Theory of Crime and Deviance*. Boston, MA: Northeastern University Press.

Akers, R.L. (1999). *Criminological Theories: Introduction and Evaluation*, 2nd edition. Los Angeles, CA: Roxbury.

Bernard, T.J. (1991). Twenty years of testing theories. *Journal of Research in Crime and Delinquency, 27*, 325–347.

Bernard, T.J., & Snipes, J.B. (1996). Theoretical integration in criminology. *Crime and Justice, 20*, 301–348.

Burgess, R.L., & Akers, R.L. (1966). A differential-association theory of criminal behavior. *Social Problems, 14*, 128–147.

Bursik, R.J. (1989). Political decision making and ecological models of delinquency: Conflict and consensus. In S.F. Messner, M.D. Krohn, & A.E. Liska (Eds.), *Theoretical Integration in the Study of Deviance and Crime* (pp. 105–117). Albany, NY: State University of New York Press.

Cao, L. (2004). *Major Criminological Theories: Concepts and Measurement*. Belmont, CA: Wadsworth.

Cuzzort, R.P. (1989). *Using Social Thought: The Nuclear Issue and Other Concerns*. New York: Mayfield.

Elliott, D.S. (1985). The assumption that theories can be combined with increased explanatory power. In R.F. Meier (Ed.), *Theoretical Methods in Criminology* (pp. 123–149). Beverly Hills, CA: Sage.

Elliott, D.S., Ageton, S.S., & Canter, R.J. (1979). An integrated theoretical perspective on delinquent behavior. *Journal of Research in Crime and Delinquency, 16*, 3–27.

Elliott, D.S., Huizinga, D., & Ageton, S.S. (1985). *Explaining Delinquency and Drug Use.* Beverly Hills, CA: Sage.

Farnworth, M. (1989). Theory integration versus model building. In S.F. Messner, M.D. Krohn, & A.E. Liska (Eds.), *Theoretical Integration in the Study of Deviance and Crime* (pp. 93–103). Albany, NY: State University of New York Press.

Farrington, D.P. (2005). The integrated cognitive antisocial potential (ICAP) theory. In D.P. Farrington (Ed.), *Integrated Developmental and Life-Course Theories of Offending: Advances in Criminological Theory*, Vol. *14* (pp. 73–91). New Brunswick, NJ: Transaction.

Gibbons, D.C. (1994). *Talking About Crime and Criminals: Problems and Issues in Theory Development in Criminology.* Englewood Cliffs, NJ: Prentice Hall.

Gottfredson, M.R., & Hirschi, T. (1990). *A General Theory of Crime.* Stanford, CA: Stanford University Press.

Hempel, C.G. (1966). *Philosophy of Natural Science.* Princeton, NJ: Princeton University Press.

Hirschi, T. (1969). *Causes of Delinquency.* Berkeley, CA: University of California Press.

Hirschi, T. (1979). Separate and unequal is better. *Journal of Research in Crime and Delinquency, 16,* 34–38.

Hirschi, T. (1989). Exploring alternatives to integrated theory. In S.F. Messner, M.D. Krohn, & A.E. Liska (Eds.), *Theoretical Integration in the Study of Deviance and Crime* (pp. 37–49). Albany, NY: State University of New York Press.

Hirschi, T. (2004). Self-control and crime. In R.F. Baumeister & K.D. Vohs (Eds.), *Handbook of Self-Regulation: Research, Theory, and Applications* (pp. 537–552). New York: Guilford Press.

Homans, G.C. (1967). *The Nature of Social Science.* New York: Harcourt, Brace, and World.

Kornhauser, R.S. (1979). *Social Sources of Delinquency: An Appraisal of Analytic Models.* Chicago, IL: University of Chicago Press.

Krohn, M.D. (1986). The web of conformity: A network approach to the explanation of delinquent behavior. *Social Problems, 32,* 455–473.

Kubrin, C.E., Stucky, T.D., & Krohn, M.D. (2009). *Researching Theories of Crime and Deviance.* New York: Oxford University Press.

Liska, A.E., Krohn, M.D., & Messner, S.F. (1989). Strategies and requisites for theoretical integration in the study of crime and deviance. In S.F. Messner, M.D. Krohn, & A.E. Liska (Eds.), *Theoretical Integration in the Study of Deviance and Crime* (pp. 1–19). Albany, NY: State University of New York Press.

Merton, R.K. (1968). *Social Theory and Social Structure.* New York: Free Press.

Moffitt, T. (1993). Life-course-persistent and adolescence-limited anti-social behavior: A developmental taxonomy. *Psychological Review, 100,* 674–701.

Nagel, E. (1961). *The Structure of Science: Problems in the Logic of Scientific Explanation.* New York: Harcourt, Brace, and World.

Nagin, D.S. (2005). *Group-Based Modeling of Development.* Cambridge, MA: Harvard University Press.

Pearson, F.S., & Weiner, N.A. (1985). Toward an integration of criminological theories. *Journal of Criminal Law and Criminology, 76,* 116–150.

Raudenbush, S.W., & Bryk, A.S. (2002). *Hierarchical Linear Models: Applications and Data Analysis Methods,* 2nd edition. Thousand Oaks, CA: Sage.

Shaw, C., & McKay, H. (1942). *Juvenile Delinquency and Urban Areas.* Chicago, IL: University of Chicago Press.

Skardhamar, T. (2010). Distinguishing facts and artifacts in group-based modeling. *Criminology, 48,* 295–320.

Stinchcombe, A.L. (1968). *Constructing Social Theories*. New York: Harcourt, Brace, and World.

Sutherland, E.H., & Cressey, D.R. (1978). *Criminology*, 10th edition. Philadelphia, PA: Lippincott.

Taagepera, R. (2008). *Making Social Sciences More Scientific: The Need for Predictive Models*. New York: Oxford University Press.

Thornberry, T.P. (1987). Toward an interactional theory of delinquency. *Criminology, 25*, 863–892.

Thornberry, T.P. (1989). Reflections on the advantages and disadvantages of theoretical integration. In S.F. Messner, M.D. Krohn, & A.E. Liska (Eds.), *Theoretical Integration in the Study of Deviance and Crime* (pp. 51–60). Albany, NY: State University of New York Press.

Thornberry, T.P. and Krohn, M.D. (2001) The development of delinquency: An interactional perspective. In S.O. White (Ed.) *Handbook of Law and Social Science: Youth and Justice* (pp. 289–306). New York: Plenum.

Thornberry, T.P., Lizotte, A.J., Krohn, M.D., Farnworth, M., & Jang, S.J. (1991). Testing interactional theory: An examination of reciprocal causal relationships among family, school, and delinquency. *Journal of Criminal Law and Criminology, 82*, 3–35.

Thornberry, T.P., Lizotte, A.J., Krohn, M.D, Farnworth, M., & Jang, S.J. (1994). Delinquent peers, beliefs, and delinquent behavior: A longitudinal test of interactional theory. *Criminology, 32*, 47–83.

Ward, J.T., Boman, J.H., & Jones, S. (2012). Hirschi's redefined self-control: Assessing the implications of the merger between social- and self-control theories. *Crime & Delinquency*. Advance online publication. doi: 10.1177/0011128712466939.

# 18

# Developmental and Life-Course Theories of Crime

## Tara Renae McGee and David P. Farrington

## Origins of the Developmental and Life-Course (DLC) Perspective

Since its rise to prominence in the late 1980s, the developmental and life-course (DLC) perspective in criminology has received increasing theoretical and empirical attention. Francis Cullen (2011), in his 2010 Sutherland address, encouraged a paradigm shift away from what he termed adolescent limited criminology (ALC). He argued that the ALC framework, under which criminology was currently operating: (1) ignored individual differences between offenders; (2) rejected the epidemiology of crime in favor of making new theories; (3) focused on the amount of variation explained by theoretical variables; (4) was based on cross-sectional self-report surveys of (mainly school based) adolescents; and (5) embraced a social justice perspective regarding how to address crime problems, while dismissing more pragmatic approaches as "administrative criminology."

Cullen argues that to move forward criminologists need to accept that life-course criminology *is* criminology; it is not just another perspective that competes with traditional theories but rather it should replace the dominant ALC framework. He argued that it is important to examine not only what happens during adolescence but also what happens before and after adolescence. He was careful to note that he was not arguing that other theories do not matter but rather that existing theories should be age-graded. Indeed when examining many of the theories within the DLC tradition, one can observe the incorporation of many traditional theories within them. Cullen (2011) highlighted the way in which Sampson & Laub (1993) cast an age-graded interpretation of social bonding theory. Similarly, elements of strain theory can be observed in Moffitt's maturity gap hypothesis (Moffitt, Caspi, Dickson,

*The Handbook of Criminological Theory*, First Edition. Edited by Alex R. Piquero.

Silva, & Stanton, 1996). Another example is Farrington's (2005a) integrated cognitive antisocial potential (ICAP) theory, which incorporates elements of traditional theories such as strain and socialization. In this way, those working within the DLC tradition can be seen to be adding an age-graded perspective to existing and newly generated knowledge within criminology.

While the DLC perspective only came to prominence in the US in the 1980s, there were many longitudinal studies that focused on aspects of key theoretical importance to DLC researchers being undertaken around the world as early as the 1940s. Key examples of these studies in the US include the Gluecks' study of delinquents and non-delinquents in Boston (Glueck & Glueck, 1934, 1950, 1968); McCord's Cambridge-Somerville Youth Study (McCord, 1992); Werner's Kauai Longitudinal Study (Werner, 1993); Eron's Columbia County Study (Lefkowitz, Eron, Walder, & Huesmann, 1977); Wolfgang's Philadelphia birth cohort studies (Wolfgang, Figlio, & Sellin, 1972); Kellam's Woodlawn project (McCord & Ensminger, 1997); Cohen and Brook's New York State Longitudinal Study (Johnson, Smailes, Cohen, Kasen, & Brook, 2004); and Elliott's National Youth Survey (Elliott, 1994). Elsewhere in the world, West & Farrington's (1973) Cambridge Study in Delinquent Development began in London in 1961 and Miller and Court's (Kolvin, Miller, Scott, Gatzanis, & Fleeting, 1990) study of boys born in Newcastle in 1947 were being conducted. There was also Magnusson and Stattin's study of children who were age 10 years in 1965, in Orebro, Sweden (Bergman & Andershed, 2009) and Pulkkinen's Jyvaskyla Longitudinal Study of children age 8–9 years in 1968 in Finland (Pulkkinen, Lyyra, & Kokko, 2009).

Despite these early studies, it was only in the 1980s that the major US funding agencies became convinced of the value of longitudinal research and funded new studies. The US Office of Juvenile Justice and Delinquency Prevention funded the three Causes and Correlates studies; the National Institute of Justice and the MacArthur Foundation funded the Program on Human Development and Criminal Behavior (see Farrington, Ohlin, & Wilson, 1986; Tonry, Ohlin, & Farrington, 1991); the National Institute of Mental Health funded Patterson; and the National Academy of Sciences organized the very influential panel which generated the two volumes on Criminal Careers and Career Criminals (Blumstein, Cohen, Roth, & Visher, 1986).

The main aim of the National Academy of Sciences panel was to review the contribution of research on offending across the life-course (Blumstein *et al.*, 1986). This process saw the explication of a number of core concepts, such as: *onset*, why people start offending; *persistence*, why people continue offending; and *desistance*, why people stop offending. Also identified were situational and contextual factors that can be observed in families and neighborhoods. These concepts remain part of the core focus of researchers working within the DLC paradigm (Piquero, Farrington, & Blumstein, 2003). A *criminal career* is defined as "the longitudinal sequence of offences committed by an individual offender" (Farrington, 1992). The criminal career approach describes the sequence of offences committed during some part of an individual's lifetime, with no necessary suggestion that offenders use their criminal activity as an important means of earning a living. Instead, the concept is intended as a means of structuring the longitudinal sequence of criminal events committed by an individual in a meaningful way. More broadly, the criminal career approach also incorporates the antecedents and outcomes of offending.

From the 1980s onwards, the injection of funding in the DLC area in the US resulted in new theories by Patterson (Patterson, DeBaryshe, & Ramsey, 1989), Loeber (Loeber, Slot, & Stouthamer-Loeber, 2008), Hawkins and Catalano (Catalano & Hawkins, 1996), Laub and Sampson (2003), and Thornberry (Thornberry & Krohn, 2005). Projects in other countries by Wikström (2006), Moffitt (2006), LeBlanc (1997a), and Farrington (2005a) also spawned new theories. These DLC theories emerged as an attempt to explain growing empirical longitudinal evidence regarding the nature of offending over the life-course, and drew on many traditional theories of offending such as strain, labeling, and rational choice. DLC theories are different from traditional theories of delinquency and crime because they tend to be more complex and multifaceted. They incorporate many different elements of traditional theories of crime but also include biological and psychological factors. DLC theories can be contrasted with general theories that argue that criminality is the result of static persistent differences between individuals. Other general theories use dynamic explanations such as those that argue that criminality is the result of social forces such as strain (Agnew, 1997). DLC theories incorporate both static and dynamic elements but differ because of their requirement to examine the phenomena longitudinally. For example the same developmental theorists argue that some individuals exhibit persistent offending due to ineffective socialization (Moffitt *et al.*, 1996; Patterson *et al.*, 1989) but also include dynamic elements by arguing that some individuals exhibit offending that is constrained to a particular time period (e.g., adolescence) and that this offending is dependent on life circumstances (Moffitt *et al.*, 1996; Patterson *et al.*, 1989). These theories are discussed in more detail later in this chapter.

## Competing Perspectives

The emergence of the DLC perspective precipitated fierce debate between those who took a cross-sectional and mostly sociological approach to the study of crime and those who were working in the DLC framework and receiving greater support in research funding. In contrast to the DLC perspective, there are models that propose that fixed individual differences between people explain delinquency and criminality (Gottfredson & Hirschi, 1990; Wilson & Herrnstein, 1985). These theorists view crime at any stage of the life-course as having the same underlying causes (for example, low self-control (Gottfredson & Hirschi, 1990) or personality (Wilson & Herrnstein, 1985)). These theorists argue that criminality at any stage of the life course is due to these time stable traits. Within this perspective DLC models are viewed as being more complex than necessary and as providing little more explanatory power than cross-sectional models (Hirschi & Gottfredson, 1995:133). Prior involvement in offending is not believed to impact on future involvement, but rather it is considered an indicator of a persisting individual difference such as low self-control (Nagin & Farrington, 1992). These competing theoretical viewpoints have been intensely debated in the academic literature, initially between Blumstein, Cohen, & Farrington (1988a, 1988b) and Gottfredson & Hirschi (1986, 1988).

Gottfredson & Hirschi (1986), argued that "the criminal career notion ... dominates discussion of criminal justice policy and ... controls expenditure of federal research funds" (213). Their main substantive argument was that individual age–crime curves were the same as the aggregate age–crime curve. Therefore, it was unnecessary to distinguish prevalence and frequency because both varied similarly with age. Between-individual differences in offending depended on a single underlying theoretical construct of self-control (Gottfredson & Hirschi, 1990) that persisted from childhood to adulthood. Persons with low self-control had a high prevalence, frequency, and seriousness of offending, an early onset, a late termination, and a long criminal career, so the predictors and correlates of any one of these criminal career features were argued to be the same as the predictors and correlates of any other. Gottfredson & Hirschi (1986) also argued that longitudinal research was unnecessary because the causes and correlates of offending (which depended on the stable underlying construct of self-control) were the same at all ages.

Blumstein, Cohen, & Farrington (1988a, 1988b) responded to the main criticisms. First, they argued that the predictors and correlates of one criminal career feature (e.g., prevalence or onset) were different from the predictors of another (e.g., frequency or desistance). Second, they pointed out that individual age–crime curves for frequency (which was constant over time for active offenders) were very different from the aggregate age–crime curve. Third, they contended that longitudinal research was needed to test many of Gottfredson & Hirschi's key hypotheses, such as the stability of self-control from childhood to adulthood. Fourth, they argued that, because of their emphasis on and experience of cross-sectional research, Gottfredson & Hirschi tried to draw conclusions about causes from between-individual differences, but the idea of cause required within-individual change over time, which could only be studied in longitudinal research. This debate has continued in the ongoing discussion between Hirschi & Gottfredson (Gottfredson, 2005; Hirschi & Gottfredson, 1995), and Sampson & Laub (1995, 2005a). The later debate centers on a number of similar themes including: stability and continuity of offending; the effect of individual choice; and the correlates of crime.

## Stability and continuity

Hirschi & Gottfredson (1995:135) argued that crime at all ages was due to the time-stable trait of self-control. An individual's level of self-control, according to this model, is acquired via socialization and fixed by about age 8 years. However, contrary to their argument, this would indicate that an individual's level of self-control is not invariant, with Hirschi & Gottfredson's model of stability across the life-course only applying to middle childhood onwards (Sampson & Laub, 1995:246). This is problematic given that there is research that shows there is change in individuals in childhood (Tremblay, 2003), adolescence (Moffitt *et al.*, 1996), and later in life (Laub & Sampson, 2003). It is, therefore, important to examine relative versus absolute stability. Over time it is possible to have relative stability in the rank ordering of people but also absolute change in the level of different variables, such as offending.

In addition, Hirschi & Gottfredson's proposed continuity of self-control across the life-course does not incorporate empirically supported phenomena such as *state-dependence* or *cumulative continuity* (Sampson & Laub, 1995:246). Nagin & Paternoster (1991) propose an effect of "state dependence" where prior delinquency is instrumental in facilitating future crimes. Sampson & Laub (1995) propose that through *cumulative continuity* "delinquency incrementally mortgages the future by generating negative consequences for life chances" (247). For example, a criminal conviction may reduce opportunities for employment and lack of employment may lead to further criminality.

## Individual choice

When self-control is conceptualized as the principle cause of crime, involvement in institutions such as schooling, employment, and marriage are not viewed as causing self-restraint (Hirschi & Gottfredson, 1995:138). Rather, individuals are believed to make the decision to change prior to their involvement with these change-producing institutions (Hirschi & Gottfredson, 1995:137). The life-course perspective recognizes that individual differences will affect decisions to participate in these institutions, but this does not mean that social mechanisms emerging from these institutions have no social significance (Sampson & Laub, 1995:249).

## Correlates of crime

According to Hirschi & Gottfredson (1995:133), the correlates of crime are universally established in both the longitudinal and cross-sectional criminological literature. They propose that this negates the need for any further longitudinal research into the causes of crime. However, far from being settled, the correlates and causes of crime provide an ongoing research endeavor within criminology. Past research on causes was based on between-individual differences but research has shown that causes from within-individual differences could be quite different. For example, while peer delinquency predicts differences in levels of delinquency between individuals, it does not predict within-individual variations (Farrington *et al.*, 2002). Much research is still needed on within-individual variation. Even assuming that the correlates have been established, there is no consensus on the ways in which these correlates bring about the outcome of criminality (Sampson & Laub, 1995:252). The ongoing debate between competing approaches to studying crime is as fervent now as it was a decade ago.[1]

Overall, the competing viewpoints are often based on theorists talking at cross-purposes. For example, Gottfredson and Hirschi focus on the relative stability in rank ordering of individuals, arguing that absolute levels of offending depend on opportunities. In contrast, others focus on absolute change. For example, Moffitt focuses on individual changes in the level of offending over time. The two ideas are not incompatible.

## Key DLC Theories

With the rise of longitudinal studies and increasingly longer follow-up times, DLC criminologists began to develop theories based on their data. These theories have been developed based on the data sets that the theorists have generated or had access to. Comparisons of the theories have been made elsewhere (Farrington, 2006) but the purpose here is to provide a brief overview of each of the theories.

### The developmental progression of antisocial behavior – Gerald Patterson

Patterson and his colleagues (1989) argue that antisocial behavior in adolescence is the result of a cumulative chain of experiences including ineffective parenting, academic failure, peer rejection, and affiliation with deviant peers. The core element of the model is poor parenting and ineffective disciplinary practices, and it is argued that these occur in the context of family disruption. Family disruption can occur because of the antisocial behavior of parents and grandparents; demographic variables related to low socioeconomic status; and/or family stress such as violence, discord, and divorce. Patterson uses the term "chimera" as a metaphor for the cumulative effects that result for a person with an antisocial trait (Patterson, 1993:918). He views antisocial behavior as symptomatic of a trait that creates an underlying dynamic process that is stable across time and impacts all interactions. However, he also recognizes that the age of onset for antisocial behavior is important and discusses the differences between early and late starters. Those individuals with a later onset have a much higher likelihood of an earlier desistance and it is argued that this is because they lack early training in antisocial behaviors. This type of argument, which identifies distinctive developmental pathways to offending, could only be proposed and tested using longitudinal data.

### Developmental pathways – Rolf Loeber

The impetus for Loeber and colleagues' (2008) pathways model arises from a recognition of the need for models which incorporate the development and accumulation of both risk and promotive factors over the life-course. A key argument of the model is that the developmental pathway for delinquency is such that individuals progress from minor to more serious forms of delinquency over time. Their model includes three escalation pathways: authority conflict; covert; and overt. In each of the three pathways, the most serious types of delinquency and violence are preceded by persistent problem behaviors at earlier stages in the pathway. One of the ways in which this model is distinct from other developmental theories is its particular focus on different types or pathways of delinquency. Other theories tend to focus on either changes in rates of delinquency or changes in and out of a delinquent status. Another distinctive consideration within this model is its emphasis on the timing of exposure to risk and promotive factors and the varying impact that they can have at different developmental stages (including recognition of the saliency of the effect, beyond the time of exposure) and the accumulation of risk factors (noting the dose-response relationship as a result of experiencing multiple risk or promotive factors).

## The social development model – David Hawkins and Richard Catalano

The social development model is one of the earliest DLC theories (Hawkins & Weis, 1985). It has been refined over time (Catalano & Hawkins, 1996; Catalano *et al.*, 2005) and also been subjected to empirical testing (Catalano *et al.*, 2005; Fleming, Catalano, Oxford, & Harachi, 2002). The central argument of this theory is that there are a range of established risk factors or predictors for antisocial behavior, but the contribution of the social development model is that it incorporates these predictors into a theory of human behavior (Catalano *et al.*, 2005). The model draws on three traditional criminological theories: social control theory; social learning theory; and differential association theory.

It is argued that children learn both pro-social and antisocial behaviors through the same socialization process. The key stages in this process include: (1) perceived opportunities for involvement and interaction with others; (2) skills for involvement and interaction; and (3) perceived reinforcement of involvement and interaction. Successfully navigating each of these stages leads to social bonding to the socializing unit. In other words, the social development model allows for divergent pathways toward socialization, one being conforming, the other being deviant and/or criminal. In short, whilst the processes of socialization are similar, the content and context of who the person is socialized with can reflect a nonconforming or deviant pathway.

More recent empirical testing of the social developmental model has shown that predictors of antisocial behavior, such as position in the social structure (gender and socioeconomic status) and constitutional factors (poor concentration, shyness, and aggressiveness), are partially mediated by the constructs of the social development model. Furthermore, the effect of external constraints (parenting, schooling, and legal constraints) on antisocial behavior is fully mediated by the constructs (Catalano *et al.*, 2005). However, Brown and his colleagues (2005) found that not all relationships were fully mediated by SDM constructs. In particular, cognitive and socioemotional skills influenced antisocial behavior directly rather than through bonding and beliefs.

## An age-graded theory of informal social control – Robert Sampson and John Laub

Sampson & Laub presented the latest articulation of their theory in their book *Shared Beginnings, Divergent Lives* (Laub & Sampson, 2003). Building on the social control theory presented in *Crime in the Making* (Sampson & Laub, 1993), they provide a revised and expanded age-graded theory of informal social control. Their theory was expanded to consider and incorporate human agency, situational influences and contexts, and the historical context. They explicitly reject trajectory and typological approaches to explaining offending over the life-course. Instead, Sampson & Laub focus on "turning points" to explain the process which allows people to engage in further offending or desist from offending. Turning points are life changes such as marriage and attachment to a spouse, joining the military, being sent to reform school, and change in neighborhood or residence.

The importance of criminogenic environments is highlighted when they discuss turning points causing the "knifing off" of individual offenders from their past and the immediate environment and the provision of supervision and social support. They argue that positive engagement with turning points brings about a change in and structure to routine activities, which allows for identify transformation, and ultimately leads to desistance from offending behavior. The element of human agency also allows individuals to use turning points as opportunities for further antisocial behavior; for example, marriage and domestic violence or employment and theft from work. Therefore, persistent offending can also be understood in the context of turning points. Persistent offending is influenced by the desire for fast money, alienation, rejection and defiance of authority, and a perception of the criminal justice system, and society/the world more generally, as unfair or corrupt (Laub & Sampson, 2003).

## Interactional theory – Terence Thornberry and Marvin Krohn

The interactional theory of Thornberry & Krohn (2005) particularly focuses on factors encouraging antisocial behavior at different ages. It is influenced by findings in the Rochester Youth Development Study (Thornberry *et al.*, 2003). They do not propose types of offenders but suggest that the causes of antisocial behavior vary for children who start at different ages. At the earliest ages (birth to 6 years) the three most important factors are neuropsychological deficit and difficult temperament (e.g., impulsiveness, negative emotionality, fearlessness, poor emotion regulation), parenting deficits (e.g., poor monitoring, low affective ties, inconsistent discipline, physical punishment), and structural adversity (e.g., poverty, unemployment, welfare dependency, a disorganized neighborhood). They also suggest that structural adversity might be one cause of poor parenting.

Neuropsychological deficits are less important for children who start antisocial behavior at older ages. At age 6 to 12 years, neighborhood and family factors are particularly salient, while at age 12 to 18 school and peer factors dominate. Thornberry & Krohn (2005) also suggest that deviant opportunities, gangs, and deviant social networks are important for onset at age 12 to 18. They propose that late starters (age 18 to 25) have cognitive deficits such as low IQ and poor school performance but that a supportive family and school environment protected them from antisocial behavior at earlier ages. At age 18 to 25, they find it hard to make a successful transition to adult roles such as employment and marriage.

The most distinctive feature of this interactional theory is its emphasis on reciprocal causation. For example, it is proposed that the child's antisocial behavior elicits coercive responses from parents, school disengagement, and rejection by peers and makes antisocial behavior more likely in the future. The theory does not postulate a single key construct underlying offending but suggests that children who start early tend to continue, both because of the persistence of neuropsychological and parenting deficits and structural adversity and because of the consequences that earlier antisocial behavior creates. Interestingly, Thornberry & Krohn also predict that late starters (age 18 to 25) will show more continuity over time than those who start during adolescence (age 12 to 18), because the late starters have more cognitive deficits. Thornberry and colleagues (Thornberry, Freeman-Gallant, & Lovegrove, 2009a; 2009b) has extended this theory to explain both intergenerational continuity and discontinuity in antisocial behavior. He suggested that the impact of the parent's antisocial behavior on the child's antisocial behavior is largely indirect, mediated by the parent's pro-social or antisocial bonding, transition to adult roles, structural adversity, stressors, and ineffective parenting.

Thornberry and colleagues tested these ideas in the Rochester Intergenerational Study (Smith, Ireland, Park, Elwyn, & Thornberry, 2011; Thornberry, Freeman-Gallant, & Lovegrove, 2009a; 2009b; Thornberry & Henry, 2013; Thornberry, Krohn, & Freeman-Gallant, 2006). Collectively this research has shown that parental antisocial behavior increases the chances that the child will also be involved in antisocial behavior, especially for mothers and fathers who have ongoing contact with their children, but interestingly, not for fathers who were largely absent. It also appears that this intergenerational effect is mediated by high levels of stress and by parenting behaviors. In general, these findings are consistent with their intergenerational theory.

## Situational action theory – Per-Olof Wikström

Wikström centers his theory on moral rule breaking. The fundamental argument is that "people are moved to action … by how they see their action alternatives and make their choices when confronted with the particularities of a setting" (Wikström, 2006:61). This theory is distinctive when compared to other developmental theories in that it draws attention to the ways in which the interaction of individual experiences and environmental features lead to crime. Wikström argues that all crimes break the moral rules that define what is acceptable in a given setting. Laws are viewed as codified moral rules, and crimes are breaches of these moral rules. The greater the extent to which one's moral rules correspond with the moral rules enacted in laws, the lower the likelihood of offending.

Wikström acknowledges that self-interest and rational choices have a role to play in explaining human action but argues that a better foundation for understanding human action is to consider it in the context of moral rules and moral contexts. In relation to agency, he argues that choices may be either habitual (determined by the setting) or deliberate (weighing up of pros and cons). Choices of crime, however, can only be made when the individual perceives that crime is a viable option for action. The theory focuses on explaining why individuals perceive crime as an option, not just why they choose crime. Overall, Wikström argues that the individual propensity to offend and exposure to criminogenic moral contexts lead to crime involvement (Wikström & Treiber, 2009). An independent test of the theory was conducted by Svensson, Pauwels, & Weerman (2010) using data from Sweden, The Netherlands, and Belgium to show that individual morality interacts with the level of self-control to produce the subsequent offending rate.

## Life-course persistent and adolescence-limited antisocial behavior – Terrie Moffitt

Moffitt developed her theoretical perspective based on the robust yet incongruous empirical facts regarding the stability of antisocial behavior across the life-course, as well as the large peak in delinquency and offending during adolescence (Moffitt, 1993; Moffitt *et al.*, 1996). To explain this she suggested that two distinct types of delinquents underlie the age–crime curve across the life-course. Moffitt developed the life-course persistent and adolescence-limited typologies of antisocial behavior and it is these typologies that have been the subject of a great deal of empirical research. Life-course persistent behavior is characterized by early neuropsychological damage followed by a history of failed social interactions and the development of antisocial behavior at an early age. On the other hand, adolescence-limited antisocial behavior is believed to be the result of individuals experiencing the maturity gap between biological and social maturity. They want adult things but cannot obtain them legitimately. Adolescents are believed to overcome this maturity gap through social mimicry of the life-course persistent individuals' behavior – who are viewed as already having access to adult roles such as an income (albeit from the underground economy), sexual relationships, and independence from parental controls.

Moffitt also states that there are individuals who abstain completely from antisocial behavior due to: (1) not experiencing the maturity gap through late onset of puberty and early onset of adult roles; (2) possessing pathological characteristics which exclude them from peer networks; and (3) a lack of opportunities for social mimicry. There are also individuals whose antisocial behavior is characterized by intermittency across the life-course. Despite the increased focus of research on Moffitt's theory, there has been very little empirical testing of these latter typologies. Moffitt's (2006) latest articulation of the theory provides a comprehensive review of the existing empirical tests of the theory and suggestions about how the theory needs to be altered in light of these tests. In this review she notes that many predictions of the theory were confirmed and discusses the need for additional categories of individuals, such as low-level chronics, who in earlier articulations of her theory she called "recoveries" but further research demonstrated that they never really recovered from their early onset antisocial behavior. She also discussed adult-onset offenders who were first arrested or convicted as adults arguing that they had previously offended but had not been caught, rather than previously abstaining from offending.

## Integrative multilayered control theory – Marc LeBlanc

LeBlanc (1997a) proposed an integrative multilayered control theory that explains the development of offending, the occurrence of criminal events, and community crime rates. This is undoubtedly the most complex of the DLC theories. The key construct underlying offending is antisocial behavior. According to LeBlanc's theory, the development of antisocial behavior depends on changes in four mechanisms of control: (1) bonding to society (attachment and commitment to family, school, peers, religion, marriage, and work); (2) self-control (especially away from egocentrism and towards "allocentrism": a hierarchical structure of personality traits); (3) modeling (pro-social or antisocial routine activities and models); and (4) constraints (external, including socialization methods, and internal, including beliefs). LeBlanc's (2009) latest statement of his theory applies the "chaos-order" paradigm of development. Accordingly, the complexity of antisocial behavior changes over time, from two types in early childhood to nine types at the end of adolescence, and to six categories during adulthood. At all ages, there are reciprocal and developmental relationships between types of antisocial behaviors, with one type leading to another. In addition, LeBlanc (2009) proposed that the course of all antisocial behaviors could be represented by three meta-trajectories: persistent, transitory, and common.

This theory has been tested using data from the Montreal Two Samples Longitudinal Study, taken from a community sample (LeBlanc, Ouimet, & Tremblay, 1988) and an adjudicated sample (LeBlanc, 1997b). LeBlanc (2006) elaborated his theory from a structural to a developmental perspective. He reviewed the psychological literature on the development of personality and self-control and identified four self-control trajectories in his samples of adolescent and adjudicated males (Morizot & LeBlanc, 2003a, 2003b). He then conceptualized and illustrated, with the chaos-order tools, an interactional model of the developmental course of antisocial behavior, social-controls, and self-controls. This interactional model was tested with the sequential co-variation strategy of analysis for longitudinal data (Loeber & Le Blanc, 1990).

## The integrated cognitive antisocial potential (ICAP) theory – David Farrington

Farrington (2005a) developed the integrated cognitive antisocial potential (ICAP) theory. For Farrington's theory, there are no types or typologies of offending or criminal trajectories. Rather, the theory focuses on antisocial potential as its key construct. Antisocial potential refers to an individual's propensity to commit antisocial acts. To explain antisocial potential, the theory draws on a range of pre-existing theories. To explain short-term within-individual variations in antisocial potential, Farrington focuses on temporal situational factors and the motivation of the individual to engage in antisocial behavior. The focus on situational and motivational factors illuminates why it is that some people commit certain offences at specific times and places. In contrast, long-term between-individual differences are explained by an individual's impulsiveness and in the context of strain, modeling, and socialization. This line of inquiry explains why it is that a person becomes an offender. The theory focuses on the long-term impact of risk factors and, similar to other developmental theories, draws attention to the importance of distinguishing between those factors that are causal rather than correlational. Similarly to Loeber's model (Loeber *et al.*, 2008), Farrington also highlights the importance of considering protective factors, but also calls attention to the problems associated with defining what constitutes a protective factor in the risk factor paradigm. This theory has been independently tested by Van Der Laan, Blom, & Kleemans (2009) with data from approximately 1500 10 to 17 year olds in the Netherlands. They found support for the theory in that that long-term individual, family, and school factors correlated with serious delinquency and the probability of serious delinquency increased with the number of factors. However, after controlling long-term factors, short-term situational factors, such as the absence of tangible guardians and using alcohol or drugs prior to the offense, were still important.

Collectively, all DLC criminology researchers agree that the *aggregate* offending pattern across the life-course shows a peak in the late teens and declines throughout adulthood. They also agree that *individual* offending trajectories follow different patterns; for example, some people offend across the entire life-course, some start as adults, others never offend. Where DLC researchers disagree is in their explanations of why we observe these individual and aggregate patterns.

## Future Directions for Research in DLC Criminology

The crucial element that is needed for the progression of DLC criminology is the formulation of theories that are composed of empirically testable postulates. Systematic examination of the key postulates of DLC theories of offending is also needed. This includes the examination of criminal careers according to both officially recorded offences and self-report offending. Examining offending also requires consideration of related behaviors such as aggression, delinquency, and antisocial behavior. Most crucially, researchers need to investigate within-individual relationships between explanatory variables and offending, since prior research has been based on between-individual relationships. Finally, theorists also need to explicitly specify findings that would disprove their theories.

Theoretical statements by each of the DLC theorists have been collated by Farrington (2005c) and the key postulates of each of the theories have been summarized and contrasted (Farrington, 2006). Critical tests and comparisons of different theories have been specified. DLC theories provide the structure for systematically examining offending across multiple data sources. Historically, all researchers have approached their data with their particular theoretical lens and as a result most data sets have only been examined to test the theory proposed by the data collector. What is needed is rigorous testing between theories and across longitudinal data sources.

Collectively, DLC theories include a broad range of factors in their competing explanations of the development of offending. Consequently, the DLC theories that have been proposed are highly contentious and are often contradictory in their explanations of offending. Rigorous testing of theories is required in order to create new knowledge about the nature of offending over the life-course. This will also provide the most accurate evidence base for policy. While there has been some testing of these theories, it has not been done in a systematic manner across multiple data sets and localities. Each of the DLC theories has been put forward by a particular group of researchers working on a particular data set. Each group of researchers brings their own particular frame of reference to their data set, which, in empirical testing, leads to the exclusion of other possible theoretical explanations. There has been very limited testing of different theories, or elements of theories, using datasets different from those on which they were developed. This represents a big problem for the DLC theories.

Another challenge for the DLC perspective is that many theorists have followed the sociological tradition of developing theories and keeping them. This is in stark contrast to a more typically psychological approach to theory development where theories are tested and revised and even disproved. A good example of theory revision in the DLC perspective is that of Moffitt's typology approach. In the early articulations of her theory (Moffitt, 1993; Moffitt *et al.*, 1996) she identified a typological grouping called "recoveries" whom she argued spontaneously recovered, by the time they had reached adolescence, from their extreme levels of antisocial behavior in early childhood. On the basis of more empirical data and extensive empirical testing by her own research group and others, she revised her theory a decade later (Moffitt, 2006). In terms of the theory of "recoveries" she argued that this label was a misnomer and that although these previously extreme antisocial individuals no longer exceeded the cut-off criteria in adolescence, they went on to have lower level chronic problems throughout their lives. Her 2006 revision of the theory collated and reviewed an extensive range of empirical evidence in relation to the key hypotheses and identified where revisions to the theory needed to be made on the basis of empirical evidence. This provides a good model for the development of theory but does not simultaneously compare the postulates of several theories against the results of several longitudinal studies.

One of the main goals of DLC theories is to predict and explain future offending. Currently the breadth of DLC theories is such that they explain everything but predict no new findings. What is needed is a thorough and simultaneous testing of all the key postulates of the DLC theories to work towards the identification of the elements of each theory that are necessary in the prediction and explanation of offending. This is important in ensuring that crime prevention and treatment policies can be based on the most rigorous and accurate information available, especially about what influences changes within individuals in offending over time.

Farrington (2005b, 2006) has identified a number of points on comparison for the testing of DLC theories.

1. What is the key construct underlying offending?
2. What factors encourage offending?
3. What factors inhibit offending?
4. Is there a learning process?
5. Is there a decision-making process?
6. What is the structure of the theory?
7. What are operational definitions of theoretical constructs?
8. What does the theory explain?
9. What does the theory not explain?
10. What findings might challenge the theory? (Can the theory be tested?)
11. Crucial tests: In what ways does the theory make different predictions from other DLC theories?

Several theorists attempted to answer these questions in his edited book (Farrington, 2005c).

## Conclusion

The DLC perspective became a major force in criminology in the late 1980s. It stands in contrast to a static, sociological perspective because it requires longitudinal data to understand the nature of offending over the life-course. Researchers within the DLC perspective have demonstrated that there are different predictors of different elements of the criminal career. They have also demonstrated that the aggregate age–crime curve and individual age–crime curves are different and that the aggregate curve may hide individual trajectories. It has also become apparent that the causes of crime can only be understood by examining within-individual change across the life-course.

There are a number of key elements that need attention in moving DLC criminology forward. We need to know more about the causes of offending: changes in X that are followed by changes in offending within individuals. We need to develop theories that make testable quantitative predictions. We need to know about the developmental sequences linking biological, individual, family, peer, school, neighborhood, and community factors with offending and antisocial behavior at different ages, and we need to know about interactive effects. We need to know about how the antisocial potential becomes the actuality of offending through situational influences.

In order to advance knowledge, DLC theories need to be refined so that they include quantitative predictions. We also need large prospective longitudinal studies with frequent assessments and within-individual analyses to test theories and causal hypotheses derived from them. To better understand crime and offending, we need more comparisons of self-reports and official records through life. The interactive effects of biological, neighborhood/community, and situational factors need to be considered simultaneously within each study. To achieve this more quickly, multiple-cohort accelerated longitudinal studies should be conducted (Tonry, Ohlin, & Farrington, 1991). When an experimental component is included in a longitudinal study, longitudinal-experimental researchers have the capacity to draw conclusions about development, risk and protective factors, effects of life events, and effects of interventions in the same project (Farrington, Ohlin, & Wilson, 1986). DLC criminology has come a long way since the 1980s but there is still much work to be done and many questions that remain unanswered. Within criminology, it will be interesting to see the extent to which the DLC perspective will indeed replace the dominant adolescent-limited criminology, as forecast by Cullen (2011).

## Note

1   For example, see Gottfredson's (2005) response to Sampson & Laub's (2005a) discussion of their life-course perspective and their response to Gottfredson (Sampson & Laub, 2005b).

## References

Agnew, R. (1997). Stability and change in crime over the life course: A strain theory explanation. In T.P. Thornberry (Ed.), *Developmental Theories of Crime and Delinquency: Advances in Criminological Theory*, Vol. 7. New Brunswick, NJ: Transaction.

Bergman, L.R., & Andershed, A.-K. (2009). Predictors and outcomes of persistent or age-limited registered criminal behavior: A 30-year longitudinal study of a Swedish urban population. *Aggressive Behavior, 35*, 164–178.

Blumstein, A., Cohen, J., & Farrington, D.P. (1988a). Criminal career research: Its value for criminology. *Criminology, 26*(1), 1–35.

Blumstein, A., Cohen, J., & Farrington, D.P. (1988b). Longitudinal and criminal career research: Further clarifications. *Criminology, 56*(1), 57–74.

Blumstein, A., Cohen, J., Roth, J., & Visher, C. (1986). *Criminal Careers and "Career Criminals"*, Vol. 1 & 2. Washington, DC: National Academy Press.

Brown, E.C., Catalano, R.F., Fleming, C.B., Haggerty, K.P., Abbott, R.D., Cortes, R.R., *et al.* (2005). Mediator effects in the social development model: An examination of constituent theories. *Criminal Behaviour and Mental Health, 15,* 221–235.

Catalano, R.F., & Hawkins, J.D. (1996). The social development model: A theory of antisocial behavior. In J.D. Hawkins (Ed.), *Delinquency and Crime: Current Theories* (pp. 149–197). New York: Cambridge University Press.

Catalano, R.F., Park, J., Harachi, T.W., Haggerty, K.P., Abbott, R.D., & Hawkins, J.D. (2005). Mediating the effects of poverty, gender, individual characteristics, and external constraints on antisocial behaviour: A test of the social development model and implications for developmental life-course theory. In D.P. Farrington (Ed.), *Integrated Developmental & Life-Course Theories of Offending: Advances in Criminological Theory,* Vol. *14* (pp. 93–123). New Brunswick, NJ: Transaction.

Cullen, F.T. (2011). Beyond adolescence-limited criminology: Choosing our future – The American Society of Criminology 2010 Sutherland Address. *Criminology, 49*(2), 287–330.

Elliott, D.S. (1994). Serious violent offenders: Onset, developmental course, and termination. *Criminology, 32,* 1–21.

Farrington, D.P. (1992). Criminal career research in the United Kingdom. *British Journal of Criminology, 32*(4), 521–536.

Farrington, D.P. (2005a). The integrated cognitive antisocial potential (ICAP) theory. In D.P. Farrington (Ed.), *Integrated Developmental and Life-Course Theories of Offending: Advances in Criminological Theory,* Vol. *14* (pp. 73–92). New Brunswick, NJ: Transaction.

Farrington, D.P. (2005b). Introduction. In D.P. Farrington (Ed.), *Integrated Developmental and Life-Course Theories of Offending: Advances in Criminological Theory,* Vol. *14* (pp. 1–14). New Brunswick, NJ: Transaction.

Farrington, D.P. (Ed.) (2005c). *Integrated Developmental and Life-Course Theories of Offending: Integrated Developmental and Life-Course Theories of Offending: Advances in Criminological Theory,* Vol. *14.* New Brunswick, NJ: Transaction.

Farrington, D.P. (2006). Building developmental and life-course theories of offending. In F.T. Cullen, J.P. Wright, & K.R. Blevins (Eds.), *Taking Stock: The Status of Criminological Theory: Advances in Criminological Theory,* Vol. *15* (pp. 335–364). New Brunswick, NJ: Transaction.

Farrington, D.P., Loeber, R., Yin, Y., & Anderson, S.J. (2002). Are within-individual causes of delinquency the same as between-individual causes? *Criminal Behaviour and Mental Health, 12,* 53–68.

Farrington, D.P., Ohlin, L.E., & Wilson, J.Q. (1986). Understanding and controlling crime: Toward a new research strategy. *Criminology, 24*(4), 799–808.

Fleming, C.B., Catalano, R.F., Oxford, M.L., & Harachi, T.W. (2002). A test of generalization of the social development model across gender and income groups with longitudinal data from the elementary school developmental period. *Journal of Quantitative Criminology, 18*(4), 423–439.

Glueck, S., & Glueck, E. (1934). *Five Hundred Delinquent Women.* New York: Alfred A. Knopf.

Glueck, S., & Glueck, E. (1950). *Unraveling Juvenile Delinquency.* New York: The Commonwealth Fund.

Glueck, S., & Glueck, E. (1968). *Delinquents and Non-Delinquents in Perspective.* Cambridge, MA: Harvard University Press.

Gottfredson, M.R. (2005). Offender classifications and treatment effects in developmental criminology: A propensity/event consideration. *Annals of the American Academy of Political and Social Science, 602*(1), 46–56.

Gottfredson, M.R., & Hirschi, T. (1986). The true value of lambda would appear to be zero: An essay on career criminals, criminal careers and selective incapacitation, cohort studies and related topics. *Criminology, 24,* 213–234.

Gottfredson, M.R., & Hirschi, T. (1988). Science, public policy, and the career paradigm. *Criminology, 26*(1), 37–55.

Gottfredson, M.R., & Hirschi, T. (1990). *A General Theory of Crime.* Stanford, CA: Stanford University Press.

Hawkins, J.D., & Weis, J.G. (1985). The social development model: An integrated approach to delinquency prevention. *Journal of Primary Prevention, 6*(2), 73–97.

Hirschi, T., & Gottfredson, M.R. (1995). Control theory and the life-course perspective. *Studies on Crime and Crime Prevention, 4*(2), 131–142.

Johnson, J.G., Smailes, E., Cohen, P., Kasen, S., & Brook, J.S. (2004). Antisocial parental behaviour, problematic parenting, and aggressive offspring behaviour during adulthood. *British Journal of Criminology, 44,* 915–930.

Kolvin, I., Miller, F.J.W., Scott, D.M., Gatzanis, S.R.M., & Fleeting, M. (1990). *Continuities of Deprivation? The Newcastle 1000 Family Study.* Aldershot: Avebury.

Laub, J.H., & Sampson, R.J. (2003). *Shared Beginnings, Divergent Lives: Delinquent Boys to Age 70.* Cambridge, MA: Harvard University Press.

LeBlanc, M. (1997a). A generic control theory of the criminal phenomenon: The structural and dynamic statements of an integrated multilayered control theory. In T.P. Thornberry (Ed.), *Developmental Theories of Crime and Delinquency: Advances in Criminological Theory,* Vol. 7 (pp. 215–285). New Brunswick, NJ: Transaction.

LeBlanc, M. (1997b). Socialization or propensity: A test of an integrative control theory with adjudicated boys. *Studies on crime and crime prevention, 6,* 200–224.

LeBlanc, M. (2006). Self-control and social control of deviant behavior in context: Development and interactions along the life course. In P.-O.H. Wikström & R.J. Sampson (Eds.), *The Social Contexts of Pathways in Crime: Development, Context, and Mechanisms* (pp. 195–242). Cambridge: Cambridge University Press.

LeBlanc, M. (2009). The development of deviant behavior, its self-regulation. *Monatsschrift für Kriminologie und Strafrechtsreform, 92,* 117–136.

LeBlanc, M., Ouimet, M., & Tremblay, R.E. (1988). An integrative control theory of delinquent behavior: A validation 1976–1985. *Psychiatry, 51,* 164–176.

Lefkowitz, M.M., Eron, L.D., Walder, L.O., & Huesmann, L.R. (1977). *Growing up to be violent: A longitudinal study of the development of aggression.* Elmsford, NY: Pergamon Press.

Loeber, R., & Le Blanc, M. (1990). Toward a developmental criminology. In M. Tonry & N. Morris (Eds.), *Crime and Justice: A Review of Research,* Vol. 12 (pp. 375–473). Chicago, IL: Chicago University Press.

Loeber, R., Slot, N.W., & Stouthamer-Loeber, M. (2008). A cumulative developmental model of risk and promotive factors. In R. Loeber, N.W. Slot, P.H. van der Laan, & M. Hoeve (Eds.), *Tomorrow's Criminals: The Development of Child Delinquency and Effective Interventions* (pp. 133–164). Burlington, VT: Ashgate.

McCord, J. (1992). The Cambridge-Somerville study: A pioneering longitudinal experimental study of delinquency prevention. In J. McCord & R.E. Tremblay (Eds.),

*Preventing Antisocial Behavior: Interventions From Birth Through Adolescence.* New York: Guilford Press.

McCord, J., & Ensminger, M.E. (1997). Multiple risks and comorbidity in an African-American population. *Criminal Behaviour and Mental Health, 7,* 339–352.

Moffitt, T.E. (1993). Adolescence-limited and life-course-persistent antisocial behavior: A developmental taxonomy. *Psychological Review, 100*(4), 674–701.

Moffitt, T.E. (2006). Life-course persistent versus adolescence-limited antisocial behavior. In D. Cicchetti & D.J. Cohen (Eds.), *Developmental Psychopathology,* 2nd edition, Vol. 3 (pp. 570–598). New York: Wiley.

Moffitt, T.E., Caspi, A., Dickson, N., Silva, P., & Stanton, W. (1996). Childhood-onset versus adolescent-onset antisocial conduct problems in males: Natural history from aged 3 to 18 years. *Development and Psychopathology, 8,* 399–424.

Morizot, J., & LeBlanc, M. (2003a). Continuity and change in personality traits from adolescence to mid-life: A 25-year longitudinal study comparing representative and adjudicated men. *Journal of Personality, 71,* 705–755.

Morizot, J., & LeBlanc, M. (2003b). Searching for a developmental typology of personality and its relations to antisocial behaviour: A longitudinal study of an adjudicated men sample. *Criminal Behaviour and Mental Health, 13,* 241–277.

Nagin, D.S., & Farrington, D.P. (1992). The stability of criminal potential from childhood to adulthood. *Criminology, 30*(2), 235–260.

Nagin, D.S., & Paternoster, R. (1991). On the relationship of past to future participation in delinquency. *Criminology, 29*(2), 163–189.

Patterson, G.R. (1993). Orderly change in a stable world: The antisocial trait as a chimera. *Journal of Consulting and Clinical Psychology, 61*(6), 911–919.

Patterson, G.R., DeBaryshe, B., & Ramsey, E. (1989). A developmental perspective on antisocial behavior. *American Psychologist, 44,* 329–335.

Piquero, A.R., Farrington, D.P., & Blumstein, A. (2003). The criminal career paradigm. In M. Tonry (Ed.), *Crime and Justice: A Review of the Research,* Vol. 30 (pp. 359–506). Chicago, IL: University of Chicago Press.

Pulkkinen, L., Lyyra, A.-L., & Kokko, K. (2009). Life success of males on non-offender, adolescence-limited, persistent, and adult-onset antisocial pathways: follow-up from age 8 to 42. *Aggressive Behavior, 35,* 117–135.

Sampson, R.J., & Laub, J.H. (1993). *Crime in the Making: Pathways and Turning Points Through Life.* Cambridge, MA: Harvard University Press.

Sampson, R.J., & Laub, J.H. (1995). Understanding variability in lives through time: Contributions of life-course criminology. *Studies on Crime and Crime Prevention, 4*(2), 143–258.

Sampson, R.J., & Laub, J.H. (2005a). A life-course view of the development of crime. *Annals of the American Academy of Political and Social Sciences, 602,* 12–45.

Sampson, R.J., & Laub, J.H. (2005b). When prediction fails: From crime-prone boys to heterogeneity in adulthood. *Annals of the American Academy of Political and Social Sciences, 602,* 73–79.

Smith, C.A., Ireland, T.O., Park, A., Elwyn, L., & Thornberry, T.P. (2011). Intergenerational continuities and discontinuities in intimate partner violence: A two-generational prospective study. *Journal of Interpersonal Violence, 26,* 3720–3752.

Svensson, R., Pauwels, L., & Weerman, F.M. (2010). Does the effect of self-control on adolescent offending vary by level of morality? A test in three countries. *Criminal Justice and Behavior, 37*(6), 732–743.

Thornberry, T.P., Freeman-Gallant, A., & Lovegrove, P.J. (2009a). The impact of parental stressors on the intergenerational transmission of antisocial behavior. *Journal of Youth and Adolescence, 38*, 312–322.

Thornberry, T.P., Freeman-Gallant, A., & Lovegrove, P.J. (2009b). Intergenerational linkages in antisocial behaviour. *Criminal Behaviour and Mental Health, 19*, 80–93.

Thornberry, T.P., & Henry, K.L. (2013). Intergenerational continuity in maltreatment. *Journal of Abnormal Child Psychology, 41*, 555–569.

Thornberry, T.P., & Krohn, M.D. (2005). Applying interactional theory to the explanation of continuity and change in antisocial behavior. In D.P. Farrington (Ed.), *Integrated Developmental and Life-Course Theories of Offending* (pp. 183–209). New Brunswick, NJ: Transaction.

Thornberry, T.P., Krohn, M.D., & Freeman-Gallant, A. (2006). Intergenerational roots of early onset substance use. *Journal of Drug Issues, 36*, 1–28.

Thornberry, T.P., Lizotte, A.J., Krohn, M.D., Smith, C.A., & Porter, P.K. (2003). Causes and consequences of delinquency: Findings from the Rochester Youth Development Survey. In T.P. Thornberry & M.D. Krohn (Eds.), *Taking Stock of Delinquency: An Overview of Findings from Contemporary Longitudinal Studies* (pp. 11–46). New York: Kluwer Academic/Plenum Publishers.

Tonry, M., Ohlin, L.E., & Farrington, D.P. (1991). *Human Development and Criminal Behavior: New Ways of Advancing Knowledge*. New York: Springer-Verlag.

Tremblay, R.E. (2003). Why socialization fails?: The case of chronic physical aggression. In B.B. Lahey, T.E. Moffitt, & A. Caspi (Eds.), *The Causes of Conduct Disorder and Juvenile Delinquency* (pp. 182–224). New York: Guilford Press.

Van der Laan, A.M., Blom, M., & Kleemans, E.R. (2009). Exploring long-term and short-term risk factors for serious delinquency. *European Journal of Criminology, 6*(5), 419–438.

Werner, E.E. (1993). Risk, resilience, and recovery: Perspectives from the Kauai Longitudinal Study. *Development and Psychopathology, 5*, 503–515.

West, D.J., & Farrington, D.P. (1973). *Who Becomes Delinquent?* London: Heinemann.

Wikström, P.-O.H. (2006). Individuals, settings, and acts of crime: Situational mechanisms and the explanation of crime. In P.-O.H. Wikström & R.J. Sampson (Eds.), *The Explanation of Crime: Context, Mechanisms and Development*. Cambridge: Cambridge University Press.

Wikström, P.-O.H., & Treiber, K. (2009). What drives persistent offending? The neglected and unexplored role of the social environment. In J. Savage (Ed.), *The Development of Persistent Criminality*. Oxford: Oxford University Press.

Wilson, J.Q., & Herrnstein, R.J. (1985). *Crime and Human Nature*. New York: Simon and Schuster.

Wolfgang, M.E., Figlio, R.M., & Sellin, T. (1972). *Delinquency in a Birth Cohort*. Chicago, IL: University of Chicago Press.

# 19

# Biosocial Bases of Antisocial and Criminal Behavior

Frances R. Chen, Yu Gao, Andrea L. Glenn,
Sharon Niv, Jill Portnoy, Robert Schug,
Yaling Yang, and Adrian Raine

## Introduction

Antisocial behavior and crime has long been a topic of interest among researchers from many different disciplines. Psychologists and sociologists have identified a myriad of social factors associated with antisocial behavior and crime, such as childhood maltreatment and low socioeconomic status (e.g., Farrington, 2000; Hill, 2003; McCord, 2001; Silva, Larm, Vitaro, Tremblay, & Hodgins, 2012). Parallel to this, a large set of biological risk factors has also been linked to antisocial behavior and crime, including autonomic underarousal, brain deficit, neuropsychological impairment, and hormone imbalance (e.g., Boccardi *et al.*, 2010; Bohnke, Bertsch, Kruk, & Naumann, 2010; Ortiz & Raine, 2004; Yang *et al.*, 2012). However, individuals are not merely isolated beings of biological assembly, nor are they pure products of social factors. Social factors and biological factors constantly interact with each other to influence individuals' behavior outcomes. Research on antisocial behavior and crime won't be complete until we break through the fences that currently separate different disciplines and more thoroughly analyze interaction effects. Hence, an interdisciplinary approach is not only helpful but also essential to further our understanding of human antisocial behavior and crime (Raine, 2002).

There are difficulties inherent in the interdisciplinary approach, both methodologically and practically. As we know, breaking through disciplinary barriers is never easy. Yet this has not intimidated some researchers. Over the past two decades, an increasing body of research on biosocial interaction has generated some productive knowledge. In this chapter, we will review empirical findings on antisocial behavior and crime using a biosocial interactive framework. This chapter is organized using the conceptual framework that specific genes result in brain alterations and physical

*The Handbook of Criminological Theory*, First Edition. Edited by Alex R. Piquero.
© 2016 John Wiley & Sons, Inc. Published 2016 by John Wiley & Sons, Inc.

abnormalities which give rise to risk factors that in turn predispose to antisocial and criminal behavior (Raine, 2008). Studies on biological risk factors will first be summarized in each of the following areas: gene, brain, neuropsychology, psychophysiology, and hormones. Within each key research area, we will draw particular attention to how these biological risk factors interact with social factors to influence antisocial behavior and crime. In doing so, we hope to provide a general overview of what has been done to date, and what needs to be done in the future under the biosocial framework to develop our knowledge on the etiology and maintenance of antisocial behavior and crime.

## Genetics

To understand the full scope of biosocial influences on antisocial behavior and crime, genetic research is one piece that cannot be omitted. Genetic research originated with the study of heritability, in which researchers statistically model genetic and environmental influences on any given observable behavior or phenotype. Most interesting to biosocial researchers would be studies that go a step beyond estimating heritability on a given behavior, and that examine gene by environment (G × E) interactions. In this section we first review studies done under G × E framework, which focus on the respective contribution of nature and nurture but not specifically emphasize the interaction between these two, then we will move on to epigenetics, which investigates interactions between molecular genetics and environmental conditions.

### Primary findings

Early adoption studies found a clear G × E interaction between children with a higher genetic risk for criminal offending (i.e. children whose biological parents had criminal records) and with adoptive parents with criminal records. That is, when raised by adoptive parents with no criminal records, even children with genetic risk were less likely to display the phenotype of criminal behavior (Cadoret, Cain, & Crowe, 1983; Cloninger, Sigvardsson, Bohman, & von Knorring, 1982; Mednick, Gabrielli, & Hutchings, 1984). On the whole, behavior genetics studies have found consistent evidence for genetic influences on different forms of crime. A meta-analysis that examined a large number of behavior genetics studies estimated 41% of antisocial behavior, comprising of illegal activity, aggression, drug use, and other socially negative behaviors, to be attributable to genetic influences, and 59% to environmental influences (Rhee & Waldman, 2002). This in itself lends support to the involvement of both nature and nurture in development of criminal behavior. This review also found that genetic effects decrease with aging, suggesting that environmental influence, including social conditions, play more of a role in criminal tendency as time goes by.

Behavior genetics studies can also provide excellent leads for further biosocial examinations of molecular genetic origins of criminal behavior. In one study, a Dutch pedigree was identified in which violence and crime was found to be highly prevalent. Researchers examined several candidate genes within this family, and found the involvement of the monoamine oxidase A gene (*MAOA*) (Brunner *et al.*, 1993). This gene codes for an enzyme involved in the breakdown of several important catecholamine neurotransmitters such as dopamine, serotonin, epinephrine, and norepinephrine. Two specific repeat variants of this gene, 2 and 5 variable number tandem repeats, were found to be associated with aggression and lower sustained attention.

## Biosocial interaction

A remarkable finding in terms of biosocial theory on the development of crime is Caspi *et al.*'s study (2002). Their examination of the monoamine oxidase A gene variant revealed that it only produced higher likelihood of criminal and aggressive behavior when environmental conditions were harsh, i.e. when the child had suffered severe abuse. Although a number of specific gene candidates have emerged in connection to crime and antisocial behavior, this finding calls into question whether it is sufficient to examine genetic variants without considering how environmental conditions may affect their expression.

An entire field of genetics has emerged to investigate interactions between molecular genetics and environmental conditions: epigenetics. Epigenetics is the study of how DNA is modified by environmental conditions, representing the molecular approach to examining the interplay between genes and environment. Several phenomena have been found that demonstrate how environmental conditions can directly affect genes. One of these is methylation, in which methyl groups become attached to DNA nucleotides, altering DNA folding, and hence attractiveness for transcription. The powerful effect of methylation profiles is illustrated by a study that found that in identical twins where one twin has schizophrenia, that twin's methylome was more similar to other individuals with schizophrenia than to his own identical twin with whom he shares 100% of his DNA sequence (Petronis *et al.*, 2003).

Epigenetic influences have also emerged in criminal behavior. For example, COMT, a gene involved in aggression and conduct disorder, has been shown to be differently methylated in identical twins as young as 5 years old (Mill *et al.*, 2006), possibly rendering them less or more inclined toward crime even at this very early stage of development. This may be one explanation for how different early life experiences influence behavior at the molecular level, setting life courses on different trajectories. Chromatin structures have also been found to be altered by drug use, potentially explaining a biological mechanism of addiction resulting directly from behavior (Robison & Nestler, 2011).

These methodologies are being applied currently to a range of candidate genes already associated with criminality, such as those involved in the dopamine, serotonin, endocrine systems, or other networks known to be involved in aggressive or delinquent behavior. With the emergence of newer and more affordable sequencing methods for both DNA and epigenetic profiles, this area of research is certain to produce a more nuanced understanding of how environmental and social conditions interact with genetics to produce changes in behavior.

# Brain – structural and functional

An increasing amount of research has been directed toward understanding the neurobiological etiology of antisocial behavior. In particular brain-imaging studies have been extremely informative in providing the empirical evidence connecting structural and functional deficiencies in several brain regions with antisocial behavior. Here we will review empirical evidence that link brain structural and functional abnormality to antisocial behavior.

## Primary findings

*Structural abnormality*   Initial lines of evidence have come from lesion studies, which have accumulated substantial evidence suggesting a causal link between damage to the frontal and temporal regions and antisocial, criminal behavior. One famous case in hand is Phineas Gage, an unfortunate railway foreman who suffered damage to his frontal lobe, most severely to the orbitofrontal cortex, in an accident involving explosives. Despite surviving such injury and proceeding to have a full recovery physically and intellectually, his personality changed dramatically and he became irresponsible, impulsive, and "psychopathic-like" (Harlow, 1999). Similar increase in antisocial tendency was observed in several other patients with frontal damage in subsequent studies (e.g. Damasio, 1994; Damasio, Tranel, & Damasio, 1990). Furthermore, antisocial characteristics, violence in particular, seem to develop when the lesion damages the medial section of the orbitofrontal cortex (Grafman *et al.*, 1996).

Another line of evidence has come from research on traumatic brain injury (TBI). This is of particular interest within the criminal justice system given the fact that the prevalence of TBI among criminal offenders is much higher than community populations. Hux *et al.* (1998) reported that half of the delinquents they studies had experienced a TBI (defined as having ever received a 'blow to the head'), and one-third of these with TBIs had suffered adverse, long-term behavioral problems including diminished attentional capacity, impaired interpersonal skills and poor school performance. Furthermore, TBI that results in a loss of consciousness is found to be significantly associated with severe violent offending behaviors in juvenile delinquents (Kenny & Lennings, 2007). One study has also shown that a history of untreated TBIs is more common in convicted violent offenders than nonviolent criminals (Leon-Carrion & Ramos, 2003).

Recent developments in brain-imaging techniques have allowed researchers to understand *in vivo* the structural brain correlates of criminal behavior using structural magnetic resonance imaging (sMRI) and diffusion tensor imaging (DTI). Consistent with lesions studies, several sMRI studies to date have found volumetric and morphological abnormalities in the prefrontal, temporal, and limbic structures in individuals with criminal, aggressive behavior. For example, Yang *et al.* (2005, 2010a) found reduced gray matter volume and thickness in the middle frontal and orbitofrontal cortex and reduced volume and surface deformations in the amygdala in unsuccessful psychopaths (i.e. psychopaths with prior criminal convictions) compared to successful psychopaths (i.e. psychopaths without convictions) and nonpsychopathic controls. One recent study showed reduced cortical thickness in the temporal lobes in criminal offenders with psychopathy compared to healthy noncriminal individuals (Howner *et al.*, 2012). For subcortical regions, Yang *et al.* (2010b) revealed reduced hippocampal and parahippocampal volumes in accused murderers with schizophrenia compared to schizophrenia patients and non-violent controls, consistent with another findings that showed abnormal hippocampal morphology in habitually violent offenders (Boccardi *et al.*, 2010). More recently, Ermer *et al.* (2012) showed decreased regional gray matter in the orbitofrontal cortex, parahippocampal, amygdala, hippocampus, temporal pole, and posterior cingulate in criminal psychopaths. Overall, these findings indicate that a decrease in gray matter volume in the brain, particularly the prefrontal, temporal and limbic structures, may contribute to risk factors which predispose to criminal offending.

In addition to sMRI, DTI is also promising, particularly in providing information regarding white matter development in the brain and the mapping of neuronal connectivity. However, very few studies have applied it to criminal samples. Among these few, the most consistent finding is reduced structural integrity in the uncinate fasciculus, the primary white matter connection between ventromedial prefrontal cortex and anterior temporal lobe, in criminal psychopaths (Graig *et al.*, 2009; Motzkin, Newman, Kiehl, & Koenigs, 2011). Most recently, using novel graph theory analysis methods, Yang *et al.* (2012) went beyond regional assessments of brain structure or connectivity and tested topological characteristics of the entire whole brain anatomical network in psychopathic individuals. They found altered interregional connectivity patterns in the frontal network in psychopaths, and also that bilateral superior frontal cortices were identified as information flow control hubs in contrast to bilateral inferior frontal and medial orbitofrontal cortices as network hubs for the controls. These studies provided initial evidence suggesting that disturbed structural connectivity, particularly within the frontal and associated areas, plays a crucial role in criminal offending.

*Functional abnormality*   A recent meta-analysis on 31 functional brain imaging studies (Yang & Raine, 2009) showed that antisocial individuals demonstrated significant reductions primarily in the functioning of the prefrontal cortex. The largest reductions have been observed in the orbitofrontal cortex, dorsolateral prefrontal cortex, and anterior cingulate.

The orbitofrontal cortex serves several functions that, when compromised, may lead to antisocial behavior. These functions include decision-making processes (Bechara, 2004), processing reward and punishment information (Rolls, 2000), understanding the emotions of others (Shamay-Tsoory et al., 2005), regulating emotions (Ochsner et al., 2005), and inhibiting responses (Vollm et al., 2006; Aron, Robbins, & Poldrack, 2004). Reductions in the functioning of the orbitofrontal cortex have been found in several antisocial subgroups, including psychopathic adults (Harenski et al., 2010), youth with callous–unemotional traits (Finger et al., 2008), and patients with intermittent explosive disorder (Coccaro, McCloskey, Fitzgerald, & Phan, 2007). One function of the orbitofrontal cortex is to track the expectation of reinforcement. Deficits in this region may result in increased frustration if an individual failed to receive a reward when expecting one, which may in turn increase the risk for frustration-based aggression (Blair, 2010).

Some studies of antisocial individuals have observed reduced functioning in the dorsolateral region of the prefrontal cortex (Schneider et al., 2000; Vollm et al., 2004), the region that is important for executive functioning (Smith & Jonides, 1999). However, several studies of psychopathic individuals have observed *increased* functioning in this region, particularly during tasks involving emotional processing (Glenn, Raine, Schug, Young, & Hauser, 2009; Gordon, Baird, & End, 2004; Intrator et al., 1997; Kiehl et al., 2001; Rilling et al., 2007). One hypothesis is that, in the absence of appropriate limbic input, psychopathic individuals may rely more on cognitive resources to process emotion-related information (Kiehl et al., 2001).

The anterior cingulate is a region that is thought to serve as a relay station of information in the brain, and is thought to be involved in effortful control, self-regulation, signaling errors, and emotional processing. Several studies have found reduced activity in this region in psychopathic individuals (Birbaumer et al., 2005; Müller et al., 2003; Rilling et al., 2007), but no volumetric reduction was observed in this particular area (Glenn, Yang, Raine, & Colletti, 2010). Because the anterior cingulate is highly connected to other brain regions that may function differently in psychopathic groups, it is hypothesized that this region may not be impaired in psychopathy, but that reduced functioning may reflect reduced input from other impaired regions.

Apart from prefrontal cortex, some subcortical brain regions are of research interest, including amygdala and striatum. The amygdala is involved in generating emotional responses (Phillips, Drevets, Rauch, & Lane, 2003), and in the formation of stimulus–reinforcement associations. Both of these processes are important for normal moral development. The amygdala has been identified as functioning differently in antisocial groups, yet whether it is found to be hypoactivite or hyperactivite seems to depend on the antisocial subgroup being studied. Studies of impulsive, reactively aggressive individuals typically demonstrate *enhanced* amygdala responding to threatening stimuli (Coccaro et al., 2007, Herpertz, Dietrich, & Wenning, 2001; Lee, Chan, & Raine 2008). In contrast, individuals with psychopathic traits consistently demonstrate *reduced* response in the amygdala during a variety of tasks (e.g., Kiehl et al., 2001; Glenn, Raine, & Schug, 2009; Birbaumer et al., 2005).

The striatum is a region involved in reward processing (O'Doherty, 2004). Kumari *et al.* (2009) found that men with a history of serious violence demonstrated less activity in this region when exposed to sustained cues threatening electric shock. Buckholtz *et al.*, (2010) found that activity in the striatum increased during the anticipation of reward. Individuals with antisocial personality disorder demonstrated increased activity in the orbitofrontal cortex, another region important in reward processing, during a reward task (Vollm *et al.*, 2010). These findings suggest that the striatum may function abnormally in antisocial individuals, but that the direction of effects may rely on the context (i.e., exposure to threat versus reward).

Together these studies highlight a number of brain regions that appear to function differently in antisocial groups. Findings may vary depending on the antisocial subgroup being studied, as well as the type of stimuli presented during the task which is used to assess brain activity.

## Biosocial interactions

There have been very few structural brain-imaging studies to date evaluating interactions between social influences and structural brain abnormalities in predisposing to criminal behavior. Among these few, several studies of young children, adolescents, and adults (Lewis, Pincus, Bard, & Richardson, 1988) have found that across the lifespan, exposure to violence and abuse in the family is the strongest factor leading to violence in individuals with neurological impairment. Alternatively, there is also evidence that social factors can act as protective factors to prevent individuals with brain damage from becoming antisocial. Mataro *et al.* (2001) describe a Spanish patient who had frontal lesion similar to that of Phineas Gage due to an accident in 1937. However, unlike Gage, he did not show an increase in antisocial, psychopathic behavior. It was suggested that such a difference in outcome may be due to the fact that patient had a family that was highly protective and caring. Overall, these findings suggest that, for structurally impaired individuals, negative social factors such as child abuse may increase the risk of one engaging in criminal behavior, whereas positive social factors such as nurturing family members may dramatically reduce such risk.

In the functional brain-imaging research area, only a few studies have examined biosocial interactions. In a sample of murderers, Raine *et al.* (1998) found that those with psychosocial deprivation early in life demonstrated greater prefrontal glucose metabolism (a measure of brain functioning) than murderers with little evidence of psychosocial deprivation. In another study, using fMRI, Raine *et al.* (2001) found that violent offenders who had suffered child abuse demonstrated reduced functioning in the right hemisphere of the brain, whereas abused individuals who refrained from violence showed greater right-hemisphere relative to left-hemisphere functioning. This is interesting in light of evidence suggesting that left-hemisphere functioning is associated with approach motivation, whereas right-hemisphere functioning is associated with withdrawal (Davidson, Putnam, & Larson, 2000). This suggests that early childhood abuse may result in different types of neurobiological deficits in individuals. When these deficits result in impairments in the withdrawal (right hemisphere) system, the tendency for violent behavior may be increased.

Although numerous brain imaging studies have now been conducted in antisocial groups, as discussed above, the majority have not examined potential interactions with environmental factors. Future evidence is sorely needed to explore the effects of structural and functional brain abnormalities in criminal offenders in interaction with social risk factors.

# Neuropsychology

Neuropsychology is the indirect study of brain dysfunction through behavioral expression. Neuropsychological investigations of crime, aggression and violence have generally involved different domains of cognitive functioning, in an attempt to understand the etiology and maintenance of antisocial behavior. Here we mainly focus on intelligence and executive functioning.

## Primary findings

Deficits in measures of general intelligence (e.g., IQ or Full Scale IQ) are the best-replicated neuropsychological correlate of antisociality, violence, and crime among non-mentally ill individuals (Wilson & Herrnstein, 1985). These findings are also echoed in individuals with psychological disorders such as schizophrenia (Schug & Raine, 2009).

Regarding different intelligence components, reduced verbal as opposed to spatial/performance IQ is widely reported among adult antisocial populations (Raine, 1993), including those with mental illness (Sreenivisan *et al.*, 2000). It has been proposed that these verbal IQ reductions index deficits in left-hemispheric functioning (Raine, 1993). Verbal IQ reductions have also been widely reported in samples of antisocial children and adolescents (Barker *et al.*, 2007; Brennan *et al.*, 2003; Raine, 1993; Teichner & Golden, 2000), and have been shown to predict later delinquency at age 18 for persistent, high-level offending beginning in preadolescence (Moffitt, Lynam, & Silva, 1994). Verbal deficits may undermine the development of self-control mechanisms based on language (Luria, 1980), leading ultimately to socialization failure (Eriksson, Hodgins, & Tengström, 2005).

Executive functioning (EF) is an umbrella term for the cognitive processes allowing for goal-oriented, contextually appropriate behavior and effective self-serving conduct (Lezak, Howieson, Loring, Hannay, & Fischer, 2004; Luria, 1980). Deficits in EF, as indicated by performance errors on neuropsychological measures of strategy formation, cognitive flexibility, or impulsivity (measures such as Stroop task, card-sorting test, Hanoi Tower test), are thought to represent frontal lobe impairment. Morgan & Lilienfeld's now-classic (2000) meta-analysis of 39 studies found overall EF deficits in antisocial individuals compared to controls, and strongest effects for the Porteus Mazes test Q score (a purported measure of impulsivity and rule-breaking) and antisociality defined by judicial status.

Studies on EF deficits in delinquent children and adolescents with conduct disorder are inconclusive, as they varied depending upon sample characteristics, control groups, assessment measures and operationalizations of EF (Moffitt & Henry, 1989; Teichner & Golden, 2000). EF deficits characterized antisocial youths in some studies (Cauffman *et al.*, 2005; Kronenberger *et al.*, 2005; Nigg *et al.*, 2004; Raine *et al.*, 2005; White *et al.*, 1994) and not in others (Moffitt *et al.*, 1994; Nigg *et al.*, 2004). This may reflect, however, the development of EF along with the ongoing myelination of the frontal cortex into adolescence and beyond (Nigg *et al.*, 2004; Raine, 2002). Furthermore, it has been proposed that antisocial behavior and EF deficits may be related developmentally: certain EF deficits may lead to an impaired ability to mentally maintain abstract ideas of ethical values and future contingencies while focusing upon immediate rewards, and the inhibition of modification of behavior in response to social feedback, which combined together predispose to antisocial behaviors (Moffitt & Henry, 1989).

EF deficits have also been associated with various antisocial groups. Studies have revealed links between EF deficits and male wife batterers and antisocial personality-disordered populations (Dolan & Park, 2002; Stanford, Conklin, Helfritz, & Kockler, 2007; Teichner, Golden, Van Hasselt, & Peterson, 2001), property offending (Barker *et al.*, 2007), reactive versus instrumental violent offenders (Broomhall, 2005), and schizophrenic compared to nonschizophrenic domestic murderers (Hanlon *et al.*, 2012). Adult psychopathy has not demonstrated consistent associations with general EF deficits (Blair & Frith, 2000; Dinn & Harris, 2000; Hiatt & Newman, 2006; Kosson, Miller, Byrnes, & Leveroni, 2007), and recent neuropsychological evidence suggests that psychopathy may be characterized more by deficits in orbitofrontal functioning (Blair *et al.*, 2006).

## Biosocial interaction

Earlier prospective neuropsychological studies have found interactions of neuropsychological/neurobiological dysfunction and adverse social/environmental influences to significantly increase levels of later violence, crime, and antisocial behaviors (Raine, 2002), and recent longitudinal evidence echoes these findings. For instance, Aguilar, Sroufe, Egeland, & Carlson (2000) found that severe psychosocial adversity before age 4, rather than biological factors (i.e., infant temperament or early neuropsychological variables) predict early-onset antisociality. Early-onset antisocials differed from others only on late childhood/adolescent neuropsychological performance. These two considered together suggest progressive cognitive dysfunction affected by adverse experience. In addition, Brennan *et al.* (2003) found the interaction of biological risk factors, including neuropsychological impairment (low vocabulary ability at age 5, poor VIQ and EF at age 15), and social risk factors (poverty, harsh discipline style), predicted later aggression in boys and girls. These authors suggest that an interaction of early social risks with later biological risks predicts persistent aggression; and that lifetime, cumulative interactions of these risks are stronger predictors of persistent aggression in boys than are risks specific to childhood or adolescence.

## Psychophysiology – Autonomic nervous system

The autonomic nervous system (ANS) serves as a link between the central nervous system and internal organs (e.g., heart, lungs, salivary glands, sweat glands) and is critically involved in the "fight or flight" response when threatened or under stress. The most frequently used measures in criminological research include heart rate and skin conductance (SC). Heart rate reflects the complex interactions between sympathetic and parasympathetic autonomic nervous system activity, while SC measures very small changes in the electrical activity of the skin and is exclusively influenced by the sympathetic autonomic nervous system.

### Primary findings

Low resting heart rate is the best-replicated biological correlate of antisocial behavior in non-institutionalized children and adolescents (Ortiz & Raine, 2004), and greater heart rate reactivity during behavioral challenge or stress tasks appears characteristic of conduct-disordered children (Kibler, Prosser, & Ma, 2004; Lorber, 2004). Low heart rate is diagnostically specific to conduct disorder, and has demonstrated predictive validity as a childhood predictor of adolescent aggression (Raine, Venables, & Mednick, 1997) and life-course persistent offending (Moffitt & Caspi, 2001). In a recent longitudinal study on delinquent male adolescents, attenuated heart rate response and stronger heart rate variability response to stress predicted higher reoffending rates 5 years later (de Vries-Bouw *et al.*, 2011).

Reduced or abnormal SC has been generally associated with a series of behavior problems and aggression, particularly in children and adolescents. For instance, low SC has been associated with conduct problems (Lorber, 2004), SC-orienting deficits have also been reported in conduct-disordered boys (Herpertz *et al.*, 2003), and reduced SC fluctuations and fear conditioning have been reported in conduct-disordered adolescents (Fairchild, Stobbe, van Goozen, Calder, & Goodyer, 2010; Fairchild, van Goozen, Strollery, & Goodyer, 2008; Herpertz *et al.*, 2005). Diminished ANS reactivity has also been found in psychopathy-prone adolescents (Fung *et al.*, 2005) and conduct-disordered children with callous–unemotional traits (Anastassiou-Hadjicharalambous & Warden, 2008; Kimonis, Frick, Fazekas, & Loney, 2006; Loney, Frick, Clements, Ellis, & Kerlin, 2003). Furthermore, some studies have suggested different autonomic correlates of externalizing behavior for females compared with males (Beauchaine, Hong, & Marsh, 2008; Murray-Close, Holland, & Roisman, 2012), and for different subtypes of aggression (Scarpa, Haden, & Tanaka, 2010). In contrast to reduced SC level and activity, enhanced ANS functioning, as indexed by higher levels of arousal, better conditioning, and higher orienting responses, may serve as biological protective factors that reduce the likelihood of becoming an adult criminal (Brennan *et al.*, 1997; Raine, Venables, & Williams, 1995, 1996).

A significant research body has accumulated to suggest that reduced or abnormal SC activity in children may be a risk factor for later antisocial behavior and criminality. Longitudinally, reduced SC arousal at age 15 has been associated with criminal offending at age 24 (Raine, Venables, & Williams, 1990), and low SC levels measured at age 11 predict institutionalization at age 13 in a sample of behavior- disordered children (Kruesi *et al.*, 1992). In addition, impaired SC fear conditioning at age 3, suggesting retarded maturation of the amygdala, has been found to be associated with aggressive behavior at age 8 as well as criminal behavior 20 years later at age 23 (Gao, Raine, Venables, Dawson, & Mednick, 2010a, 2010b). Furthermore, prospective studies have indicated that abnormal SC responses (i.e., longer half-recovery time, which reflects a closed attentional stance to the environment) to aversive stimuli as early as age 3 predispose to psychopathic personality in adulthood (Glenn, Raine, Venables, & Mednick, 2007).

## Biosocial interaction

Psychophysiological risk factors may interact with psychosocial variables in predisposing certain individuals to antisocial and criminal behavior. A number of studies have found that psychophysiological factors, particularly measures of SC and heart rate, show stronger relationships to antisocial behavior in those from benign social backgrounds that lack the classic psychosocial risk factors for crime (e.g., Hemming, 1981; Raine & Venables, 1981). In a longitudinal study, low heart rate at age 3 years has been found to predict aggression at age 11 years in children from high but not low social classes (Raine *et al.*, 1997). These findings, as argued by the "social push" hypothesis, suggest that psychophysiological risk factors may assume greater importance when social predispositions to crime are minimized. In contrast, social causes may be more important explanations of antisocial behavior in those exposed to adverse early home conditions (Raine, 2002).

Alternatively, the "dual-hazard" effect has been documented in the psychophysiological research of antisocial behavior (Dierckx *et al.*, 2011; Farrington, 1997; Katz, 2007; Murray-Close & Rellini, 2012; Scarpa, Tanaka, & Haden, 2008; Sijtsema, Shoulberg, & Murray-Close, 2011). For example, boys with low resting heart rate have been found more likely to be rated as aggressive by their teachers if their mother was pregnant as a teenager, if they were from a low social class family, or if they were separated from a parent before age 10. They are also more likely to become adult violent criminals if they also have a poor relationship with their parents and come from a large family (Farrington, 1997). In a community sample of children, community violence victimization was found to be positively related to proactive aggression only in children with low heart rate, and witnessed community violence was positively related to reactive aggression only in conditions of high heart rate variability (Scarpa *et al.*, 2008). Lower heart rate was found to be associated with antisocial behavior in adolescents, but only in those affiliating with bullies (Sijtsema *et al.*, 2013). These findings are in line with the biosocial theories of crime which predict that negative social environments combining with deficits in biological functioning predispose to criminal outcome (Mednick & Christiansen, 1977).

In summary, psychophysiological risk factors may interact with psychosocial variables in predisposing individuals to antisocial and criminal behavior. Certain psychophysiological measures, including heart rate activity, can be recorded relatively easily (e.g., using portable equipment or taking a pulse), and as such they are especially valuable to the criminologists who are attempting to explore the biosocial etiology of crime.

## Hormones

Hormones are molecules that are released into the bloodstream and travel throughout the body, coordinating complex processes like growth and metabolism. Although several hormones have been examined in a criminological context, cortisol and testosterone, which we will now turn to, are the best-studied hormones in relation to antisocial behaviors and crime.

### Primary findings

The release of cortisol is regulated by the hypothalamic–pituitary–adrenocortical (HPA) axis, which is activated by psychological stressors (Dickerson & Kemeny, 2004). Low basal cortisol has been associated with adolescent conduct disorder (Pager, Gardner, Rubin, Perel, & Neal, 2001) and with aggression both in adolescents (McBurnett, Lahey, Rathouz, & Loeber, 2000) and in adults (Bohnke, Bertsch, Kruk, & Naumann, 2010). Though fewer studies have examined basal cortisol in relation to offending, results of these few have been largely consistent with studies of aggression and conduct disorder. Brewer-Smyth, Burgess, & Shults (2004) found that morning basal cortisol levels were lower in violent female inmates than in non-violent female inmates. Cima, Smeets, & Jelicic (2008) found that cortisol levels were lower throughout the day in psychopathic criminals than in non-psychopathic criminals. Together, these findings suggest a possible disruption in the stress-response systems of criminal and other antisocial individuals. However, some results have been inconsistent (Scarpa, Fikretoglu, & Luscher, 2000; Soderstrom *et al.*, 2004), pointing to the need for research that examines the source of variation in findings. It was proposed that the relationship between cortisol and antisocial behavior might differ across life-span (Alink *et al.*, 2008), but more studies are required to test it.

Both pre- and post-natal levels of testosterone have also been associated with antisocial behavior, but the effects of testosterone on behavior vary at different development stages (Mazur & Booth, 1998). During fetal development, testosterone exerts an organizational influence on the brain, with higher testosterone level corresponding to a more masculine configuration of the nervous system (Breedlove, 1994). Postnatal markers of prenatal testosterone exposure, such as the second to fourth digit ratio (2d:4d) of the hand, have allowed researchers to examine the influence of prenatal hormones on later antisocial behavior without performing unnecessarily invasive medical procedures. Lower 2d:4d is consider to indicate higher levels of prenatal testosterone (Manning, Scutt, Wilson, & Lewis-Jones, 1998). Low 2d:4d have been associated with aggression (Hampson, Ellis, & Tenk, 2008), dating violence (Cousins, Fugère, & Franklin, 2009), and externalizing behavior problems in children (Liu, Portnoy, & Raine, 2012), despite some inconsistent findings (Austin, Manning, McInroy, & Matthews, 2002). A recent meta-analysis found a small negative association between 2d:4d and aggression in males, but not in females (Hönekopp & Watson, 2011). These results indicate that early prenatal testosterone exposure may have certain influence on later antisocial behavior by affecting early nervous system development.

Post-natal circulating testosterone is thought to influence antisocial behavior by activating the hormone receptor structures established prenatally (Mazur & Booth, 1998). High circulating testosterone levels were observed in violent offenders (Dabbs, Carr, Frady, & Riad, 1995), in men convicted of rape (Giotakos, Markianos, Vaidakis, & Christodoulou, 2004), and in men convicted of premeditated homicide (Dabbs, Riad, & Chance, 2001). One key issue is whether any observed relationship between testosterone and antisocial and criminal behavior is causal. A series of double-blind, placebo controlled trials found that administering doses of testosterone increased aggression (Pope, Kouri, & Hudson, 2000), decreased fear (Hermans, Putman, Baas, Koppeschaar, & van Honk, 2006; van Honk, Peper, & Schutter, 2005), and reduced empathy (Hermans, Putman, & van Honk, 2006; van Honk *et al.*, 2011) in laboratory settings. These findings, at the very least, are suggestive that testosterone causally influences aggression, as well as levels of empathy and fear, both of which are well-replicated correlates of antisocial behavior (Jolliffe & Farrington, 2004; van Goozen, Snoek, Matthys, van Rossum, & van Engeland, 2004).

In addition to considering the independent effects of testosterone and cortisol on antisocial behavior, the importance of examining interactions between multiple hormones has been increasingly acknowledged (Mehta & Josephs, 2010). Several studies have found an association between increased testosterone and antisocial behavior, but only amongst individuals with low levels of cortisol (Dabbs, Jurkovic, & Frady, 1991; Popma *et al.*, 2007). These results indicate that cortisol may moderate the relationship between testosterone and antisocial behavior, which possibly explains some of the aforementioned inconsistent results in testosterone.

## Biosocial interactions

The study of hormones provides a promising avenue for biosocial research due to its close relation with individual's surroundings. Researchers have started to examine interactions between hormones and the social environment on antisocial behavior. Dabbs & Morris (1990), for instance, found that testosterone was more strongly related to antisocial behavior amongst low SES subjects. Because testosterone and cortisol are affected by adverse social conditions (Mazur & Booth, 1998; Susman, 2006), other researchers have examined whether hormone levels mediate the relationship between psychosocial adversity and antisocial behavior. Tarter *et al.* (2009) found that the proportion of vacant dwellings in boys' neighborhoods was positively associated with their concurrent testosterone levels. Increased testosterone levels in turn predicted assaultive behavior at 12–14 years, which was associated with later antisocial behavior and cannabis use. These results suggest that elevated testosterone may partly underlie the association between neighborhood adversity and later antisocial outcomes.

O'Neal *et al.* (2010) examined the association between social environment, hormone levels, and antisocial behavior through a randomized controlled trial of a family intervention amongst preschoolers at high risk for antisocial behavior. In analyses of a subsample of low-warmth families, they found that cortisol levels in anticipation of a social challenge increased from pre-intervention levels in the experimental group, but decreased in the control group, and the experimental group also displayed decreased aggression. Importantly, cortisol change from pre-intervention level mediated the effect of the intervention on aggression. These results provide preliminary evidence that early family adversity may have an effect on cortisol response to social challenge, which in turn may influence aggression.

These findings highlight the importance of considering hormones in the context of the social environment in order to best understand the etiology of antisocial behavior. Because some hormones can be relatively easily measured through saliva samples, the assessment of hormones may provide a promising opportunity for criminologists interested in biosocial interaction.

## Conclusions

Research investigating crime, violence and antisocial behavior has found substantial evidence for biological contributions to crime causation. Structural brain-imaging studies on individuals with criminal and aggressive behavior have revealed volumetric and morphological abnormalities in the prefrontal, temporal, and limbic structures, as well as disturbed structural connectivity, particularly within the frontal and associated areas. There is also a large body of research highlighting a number of brain regions that appear to function differently in antisocial groups, including the orbitofrontal cortex, dorsolateral prefrontal cortex, anterior cingulate, and subcortical brain region, including the amygdala and striatum. Individuals with high aggression, antisociality, and criminal behaviors show deficits in general IQ and the verbal IQ component, as well as numerous neuropsychological measures of executive functioning. Psychophysiological studies indicate that underarousal and reduced responsivity, as indexed by low resting heart rate and skin conductance, are among the most well-replicated correlates of aggression and antisocial behaviors. In addition, low basal cortisol levels and high pre- and post-natal levels of testosterone have been observed amongst antisocial individuals. Genetics studies estimate that 41% of antisocial behavior can be attributable to genetic influences, and 59% to environmental influences. Recent genetic studies have started to examine specific gene candidates such as *MAOA* (coding for monoamine oxidase-A) in connection to crime and antisocial behavior.

Studies that look into the interaction between biological risk factors and social factors, while still accumulating, have shed some light on the biosocial bases of antisocial and criminal behavior. Most of these studies focus on adverse social/environmental influences, including, but not limited to, childhood maltreatment, being born into a low social class family, or separation from parents before age 10. Results from these studies have found a dual hazard effect, that is, adverse social factors interacting with biological risk factors generate larger effects than their simple additive effects. In addition, findings adopting another approach to examine the biosocial interaction on crime have been documented. These studies measure biological activity, such as heart rate, brain regional glucose metabolism of violent offenders from "good homes" (i.e. without social deprivation) in comparison with those of offenders from "bad homes" (i.e., with social deprivation). Initial evidence is supportive of "social push" hypothesis, which suggests that when the "social push" towards crime is weaker, biological risk factors are more salient.

Taken together, the most fruitful biosocial research on antisocial behavior and crime to date is concentrated in the field of psychophysiology. Some rigorous experiments have started to emerge in hormone research examining the possible mediation role of hormone imbalance on the relationship between psychosocial adversity and antisocial behavior. However, relatively few empirical biosocial examinations in brain research exist to date. Given the nature of biosocial interactions, research that only emphasizes social risk factors or biological factors risks missing important pieces to complete the puzzle – any revealed main effect, whether social or biological, is potentially qualified by the interaction. As noted before, many psychophysiological measures like heart rate and skin conductance, and also hormone measures, are relatively easy to conduct and relatively easy to process. Consequently these can be a very good starting point for social researchers who want to include biological measures into their studies.

Our understanding of the biosocial bases of antisocial behavior and crime is far from comprehensive. In order to develop our knowledge in antisocial behavior and crime under the biosocial framework, not only do we need research that examines the biological mechanisms, we also need to have more direct and refined tests of biosocial interactions within each research area. Taken one step further, this field can also benefit from research that crosses these domains and combines different biological systems, such as unifying autonomic nervous system, endocrine system, and central nervous system measures. After all, these biological systems work in a coordinated fashion and interact with the external environment – the social environment. It is such interactions that shape all human behavior – including anti-social and criminal behavior. We believe that genuine advances in understanding and ultimately preventing such complex forms of behavior will only result from focused and concerted biosocial research efforts.

# References

Aguilar, B., Sroufe, L.A., Egeland, B., & Carlson, E. (2000). Distinguishing the early-onset/persistent and adolescence-onset antisocial behavior types: From birth to 16 years. *Development and Psychopathology, 12*, 109–132.

Alink, L.R., van Ijzendoorn, M.H., Bakermans-Kranenburg, M.J., Mesman, J., Juffer, F., & Koot, H.M. (2008). Cortisol and externalizing behavior in children and adolescents: Mixed meta-analytic evidence for the inverse relation of basal cortisol and cortisol reactivity with externalizing behavior. *Developmental Psychobiology, 50*(5), 427–450. doi: 10.1002/dev.20300.

Anastassiou-Hadjicharalambous, X., & Warden, D. (2008). Physiologically-indexed and self-perceived affective empathy in conduct-disordered children high and low on callous-unemotional traits. *Child Psychiatry and Human Development, 39*, 503–517.

Aron, A.R., Robbins, T.W., & Poldrack, R.A. (2004). Inhibition and the right inferior frontal cortex. *Trends in Cognitive Science, 8*(4), 170–177.

Austin, E.J., Manning, J.T., McInroy, K., & Matthews, E. (2002). A preliminary investigation of the association between personality, cognitive ability and digit ratio. *Personality and Individual Differences, 33*, 1115–1124.

Barker, E.D., Séguin, J.R., White, H.R., Bates, M.E., Lacourse, E., Carbonneau, R., *et al.* (2007). Developmental trajectories of male physical violence and theft: Relations to neurocognitive performance. *Archives of General Psychiatry, 64*, 592–599.

Beauchaine, T.P., Hong, J., & Marsh, P. (2008). Sex differences in autonomic correlates of conduct problems and aggression. *Journal of American Academy of Child and Adolescent Psychiatry, 47*, 788–796.

Bechara, A. (2004). The role of emotion in decision-making: Evidence from neurological patients with orbitofrontal damage. *Brain and Cognition, 55*(1), 30–40.

Birbaumer, N., Viet, R., Lotze, M., Erb, M., Hermann, C., Grodd, W., *et al.* (2005). Deficient fear conditioning in psychopathy: A functional magnetic resonance imaging study. *Archives of General Psychiatry, 62*(7), 799–805.

Blair, R.J.R. (2006). The emergence of psychopathy: Implications for the neuropsychological approach to developmental disorders. *Cognition, 101*, 414–442.

Blair, R.J.R. (2010). Psychopathy, frustration, and reactive aggression: The role of ventromedial prefrontal cortex. *British Journal of Psychology, 101*, 383–399. doi: 10.1348/000712609x418480.

Blair, J., & Frith, U. (2000). Neurocognitive explanations of the antisocial personality disorders. *Criminal Behaviour and Mental Health, 10*, S66–S81.

Boccardi, M., Ganzola, R., Rossi, R., Sabattoli, F., Laakso, M.P., Repo-Tiihonen, E., *et al.* (2010). Abnormal hippocampal shape in offenders with psychopathy. *Human Brain Mapping, 31,* 438–447.

Bohnke, R., Bertsch, K., Kruk, M.R., & Naumann, E. (2010). The relationship between basal and acute HPA axis activity and aggressive behavior in adults. *Journal of Neural Transmission, 117*(5), 629–637. doi: 10.1007/s00702-010-0391-x.

Breedlove, S.M. (1994). Sexual differentiation of the human nervous system. *Annual Review of Psychology, 45,* 389–418. doi: 10.1146/annurev.ps.45.020194.002133.

Brennan, P.A., Hall, J., Bor, W., Najman, J.M., & Williams, G. (2003). Integrating biological and social processes in relation to early-onset persistent aggression in boys and girls. *Developmental Psychology, 39,* 309–323.

Brennan, P.A., Raine, A., Schulsinger, F., Kirkegaard-Sorensen, L., Knop, J., Hutchings, B., *et al.* (1997). Psychophysiological protective factors for male subjects at high risk for criminal behavior. *American Journal of Psychiatry, 154,* 853–855.

Brewer-Smyth, K., Burgess, A.W., & Shults, J. (2004). Physical and sexual abuse, salivary cortisol, and neurologic correlates of violent criminal behavior in female prison inmates. *Biological Psychiatry, 55*(1), 21–31. doi: 10.1016/s0006-3223(03)00705-4.

Broomhall, L. (2005). Acquired sociopathy: A neuropsychological study of executive dysfunction in violent offenders. *Psychiatry, Psychology, and Law, 12,* 367–387.

Brunner, H.G., Nelen, M., Breakefield, X.O., Ropers, H.H., & Vanoost, B.A. (1993). Abnormal behavior associated with a point mutation in the structural gene for monoamine oxidase A. *Science, 262,* 578–580.

Buckholtz, J.W., Treadway, M.T., Cowan, R.L., Woodward, N.D., Benning, S.D., Li, R., *et al.* (2010). Mesolimbic dopamine reward system hypersensitivity in individuals with psychopathic traits. *Nature Neuroscience, 13,* 419–421.

Cadoret, R.J., Cain, C.A., & Crowe, R.R. (1983). Evidence for gene–environment interaction in the development of adolescent antisocial behavior. *Behavior Genetics, 13,* 301–310.

Caspi, A., McClary, J., Moffiett, T.E., Mill, J., Martin, J., Craig, I.Q., *et al.* (2002). Role of genotype in the cycle of violence in maltreated children. *Science, 297,* 851–854.

Cauffman, E., Steinberg, L., & Piquero, A.R. (2005). Psychological, neuropsychological and physiological correlates of serious antisocial behavior in adolescence: The role of self-control. *Criminology: An Interdisciplinary Journal, 43*(1), 133–176. doi:10.1111/j.0011-1348.2005.00005.x.

Cima, M., Smeets, T., & Jelicic, M. (2008). Self-reported trauma, cortisol levels, and aggression in psychopathic and non-psychopathic prison inmates. *Biological Psychology, 78*(1), 75–86. doi: 10.1016/j.biopsycho.2007.12.011.

Cloninger, C.R., Sigvardsson, S., Bohman, M., & von Knorring, A.I. (1982). Predisposition to petty criminality in Swedish adoptees: II. Cross-fostering analysis of gene–environment interaction. *Archives of General Psychiatry, 39,* 1242–1247.

Coccaro, E.F., McCloskey, M.S., Fitzgerald, D.A., & Phan, K.L. (2007). Amygdala and orbitofrontal reactivity to social threat in individuals with impulsive aggression. *Biological Psychiatry, 62,* 168–178.

Cousins, A.J., Fugère, M.A., & Franklin, M. (2009). Digit ratio (2D:4D), mate guarding, and physical aggression in dating couples. *Personality and Individual Differences, 46*(7), 709–713. doi: 10.1016/j.paid.2009.01.029.

Dabbs, J.M., Carr, T.S., Frady, R.L., & Riad, J.K. (1995). Testosterone, crime, and misbehavior among 692 male prison inmates. *Personality and Individual Differences, 18*(5), 627–633.

Dabbs, J.M., Jurkovic, G.J., & Frady, R.L. (1991). Salivary testosterone and cortsiol among late adolescent male offenders. *Journal of Abnormal Child Psychology, 19*(4), 479–478.

Dabbs, J.M., & Morris, R. (1990). Testosterone, social class, and antisocial behavior in a sample of 4,462 men. *Psychological Science, 1*(3), 209–211.

Dabbs, J.M., Riad, J.K., & Chance, S.E. (2001). Testosterone and ruthless homicide. *Personality and Individual Differences, 31*, 599–603.

Damasio, A. (1994). *Descartes' Error: Emotion, Reason, and the Human Brain.* London: Vintage.

Damasio, A.R., Tranel, D., & Damasio, H. (1990). Individuals with sociopathic behavior caused by frontal damage fail to respond autonomically to social stimuli. *Behavioural Brain Research, 41*, 81–94.

Davidson, R.J., Putnam, K.M., & Larson, C.L. (2000). Dysfunction in the neural circuitry of emotion regulation – a possible prelude to violence. *Science, 289*, 591–594.

de Vries-Bouw, M., Popma, A., Vermeiren, R., Doreleijers, T.A.H., Van de Ven, P.M., & Jansen, L.M.C. (2011). The predictive value of low heart rate and heart rate variability during stress for reoffending in delinquent male adolescents. *Psychophysiology, 48*, 1596–1603.

Dickerson, S.S., & Kemeny, M.E. (2004). Acute stressors and cortisol responses: A theoretical integration and synthesis of laboratory research. *Psychological Bulletin, 130*(3), 355–391. doi: 10.1037/0033-2909.130.3.355.

Dierckx, B., Tulen, J.H.M., Tharner, A., Joddoe, V.W., Hofman, A., Verhulst, F.C., *et al.* (2011). Low autonomic arousal as vulnerability to externalizing behavior in infants with hostile mothers. *Psychiatry Research, 185*, 171–175.

Dinn, W.M., & Harris, C.L. (2000). Neurocognitive function in antisocial personality disorder. *Psychiatry Research, 97*, 173–190.

Dolan, M., & Park, I. (2002). The neuropsychology of antisocial personality disorder. *Psychological Medicine, 32*, 417–427.

Eriksson, A., Hodgins, S., & Tengström, A. (2005). Verbal intelligence and criminal offending among men with schizophrenia. *International Journal of Forensic Mental Health, 4*, 191–200.

Ermer, E., Cope, L.M., Myalakanti, P.K., Calhoun, V.D., & Kiehl, K.A. (2012). Aberrant paralimbic gray matter in criminal psychopathy. *Journal of Abnormal Psychology, 12*, 649–658.

Fairchild, G., Stobbe, Y., van Goozen, S.H.M., Calder, A.J., & Goodyer, I.M. (2010). Facial expression recognition, fear conditioning, and startle modulation in female subjects with conduct disorder. *Biological Psychiatry, 68*, 272–279.

Fairchild, G., van Goozen, S.H.M., Strollery, S.J., & Goodyer, I.M. (2008). Fear conditioning and affective modulation of the startle reflex in male adolescents with early-onset or adolescence-onset conduct disorder and healthy control subjects. *Biological Psychiatry, 63*, 279–285.

Farrington, D.P. (1997). The relationship between low resting heart rate and violence. In A. Raine, P.A. Brennan, D.P. Farrington, & S.A. Mednick (Eds.), *Biosocial Bases of Violence* (pp. 89–106). New York: Prenum Press.

Farrington, D.P. (2000). Psychosocial predictors of adult antisocial personality and adult convictions. *Behavior Sciences and the Law, 18*, 605–622.

Finger, E.C., Marsh, A.A., Mitchell, D.G., Reid, M.E., Sims, C., Budhani, S., *et al.* (2008). Abnormal ventromedial prefrontal cortex function in children with psychopathic traits during reversal learning. *Archives of General Psychiatry, 65*, 586–594.

Fung, M.T., Raine, A., Loeber, R., Lynam, D.R., Steinhauer, S.R., Venables, P.H., *et al.* (2005). Reduced electrodermal activity in psychopathy-prone adolescents. *Journal of Abnormal Psychology, 114*, 187–196.

Gao, Y., Raine, A., Venables, P.H., Dawson, M.E., & Mednick, S.A. (2010a). Association of poor childhood fear conditioning and adult crime. *American Journal of Psychiatry, 167*, 56–60.

Gao, Y., Raine, A., Venables, P.H., Dawson, M.E., & Mednick, S.A. (2010b). Reduced electrodermal fear conditioning from ages 3 to 8 years is associated with aggressive behavior at age 8 years. *Journal of Child Psychology and Psychiatry, 51*, 550–558.

Giotakos, O., Markianos, M., Vaidakis, N., & Christodoulou, G.N. (2004). Sex hormones and biogenic amine turnover of sex offenders in relation to their temperament and character dimensions. *Psychiatry Research, 127*(3), 185–193. doi: 10.1016/j.psychres.2003.06.003.

Glenn, A.L., Raine, A., & Schug, R.A. (2009). The neural correlates of moral decision-making in psychopathy. *Molecular Psychiatry, 14*, 5–6.

Glenn, A.L., Raine, A., Schug, R.A., Young, L., & Hauser, M. (2009). Increased DLPFC activity during moral decision-making in psychopathy. *Molecular Psychiatry, 14*, 909–911.

Glenn, A.L., Raine, A., Venables, P.H., & Mednick, S.A. (2007). Early temperamental and psychophysiological precursors of adult psychopathic personality. *Journal of Abnormal Psychology, 116*, 508–518.

Glenn, A.L., Yang, Y., Raine, A., & Colletti, P. (2010). No volumetric differences in the anterior cingulate of psychopathic individuals. *Psychiatry Research Neuroimaging, 183*, 140–143.

Gordon, H.L., Baird, A.A., & End, A. (2004). Functional differences among those high and low on a trait measure of psychopathy. *Biological Psychiatry, 56*, 516–521.

Grafman, J., Schwab, K., Warden, D., Pridgen, A., Brown, H.R., & Salazar, A.M. (1996). Frontal lobe injuries, violence, and aggression: A report of the Vietnam Head Injury Study. *Neurology, 46*, 1231–1238.

Graig, M.C., Catani, M., Deeley, Q., Latham, R., Daly, E., Kanaan, R.A.A., *et al.* (2009). Altered connections on the road of psychopathy. *Molecular Psychiatry, 14*, 946–953.

Hampson, E., Ellis, C.L., & Tenk, C.M. (2008). On the relation between 2D:4D and sex-dimorphic personality traits. *Archives of Sexual Behavior, 37*(1), 133–144. doi: 10.1007/s10508-007-9263-3.

Hanlon, R.E., Coda, J.J., Cobia, D., & Rubin, L.H. (2012). Psychotic domestic murder: Neuropsychological differences between homicidal and nonhomicidal schizophrenic men. *Journal of Family Violence, 27*, 105–113.

Harenski, C.L., Harenski, K.A., Shane, M.S., & Kiehl, K.A. (2010). Aberrant neural processing of moral violations in criminal psychopaths. *Journal of Abnormal Psychology, 119*, 863–874.

Harlow, J.M. (1999). Passage of an iron rod through the head. *Journal of Neuropsychiatry and Clinical Neurosciences, 11*, 281–283.

Hemming, J.H. (1981). Electrodermal indices in a selected prison sample and students. *Personality and Individual Differences, 2*, 37–46.

Hermans, E.J., Putman, P., Baas, J.M., Koppeschaar, H.P., & van Honk, J. (2006). A single administration of testosterone reduces fear-potentiated startle in humans. *Biological Psychiatry, 59*(9), 872–874. doi: 10.1016/j.biopsych.2005.11.015.

Hermans, E.J., Putman, P., & van Honk, J. (2006). Testosterone administration reduces empathetic behavior: A facial mimicry study. *Psychoneuroendocrinology, 31*(7), 859–866. doi: 10.1016/j.psyneuen.2006.04.002.

Herpertz, S.C., Dietrich, T.M., & Wenning, B. (2001). Evidence of abnormal amygdala functioning in borderline personality disorder. *Biological Psychiatry, 50*, 292–298.

Herpertz, S.C., Mueller, B., Qunaibi, M., Lichterfeld, C., Konrad, K., & Herpertz-Dahlmann, B. (2005). Responses to emotional stimuli in boys with conduct disorder. *American Journal of Psychiatry, 162*, 1100–1107.

Herpertz, S.C., Mueller, B., Wenning, B., Qunaibi, M., Lichterfeld, C., & Herpertz-Dahlmann, B. (2003). Autonomic responses in boys with externalizing disorders. *Journal of Neural Transmission, 110*, 1181–1195.

Hiatt, K.D., & Newman, J.P. (2006). Understanding psychopathy: The cognitive side. In C.J. Patrick (Ed.), *Handbook of Psychopathy* (pp. 334–352). New York: Guilford Press.

Hill, J. (2003). Early identification of individuals at risk for antisocial personality disorder. *British Journal of Psychiatry, 182*, 11–14.

Hönekopp, J., & Watson, S. (2011). Meta-analysis of the relationship between digit-ratio 2D:4D and aggression. *Personality and Individual Differences, 51*(4), 381–386. doi: 10.1016/j.paid.2010.05.003.

Howner, K., Eskildsen, S.F., Fischer, H., Dierks, T., Wahlund, L.O., Jonsson, T., et al. (2012). Thinner cortex in the frontal lobes in mentally disordered offenders. *Psychiatry Research, 203*, 126–131.

Hux, K., Bond, V., Skinner, S., Belau, D., & Sanger, D. (1998). Parental report of occurrences and consequences of traumatic brain injury among delinquent and non-delinquent youth. *Brain Injury, 12*(8), 667–681.

Intrator, J., Hare, R.D., Stritzke, P., Brichtswein, K., Dorfman, D., & Harpur, T. (1997). A brain imaging (single photon emission computerized tomography) study of semantic and affective processing in psychopaths. *Biological Psychiatry, 42*, 96–103.

Jolliffe, D., & Farrington, D.P. (2004). Empathy and offending: A systematic review and meta-analysis. *Aggression and Violent Behavior, 9*(5), 441–476. doi: 10.1016/j.avb.2003.03.001.

Katz, L.F. (2007). Domestic violence and vegal reactivity to peer provocation. *Biological Psychology, 74*(2), 154–164.

Kenny, D.T., & Lennings, C.J. (2007). The relationship between head injury and violent offending in juvenile detainees. *Contemporary Issues in Crime and Justice, 107*, 1–15.

Kibler, J.L., Prosser, V.L., & Ma, M. (2004). Cardiovascular correlates of misconduct in children and adolescents. *Journal of Psychophysiology, 18*, 184–189.

Kiehl, K.A., Smith, A.M., Hare, R.D., Mendrek, A., Forster, B.B., & Brink, J. (2001). Limbic abnormalities in affective processing by criminal psychopaths as revealed by functional magnetic resonance imaging. *Biological Psychiatry, 50*, 677–684.

Kimonis, E.R., Frick, P.J., Fazekas, H., & Loney, B.R. (2006). Psychopathy, aggression, and the processing of emotional stimuli in non-referred girls and boys. *Behavioral Sciences and the Law, 24*, 21–37.

Kosson, D.H., Miller, S.K., Byrnes, K.A., & Leveroni, C.L. (2007). Testing neuropsychological hypotheses for cognitive deficits in psychopathic criminals: A study of global-local processing. *Journal of the International Neuropsychological Society, 13*, 267–276.

Kronenberger, W.G., Mathews, V.P., Dunn, D.W., Wang, Y., Wood, E.A., Giauque, A.L., et al. (2005). Media violence exposure and executive functioning in aggressive and control adolescents. *Journal of Clinical Psychology, 61*(6), 725–737.

Kruesi, M.J.P., Hibbs, E.D., Zahn, T.P., Keysor, C.S., Hamburger, S.D., Bartko, J.J., *et al.* (1992). A 2-year prospective follow-up study of children and adolescents with disruptive behavior disorders. *Archives of General Psychiatry, 49*, 429–435.

Kumari, V., Das, M., Taylor, P.J., Barkataki, I., Andrew, C., Sumich, A., *et al.* (2009). Neural and behavioral responses to threat in men with a history of serious violence and schizophrenia or antisocial personality disorder. *Schizophrenia Research, 110*, 47–58.

Lee, T.M.C., Chan, S.C., & Raine, A. (2008). Strong limbic and weak frontal activation to aggressive stimuli in spouse abusers. *Molecular Psychiatry, 13*, 655–656.

Leon-Carrion, J., & Ramos, F.J.C. (2003). Blows to the head during development can predispose to violent criminal behavior: Rehabilitation of consequences of head injury is a measure for crime prevention. *Brain Injury, 17*, 207–216.

Lewis, D.O., Pincus, J.H., Bard, B., & Richardson, E. (1988). Neuropsychiatric, psychoeducational, and family characteristics of 14 juveniles condemned to death in the United States. *American Journal of Psychiatry, 145*, 584–589.

Lezak, M.D., Howieson, D.B., Loring, D.W., Hannay, H.J., & Fischer, J.S. (2004). *Neuropsychological Assessment*, 4th edition. New York: Oxford University Press.

Liu, J., Portnoy, J., & Raine, A. (2012). Association between a marker for prenatal testosterone exposure and externalizing behavior problems in children. *Developmental Psychopathology, 24*(3), 771–782. doi: 10.1017/S0954579412000363.

Loney, B.R., Frick, P.J., Clements, C.B., Ellis, M.L., & Kerlin, K. (2003). Callous-unemotional traits, impulsivity and emotional processing in adolescents with antisocial behavior problems. *Journal of Clinical Child & Adolescent Psychology, 32*, 66–80.

Lorber, M.F. (2004). Psychophysiology of aggression, psychopathy, and conduct problems: A meta-analysis. *Psychological Bulletin, 130*, 531–552.

Luria, A. (1980). *Higher Cortical Functions in Man*, 2nd edition. New York: Basic Books.

Manning, J.T., Scutt, D., Wilson, J., & Lewis-Jones, D.I. (1998). The ratio of 2nd to 4th digit length: A predictor of sperm numbers and concentrations of testosterone, luteinizing hormone and oestrogen. *Human Reproduction, 13*(11), 3000–3004.

Mataro, M., Jurado, M.A., Garcia-Sanchez, C., Barraquer, L., Costa-Jussa, F.R., & Junque, C. (2001). Long-term effects of bilateral frontal brain lesion 60 years after injury with an iron bar. *Archives of Neurology, 58*, 1139–1142.

Mazur, A., & Booth, A. (1998). Testosterone and dominance in men. *Behavioral and Brain Sciences, 21*, 353–397.

McBurnett, K., Lahey, B.B., Rathouz, P.J., & Loeber, R. (2000). Low salivary cortisol and persistent aggression in boys referred for disruptive behavior. *Archives of General Psychiatry, 57*, 38–43.

McCord, J. (2001). Psychosocial contributions to psychopathy and violence. In A. Raine & J. Sanmartin (Eds.), *Violence and Psychopathy* (pp. 141–170). New York: Kluwer Academic.

Mednick, S.A., & Christiansen, K.O. (1977). *Biosocial Bases of Criminal Behavior*. New York: Gardner Press.

Mednick, S.A., Gabrielli, W.F., & Hutchings, B. (1984). Genetic influence in criminal convictions: Evidence from an adoption cohort. *Science, 224*, 891–894.

Mehta, P.H., & Josephs, R.A. (2010). Testosterone and cortisol jointly regulate dominance: Evidence for a dual-hormone hypothesis. *Hormones and Behavior, 58*(5), 898–906. doi: 10.1016/j.yhbeh.2010.08.020.

Mill, J., Dempster, E., Caspi, A., Williams, B., Moffitt, T., & Craig, I. (2006). Evidence for monozygotic twin (MZ) discordance in methylation level at two CpG sites in the promoter region of the catechol-O-methyltransferase (COMT) gene. *American Journal of Medical Genetics: Part B. Neuropsychiatric Genetics, 141B*, 421–425.

Moffitt, T.E., & Caspi, A. (2001). Childhood predictors differentiate life-course persistent and adolescence-limited antisocial pathways among males and females. *Development and Psychopathology, 13*, 355–375.

Moffitt, T.E., & Henry, B. (1989). Neuropsychological assessment of executive functions in self-reported delinquents. *Development and Psychopathology, 1*, 105–118.

Moffitt, T.E., Lynam, D.R., & Silva, P.A. (1994). Neuropsychological tests predicting persistent male delinquency. *Criminology, 32*, 277–300.

Morgan, A.B., & Lilienfeld, S.O. (2000). A meta-analytic review of the relationship between antisocial behavior and neuropsychological measures of executive function. *Clinical Psychology Review, 20*, 113–136.

Motzkin, J.C., Newman, J.P., Kiehl, K.A., & Koenigs, M. (2011). Reduced prefrontal connectivity in psychopathy. *Journal of Neuroscience, 31*, 17348–17357.

Müller, J.L., Sommer, M., Wagner, V., Lange, K., Taschler, H., Roder, C.H., et al. (2003). Abnormalities in emotion processing within cortical and subcortical regions in criminal psychopaths: Evidence from a functional magnetic resonance imaging study using pictures with emotional content. *Biological Psychiatry, 54*, 152–162.

Murray-Close, D., Holland, A.S., & Roisman, G.I. (2012). Autonomic arousal and relational aggression in heterosexual dating couples. *Personal Relationships, 19*(2), 203–218.

Murray-Close, D., & Rellini, A.H. (2012). Cardiovascular reactivity and proactive and reactive relational aggression among women with and without a history of sexual abuse. *Biological Psychology, 89*(1), 54–62.

Nigg, J.T., Glass, J.M., Wong, M.M., Poon, E., Jester, J., Fitzgerald, H.E., et al. (2004). Neuropsychological executive functioning in children at elevated risk for alcoholism: Findings in early adolescence. *Journal of Abnormal Psychology, 113*, 302–314.

Ochsner, K.N., Beer, J.S., Robertson, E.R., Cooper, J.C., Gabrieli, J.D.E., Kihsltrom, J.F., et al. (2005). The neural correlates of direct and reflected self-knowledge. *NeuroImage, 28*(4), 797–814.

O'Doherty, J. (2004). Reward representations and reward-related learning in the human brain: Insights from neuroimaging. *Current Opinion in Neurobiology, 14*, 769–776.

O'Neal, C.R., Brotman, L.M., Huang, K., Gouley, K.K., Kamboukos, D., Calzada, E.J., et al. (2010). Understanding relations among early family environment, cortisol response, and child aggression via a prevention experiment. *Child Development, 81*(1), 290–305.

Ortiz, J., & Raine, A. (2004). Heart rate level and antisocial behavior in children and adolescents: A meta-analysis. *Journal of American Academy of Child and Adolescent Psychiatry, 43*, 154–162.

Pager, K., Gardner, W., Rubin, R.T., Perel, J., & Neal, S. (2001). Decreased cortisol levels in adolescent girls with conduct disorder. *Archives of General Psychiatry, 58*, 297–302.

Petronis, A., Gottesman, I.I., Kan, P., Kennedy, J.L., Basile, V.S., Paterson, A.D., et al. (2003). Monozygotic twins exhibit numerous epigenetic differences: Clues to twin discordance? *Schizophrenia Bulletin, 21*, 169–178.

Phillips, M.L., Drevets, W.C., Rauch, S.L., & Lane, R. (2003). Neurobiology of emotion perception I: The neural basis of normal emotion perception. *Biological Psychiatry, 54*, 504–514.

Pope, H.G., Jr., Kouri, E.M., & Hudson, J.I. (2000). Effects of supraphysiologic doses of testosterone on mood and aggression in normal men: A randomized controlled trial. *Archives of General Psychiatry, 57*(2), 133–140; discussion 155–136.

Popma, A., Vermeiren, R., Geluk, C.A., Rinne, T., van den Brink, W., Knol, D.L., *et al.* (2007). Cortisol moderates the relationship between testosterone and aggression in delinquent male adolescents. *Biological Psychiatry, 61*(3), 405–411. doi: 10.1016/j. biopsych.2006.06.006.

Raine, A. (1993). *The Psychopathology of Crime: Criminal Behavior as a Clinical Disorder.* San Diego, CA: Academic Press.

Raine, A. (2002). Biosocial studies of antisocial and violent behavior in children and adults: A review. *Journal of Abnormal Child Psychology, 30*, 311–326.

Raine, A. (2008). From genes to brain to antisocial behavior. *Current Directions in Psychological Science, 17*(5), 323–328.

Raine, A., Moffitt, T.E., Caspi, A., Loeber, R., Stouthamer-Loeber, M., & Lynam, D. (2005). Neurocognitive impairments in boys on the life-course persistent antisocial path. *Journal of Abnormal Psychology, 114*, 38–49.

Raine, A., Park, S., Lencz, T., Bihrle, S., Lacasse, L., Widom, C.S., *et al.* (2001). Reduced right hemisphere activation in severely abused violent offenders during a working memory task: An fMRI study. *Aggressive Behavior, 27*, 111–129.

Raine, A., Stoddard, J., Bihrle, S., & Buchsbaum, M.S. (1998). Prefrontal glucose deficits in murderers lacking psychosocial deprivation. *Neuropsychiatry, Neuropsychology, and Behavioral Neurology, 11*, 1–7.

Raine, A., & Venables, P.H. (1981). Classical conditioning and socialization – A biosocial interaction. *Personality and Individual differences, 2*, 273–283.

Raine, A., Venables, P.H., & Mednick, S.A. (1997). Low resting heart rate age 3 years predisposes to aggression at age 11 years: Evidence from the Mauritius Child Health Project. *Journal of American Academy of Child and Adolescent Psychiatry, 36*, 1457–1464.

Raine, A., Venables, P.H., & Williams, M. (1990). Relationships between CNS and ANS measures of arousal at age 15 and criminality at age 24. *Archives of General Psychiatry, 47*, 1003–1007.

Raine, A., Venables, P.H., & Williams, M. (1995). High autonomic arousal and electrodermal orienting at age 15 years as protective factors against criminal behavior at age 29 years. *American Journal of Psychiatry, 152*, 1595–1600.

Raine, A., Venables, P.H., & Williams, M. (1996). Better autonomic conditioning and faster electrodermal half-recovery time at age 15 years as possible protective factors against crime at age 29 years. *Developmental Psychology, 32*, 624–630.

Rhee, R.H., & Waldman, I.D. (2002). Genetic and environmental influences on antisocial behavior: A meta-analysis of twin and adoption studies. *Psychological Bulletin, 128*, 490–529.

Rilling, J.K., Glenn, A.L., Jairam, M.R., Pagnoni, G., Goldsmith, D.R., Elfenbein, H.A., *et al.* (2007). Neural correlates of social cooperation and non-cooperation as a function of psychopathy. *Biological Psychiatry, 61*, 1260–1271.

Robison, A.J., & Nestler, E.J. (2011). Transcription and epigenetic mechanisms of addiction. *Nature Reviews and Neuroscience, 12*, 623–637.

Rolls, E.T. (2000). The orbitofrontal cortex and reward. *Cerebral Cortex, 10*, 284–294.

Scarpa, A., Fikretoglu, D., & Luscher, K. (2000). Community violence exposure in a young adult sample: II. Psychophysiology and aggressive behavior. *Journal of Community Psychology, 28*(4), 417–425.

Scarpa, A., Haden, S.C., & Tanaka, A. (2010). Being hot-tempered: Autonomic, emotional, and behavioral distinctions between childhood reactive and proactive aggression. *Biological Psychology, 84*, 488–496.

Scarpa, A., Tanaka, A., & Haden, S.C. (2008). Biosocial bases of reactive and proactive aggression: The roles of community violence exposure and heart rate. *Journal of Community Psychology, 36*(8), 969–988.

Schneider, F., Habel, U., Kessler, C., Posse, S., Grodd, W., & Muller-Gartner, H.W. (2000). Functional imaging of conditioned aversive emotional responses in antisocial personality disorder. *Neuropsychobiology, 42*, 192–201.

Schug, R.A., & Raine, A. (2009). Comparative meta-analyses of neuropsychological functioning in antisocial schizophrenic persons. *Clinical Psychology Review, 29*, 230–242.

Shamay-Tsoory, S.G., Tomer, R., Berger, B.D., Goldsher, D., & Aharon-Peretz, J. (2005). Impaired "affective theory of mind" is associated with right ventromedial prefrontal damage. *Cognitive Behavioral Neurology, 18*(1), 55–67.

Sijtsema, J.J., Shoulberg, E.K., & Murray-Close, D. (2011). Physiological reactivity and different forms of aggression in girls: Moderating roles of rejection sensitivity and peer rejection. *Biological Psychology, 86*, 181–192.

Sijtsema, J.J., Veenstra, R., Lindenberg, S., van Roon, A.M., Verhulst, F.C., Ormel, J., *et al.* (2013). Heart rate and antisocial behavior: Mediation and moderation by affiliation with bullies. *The TRAILS study. Journal of Adolescent Health, 52*, 102–107.

Silva, T.C., Larm, P., Vitaro, F., Tremblay, R.E., & Hodgins, S. (2012). The association between maltreatment in childhood and criminal convictions to age 24: A prospective study of a community sample of males from disadvantaged neighborhoods. *European Child & Adolescent Psychiatry, 21*(7), 403–413.

Smith, E.E., & Jonides, J. (1999). Storage and executive processes in the frontal lobes. *Science, 283*, 1657–1661.

Soderstrom, H., Blennow, K., Forsman, A., Liesivuori, J., Pennanen, S., & Tiihonen, J. (2004). A controlled study of tryptophan and cortisol in violent offenders. *Journal of Neural Transmission, 111*(12), 1605–1610. doi: 10.1007/s00702-004-0219-7.

Sreenivasan, S., Kirkish, P., Shoptaw, S., Welsh, R.K., & Ling, W. (2000). Neuropsychological and diagnostic differences between recidivistically violent not criminally responsible and mentally ill prisoners. *International Journal of Law and Psychiatry, 23*(2), 161–172.

Stanford, M.S., Conklin, S.M., Helfritz, L.E., & Kockler, T.R. (2007). P3 amplitude reduction and executive function deficits in men convicted of spousal/partner abuse. *Personality and Individual Differences, 43*, 365–375.

Susman, E.J. (2006). Psychobiology of persistent antisocial behavior: Stress, early vulnerabilities and the attenuation hypothesis. *Neuroscience and Biobehavioral Reviews, 30*(3), 376–389. doi: 10.1016/j.neubiorev.2005.08.002.

Tarter, R.E., Kirisci, L., Gavaler, J.S., Reynolds, M., Kirillova, G., Clark, D.B., *et al.* (2009). Prospective study of the association between abandoned dwellings and testosterone level on the development of behaviors leading to cannabis use disorder in boys. *Biological Psychiatry, 65*(2), 116–121. doi: 10.1016/j.biopsych.2008.08.032.

Teichner, G., & Golden, C.J. (2000). The relationship of neuropsychological impairment to conduct disorder in adolescence: A conceptual review. *Aggression and Violent Behavior, 5*, 509–528.

Teichner, G., Golden, C.J., Van Hasselt, V.B., & Peterson, A. (2001). Assessment of cognitive functioning in men who batter. *International Journal of Neuroscience, 111*(3–4), 241–253.

van Goozen, S.H.M., Snoek, H., Matthys, W., van Rossum, I., & van Engeland, H. (2004). Evidence of fearlessness in behaviourally disordered children: A study on startle reflex modulation. *Journal of Child Psychology and Psychiatry, 45*(4), 884–892.

van Honk, J., Peper, J.S., & Schutter, D.J. (2005). Testosterone reduces unconscious fear but not consciously experienced anxiety: Implications for the disorders of fear and anxiety. *Biological Psychiatry, 58*(3), 218–225. doi: 10.1016/j.biopsych.2005.04.003.

van Honk, J., Schutter, D.J., Bos, P.A., Kruijt, A.W., Lentjes, E.G., & Baron-Cohen, S. (2011). Testosterone administration impairs cognitive empathy in women depending on second-to-fourth digit ratio. *Proceedings of the National Acadamy of Sciences of the United States of America, 108*(8), 3448–3452. doi: 10.1073/pnas.1011891108.

Vollm, B., Richardson, P., McKie, S., Elliot, R., Deakin, J.F., & Anderson, I.M. (2006). Serotonergic modulation of neuronal responses to behavioural inhibition and reinforcing stimuli: An fMRI study in healthy volunteers. *European Journal of Neuroscience, 23*(2), 552–560.

Vollm, B., Richardson, P., McKie, S., Reniers, R., Elliot, R., Anderson, I.M., *et al.* (2010). Neuronal correlates and serotonergic modulation of behavioral inhibition and reward in healthy and antisocial individuals. *Journal of Psychiatric Research, 44,* 123–131.

Vollm, B., Richardson, P., Stirling, J., Elliot, R., Dolan, M., Chaudhry, I., *et al.* (2004). Neurobiological substrates of antisocial and borderline personality disorders: Preliminary result of a functional MRI study. *Criminal Behavior and Mental Health, 14,* 39–54.

Yang, Y., & Raine, A. (2009). Prefrontal structural and functional brain imaging findings in antisocial, violent, and psychopathic individuals: A meta-analysis. *Psychiatry Research, 174,* 81–88.

Yang, Y., Raine, A., Colletti, P., Toga, A.W., & Narr, K.L. (2010a). Morphological alterations in the prefrontal cortex and the amygdala in unsuccessful psychopaths. *Journal of Abnormal Psychology, 119,* 546–554.

Yang, Y., Raine, A., Han, H., Schug, R.A., Toga, A.W., & Narr, K.L. (2010b). Reduced hippocampal and parahippocampal volumes in murderers with schizophrenia. *Psychiatry Research, 182,* 9–13.

Yang, Y., Raine, A., Joshi, A.A., Joshi, S., Chang, Y.T., Schug, R.A., *et al.* (2012). Frontal information flow and connectivity in psychopathy. *British Journal of Psychiatry, 201,* 408–409.

Yang, Y., Raine, A., Lencz, T., Bihrle, S., Casse, L., & Colletti, P. (2005). Volume reduction in prefrontal gray matter in unsuccessful criminal psychopaths. *Biological Psychiatry, 57,* 1103–1108.

White, J.L., Moffitt, T.E., Caspi, A., Jeglum, D., Needles, D.J., & Stouthamer-Loeber, M. (1994). Measuring impulsivity and examining its relationship to delinquency. *Journal of Abnormal Psychology, 103,* 192–205.

Wilson, J.Q., & Herrnstein, R. (1985). *Crime and Human Nature.* New York: Simon and Schuster.

# 20

# From Theory to Policy
# and Back Again

## Scott H. Decker

This chapter assesses the reciprocal relationship between theory and policy in criminology. The central argument of the chapter is that good policy needs good theory and that good theory finds its ultimate test in its application to policy and practice. We begin with the simple premise expressed by Kurt Lewin in 1945 that, "Nothing is a practical as a good theory." Lewin's observation has been central to research and development within management, psychology, sociology and other social sciences that have both a theoretical and applied component. To date, however this position has received a good deal less attention in criminology. The chapter argues that there is a solid foundation for strengthening the reciprocal relationship between theory and policy in criminology and builds on past work that has attempted to lay that foundation. We see this as an important and logical next step for criminology as it attempts to become more scientific as a discipline as it seeks to influence criminal justice policy, practice, and programs.

In the course of this review, we examine two key intersections of theory and policy in criminology and discuss how each benefitted from the intersection. Each of these examples provides an assessment of the reciprocal relationship between theory and policy. The first of these is the examination of theories of group process in gangs. The second example is the desistance process from gangs. We choose these because many of the central theories of crime and delinquency stem from attempts to explain gang behavior in the 1960s, much of which occurred in conjunction with action programs to address delinquent and gang behavior. The well-known theoretical work of Walter Miller, James F. Short Jr., and Richard Cloward and Lloyd Ohlin emerged from large-scale programmatic efforts to curb crime and delinquency. We extend this foundation work to contemporary gang research in group process and desistance because of the importance of those two concepts to broader criminological

*The Handbook of Criminological Theory*, First Edition. Edited by Alex R. Piquero.
© 2016 John Wiley & Sons, Inc. Published 2016 by John Wiley & Sons, Inc.

theory, and in doing so note the disjuncture between theory, research and policy in this area. This examination serves as an example both of the potential for integrating theory with policy, as well as the pitfalls when theory and policy run on parallel tracks. This chapter places the theory–policy intersection in a broader scientific context, noting the expanded approach to this nexus in other disciplines, including medicine, social work practice, and other social sciences. It is our view that the closer alignment of theory and policy will make criminology a more scientific discipline and lead to more efforts to develop solid propositions of criminal behavior that are testable through empirical examination in a host of settings, including tests in programs, policies, or practices. We also examine the growing attention paid to "translational criminology," (Laub, 2012) a focus that other disciplines have been more advanced in examining than has criminology. This deficiency in criminology is particularly notable despite the work of earlier pioneers such as Allen Liska, who argued for the fuller integration of theory, research and policy. The issue – the disjuncture between theory, research, and policy – was highlighted most clearly in a recent overview (Sampson, Winship, & Knight, 2013). This review of six recent policy innovations in criminology led the authors to conclude that the status of policy in criminology is deficient in part because of the lack of attention to "causal claims" in criminology. We begin the chapter with a general discussion of the parameters and characteristics of theory. This general discussion is then tied to criminological theory. From there we link the discussion of theory to practice and policy. The chapter concludes with observations about the future prospects of applied theory in criminology and current developments in translational and public criminology.

## From Theory to Policy

The general characteristics of theory are well reviewed in most methods or theory texts. However, it is rare to find them integrated with discussions of the outline of policies or programs. We begin this section of the chapter by discussing the general characteristics of theory. At its heart, a theory is an organizational schema, a means of putting a disparate group of observations and expectations into a more organized structure. As such, this fulfills one of the first goals of science, developing an organizational taxonomy of key variables and relationships. The need for theory to serve as a classifying framework is quite important and not to be neglected. But theories must also recognize the patterns and modal categories of behavior in ways that help to predict relationships that may be related but are yet to be tested or observed. Theory should also serve as a means of suggesting and directing future research. A key general characteristic of theory, one that is often overlooked, is its role in suggesting future directions for intervention into changing the behavior of individuals, groups, or social institutions. This discussion of the broad scope of theory can be crystallized in the search for the answer to the question "why"; that is, a good theory ought to provide directions about why actions, structures, and events occur (Sutton & Staw, 1995).

But discussions of the general characteristics of theories beg the question of what a theory is. A theory is a set of logically interrelated propositions. Some have referred to propositions as the "mortar" that holds the bricks of theory together, with the bricks being the variables. Propositions generally take one of two forms, either as hypotheses that state an expected relationship among or between variables, or as an empirical generalization drawn from empirical research. Propositions are constructed of variables, each of which must be defined in both nominal and operational terms. The operational definitions of variables comprise the building blocks of measurement, indicating how, in a precise way, a variable is to be measured. Theories may be built in multiple ways, either deductively from conceptualization to empirical reality, or by inductive observations from which theoretical propositions are developed. The value of a theory lies in both internal and external measures. Internally, theories must be parsimonious, logically consistent, explain phenomena of reasonable breadth, and be falsifiable. The external measure of a theory lies in its accuracy in predicting behavior and ultimately – we argue – its usefulness is suggesting policy, programs, or practice. However, as this chapter attempts to make clear, there has been altogether too little attention directed at the last goal – improving policy, practice, or programs.

Theory can be constructed, tested and applied at a multitude of levels. Grand theories attempt to explain large-scale phenomenon such as evolutionary social change or differences in levels of crime between nations. These theories are important for understanding large patterns or trends but tend to have less utility in their application to policies, programs, or patterns. Mid-range theories organize knowledge about smaller units of analysis such as groups of offenders, social classes, or neighborhoods. These are among the most common theoretical approaches in criminology. Finally, micro-range theories examine the behavior of individuals, and as such are employed quite frequently in criminology, particularly in studies that rely on self-reported measures of delinquency or survey methods.

The "theory process" is comprised of three stages. The first stage of the theory process is theory *development*. In this stage, key variables are identified, their measurement identified, links between variables are developed into propositions, and the internal logical consistency of the theory is tested. The second stage of the theory process is the *testing* of the theory. Here measures of the key variables are tested for their measurement properties including logical consistency, internal and external validity, and parsimony. The final stage of the theory process is the *application* of the theory to a social setting. In this process, an effort is made to manipulate independent variables to produce changes in outcome measures.

The application of this process in criminology has enjoyed, at best a mixed history. Despite the intellectual debt owed by criminologists to the work of Robert K. Merton, the theory process is often hard to discern in criminological work. This is not a recent phenomenon. Indeed, in 1987 Gibbs lamented the current "State of Criminological Theory." Allan Liska wrote persuasively (though apparently not persuasively enough) about the need to link theory, policy, and research. In a recent discussion, Sampson and colleagues (2013) argued for increasing sophistication in the appreciation of calls for causality in theory development and research, particularly in light of the "what works" and evidence-based intervention orientation currently gripping the discipline.

Despite the observation that there are links between theory, research, and policy are lacking in criminology, there are several places where the linkages are obvious and can be exploited. The Office of Juvenile Justice and Delinquency Prevention (OJJDP) has underscored the importance of logic models in program development. A logic model is an explicit statement of how a program or policy should work and where it intersects – explicitly and directly – with what research findings tell us about behavior. The requirement that applied program research acknowledge the links between variables based on prior research is a solid means of attempting to insure that program interventions are built on a solid basis of research knowledge, that links between program activities and behavior are explicit, and that program activities are linked. None of this is to say that a logic model guarantees that a testable set of propositions will be developed, tested, and followed. Indeed, much of the experience in attempting to use a logic model, particularly in the area of gang prevention and intervention, has not led to successful or effective implementation of programs. But the development of logic models is an important recognition of the role that theory must play in research and practice and how theory can be successfully integrated with practice.

The logic model in Figure 20.1 illustrates the complementarity between a logic model and the ordered set of propositions in a theory. Both contain many of the same elements, including the identification of the topic of study (problem), key variables, outputs, and the interrelationship between the parts of the intervention. These logic models were explicitly developed to reflect how programs should work, but are easily adapted to integrate criminological theories.

## Specific Applications of Theory to Policy

### Gang theory, gang research, and gang practice

In a recent review of the relationship between research on gangs and gang policy, programs, and interventions, Maxson (2013) pointed out the discordance between the two realms. Specifically, she noted that much of the response to gangs either failed to account for research findings or used them inappropriately. "Efforts to effectively control gang crime and violence and to reduce rates of joining gangs have been stymied by program models based on misconceptions about gang contours and dynamics, the failure to adequately implement programs as designed, and the lack of systematic, independent evaluations that could generate sufficient documentation of what works and what does not" (159). This failure to incorporate research findings adequately and accurately into the response to gangs is as much a failure on the part of researchers as it is on the part of policy-makers and program leaders. Perhaps part of the reason for this condition is the lack of good theories to account

**Problem**

The problem is defined in relation to a mission and in the case of OJJDP must be one of the following:
1. Juvenile Delinquency;
2. Youth victimization;
3. Improving systems/programs to address either problem 1 or 2 above.

**Subproblems**

This is the specific problem that the program/initiative will address.

**What is the problem or issue that the program/initiative is designed to address?**

**Activities**

A general listing of the program efforts (events and actions) conducted to achieve its objective(s).

**What will the program do? For example, does the program offer direct prevention or intervention services to youth or families, conduct needs assessments, or provide training or technical assistance?**

**Output measures**

These are measures of the program/initiatives process or implementation. The data demonstrate the implementation of the program/initiative's activities.

**What did the program produce? Measures commonly include the numbers of youth and/or families served, number of service hours completed, and numbers of hours of training provided.**

**Outcome measures**

Short term

These are quantitative measures of the initial results of the program. They are typically measured as of the end of the program. This typically includes changes in knowledge, attitudes and awareness.

**How, and how much, have participants (or participating entities) changed by the end of the program/ initiative?**

Long term

These are quantitative measures of the longer results of the program. They are measured six to 12 months post-program. This typically includes changes in behaviors, practices, decision-making. It may also include changes in social conditions (e.g., local arrest rates).

**What changes are exhibited by participants (or participating entities) approximately six to 12 months after participating in the program/initiative?**

**Goals**

The goal must be defined in relation to agency-level goals which are, for OJJDP:
**1.** Prevent and reduce delinquent behavior and victimization;
**2.** Promote public safety by encouraging accountability for acts of delinquency;
**3.** Address juvenile crime and victimization by supporting effective programs and practices.

**Objective(s)**

A specific and measurable statement regarding what the program/ initiative will accomplish **What will the program achieve?**

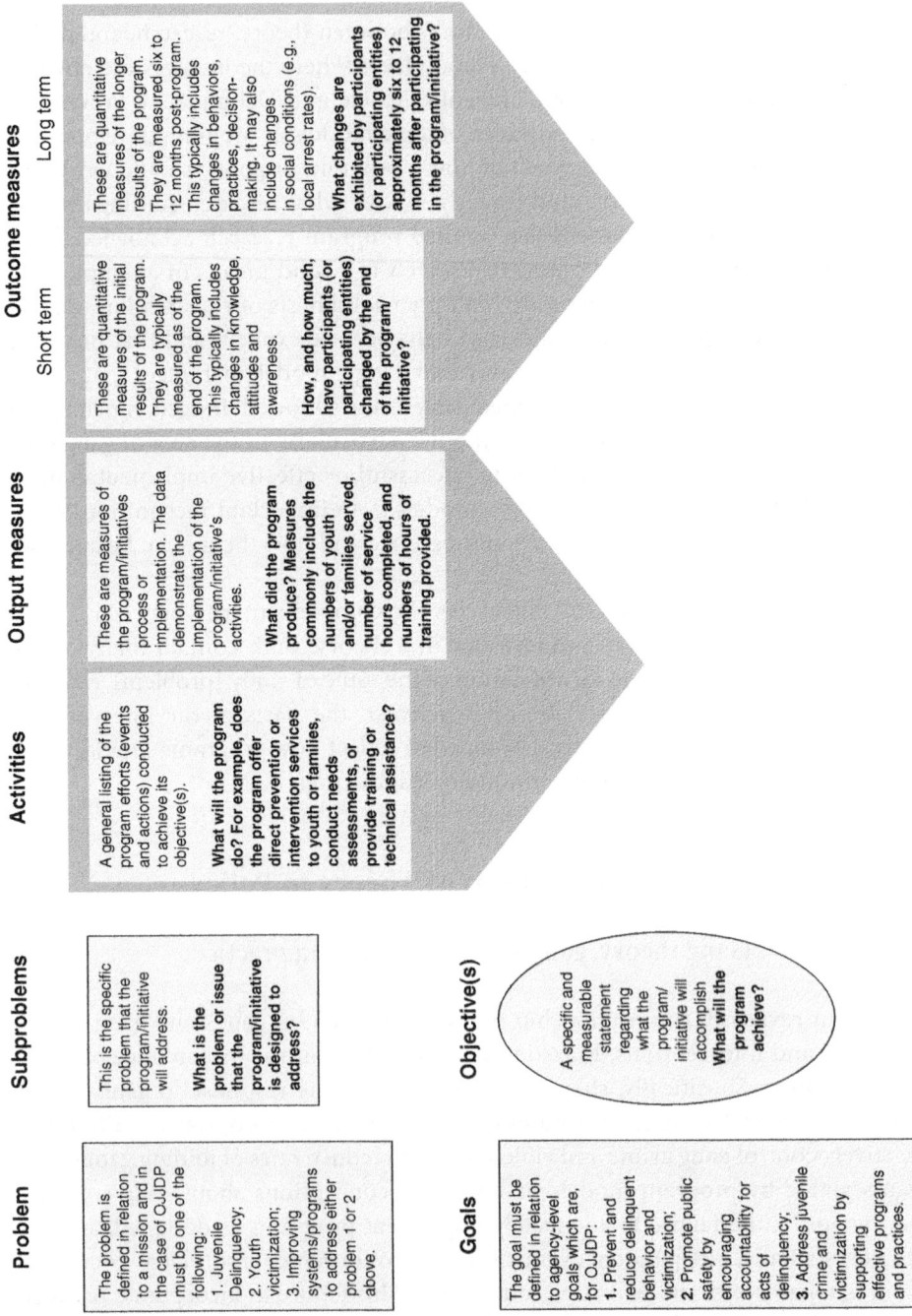

**Figure 20.1**   Generic Logic Model. The text in each block should be used to guide the development of a project-specific logic model.

for how people join gangs, why they do what they do as members and how they leave a gang. Maxson notes three additional areas of progress in gang findings: (1) the growth and spread of gangs across the country; (2) the fact that even in the "worst" gang neighborhoods a minority of youths join a gang and the majority of those who do stay in the gang for a year or less; and (3) gang membership contributes to elevated levels of offending. While as Maxson notes the research support for each of these observations is quite strong, the theory of why each of these is the case is much less developed (McGloin & Decker, 2010). Indeed, the first two points suggest that theories of social diffusion and change may explain the growth of gangs and affiliational patterns of gang membership.

While theories of collective behavior, networks, and the adoption of innovations abound in the social sciences, criminologists have been slow to integrate theories outside the narrow confines of "criminological theory" (Decker, Melde, & Pyrooz, 2012). But it is also the case that theories available within criminology have not been fruitfully applied to account for the "why" question for each of these summarized points of research. The third point, that gangs seem to enhance crime during membership, argues for explanations of group process and network influence. Again, gang researchers and theorists largely have been reticent to integrate theories in their explanations, either as testable hypotheses before conducting research or inductively following the research process. We illustrate the current shortcomings in theorizing about gangs with two specific examples. The first is a discussion of theories about "group process" and the second is a discussion of the process of leaving the gang. In each case, the lack of good theory has hindered the advance of solid research, and led to a failure in policy, illustrating the central point of this chapter, that there is a strong reciprocal relationship between good theory and good policy.

Nearly 30 years ago, James F. Short Jr. (1985) wrote about the need for criminologists to specify more accurately the level of theory they were working with. He demonstrated that while there was considerable theoretical development at the macro and individual levels, the field lacked adequate theories of groups. Ironically, this observation was illustrated in the use of concepts of group process in explaining gang and gang member behavior. McGloin & Decker (2010) echoed this observation 25 years later, noting that group-level explanations played an important role in helping to account for the gang processes that were observed in a number of settings. Specifically, they underscored the reasons why gang membership increases criminal involvement, why the Boston Gun Project may have attained success, and why RICO prosecutions of gang members seemed to be unsuccessful. In each case, the group process within the gang served to unify them in the face of opposition from an opposing group. However, the mechanisms by which that process is ignited, cooled, or spread have not been well specified in theory and, as a consequence, not examined empirically. However, help is on the way and is drawn from theory outside criminology. Specifically, Karen Hennigan and her colleagues have introduced tenets of social identity theory, particularly entitativity, into the study of group process in gangs (Hennigan & Spanovic, 2012; Vasquez, Lickel, & Hennigan, 2010). Paying particular attention to the role that group membership plays in creating and sustaining a social identity, they note that the perceptions and actions of opposing groups play a significant role in the creation of an individual's self-concept. A key part of that self-concept is entitativity, which they describe as "the perceptual side of group cohesiveness" (135) and functions as a means of assessing the degree to which a group is cohesive, measured by the commitment of its members to a shared set of goals, traits, and values (135). The more an opposing group is perceived to be strongly united and cohesive, the greater levels of entitativity will be held against that group. Because such groups are viewed as more proximate and credible threats to one's own group, they are more likely to generate collective action. Hennigan and her colleagues have identified the potential "spark" that escalates gang violence and retaliation in some cases and fails to do so in others. It is important for the purposes of this chapter to point out that this advance in theory – which is important to the understanding of gangs as well as other groups such as terror groups, drug smugglers, human traffickers, and organized crime – came from outside mainstream criminology.

The lack of solid theory development about gangs, gang members, and gang crime hinders the development of solid policy as well. Hundreds of millions of dollars have been spent by federal, state, and local units of government and non-governmental organizations in responding to gangs. The goal of such expenditures is to produce reductions in the number of gangs, gang members, and gang crimes. Despite this, the focus of gang research has been on why individuals join gangs and what they do whilst gang members; very little attention has been focused on the process of leaving gangs or desisting from involvement in gang activity, especially crime. As Klein & Maxson (2006:154) observed "Surprisingly little research has been conducted on gang desistance and the processes of leaving gangs." The disjuncture between the study of gang joining and what gang-intervention programs are oriented toward (leaving gangs or desistance) can be effectively bridged by better attention to theory. That is, a theory of gang joining would be different than a theory of gang leaving. In addition, the majority of work on disengagement from gangs prior to the last two or three years has been descriptive, isolated from research and theory on disengagement from other types of crime, and atheoretical (Decker & Lauritsen, 2002; Hagedorn, 1988; Moore, 1991). This work has focused on motives or methods of leaving the gang without reliance on a theory of disassociation from a group (Pyrooz & Decker, 2011; Pyrooz, Decker, & Webb, 2011). Some recent progress in accounting for disengagement from gangs has been made through integrating theoretical perspectives outside the gang literature that explain leaving other deviant or marginalized groups. Following the lead of Ebaugh (1988), Healey (2010), and Kazemian (2007), this research has integrated examples of disengaging from other forms of crime, sought a more theoretical basis for its explanation, and employed data more suitable to accounting for individual change. Below, we sketch out some of the key elements in understanding the process of disengaging from gangs.

The theoretical perspective most appropriate to addressing disengagement from gangs, ironically, is linked to the Chicago School (of which Thrasher the godfather of gang studies was a part) and has been employed to account for delinquent involvement and desistance (Shaw, 1930). Disengagement from groups involved in crime, such as a gang, can be conceptualized as the product of age-graded informal social control, cognitive transformation, identity reformulation, peer relationships, and role sets. These are theoretical approaches that are appropriate for the explanation of group behavior across a diverse set of groups. Because of this, these theoretical constructs address both the process of leaving the group as well as the reductions in crime associated with leaving the group. A key factor in the appreciation of disengagement from gangs is the fact that "group involvement" is often inversely related to age. It is a characteristic of youth and adolescents to belong to groups, and group offending is a well-established correlate of youthful behavior (Schaefer, Rodriguez, & Decker, 2013) as they are less entrenched in behavioral patterns and generally not subject to the positive effects of marriage and a job. As a consequence, younger offenders are more subject to sudden changes in offending patterns that lead to quicker desistance rather than the gradual processes involved with employment and marriage, suggesting that theories of desistance and disengagement derived from observations of adults are less likely to apply to young people. As a consequence theories of gang departure, particularly those associated with younger gang members, must account for more sudden departures from lives of crime and gang involvement than for older offenders.

Certain key elements of the life-course framework can be applied to account for gang leaving because gang membership follows patterns comparable to crime in the life-course: individuals join (onset), persist (continuity), and leave (desistance) gangs (Piquero, Farrington, & Blumstein 2003; 2007). Onset and termination of membership are the points where an individual identifies and de-identifies with their gang and are generally consistent with a life-course theory approach (Elder, 1985; Sampson & Laub, 1993). The onset and termination of gang membership are important because they act as transitions between different lifestyles. As such, these transitions are important events that create new opportunities while closing out earlier ones and, as turning-points, are key to understanding larger changes in the life-course (Laub, Sampson, & Sweeten, 2007:314). Such events change lives in significant ways and as such gang membership acts as a turning point (Melde & Esbensen, 2012; Thornberry *et al.*, 2003).

Gang membership functions as a "pathway or line of development over the life span" Sampson & Laub (1993:8). The period between onset and termination delineate gang membership trajectories. However, there are processes in these turning-points as they are not random and have empirical antecedents that are typically related to a theoretical concept that Pyrooz and colleagues have come to call *gang embeddedness*, which refers to "individual immersion in enduring deviant network …. reflecting varying degrees of involvement identification, and status among gang members" (Pyrooz, Sweeten, & Piquero, 2012:5). Gang embeddedness is a theoretical construct comprised of five items, including contact or time spent with the gang, the importance an individual affords to the gang, the number of out-group or non-gang friendships, individual position within the gang, and participation in acute gang activities such as assaults. Based on role-immersion theory, the time prior to joining a gang and after leaving the gang would display lower levels of gang embeddedness than during periods of active gang membership. It is also the case that gang embeddedness is predicted to have criminological consequences and will entangle individuals in the gang life by the interaction of group process with embeddedness. Thus some youth are "pushed" into gang activities on the "front end," and "pulled" back into gang activities on the "back end."

The operational definition of gang desistance is the declining probability of gang membership. The elements of this definition come from the research and theory on desistance from crime (Bushway *et al.*, 2001; Kazemian, 2007; Maruna, 2001; Massolgia, 2006). Gang desistance can occur before or after identification as a gang member, but true desistance from gangs does not occur until the probability of gang membership approaches zero. This theoretical expectation emphasizes the processual nature of desistance from gang membership, one that Pyrooz & Decker (2013) have described as a teeter-totter.

The process of desisting from gang membership reflects life-course desistance concepts such as "knifing off" and desistance as a "developmental process" (Bushway, Piquero, Broidy, Cauffman, & Mazerolle, 2001; Jacques & Wright, 2008, Maruna, 2001). Maruna & Roy (2007) described aspects of the knifing-off process that involve the elimination of manners, social roles including associates, disadvantage, stigma, and opportunities from an earlier time in the life-course. In the context of gang life, knifing off applies to the process of severing ties with gang associates and thus eliminating (or reducing) opportunities to engage in crime. Decker & Lauritsen (2002) identified such abrupt changes as moving from one's neighborhood or moving to another city. Neighborhood ties are particularly important in this process (Schaefer *et al.*, 2013), as these influences can linger beyond the decision to quit the gang and, like tentacles, make it difficult for a gang member to disengage from their previous lifestyle, friends, and activities. Decker & Lauritsen (2002) describe a second pattern of desisting from the gang which involves developing beliefs and commitments that are contrary to those held by the gang. In these cases there is no sudden knifing off, more of a gradual erosion of the ties held over an individual as their allegiance and alliances shift to new, non-gang groups.

## Concluding Thoughts on the Future of Policy and Theory in Criminology

A unified approach to theory, research, and practice is long overdue in criminology. Even a cursory examination of disciplines with an applied component shows that such an integration, though not always perfect, has paid dividends. This can be seen in medicine, nursing, public health, psychology, and a host of other applied sciences with a theoretical foundation. Indeed, the strongest intellectual forbear of criminology, sociology, is an important part of several of these approaches. Many of the theoretical perspectives that provide the foundation for public health come from the same intellectual roots as those of criminology. This is not an indictment of those who work to develop theory further; indeed, good theory is the starting point in enhancing the quality of programs, policies, and practices. This view is an exhortation to expand the contours of theory beyond their current limitation. Greenwald (2012) observed that awards in science (particularly Nobel awards in physics, chemistry, and medicine) were more likely to be awarded for advances in methods than theory. He argues that a stronger integration of theory with methods can advance theory while advancing our understanding of complex phenomena. There is limited information in criminology to address this issue. The nearest analogy is the Stockholm Prize, an international award for research in Criminology first granted in 2006. The winners to date include:

2006: John Braithwaite and Friedrich Losel
2007: Alfred Blumstein and Terrie Moffitt
2008: David Olds and Jonathan Shepherd
2009: John Hagan and Raúl Zaffaroni
2010: David Weisburd
2011: John Laub and Robert J. Sampson
2012: Jan van Dijk
2013: David P. Farrington
2014: Daniel S. Nagin and Joan Petersilia

The majority of these individuals have made contributions to practice, policy, or programs (Braithwaite, Losel, Blumstein, Olds, Weisburd, Laub, Sampson, van Dijk, Farrington, and Petersilia). Indeed many of these individuals are represented in Sampson *et al.*'s (2013) review of "policy relevant criminology." All have brought sophisticated methodologies to criminology and contributed to making it a far more scientific discipline than when their careers began. Interestingly, this group includes several of the most important theorists of the discipline in the past two decades, either leading or making key contributions to the dominant conceptual perspectives of the time, including life-course and developmental criminology, neighborhoods and crime, the role of social capital in crime control, reintegrative shaming, deterrence, and communication. Arguably, a number of the Stockholm Prize winners have made more significant contributions to practice (Olds, Petersilia, and Zaffaroni) than to research, changing the practice of criminology in significant ways. It would appear that criminology has leadership at the top in the integration of theory, method, and policy, but perhaps the "rank and file" have yet to grasp the significance of such an integration.

Evidence of the lack of broad integration of theory and policy among the rank and file in criminology can be found in the training of young criminologists. The American Society of Criminology (ASC) maintains a bank of syllabi from various programs across the country. While hardly a systematic sample, the results of reviewing the syllabi from "Criminological Theory" are instructive. Of the 13 syllabi on the website, only two mention policy in a substantive way (though almost all mention a policy on plagiarism or class attendance). One of those two syllabi devotes

a 75-minute class period to the critical evaluation of "criminology and public policy"
and the other lists as a learning objective the evaluation of criminal justice policy
based on [a student's] "theoretical knowledge and their understanding of the causes
and correlates of crime and delinquency." Similarly, the Academy of Criminal Justice
Sciences (ACJS) in their accreditation guidelines lists as requirements for a successful accreditation separate courses on criminological theory and a course in the
administration of justice that includes policy as one of a multitude of foci. John
Klofas, Natalie Hipple, and Ed McGarrell (2010) made a similar observation in the
recent book, *The New Criminal Justice: American Communities and the Changing
World of Crime Control*. It is their contention that criminology neither trains nor
rewards researchers for their integration of theory and policy. Dan Mears (2010)
also argues that the state of criminology, evaluation, policy, and theory, would be
improved by stronger integration of the three. This goal can be accomplished by
increased accountability of criminologists to each other, the public, and the agencies
which practice criminal justice.

Given the apparent growing consensus regarding the virtues of integration, it is
no surprise that there is progress on the horizon. The first of this can be found in the
"public criminology" movement. While this effort has a number of champions,
Chris Uggen at the University of Minnesota is perhaps its best representative.[1] Uggen
argues that criminologists have a responsibility to explicitly bring the results of their
research to the public and the agencies that practice criminal justice because
their research bears on and affects such practice. Examples of the practice of public
criminology can be seen in Uggen's frequent blogs, Opinion-Editorials in newspapers,
appearances at public discussions of criminal justice issues, and testimony before
legislative and policy-making bodies. There are similar groups working on "Public"
History, Economics, Political Science, Psychology, and Anthropology among others.
The movement of social sciences into the public arena is likely to increase accountability and cause criminologists, among others, to more carefully address the
integration of theory and practice. Public criminology implies a multitude of roles
for criminologists; some are supportive, others are critical.

Supportive roles include the growing number of formal opportunities to work as
a research partner with a criminal justice agency. Police departments were involved
in such efforts earlier than other segments of the criminal justice system and the
work of George Kelling and James Q. Wilson remains among the strongest examples
of such a partnership. More formally, Weed and Seed (dating from the early 1990s)
is among the earliest examples of an attempt to institutionalize such a role.
Contemporary examples of this include the National Institute of Justice's Researcher/
Practitioner Partnerships,[2] the research partner relationship specified as a required
part of the Project Safe Neighborhoods initiative, and the researcher role in the
Smart Policing Initiative.[3] In these relationships, researchers – typically criminologists with a university affiliation – develop a close relationship with a criminal justice
agency, provide process and outcome evaluation, and advise the agency on the
progress and impact of a program, policy, or practice. In return, the agency or
agencies involved provides access to their data. Such relationships provide ample

opportunity for criminologists to sway the course of public policy, guide interventions toward more scientifically sound foundations, and test criminological theory. An excellent example of this can be found in the work that has been done in focused deterrence. Such work stems from attention to hotspots[4] that dates (at least) to the 1980s but was more formally developed by Anthony Braga and colleagues. Under Braga's leadership, the Boston Police department identified both high-crime areas (hotspots) and high-rate offenders within those areas and targeted both (areas and persons) with increased police attention and the threat (i.e., focused deterrence) of increased police attention if levels of violence continue at high levels. Braga and colleagues worked as partners with the Boston Police department, Suffolk County Probation, a clergy group, and others to develop a deterrence message and deliver it in a way that was consistent with principles of deterrence such as certainty, severity, and celerity.

However, not all of public criminology involves criminologists working in concert with criminal justice agencies. The work of Mark Mauer and the Sentencing Project offers another example of how criminologists can work publicly to change policies, programs, and practices by the use of research and advocacy designed to change public opinion. A number of criminologists choose to write opinion pieces for influential public outlets including newspapers, blogs, and magazines as well as speaking at public gatherings. In other cases, criminologists debate issues of crime and criminal justice control policy with officials of the criminal justice system or local politics. We argue in this chapter that such efforts to extend the boundaries of criminal justice are strengthened when they integrate both principles of criminological theory as well as findings from research.

The second area of progress in the integration of theory with practice is the growth of the "What Works" literature, though this has hardly been a seamless process without its detractors. Beginning with Robert Martinson's influential 1974 essay, there has been an ongoing controversy regarding the impact of rehabilitation in prison. While many have accepted the conclusion that "nothing works" in rehabilitating offenders, the issue is a good deal more complicated, as Cullen and his colleagues have convincingly shown in several contexts (Cullen & Gendreau, 1989; Cullen, Smith, Lowenkamp, & Latessa, 2009). One of the complications is the lack of broader context for understanding the role, impact, and varieties of correctional rehabilitation. Spurred by Cullen's commitment to and understanding of criminological theory, he and his colleagues have provided an important alternative to the conclusion that "nothing works." Interestingly, this alternative has found a welcome audience among practitioners, those who know the evaluation literature best, and the growing body of meta-evaluations of program and policy effects. The net result of this resurgence in the search for "what works" has spawned a number of government, university, and advocacy based websites and groups. These groups include the Campbell Collaboration,[5] the Center for Evidence-Based Crime Policy,[6] whose leader David Weisburd recently won the Stockholm Prize, the DOJ website Helping America's Youth,[7] and its successor Crime Solutions.[8] In addition, the National Institute of Justice has aggressively published review essays of what works, including a multidisciplinary collaborative volume with the Centers for Disease Prevention on gang prevention (Ritter, Simon, & Mahendra, 2013). This partnership approach between researchers and the Justice Department was piloted by Lawrence Sherman and his colleagues at the University of Maryland in 1997. These efforts have given prominence to approaches that integrate research and researchers with policy and practice and offer hope for the future integration of theory with policy. When such a fuller integration of the two occurs, it will be to the benefit of both.

## Notes

1 See http://thesocietypages.org/pubcrim/author/chris/ (accessed May 11, 2015).
2 See https://www.ncjrs.gov/pdffiles1/nij/sl000886.pdf (accessed May 11, 2015).
3 See http://www.smartpolicinginitiative.com/ (accessed May 11, 2015).
4 I am grateful to my colleague Cody Telep for pointing out the early work of John Schnelle and his colleagues in 1977, who may be credited with the first use of such an approach to policing.
5 Campbell Collaboration www.campbellcollaboration.org (accessed May 11, 2015).
6 Center for Evidence-Based Crime Policy, www.cebcp.org (accessed May 11, 2015).
7 DOJ website Helping America's Youth (now youth.gov) www.helpingamericasyouth.gov (accessed May 11, 2015).
8 Crime Solutions www.crimesolutions.gov (accessed May 11, 2015).

## References

Bushway, S.D., Piquero, A.R., Broidy, L.M., Cauffman, E., & Mazerolle, P. (2001). An empirical framework for studying desistance as a process. *Criminology, 39*, 491–516.
Cullen, T.T., Smith, P., Lowenkamp, C.T., & Latessa, E.J. (2009). Nothing works revisited: Deconstructing Farabee's "Nothing Works." *Victims and Offenders, 4*, 101–123.
Cullen, F., & Gendreau, P. (1989). The effectiveness of correctional rehabilitation. In L. Goodstein & D.L. MacKenzie (Eds.), *The American Prison: Issues in Research and Policy* (pp. 23–44). New York: Plenum.
Decker, S.H., & Lauritsen, J. (2002). Leaving the gang. In C.R. Huff (Ed.), *Gangs in America*, 3rd edition (pp. 51–70). Thousand Oaks, CA: Sage.
Decker, S.H., Melde, C., & Pyrooz, D.C. (2013). What do we know about gangs and gang members, and where do we go from here? *Justice Quarterly, 30*, 369–402.
Ebaugh, H. (1988). *Becoming an Ex: The Process of Role Exit*. Chicago, IL: University of Chicago Press.
Elder, G.H. (1985). Perspectives on the life course. In G.H. Elder (Ed.), *Life-Course Dynamics: Trajectories and Transitions, 1968–1080* (pp. 23–49). Ithaca, NY: Cornell University Press.
Gibbs, J.P. (1987). The state of criminological theory. *Criminology, 25*, 821–840.
Greenwald, A.G. (2012). There is nothing so theoretical as a good method. *Association for Applied Psychological Science, 7*, 99–108.
Hagedorn, J. (1988). *People and Folks: Gangs, Crime and the Underclass in a Rustbelt City*. Chicago, IL: Lake View Press.

Healy, D. (2010). *The Dynamics of Desistance*. London: Willan.

Hennigan, K., & Spanovic, M. (2012). Gang dynamics through the lens of social identity theory. In F. Esbensen & C. Maxson (Eds.), *Youth Gangs in International Perspective: Findings from the Eurogang Program* (pp. 127–149). New York: Springer.

Jacques, S., & Wright, R. (2008). The victimization-termination link. *Criminology, 46*, 1009–1038.

Kazemian, L. (2007). Desistance from crime: Theoretical, empirical, methodological, and policy considerations. *Journal of Contemporary Criminal Justice, 23*, 5–27.

Klein, M., & Maxson, C.L. (2006). *Street Gang Patterns and Policies*. New York: Oxford University Press.

Klofas, J., Hipple, N., & McGarrell, E. (2010). *The New Criminal Justice: American Communities and the Changing World of Crime Control*. New York: Routledge.

Laub, J.H. (2012). Translational criminology. *Translational Criminology*, Fall, 4–5.

Laub, J., Sampson, R.J., & Sweeten, G. (2007). Assessing Sampson and Laub's life-course theory of crime. In F.T. Cullen, J.P. Wright, & K. Blevins (Eds.), *Taking Stock: The Status of Criminological Theory* (pp. 313–334). New Brunswick, NJ: Transaction.

Lewin, K. (1945). The Research Center for Group Dynamics at the Massachusetts Institute of Technology. *Sociometry, 6*, 126–135.

Maruna, S. (2001). *Making Good: How Ex-Convicts Reform and Rebuild Their Lives*. Washington, DC: American Psychological Association.

Maruna, S., & Roy, K. (2007). Amputation or reconstruction?: Notes on the concept of "knifing off" and desistance from crime. *Journal of Contemporary Criminal Justice, 22*, 1–21.

Martinson, R. (1974). What works? – Questions and answers about prison reform. *The Public Interest, 35*, 22–54.

Massolgia, M. (2006). Desistance or displacement? The changing patterns of offending from adolescence to young adulthood. *Journal of Quantitative Criminology, 22*, 215–239.

Maxson, C. (2013). Street gangs: How research can inform policy. In J.Q. Wilson & J. Petersilia (Eds.), *Crime and Public Policy* (pp. 158–182). New York: Oxford University Press.

McGloin, J., & Decker, S.H. (2010). Theories of gang behavior and public policy. In H. Barlow & S.H. Decker (Eds.), *Criminology and Public Policy: Putting Theory to Work* (pp. 150–166). Philadelphia: Temple University Press.

Mears, D.P. (2010). *American Criminal Justice Policy: An Evaluation Approach to Increasing Accountability and Effectiveness*. New York: Cambridge University Press.

Melde, C., & Esbensen, F.-A. (2011). Gang membership as a turning point in the life course. *Criminology, 49*, 513–552.

Moore, J. (1991). *Going Down to the Barrio*. Philadelphia: Temple University Press.

Piquero, A., Farrington, D.P., & Blumstein, A. (2003). The criminal career paradigm: Background and recent developments. In M. Tonry (Ed.), *Crime and Justice: A Review of Research*, Vol. 30 (pp. 359–506). Chicago, IL: University of Chicago Press.

Piquero, A.R., Farrington, D.P., & Blumstein, A. (2007). *Key Issues in Criminal Career Research*. New York: Cambridge University Press.

Pyrooz, D.C., & Decker, S.H. (2011). Motives and methods for leaving the gang: Understanding the process of gang desistance. *Journal of Criminal Justice, 39*, 417–425.

Pyrooz, D.C., Decker, S.H., & Webb, V.J. (2014). The ties that bind: Desistance from gangs. *Crime and Delinquency, 60*, 491–516.

Pyrooz, D.C., Sweeten, G., & Piquero, A.R. (2012). Continuity and change in gang membership and gang embeddedness. *Journal of Research in Crime and Delinquency, 50*, 239–271.

Ritter, N., Simon, T.R., & Mahendra, R.R. (2013). *Changing Course: Preventing Gang Membership*. Washington, DC: National Institute of Justice.

Sampson, R.J., Winship, C., & Knight, C. (2013). Overview of "Translating Causal Claims: Principles and Strategies for Policy-Relevant Criminology." *Criminology and Public Policy, 12*, 1–30.

Sampson, R.J., & Laub, J.H. (1993). *Crime in the Making: Pathways and Turning Points Through Life*. Cambridge, MA: Harvard University Press.

Schaefer, D., Rodriguez, N., & Decker, S.H. (2013). The role of neighborhood context in youth co-offending. *Criminology, 51*, 1–23.

Schnelle, J.F., Kirchner, R.E., Casey, J.D., Uselton, P.H., & NcNees, M.P. (1977). Patrol evaluation research: A multiple-baseline analysis of saturation police patrolling during day and night hours. *Journal of Applied Behavior Analysis, 10*, 33–40.

Shaw, C. (1930). *The Jack-Roller*. Chicago, IL: University of Chicago Press.

Sherman, L., Bushway, S., Eck, J., Gottfredson, D., MacKenzie, D., & Reuter, P. (1997). *Preventing Crime: What Works, What Doesn't, What's Promising: A Report to the United States Congress*. Washington, DC: National Institute of Justice.

Short, J.F. (1985). The level of explanation problem. In R. Meier (Ed.), *Theoretical Methods in Criminology* (pp. 51–72). Beverly Hills, CA: Sage.

Sutton, R.I., & Staw, B.M. (1995). What theory is not. *Administrative Science Quarterly, 40*, 371–384.

Thornberry, T., Krohn, M.D., Lizotte, A., Smith, C.A., & Tobin, K. (2003). *Gangs and Delinquency in Developmental Perspective*. New York: Cambridge University Press.

Vasquez, E.A., Lickel, B., & Hennigan, K. (2010). Gangs, displaced, and group-based aggression. *Aggression and Violent Behavior, 15*, 130–140.

# 21

# How Do Criminologists Interpret Statistical Explanation of Crime? A Review of Quantitative Modeling in Published Studies

David Weisburd, Breanne Cave, and Alex R. Piquero

## Introduction

The issue of explanatory power has strong relevance for theory in criminology. How well a statistical model predicts crime (generally summarized in a measure of the amount of variance explained, or $R^2$) can be an important measure of the comprehensiveness of a theory in explaining a crime problem, or of the extent to which a theoretical perspective provides only a partial explanation for the variability in crime. Explanatory power is at the heart of our ability to say that a theory explains the phenomena under study. If a theory explains very little of the variability in the empirical data that we have available, how can we say that the theory is an important one for understanding those data?

Moreover, how much we explain has implications for our ability to have faith in the specific impacts of variables and the theories that they represent in statistical models. A measure or construct that is excluded from a statistical model of outcomes, whether because it is not known or not measured, can have an important impact on the variables that are included. This "omitted variable bias" is an often neglected limitation of multivariate statistical models, but one that is strongly related to how well we explain the phenomenon under study. If our models have relatively low explanatory power it is reasonable to assume that important factors have been missed. The exclusion of these variables in turn, may lead us to under- or over-estimate the importance of the factors that we have measured and included in our models.

Thus, variance explained provides one method for assessing the state of the criminological theory in criminology.[1] In a previous paper (Weisburd & Piquero, 2008) we asked how well criminologists are doing in developing multivariate models to

*The Handbook of Criminological Theory*, First Edition. Edited by Alex R. Piquero.
© 2016 John Wiley & Sons, Inc. Published 2016 by John Wiley & Sons, Inc.

explain crime by reviewing research studies in what most criminologists would define as the most important journal in criminological science, *Criminology*. Specifically, we examined all articles published in *Criminology* from 1968 through 2005 that used multivariate modeling approaches to test criminological theories. Among our key findings we showed that the overall level of variance explained was low, with researchers often leaving 80 or 90% of variance unexplained; and there has been a lack of improvement in explanation over time.

In this paper, we attempt to extend what we have learned about empirical tests of criminological theory by focusing on "how" variance explained was used in the papers we reviewed. Simply stating that variance explained was measured, does not tell us whether and how researchers used the idea of explained variance to understand their findings. In papers that reported variance explained, was it simply presented as a statistical number with little discussion? Or was there substantive examination of what variance explained meant to the findings in the study, and how the study related to other research in this area? This seems a particularly important question, as variance explained can give insight into how well models within a study compare, as well as to how explanation in a specific context compares to other studies. It can also provide insight into whether there is likely to be bias in the impacts of variables observed. We begin our paper by discussing variance explained and its importance for evaluating multivariate modeling. We then turn to how we collected data for the original study, and added to it for the present paper. Our findings reinforce our earlier observations regarding the limited attention paid to variance explained as a tool for assessing criminological theory. About a third of the papers that reported $R^2$ simply said nothing about it, and seldom were discussions more than a few sentences. When $R^2$ was discussed substantively it was generally used to compare statistical models within a study. Seldom is $R^2$ used by researchers to consider the broader implications of their work for theoretical explanation across studies. Moreover, there is very little consideration of the implications that $R^2$ has for the validity of estimates observed in a study. In concluding, we consider the implications of these findings for advancing empirical studies of criminological theory.

## Variance Explained and Its Importance for Evaluating Multivariate Modeling

Though oftentimes misused (Maltz, 1994), multivariate modeling has been a critical tool in the development of criminology as a science (Weisburd, 2001). By multivariate modeling, we mean a statistical approach to gaining knowledge about crime that tries to identify the broad array of factors (i.e. the independent variables) that influence crime outcomes (the dependent variable) and allows for the comparison of the specific effects of the factors that are studied. For example, criminologists have long been interested in understanding why juveniles initially become involved in crime, and why some persist in crime while others desist from crime (Shaw & McKay, 1932; Wolfgang, Figlio, & Sellin, 1972; Blumstein *et al.*,

1986; Piquero, Farrington, & Blumstein, 2003). In using multivariate modeling, a researcher will typically begin by identifying the array of factors that are believed to influence involvement in crime among juveniles and then collect information on those factors (i.e., the independent variables, or $X_i$) and criminal involvement (i.e., the dependent variable, or $Y$). Typically the researcher will fit a linear model that includes a constant $(B_0)$:

$$Y = B_0 + B_1 X_1 \ldots + B_i X_i$$

Such models assume a causal relationship between the independent and dependent variables, though in practice researchers often use cross-sectional data in which such an assumption is made but cannot be proved. Importantly, this model, which may include a large number of independent variables, is seen as providing a description of the broad array of factors that influence juvenile involvement in crime.

The use of multivariate modeling to advance science provides a framework for understanding the complex variables that influence crime outcomes. At the same time, it generally allows for measurement of how well such models explain the phenomena under study. In the colloquial sense, multivariate modeling not only provides information regarding the influences of specific factors that relate to crime, but also enables us to ask how well criminologists are doing overall in explaining crime. This is because statistical modeling generally allows us to assess not just how each factor influences the phenomenon of interest, but also how the accumulation of factors improves our predictions above what would be the case if we did not have information about them. In most cases, this assessment is defined as "percent of variance explained" ($R^2$).

Percent of variance explained takes into account two main sources of variation in a regression model. One source is the total variability that exists in the sample we are examining or the "total sum of squares" $(\sum(Y_i - \bar{Y})^2)$. That variation is measured in terms of the difference between the observed values of $Y$ and the mean of $Y$ (our best estimate of $Y$ absent the regression model). The second source of variation in $R^2$ is the "explained sum of squares" $(\sum(\hat{Y}_i - \bar{Y})^2)$. This represents the improvement in prediction(s) that is gained from estimating our regression model. Percent of variance explained in a simple linear regression model is gained by estimating the proportion of the "total sum of squares" that is accounted for by the "explained sum of squares":

$$R^2 = \frac{\sum(\hat{Y}_i - \bar{Y})^2}{\sum(Y_i - \bar{Y})^2}$$

The importance of this ratio is that it allows us to estimate how much the regression model improves our ability to predict the outcomes observed. If the percent of variance explained is very high it suggests that the goodness of fit of our model to the data is very good. A low $R^2$ implies that the model estimated is not adding much beyond what we already know from calculating the mean for the dependent variable. Variance explained in this sense, provides a direct assessment of how well our model, and by implication our theories,[2] explain the phenomenon being examined. If systematic factors influence the occurrence of crime, and criminological theory has been successful in identifying such factors, we would expect that the percent of variance explained in regression modeling would, on average, be very high.

The approach we have described so far applies to linear models relying on an Ordinary Least Squares (OLS) Regression framework. Other multivariate methods such as 2-Stage Least Squares (2SLS), Tobit regression, or count models (Poisson or Negative Binomial) also use a direct application of the variance-explained approach. However, in the case of specific types of nonlinear regression, the development of measures of explained variance is less clear. For example, while there is no direct $R^2$ measure for logistic regression, a number of "pseudo $R^2$" measures have been proposed. Importantly, in these cases statisticians have tried to develop measures that are comparable to the variance explained coefficient in the linear model. While caution should be used in making such comparisons, 95% of the studies we reviewed used traditional linear model $R^2$ coefficients.

## Variance explained and correct model specification

It is intuitively obvious why we want the explained variance in a regression model to be large, since it represents the ability of our theory as represented by our model to explain the phenomenon under study. But a high or low $R^2$ can also be used as an indicator of the success of a model in meeting one of the central assumptions in multiple regression: "correct model specification." Its principal component is that all "independent" or predictor variables that have an impact on the outcome we seek to explain (the dependent variable) must be included in the statistical models that are estimated (Weisburd & Britt, 2014).[3] When this assumption is violated it is difficult to have confidence either in the predictions developed from a regression model, or in the regression coefficients that are gained for specific independent variables.

If the model estimated by a researcher has a variance explained of 10 or 20%, it would seem very difficult to argue that all systematic causes of Y have been included in the model. While it is always possible that the vast majority of the "unexplained variance" is not systematic and that, accordingly, important variables have not been omitted, such an assumption becomes tenuous when $R^2$ is very low. In this context, Pedhauser (1982:36) argues that this assumption may be "highly questionable" when the independent variables explain "a relatively small proportion of the variance in Y." Even if a regression model meets a much higher standard of explained variance, such as 40 or 50%, it still may be unreasonable to assume that all of the unexplained variance is random and not composed at least in part of systematic factors excluded from the regression.

The assumption that we have not excluded important independent variables has important implications for our ability to trust the predictions provided by a model, or of the effects of specific variables on a crime outcome. If for example, a variable was an important factor in predicting crime, but it was not included in the regression model estimated (either because the factor was unmeasured or unknown) the regression model is not likely to provide accurate predictions of Y. Regression models cannot take into account and adjust outcomes for a measure that is not accounted for or measured incorrectly.

The problem of model misspecification has a second and equally important implication for multivariate analyses. If an omitted variable is related in some way to a factor included in the model, then the estimate of the coefficient for the included factor will be biased.[4] An example of this would be a model in which a prison term was used to predict future recidivism. It is well known that the likelihood of gaining a prison term is related to the seriousness of an offender's prior record, and that the seriousness of a prior record is in turn strongly related to future recidivism (Blumstein *et al.*, 1983). The estimation of a regression model including imprisonment but excluding prior record would result in a biased estimate of the regression coefficient for imprisonment. This is because the effect of imprisonment is confounded with that of prior record.[5] A finding that prison increases recidivism in this case, for example, might be the result of the fact that those who gained prison sentences had more serious prior records and because of that were more likely to recidivate in the first place. If prior record is omitted from estimation of the model, then the regression will mistakenly attribute a causal effect to imprisonment that is due instead to the confounding of imprisonment and prior record. Multivariate modeling provides a statistical tool for correcting this problem, but this also means that when a relevant predictor of the dependent variable is either unmeasured or unknown, and that predictor is related to a variable included in the model, the regression estimate for the included variable will be over- or underestimated in some way.

Incorrect model specification can thus have a very important impact on our ability to define valid results in multiple regression. Indeed, it may be defined as one of the primary problems and central dilemmas of multivariate modeling (Mustard, 2003; Weisburd, 2010), the other being sample selection bias, such as that caused by the continual analysis of conviction databases to make inference about discretion in the system as a whole (Bushway, 2007). Most statistical manipulation is an attempt to do something about this problem. Because researchers recognize that they cannot correctly predict outcomes or identify correctly the influence of specific variables on an outcome without taking into account a series of relevant independent variables, they utilize multivariate methods. Nonetheless, in the end, the assumption of correct model specification may challenge the validity of the conclusions reached.

## The limitations of $R^2$ as an indicator of how much we explain and of omitted variable bias

A number of scholars have warned against over reliance on $R^2$ in coming to conclusions about the strength of theoretical models (e.g., see Cramer, 1987; Duncan, 1975; Lieberson, 1985; Moksony, 1990). We want to raise at the outset some specific cautions regarding the use of $R^2$ that should be kept in mind throughout our essay.

An important statistical problem in using $R^2$ as a measure for how well multivariate models explain crime was raised by James Barrett (1974) more than three decades ago. Barrett noted that two models which fit the data with approximately the same accuracy can provide different outcomes for $R^2$. This is the case because the value of $R^2$ is influenced not just by the fit of the model to the data, but also by the "steepness of the regression surface." Barrett notes:

> [I]n analyzing two or more sets of data, predictions for a regression equation based on a steep regression surface with a larger $R^2$ might not be more precise (and could be less precise) then the predictions based on an equation with a surface not so steep with a smaller $R^2$." (Barrett, 1974:19)

In practice this limitation may not be a serious one for our purposes since it suggests that a model in which the measures more strongly impact the outcome will have a larger $R^2$ than one in which the measures together have less strength in predicting the outcome. At the same time, it is important to keep in mind that $R^2$ takes into account both the strength of the model in predicting the data and the extent to which the predictions fit the observed distribution of the data.[6]

We think it also important to note that the nature of the distribution of the dependent variable can also affect the estimates of $R^2$ that are gained (see also Blalock, 1964; Weisberg, 1985).[7] For example, Ranney & Thigpen (1981) show that when the values of the dependent variable are spread more widely, $R^2$ values will increase even when the basic relationships in the data are similar. They also note, in this regard, that as sample size increases, $R^2$, all else being equal, will decrease, in part because a larger sample size naturally leads to greater variability. This later change is not likely to have large influence on $R^2$ values, though an increase in the range of values can have much larger impacts, especially in models which already have a very high $R^2$. We have no reason to believe that the range of values varies systematically in studies of crime, and beyond this, $R^2$ values in criminology are seldom at the very highest ranges (e.g., above 0.70, see Weisburd & Piquero, 2008).

Finally, we think it important to point out that a low $R^2$ in itself does not necessarily mean that findings are unimportant; in fact, in some cases "less could be better" (Lieberson, 1985:94). Nor does a large $R^2$ necessarily justify a conclusion that the theory tested has strong explanatory power. In some cases, small effects may have considerable substantive importance. As Abelson (1985:129) notes, sometimes percentage of variance explained is a misleading index of influence where there are tiny influences that produce meaningful outcomes. However, when a model overall has a relatively small $R^2$ it naturally leads to the question of whether a researcher has left out important sources of explanation. In turn, as we pointed out earlier, such omitted variables can lead to serious biases in the estimates of variables that we do examine.

A large $R^2$, in turn, can sometimes be as much a statistical manipulation as an indication of model strength (King, 1986; Moksony, 1990). For example, the use of prior delinquency to predict current delinquency does not get at the underlying causes of delinquency per se but merely reflects the reality that prior behavior is a good predictor of present behavior. The addition of variables measuring prior crime or delinquency in the absence of the original causes of such behavior, however, will result in high $R^2$ values. This approach is particularly common in models using time-related data, where measures of the outcome in prior time periods are naturally included as part of the statistical model estimates. However, where a model is not correctly specified, such measures will likely include significant bias meaning that our estimate of the independent effect of prior crime or delinquency will be highly questionable.[8]

## The Study

Our discussion so far points to the ways in which variance explained can provide a method for assessing the development of science in criminology. In our original work, we set out to examine the amount and extent of explanatory power in statistical models of crime, i.e., how well we are doing in practice and whether some areas are more promising than others. In this paper we extend that work by looking more carefully at "how" variance explained is used in the 169 papers identified in the prior study.

Our first choice in developing a data set for the prior study was to decide how to identify studies that would be representative of the state of the field of criminology. While we could have drawn a sample from all "crime studies" we thought at the outset that such an approach would be too cumbersome. Not only would we have to scan a very large group of journals, but there would be disagreement as to which studies actually fall within the scope of the field of criminology and which journals to include. Given this, we decided to focus on a specific journal that could be seen as representing the field of criminology over time. The obvious choice for this purpose was *Criminology*, the official journal of the American Society of Criminology (ASC). The ASC is the main professional organization for American criminologists (with strong participation of criminologists from around the world), and in this context its flagship journal can be seen to represent professional criminological research over the last four decades.

Aside from *Criminology* being the main journal of the American Society of Criminology, its citation count and impact score are quite high and rival those of leading journals in other fields. For example, the journal rankings for 2004 (the date of our original data collection) from the Institute for Scientific Information (ISI) identify *Criminology* as the leading professional journal in the field of criminology (first out of 22), sixth of 96 in the field of sociology, and 29th of 101 in the field of law. *Criminology* is consistently used in publication and citation count studies and regarded, qualitatively, as the leading journal in the field (Cohn & Farrington, 2007; Rice, Cohn, & Farrington, 2005; Sorenson & Pilgrim, 2002; Sorenson, Snell, & Rodriguez, 2006; Steiner & Schwartz, 2006).

## Methodology for identifying and coding papers

For a study to be included in our sample it must have been published in *Criminology* and use multivariate statistical modeling to explain crime, delinquency, or other deviant behaviors within some theoretical context. Specifically, (1) the study must use statistical modeling in capturing the targeted phenomenon;[9] (2) the study needs to focus on one of the following units of analysis: individual, groups of individuals, organizations, or geographic area (i.e., public funding or sentencing length is not eligible as the outcome of interest); and (3) the study must report statistics that are more sophisticated than pure correlation or cross-tabulation as we are interested in statistical models that define a (causal) relationship between the independent and dependent variables.

We had a research team of four coders who were advanced graduate students who had completed requisite training in criminological theory, methods, and statistics code data for the original study (for details see Weisburd & Piquero, 2008). For the current study we had two coders who added a series of measures to the data base that reflected the specific usage of $R^2$ in the papers examined (see Appendix 1). We also collected qualitative data so we could provide illustration of our findings.

During the time period covered by our coding (1968–2005), *Criminology* published 1,306 total articles, and 259 of these included some quantitative test of criminological theory. Of these 259 papers, 207 included multivariate modeling with some type of statistic of goodness of fit or variance explained. Most of the 52 papers dropped at this stage included tests of theory that did not use multivariate modeling approaches. However, this attrition included some cases where authors simply did not report explained-variance indicators even though such statistics could be calculated. Of the 207 relevant papers, 38 included goodness of fit measures which could not be converted to or compared to $R^2$. Chi-Square statistics, or log-likelihood measures were common in this category, as were fit statistics for multilevel models. Our final sample thus included 169 unique articles, or 81% of the 207 relevant papers we identified.

## Results: How Do Criminologists Use $R^2$?

In our original study we drew a number of substantive findings from our examination of $R^2$ in published studies. These included:

1. The reporting of $R^2$ measures began to grow in use in *Criminology* in the 1980s until the end of the 1990s. There appears to be a decline in the number and proportion of papers using $R^2$ after 2002.
2. It is clear that most crime studies explain less than 50% of the variance beyond the threshold criterion (the mean of *Y* for linear models), and many of the models leave 80–90% of the variance unaccounted for.

3.  Beginning in the mid 1980s and continuing throughout the remainder of the time series, $R^2$ values are concentrated in a rather tight range between 0.20 and 0.40, without clear indications of improvement over time.

We argued that these findings point more generally to the failure of criminologists to take advantage of variance explained to understand both the progression of knowledge in our field, as well as whether our models are strong enough to place confidence in the outcomes we identify. If we were developing as a science in our understanding of the causes of crime, we would have expected to see improvement over time in $R^2$ values. That was not observed in these data. Moreover, the fact that $R^2$ is often very low in these models suggests that it is difficult to rule out omitted variable biases, and this raises important questions regarding how much confidence we can place in the specific findings reported. Our earlier study did not assess the extent examine the extent to which variance explained is substantively examined in these papers, and how $R^2$ is used in interpretation of results. Perhaps most importantly, we had not examined whether authors considered the implications of the $R^2$ values reported in understanding the validity of their findings and their implication for understanding the strength of the theories examined. We turn to those questions below.

*Was $R^2$ substantively discussed in the text of the paper?*   A key question for us is whether researchers discussed variance explained in the paper, and how much attention they paid to the statistic. Our first finding is that in about a quarter of the papers that included $R^2$ in tables it is not discussed at all in the text. It is simply reported in the table as a statistic without any interpretation in the text. The fact that a quarter of the papers that report $R^2$ include no discussion of variance explained whatsoever suggests that many researchers are not considering at all the implications of variance explained statistics, but are simply including it mechanically as a piece of information on tables. Perhaps this is the case because it is reported routinely in statistical software programs. But researchers in this case are simply going through the motions and not giving weight to the implications of variance explained findings.

Importantly, there is not an indication that researchers are more likely to discuss $R^2$ when the results are stronger. Looking at the largest $R^2$ values reported in the papers, there is very little difference between papers that included a discussion of $R^2$ in the text and those that did not (see Table 21.1). While on average the papers that reported variance explained with no further discussion had a later average publication date than papers that did provide some discussion of variance explained, the difference was not statistically significant. We clearly do not have any evidence that there is a growing sophistication of criminologists in quantitative criminology in their discussion of variance explained statistics.

Looking at the 130 papers that included discussion of $R^2$ according to the amount of discussion that they devoted to variance explained, there is considerable variation (see Table 21.2). We divide the studies into three categories. In the first there is simply a sentence statement about variance explained; the second a discussion that lasts through a paragraph; and in a third a discussion across multiple paragraphs.

**Table 21.1**   Discussion of variance explained by year and largest $R^2$ value ($n$ = 169)

| Mean (SD) | % | N | Year | Largest $R^2$ |
|---|---|---|---|---|
| Studies that discuss $R^2$ | 76.9 | 130 | 1991.43 | 0.46 |
| | | | (7.93) | (0.24) |
| Studies with no discussion | 23.1 | 39 | 1994.00 | 0.48 |
| | | | (9.13) | (0.26) |

**Table 21.2**   Length of discussion of $R^2$ by year and largest $R^2$ value ($n$ = 130)

| | % | Year | Largest $R^2$ |
|---|---|---|---|
| One sentence in text | 16.4 | 1993.57 | 0.48 |
| | | (6.49) | (0.27) |
| Single paragraph | 48.4 | 1990.82 | 0.48 |
| | | (7.37) | (0.23) |
| Multiple paragraphs | 35.2 | 1991.43 | 0.47 |
| | | (7.93) | (0.24) |

About 16% of the papers simply include a one-sentence statement, which does not suggest much interpretation of the $R^2$ statistic, but usually a restatement of the result in a table. For example, Costello & Vowell (1999:832) discuss their findings regarding the influence of social bonds and friends' delinquency with a simple summary: "this model accounts for 40.4% of the variance in delinquency." Almost half of the studies that included a discussion of variance explained did this in the context of a single paragraph. Generally, paragraph discussions do not go much beyond reporting the $R^2$ statistics (as is the case in one-sentence descriptions), often times simply noting the size of $R^2$ values across multiple models or the contributions of individual variables to variance explained in the model as a whole. For example, Haynie & McHugh (2003) compare the variance explained by four models developed in their article:

> Model 2 accounts for 7% less variation in respondents' deviance than did model 1 ($R^2$ – .10 versus .17 in model 1) and suggests that mutual friends' deviance may be less closely associated with an adolescent's behavior than the deviance of his/her sibling. Model 3 focuses on unique friends' deviance and indicates that each unit increase in friends' deviance is associated with a 0.63 increase in respondents' deviance. Moreover, this appears to be the best fitting model since it accounts for 20% of the variation in deviance, indicating that unique friends' deviance may be more important than either sibling or mutual friends' deviance... Model 4 is the best fitting model and is able to account for a little over a quarter of the variation in a respondent's deviance. (375–379).

A third of the papers (where $R^2$ is discussed in the text) include more in-depth discussions of variance explained across multiple paragraphs. Reflecting a typical discussion, Woolredge & Thistlethwaite (2003) interpret their findings concerning

**Table 21.3**  Uses of variance explained (*n* =130)

|  | *n* | % |
|---|---|---|
| Compare models developed within a single study | 101 | 59.8 |
|     Different dependent variables | 52 | 51.5 |
|     Different groups | 23 | 22.8 |
|     Different theories | 23 | 22.8 |
|     Other | 6 | 5.9 |
|     Different time periods | 5 | 5.0 |
|     Different statistical modeling techniques | 4 | 4.0 |
| Compare current study to models in previous research | 29 | 17.2 |

race and intimate assault by describing the variance explained by several different models and comparing the variance explained in these models to that in previous research. They also discuss the differences and similarities between the proportions of explained variance and suggest explanations for the performance of their models relative to those presented by previos researchers in similar studies. In another example, Rowe & Farrington (1997) present an analysis of the changes in variance explained between models in order to assess whether the variance explained in the full model differs significantly from the base model.

Again, we have no indication that there is more discussion of variance explained in papers that had higher $R^2$s. There is not a significant difference among the categories, and overall the $R^2$ s are very similar in magnitude.

In sum, in about a quarter of the papers we examined there is no discussion of $R^2$ statistics at all. In those papers that discussed $R^2$ in the text (or in a table) about 15% include a single sentence describing the results. In about half of the papers there is a paragraph discussion, but again this generally does not go beyond description of the results. We do not find significant differences in the amount of discussion of variance explained over time or according to the amount of variance explained by models within a study.

*What is the specific use of $R^2$ when it is discussed?*    We are not only interested in how long a discussion there is of variance explained in these papers, we also wanted to understand how variance explained was used when it was discussed. We identified two main uses of $R^2$ in the papers. The first, which was much more common, was to compare models within a study (see Table 21.3). In about 60% of the studies researchers employed $R^2$ to make statements about how well one model in a paper compared to another.

The most common use of this type was to compare alternative dependent variables (51.5%). For example, Agnew & White (1992) test general strain theory's capacity to predict both delinquency and drug use by juveniles. About 22.8% of the studies use variance explained to compare the model fit across different subgroups. For example, LaGrange & Silverman (1999) compare control and opportunity theory's capacities to explain differences in delinquency between boys and girls.

Boritch & Hagan (1990) compare arrests rates for men and women for different types of offenses. A similar proportion of studies used statistical modeling to compare different theoretical specifications. For example, Makkai & Braithwaite (1991) compare models developed from opportunity, control, subcultural, and differential association theories to explain nursing home compliance with regulatory laws. In these cases the fit of the model is often critical to the narrative of the study. Variance explained becomes a tool to argue whether one specification or theoretical perspective fits the data better than another. It is rare in our data for researchers to compare different statistical modeling techniques or different time periods.

In only 17% of the studies do we find that authors use $R^2$ to compare how well their models predict crime in comparison to previous studies. This is a particularly important finding because it suggests that researchers seldom put the explanatory power of the models they examine in the context of the development of explanation in a specific field that they are working in. A good example of how such interpretation might aid in interpreting study results is provided by Longshore *et al.* (1996) in their study of the construct validity of self-control measures. They argue: "The $R^2$s for the self-control scale were generally lower than those found by Grasmick *et al.* (1993) in similar analyses. However, in our analyses, it was often the self-control scale or subscale that accounted for most of the explained variance in crime" (221).

One of the key questions asked in our original work was whether criminologists' ability to explain variance over time has increased. We found that variance explained did not change over time, suggesting that criminologists' ability to explain crime had not improved over time (Weisburd & Piquero, 2008). An intriguing question is whether there is variability depending on how researchers used variance explained. Over time have $R^2$s improved for researchers who used $R^2$ to compare models within a study, as compared to between studies? One approach to answering this question is to consider the correlation between publication date and the highest reported measure of variance explained within these groups. If the correlation coefficient is positive, then the variance explained in the studies in the sample is on average greater for studies with later publication dates. If it is negative, then this implies that that the highest reported variance explained in studies is on average lower in more recently published articles.

Table 21.4 shows the correlation between year of publication and variance explained for the main uses of $R^2$ we have identified. As the table shows, there was a non-significant negative relationship between publication date and highest reported variance explained for studies that compare models within studies and studies that compare models to previous research. Looking at the types of comparisons within models, we can see that the strongest correlation is that between variance explained and publication year in papers that compared models as they applied to different dependent variables. In contrast, the relationship was positive (although not statistically significant) for research that compared measures of variance explained for different groups of research subjects or theories. We cannot draw strong conclusions from this analysis. But it would seem reasonable to conclude that this only

**Table 21.4** Correlation between publication year and variance explained

|  | *n* | *Coefficient* |
|---|---|---|
| All studies | 169 | -0.086 |
| Comparisons to previous research | 29 | -0.177 |
| Model comparison studies | 101 | -0.109 |
|    Dependent variables | 52 | -0.312* |
|    Groups | 23 | 0.019 |
|    Theories | 23 | 0.151 |

*$p < .05$; *$p < .01$; *$p < .001$

reinforces the conclusion Weisburd & Piquero (2008) reached that explanation has not improved over time.

Another key concern in our paper is whether researchers used $R^2$ to assess whether they could assume strong validity for the parameter estimates they observed in the paper. As we noted earlier, if $R^2$ values are lower we might suspect that there are important variables that are omitted from the analysis. And such variables might be correlated with key variables included in the model, in this case key variables that explain crime. Our measure is straightforward. Did the study include a discussion of the implications of the $R^2$ observed for the issue of omitted variable bias? Reference to $R^2$ in the discussion section of a paper which simply notes that there are always such problems was not sufficient. Our concern here was a link between $R^2$ and the validity of parameter estimates in the models.

We found only four papers that included any discussion of the implications of variance explained for the completeness of the models in terms of the variables included in the analysis. For example, Simcha-Fagan & Schwartz (1986) note that:

> The findings suggest (as indicated in part by the amount of variance accounted for in the endogenous variables shown in Table 3) that the model proposed satisfactorily taps social forces generated "within the community" and which account for self-reported measures of delinquency (695).

In two studies, the authors specifically pointed to variance explained as an indication that more variables should be included to improve model performance (Bailey, 1998; Curry & Spergel, 1988). In the fourth study, the authors used the magnitude of the proportion of explained variance in the model to argue that the more parsimonious model developed from differential association theory is preferable to a more complex model suggested by social learning theory (Orcutt, 1987). These studies did consider variance explained when determining the completeness of the array of variables that they considered in their analysis. However, the issue of omitted variable bias is not addressed directly even among studies that relate the magnitude of the observed variance explained to the decisions that the authors made to include or exclude specific variables in the analysis.

## Discussion and Conclusions

We think that our examination of "how" criminologists "use" $R^2$ in quantitative modeling of criminological theory, adds important new data to our previous findings (Weisburd & Piquero, 2008). What we learn only reinforces the concerns raised in the earlier study. In about 40% of the papers that we examined there is simply no discussion of $R^2$ in the paper, or a single sentence that reports the $R^2$ findings. Seldom is a discussion of $R^2$ in depth, and we find no real changes in this over time. Commonly, $R^2$ is used to compare models in a single study. It is seldom used to compare the strength of models across studies, or to consider whether omitted variable bias should be a concern in interpreting results.

What does this say about the uses of $R^2$ in quantitative studies of criminological theory? Why might discussions be so limited in published studies? The most positive take we can bring to these data is that criminologists generally are well aware of the constraints of variance explained as a measure of how well a model is doing. A low $R^2$ does not mean that the individual variable effects in the model are not important, a high $R^2$ does not mean that it is important. For example, studies in medicine can have very small variance explained, but can have significant implications for public health across large populations. In this regard Rosenthal (1990) showed that although aspirin cut the risk of a heart attack approximately in half, it explained only 0.0011 of the variance (0.11%). As we noted earlier, in some studies high $R^2$s are achieved simply by including time 1 crime data as a parameter for explaining time 2 outcomes. In that case much of the variance is explained simply by the fact that the past is the best predictor of the future. It does not imply that we are getting at the core underlying causes of crime.

Nor can one assume that a theory is lacking simply because of a low $R^2$ or that it is persuasive because of a high $R^2$. There are many ways to evaluate a theory, and sometimes variance explained is not the ideal or even correct one. As Lieberson (1985:117) notes the finding that variance explained is not very high "…is not necessarily due to the operation of other forces or problems with the data."

> It is certainly possible that the theory is wrong or incomplete or the data inadequate, but it is also necessary to consider whether the criterion for the maximum proportion is in error. Obviously, the amount of variation that a theory expects to explain cannot be a figure that is arrived at by a subjective or post hoc statement conveniently made equal to the actual proportion accounted for. Appropriately rigorous criteria must be used. One must keep in mind, however, that in many cases an analysis of the variance explained, goodness-of-fit, or other statistical procedure used to account for variability, is not at all an appropriate step for evaluating the theory.

Moreover, $R^2$ is in some sense very much a product of the particular sample examined. $R^2$ does not provide a parameter estimate for how well a specific theory explains the data, it provides an estimate of how well the distribution of the data in a specific sample explains the dependent variable examined. Of course, we estimate a sampling distribution for $R^2$, implying that we are concerned with whether the model can explain the data in the population distribution. But nonetheless, for this reason and those noted earlier, it is not a simple and straightforward process to extrapolate from the variance explained value in a sample to how a theory works across populations.

Perhaps researchers in this regard recognize the complexity of drawing inferences from variance explained and accordingly say little about it in published studies. Our reading of the studies does not suggest such a sophisticated critique of variance explained. We find little evidence of placing variance explained in context, and the fact that it is reported suggests that it is considered a statistic that should be interpreted. Variance explained provides a concrete method for gaining information about how well a theory fits the data the researcher is examining. A full discussion of variance explained in this context seems to us a key element of discussion of how well that theory explains crime. Our data do not imply that criminologists are excluding discussion of variance explained because $R^2$ values are low, or that they are including such discussion because $R^2$ values are high. It appears to be the case that criminologists are simply ignoring the implications of variance explained for how well models explain crime.

This in turn is troubling for criminology if we are trying to assess how well we are doing as a discipline. In our previous paper (Weisburd & Piquero, 2008) we argued that criminologists need to pay more attention to variance explained statistics in interpreting how well they are doing in explaining crime. In this paper we see that even when $R^2$ is reported in published studies, it is often reported mechanically, and little consideration is given to the implications of $R^2$ values for the strength or weaknesses of theoretical perspective. We suspect that this is the case in part because criminologists who develop quantitative studies of criminological theory are used to speaking to each other rather than to people outside our discipline. An $R^2$ of 0.15 or 0.20 is common in some areas of study in criminology. If it is common, there is nothing surprising about getting such results over and over again. And indeed, the finding that models over time are not explaining more of the variability only reinforces this complacency (Weisburd & Piquero, 2008). Perhaps researchers are not addressing the implications of variance explained for how well theories across studies explain crime because there is so little variability across studies within an area and across studies over time. Interestingly, the most common use of variance explained is to compare models within a study, suggesting again that criminologists recognize the validity of $R^2$ for the purpose of making comparisons.

Even if researchers are concerned about using variance explained as a statement about how well models explain crime, or observe little variability to speak of across studies, why is it that they don't use $R^2$ as a way of considering the threats of excluded variable bias. When variables are omitted from a multivariate model because they are unknown or unmeasured, and they are related to key theoretical variables, those measures will include some degree of bias. How much bias depends on the correlations between the omitted variables and the outcome and the omitted variables and the parameter of interest (Weisburd, 2010).

It may be that much of the variance we leave unexplained is in fact random, and thus neither affects the validity of our predictions nor estimates of specific parameters in our models. Causes of individual criminality, for example, may be so individualistic and varied, and found in such different places over the life-course, that it is very difficult for scholars to identify them or for public policy makers to use them to develop crime prevention policies (Weisburd & Waring, 2001). The causes of criminality in this context may be similar to the causes of changes in weather or other phenomena for which long range forecasts are difficult. The chain of causal events involves many factors that can have varied effects and thus makes long-term prediction difficult (Laub & Sampson, 2003).[10] In this context, if we could *only* explain 20% of the variance in human decision-making, and a statistical study using some constellation of variables had an $R^2$ of 0.19, we would have almost a perfectly fitting theoretical model as applied to the data.[11]

It may also be that low explained variance is more a function of poor methodology / measurement than some limitation in the state of criminological theory. This does not add confidence to the believability of our statistical models, but it would suggest that the problem lies not in our theories but in our data and measurement. Most "tests" of theories are limited. This is especially true when secondary data are used, and key theoretical constructs are measured with two or three items. Very rarely do scholars undertake primary data collection in which studies are designed to measure *all aspects of a theory*.[12] In short, then, theories are rarely measured completely or with fully defensible measures. As a result, the capacity of theories to explain variation is hampered. Maltz (2007) argues in this regard, that people are so inherently different that we would expect them to behave differently in the same circumstances. Thus, by taking the average value of their varying characteristics to develop theories (about what the average offender looks like), we risk conflating individuals who are deviant (well off the mean) but who are usually deviant in different ways (Maltz, 1994).

Accordingly, the problem with low variance explained may be less with the theories that criminologists construct than it is with the field's capacity to measure and empirically assess them.[13]

Irrespective of these caveats, we think it unreasonable to assume that models that leave 80 or 90% of the variance unexplained have identified the major causes of outcomes of interest. And as we noted earlier, if such unknown or unmeasured causes of Y are related to an independent variable of interest, the result is that our estimate of that independent variable of interest will be biased. As Pedhauser (1982:36) remarks:

> Assume, for example, that the proportion of variance due to a regression is .10, that is, that 10 percent of the variance is accounted for. Such a finding would be considered by most researchers in the social sciences as meaningful and being of medium magnitude... But since 90 percent of the variance is unaccounted for, it is very questionable that of all of the variables "responsible" for this percentage of the variance none is related to X [the included independent variable].

It seems reasonable to discuss with strong caution models that explain only 10 or 20% of variance, but what about models that explain between 30 and 50%? Of course there can be no blanket rule, since the validity of such models is dependent on how much of unexplained variance is due to random error. Conversely, shouldn't researchers who explain substantial parts of the variability observed tell us that this has more positive implications for the validity of their findings?

Our data suggest simply that quantitative studies of criminological theory are drawing very few conclusions from statistical portraits of how well their models explain crime. We think that such omissions limit our ability to specify how well we are doing at explaining crime and how much confidence we can put in our estimates of the impacts of dimensions of theories about crime.

## Acknowledgement

We would like to thank Sarah Calhoun for her assistance in designing the instruments and coding the studies

## Notes

1  We are not suggesting that this is the only method for taking stock of theoretical advancement. More traditional narrative reviews (Bernard, 1990) or meta analyses of effects of specific variables across studies (Pratt & Cullen, 2005) provide examples of other approaches that criminologists have used to examine related questions.

2  To be sure, a low $R^2$ does not mean that the theory is problematic. For example, the empirical test may be poorly specified, the test may include poor measures of the key theoretical constructs, researchers may have only assessed part of the theory (and some results may yield support for that part of the theory). See later for a more detailed discussion of these issues.

3  It also assumes that the variables included are measured correctly, and included in their correct form.

4  The traditional regression assumption may be expressed by noting that the error term and the included independent or predictor variables are independent. When a relevant predictor is excluded that is related to an included independent variable its effect is found in the error term which thus becomes correlated with the independent variable of interest. For a discussion of this assumption in regression see Pedhauser (1982, Chapter 2) and Weisburd & Britt (2014, Chapter 16).

5  This is illustrated in the equation for a simple regression with two independent variables. When the correlations between $X_1$ and $X_2$, and $X_2$ and $Y$, are greater or less than 0 the coefficient $b$ will be impacted: $b_{x_1} = \left( \dfrac{r_{y,x_1} - (r_{y,x_2} r_{x_1,x_2})}{1 - r_{x_1,x_2}^2} \right) \left( \dfrac{s_y}{s_{x_1}} \right)$

6  Anscombe (1973) makes a similar point but does so visually and quantitatively – with an $R^2$ of .667 no less.

7   Duncan (1975:55–66) has observed that the variance and range of both the dependent and independent variables, which likely vary from setting to setting (and dataset to dataset), will affect the relative importance attributed to each independent variable (see also Lieberson, 1985:117).

8   The likelihood of bias in the estimate of the measure of prior crime or delinquency is very high because it is likely to be related to unmeasured causes of present delinquency.

9   As noted at the outset, our interest is in studies using nonexperimental data and statistical modeling to understanding the causes of crime. In this context, we exclude from our analyses experimental studies that use random allocation as a method for isolating specific variable effects.

10  In this context it may be that, in certain instances, observing the variables in a weather map is more informative than being given the probability of rain, and as such, moving from model development to methods that portray variables in maps or graphs (EDA) may generate important (and new) hypotheses (Maltz, 2007).

11  Because we simply do not know how much variance is at all explainable so to say, there may be little to gauge such estimates against.

12  For a rare exception, see Akers *et al.* (1979), who measured fifteen dimensions of social learning theory, and generated explained variance estimates of over 50%.

13  Some may also observe that no one "model" – or study – can incorporate detailed measures of all dimensions of all major theories. As a result, no one model can ever truly indicate what the true capacity of our theoretical models – when taken together – is to explain crime. This may be why some scholars prefer meta-analysis, which can tell us across all studies what the effect size of each dimension of each theory is. When lined up as a roster of predictors, one can get a sense of what our theories can tell us empirically. More generally, as some scholars have observed, the challenge with explaining and predicting crime is that, in all likelihood, Gottfredson & Hirschi (1990) notwithstanding, it has a number of (causal) influences at various levels of analysis (biological, psychological, family, community, situational, economic, etc.). When this is compounded with our inability to accurately measure the dependent variable, some may view a median $R^2$ of 0.37 as quite impressive.

# References

Abelson, R.P. (1985). A variance explanation paradox: When a little is a lot. *Psychological Bulletin, 97,* 129–133.

Agnew, R.L., & White, H.R. (1992). An empirical test of general strain theory. *Criminology, 30,* 475–499.

Akers, R.L., Krohn, M.D., Lanza-Kaduce, L., & Radosevich, M. (1979). Social learning and deviant behavior: A specific test of a general theory. *American Sociological Review, 44,* 636–655.

Anscombe, F.J. (1973). Graphs in statistical analysis. *The American Statistician, 27,* 17–21.

Bailey, W.C. (1998). Deterrence, brutalization, and the death penalty: Another examination of Oklahoma's return to capital punishment. *Criminology, 36,* 711–733.

Barrett, J. (1974). The coefficient of determination – Some limitations. *The American Statistician, 28,* 19–20.

Bernard, T.J. (1990). Twenty years of testing theories: What have we learned and why? *Journal of Research in Crime and Delinquency, 27,* 325–347.

Blalock, H.M., Jr. (1964). *Causal Inferences in Non-Experimental Research*. Chapel Hill, NC: University of North Carolina Press.

Blumstein, A., Cohen, J., Martin, S.E., & Tonry, M.H. (1983). *Research on Sentencing: The Search for Reform*, Vol. *1*. Washington, DC: National Academies Press.

Blumstein, A., Cohen, J., Roth, J.A., & Visher, C.A. (1986). *Criminal Careers and "Career Criminals."* Washington, DC: National Academies Press.

Boritch, H., & Hagan, J. (1990). A century of crime in Toronto: Gender, class, and patterns of social control, 1859 to 1955. *Criminology*, *28*, 567–599.

Bushway, S. (2007). Personal communication. February 15.

Cohn, E., & Farrington, D.P. (2007). Changes in scholarly influence in major American criminology and criminal justice journals between 1986 and 2000. *Journal of Criminal Justice Education*, *18*, 6–34.

Costello, B.J., & Vowell, P.R. (1999). Testing control theory and differential association: A reanalysis of the Richmond Youth Project data. *Criminology*, *37*(4), 815–842. doi:10.1111/j.1745-9125.1999.tb00506.x.

Cramer, J.S. (1987). Mean and variance of $R^2$ in small and moderate samples. *Journal of Econometrics*, *35*, 253–266.

Curry, G.D., & Spergel, I.A. (1988). Gang homicide, delinquency, and community. *Criminology*, *26*, 381–405.

Duncan, O.D. (1975). *Introduction to Structural Equation Models*. New York: Academic Press.

Gottfredson, M.R., & Hirschi, T. (1990). *A General Theory of Crime*. Stanford, CA: Stanford University Press.

Grasmick, H.G., Tittle, C.R. Bursik, R.J., & Arneklev, B.J. (1993). Testing the core empirical implications of Gottfredson and Hirschi's General Theory of Crime. *Journal of Research in Crime and Delinquency*, *30*(5): 5–29.

Haynie, D.L., & McHugh, S. (2003). Sibling deviance: In the shadows of mutual and unique friendship effects. *Criminology*, *41*, 355–392.

King, G. (1986). How not to lie with statistics: Avoiding common mistakes in quantitative political science. *American Journal of Political Science*, *30*, 666–687.

LaGrange, T.C., & Silverman, R.A. (1999). Low self-control and opportunity: Testing the general theory of crime as an explanation for gender differences in delinquency. *Criminology*, *37*, 41–72.

Laub, J.H., & Sampson, R.J. (2003). *Shared Beginnings, Divergent Lives*. Cambridge, MA: Harvard University Press.

Lieberson, S. (1985). *Making it Count: The Improvement of Social Research and Theory*. Berkeley, CA: University of California Press.

Longshore, D., Turner, S., & Stein, J.A. (1996). Self-control in a criminal sample: An examination of construct validity. *Criminology*, *34*(2): 209–228.

Makkai, T., & Braithwaite, J. (1991). Criminological theories and regulatory compliance. *Criminology*, *29*(2), 191–220. doi:10.1111/j.1745-9125.1991.tb01064.x.

Maltz, M.D. (1994). Deviating from the mean: The declining significance of significance. *Journal of Research in Crime and Delinquency*, *31*, 434–463.

Maltz, M.D. (2007). Personal communication. April 24.

Moksony, F. (1990). Small is beautiful: The use and interpretation of $R^2$ in social research. *Szociologiai Szemle*, Special Issue, 130–138.

Mustard, D.B. (2003). Reexamining criminal behavior: The importance of omitted variable bias. *The Review of Economics and Statistics*, *85*, 205–211.

Orcutt, J.D. (1987). Differential association and marijuana use: A closer look at Sutherland (with a little help from Becker). *Criminology, 25,* 341–358.

Pedhauser, E.J. (1982). *Multiple Regression in Behavioral Research: Explanation and Prediction,* 2nd edition. New York: Holt, Rinehart, and Winston.

Piquero, A.R., Farrington, D.P., & Blumstein A. (2003). The criminal career paradigm. In M. Tonry (Ed.), *Crime and Justice: A Review of Research,* Vol. *30.* Chicago, IL: University of Chicago Press.

Pratt, T.C., & Cullen, F.T. (2005). Assessing macro-level predictors and theories of crime: A meta-analysis. *Crime and Justice, 32,* 373–450.

Ranney, G.B., & Thigpen, C.C. (1981). The sample coefficient of determination in simple linear regression. *The American Statistician, 35,* 152–153.

Rice, S., Cohn, E.G., & Farrington, D.P. (2005). Where are they now? Trajectories of publication "stars" from American criminology and criminal justice programs. *Journal of Criminal Justice Education, 16,* 244–264.

Rosenthal, R. (1990). How are we doing in soft psychology? *American Psychologist, June,* 775–777.

Rowe, D.C., & Farrington, D.P. (1997). The familial transmission of criminal convictions. *Criminology, 35*(1), 177–202. doi:10.1111/j.1745-9125.1997.tb00874.x.

Shaw, C., & McKay, H. (1932). *Juvenile Delinquency and Urban Areas.* Chicago, IL: University of Chicago Press.

Simcha-Fagan, O., & Schwartz, J.E. (1986). Neighborhood and delinquency: An assessment of contextual effects. *Criminology, 24,* 667–703.

Sorenson, J.R., & Pilgrim, R. (2002). The institutional affiliations of authors in leading criminology and criminal justice journals. *Journal of Criminal Justice, 30,* 175–182.

Sorensen, J., Snell, C., & Rodriguez, J.J. (2006). An assessment of criminal justice and criminology journal prestige. *Journal of Criminal Justice Education, 17*(2), 297–322. doi:10.1080/10511250500336203.

Steiner, B., & Schwartz, J. (2006). The scholarly productivity of institutions and their faculty in leading criminology and criminal justice journals. *Journal of Criminal Justice, 34,* 393–400.

Weisberg, S. (1985). *Applied Linear Modeling.* New York: John Wiley and Sons.

Weisburd, D. (2001). Magic and science in multivariate sentencing models: Reflections on the limits of statistical methods. *Israel Law Review, 35,* 225–248.

Weisburd, D. (2010). Justifying the use of non-experimental methods and disqualifying the use of randomized controlled trials: Challenging folklore in evaluation research in crime and justice. *Journal of Experimental Criminology, 6*(2), 209–227. doi: 10.1007/s11292-010-9096-2.

Weisburd, D., & Britt, C. (2014). *Statistics in Criminal Justice,* 4th edition. New York: Springer.

Weisburd, D., & Piquero, A.R. (2008). How well do criminologists explain crime? Statistical modeling in published studies. *Crime and Justice, 37*(1), 453–502. doi: 10.1086/524284.

Weisburd, D., & Waring, E. (2001). *White-Collar Crime and Criminal Careers.* New York: Cambridge University Press.

Wolfgang, M.E., Figlio, R.M., & Sellin, T. (1972). *Delinquency in a Birth Cohort.* Chicago, IL: University of Chicago Press.

Woolredge, J., & Thistlethwaite, A. (2003). Neighborhood structure and race-specific rates of intimate assault. *Criminology, 41*(2): 393–422

# 22

# Situational Theory: The Importance of Interactions and Action Mechanisms in the Explanation of Crime

## Per-Olof H. Wikström and Kyle Treiber

The idea that human action (such as acts of crime) is fundamentally an outcome of the interaction between kinds of people and kinds of environments is far from new. Kurt Lewin, often regarded as the father of social psychology, argued that this interaction was central to the understanding and explanation of human action. According to Lewin, "every scientific psychology must take into account whole situations, *i.e.*, the state of both person and environment" (1936:12). For Lewin, the *situation*[1] – the combination of a particular person (in a particular state) and a particular environment (in a particular state) – explains why a person acts as he or she does (ibid. 30).[2]

*Situational theories* of crime focus on explaining *why* crime events happen. They pay particular attention to the explication of *how* interactions between people and environments *move* people to engage in acts of crime. They can be distinguished from *individual and developmental theories* (which focus on why people come to have certain and varying crime propensities) and *environmental theories* (which focus on why environments come to have certain and varying criminogenic inducements).

In this chapter we discuss the importance of situational analysis for the advancement of knowledge about the causes of crime. We argue that situational analysis should, in fact, form the core of criminological theory. And yet proper situational theories are a rarity in criminology; although many criminological theories pay lip-service to the importance of the person–environment interaction, most concentrate on explaining what makes people crime-prone (e.g., a poor ability to exercise self-control) *or* what aspects of environments make them criminogenic (e.g., a poor collective efficacy). This is problematic because compelling developmental and environmental explanations depend on adequate situational analysis.

*The Handbook of Criminological Theory*, First Edition. Edited by Alex R. Piquero.
© 2016 John Wiley & Sons, Inc. Published 2016 by John Wiley & Sons, Inc.

Without accurately understanding what moves people to engage in acts of crime, it is difficult to convincingly identify (and understand the role of) key causally relevant personal and environmental factors implicated in crime causation.

A proper situational explanation of crime requires a well developed *action theory* that details how (the process by which) the interaction between kinds of people and kinds of settings (environments) triggers particular kinds of acts of crime. A situational theory is a theory that specifies which combinations of what personal and environmental factors (*interactions*) initiate what processes (*action mechanisms*) that bring about the crime event; hence a situational analysis is one that investigates and explicates such factors and processes.

We will set the stage by briefly discussing common pitfalls in defining the concept of situation (particularly the conflation of *situation* and *immediate environment*). Most so-called situational theories ignore the role of individual differences in action and focus only on the influence of the immediate environment. We argue that at the core of a proper situational analysis lies the explication of the *interaction* between kinds of people and kinds of immediate environments and the specification of the *mechanism* that links people and their immediate environment to their actions.

We then turn to discussing *Routine Activity Theory* (RAT), and particularly its interactional model which emphasizes the convergence of people and their immediate environments in crime causation. We will argue that despite its contribution in drawing attention to the role of the person–environment interaction in crime causation, routine activity theory fails to adequately and clearly expound the key concepts of its interactional model (motivated offenders, suitable targets and lack of guardianship) and their relationships, leaving the role of individual differences particularly underdeveloped. Moreover, we argue that routine activity theory fails to provide a properly integrated action mechanism which explains how the convergence materializes in crime, other than (at times) generally alluding to crimes as self-interested and rational. We conclude that routine activity theory is a missed opportunity to address the role and significance of the person–environment interaction in crime causation.

We then move on to introduce *Rational Choice Theory* (RCT) and discuss its application in criminology, specifically the version forwarded by Derek Cornish and Ronald Clarke. We consider whether this version provides an adequate action mechanism for criminological theories such as routine activity theory. We acknowledge the important contribution rational choice theory makes to criminological theorizing in proposing a much-needed action-mechanism. However, we question several of its key features, namely its common assumption that self-interest is the principle driving force behind human action, and its neglect of more automated, habitual action choice processes, as well as its poor treatment of the role of individual differences. We conclude that rational choice theory is not a good enough action theory to adequately explain how the person–environment interaction moves people to engage in acts of crime.

We then consider whether combining routine activity theory's interactional model with rational choice theory's proposed action mechanism will provide an adequate situational theory of crime causation. We conclude that these two sets of theories have not yet been properly integrated and question whether this is the best avenue to create a proper situational theory of crime causation, particularly as neither theory adequately addresses individual differences and the interaction of personal propensities and environmental inducements.

Finally, we turn to *Situational Action Theory* (SAT), a theory that aims to integrate into an adequate action theory key insights from criminology and relevant behavioral sciences regarding the role of personal propensities and environmental inducements in human action. Situational action theory proposes that people are essentially rule-guided creatures. The cornerstone of the theory is that people are the source of their actions but the causes (triggers) of their actions are situational; particular combinations of kinds of people (with particular personal propensities) and kinds of settings (with particular environmental inducements) promote the perception and choice of particular action alternatives in response to particular motivations (temptations or provocations), some of which may result in actions that break the rules of the law. We suggest that situational action theory provides a more realistic and constructive alternative for a situational theory of crime causation than either the interactional model of routine activity theory or rational choice theory, or their combination.

## The Ambiguous Concept of Situation: Conflating Immediate Environment and Situation

Birkbeck & LaFree point out that "precise definition and operationalization of the situation is difficult," but note that the concept of situation "generally refers to the *immediate* setting in which behavior occurs" (1993:115; italics in original). Many scholars, it seems, equate *situation* with the *immediate environment* and make a clear distinction between the actor and the situation (i.e., the immediate environment) in the explanation of behavior. For example, Wortley defines a situation as "a setting in which behaviour occurs" (2012:186).[3] As a consequence, *situational analysis* typically refers to analyses of how the immediate environment influences particular actions rather than how the person–environment interaction results in particular actions.

The common practice of defining the situation as the immediate environment means that the concepts of situation and (immediate) environment get conflated. Arguably, a proper *situational analysis of action* requires a clear definition and specification of the relationships between key concepts such as the person, setting (immediate environment), situation and action (Wikström, 2004). To clearly distinguish the immediate environment from the situation, we submit that a situation should be understood as the *outcome* of the interaction between a person and his or her immediate environment: the motivation and the perception of action alternatives (on which basis people make choices) that emerge from the combination of a particular person in a particular environment. The situation is thus neither the person (his or her traits and state) nor the immediate environment (its characteristics and state) but the motivations and perceptions of action alternatives that arise from their particular combination. The *situational mechanism* that brings about action (or inaction) is the perception–choice process that is a result of the person and environment interaction (Wikström, 2006).

## Routine Activity Theory: A Missed Opportunity?

... The probability that a violation will occur at any specific time and place might be taken as a function of the convergence of likely offenders and suitable targets in the absence of capable guardians (Cohen & Felson, 1979).

Situational theory and analysis focuses on how the *person–environment interaction* triggers people to act in one way or another. Person–environment interactions occur as a result of specific person–environment intersections. In the late 1970s and early 1980s a number of influential criminological theories were forwarded suggesting the importance of these intersections and their relation to broader social conditions and patterns of crime, e.g., routine activity theory (Cohen & Felson, 1979; Felson & Cohen, 1980), life-style theory (Hindelang, Gottfredson, & Garofalo, 1978) and crime pattern theory (Brantingham & Brantingham, 1981, 1993). Here we will focus on the contribution of routine activity theory.

Routine activity theory (RAT) was originally proposed to explain societal changes in (direct-contact predatory) crime rates. Routine activities refer to regular patterns of human activities in society (e.g., recurrent spatial and temporal patterns in family, work and leisure activities) that "provide for basic population and individual needs" (Cohen & Felson, 1979:593). The main idea of RAT is that changes in societal routine activities impact the rate of convergence of likely offenders, suitable targets and capable guardians – i.e., opportunities for crime – which in turn cause changes in societal crime rates (Cohen & Felson, 1979; Felson & Cohen, 1980). The argument seems straightforward: more opportunities cause more crime; fewer opportunities cause fewer crimes. It is therefore no great surprise that RAT is often referred to as an *opportunity theory*.

Routine activity theory thus advances two important key ideas:

1. The structure of routine activities in a society influences what kinds of opportunities emerge, and changes in a society's routine activities cause changes in the kinds of opportunities people confront.
2. People act in response to opportunities (including when they commit acts of crime); therefore the kinds of opportunities they encounter in their daily lives influence their crime involvement (and as a result a society's crime rate), and changes in people's exposure to opportunities may lead to changes in their crime involvement (and consequently changes in a society's crime rate).

## The interactional model

The interactional model of RAT proposes that an act of crime occurs as a result of a (crime) opportunity – the convergence of a motivated/likely offender,[4] a suitable target and a lack of guardianship (supervision) (Cohen & Felson, 1979; Felson & Cohen, 1980). Cohen & Felson argue that each successful (direct-contact predatory[5]) crime requires "an *offender* with both criminal inclinations and the ability to carry out those inclinations, a person or object providing a *suitable target* for the offender, and the *absence of guardians* capable of preventing violations" (1979:590; italics in original). They also argue that "the lack of any of these elements normally is sufficient to prevent such violations from occurring" (ibid., 590). More recently these elements have been referred to as "almost-always elements of a criminal act" (Felson & Boba, 2010:28).

The key concepts of RAT are vaguely defined and their relationships not very well specified, which causes analytical problems and difficulties for theory-testing (and falsification). Felson & Boba (2010:28) state that "anybody might commit a crime," and Clarke & Felson (1993:2) define a motivated offender as "anybody who for any reason might commit a crime." A suitable target is defined as "any person or thing that draws the offender toward a crime," such as "a car that invites him to steal it, some money that he could easily take, somebody who provokes him into a fight, or somebody who looks like an easy purse-snatch" (Felson & Boba, 2010:28). According to Felson & Boba, "the most significant guardians in society are ordinary citizens going about their daily routines" and "usually, you are the best guardian for your own property" (ibid., 28). However, in a more recent publication it is argued that "guardianship implies that someone *else* is watching who could assist in the event of attempting a criminal act" and that guardianship "involves the presence of others" (Hollis, Felson, & Welsh, 2013:74; italics in original). Guarding one's own property is thus not a question of guardianship but of target hardening (ibid., 73–74), which is seen as an aspect of target suitability. As for the relationship between the elements, Felson & Boba say that "the guardian differs from the offender and target, because the absence of a guardian is what counts" (2010:28). Recognizing the definitional problems of what constitute guardianship and how this concept relates to the other elements of the interactional model, Hollis, Felson, and Welsh suggest that "guardianship can be defined as the presence of a human element which acts – whether intentionally or not – to deter the would-be offender from committing a crime against an available target" (2013:76). Whether this definition makes things conceptually clearer can be debated.

This interactional model of RAT presents the embryo of a situational model. It stipulates under what supposedly (almost-always) necessary conditions crime is likely to happen, but does not properly explain how (through what process). Although Felson & Boba (2010:25–27) talk about the chemistry of crime[6] (indicating that something happens that may cause an act of crime when a motivated offender is mixed with a suitable target without capable guardianship), RAT posits no definite mechanism linking motivated offenders, suitable targets, capable guard-ians, and acts of crime other than loosely alluding to its being "consistent with the economic notion of individual choice given calculation of costs, risks, benefits, etc." (Felson & Cohen, 1980:403). More recently, Hollis, Felson, & Welsh have declared that "the theory is based on a rational choice perspective" (2013:66). However, routine activity and rational choice theories have, as far as we know, never been formally integrated. For example, Clarke & Felson point out that the concept of rationality is only implicit in RAT (1993:8–9) and Felson states that "the routine activity approach implied a decisional offender, but did not make the decision process explicit" (2008:73).

Hence, the interactional model of RAT is a primarily predictive, but not a truly explanatory model. It says more about *where* and *when* crimes are likely to occur (i.e., crimes occur at places and times where motivated offenders, suitable targets and a lack of guardianship converge)[7] than about *why* crime is likely to happen (i.e., why and how the proposed convergence supposedly creates acts of crime). Arguing that if someone is motivated to commit a crime and faces a suitable target lacking adequate guardianship, he or she will commit an act of crime does not take us very far towards understanding what *causes* that crime, or the role of the environment. For example, it does not explain why some people, but not others, commit an act of crime in response to (particular) suitable targets lacking guardianship; why some targets are suitable to some people, but not others; or why some forms of guardianship, but not others, influence some people's, but not others', crime involvement.

## The neglect of individual differences

The role of individual differences in crime propensity is particularly poorly treated in RAT, which is perhaps understandable considering "the routine activity approach offered a thought experiment: to see how far one could go in explaining crime trends without ever discussing any of the various theories about criminal motivation"[8] (Clarke & Felson, 1993:2). Cohen & Felson even state in their original formulation of routine activity theory that "unlike many criminological inquires, we do no examine why individuals or groups are inclined criminally, but rather we take criminal inclination as given" (1979:589). Hence, the theory recognizes dispositional differences in the guise of motivated (and presumably unmotivated) offenders,[9] but pays attention only to those who are responsive to criminal opportunities. Thus RAT can essentially ignore personal differences, make general assumptions about likely offenders (e.g., their preferences), and focus instead on immediate environ-mental factors.

This basic neglect of the role of individual differences in crime causation may be considered a major shortcoming of RAT which undermines its aim to explain the role of the environment, as there are no environmental features that cause all individuals to act in exactly the same way, nor, as Felson & Boba correctly observe, does "everybody respond exactly the same to any given environmental cue" (2010: 53). Thus, although routine activity theory may at first glance appear to be an interaction theory (stressing the role in crime causation of the intersection of likely offenders and suitable targets lacking capable guardianship), a closer examination reveals that it basically is (and has been applied as) a theory about particular environmental influences (i.e., the presence of suitable targets in the absence of guardianship) on the occurrence of crime events by motivated offenders (i.e., people who for whatever reason might commit a crime).

Rational choice has been suggested as a possible action mechanism which may link opportunities to crime, although so far this has amounted to arguing rational choice and routine activity theory are compatible (e.g., Felson, 2008:73; Felson & Cohen, 1980:403) and therefore might be integrated rather than actually suggesting in any detail how they can be. The question remains whether combining routine activity and rational choice theories would provide a proper situational theory of crime causation.

## Rational Choice Theory: A Good-Enough Theory?

The rational choice perspective takes the view that crimes are purposive and deliberate acts, committed with the intention of benefiting the offender (Cornish & Clarke, 2008).

Situational theory and analysis not only emphasizes the importance of the person–environment interaction in explaining action, but crucially also understanding the *mechanism* (process) that moves people to act in one way or another when confronted with a particular setting. To explain how the interactive process initiated by the person–environment intersection brings about action requires an action theory.

Rational choice theory is a prime example of a theory aiming to specify *what* moves people to action (e.g., Coleman & Fararo, 1992; Simon, 1997; Wittek, Snijders, & Nee, 2013). At the core of rational choice theory is the idea that the action choices people make are aimed at optimizing outcomes in relation to their preferences. To be rational is thus to decide upon a course of action which the actor feels is optimal given the circumstances and his or her preferences. It is often (at least implicitly) assumed that people share a universal preference to maximize personal advantage (particularly material gain). Optimizing outcomes generally means choosing the action alternative with the most favorable balance between costs and benefits. However, the assumption about how elaborate such calculations are differs among rational choice theorists. For example, Simon (1997:17) distinguishes between global (neoclassical) and bounded rationality. Global rationality "assumes that the decision maker has a comprehensive, consistent utility function, knows all the alternatives that are available for choice" and "can compute the expected value of utility associated with each alternative" while bounded rationality "is consistent with our knowledge of actual human choice behavior" and "assumes that the decision maker must search for alternatives, has egregiously incomplete and inaccurate knowledge about the consequences of actions, and chooses actions that are expected to be satisfactory (attain targets while satisfying constraints)."

## Clarke and Cornish's application of rational choice theory

Developed in the early 1980s (e.g., Clarke & Cornish, 1985) as a practical rather than an explanatory tool "specifically intended to assist policy thinking" (Clarke, 2014b:xi) and "to underpin situational prevention" (Clarke, 2012:3), Derek Cornish and Ronald Clarke's version of rational choice theory (hereafter RCT[10]) aspires to be what they designate *good-enough theory*; an explanation which values simplicity over specificity and practicality over precision (Clarke, 2004; Cornish & Clarke, 2008). The main propositions of Cornish & Clarke's rational choice theory are that people's action decisions, including their decisions to commit acts of crime, are (1) purposeful, intended to obtain a desired outcome, primarily of hedonistic benefit to the actor; (2) freely chosen based on a utilitarian hierarchy of preferences; and (3) rational, involving at least some calculation of expected cost and benefits with the aim of maximizing the utility of both the desired ends and the chosen means. This means that when a person takes part in a setting, he or she will commit an act of crime if his or her assessment of the circumstances leads him or her to believe it would obtain a desired outcome and the expected gains would outweigh the potential costs. His or her chosen methods are then guided and constrained by rational considerations.

The application of this decision making framework to the explanation of criminal events has made a significant contribution to the study of crime by taking into account the cognitive process through which personal and environmental factors directly influence criminal action. At the point of action (the *event decision*) Cornish & Clarke see this process as being driven primarily by features of the setting and circumstances, which determine, through rational processes, if and by what means an act of crime is carried out. Personal characteristics are more implicated in *involvement decisions* which occur prior to a person's entrance into a particular setting and determine, again through rational processes, whether or not a person recognizes an act of crime as a means of satisfying his or her needs or desires.

This two step process of criminal decision making – involvement decisions through which a person rationally decides he or she would commit a crime given the right conditions, and event decisions through which a person rationally decides the conditions are right to commit an act of crime and how to go about doing so – is consistent with Cornish & Clarke's depiction of criminal activity as a step-by-step process requiring rational choices at each decision point (Leclerc & Wortley, 2014). Once a person decides he or she is ready to commit a crime and the conditions for doing so manifest, criminal behavior often follows a *crime script* – a step-by-step procedure which guides the action process from rational decision to rational decision through crime commission (and its aftermath) (Cornish & Clarke, 2008).

Clarke & Cornish not only see individual acts of crime as comprised of sequential stages, but likewise criminal careers, and suggest that different explanatory models may be required for each of three stages: initiation, through which the would-be offender acquires a *readiness* to offend (comes to see crime as a solution to his or her needs given the right circumstances); habituation, during which the repercussions of successful crime involvement (e.g., increasing crime-relevant knowledge and skills, and changes in lifestyle and values) bolster offending as the rational choice for action; and desistance, during which the repercussions of unsuccessful crime involvement, as well as changes in life circumstances, make crime commission less appealing. Cornish & Clarke seem to confuse content with mechanism, however (Cornish & Clarke, 2008); while the *content* (e.g. relevant skills, experiences and consequences) driving action decisions during initiation, habituation, and desistance may differ, the proposed decision making *process* itself does not change – according to RCT it remains rational.

Cornish & Clarke likewise suggest that different types of crime may require different explanations, i.e., that criminal decision-making is crime-specific (2008:26). But, although the factors which influence, for example, a person's readiness to rape and the settings and circumstances amenable to rape are significantly different from those associated with tax evasion, the difference is again one of content, not process. Rape and tax evasion, according to RCT, have at least one thing in common – they are rationally chosen.


## Key assumptions

Cornish & Clarke's model of rational decision making relies on a number of assumptions. The first set of assumptions relates to the desired outcome of the decision process. Generally, this is seen to be something of benefit to the actor (often material gain, but also more visceral rewards like positive emotions and the gratification of physical appetites). Self-interested motives are taken for granted, although a rational choice framework does not require them (see e.g., Elster, 2007:193). Preferences are also presumed to be broadly universal (presumably everybody desires money, status, sexual gratification, etc.). To what extent these preferences are equal in magnitude as well as valence is not always specified, but often presumed to also be at least roughly generalizable.

The second set of assumptions relates to the costs–benefits calculation at the heart of RCT. Like preferences, costs and benefits are generally presumed, in themselves, to be universally valued (although different costs and benefits may be relevant to different actors, and different actors may stand to gain or lose more than others). Hence, RCT implies that the nature and outcomes of these calculations can be specified based on information about the setting and circumstances, and therefore predicted, and potentially manipulated.

A third set of assumptions relates to the bounded nature of rationality. Actors do not usually (if ever), possess perfect knowledge regarding outcomes, or perfect evaluative capacities; rather, they tend to work with limited and sometimes distorted information (Simon, 1997). However, regardless of the extent and reliability of the knowledge informing the decision process, much of the process itself is seen to be rational (Clarke & Cornish, 1985:164).

A final set of assumptions has to do with involvement decisions, i.e., how people select an act of crime as an action they are ready to pursue once they encounter the right circumstances (i.e., opportunity). This decision, according to RCT, takes place before the person enters the setting in which the crime actually happens, and is influenced by personal background factors (such as sex, temperament, and broken homes), which influence his or her generalized needs (e.g., money, sex, or excitement), and previous experiences and learning (which include, for example, moral attitudes and experiences of crime), which, in turn, influence whether or not he or she recognizes an act of crime as a means of satisfying those needs (Clarke & Cornish, 1985; Cornish & Clarke, 2014).

This means that at the point of action the decision process is merely concerned with the practical considerations of carrying out the action and reaping its rewards (or costs). It also implies that people take their criminal motivation[11] with them, monitoring their environments for the right conditions (opportunity) to offend. Cornish & Clarke (e.g., 2003:56) describe such people as predatory offenders, opportunity theories' "model or ideal" offender type. All told, "the rational choice perspective has little to say about the construction of motives, desire and preferences" (Cornish & Clarke, 2003:87) and "the nature of the offender" (Cornish & Clarke, 2008:39). Instead, it remains focused on decision processes at the point of action, when settings and circumstances signal to the would-be offender "the existence of opportunities to carry out the offense he or she… has already decided to do once the circumstances are right" (Cornish & Clarke, 2003:59). The costs–benefits analyses concerning how to carry out the action (event decisions) are therefore free from "questions of needs and motives, moral scruples and readiness" which "have already been addressed" (Cornish & Clarke, 2008:31)[12] in a *standing decision* to engage in the particular type of crime.

## An inadequate action mechanism

The rational choice perspective has been instrumental in drawing the attention of criminologists to decision-making and its importance in linking people and environments to acts of crime. However, there are several fundamental problems with RCT's specification which mean that it is questionable whether it is, as Clarke & Cornish suggest, a good-enough theory.

The first of these problems is rational choice theory's assumption that the main orienting force behind human action is self-interest. Growing evidence suggests that human social behavior is too complex to be governed by this simplistic principle. Rather, social behavior is to a large extent rule-guided (e.g., Bunge & Wallis, 2008; Lyons, Young, & Keil, 2007; Wellmans & Miller, 2008) and, therefore, best explained and analyzed as such.

RCT does not see rules of conduct as particularly relevant to the offending of its default predatory offenders, but it does not completely overlook their influence on at least some offenders, in particular those it dubs *mundane offenders*. Moral scruples may destabilize the readiness of this less ideal type of offender to offend, causing them to be "more selective, revisable and tentative" (Cornish & Clarke, 2003:63), primarily through the association of rule-breaking with negative consequences, including shame and guilt. "It is not immediately apparent" to Cornish & Clarke (ibid., 67) "how moral considerations could be brought to bear with much force at any later point" in criminal decision-making, but they do acknowledge that establishing codes of behavior may signal, through perceptible changes in the setting (e.g., notices, interventions), that actions are less permissible or excusable, potentially affecting moral inhibitions or neutralizations (ibid., 68). Generally, however, as noted previously, Cornish & Clarke see issues of morality as something which is dealt with prior to the point of action and part of one's criminal disposition (Cornish & Clarke, 2008). Hence the mundane offender may represent "merely a rather more complex version of the predatory one" (Cornish & Clarke, 2003:65) which does not offend as prolifically, tends to commit "ambiguously criminal acts" (ibid., 62) and is therefore not nearly as gratifying to study from an RCT perspective.

Rational choice theory's second major shortcoming is its failure to take into account more automatic processes of choice which do not follow a rational design. RCT's version of habituation refers to the continuation of crime involvement and the inclusion of previous experience with crime in the rational calculus; in other words, the entrenchment of the standing decision to offend (criminal readiness) as well as the acquisition of relevant knowledge and skills (Cornish & Clarke, 2008). This expands the conditions which a motivated offender sees as opportunities to offend, but does not change the rational nature by which he or she chooses when, where and how to carry out the offence. Traditionally, habituation refers to the automation of action decisions such that the person skips over rational deliberation regarding potential interference and consequences and dives straight into the action. While this automaticity may be acquired subsequent to rational calculations in previous situations, once it is triggered those considerations do not influence the action until interferences or consequences manifest, typically after the action is initiated.

One major difference between habitual and rational choices is that when people make habitual choices, they perceive only one potent alternative for action, which is then automatically chosen. Rationality, on the other hand, requires the perception of more than one potent action alternative because to choose the best alternative requires making a genuine choice between more than one alternative. Habits draw on past actions and experienced outcomes, while rational deliberation focuses on the future and expected outcomes. The latter involves more uncertainty and requires more cognitive effort, but is bespoke; the former is faster and more efficient, but lacks reflective flexibility (see further, Wikström, 2006). Thus, habituation (in the traditional sense) avoids the heavy demands of rationality. There is good reason to believe that habitual processes underlie much of human action (e.g., Bargh, 1997; Wood & Quinn, 2005; Verplanken & Wood, 2006), and that much crime (for example, many instances of violent crimes, minor thefts, and traffic violations) may be a result of habitual responses rather than rational decision-making. Moreover, there are good reasons to believe that persistent offending may include strong elements of habit.

Rule-guidance does not preclude rationality from all decision processes, but much human action is guided by automated rule-following which saves the decision maker much of the cognitive time and effort required by consistently applying rational choices in everyday life. As Davidson (2004:107) observes, "most of our actions are not preceded by any conscious reasoning and deliberation. We don't usually 'form' intentions, we just come to have them." Not only does this have implications for predicting decision-making outcomes, but also for practical efforts to influence those outcomes (i.e., crime prevention), the purported focus of Cornish & Clarke's rational choice theory.

RCT likes to invoke the concept of bounded rationality to account for aspects of decision making which lie beyond its presumably rational core, but its "focus remains on the vestiges of rationality that remain" (Wortley, 2012:245). However, Smith & Clarke (2012:294) argue that "undue attention" to irrational aspects of behavior may lead to the neglect of important rational elements. Until we fully understand the extent to which criminal decision-making is rational or irrational (i.e., non-deliberative), however, we cannot say where that attention is best placed.

## The situational model

Essentially, RCT argues that when a person engages with an action setting, if he or she is ready (motivated) to commit an act of crime, he or she decides through a (bounded) rational process whether that act can be successfully carried out given the setting and circumstances. Cornish & Clarke (2003:50) interpret this interaction between offenders and their environments as that of motivation and opportunity, motivation being something a person brings to the setting (a readiness),[13] and opportunity something which the setting presents to the person. This explains why RCT divides criminal decision-making into involvement decisions (those determining criminal readiness) and event decisions (those determining in which settings and circumstances crimes occur). Yet there is a sound argument for the proposition that motivation (understood as goal-directed attention) and (perceived) opportunity are situational concepts, outcomes of the interaction between a person and a setting at the point of action, and not intrinsic features of the person (propensities) and setting (inducements) respectively.

Cornish & Clarke developed RCT as "a heuristic device or conceptual tool rather than conventional criminological theory" (2008:24). Despite its name, the question of whether or not people make rational decisions is not (according to Cornish & Clarke, 2008:41) the main focus of RCT. To them, even if it lacks rigor in its specification, RCT is a good-enough theory if it achieves its practical aims: if crime events can be effectively prevented through methods aimed at offenders who are presumed to be making rational choices, then RCT is good enough.

We believe, however, that Herbert Simon, the father of bounded rationality, is correct in positing that if we want to adequately explain and predict behavior, a theory like Cornish & Clarke's version of rational choice theory which primarily focuses on substantive (instrumental) rationality[14] "will not do the job" (Simon, 1997:19). "It is, of course, a great pity," Simon notes; "if it would, we would be spared a tiresome inquiry into the sociology and psychology of human decision making" (ibid., 19). Such an inquiry is, however, necessary in regards to "most situations of practical interest" (ibid., 19).

## Opportunity theory: Combining routine activity and rational choice theories

In 1993, Clarke & Felson made the marriage of routine activity and rational choice theory official, stating that rationality is implicit in RAT and arguing they are "compatible and, indeed, mutually supportive" despite "differing in scope and purpose" (Clarke & Felson, 1993:1). Key differences which they highlight include the efforts of RCT to explain criminal dispositions (motivated offenders) and particularly the fact that RAT takes a macro perspective, looking at crime events from population level, while RCT takes a micro perspective, looking at crime events from the personal level (i.e., the perspective of the motivated offender). Subsequently, Felson & Clarke adopted the slogan "*opportunity makes the thief*" (e.g., Felson & Clarke, 1998), although a scrutiny of their reasoning suggests that "*thieves take opportunities*" would probably be more fitting.

Although never formally integrated, routine activity theory, bolstered by rational choice, represents the closest criminological theorists have traditionally come to a situational analysis of crime. We have highlighted routine activity theory's interactional model, which emphasizes the convergence of people and settings, and its contribution to criminological theorizing by drawing attention to the importance of the person–environment interaction, but we have also highlighted serious weaknesses in the model, particularly its lack of attention to, and interest in, the role of the actor and his or her personal characteristics, and its failure to clearly define and explain how the interaction of the key components – motivated offenders, suitable targets, and lack of guardianship – lead to crime involvement, except by falling back upon notions of rational choice. We have gone on to describe Cornish & Clarke's version of rational choice theory, highlighting its significant contribution of drawing attention to the need for an action mechanism – proposed as a rational choice process – linking people and their environments to their actions, but questioned several of its key assumptions, namely those relating to human nature as self-interested, which we argue overlooks our social tendencies, and human action as characteristically considered and effortful, which we argue overlooks more automated decision processes. Considering that RAT is founded on the notion of routine activities (i.e., common habits), and routines have been argued to arise from constraining rules and resources (e.g., Wikström & Sampson, 2003) it is surprising that deliberation-heavy, self-interested rational calculations have been highlighted as the most appropriate action mechanism for routine activity theory.

## Situational Action Theory: A Better Alternative?

> Acts of crime happen because people perceive them as a morally acceptable action alternative given the circumstances (and there is no relevant and strong enough deterrent) or fail to adhere to personal morals (i.e., fail to exercise self-control) in circumstances when they are externally incited to act otherwise. (Wikström & Treiber, forthcoming).

Situational action theory (SAT) is a dynamic theory of crime causation. It stresses the importance of the person–environment interaction and the need to properly understand and explicate the action mechanism that links people and their immediate environments to their actions (including their acts of crime). The theory aims to overcome the fragmentation and poor integration of key criminological (and supporting behavioral science) insights about the role and interplay of relevant personal propensities and environmental inducements in crime causation and its dependence on the wider social context. SAT was initially presented in the early 2000s (e.g., Wikström, 2004, 2005, 2006) and has been further developed and refined ever since (e.g., Wikström, 2010, 2011, 2014; Wikström et al., 2012:3–43; specifically about the neuroscientific basis of SAT, see Treiber, 2011).

Situational action theory is based on four key propositions about the sources of human action:

1.  Action is ultimately an outcome of a perception–choice process.
2.  This perception–choice process is initiated and guided by relevant aspects of the person–environment interaction.
3.  Processes of social and self-selection place kinds of people in kinds of settings (creating particular kinds of interactions).
4.  What kinds of people and what kinds of environments are present (and to what extent) in a jurisdiction is the result of historical processes of personal and social emergence (setting the stage for the potential personal and environmental input into human interactions).

Propositions 1 and 2 refer to the *situational model* of SAT, while propositions 3 and 4 refer to the *social model* of SAT. How the situational and social models are linked is illustrated in Figure 22.1.[15] In this chapter we focus on the situational model at the core of SAT's explanation of human action and crime, and contrast it with the previously discussed opportunity theories (i.e., Cohen & Felson's routine activity theory and Cornish & Clarke's version of rational choice theory).

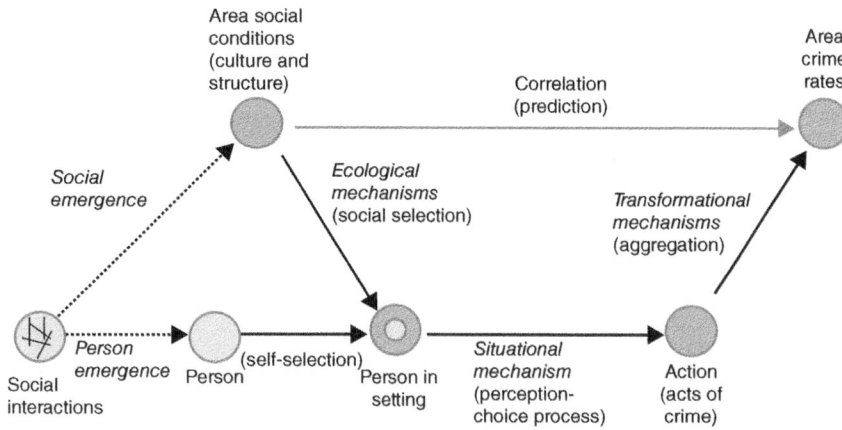

**Figure 22.1** Situational Action Theory: Key proposed mechanisms. *Source:* Wikström P-O H. (2011). "Does Everything Matter? Addressing the Problem of Causation and Explanation in the Study of Crime." In J. McGloin, C. J. Sullivan, and L. W. Kennedy (Eds.), *When Crime Appears. The Role of Emergence.* London. Routledge.

## The concepts of *situation* and *situational mechanism*

SAT insists that people are the *source* of their actions (people perceive, choose, and execute their actions) but that the *causes* of their actions are situational (people's particular perception of action alternatives, process of choice and execution of action are triggered and guided by the relevant input from the person–environment interaction).

A *situation* is defined as "the perception of action alternatives in response to a certain motivation." What motivations (temptations or provocations) arise and what action alternatives a particular person perceives in response to those motivations is a result of his or her active engagement with the particular setting (immediate environment). Importantly, the situation represents neither the person nor the setting but the outcome of their combination; a person's particular action propensities are triggered by specific features of a setting, and a setting's particular action inducements are made relevant by a person's specific propensities.

People make action choices on the basis of their motivations and perception of action alternatives. The *situational mechanism* that links people and their settings (immediate environments) to their actions is the *perception–choice process*. This is the process that brings about action (or inaction); particular kinds of people in particular settings perceive particular action alternatives and make particular choices in response to the motivations they experience. Factors that (directly as *causes*, or indirectly as *causes of the causes*) influence the perception–choice process are those that have causal relevance in the explanation of human action (see further Wikström, 2011).

## The situational model: The PEA hypothesis

The core hypothesis of SAT's situational model for the explanation of action (including acts of crime) is as follows: for any particular motivation (temptation or provocation), the resulting action ($A$) is an outcome of a perception–choice process ($\rightarrow$) that results from the interaction ($\times$) between relevant personal propensities ($P$) and exposure to relevant setting inducements ($E$).

$$P \times E \rightarrow A$$

The perception–choice process ($\rightarrow$) may be more or less automated depending on the circumstances (as discussed further below). Changes in people's action are a result of changes in their propensities or exposure, or both. The key elements of the PEA hypothesis are defined in Table 22.1.

Few criminological theories (including routine activity[16] and Cornish & Clarke's version of rational choice theory) pay much attention to what it is they aim to explain (i.e., crime). This is problematic because to explain something we first need to be clear about what it is we aim to explain. A cause has to be a cause of *something* and an explanation has to explain *something*. Clearly, defining what it is we aim to explain when we theorize about the causes of crime helps delimit what personal and environmental factors and what interactional action processes may be causally relevant.

Situational action theory asserts that humans are essentially rule-guided creatures, and society (social order) is based on shared rules of conduct (see further Wikström, 2010). SAT defines and analyzes acts of crime as *moral actions*, that is, "actions which are guided by value-based rules of conduct specifying what is the right or wrong thing to do (or not do) in response to particular motivations in particular circumstances." Acts of *crime* are defined as "breaches of rules of conduct stated in

**Table 22.1**  Definitions of key elements of the PEA hypothesis.

| | |
|---|---|
| **Person** | A body with a biological and psychological make-up, experiences and agency (powers to make things happen intentionally) |
| **Setting** | The part of the environment (the configuration of objects, people and events) a person can access with his or her senses (e.g., see, hear, feel) at a particular moment in time, including any media present (e.g., internet) |
| **Motivation** | Goal-directed attention (e.g., temptation, provocation) |
| **Personal propensities** | A person's (somewhat stable) tendencies to act in certain ways in response to particular environmental incitements |
| **Setting inducements** | Particular environmental conditions and events that tend to activate particular propensities |
| **Exposure** | A person in a setting |
| **Action** | Bodily movements under a person's guidance (e.g., speaking, hitting) |

law," and this is what all acts of crime, in all places, at all times, have in common. SAT asserts that there is no principle difference between explaining acts of crime and rule-breaking more generally; the same process which explains why people follow or break the rules of law should also explain why people break other kinds of moral rules (e.g., informal social norms). To explain acts of crime is to explain why people break rules of conduct stated in law.

Against this background (crime as rule-breaking behavior), SAT proposes that people's *crime propensity* is largely dependent on their law-relevant *personal morals* (internalized rules of conduct including supporting moral emotions such as shame and guilt) and their *ability to exercise self-control* (their ability to withstand external pressure to act against their own personal morals). People are seen as varying from highly crime averse (for whom few if any acts of crime are regarded as morally acceptable) to highly crime prone (for whom many if not most acts of crime are seen as morally acceptable). The closer a person's personal morals are to the rules of conduct stated in law, the less prone he or she is to violate these rules. The stronger a person's ability to exercise self-control, the less likely he or she is to be enticed to act contrary to his or her own personal morals.

Settings vary strongly in their criminogenic features. SAT proposes that the criminogeneity of a setting depends on the moral context (the moral norms and their enforcement) of the opportunities it provides and/or the frictions it generates. Settings are *criminogenic* to the extent that their (perceived) moral norms, and their level of enforcement, encourage (or do not discourage) acts of crime in response to the opportunities they provide and/or the frictions they create.[17] A *criminogenic setting* is thus a setting in which the (perceived) moral context encourages (or at least does not discourage) particular acts of crime in response to its particular opportunities or frictions. Acts of crime are most likely to occur when a crime prone person intersects with a criminogenic setting.

## The key elements and steps of the action process in crime causation

SAT's action process of crime causation and its key elements are illustrated in Figure 22.2. Motivation is what initiates the action process. *Motivation* is a situational concept and may be defined as "goal-directed attention." Two main kinds of motivation are temptation and provocation. *Temptation* occurs when there is an opportunity to satisfy a desire (want, need) or to honor a commitment. *Provocation* occurs when people encounter frictions (unwanted interferences) that cause upset or anger.

What kind of desires a person has (which in some cases may show short-term temporal variation due to saturation effects) depends on his or her biological needs and socially developed preferences. What kinds of commitments a person has entered into depends on his or her social circumstances (e.g., the kind and content of his or her social network and the activities they are engaged in). What kinds of frictions cause upset and anger depends on socially developed and biologically grounded sensitivities. A person's preferences, commitments and sensitivities

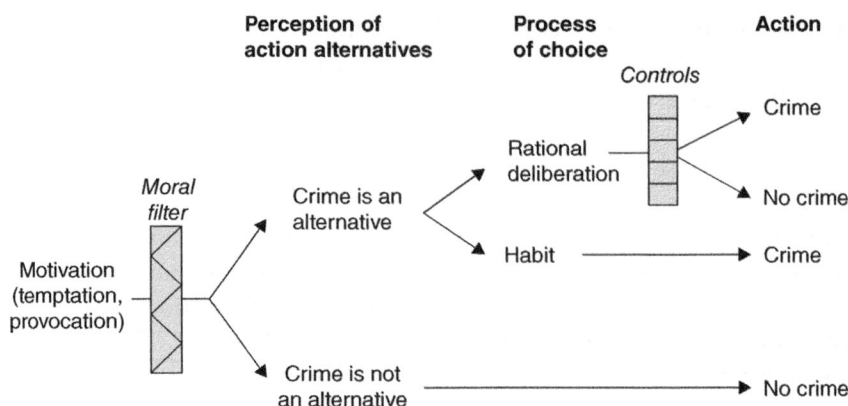

**Figure 22.2**   Key elements and steps in the situational process of SAT. *Source:* Wikström P-O H. (2011). "Does Everything Matter? Addressing the Problem of Causation and Explanation in the Study of Crime." In J. McGloin, C. J. Sullivan, and L. W. Kennedy (Eds.), *When Crime Appears. The Role of Emergence.* London. Routledge.

determine what kinds of opportunities and frictions are relevant for creating temptations and provocations. Motivation is the reason for action; we act because we are tempted or provoked to do so.

However, there are many different possible action alternatives in response to a particular motivation (of which one is inaction). What *action alternatives* a person perceives in relation to a specific temptation or provocation (and whether or not these alternatives include an act of crime) depends on his or her relevant personal morals and the (perceived) relevant moral norms of the setting in which he or she takes part. People vary in their relevant personal morals, settings vary in their (perceived) relevant moral norms, and their interaction will guide what kinds of action alternatives a person perceives as potential responses to a temptation or provocation. The application of relevant personal morals and perceived relevant moral norms of the setting to a particular motivation (temptation or provocation) is referred to in SAT as *the moral filter* (defined as "the moral rule-induced selective perception of action alternatives in relation to a particular motivation").

People make *choices* ("form intentions to act in a certain way") among the action alternatives they perceive in relation to a particular motivation (temptation or provocation). The process of choice is *only* relevant in crime causation if at least one of the perceived action alternatives involves an act of crime. If the person does not see crime as an action alternative there will be no crime and the process of choice and controls (the ability to exercise self-control and deterrence) will lack explanatory relevance. In this case the person does not choose not to commit an act of crime, nor does he or she refrain from crime because of the influence of controls. He or she just does not see an act of crime as an option.[18]

People's process of choice is predominantly habitual or deliberate (on dual thought-processes generally see, e.g., Evans & Frankish, 2009; Kahneman, 2003).[19]

Sometimes, people commit crimes out of habit; at other times their crimes are an outcome of a (more or less elaborate) rational deliberation. When people commit crime out of habit, controls play no role in the process of choice.

*Habitual* (or automated) *choices* are based on the application of a person's moral habits (automated rules of conduct) to a temptation or provocation. When acting out of habit, a person acts as he or she normally does in response to a particular motivation in a particular kind of setting without giving it much thought. Habitual choices are likely when people act in familiar circumstances where there is a close correspondence between their personal morals and the (perceived) moral norms of the setting. Habitual choices may also be likely in highly stressful and emotionally charged circumstances (even if the setting is unfamiliar). A habitual choice involves seeing only *one* potent alternative for action (although the actor may be loosely aware in the back of his or her mind that there are other alternatives). Habitual choices are oriented towards the past; "the control of action is outsourced to the environment so that sequences of prior action are triggered automatically by the appropriate circumstance" (Verplanken & Wood, 2006:93).

*Deliberate* (or reasoned) *choices* involve some assessment of the pros and cons of *more than one* potent alternative for action (which may include the choice to do nothing) and may also involve elements of problem-solving. People apply *free will* when they deliberate because there is no predetermined alternative for action. However, and importantly, it is free will constrained by the action alternatives a person perceives. Deliberation is future-oriented; "deliberation does not refer to the past but only to the future and what is possible" (Aristotle, 1999:149). Deliberate choices are most likely in unfamiliar circumstances and circumstances in which personal morals and the perceived moral norms of the setting provide conflicting or unclear rule-guidance (e.g., the person is uncertain what moral norms apply in the setting). They are *rational* in the sense that the person aims to select the best out of the action alternatives perceived. However, SAT does not view personal advantage as the basis for making a rational choice. Rather, what the actor regards as the "best alternative" is fundamentally a question of what he or she sees as *a morally acceptable means* to best satisfy a particular temptation or respond to a specific provocation given the circumstances (i.e., the most beneficial, pleasing or proportionate alternative within the constraints of what he or she regards as morally acceptable given the circumstances). SAT thus asserts that people's action choices are essentially rule-guided and not primarily driven by self-interest (i.e., by a wish to optimize personal advantage).[20] Whether or not a crime will occur is dependent on the outcome of the actor's assessment of the pros and cons of different perceived criminal and other action alternatives.

Only when people deliberate may *controls* play a role in the process of choice. *Control* is conceptualized in SAT as a situational process and is defined as "the process by which a person manages conflicting rule-guidance in his or her choice of action in relation to a particular motivation." Control processes may be internal (self-control) or external (deterrence) in origin. When people deliberate, self-control helps people comply with their own personal moral rules, while deterrence impels people to comply with the moral norms of a setting.

*Self-control* is defined as "the process by which a person succeeds in adhering to a personal moral rule when it conflicts with the (perceived) moral norms of a setting."[21] The typical example here is withstanding peer pressure when challenged to act against one's own personal morals.

*Deterrence* is defined as "the process by which the (perceived) enforcement of a setting's (perceived) moral norms (by creating concern or fear of consequences) succeeds in making a person adhere to the moral norms of the setting even though they conflict with his or her personal moral rules." The typical example here is when people who find a particular crime acceptable refrain from crime because environmental cues (such as the presence of police officers, guard dogs, or CCTV cameras) create concern or fear of the consequences. If the moral norms of the setting are in conflict with the rules of conduct stated in law, a high level of deterrence may be criminogenic (as may be the case, for example, in gangland settings when gang members enforce certain norms that conflict with the law).

The extent to which people commit crime (or different types of crime) out of habit or after some deliberation is largely unknown. However, since human actions to a large extent are habitual it would be surprising if there were not important elements of habit in peoples' criminality (particularly in their persistent criminality).

## Contrasting key assumptions of SAT and opportunity theory (RAT + RCT)

Situational action theory posits that all people share a natural inclination to be rule-guided and therefore to act in accordance with personal rules of conduct and the behavioral norms of the settings in which they take part. This rule-guided behavior may not accord with the optimization of self-interested action outcomes through the maximization of personal gains and the minimization of personal costs, which is the hallmark of rational choice theory and theories like routine activity theory which rely on it as an action mechanism (Clarke, 2005, 2014a; Cornish & Clarke, 1986; Felson, 2006). While SAT does not deny that people at times may act to achieve gains and avoid costs, it posits they do so within the context of rule-guided choice.

SAT questions the assumption that human action is fundamentally self-interested. Human behavioral goals, especially in the social domain, are far more complicated, as are human perceptions of the value and relevance of expected outcomes. Ultimately, assuming people are generally self-interested, coupled with the additional assumption that people share similar preferences, does not contribute much to the understanding of differences in behavior. It is also an assumption that is almost impossible to falsify; "no example of an altruistic action can refute the view that there was an egoistic motive hidden behind it" (Popper [1956]1985:xx).

Because RAT and RCT assume self-interest and construe crimes as acts which provide quick, easy means of satisfying normal human desires or needs, they automatically presume, like control theories (e.g., Hirschi, 1969:34), that people have a relatively constant incentive to break rules of conduct, and hence find rule-breaking "unproblematic" (Clarke, 2005). SAT, on the other hand, assumes that because people are naturally inclined to follow rules of conduct, most people, most of the time, prefer to abide by them. Of course, not all people will agree with and care equally about following different rules; in fact, disagreeing with or not caring much about a particular rule is one major reason why people break rules of conduct (such as the law).

This does not mean SAT thinks controls (i.e., self-control and deterrence) are unimportant for crime causation. On the contrary, SAT highlights controls as key factors which may influence the process of choice. However, SAT emphasizes the fact that the relevance of controls is conditional: controls are relevant to crime involvement only when personal and environmental rule-guidance conflicts and people deliberate over whether or not to choose rule-breaking as their response to a particular motivator.

If people are naturally rule-guided, it makes sense that societies (communities) are based on shared rules of conduct. Such societal or community structures make less sense from a rational, self-interested perspective; why would we create a social structure at odds with our nature? Shared rules of conduct help members of a society or community predict others' behaviors, and responses to their own behaviors, and to act pro-socially. Crucially, societal *patterns* of human activities (routine activities) are much more easily explained by the assumption that people are rule-following creatures, than that their actions are primarily undertaken in pursuit of their self-interest.

Criminological theories rarely address the choice process, and those which do focus on the choice between alternatives and neglect the important first step of perceiving alternatives amongst which to choose. RAT does so because, for the most part, it ignores individual differences by focusing only on "likely" or "motivated offenders," who, it assumes, will perceive crime as an alternative whenever an opportunity presents itself. RCT provides more background, suggesting "motivated offenders" have already chosen crime as an alternative via a rational decision process prior to the point of action (made a standing decision to commit some kind of crime), but maintain that at the point of action the actor simply decides whether the circumstances are right.

Both of these perspectives seem to conflate motivation (goal-directed attention) and propensity (a personal tendency to behave in certain ways in response to particular motivations). SAT sees motivation as a situational concept, arising from the interaction between people's desires, commitments, and sensitivities, and settings' opportunities and frictions; and initiating the perception–choice process leading to action. Therefore, different people will respond differently to different motivators in different settings, and their goal-directed attention in a given situation cannot be predicted purely from their personal characteristics and experiences prior to their intersection with the action setting.

Because RAT presupposes criminal motivation as a precondition of criminal opportunities (the convergence of a motivated offender with suitable targets and a lack of guardianship) it sees the role of the setting in crime involvement as instrumental, setting the scene, as it were, for the act of crime to unfold. It is not interested in how settings influence different kinds of people (i.e., those who are not "motivated offenders"). SAT sees settings as playing a much more active role in people's perceptions and choice of preferred action, and emphasizes the critical importance of people's differential susceptibility to particular crime inducements, which lies at the core of the person–environment interaction.

Consequently, RAT and SAT focus on different key features of the setting. SAT focuses on the moral context of opportunities and frictions – the action-relevant moral norms of the setting and their level of enforcement – and how it influences the perception–choice process. Weak law-relevant moral norms may encourage, or at least not discourage, people to see crime as an action alternative. Weak enforcement of the rules of law means that if a person sees crime as an alternative, the setting may not exhibit strong enough external controls to deter him or her from choosing that alternative.

RAT focuses on suitable targets and (the absence of) capable guardians as key environmental influences, but these are poorly conceptualized (e.g., Madero-Hernandez & Fisher, 2012:7–8), especially in regards to their role in the action process. Essentially, suitable targets represent motivators (opportunities that may cause temptation or even sources of friction causing provocation), and capable guardians represent sources of supervision (deterrents). RAT implicitly, and sometimes even explicitly, assumes they exert a similar influence on all people (or even all motivated offenders), in line with the opportunity theory slogan "opportunity makes the thief." SAT, on the other hand, highlights the fact that in many situations, motivators or controls may be irrelevant because people have different desires, commitments and sensitivities, won't perceive crime as an alternative because of their personal morality and/or the moral norms of the setting, or make habitual choices.

The inclusion of habitual choices in the action decision process also sets SAT apart from RAT and RCT. Although RCT discusses habituation, as described above, as standing decisions, it does not fully engage with the idea of automatic, involuntary processes of choice. SAT, on the other hand, emphasizes the importance of these processes for guiding everyday decisions and potentially many decisions relating to crime involvement.

## Testability

According to Popper (1963) "the criterion of the scientific status of a theory is its falsifiability, or refutability, or testability." To be assessed and refined, theories must be testable. To be testable, a theory must have unambiguous predictions (testable consequences) that can be derived and empirically investigated. We argue that routine activity theory suffers from a lack of clear testable implications due to a lack of specificity in its key concepts and their relationships. Cornish & Clarke's RCT is explicitly uninterested in testability as it is more concerned with practical rather than scientific merit.

Most empirical studies of routine activity theory have analyzed the macro-level relationship between routine activities and crime rates. To operationalize routine activities, these studies tend to rely on crude proxy measures, such as sociodemographic features (e.g., indices of household characteristics to indicate levels of guardianship; see Cohen, Felson & Land, 1980) or land-use variables (e.g., to indicate place routine activities; see Rhodes & Conly, 1981; Felson, 1987), typically at the aggregate level (e.g., national, regional or neighborhood). A meta-analysis reports moderate empirical support for routine activities as a macro-level predictor of crime rates (Pratt & Cullen, 2005). However, aggregate level data may not be appropriate for testing RAT as micro-level processes lie at the core of its explanation of crime (Eck, 1995); hence, a true test of RAT would need to investigate the interaction of its key elements.

Bursik & Grasmick (1993) pointed out some time ago that the interactional model of RAT (i.e., the proposition that the *convergence* of a motivated offender and a suitable target in the absence of a capable guardian *creates* acts of crime) has never been convincingly tested (see also Eck, 1995). As far as we are aware, this statement still holds true. While this may seem surprising considering RAT's popularity, it is less surprising when you consider that RAT research suffers from a number of limitations, in particular loosely defined concepts (and consequently poor empirical indicators) and a lack of specification of the relationships between factors (and consequently a lack of explicit predictions) (see, e.g., Madero-Hernandez & Fisher, 2012:7). How does one empirically test a theory which argues that crime events ("any identifiable behavior that an appreciable number of governments has specifically prohibited and formally punished") are an outcome of the convergence of a motivated offender ("anybody who for any reason might commit a crime"), a suitable target ("any person or thing that draws the offender toward a crime") in the absence of a capable guardian ("a human element which acts… to deter the would-be offender from committing a crime against an available target")? Each of its key concepts not only lacks specificity, but is also in part defined by its effects on the actor or action. For example, a target is suitable *because* it draws a person towards committing a crime. This suggests that a target may be suitable for some people but not others – how do we then specify (and operationalize) what characterizes a suitable targets without better specifying what characterizes motivated (and, by contrast, unmotivated) offenders?

As for Cornish & Clarke's rational choice theory, Clarke even argues that the theory "was never intended to be 'tested' in the way criminologists routinely attempt to test a theory's validity by making predictions from the theory and seeing whether these predictions can be falsified by empirical data" (2014:xii). In fact, Clarke goes as far as to claim that "it is self-evidently true that offenders commit crimes in order to obtain some benefits" and therefore the theory "cannot be falsified by being 'tested to destruction'"[22] (ibid., xii). We agree with Popper (1963) that "irrefutability is not a virtue of a theory (as people often think) but a vice"; "a theory which is not refutable by any conceivable event is non-scientific."

Testability is a core aim of situational action theory, which has been developed alongside an in-depth longitudinal study specifically designed to test it (e.g., Wikström *et al.*, 2012). Thus SAT posits clear definitions for its key concepts and explicitly models how they are interrelated in explaining acts of crime. As a consequence, SAT has clear testable implications, and is thus more open to refutation, but also refinement.

## Conclusion

Criminological research has two well-documented and frequently replicated core findings:

1.  The distribution of crime in the population is highly skewed – a small minority of people are responsible for a majority of crimes (e.g., Piquero, Farrington & Blumstein, 2007:17–19; Wikström, 1990; Wikström *et al.*, 2012:113–117; Wolfgang, Figlio & Sellin, 1972).
2.  Crime events (and particular types of crime events) tend to be concentrated in space and time – sometimes referred to as hotspots (Baldwin & Bottoms, 1976; Sherman, Gartin, & Buerger, 1989; Weisburd, Morris, & Groff, 2009; Wikström, 1991; Wikström *et al.*, 2012:192).

Criminological theories tend to focus on explaining one or the other of these findings; rarely do they consider how both may be explained within a common theoretical framework. And yet, arguably, neither can be explained without taking the other into consideration. For example, the particular crime distribution in a population is dependent on how people's crime propensities and exposure to criminogenic settings are distributed in that population, and, crucially, how they combine.

Criminology has for some time lacked a truly situational theory of crime causation, evidenced by its confused usage of the term "situation" and its failure to address the two major foci of a situational theory: the interaction between people and settings, and the situational mechanism which links them to action. We have suggested that opportunity theory (a combination of routine activity theory and Cornish & Clarke's version of rational choice theory) is the closest criminologists in past decades have come to a situational theory, and considered the contributions and shortcomings of both theories' situational analysis of the causes of crime. We have highlighted RAT's contribution to criminological theory through its emphasis on the convergence of people and place, but criticized its lack of conceptual clarity, especially in regards to individual differences, and its failure to posit a situational mechanism explaining how the convergence it describes leads to crime. We have likewise highlighted RCT's contribution to criminological theory through its emphasis on (rational) decision-making as a situational mechanism linking people and settings to action, but criticized a number of the assumptions upon which RCT relies, including the assumption that people are self-interested, and the fact that RCT tacitly overlooks more automated decision processes.

Both RAT and RCT have criticized criminological theorizing for focusing on the distribution of crime in the population (crime propensity) and used this as a rationale for focusing on the distribution of crime in space and time (criminogenic features of the environment), though it is difficult to see any strong rationale for why either of these two key insights should be ignored. As a consequence, situational theories have become synonymous with opportunity theories in criminology, despite the fact that the latter are essentially concerned with how the immediate environment incites people (motivated offenders) to engage in acts of crime, and say little to nothing about the role of the offender and the person–environment interaction.

Arguably, a proper explanation of the causes of crime needs to take both differential crime propensity and differential criminogeneity of places into account. SAT aims to provide a detailed, testable framework explaining crime as the outcome of a perception–choice process guided by the interaction of personal moral rules and the moral rules of the setting and their levels of enforcement (controls). We have argued that it provides an alternative situational theory to opportunity theory, offering greater conceptual and analytical clarity in regards to the interaction between people and settings and the action mechanism which links them to acts of crime.

## Notes

1   Lewin distinguishes between momentary and life situations, the latter referring to the social context of the person in question (e.g., his or her family and work circumstances) and serving as the "background" to the momentary situation, i.e., the combination of the states of a person and of his or her environment that brings about particular actions (see Lewin, 1936:22–23).

2   This was famously captured in the formula $B = f(S)$, where $B$ stands for *behavior* and $S$ for *situation*, and where Lewin defined situation ($S$) as $f(P,E)$, where $P$ stands for *person* and $E$ for *environment* (Lewin, 1936:12).

3   He specifies that "situations have both spatial and temporal dimensions: they are specific locations at particular points in time. Situational factors include tangible elements such as the physical aspects of the immediate environment and the behaviour of the people who are present. Somewhat less tangibly, situations can also refer to a state of affairs or set of circumstances at a given moment" (Wortley, 2012:186).

4   The concepts of *likely* and *motivated offender* seems to be used interchangeably by authors writing in the routine activity tradition. In this chapter we will also use the two concepts interchangeably.

5   The scope of the theory has subsequently been extended to include all kinds of crime (e.g., Felson & Boba, 2010).

6   However, in an earlier publication Felson argues that viewing crime in terms of physical science concepts such as chemistry is "too mechanical" and that he now prefers to think about crime in terms of life sciences because "it does allow choices and alternatives, basic to our concept of life itself" (2008:76). The concepts of choices and alternatives are central to Situational Action Theory (e.g., Wikström, 2004, 2006), which is discussed later in this chapter.

7   As a predictive model, we would argue that Brantingham & Brantingham's (1993) Crime Pattern Theory is conceptually much clearer and analytically stronger when it comes to explicating the reasons for where and when crime will occur.

8   Which probably more adequately should read "theories of criminal propensity" rather than "theories of criminal motivation."

9   "Without denying the importance of factors motivating offenders to engage in crime, we have focused specific attention upon violations themselves and the prerequisites for their occurrence" (Cohen & Felson, 1979:605).

10  Cornish & Clarke prefer *perspective* to *theory* but we feel the latter is more appropriate considering its general applications.

11  Which may more adequately be labeled *propensity* (a somewhat stable tendency to react in particular ways to particular environmental inducements).

12  In response to criticism, RCT has considered the role of *precipitators* which may influence motivation at the point of action, as well as moral features of environments, such as *permissibility* and *excusability*, although Cornish & Clarke argue that these complications of the original RCT framework may be limited in their applicability and hence general relevance (Cornish & Clarke, 2003).

13  Again, which may be more adequately labeled propensity (i.e., a somewhat stable tendency to act in a certain way in response to particular environmental inducements).

14  Substantive rationality "is a theory of decision environments (and utility functions), but not of decision-makers" and ignores "*how* the decision-maker generates alternatives and compares them" (Simon, 1997:18; italics in original).

15  The figure is a version of what is sometimes called a Coleman diagram (or a "Coleman boat" or "bath tub"). However, the terminology and content is very different from that used by Coleman (1990:1–23).

16  Felson does define crime as "any identifiable behavior that an appreciable number of governments has specifically prohibited and formally punished" (2006:35), but this definition does not give much guidance to what a theory of crime causation should explain. For example, it is hardly helpful to assert that an identifiable behavior that an appreciable number of governments has specifically prohibited and formally punished will occur when a motivated offender and a suitable target converge in the absence of a capable guardian. In other words, Felson's definition of crime is pointless even in relation to his own theory.

17  If a setting has a high level of enforcement of moral norms promoting acts of crime in response to its particular opportunities or frictions, this enforcement is criminogenic.

18  Based on the assumption that people are essentially rule-guided creatures and social order is based on shared rules of conduct, SAT proposes that most people in most circumstances (in most societies at most times) do not see crime as an action alternative in response to the motivations they experience. This assumption is supported by the fact that most studies show that the distribution of crime in the population is highly skewed; the overwhelming majority of the population rarely gets involved in crime.

19  Although in longer action sequences it may drift between habitual and deliberate influences.

20  Whether or not people aim to maximize personal advantage in their deliberate choices of action alternatives in a particular circumstance is a question of moral judgment (dependent on the actor's relevant personal morals and the perceived relevant moral norms of the setting in which he or she takes part).

21   Self-control is generally defined in criminological theory as an individual characteristic (e.g., Gottfredson & Hirschi, 1990). SAT differentiates between "the ability to exercise self-control" (as part of what determines a person's crime propensity) and "exercising self-control" (as a situational process).

22   In the original the quote includes the word "being" twice: "cannot be falsified by being 'being tested to destruction.'" Assuming this to be a mistake, we have deleted one "being" from the quote.

# References

Aristotle (1999). *Nicomachean Ethics*. trans. M. Ostwald. Englewood Cliffs, NJ: Prentice Hall.

Baldwin, J., & Bottoms, A.E. (1976). *The Urban Criminal*. London: Tavistock.

Bargh, J. (1997). The automaticity of everyday life. In J. Bargh & R. Wyer (Eds.), *The Automaticity of Everyday Life. Advances in Social Cognition*, Vol. 10. Mahwah, NJ: Lawrence Erlbaum.

Birkbeck, C., & LaFree, G. (1993). The situational analysis of crime and deviance. *Annual Review of Sociology, 19*, 113–137.

Brantingham, P.L., & Brantingham, P.J. (1981). Notes on the geometry of crime. In P.J. Brantingham & P.L. Brantingham (Eds.), *Environmental Criminology* (pp. 27–54). London: Sage.

Brantingham, P.L., & Brantingham, P.J. (1993). Environment, routine, and situation: Toward a Pattern theory of crime. In R.V. Clarke & M. Felson (Eds.), *Routine Activity and Rational Choice: Advances in Criminological Theory*, Vol. 5 (pp. 259–294). New Brunswick, NJ: Transaction.

Bunge, S., & Wallis, D. (2008). *Neuroscience of Rule-Guided Behavior*. Oxford: Oxford University Press.

Bursik, R., & Grasmick, H. (1993). *Neighborhoods and Crime: The Dimensions of Effective Community Control*. New York: Lexington Books.

Clarke, R. (2004). Technology, criminology and crime science. *European Journal on Criminal Policy and Research, 10*, 55–63.

Clarke, R. (2005). Seven misconceptions of situational crime prevention. In N. Tilley (Ed.), *Handbook of Crime Prevention and Community Safety*. Collumpton: Willan.

Clarke, R. (2012). Opportunity makes the thief. Really? And so what? *Crime Science, 1*(3).

Clarke, R. (2014a). Affect and the reasoning criminal: Past and future. In J.-L. van Gelder, H. Elffers, D. Reynald, & D. Nagin (Eds.), *Affect and Cognition in Criminal Decision Making* (pp. 20–41). London: Routledge.

Clarke, R. (2014b). Introduction. In D. Cornish & R. Clarke (Eds.), *The Reasoning Criminal: Rational Choice Perspectives on Offending* (pp. ix–xvi). Piscataway, NJ: Transaction.

Clarke, R., & Cornish, D. (1985). Modelling offenders' decisions: A framework for research and policy. *Crime and Justice, 6*, 147–185.

Clarke, R., & Felson, M. (1993). *Routine Activity and Rational Choice. Advances in Criminological Theory*, Vol. 5. Piscataway, NJ: Transaction.

Cohen, L., & Felson, M. (1979). Social change and crime rate trends: A routine activity approach. *American Sociological Review, 44*(4), 588–608.

Cohen, L., Felson, M., & Land, K. (1980). Property crime rates in the United States: A macrodynamic analysis, 1947–1977 with ex ante forecasts for the mid-1980s. *American Journal of Sociology, 86*, 90–118.

Coleman, J. (1990). *Foundations of Social Theory*. Cambridge, MA: Belknap Press.

Coleman, J., & Fararo, T. (1992). Introduction. In J. Coleman & T. Fararo (Eds.), *Rational Choice Theory: Advocacy and Critique*. Newbury Park, CA: Sage.

Cornish, D., & Clarke, R. (1986). *The Reasoning Criminal: Rational Choice Perspectives on Offending*. New York: Springer-Verlag.

Cornish, D., & Clarke, R. (2003). Opportunities, precipitators and criminal decisions: A reply to Wortley's critique of situational crime prevention. *Crime Prevention Studies*, 16, 41–96.

Cornish, D., & Clarke, R. (2008). The rational choice perspective. In R. Wortley & L. Mazerolle (Eds.), *Environmental Criminology and Crime Analysis* (pp. 21–47). Oxford: Routledge.

Cornish, D., & Clarke, R. (2014). *The Reasoning Criminal: Rational Choice Perspectives on Offending*. Piscataway, NJ: Transaction.

Davidson, D. (2004). *Problems of Rationality*. Oxford: Clarendon Press.

Eck, J. (1995). Examining routine activity theory: A review of two books. *Justice Quarterly*, 12, 783–797.

Elster, J. (2007). *Explaining Social Behavior: More Nuts and Bolts For the Social Sciences*. Cambridge: Cambridge University Press.

Evans, J., & Frankish, K. (2009). *In Two Minds: Dual Processes and Beyond*. Oxford: Oxford University Press.

Felson, M. (1987). Routine activities and crime prevention in the developing metropolis. *Criminology*, 25, 911–931.

Felson, M. (2006). *Crime and Nature*. Thousand Oaks, CA: Sage.

Felson, M. (2008). Routine activity approach. In R. Wortley & L. Mazerolle (Eds.), *Environmental Criminology and Crime Analysis* (pp. 70–77). Oxford: Routledge.

Felson, M., & Boba, R. (2010). *Crime and Everyday Life*. London: Sage.

Felson, M., & Clarke, R. (1998). *Opportunity Makes the Thief: Practical Theory for Crime Prevention*. London: Home Office, Policing and Reducing Crime Unit, Research, Development and Statistics Directorate.

Felson, M., & Cohen, L. (1980). Human ecology and crime: A routine activity approach. *Human Ecology*, 8(4), 389–406.

Gottfredson, M., & Hirschi, T. (1990). *A General Theory of Crime*. Stanford, CA: Stanford University Press.

Hindelang, M.J., Gottfredson, M., & Garofalo, J. (1978). *Victims of Personal Crime: An Empirical Foundation for a Theory of Personal Victimization*. Cambridge, MA: Ballinger.

Hirschi, T. (1969). *Causes of Delinquency*. Berkeley, CA: University of California Press.

Hollis, M., Felson, M., & Welsh, B. (2013). The capable guardian in routine activities theory: A theoretical and conceptual reappraisal. *Crime Prevention & Community Safety*, 15(1), 65–79.

Kahenman, D. (2003). A perspective on judgment and choice: Mapping bounded rationality. *American Psychologist*, 58, 697–720.

Leclerc, B., & Wortley, R. (2014). The reasoning criminal: Twenty-five years on. In B. Leclerc & R. Wortley (Eds.), *Cognition and Crime: Offender Decision Making and Script Analyses* (pp. 1–11). Oxford: Routledge.

Lewin, K. (1936). *Principles of Topological Psychology*. New York: McGraw-Hill.

Lyons, D., Young, A., & Keil, F. (2007). The hidden structure of overimitation. *Proceedings of the National Academy of Sciences*, 104(50), 19751–19756.

Madero-Hernandez, A., & Fisher, S. (2012). Routine activity theory. In F.T. Cullen & P. Wilcox (Eds.), *The Oxford Handbook of Criminological Theory*. Oxford: Oxford University Press.

Piquero, A., Farrington, D., & Blumstein, A. (2007). *Key Issues in Criminal Career Research: New Analyses of the Cambridge Study in Delinquent Development.* Cambridge: Cambridge University Press.

Popper, K. (1963). *Conjectures and Refutations: The Growth of Scientific Knowledge.* London: Routledge.

Popper, K. (1985[1956]). *Realism and the Aim of Science.* Trans. W. Bartley. London: Routledge.

Pratt, T., & Cullen, F. (2005). Assessing macro-level predictors and theories of crime: A meta-analysis. In M. Tonry (Ed.), *Crime and Justice: A Review of Research,* Vol. *32* (pp. 373–450). Chicago, IL: University of Chicago Press.

Rhodes, W., & Conly, C. (1981). Crime and mobility: An empirical study. In P. Brantingham & P. Brantingham (Eds.), *Environmental Criminology.* Beverly Hills, CA: Sage.

Sherman, L., Gartin, P., & Buerger, M. (1989). Hot spots of predatory crime: Routine activities and the criminology of place. *Criminology, 27*(1), 27–55.

Simon, H. (1997). *An Empirically Based Microeconomics.* Cambridge: Cambridge University Press.

Smith, M., & Clarke, R. (2012). Situational crime prevention: Classifying techniques using "good enough" theory. In B. Welsh & D. Farrington (Eds.), *The Oxford Handbook of Crime Prevention* (pp. 291–315). Oxford: Oxford University Press.

Treiber, K. (2011). The neuroscientific basis of situational action theory. In K. Beaver & A. Walsh (Eds.), *The Ashgate Research Companion to Biosocial Theories of Crime* (pp. 213–246). Surrey: Ashgate.

Verplanken, B., & Wood, W. (2006). Interventions to break and create consumer habits. *Journal of Public Policy & Marketing, 25*(1), 90–103.

Weisburd, D., Morris, N., & Groff, E. (2009). Hot spots of juvenile crime: A longitudinal study of arrest incidents at street segments in Seattle, Washington. *Journal of Quantitative Criminology, 25,* 443–467.

Wellmans, H., & Miller, J. (2008). Including deontic reasoning as fundamental to theory of mind. *Human Development, 51,* 105–135.

Wikström, P-O H. (1990). Age and crime in a Stockholm cohort. *Journal of Quantitative Criminology, 6*(1), 61–84.

Wikström, P-O H. (1991). *Urban Crime, Criminals and Victims.* New York: Springer-Verlag.

Wikström, P-O H. (2004). Crime as alternative: Towards a cross-level situational action theory of crime causation. In J. McCord (Ed.), *Beyond Empiricism: Institutions and Intentions in the Study of Crime* (pp. 1–38). New Brunswick, NJ: Transaction.

Wikström, P-O H. (2005). The social origins of pathways in crime: Towards a developmental ecological action theory of crime involvement and its changes. In D. Farrington (Ed.), *Integrated Developmental and Life-Course Theories of Offending. Advances in Criminological Theory,* Vol. *14* (pp. 211–246). New Brunswick, NJ: Transaction.

Wikström, P-O H. (2006). Individuals, settings, and acts of crime: Situational mechanisms and the explanation of crime. In P-O H. Wikström & R.J. Sampson (Eds.), *The Explanation of Crime: Context, Mechanisms and Development* (pp. 61–107). Cambridge: Cambridge University Press.

Wikström, P-O H. (2010). Explaining crime as moral actions. In S. Hitlin & S. Vaisey (Eds.), *Handbook of the Sociology of Morality* (pp. 211–239). New York: Springer-Verlag.

Wikström, P-O H. (2011). Does everything matter? Addressing problems of causation and explanation in the study of crime. In J.M. McGloin, C.J. Silverman, & L.W. Kennedy (Eds.), *When Crime Appears: The Role of Emergence* (pp. 53–72). New York: Routledge.

Wikström, P-O H. (2014). Why crime happens: A situational action theory. In G. Manzo (Ed.), *Analytical Sociology: Actions and Networks* (pp. 74–94). Sussex: Wiley.

Wikström, P-O H., & Treiber, K. (forthcoming). A dynamic and analytical approach to crime prevention. In. B. Teasdale, & M.S. Bradley (Eds.). *Preventing Crime and Violence. Advances in Prevention Science*, Vol. 2. London: Springer.

Wikström, P-O H., Oberwittler, D., Treiber, K., & Hardie, B. (2012). *Breaking Rules: The Social and Situational Dynamics of Young People's Urban Crime*. Oxford: Oxford University Press.

Wikström, P-O H., & Sampson, R. (2003). Social mechanisms of community influences on crime and pathways in criminality. In B. Lahey, T. Moffitt, & A. Caspi (Eds.), *The Causes of Conduct Disorder and Serious Juvenile Delinquency*. New York: Guilford Press.

Wittek, R., Snijders, T., & Nee, V. (2013). Introduction: Rational choice social research. In R. Wittek, T. Snijders, & V. Nee (Eds.), *The Handbook of Rational Choice Social Research*. Stanford: Stanford University Press.

Wolfgang, M., Figlio, R., & Sellin, T. (1972). *Delinquency in a Birth Cohort*. Chicago, IL: University of Chicago Press.

Wood, W., & Quinn, J. (2005). Habits and the structure of motivation in everyday life. In J. Forgas, K. Williams, & S. Laham (Eds.), *Social Motivation: Conscious and Unconscious Processes* (pp. 55–70). Cambridge: Cambridge University Press.

Wortley, R. (2012). Exploring the person-situation interaction in situational crime prevention. In N. Tilley & G. Farrell (Eds.), *The Reasoning Criminologist: Essays in Honour of Ronald V. Clarke* (pp. 184–193). London: Routledge.

# 23

# Macro-Level Theory: A Critical Component of Criminological Exploration

## Eric P. Baumer and Ashley N. Arnio

### Introduction

Criminological theories often are classified by "levels of explanation," with perhaps the most significant distinction coming between macro-level perspectives and micro-level (or individual-level) perspectives (Akers & Sellers, 2012; Rosenfeld, 2011; Sutherland, 1947).[1] Such classifications can be useful, as they provide a means by which the research questions that define a discipline's subject matter may be subdivided. Further, these sorts of classification schemes can assist a community of scholars in organizing large and complex literatures. In criminology, it is clear that the macro–micro distinction has had many beneficial consequences; there are vibrant strands of both macro- and micro-level theoretical and empirical scholarship (e.g., Sampson & Lauritsen, 1994), and also growing interests in integrating insights across levels (e.g., Miethe & Meier, 1994; Meier, Kennedy, & Sacco, 2001; Messner, 2012; Messner, Krohn, & Liska, 1989; Wilcox, Land, & Hunt, 2003). However, there are also drawbacks to classifying complex theoretical ideas into such broad categories; in particular, there is a risk that the categories themselves become unnecessarily rigid, forcing scholars to frame iterations of theories to fit the macro–micro classification scheme and therefore limiting theoretical progress rather than allowing it to flourish. In our judgment, this has been one of the unfortunate consequences of the macro–micro distinction applied in assessments of criminological theory, and it provides an important backdrop to the subject matter of this chapter – an overview of *macro*-level theory.

The macro–micro distinction drawn in the criminological theoretical literature often has yielded a mischaracterization of the focus, purpose, and breadth of macro-level inquiry, while also framing macro- and micro-level perspectives as oriented

*The Handbook of Criminological Theory*, First Edition. Edited by Alex R. Piquero.
© 2016 John Wiley & Sons, Inc. Published 2016 by John Wiley & Sons, Inc.

toward fundamentally different questions and as largely incompatible with one another. Though this is perhaps an expected outcome given the "competition orientation" that historically has governed theoretical developments in criminology (Hirschi, 1989), we believe that it may have unnecessarily constrained the depth and power of proposed explanations. In short, though it has had some positive benefits, the macro–micro divide in criminology seems to have contributed to misperceptions that macro-level theories are not pertinent to explaining criminal behavior among individuals, and that micro-level theories are not relevant to explaining differences in criminal behavior across social collectivities. Despite positive signs to the contrary (Coleman, 1986; Matsueda, 2013a), such views continue to populate the theoretical landscape, with a relatively strong distinction made in many contemporary theoretical texts between macro- and individual-level perspectives, and continued reference to how these approaches are directed at different questions. Two overarching objectives of our chapter are to counter unproductive distinctions between macro- and individual-level theories, and to minimize the parochialism that could emerge from a theoretical contribution that focuses exclusively on one of these approaches.

With this backdrop in mind, we begin our review by highlighting the common ground between macro- and micro-level inquiries, while also delineating what we see as the defining elements of macro-level criminological theory. We advance the position that most macro- and micro-level theories are directed at explaining the same outcome – variability in criminal behavior – while emphasizing unique explanatory variables. In light of this commonality and their complementary contributions, we emphasize that both macro- and micro-level perspectives are critical for developing a comprehensive understanding of criminal behavior. After laying this important conceptual foundation, we review the basic causal arguments advanced in several macro-level theories. Given that these perspectives have been reviewed elsewhere, including in some cases other chapters in this volume, we present succinct overviews rather than in-depth discussions. We focus more attention, however, on situating macro-level theories within a conceptual framework that seems well-suited for illuminating parallels with and potential connections to individual-level theories. We close by suggesting ways in which macro- and micro-level theories can be improved by joining forces to advance important developments in multilevel theoretical inquiry (e.g., Miethe & Meier, 1994; Messner, 2012; Wilcox *et al.*, 2003).[2]

## Common Ground and Distinguishing Features

Macro- and micro-level theories are frequently described as addressing fundamentally different questions, with micro-level theories seeking to advance understanding of why individuals engage in crime, and macro-level theories devoted instead to explaining variation across social or geographic areas in rates of crime (Brown, Esbensen, & Geis, 2013; Tibbets, 2012; Vito & Maahs, 2012). Perhaps because of the tendency to draw such heavy lines of demarcation, there have been intense debates in which strong arguments are advanced in favor of macro- *or* micro-level explanations (c.f., Agnew, 1987; Bernard, 1987a, b). We appreciate the historical significance of such debates but, as noted above, the position that frames this chapter is quite different.

Our view is that although macro- and individual-level theories tend to be applied in different settings and for what often are characterized as different purposes, in most instances they address the same fundamental issue: Which factors increase or decrease criminal behavior (see also Akers & Sellers, 2012)? As we elaborate below, although macro- and individual-level theories emphasize different types of explanatory factors or, to use Coleman's (1986) language, their critical ingredients occupy different corners of the "boat" (see Sampson, 2012), their basic purposes are quite similar. These purposes are sometimes expressed in ways that look different, but both macro- and micro-level theories of crime are concerned with illuminating the conditions that render crime and victimization to be more common and/or more frequent among individuals exposed to different conditions. Further, both types of perspectives are concerned with identifying factors that affect criminality and/or the occurrence of crime among those criminally inclined. Thus, macro- and micro-level theories in criminology share a common focus; they simply emphasize different types of explanatory factors.

It is unclear to us why many theoretical discussions seem to underappreciate this common ground between macro- and micro-level explanations. Perhaps it is a collateral consequence of historical tensions that emerged in debates over whether non-normative behaviors emanate from internal malfunctions or from external environmental conditions (e.g., Durkheim, 1951[1897]; Lombroso, 2006[1896–97]). Alternatively, it could be a function of the territoriality that has been attributed to theoretical developments in criminology (Hirshi, 1989), or maybe it stems from the unavailability – until quite recently – of multilevel data on individuals situated within different macro-level "contexts," which makes more obvious the common ground shared by macro- and micro-level perspectives. Irrespective of whether these broader considerations have merit, it seems likely that at least part of the reason that macro- and micro-level theories are considered as different classes of explanations relevant to distinct questions or problems is because of ambiguity about units of analysis, the meaning of aggregate or "group-level" measures of crime and victimization *vis-à-vis* individual-level measures of these behaviors, and more general confusion associated with moving *between* micro- and macro-levels of explanation (Matsueda, 2013a).

Discussions of macro-level theory are often synonymous with references to fully macro-level research designs (e.g., analyses conducted across social collectivities or geographic areas), and we fear that this has led many to conclude – in our view, incorrectly – that the distinguishing feature of macro-level theory is that it relies on a different unit of analysis (e.g., neighborhoods, cities, nations) than is the case with individual-level theories, and thus by implication that the two types of theories address different substantive questions. It is true that macro-level theories often are assessed with aggregate-level research designs for which the units of analysis are geographic areas defined in various ways, with crime and/or victimization measured as rates (see Pratt & Cullen, 2005). But, this methodological approach is not a necessary means by which to assess their causal arguments (Baumer, 2007), nor is it the feature that distinguishes them theoretically from micro-level perspectives. Liska (1990) provides a rich discussion of why this is the case, building on Lazarsfeld & Menzel's (1961) conceptual scheme that organizes group-level variables in terms of their defining properties.

As Liksa (1990) explains, Lazarsfeld & Menzel (1961) distinguish between analytical (i.e., aggregate) attributes, which reflect mathematically derived summaries of social collectivities or places based on the statistical aggregation of individual analogues within them, and global (i.e., emergent) and structural group properties, which refer to unique aggregate conditions that do not have individual-level analogues (i.e., they cannot be reduced to the sum of their parts or measured by combining individual-level responses). In our view, crime and victimization rates for a given group or geographic area, which represent the aggregated sum of individual criminal acts within them divided by a quantity that captures the relative crime potential (usually the population size), are good examples of analytical or aggregate properties, as defined by Lazarsfeld & Menzel (1961). As we elaborate below, the same logic does not apply to most of the group or place properties emphasized as explanatory variables in macro-level criminological theories, which should be instead viewed as structural or global attributes (see also Messner & Rosenfeld, 1994; Sampson, 2012). The key point we wish to emphasize at this juncture is that the most common dependent variables implied in macro-level theories of crime (e.g., crime and victimization rates) are, to use the language applied by Lazarsfeld & Menzel (1961), analytical properties that represent the aggregation of individual criminal acts. This illuminates the important common ground that we believe underlies macro- and micro-level theoretical frameworks in criminology – the focus on highlighting how selected attributes make criminal acts more (or less) likely by increasing criminality (i.e., criminal propensity) and/or by structuring situations or opportunities for criminal acts or events to unfold.

Setting aside this commonality for a moment, how do macro- and micro-level frameworks differ? What are their distinguishing features? Put simply, it is in the nature of the explanatory factors they emphasize. Whereas micro-level perspectives highlight attributes of individuals and interpersonal interactions, the defining feature of macro-level theories is their focus on the "bigger picture" (Rosenfeld, 2011), explanatory factors that represent properties of social collectivities and/or geographic areas, (e.g., neighborhoods, counties, states, and nations). Some of the attributes considered (e.g., economic disadvantage) are common to several macro-level criminological perspectives, but as we elaborate below a large number and wide variety of group- or place-level conditions (e.g., racial and ethnic heterogeneity, residential instability, social disorganization, differential social organization, collective efficacy, anomie, and high levels of strain) have been encompassed within the literature. Further, in many instances, the explanatory factors highlighted in macro-level theories are conceptualized as structural or global attributes, emerging as conditions that reflect group-level products of a complex integration of attitudes and interactions that cannot be reduced to individual attributes. The next section delves deeper into the major macro-level perspectives that have emerged in criminology, briefly illuminating the key explanatory conditions they emphasize, summarizing the logic of their core causal arguments, and organizing them into a conceptual scheme that contrasts their relative focus on mechanisms of constraint, motivation/ propensity, and opportunity/situational attributes that may be conducive to crime. Before doing so, however, we want to reiterate three implications of our discussion for both the common ground that exists between macro- and micro-level theoretical arguments and the unique features that define macro-level theories.

First, conceiving crime and victimization rates as "analytical variables" (see Liska, 1990), while emphasizing the distinctive focus of macro-level theories on explanatory factors that reflect properties of social collectivities and/or places, should make it apparent that we are not advancing a position that macro-level theories are simply aggregations of individual-level arguments, a position that is sometimes referenced as methodological-individualism (Sutherland, 1947). Instead, our view of macro-level theory is sensitive to the important nuances and complexities associated with the macro–micro distinction in other fields (Coleman, 1986), and is consistent with arguments that affirm the potentially profound role of group- and place-based social context for involvement in crime (e.g., Rosenfeld, 2011; Sampson, 2012).

Second, acknowledging flexibility in the level of measurement for crime in assessing macro-level theories while also highlighting the distinctive feature of macro-level theory – its emphasis on attributes of social collectivities as explanatory variables – reveals that both aggregate- and multilevel analytical designs are appropriate for assessing macro-level theories. Multilevel designs (e.g., individuals nested within places) are perhaps ideal because they permit an assessment of how involvement in crime might vary across places as a function of global or structural contextual attributes while accounting for differences across places in population composition. Additionally, multilevel research approaches make possible analyses that explore the role of both micro- and macro-level intervening variables and theoretically informed cross-level interactions that may shape not only criminality but also the occurrence of criminal acts (Meier *et al.*, 2001). The "analytical" measurement characteristic of crime rates for groups or places also means that aggregate-level designs are suitable for evaluating the core relationships that form the basis of most macro-level theories (Baumer, 2007; Liska, 1990).

Third, though much of the remainder of our chapter is focused exclusively on macro-level theories, our hope is that by clarifying both the common ground that they share with micro-level perspectives (i.e., their mutual attention to explaining differential involvement in crime) and the unique explanatory elements they emphasize (i.e., properties of social collectivities and/or geographic areas), the possibilities for theoretical integration are made more obvious. Rather than being incompatible, macro-level and individual-level theories have much to offer one another (Rosenfeld, 2011; Wilcox *et al.*, 2003), a theme to which we return after more clearly delineating the defining features of macro-level theories and providing an overview of the most commonly applied perspectives.

# Organizing and Evaluating Macro-Level Theories of Crime

## General considerations

Other chapters in this volume provide detailed descriptions of selected theories frequently classified as macro-level perspectives (e.g., social disorganization, general deterrence, routine activities). Additionally, there are several previously published overviews that cover these and other pertinent frameworks (e.g., Adler & Laufer, 1995; Akers & Sellers, 2012; Baumer, 2007; Kubrin & Weitzer, 2003; Messner & Rosenfeld, 1994; Miller, 2014). We provide a review of macro-level theory and research in this section as well, but with a different purpose. Specifically, we focus on outlining the basic causal arguments contained in these perspectives in a succinct manner, while devoting greater attention to organizing them within a conceptual framework that has been developed and applied constructively to individual-level theories (Tittle, 1995). This conceptual scheme situates theories on the basis of their primary causal emphasis on mechanisms of constraint, motivation/propensity, and opportunity/situational attributes, while also evaluating them in terms of the adequacy of the explanations they propose. We couple with this approach a summary of key issues and knowledge related to assessing the empirical validity of macro-level theories. This strategy permits a comprehensive overview of macro-level theory and research, while also illuminating the broad similarities and distinctions that emerge across perspectives and providing a strong foundation for our discussion of future theoretical inquiry, which is the focus of our closing section.

Before turning to our review, we feel obliged to acknowledge the ambiguity that exists about what constitutes the landscape of macro-level theory. To put it more bluntly: there does not appear to be a strong consensus in the field regarding the perspectives that encompass macro-level theoretical inquiry. Some classic frameworks are routinely considered in theoretical reviews (e.g., social disorganization, anomie, and general deterrence), but others often are given relatively little consideration (e.g., differential social organization). Additionally, some more recently developed frameworks have gained sufficient traction in the literature to garner fairly consistent attention as macro-level theories (e.g., institutional anomie theory, collective efficacy, and routine activities), but others are less consistently encompassed and, in some ways underappreciated, in macro-level theoretical discussions (e.g., the systemic model, macro-level general strain, structural economic strain, social structure and social learning, and crime pattern theory). We recognize that there are many possible reasons for the noted ambiguity that characterizes the macro-level theoretical terrain within criminology. Sometimes, newer perspectives are encompassed within classic frameworks rather than discussed separately. For example, the systemic model and, to a lesser extent routine activities theory, are sometimes encompassed within overviews of social disorganization. Additionally, there may be legitimate disagreements about whether some arguments advanced in the literature regarding the relevance of selected attributes of social collectivities and/or places constitute fully developed *theories*. We acknowledge this ambiguity not because we have strong views about what ought to be considered in overviews of macro-level theoretical inquiry or to be critical of previous reviews, but rather simply to admit that the range of perspectives considered in our assessment is somewhat arbitrary. We have sought to be comprehensive, but appreciate that there are other legitimate ways to organize the macro-level theoretical literature.

## The relative causal focus of macro-level theories

In an important critique of existing theoretical frameworks, Tittle (1995) notes that a productive way of thinking about the utility of criminological theories is to consider the degree to which they encompass the different causal elements that are relevant to most forms of criminal behavior. He emphasizes in this regard several pertinent types of causal mechanisms, but in our judgment those most germane for organizing macro-level theories are: (a) motivation or propensity for criminal behavior; (b) constraints to criminal behavior; and (c) the role of opportunities or situations for generating crime. Tittle's (1995) recognition of these causal elements is not unique (e.g., Cohen & Felson, 1979), but his systematic application of the resulting conceptual scheme for organizing the utility of criminological theories is notable. His review focuses on individual-level theories, however.[3] Though others have considered somewhat comparable issues for selected macro-level theories (Messner & Rosenfeld, 1994), we think a more systematic assessment that applies the framework formalized by Tittle (1995) in a comprehensive manner may prove valuable for illuminating both the relative strengths and weaknesses of macro-level theories and for identifying parallels to individual-level perspectives. Thus, we use this framework as a guide for the overview of macro-level theories discussed below.

We acknowledge that the distinction between motivation, constraint, and opportunity-situational factors can be ambiguous. The nuances found within the definitions of these causal elements often are taken for granted. As adopted in our review, properties of social collectivities and/or places that represent forces which increase the general propensity for, or drive towards, criminal behavior are considered "motivational" factors, while properties that prevent or limit participation in criminal behavior either by reducing criminality or by curtailing action by those contemplating illicit conduct are elements of "constraint." This distinction is typically a straightforward one, and in most instances macro-level theories can be readily classified as emphasizing one or both of these mechanisms. Less clear, in our view, is how to conceive of what we have referred to as "opportunities and situational attributes." In some respects, opportunities and situations for crime are ubiquitous; in virtually all social collectivities and places there are an abundant supply of people to assault and property to steal, and situations in which criminal behavior may flourish also are plentiful. However, as most typically used in macro-level theories, opportunities and situations refer not merely to the presence of a potential crime target or a setting that may serve as a location for crime committed by appropriately motivated and unconstrained persons (Warr, 2001). Instead, when opportunity/situational attributes are considered as distinct sets of properties in macro-level theories, which as we elaborate below is not very common, they tend to be implemented in a manner that is not wholly independent of motivation and constraint.

Within selected macro-level theories (e.g., routine activities and crime pattern theory), opportunities and situations are most frequently considered as features of places and settings that influence the occurrence of crime both by structuring access to the raw materials of crime (e.g., exposure to criminals, the presence of more people or places that might serve as crime targets, etc.), and by providing differential forms of regulation (e.g., the presence of police, bystanders, and/or CCTVs) and/ or enticements or provocations (e.g., an attractive or lucrative target) that affect the probability of crime (Meier *et al.*, 2001). Nevertheless, though opportunity/ situational theories often are credited with emphasizing mechanisms of constraint, they usually are classified as being silent on criminal motivation, presumably since the enticing or provocational elements they tend to emphasize are not routinely considered as motivational attributes, at least as typically referenced in the theoretical literature. Katz (1988) suggests that this may be because many criminological theories focus on *background* factors that serve to motivate or constrain behavior in a general sense, while neglecting the *foreground* conditions that influence crime, including the nature of opportunities and situations which can serve to motivate or constrain behavior in the immediate moments before and during a criminal event. We draw attention to this distinction to acknowledge that, while we follow the lead of others in classifying opportunity theories as being neglectful of "motivation," this is true only in the context of the specific definition of motivation applied in our assessment (and most others) of criminological theories.

With the above caveats outlined, we now present in Table 23.1 a summary of the primary explanatory emphasis of thirteen macro-level theoretical perspectives that, in our judgment, present distinct arguments. Admittedly, in some cases the listed perspectives overlap substantially (e.g., collective efficacy, the systemic model, and social disorganization; anomie and institutional anomie; differential social organization and social structure and social learning) and the more recent statements are probably better thought of as important theoretical elaborations rather than wholly distinct perspectives. Additionally, there are developing perspectives, such as theories of social support/altruism (Chamlin & Cochran, 1997; Cullen, 1994), government legitimacy (LaFree, 1998; Roth, 2009), and multilevel contextual models (Messner, 2012; Wilcox *et al.*, 2003) that would be included in any effort to generate an exhaustive list of potentially useful macro-level ideas or frameworks. We necessarily had to make some arbitrary choices to render the task manageable; we limited our scope to macro-level theories for which there are clear statements and fairly consistent attention in the empirical literature, fully recognizing that alternative choices could be defended, and hoping that readers will consider our review a commencement to rather than a concluding statement on these matters.

**Table 23.1**  Primary Explanatory Focus of Macro-Level Theories of Crime

| Theoretical Perspective and Representative Statements | Primary Theoretical Emphasis | | |
| --- | --- | --- | --- |
| | *Constraint* | *Motivation/ Propensity* | *Situations/ Opportunities* |
| Modern Deterrence (Zimring & Hawkins, 1973; Gibbs, 1975) | ✓ | | |
| Social Disorganization (Shaw & McKay, 1942) | ✓ | | |
| Systemic Model (Bursik & Grasmick, 1993) | ✓ | | |
| Collective Efficacy (Sampson, 2006) | ✓ | | |
| Structural Economic Strain (Blau & Blau, 1982) | | ✓ | |
| Macro-Level General Strain (Agnew, 1999) | ✓ | ✓ | |
| Anomie (Merton, 1938) | ✓ | ✓ | |
| Institutional Anomie (Messner & Rosenfeld, 1994, 2013) | ✓ | ✓ | |
| Differential Social Organization (Sutherland, 1947; Matsueda, 2010) | ✓ | ✓ | |
| Social Structure and Social Learning (Akers, 1998, 2009) | ✓ | ✓ | |
| Contextualized Subculture (Sampson & Wilson, 1995) | ✓ | ✓ | |
| Crime Pattern Theory (Brantingham & Brantingham, 1995) | | | ✓ |
| Routine Activities/Lifestyle (Cohen & Felson, 1979; Miethe, Hughes, & McDowall, 1991) | ✓ | | ✓ |

Table 23.1 reveals that based on our reading of macro-level theoretical perspectives, many theories emphasize exclusively elements of "constraint" *or* elements of "motivation." The first four perspectives listed – modern deterrence theory, social disorganization, the systemic model, and collective efficacy theory – describe causal processes that highlight how selected features of social collectivities or places yield variation in crime primarily by shaping the degree of constraint to which potential offenders are exposed.[4] These theories are best described in general terms as control theories, and as such they take the motivation for criminal behavior for granted, or at least they do

not contain causal arguments directed at explaining the sources of drives or provocations for crime. Instead, these perspectives focus on how properties of social collectivities and places yield lower levels of criminal involvement through their capacity to regulate or constrain behavior, though they emphasize different types of macro-level properties and unique causal mechanisms for why they might yield less crime.

Modern depictions of general deterrence theory (e.g., Gibbs, 1975; Zimring & Hawkins, 1973) emphasize the regulatory potential of prevailing sanctions for law violation that are present in different social contexts. The basic logic of the theory is that crime will be less prevalent where the certainty, severity, and swiftness of legal sanctions are higher, because the latter imbue greater perceived costs to those contemplating criminal behavior. Thus, the key macro-level constructs in the theory reflect objective conditions of social collectivities such as the probability of detection by police and the quality and quantity of sanctions applied to those whose criminal behavior is discovered. Often, deterrence is intertwined with rational choice theory to acknowledge the utilitarian foundations of the theory (e.g., Akers & Sellers, 2012), a conception that emphasizes not only the costs attached in a given environment to specified actions but also the potential benefits or rewards that may serve as a motivating factor for such actions. Still, macro-level applications of rational choice theory within criminology remain somewhat scattered and are most typically subsumed within other frameworks. Thus, while some studies of crime explicitly reference both costs (e.g., sanctions) and rewards (e.g., access to income generating roles, actual earnings) as potentially important properties of social collectivities (Gould, Weinberg, & Mustard, 2002; Grogger, 2006; Raphael & Winter-Ebmer, 2001), usually under the umbrella of classic economic theory (Becker, 1968), these ideas are most typically manifested in theoretical discussion of macro-level explications of other perspectives, such as routine activities theory, which we review below.

Classic social disorganization theory (Shaw & McKay, 1942) and contemporary elaborations of this framework, including the systemic model (Bursik & Grasmick, 1993; Kasarda & Janowitz, 1974) and collective efficacy theory (Sampson, Morenoff, & Earls, 1999; Sampson, Raudenbush, & Earls, 1997), also emphasize mechanisms of constraint. Social disorganization theory emerged from efforts to explain why levels of crime tend to be significantly more prevalent in neighborhoods characterized by high levels of poverty, population turnover, and ethnic heterogeneity. The explanation for this puzzle provided by Shaw & McKay (1942) integrates ideas reflected in a wide variety of criminological theories, including some that highlight social sources of criminal motivation (e.g., strain, differential social organization/cultural transmission), but the central thesis extracted from their work focuses on the degree to which social collectivities are organized in a manner that facilitates the realization of common goals, including relatively low levels of crime, through effective regulatory mechanisms (Bursik, 1988; Kornhauser, 1978). Thus, Shaw & McKay suggested that social collectivities exhibiting structural conditions such as high rates of poverty, population turnover, and ethnic heterogeneity experience more crime because they do not possess the density of social network ties or strength of informal social controls thought to be critical for regulating crime (Kubrin & Weitzer, 2003). Social disorganization is therefore conceived most commonly as an emergent property of social collectivities, manifested in weak social ties, low levels of involvement in community organizations and institutions, and limited attention to monitoring public spaces and interpersonal interactions that can yield illicit conduct (Sampson & Groves, 1989). These conditions are posited to increase the likelihood of crime both because they yield less surveillance of social behavior and because they impede the capacity for communities to reinforce conventional norms of conduct (Bursik, 1988).

Contemporary elaborations of social disorganization theory have detailed in more explicit terms the importance of different types of social ties in generating community social organization, the utility of both informal and formal regulatory processes, and the important distinction between the capacity for social control and its realization through purposive social action (Bursik & Grasmick, 1993; Sampson *et al.*, 1997). Bursik & Grasmick (1993) concur with Shaw & McKay's basic argument that cohesive social networks are vital for stimulating neighborhood-based informal social controls, but they also make a persuasive case about the importance of ties that span local neighborhood boundaries, and particularly those that are built with broader political and economic institutions. Such external ties can, according to Bursik & Grasmick's (1993) systemic model, yield important public controls for neighborhoods, including formal social controls that can accrue from solid relations with law enforcement agencies. Sampson *et al.* (1997, 1999) also adopt the basic social disorganization framework that has been extracted from Shaw & McKay, but they clarify the process through which dense neighborhood ties can effectively serve to regulate criminal behavior, illuminating the importance of "collective efficacy" (see also Kirk, 2010). Sampson and colleagues suggest that dense, cohesive social networks are necessary but not always sufficient properties for facilitating neighborhood social control. Collective efficacy – mutual trust and shared commitments to actively engaging in social control – is advanced as a global property of communities that is critical for activating the crime constraining potential for strong social ties (Sampson, 2006). The noted elaborations of social disorganization theory have significantly sharpened the theoretical logic implied and have stimulated a significant volume of contemporary research, but they have not deviated sharply from social disorganization's focus on constraint as the primary mechanism through which criminal behavior is regulated.

In contrast to the "constraint" focus of general deterrence and social disorganization perspectives, one of the "structural strain theories" included in Table 23.1 is classified exclusively as emphasizing motivational arguments, though we acknowledge some ambiguity about this designation. The general thrust of structural strain theories is that selected undesirable conditions within social collectivities (e.g., economic inequality or other aversive stimuli) tend to stimulate negative emotional states for which criminal behavior may emerge as a remedy that is deemed suitable (Ousey, 2010). The structural economic strain argument advanced by Blau and colleagues (Blau & Blau, 1982; Blau & Schwartz, 1984) emphasizes the potentially adverse consequence of population heterogeneity, and in particular high rates of economic inequality, for stimulating violent behavior (see also Stolzenberg, Eitle, & D'Alessio, 2006). This framework acknowledges the importance of opportunity in terms of providing the interpersonal interactions, or social contact, required for violence (Blau, 1977; Messner & Golden, 1992), and it also draws connections to macro-level conditions associated with constraint, such as social disorganization and anomie. However, the central tenet of the theoretical argument proposed by Blau and colleagues is that the presence of high levels of economic inequality (especially ascriptive inequality) in a social collectivity may "foster conflict and violence because such conditions yield resentment, frustration, hopelessness, and alienation… [which in turn leads to a] sense of injustice, discontent, and distrust" (Blau & Blau, 1982:119). Thus, while Blau and colleagues make reference to opportunity and constraint, the most fully developed component of their argument links high levels of inequality to increased criminality through heightened motivation for offending that arises in response to negative emotions.

We conclude that several other perspectives emphasize macro-level properties relevant to both constraint and motivation, including macro-level general strain, anomie, institutional anomie, differential social organization, social structure and social learning, and contextualized subcultural theory. However, like the theories already reviewed, these perspectives do not prescribe an independent central role for the differential opportunities/situations that emerge across social collectivities and which may have implications for crime.

Agnew (1999) builds on the logic of structural strain theory described above, but expands on the breadth of macro-level properties that may enhance motivations towards crime and also integrates elements of that can serve to constrain such motivation. He argues that through both selection and causal pathways, social collectivities tend to exhibit variation on a variety of different forms of structural strain, including economic inequality but also high levels of other forms of social cleavages, family disruption, child maltreatment, incivilities, and crime. According to Agnew (1999), these macro-level conditions stimulate negative emotional affect (e.g., anger and frustration) both among those who experience strains directly, and among others exposed to them "vicariously." The net result is a larger fraction of persons who experience negative emotional states; these individuals may turn to crime in response, and they also may stimulate crime among others through interpersonal interactions. Thus, Agnew (1999) identifies several dimensions of strain and stress as potentially important collective features that may generate negative emotions that motivate persons to engage in crime. He also notes, however, that social collectivities can supply a variety of mechanisms that regulate, or constrain, the tendency for high levels of community strain to yield negative emotions and criminal behavior. Agnew (1999) focuses primarily on how social collectivities can serve as importance sources of social support and social control that can lessen the likelihood that high levels of strain translate into negative emotions and/or that criminal behavior is used as a "coping mechanism" for negative emotions.

The dual role of "motivation" and "constraint" is developed more fully, in our judgment, within classic and contemporary anomie theories (Merton, 1938; Messner & Rosenfeld, 1994, 2013). Merton (1938, 1968) advances a theory of deviance that highlights elements of both cultural structure and social structure. In Merton's theory, the cultural structure serves as the primary source of both the motivation to pursue valued goals and the degree of constraint attached to doing so (Messner,

1988), while the social structure is conceived mainly as dictating the range of choices available for satisfying culturally assimilated goals through legitimate means (Baumer, 2007; Stinchcombe, 1975). Most important for our purposes is the cultural structure, which Merton describes as a global property of social collectivities that integrates two elements, or functions: (1) it prescribes the goals and values to which people should strive; and (2) it defines norms that govern the means by which valued goals should be pursued. In this fashion, according to Merton's anomie theory, culture generates both the motives for purposive action directed at goal achievement and a normative context that can serve to regulate such action, or in other words constrain the use of illicit conduct to achieve desired goals.

Though it is not frequently highlighted, the social structure within Merton's theory also can be viewed as a global feature of social collectivities that may constrain behavior. Specifically, Merton (1938) suggests that access to normative roles for pursuing culturally valued goals can condition the deviance producing tendencies of a cultural context that strongly emphasizes goal attainment without a comparatively strong focus on normative means (Baumer & Gustafson, 2007). This feature of Merton's theory often is described in terms of how limited access to normative roles can strengthen the possibility of illicit responses, but another view is that abundant access to such roles may lessen (i.e., constrain) the use of illegitimate means to attain valued goals.

Messner & Rosenfeld (1994) integrate the fundamental causal logic implied in Merton's theory (i.e., that cultural contexts provide the impetus for the goals to which people strive while also providing normative constraints to the means used to pursue such goals) in their argument for American exceptionalism in levels of instrumental violence, which has been subsequently labeled institutional anomie theory (IAT). Thus, IAT also is a macro-level theoretical perspective that has clear relevance to both motivation and constraint for criminal behavior. However, Messner & Rosenfeld (1994) significantly expand on Merton's arguments regarding the role of the social structure in regulating, or constraining, how people respond to culturally induced motivations toward illegitimate conduct and weak cultural constraints for such conduct. They do so by highlighting the role of social institutions (e.g., the economy, family, polity, and education) and, in particular, how the relative strength of such institutions is both an important source and consequence of the prevailing cultural structure within a social collectivity and a critical factor in shaping how people respond to it. In this fashion, Messner & Rosenfeld (1994, 2013) follow Merton in attributing an important regulatory function to the social structure that defines social collectivities, but they clarify and expand this argument significantly by emphasizing the importance of strong noneconomic social institutions, which in IAT are critical for providing socialization to counteract (i.e., moderate) cultural messages that may increase illicit conduct and for increasing exposure to external social controls and social support.

At their core, classic and contemporary anomie theories highlight cultural context and the socialization that emerges from it as key sources of motivation and constraint for social behavior. In our judgment, Sutherland's (1947) differential social organization argument implies a similar general argument, though it is rooted in a different conception of the normative order and emphasizes more specific elements of socialization. Specifically, while anomie theory generally assumes that social collectivities are characterized by normative consensus, Sutherland (1947) noted how advanced societies, in which there is a complex division of labor and social roles, tend to possess conflicting normative orders in which, as Matsueda (2010:898) puts it, "some groups define the law as a set of rules to be followed under all circumstances, while others define the law as a set of rules to be violated under certain circumstances." While Sutherland viewed most social collectivities as organized in this fashion to some extent, he also advanced the idea that there are important differences in organization across social collectivities, whereby the relative presence and influence of norms supportive of law violation and norms supportive of law abiding conduct vary across groups or places (e.g., neighborhoods). According to Sutherland (1947), variation in criminal behavior is largely the result of differential exposure (i.e., differential association) to normative messages in favor of or against law violation. This socialization process is a critical ingredient of Sutherland's individual-level differential association theory, but he also extended the logic to suggest that crime levels will co-vary with what he ultimately labeled "differential social organization." Specifically, Sutherland (1947) argued that crime rates should be expected to be higher in social collectivities in which there is greater normative support for law violation (relative to support for law abiding behavior), and lower in social collectivities in which there is greater normative support for law abiding behavior (than for law violation). Thus, though they differ in important ways, we see a parallel between the logic of Sutherland's differential social organization theory and the anomie perspective described above; both emphasize the importance of socialization processes in generating crime, conceiving cultural context as a global or structural property that contributes to the types of social actions people value and in which they participate.

While Sutherland's notion of differential social organization and crime represents an important, and in our view under-appreciated component of macro-level theoretical inquiry, it was largely underdeveloped. Matsueda (2006) makes a persuasive case that Sutherland's conception of social organization was relatively narrow and simplistic and was not sufficiently developed to explicate the full range of processes and mechanisms that might link different types of social organization to variability in crime across social collectivities. Others have drawn on the logic of Sutherland's arguments in contemporary discussions of how differences in norms across social collectivities may affect the quality and quantity of crime. Matsueda (2006, 2010) elaborates directly on the macro-level implications of Sutherland's differential social organization argument, yielding a more general portrait of how different types of social organization can shape levels of crime. Akers (1998, 2009) also adopts the same basic logic that is evident in the macro-level interpretation of Sutherland's theory in what has been termed a "social structure and social learning" theory, though he significantly expands on the ways in which social collectivities can represent unique "learning environments" that influence participation in criminal behavior. Like Sutherland, Akers (1998) acknowledges that groups and places vary in the extent to which they are organized around norms supportive of or against illicit conduct. However, Akers (1998) also highlights how social collectivities may differ in other ways that have implications for how people are socialized and the volume of crime that emerges, including patterns of positive and negative reinforcement for criminal behavior and the presence of criminal role models.

Other scholarship has wedded ideas from differential social organization and social disorganization perspectives to illuminate contemporary links between structural disadvantages, weakened social ties and informal social control, and cultural adaptations that enhance the likelihood of crime (Anderson, 1999; Sampson & Wilson, 1995). Perhaps most notably, in what has been termed a "contextualized subculture" perspective (e.g., Bartusch, 2010), Sampson & Wilson (1995) suggest that ecologically concentrated structural disadvantages, such as high levels of poverty, family disruption, and population turnover weaken the capacity for dense networks and effective institutions and organizations to develop in communities. These community conditions may yield elevated crime because they tend to dampen resident participation in informal social control efforts, and also because they isolate people from conventional role models and promote adaptation to norms about how to navigate life and interactions within highly disadvantaged social contexts. This cultural adaptation illuminates a weakening of conventional norms, which often are unviable for securing safety and survival in highly disadvantaged community contexts (see also Anderson, 1999).

Sampson & Wilson (1995:50–51) make clear that while the cultural attenuation to which they refer does not yield a competing subculture, it can yield a normative environment in which criminal behavior is "less than fervently condemned" and in which there are relatively high levels of crime and violence and "criminal" role models who may shape how others adapt to specific interpersonal interactions within disadvantaged contexts. As Sampson & Wilson (1995) put it, "in structurally disorganized slum communities...crime, disorder, and drug use are...expected as a part of everyday life...[which in turn]...appear to influence the probability of criminal outcomes and harmful deviant behavior (50). The latter occurs, they suggest, because people who reside in structurally disadvantaged communities "are more likely to witness violent acts, to be taught to be violent by exhortation, and to have role models who do not adequately control their own impulses or restrain their own anger. Accordingly, given the availability of and easy access to firearms, knives, and other weapons, adolescent experiments with macho behavior often have deadly consequences" (51–52). Importantly, this argument conceives of cultural adaptations as ecologically structured and situational, rather than omnipresent and permanent, and it locates their source in structurally disadvantaged community conditions. Anderson (1999) adopts a similar conception of the sources and nature of cultural adaptations that often emerge in communities with very high levels of economic and social disadvantage, but he outlines in more concrete terms the content of such adaptations. Specifically, he argues that social and economic isolation gives rise to cultural norms that provide differential exposure to definitions (i.e., the code of the street) about the proper or valued ways in which to present oneself in public (e.g., to "campaign for respect) and to react when involved in an interpersonal confrontation. For Anderson (1999), an important mechanism through which social isolation is linked to the emergence of "street codes" is a weakened belief in the capacity of police and other criminal justice representatives to effectively help residents resolve interpersonal conflicts, a theme that also is prominent in recent scholarship that emphasizes high levels of legal cynicism as an important source and component of cultural adaptations that increase criminal behavior (Kirk & Papachristos, 2011; Sampson & Bartusch, 1998).

None of the aforementioned theories have much, if anything, to say about the relevance of opportunity/situational attributes of social collectivities and/or places for generating differential involvement in crime. In contrast, the final three macro-level theories included in Table 23.1 emphasize "opportunity/situational" attributes, sometimes in apparent isolation (e.g., crime pattern theory) and in other cases in conjunction with a clear dual emphasis on differential patterns of constraint across social collectivities (e.g., routine activities theory). These perspectives do not encompass in their explanations features of social collectivities that influence motivation for criminal behavior, at least in the general (non-situational) sense in which motivation is typically referenced in the theoretical literature. To be sure, most of these theories acknowledge the relevance of a higher volume of "motivated offenders" for the rate of crime that is generated in or attracted to a given social collectivity, but they do not encompass an explanation for why such differences emerge aside from the presence of desirable opportunities and situations that might attract offenders or serve as provocations for those generally inclined towards criminality. Nonetheless, their emphasis on opportunity structures is a valuable addition and one that is notably absent in many other perspectives that more often guide macro-level empirical inquiry.

Crime pattern theory (Brantingham & Brantingham, 1995, 2011) outlines several principles that govern the routine activities of potential offenders and victims, and the choices they make when confronted with a "triggering event" or when a given situation fits an offender's "crime template." The theory thus references multiple levels of explanation, including micro-level decisions by victims and offenders, and macro-level attributes that can shape the degree to which they interact and govern the decisions they make when such interaction occurs (Malm, 2010). The latter are most central to the macro-level theoretical implications of crime pattern theory. Specifically, this perspective suggests that social collectivities or areas that possess more crime opportunities (e.g., people and goods) will tend to exhibit the highest rates of crime. Brantingham and Brantingham (1995:7–9) note that crime opportunities can come in the form of "crime generators," which concentrate in dense spatial areas a large volume of potential targets for crime and increase the likelihood that offenders are exposed to them (e.g., shopping malls, large entertainment venues), and "crime attractors," which tend to concentrate persons who may be more inclined toward criminal behavior (e.g., drug markets, red-light districts). The latter also is a prominent theme in perspectives that focus on the crime generating potential of incivilities, including but not limited to "broken windows" (Skogan, 1990; Taylor, 2001;

Wilson & Kelling, 1982), though these frameworks suggest that incivilities may yield more crime not only because they tend to attract offenders, but also because they often suppress levels of constraint by, for example, promoting withdrawal from community residents who might otherwise serve an important social control function.

While crime pattern theory and related perspectives reference the importance of offender motivation and the role of constraint in shaping whether opportunities yield crime, these themes are, in our judgment, more fully developed in two other contemporary theories – routine activities theory and lifestyle theory – both of which have been linked to a more general opportunity theory of crime (e.g., Cohen, Kluegel, & Land, 1981).[5] Routine activities theory has been used to explain individual-level differences in victimization and offending (Miethe, Stafford & Long, 1987; Osgood *et al.*, 1996) and macro-level differences in crime across time and space (Cohen & Felson, 1979). Additionally, noteworthy extensions have been advanced that integrate these approaches, illuminating the inherent multilevel implications of the theory (Sampson & Wooldredge, 1987; Wilcox *et al.*, 2003). Routine activities theory emphasizes the importance of attractive targets in generating crime (i.e., opportunities), but also acknowledges the critical role played by levels of guardianship (i.e., constraint) and the presence of "motivated offenders." The latter is not explained within most presentations of the theory, however (but see Osgood *et al.*, 1996). Thus, from the vantage point of routine activities theory, differences in levels of crime across social or geographic collectivities are not a function of variation in conditions that may increase or reduce criminality. Rather, as Miethe, Hughes, & McDowall (1991:166) summarize nicely, routine activities/lifestyle theories posit that macro-level differences in crime rates emerge primarily as a function of variation in "the exposure of potential victims to dangerous locales, the supply of attractive targets, and the level of protection or guardianship." The first of these elements parallels the concepts of crime generators and attractors, which are prominent in crime pattern theory. Most explications of routine activities theory highlight the latter two, however, which shines a light on the salience of the opportunity structure and level of constraint for explaining differences in crime across social collectivities. In essence, the key predictions that arise from this theory for macro-level inquiry is that crime rates will be highest where offenders tend to congregate, where materially and symbolically attractive crime targets or situations are more plentiful, and where people or technology (e.g., alarms, security devices, video cameras) provide relatively few impediments to or little monitoring of the actions of those contemplating criminal conduct. Thus, this perspective illuminates a prominent role for both the nature of opportunities/situations and the level of constraint for generating macro-level differences in criminal behavior.

Viewed as a whole, none of the theories included in Table 23.1 encompasses clear attention to all three of the considered mechanisms – motivation, constraint, and opportunity. As suggested earlier, this is the case in part because macro-level theories that emphasize constraint and/or motivational forces tend to be directed at explaining criminality (i.e., the potential or heightened probability for involvement in crime), whereas perspectives that integrate opportunity/situational attributes are directed at explaining the occurrence of criminal acts or events among persons who might bring varying levels of motivation and/or constraint for crime to a given situation (Miethe & Meier, 1994).[6] This is generally true of individual- or micro-level theories as well, of course, and we elaborate below on how this distinction offers some potentially useful ground on which to develop integrated macro-level theoretical perspectives. Beyond this matter, though, the "empty" cells in Table 23.1 reveal that all of the macro-level theories considered could be enhanced with further development, an issue the forms the focus of our closing remarks. But first we want to step back a bit and comment on the "adequacy" and empirical validity of macro-level theories. Our discussion here is general in scope, rather than a theory-by-theory account. Though we do make reference to specific theories where warranted, it seems particularly valuable at this stage of macro-level theoretical development to consider these matters from a more general standpoint, identifying common themes that apply across perspectives. More detailed assessments of the theoretical adequacy and empirical validity of individual macro-level perspectives can be located elsewhere (e.g., Akers & Sellers, 2012; Cullen, Wright, & Blevins, 2011; Kubrin, Stucky, & Krohn, 2008; Messner & Rosenfeld, 2013).

## The theoretical and empirical adequacy of macro-level theories

There are many potentially useful ways to evaluate criminological theories, but the two pillars that we find most important are theoretical adequacy (Tittle, 1995) and empirical validity (Akers & Sellers, 2012). Tittle (1995) advances a uniform means by which to judge the adequacy of criminological theories, emphasizing in this regard their relative comprehensiveness, precision, and depth. Briefly, comprehensiveness refers to how exhaustive the explanatory factors identified in a given perspective are in relation to the full universe of causal elements that have been emphasized in the theoretical and empirical literature (Tittle, 1995). The more unique types of causal mechanisms considered, the more comprehensive the theory. Precision is defined as the degree to which theories "identify the contingencies that influence the strength with which the causal processes operate, the form of the causal effect, and the time lag between the occurrence of the cause and the expected effect" (35), whereas depth concerns the degree to which they "fully spell out the logical connections among their variables...[including the possibility of] reciprocality" (46). Thus, a theory that addressed matters of functional form, conditional effects, and the time frame over which the influence of key macro-level properties unfolds would be considered more precise, and one that explained both the causes and consequences of those factors would be deemed to have greater depth.[7] Applying this evaluative scheme to macro-level theories strikes us as an efficient and effective means by which to summarize the relative strengths and weaknesses of existing macro-level theories and, more important, to illuminate the key ways in which they could be improved.

What can be said regarding the comprehensiveness of macro-level theories of crime? We think it is instructive to begin by reiterating a broader view of criminological theory that traverses levels of analysis (i.e., macro- and micro-levels), which reveals that macro-level theoretical perspectives offer something unique that micro-level theories do not: an emphasis on properties of social collectivities and/or geographic areas that may influence criminal propensity and/or crime (Rosenfeld, 2011). A significant volume of research has affirmed the significant influence of many of the social contextual conditions emphasized in macro-level theories, which underscores their relevance for formulating highly comprehensive explanations of crime. At the same time, though, it is certainly the case that there is notable variability in comprehensiveness across macro-level perspectives.

Some perspectives that emphasize similar causal mechanisms (e.g., only constraint, or constraint and motivation) exhibit variation in comprehensiveness, but the more readily visible differences are found between those that emphasize a different range of such mechanisms (e.g., only constraint vs. constraint and motivation or constraint and opportunity). Indeed, the consideration of comprehensiveness overlaps in a notable way with the classification scheme adopted in Table 23.1; perspectives that address fewer of the referenced elements will tend to be less comprehensive than those that include more of them. Thus, at least in terms of relative attention to the broad categories of causal mechanisms around which our review is organized, frameworks that encompass explanations of offender motivation and constraint (e.g., classic and contemporary anomie theories, general strain theories, and perspectives that highlight differential social organization) or elements of opportunity and constraint (e.g., routine activities theory) are more comprehensive than frameworks that focus primarily on only one of these mechanisms (e.g., general deterrence, social disorganization theory, structural economic strain, and crime pattern theory). Part of this assessment parallels the conclusions drawn by others who have classified a smaller range of macro-level perspectives. In particular, Messner & Rosenfeld (1994) reach a similar conclusion in their review of anomie and social disorganization theories, arguing that the former offers a more comprehensive explanation than the latter. However, it is important to recognize that some of the earliest descriptions of social disorganization were, in many respects, more comprehensive than the version that has formed the focus of much contemporary work. As Kubrin *et al.* (2008) note, Shaw & McKay (1942) developed arguments both for how neighborhood social environments were critical for regulating conduct, and for how they can under some circumstances provide a differential system of values to which people are exposed and which can shape criminal propensity. The latter arguments were not very fully developed in Shaw & McKay's writings, and some have argued that they are logically inconsistent with other components of Shaw and McKay's social disorganization model (Kornhauser, 1978), but nonetheless it is important to highlight that their more comprehensive "mixed" theory has resurfaced in a more nuanced and elaborate manner in contemporary arguments (i.e., "contextualized subcultural theory").

While common depictions of social disorganization theory have been described here as less comprehensive than several other popular frameworks, contemporary scholarship has contributed significantly to enhancing the theory's depth. Substantial attention has been devoted to clearly specifying and elaborating the underlying causal logic of social disorganization, with particular attention to illuminating the implied intervening mechanisms (Bursik, 1988; Kubrin & Weitzer, 2003; Sampson & Groves, 1989). The same can be said of contemporary elaborations of social disorganization theory (e.g., the systemic model, collective efficacy theory). A similar process has unfolded for general deterrence theory (e.g., Zimring & Hawkins, 1973), classic and contemporary anomie theories (Baumer, 2007; Messner, 1988; Messner & Rosenfeld, 1994), and macro-level general strain theory (Agnew, 1999). In our judgment, all of the aforementioned perspectives possess relatively high levels of theoretical depth, while theories that emphasize differential social organization and routine activities remain less well developed, especially in terms of the depth of the explanatory models proposed. However, recently developed integrated perspectives relevant to both differential social organization (Akers, 1998; Matsueda, 2006; Sampson & Wilson, 1995) and routine activities theory (Meier *et al.*, 2001; Wilcox *et al.*, 2003) have made notable progress in addressing this deficiency.

We see fewer differences across macro-level perspectives in terms of precision. This is not because most of them are highly precise, however. In contrast, like criminological theories more generally (see Tittle, 1995), macro-level theoretical statements rarely specify clearly matters such as the time lag, functional form, the expected magnitude of the effects observed for key constructs, and the possibility of contingent causal impacts. Most macro-level theoretical statements are silent on the assumed time period over which proposed relationships will emerge, though this often is an issue explored in empirical research. With respect to functional form, linearity is commonly assumed in macro-level models, but it is often unclear whether this is by design or a simplifying assumption made by researchers who embark on empirical tests. Most typically, macro-level theories posit relationships without a clear reference to functional form. It is more common for macro-level theoretical statements to specify, or at least imply, conditional effects for key causal variables. For instance, Cohen & Felson (1979:604) suggest that crime generating tendencies of the presence of many attractive targets and low levels of guardianship are likely to be inherently multiplicative in nature. Similarly, Zimring & Hawkins (1973) specify a large number of attributes that may condition the influence of aggregate differences in objective sanctions on offending. More recently, Agnew (1999) has highlighted several ways in which the impact of community differences in strain may be moderated, and several scholars have documented the highly contingent nature of causal arguments in both classic and contemporary anomie theories (e.g., Baumer & Gustafson, 2007; Chamlin & Cochran, 1995; Savolainen, 2000).

This assessment of theoretical adequacy should not be interpreted as an indictment against macro-level theory. Instead, as we have tried to emphasize, the weaknesses to which we have drawn attention are common deficiencies with criminological theories more generally – both individual and macro-level. More important, considerations of comprehensiveness, depth, and precision point to concrete ways in which macro-level theories could be enhanced, a theme to which we return below in our closing section. Before doing so, however, we want to comment on the empirical status of macro-level theories. After all, even the most "adequate" theory in terms of the comprehensiveness, precision, and depth may not be highly useful if the tentative answer it provides is an inaccurate portrayal compared to observed crime patterns (Akers & Sellers, 2012). Given the scope of this chapter, our review of relevant research is necessarily quite general in orientation, focusing on broad considerations of the key issues associated with testing macro-level theories rather than an exhaustive review of individual studies. We also comment on what we see as the greatest needs for enhancing empirical assessments of macro-level theory.

The empirical literature has documented quite convincingly, in our view, that crime and criminality vary significantly across social collectivities and/or geographic areas, and that several different macro-level properties or conditions are linked systematically to that variability (for reviews, see Baumer, 2008; Bursik & Grasmick, 1993; Messner & Rosenfeld, 2006; Ousey, 2000; Pratt & Cullen, 2005; Sampson, Morenoff, & Gannon-Rowley, 2002). This evidence comes from both macro- and multilevel research designs, and it underscores the importance of macro-level explanatory variables within the broader umbrella of criminological theory (Rosenfeld, 2011). At the same time, though, a careful reading of the criminological literature relevant to macro-level theory yields ambiguous conclusions regarding the degree of empirical validity that can be attributed to specific perspectives. A key reason is that, largely because of gaps in data infrastructure, empirical assessments of macro-level theories tend to fall short of providing a very strong test of core theoretical arguments. To be sure, many valuable macro-level studies have been produced during the past several decades, and they often yield important empirical insights about the ecological conditions associated with elevated levels of crime. However, while many such studies encompass variables, often labeled as "structural conditions" (e.g., poverty rates, percent unemployed, the prevalence of female-headed households, divorce rates, racial composition), that are components of specified macro-level theories, it is not readily apparent which theories these variables reference. Several theories draw attention to indicators of economic deprivation, including unemployment and poverty rates, as properties that may promote crime (e.g., social disorganization, differential social organization, structural economic strain, macro-level general strain, and contextualized subculture). These and other theories (e.g., routine activities theory and anomie theory) also can be applied to account for the tendency of crime to be more prevalent in social collectivities in which there is greater family disruption. Which theory is supported, then, by studies that yield evidence that economic deprivation and family disruption are associated with elevated crime rates? In our judgment, it is very difficult to answer that question.

It is important to acknowledge that the empirical literature likely has focused on assessing the influence on crime of macro-level factors such as economic deprivation, family disruption, racial context, and income inequality because those conditions are measured on a consistent basis, not because they are considered as the key constructs identified in macro-level theoretical frameworks. Indeed, from our vantage point the major limit of much of the existing research available for assessing the empirical validity of macro-level theories is not what they include, but rather what they omit. Many assessments of macro-level theories do not include direct measures of the key constructs emphasized as proximate conditions in those perspectives (e.g., levels of social disorganization, informal social control, guardianship, anomie, perceived risk, differences in value commitments, etc.), which limits their relevance for judging the validity of the proposed theoretical arguments. Of course, we are not the first to highlight this general limitation of macro-level theoretical assessments. Sampson & Groves (1989) noted that despite more than four decades of research linked to social disorganization theory, the bulk of that research was not highly relevant because it omitted the proximate causes of crime implied in the theory, which they defined as density of local networks, organizational participation, and presence of unsupervised peer groups. Similarly, Bernard (1987a) and Messner (1988) argued that the large volume of studies published in the aftermath of Merton's (1938) original statement of anomie theory bore little resemblance to the macro-level causal logic implied in the theory. More recently, Kleck *et al.* (2005) pointed out that while many studies claiming to test general deterrence theory have considered the relationship between objective punishment levels and crime, none had assessed the core causal argument posited in the theory – whether objective levels of punishment influence crime by shaping perceived punishment risk.

The two issues we have emphasized in relation to empirical research on macro-level theories – a predominant focus on "structural indicators" that are relevant to many different perspectives, but usually not the critical ingredients and not easily attributed to specific frameworks, and the omission of the proximate conditions that serve as core constructs – mean that it is precarious at present to draw strong conclusions about empirical validity. Thus, while we find significant value in a recent meta-analysis of macro-level studies by Pratt & Cullen (2005), which reveals compelling evidence for the consistency and strength of several macro-level properties, we urge caution in accepting the conclusions it advances about the implications of those findings for the relative degree of support for different macro-level theories. With a few notable exceptions, Pratt & Cullen's (2005) assessment of the empirical evidence is limited to "structural indicators" that are implicated in several theories, but do not represent the core constructs of those theories. As Pratt & Cullen (2005:430) acknowledge, "many of the macro-level predictors of crime assessed in this study cut across multiple theories" and, further, "meta-analysis is not designed to settle the debates surrounding which theories may claim ownership over particular variables."

We strongly echo others in calling for more direct assessments of macro-level theoretical arguments (Baumer & Gustafson, 2007; Kubrin *et al.*, 2008; Messner, 1988; Ousey, 2000; Sampson, 2012), and we are heartened by significant developments in that direction over the past few decades. Sampson & Groves (1989) offered the first clear assessment of the core causal arguments of social disorganization theory just over 25 years ago, which has subsequently spawned many comparable efforts, including several studies of neighborhood social organization and crime (for reviews, see Sampson, *et al.*, 2002; Sampson, 2012). Similarly, others have developed data and empirical analyses to examine more explicitly some of the core arguments contained in classic and contemporary anomie theories (e.g., Baumer & Gustafson, 2007), macro-level general strain (Brezina, Piquero, & Mazzerolle, 2001), general deterrence (Kleck *et al.*, 2005), and arguments that are central to differential social organization theories (Kirk & Papachristos, 2011; Sampson & Bartusch, 1998; Stewart & Simons, 2006). These studies and others like them contribute substantially to what we can learn about the empirical validity of macro-level theories, and as the volume of such research grows we will be in a better position to draw definitive conclusions about the relative empirical status of different perspectives. Of course, a major impediment to developing a broader base of highly relevant empirical evidence on macro-level theory is the relatively barren data infrastructure for doing so. A thorough evaluation of the empirical validity of many macro-level theories requires rich data on the collective values, routines, customs, and behaviors that manifest across social collectivities. While there have been notable advances in gathering such data in the last two decades, further efforts are needed to generate a more solid foundation from which to evaluate the validity of many macro-level theories.

## Concluding Thoughts

In this chapter, we first set out to delineate both the common ground between macro- and micro-level inquiries and the unique elements offered by macro-level perspectives. We advanced the position that, contrary to many depictions, macro- and micro-level theories are both directed at explaining variability in criminal behavior. Where they differ is in the types of explanatory variables emphasized: micro-level perspectives emphasize attributes of individuals and interpersonal interactions, while macro-level theories focus on explanatory factors that represent properties of social collectivities and/or geographic areas, variously defined. Given that macro- and micro-level theories address comparable outcomes from unique angles, we argued that integrating these perspectives is a promising way to enhance the reach of criminological theory. Further, our assessment of the relative causal emphasis contained in macro-level theoretical perspectives and the adequacy of those perspectives reveal insights into the type of theoretical integration that may prove most useful for enhancing both macro- and micro-level frameworks. We illuminate this further below, but first we want to highlight ways in which macro-level theories more specifically might be improved.

Drawing on a conceptual framework developed by Tittle (1995), we documented that macro-level theories differ notably in their degree of comprehensiveness. Specifically, some macro-level perspectives focus primarily on how differences across social collectivities in levels of constraint are the key to understanding variation in crime, with others focusing on differences in conditions that shape criminal propensity or the presence of opportunities and situations that are conducive to crime. Several macro-level theories emphasize two of the aforementioned causal mechanisms, but none in our judgment clearly encompasses all three. We suggested that one possible reason for this gap is that macro-level theories that emphasize constraint and/or motivational forces tend to be directed at explaining criminality (i.e., the potential or heightened probability for involvement in crime), whereas perspectives that integrate opportunity/situational attributes are directed at explaining the occurrence of criminal acts or events among persons who might bring varying levels of motivation and/or constraint for crime to a given situation. In light of this, we conclude that integrating macro-level perspectives that address criminal propensity with those that concentrate on why and how such propensities translate into crime would be most valuable (see also Meier *et al.*, 2001). Doing so would address important limitations of frameworks that describe well why some people develop propensities for crime, but cannot easily explain why most of such people spend the vast majority of their lives not acting on those propensities (e.g., anomie and differential social organization theories). This type of integration also would help to broaden the reach of theories such as classic social disorganization and its contemporary elaborations, which document that high levels of crime tend to emerge in contexts with relatively little informal social control, but do not account for why some decide to offend when community constraints are weakened while most do not, or why conformity to conventional actions is the predominant norm even in social collectivities that exert very weak social controls.

Greater attention to integrating macro-level theories that attend to mechanisms of constraint, motivation, and opportunity/situations could yield a more comprehensive framework for how the properties of social collectivities and/or places yield variability in criminal behavior. Such an approach would be particularly useful with significant attention to matters of theoretical depth and precision (Tittle, 1995). As we noted in our review, while there have been significant strides in the contemporary literature in regards to more clearly spelling out the logical connections among key constructs specified in macro-level theories (i.e., they possess considerable theoretical depth), most of the frameworks we considered could be enhanced with greater clarity regarding the nature of implied causal effects (i.e., time lags and functional form) and potentially important contingencies. Reworking existing macro-level theories with these matters in mind as part of the suggested integration process would go far in expanding the reach of macro-level inquiry.

A perhaps even more valuable avenue for future theoretical development would be the integration of macro- and micro-level theories with scope conditions that encompass both criminality and crime. Thoughtful integration of some of the macro-level theories along the lines suggested above could yield a more comprehensive framework, but a broader reading of the criminological literature underscores that both macro- and micro-level attributes are important for shaping criminal propensity, the effective constraints to which people are subjected, and how opportunities and situations are experienced and interpreted (Meier *et al.*, 2001).

Thus, considering both macro- and micro-level explanatory variables would be preferable. Though there are good examples of multilevel theoretical development in the literature (e.g., Baumer, 2007; Matsueda, 2013b; Messner, 2012; Sampson & Wooldredge, 1987; Wilcox *et al.*, 2003), most of these do not fully integrate the three types of causal mechanisms on which we have focused. Instead, while they represent important integrated frameworks, they retain a focus on explaining either criminality or crime. One exception is Miethe & Meier (1994:65), who have proposed a heuristic theoretical model that provides a compelling sketch of what a more comprehensive integrated multilevel framework might look like. Their model reflects an "end-to-end" integration of general macro-level and micro-level arguments (e.g., Messner *et al.*, 1989) that blends attributes relevant to mechanisms of motivation, constraint, and opportunities, while also accounting for both the development of criminal propensities and the emergence of crime events. Further refining this model in the context of existing macro- and micro-level theories strikes us as a very promising avenue of future inquiry, as would parallel developments that draw on some of the other frameworks reviewed herein.

## Notes

1  As most frequently applied within criminology, "macro-level" encompasses perspectives that emphasize attributes of entire social systems, but also subnational communities and local neighborhoods; "micro-level" is often used interchangeably with "individual-level," but also is sometimes applied to reference theories that highlight defining features of "situations" and "interactions" (Short, 1998). We focus on the most common distinction made in the field, between macro-level and individual-level frameworks, using micro-level interchangeably with the latter.

2  To keep the task manageable, we focus our review on theories of crime. There also is an important, vibrant body of theory and research that addresses macro-level sources of the creation and application of law and social control that we encourage readers to consult (see Liska, 1992).

3  Tittle (1995) suggests that none of the classic theories of delinquency includes all three theoretical elements. Specifically, he asserts that differential association, strain, labeling and Marxist theories emphasize motivational factors, while social control is exclusively focused on elements of constraint. In contrast, he classifies rational choice models as inclusive of causal factors relevant to both motivation and constraint, and routine activities theory as encompassing both constraint and opportunities.

4  As Bursik & Grasmick (1993) note, such mechanisms can shape the behavior of both residents and non-residents of a socially or geographically defined context.

5  To simplify the presentation, we use the more frequently adopted descriptor of "routine activities theory."

6  We use the terms "acts" and "events" interchangeably for convenience, but see Meier *et al.* (2001) for a rich discussion of the potentially important distinction.

7  Theories also often are judged on the "breadth" of their scope (Tittle, 1995). We agree that this is an important element for describing theories, and thus we note where appropriate important differences across perspectives in the types of behaviors to which macro-level

theories are relevant. But we do not make qualitative judgments in our review about the relative utility of different degrees of breadth because, in our judgment, the utility of theoretical breadth in macro-level theories is not highly variable and is far less important than matters of comprehensiveness, precision, and depth.

# References

Adler, F., & Laufer, W.S. (Eds.) (1995). *The Legacy of Anomie Theory: Advances in Criminological Theory*, Vol. 6. New Brunswick, NJ: Transaction.

Agnew, R. (1987). On "testing structural strain theories." *Journal of Research in Crime and Delinquency*, 24(4), 281–286.

Agnew, R. (1999). A general strain theory of community differences in crime rates. *Journal of Research in Crime and Delinquency*, 36(2), 123–155.

Akers, R.L. (1998). *Social Learning and Social Structure: A General Theory of Crime and Deviance*. Boston, MA: Northeastern University Press.

Akers, R.L. (2009). *Social Learning and Social Structure: A General Theory of Crime and Deviance*, Paperback edition. New Brunswick, NJ: Transaction.

Akers, R.L., & Sellers, C.S. (2012). *Criminological Theories: Introduction, Evaluation and Application*, 6th edition. New York: Oxford University Press.

Anderson, E. (1999). *Code of the Street: Decency, Violence, and the Moral Life of the Inner City*. New York: W.W. Norton.

Baumer, E.P. (2007). Untangling research puzzles in Merton's multilevel anomie theory. *Theoretical Criminology*, 11(1), 63–93.

Baumer, E.P. (2008). An empirical assessment of the contemporary crime trends puzzle: A modest step toward a more comprehensive research agenda. In Committee on Law and Justice, National Research Council of the National Academies, *Understanding Crime Trends: Workshop Report* (pp. 127–176). Washington, DC: National Academies Press.

Baumer, E.P., & Gustafson, R. (2007). Social organization and instrumental crime: Assessing the empirical validity of classic and contemporary anomie theories. *Criminology*, 45(3), 617–663.

Becker, G.S. (1968). Crime and punishment: An economic approach. *The Journal of Political Economy*, 76(2), 169–217.

Bartusch, D.J. (2010). Sampson, Robert J., and William Julius Wilson: Contextualized subculture. In F.T. Cullen & P. Wilcox (Eds.), *Encyclopedia of Criminological Theory* (pp. 813–815). Thousand Oaks, CA: Sage.

Bernard, T.J. (1987a). Testing structural strain theories. *Journal of Research in Crime and Delinquency*, 24(4), 262–280.

Bernard, T.J. (1987b). Reply to Agnew. *Journal of Research in Crime and Delinquency*, 24(4), 287–290.

Blau, P.M. (1977). *Inequality and Heterogeneity: A Primitive Theory of Social Structure*. New York: Free Press.

Blau, J.R., & Blau, P.M. (1982). The cost of inequality: Metropolitan structure and violent crime. *American Sociological Review*, 47(1), 114–129.

Blau, P.M., & Schwartz, J.E. (1984). *Crosscutting Social Circles: Testing a Macrostructural Theory of Intergroup Relations*. Orlando, FL: Academic Press.

Brantingham, P.J., & Brantingham, P.L. (2011). Crime pattern theory. In R. Wortley & L.G. Mazerolle (Eds.), *Environmental Criminology and Crime Analysis* (pp. 78–93). New York: Routledge.

Brantingham, P.L., & Brantingham, P.J. (1995). Criminality of place: Crime generators and crime attractors. *European Journal on Criminal Policy and Research, 3*(3), 5–26.

Brezina, T., Piquero, A.R., & Mazerolle, P. (2001). Student anger and aggressive behavior in school: An initial test of Agnew's macro-level strain theory. *Journal of Research in Crime and Delinquency, 38*(4), 362–386.

Brown, S.E., Esbensen, F., & Geis, G. (2013). *Criminology: Explaining Crime and Its Context,* 8th edition. Waltham, MA: Elsevier.

Bursik, R.J. (1988). Social disorganization and theories of crime and delinquency: Problems and prospects. *Criminology, 26*(4), 519–551.

Bursik, R.J., & Grasmick, H.G. (1993). *Neighborhoods and Crime: The Dimensions of Effective Community Control.* New York: Lexington Books.

Chamlin, M.B., & Cochran, J.K. (1995). Assessing Messner and Rosenfeld's institutional anomie theory: A partial test. *Criminology, 33*(3), 411–429.

Chamlin, M.B., & Cochran, J.K. (1997). Social altruism and crime. *Criminology, 35*(2), 203–228.

Cohen, L.E., & Felson, M. (1979). Social change and crime rate trends: A routine activity approach. *American Sociological Review, 44*(4), 588–608.

Cohen, L.E., Kluegel, J.R., & Land, K.C. (1981). Social inequality and predatory criminal victimization: An exposition and test of a formal theory. *American Sociological Review, 46*(5), 505–524.

Coleman, J.S. (1986). Social theory, social research, and a theory of action. *American Journal of Sociology, 91*(6), 1309–1335.

Cullen, F.T. (1994). Social support as an organizing concept for criminology. *Justice Quarterly, 11*(4), 527–559.

Cullen, F.T., Wright, J.P., & Blevins, K.R. (Eds.) (2011). *Taking Stock: The Status of Criminological Theory: Advances in Criminological Theory,* Vol. 15. New Brunswick, NJ: Transaction.

Durkheim, É. (1951[1897]). *Suicide: A Study in Sociology.* Trans. by J.A. Spaulding & G. Simpson. New York: Free Press.

Gibbs, J.P. (1975). *Crime, Punishment, and Deterrence.* New York: Elsevier.

Gould, E.D., Weinberg, B.A., & Mustard, D.B. (2002). Crime rates and local labor market opportunities in the United States: 1979–1997. *The Review of Economics and Statistics, 84*(1), 45–61.

Grogger, J. (2006). An economic model of recent trends in violence. In A. Blumstein & J. Wallman (Eds.), *The Crime Drop in America,* revised edition. New York: Cambridge University Press.

Hirschi, T. (1989). Exploring alternatives to integrated theory. In S.F. Messner, M.D. Krohn, & A.E. Liska (Eds.), *Theoretical Integration in the Study of Deviance and Crime: Problems and Perspectives* (pp. 37–49). Albany, NY: State University of New York Press.

Kasarda, J.D., & Janowitz, M. (1974). Community attachment in mass society. *American Sociological Review, 39*(3), 328–339.

Katz, J. (1988). *Seductions of Crime: Moral and Sensual Attractions in Doing Evil.* New York: Basic Books.

Kirk, D.S. (2010). Sampson, Robert J.: Collective efficacy theory. In F.T. Cullen & P. Wilcox (Eds.), *Encyclopedia of Criminological Theory* (pp. 802–805). Thousand Oaks, CA: Sage.

Kirk, D.S., & Papachristos, A.V. (2011). Cultural mechanisms and the persistence of neighborhood violence. *American Journal of Sociology, 116*(4), 1190–1233.

Kleck, G., Sever, B., Li, S., & Gertz, M. (2005). The missing link in deterrence research. *Criminology, 43*(3), 623–660.

Kornhauser, R.R. (1978). *Social Sources of Delinquency: An Appraisal of Analytic Models.* Chicago, IL: University of Chicago Press.

Kubrin, C.E., Stucky, T.D., & Krohn, M.D. (2008). *Researching Theories of Crime and Deviance.* New York: Oxford University Press.

Kubrin, C.E., & Weitzer, R. (2003). New directions in social disorganization theory. *Journal of Research in Crime and Delinquency, 40*(4), 374–402.

LaFree, G.D. (1998). *Losing Legitimacy: Street Crime and the Decline of Social Institutions in America.* Boulder, CO: Westview Press.

Lazarsfeld, P.F., & Menzel, H. (1961). On the relation between individual and collective properties. In A. Etzioni (Ed.), *Complex Organizations: A Sociological Reader* (pp. 499–516). New York: Holt, Reinhart, and Winston.

Liska, A.E. (1990). The significance of aggregate dependent variables and contextual independent variables for linking macro and micro theories. *Social Psychology Quarterly, 53*(4), 292–301.

Liska, A.E. (Ed.) (1992). *Social Threat and Social Control.* Albany, NY: State University of New York Press.

Lombroso, C. (2006[1896–97]). *Criminal Man.* Trans, by M. Gibson & N.H. Rafter. Durham, NC: Duke University Press.

Malm, A.E. (2010). Brantingham, Patricia L., and Paul J. Brantingham: Environmental criminology. In F.T. Cullen & P. Wilcox (Eds.), *Encyclopedia of Criminological Theory* (pp. 114–118). Thousand Oaks, CA: Sage.

Matsueda, R.L. (2006). Differential social organization, collective action, and crime. *Crime, Law, and Social Change, 46*(1–2), 3–33.

Matsueda, R.L. (2010). Sutherland, Edwin H.: Differential association theory and differential social organization. In F.T. Cullen & P. Wilcox (Eds.), *Encyclopedia of Criminological Theory* (pp. 898–906). Thousand Oaks, CA: Sage.

Matsueda, R.L. (2013a). The macro–micro problem in criminology revisited. *The Criminologist, 38*(1), 1–7.

Matsueda, R.L. (2013b). Rational choice research in criminology: A multi-level approach. In R. Wittek, T. Snijders, & V. Nee (Eds.), *Handbook of Rational Choice Social Research* (pp. 283–321). Stanford, CA: Stanford University Press.

Meier, R.F., Kennedy, L.W., & Sacco, V.F. (Eds.) (2001). *The Process and Structure of Crime: Criminal Events and Crime Analysis: Advances in Criminological Theory,* Vol. 9. New Brunswick, NJ: Transaction.

Merton, R.K. (1938). Social structure and anomie. *American Sociological Review, 3*(5), 672–682.

Merton, R.K. (1968). *Social Theory and Social Structure.* New York: Free Press.

Messner, S.F. (1988). Merton's "social structure and anomie": The road not taken. *Deviant Behavior, 9*(1), 33–53.

Messner, S.F. (2012). Morality, markets, and the ASC: 2011 presidential address to the American Society of Criminology. *Criminology, 50*(12), 5–25.

Messner, S.F., & Golden, R.M. (1992). Racial inequality and racially disaggregated homicide rates: An assessment of alternative theoretical explanations. *Criminology, 30*(3), 421–448.

Messner, S.F., Krohn, M.D., & Liska, A.E. (1989). *Theoretical Integration in the Study of Deviance and Crime: Problems and Prospects.* Albany, NY: State University of New York Press.

Messner, S.F., & Rosenfeld, R. (1994). *Crime and the American Dream*. Belmont, CA: Wadsworth.

Messner, S.F., & Rosenfeld, R. (2006). The present and future of institutional anomie theory. In F.T. Cullen, J.P. Wright, & K.R. Blevins (Eds.), *Taking Stock: The Status of Criminological Theory: Advances in Criminological Theory*, Vol. *15* (pp. 127–148). New Brunswick, NJ: Transaction.

Messner, S.F., & Rosenfeld, R. (2013). *Crime and the American Dream*, 5th edition. Belmont, CA: Wadsworth.

Miethe, T.D., Hughes, M., & McDowall, D. (1991). An evaluation of alternative theoretical approaches. *Social Forces, 70*(1), 165–185.

Miethe, T., & Meier, R.F. (1994). *Crime and its Social Context: Toward an Integrated Theory of Offenders, Victims, and Situations*. Albany, NY: State University of New York Press.

Miethe, T.D., Stafford, M.C., & Long, J.S. (1987). Social differentiation in criminal victimization: A test of routine activities/lifestyle theories. *American Sociological Review, 52*(2), 184–194.

Miller, J.M. (Ed.) (2014). *The Encyclopedia of Theoretical Criminology*. Malden, MA: Wiley-Blackwell.

Osgood, D.W., Wilson, J.K., O'Malley, P.M., Bachman, J.G., & Johnston, L.D. (1996). Routine activities and individual deviant behavior. *American Sociological Review, 61*(4), 635–655.

Ousey, G.C. (2000). Explaining regional and urban variation in crime: A review of research. In G.D. LaFree (Ed.), *Criminal Justice 2000*, Vol. *1: The Nature of Crime: Continuity and Change* (pp. 261–308). Washington, DC: National Institute of Justice.

Ousey, G.C. (2010). Inequality and crime. In F.T. Cullen & P. Wilcox (Eds.), *Encyclopedia of Criminological Theory* (pp. 473–476). Thousand Oaks, CA: Sage.

Pratt, T.C., & Cullen, F.T. (2005). Assessing macro-level predictors and theories of crime: A meta-analysis. In M.H. Tonry (Ed.), *Crime and Justice: A Review of Research*, Vol. *32* (pp. 373–450). Chicago, IL: University of Chicago Press.

Raphael, S., & Winter-Ebmer, R. (2001). Identifying the effect of unemployment on crime. *Journal of Law and Economics, 44*, 259–283.

Rosenfeld, R. (2011). The big picture: 2010 presidential address to the American Society of Criminology. *Criminology, 49*(1), 1–26.

Roth, R. (2009). *American Homicide*. Cambridge, MA: Harvard University Press.

Sampson, R.J. (2006). Collective efficacy theory: Lessons learned and directions for future inquiry. In F.T. Cullen, J.P. Wright, & K.R. Blevins (Eds.), *Taking Stock: The Status of Criminological Theory: Advances in Criminological Theory*, Vol. *15* (pp. 149–167). New Brunswick, NJ: Transaction.

Sampson, R.J. (2012). *Great American City: Chicago and the Enduring Neighborhood Effect*. Chicago: IL: University of Chicago Press.

Sampson, R.J., & Bartusch, D.J. (1998). Legal cynicism and (subcultural?) tolerance of deviance: The neighborhood context of racial differences. *Law and Society Review, 32*(4), 777–804.

Sampson, R.J., & Groves, W.B. (1989). Community structure and crime: Testing social-disorganization theory. *American Journal of Sociology, 94*(4), 774–802.

Sampson, R.J., & Lauritsen, J.L. (1994). Violent victimization and offending: Individual-, situational-, and community-level risk factors. In A.J. Reiss & J.A. Roth (Eds.), *Understanding and Preventing Violence: Social Influences on Violence*, Vol. *3* (pp. 1–114). Washington, DC: National Academies Press.

Sampson, R.J., Morenoff, J.D., & Gannon-Rowley, T. (2002). Assessing "neighborhood effects": Social processes and new directions in research. *Annual Review of Sociology*, *28*, 443–478.

Sampson, R.J., Morenoff, J.D., & Earls, F. (1999). Beyond social capital: Spatial dynamics of collective efficacy for children. *American Sociological Review*, *64*(5), 633–660.

Sampson, R.J., Raudenbush, S.W., & Earls, F. (1997). Neighborhoods and violent crime: A multilevel study of collective efficacy. *Science*, *277*, 918–924.

Sampson, R.J., & Wilson, W.J. (1995). Toward a theory of race, crime, and urban inequality. In J. Hagan & R. Peterson (Eds.), *Crime and Inequality* (pp. 37–54). Stanford, CA: Stanford University Press.

Sampson, R.J., & Wooldredge, J.D. (1987). Linking the micro- and macro-level dimensions of lifestyle – Routine activity and opportunity models of predatory victimization. *Journal of Quantitative Criminology*, *3*(4), 371–393.

Savolainen, J. (2000). Inequality, welfare state, and homicide: Further support for the institutional anomie theory. *Criminology*, *38*(4), 1021–1042.

Shaw, C.R., & McKay, H.D. (1942). *Juvenile Delinquency and Urban Areas*. Chicago, IL: University of Chicago Press.

Short, J.F. (1998). The level of explanation problem revisited – The American Society of Criminology 1997 presidential address. *Criminology*, *36*(1), 3–36.

Skogan, W.G. (1990). *Disorder and Decline: Crime and the Spiral Decay in American Neighborhoods*. Berkeley, CA: University of California Press.

Stewart, E.A., & Simons, R.L. (2006). Structure and culture in African American adolescent violence: A partial test of the "code of the street" thesis. *Justice Quarterly*, *23*(1), 1–33.

Stinchcombe, A.L. (1975). Merton's theory of social structure. In L.A. Coser (Ed.), *The Idea of Social Structure: Papers in Honor of Robert K. Merton* (pp. 11–13). New York: Harcourt Brace Jovanovich.

Stolzenberg, L., Eitle, D., & D'Alessio, S.J. (2006). Race, economic inequality, and violent crime. *Journal of Criminal Justice*, *34*, 303–316.

Sutherland, E.H. (1947). *Principles of Criminology*, 4th edition. Chicago, IL: J.B. Lippincott.

Taylor, R.B. (2001). *Breaking Away From Broken Windows: Baltimore Neighborhoods and the Nationwide Fight against Crime, Grime, Fear and Decline*. Boulder, CO: Westview Press.

Tibbets, S.G. (2012). *Criminological Theory: The Essentials*. Thousand Oaks, CA: Sage.

Tittle, C.R. (1995). *Control Balance: Toward a General Theory of Deviance*. Boulder, CO: Westview Press.

Vito, G.F., & Maahs, J.R. (2012). *Criminology: Theory, Research, and Policy*, 3rd edition. Sudbury, MA: Jones & Bartlett.

Warr, M. (2001). Crime and opportunity: A theoretical essay. In R.F. Meier, L.W., Kennedy, & V.F. Sacco (Eds.), *The Process and Structure of Crime: Criminal Events and Crime Analysis: Advances in Criminological Theory*, Vol. 9 (pp. 65–94). New Brunswick, NJ: Transaction.

Wilcox, P., Land, K.C., & Hunt, S.A. (2003). *Criminal Circumstance: A Dynamic Multicontextual Criminal Opportunity Theory*. Hawthorne, NY: Aldine de Gruyter.

Wilson, J.Q., & Kelling, G.L. (1982). Broken windows: The police and neighborhood safety. *Atlantic Monthly*, *249*(3), 29–38.

Zimring, F.E., & Hawkins, G.J. (1973). *Deterrence: The Legal Threat in Crime Control*. Chicago, IL: University of Chicago Press.

# 24

# What International Research Has Told Us About Criminological Theory

Olena Antonaccio* and Ekaterina V. Botchkovar

Why do people commit crimes? There are many competing theories that provide a variety of answers to this question. Some of these theories are complex, whereas others are more parsimonious; some struggle for describing a number of contingencies thought to influence their causal mechanisms, and others forgo conditional influences completely (Tittle, 1995). Most importantly, although virtually all of these theories emerged in the US and other Western societies, it is assumed, if not asserted, that their explanation of crime would hold across time and space.

For years, theories of criminal behavior were scrutinized on the basis of Western data, and the criteria for the generality of their predictions were set to vary within the borders of the Western world. Thus, to be perceived general, a theory of criminal behavior was to explain a variety of illegal behaviors in individuals of varying criminality and demographic characteristics. New empirical studies investigating the relevance of criminological theories to crime in the settings other than the US and a few other English-speaking countries have challenged this view. Although a few tests of the US-based theories with data from Western Europe and Asia appeared in the early 1990s (e.g., Junger-Tas, 1992; Tanioka & Glaser, 1991), the situation radically shifted at the beginning of the 21st century when new data from a variety of sociocultural settings became available to the students of criminological theory. As a result, in the last decade, scholars have tested a number of theories of crime and deviance in non-English-speaking Western and non-Western settings. Preliminary findings suggest that some theories perform better than others in unusual sociocultural contexts, that some settings may share structural and/or cultural characteristics altering the outcomes predicted by these theories, and that the culture of a

*The authors contributed equally to this manuscript

*The Handbook of Criminological Theory*, First Edition. Edited by Alex R. Piquero.
© 2016 John Wiley & Sons, Inc. Published 2016 by John Wiley & Sons, Inc.

setting may have an important conditional influence on the causal mechanisms of some theoretical accounts of criminal behavior. While accumulated evidence is still too scarce and scattered to draw definitive conclusions, it is clear that, to answer the question of why people *around the world* commit crimes, extant theories will need to entertain the role of larger sociocultural contexts as a potential contingency for the processes they describe.

This chapter reviews and compares the results of research from Western and non-Western countries, focusing on several theories that seem to have received the most testing in foreign contexts. For the sake of simplicity, these theories are placed in four broad groups: strain, social learning, control, and "other" theories. Although some theoretical explanations of crime rates and criminal victimization have been evaluated in international settings, this analysis is limited to individual-level theories of criminal behavior.

## Strain Theories

### General strain theory

In the last two decades, general strain theory (GST; Agnew, 1992, 2006a) has become one of the most popular theoretical accounts of criminal behavior. According to GST, criminal behavior is a product of anger and related negative emotions resulting from unpleasant conditions and events (strains) often encountered by individuals (Agnew, 1992). The theory recognizes that people regularly face situations they dislike but choose to cope conventionally. Thus, it identifies multiple factors, including objective and subjective properties of strains, as well as individual characteristics, likely to affect the probability that strain would result in criminal conduct (Agnew, 1992).

Although GST boasts a solid body of evidence supporting its premises, most of its tests draw on North American data elicited from juveniles or young adults (e.g. Baron, 2004; Broidy, 2001). In these studies, strains have been found to explain a variety of illegal/deviant behaviors, ranging from general delinquency (Brezina, 1996) and white-collar crime (Langton & Piquero, 2007) to drunk driving (Capowich, Mazerolle, & Piquero, 2001) and self-harm (Hay & Meldrum, 2010). Strains have been shown to vary in their criminogenic potential (see Agnew, 2006b for review) but more research is needed to establish exact patterns of relationships between specific strains and crime. The precise nature of the relationship between strain, negative affect, and criminal conduct is also yet to be established, with some studies confirming an intervening role of negative affect (e.g. Tittle, Broidy, & Getz, 2008) and some not (e.g., Baron, 2004; Hay & Meldrum, 2010). Finally, only some contingencies specified by GST have been investigated, and findings of this research are often inconclusive (see Agnew, 2006b for review).

Recently, this body of literature has been supplemented with studies investigating the potential of GST to explain criminal behavior in other countries. Accumulated evidence suggests that strain is associated with delinquency in some western non-English-speaking countries, including Belgium (Beeck, Pauwels, & Put, 2012), Italy (Froggio & Agnew, 2007), and Iceland (Sigfusdottir & Silver, 2009; Sigfusdottir, Kristjansson, & Agnew, 2012), as well as in the non-Western settings, such as China (Bao *et al.*, 2004; Liu & Lin, 2007; Cheung & Cheung, 2010), Taiwan (Lin *et al.*, 2014), Philippines (Maxwell, 2001), South Korea (Morash & Moon, 2007; Moon *et al.*, 2009; Moon, Blurton, & McCluskey, 2010), Turkey (Özbay, 2011), Lithuania, Romania, Bulgaria, Latvia (Sigfusdottir, Kristjansson, & Agnew, 2012), and Ukraine (Botchkovar, Tittle, & Antonaccio, 2009). Although negative emotions have been shown to mediate the relationship between strain and crime (Botchkovar, Tittle, & Antonaccio, 2009; Beeck, Pauwels, & Put, 2012), the paucity of studies in non-English speaking countries that include measures of negative affect makes it impossible to draw any firm conclusions about their role in the strain–crime relationship. Finally, in some settings, the strain–crime link appears to be subject to conditional influences such as the subjective evaluation of an event as stressful (Froggio & Agnew, 2007), presence of delinquent peers (Morash & Moon, 2007), and coping strategies employed in the past (Botchkovar, Tittle, & Antonaccio, 2013).

While GST appears to fare moderately well both in the Western and non-Western context, some preliminary findings from Asian countries and Eastern/Southern Europe hint that not all cultural settings are equally receptive to the processes described by GST, and that the relevance of some strains to crime may be culture dependent. For instance, measured broadly, strain is, at best, weakly related to criminal behavior and heavy drinking in Russia (Botchkovar & Broidy, 2013a; Botchkovar & Hughes, 2010; Botchkovar *et al.*, 2009). Strain also predicts few deviant behaviors among young Turkish adults (Özbay, 2011), and it is unimportant for crime in Greece (Botchkovar *et al.*, 2009) and India (Hartjen & Kethineni, 1999). In an attempt to explain the relative resilience to strain among Russians, Botchkovar & Broidy (2013a) rely on the unique situation of Russia to suggest that chronic exposure to strain may eventually reduce its criminogenic potential. It is possible that the absence of or weak relationship between strain and deviance in Greece, Turkey and India could also be explained by contextual factors.

Equally interesting are the results of studies teasing out associations between specific strains and deviance. In a series of studies involving South Korean youth, contrary to theoretical expectations, Moon and colleagues (Morash & Moon, 2007; Moon, Blurton, & McCluskey, 2008) show a consistent preventive effect of parental punishment, a likely source of strain, on delinquent behavior. Similar findings are observed in Chinese male students by Cheung & Cheung (2010), whereas Maxwell (2001) reports no association between harsh parenting (i.e. spanking) and delinquency in Filipino youth. Although this pattern of findings in Asian studies is yet to be explained, Moon, Blurton, & McCluskey (2008) speculate that harsh parenting may have a deterrent rather than crime provoking effect on delinquency in the context of South Korea where such parenting strategies are widely accepted. Finally, Lin (2011) reports that educational and financial goal-related strains fare modestly well as predictors of delinquency in Taiwan, but not in the US (see Liu & Lin, 2007 for similar findings in China). Moreover, Lin's study also shows that comparable strains may produce different outcomes in the US and Taiwan. This curious finding suggests that not only evaluation of strains, but also choices of coping strategies may be culture-dependent.

## Control Theories

### Social control theory

Social control theory proposes that delinquents who fail to maintain strong social bonds are more likely to engage in delinquent behavior (Hirschi, 1969). According to Hirschi (1969), there are four elements of the social bond: attachment, commitment, involvement, and belief. Attachment corresponds to the affective ties formed with significant others such as parents and peers. Commitment is investment in conventional activities, which can be lost if a deviant act is committed. The third element is involvement in conventional activities that keep individuals too busy to engage in crime. Finally, belief or the extent of internalization of societal rules and norms is the fourth element of the social bond. Originally, Hirschi's social control theory was proposed as a theory of juvenile delinquency but, since then, it has been also extended to explain involvement in crime over the life course in Sampson & Laub's (1993) age-graded theory of informal social control.

*Cross-national research on social control theory*   Hirschi's (1969) social control theory has been extensively tested in numerous empirical studies, with most emanating from English-speaking countries. These studies find evidence supporting the link between some elements of the social bond (especially attachment and commitment to school and family as well as conventional beliefs) and different types of crime and delinquency, although observed effects sizes are moderate (e.g., Chapple, McQuillan, & Berdahl, 2005; Doherty, 2006; Sampson & Laub, 1993) and often attenuated when other predictors of delinquency (i.e. delinquent peers) are taken into consideration (Kempf, 1993).

Using various random and non-random samples of adolescents from Western European, but non-English–speaking, countries such as Belgium and Switzerland (Egli *et al.*, 2010; Junger-Tas, Marshall, & Ribeaud, 2003), France (Hartjen & Priyadarsini, 2003), Iceland (Bernburg & Thorlindsson, 1999), Netherlands (Junger-Tas, 1992; Junger & Marshall, 1997; Junger-Tas, Marshall, & Ribeaud, 2003), Finland, Italy, Portugal, Spain (Junger-Tas, Marshall, & Ribeaud, 2003) and Sweden (Svensson, 2003; Torstensson, 1990), new studies report results similar to those in the Anglo-American nations. Although they find that some types of social bonds, such as parental attachment and supervision, school attachment, and belief, impact various types of juvenile delinquency, the effects of those predictors are relatively weak. Notably, several of these studies also investigate whether gender or ethnicity moderate effects of social bonds on juvenile crime and delinquency (Hartjen & Priyadarsini, 2003; Junger & Marshall, 1997; Junger-Tas, Ribeaud, & Cruyff, 2004).

Supporting the theory, they conclude that crime-preventive qualities of social bonds are not substantially different for boys and girls in several Western European countries or for adolescents of variable ethnic origins in the Netherlands, and that group differences in levels of social controls account for some of observed gender/ethnic gaps in delinquency. However, this research also suggests that group differences in the strength of social controls may be culturally determined. For example, in the Netherlands, Turkish parents exercise tight control over both boys and girls, whereas Moroccan parents strongly control their daughters but not their sons (Junger-Tas, Ribeaud, & Cruyff, 2004).

A number of studies have put Hirschi's social control theory to test in non-Western nations, including Bolivia (Meneses & Akers, 2011), China (Chui & Chan, 2011; Sheu 1988; Wang *et al.*, 2002; Zhang & Messner, 1996), India (Hartjen & Kethineni, 1999), Israel (Cohen & Zeira, 1999; Shechory & Laufer 2008), Japan (Kobayashi & Fukushima, 2012; Tanioka & Glaser, 1991), the Philippines (Shoemaker, 1994), South Korea (Hwang & Akers, 2003; Kim, Kwak, & Yun, 2010), and Turkey (Özbay & Özcan, 2006). Using nonrandom samples of youth or school/college students (cf. Kim *et al.*, 2010), this research reports that some dimensions of social bonds, such as parental attachment and monitoring, school commitment, and belief, are associated with lower levels of juvenile delinquency in non-Western samples (but see Cohen & Zeira, 1999).

However, the effects of some social bonds, especially family supervision and school commitment, on juvenile delinquency appear to be more robust than commonly observed in the research with Western samples withstanding the competition from rival predictors of delinquency (e.g., Fukushima, Sharp, & Kobayashi, 2009; Hartjen & Kethineni, 1999; Hwang & Akers, 2003; Kobayashi & Fukushima, 2012; Özban & Özcay, 2008; Shoemaker, 1994; Wang & Jensen, 2003; Wang *et al.*, 2002; Zhang & Messner, 1996). Some of these differences may be interpreted as indicative of support for a stronger emphasis on familial and educational institutions in the Asian culture (Kim *et al.*, 2010; Zhang & Messner, 1996). In addition, some of this non-Western research indicates that social bond variables may account for more variation in boys' delinquency than girls' and may not be applicable at all to Filipino or Indian girls (Hartjen & Kethineni, 1999; Özban & Özcay, 2008; Shoemaker, 1994).

*Cross-national research on age-graded theory of informal social control*   Studies testing the age-graded theory of informal social control in the US have produced equivocal findings. Whereas some research has shown that ties to spouses or work or motherhood might prevent criminal activity (Kreager, Matsueda, & Erosheva, 2010; Sampson & Laub, 2003, Sampson, Laub & Wimer, 2007), other relevant studies have reported conditional (e.g., only for men) or non-significant crime-reducing effects of marriage, cohabitation, or motherhood (e.g., Horney, Osgood & Marshall, 1995; King, Massoglia & Macmillan, 2007; Giordano, Cernkovich & Rudolph, 2002), suggesting that such influences may be highly contingent on many factors including cultural contexts. Yet, so far there has been very little additional research on this topic in other cross-cultural contexts. The two applications of age-graded theory of informal social control to Western non-English speaking countries are the studies by Blokland & Nieuwbeerta (2005) and Savolainen (2009). While the research by Blokland & Nieuwbeerta (2005), using the Dutch data from both males and female, finds a significant impact of marriage on reducing convictions (but not self-reported crime) that differs across offender groups, the study of Savolainen (2009), employing a sample of Finnish recidivists, reports crime-protective effects of not only marriage and work but also cohabitation and parenthood, which have not been commonly documented in the US-based research previously. The latter research attributes these observed effects to specific cultural norms in Finland bearing on union formation and universal governmental benefits for families with young children.

Only one study drawing on age-graded theory of informal social control has been conducted in a non-Western, Asian context, using a sample of young workers from Tianjin, China, and it proposes that distinctive features of work units in China in the 1980s might make ties to these units especially salient in the life of Chinese workers (Zhang & Messner, 1999). Supporting this hypothesis, the research finds that strong bonds to work unit among workers are associated with a reduced likelihood of imprisonment. Finally, some relevant findings from the study by Antonaccio *et al.* (2010) indicate that protective effects of the marital status might be sensitive to societal contexts. The researchers report no significant protective effect of marriage on deviance in Russia and Ukraine, but they observe the expected relationship in Greece. Overall, albeit scarce, evidence originating in non-English speaking countries appears to confirm that effects of adult social bonds may depend on specific sociocultural environments.

## A general theory of crime

A general theory of crime or self-control theory (Gottfredson & Hirschi, 1990) proposes that inability to appreciate long-term consequences of one's actions, or weak self-control, is the sole cause of all types of deviant behavior. A product of ineffective upbringing by caregivers who fail to recognize and punish misbehavior of their children early, self-control is argued to develop by approximately 8–9 years old and remain relatively stable after that. Interestingly, the theory considers self-control to be a truly general predictor of crime, arguing, "Our approach… assumes… that cultural variability is not important in the causation of crime, and that a single theory of crime can encompass the reality of cross-cultural differences in crime rates" (Gottfredson & Hirschi, 1990:174–175).

The theory remains one of the most popular accounts of deviant behavior, and its key premises have been investigated in numerous cultural settings. Research has focused on various elements of the theory, ranging from assessment of the psychometric characteristics of the self-control scale (e.g. Piquero & Rosay, 1998) and the stability of self-control (Hay & Forrest, 2006) to the relationship between self-control and deviance (Pratt & Cullen, 2000) and the origins of self-control (Nofziger, 2008).

Most of this research, however, is limited to a small number of English-speaking countries: the US (Pratt & Cullen, 2000), Canada (e.g. Nakhaie, Silverman, & LaGrange, 2000; Keane, Maxim, & Teevan, 1993), England (Wikström & Svensson, 2010), and New Zealand (e.g. Caspi *et al.*, 1994), where self-control has been found to predict a range of deviant acts across demographic groups (Tittle *et al.*, 2003), longitudinal and cross-sectional designs (see Pratt & Cullen, 2000), and in the samples of varying criminality (e.g. Pogarsky, 2007). Accumulated evidence from the US also links self-control to childrearing (e.g. Nofziger, 2008), although self-control does not always mediate the relationship between parenting and misconduct (e.g. Latimore, Tittle, & Grasmick, 2006).

Somewhat less frequent are the tests of self-control theory in other Western and non-Western countries. Extant studies suggest, however, that the association between self-control and crime holds in Finland (Pulkkinen & Hamalainen, 1995), Germany (Seipel & Eifler, 2010), Switzerland (Ribeaud & Eisner, 2006; Vazsonyi & Klanjsek, 2008), Sweden (Svensson, Pauwels, & Weerman, 2010), the Netherlands (Vazsonyi *et al.*, 2001), Spain (Romero *et al.*, 2003), and several other non-English speaking countries (Rebellon *et al.*, 2008; see Marshall & Enzmann, 2012). Self-control has also been reported to predict acts of deviance in Eastern and Southern European countries, such as Russia (Tittle & Botchkovar, 2005a, 2005b; Tittle *et al.*, 2010), Ukraine (Antonaccio & Tittle, 2008), Greece (Tittle *et al.*, 2010), Turkey (Özbay, 2008; Özbay & Koksoy, 2009), Bosnia and Herzegovina (Klanjsek, Vazsonyi, & Trejos, 2012), Slovenia (Vazsonyi, Trejos, Castillo, & Huang, 2006), Serbia, Hungary (Vazsonyi *et al.*, 2001; see also Rebellon *et al.*, 2008), Romania, and Lithuania (Rebellon *et al.*, 2008). Albeit scarce, some evidence suggests that self-control may also explain acts of deviance in such rare research locations as Central/South America (Marshall & Enzmann, 2012; Meneses & Akers, 2011; Rebellon *et al.*, 2008) and South Africa (Rebellon *et al.*, 2008). Across these settings, self-control has been found to predict various types of deviance, including property offending and violence (Tittle & Botchkovar, 2005a; Rebellon *et al.*, 2008), piracy, cheating and bribery (Vazsonyi & Klanjsek, 2008), risky sexual behavior, drug and alcohol use (Klanjsek, Vazsonyi, & Trejos, 2012; Meneses & Akers, 2011), and it performs quite well as a predictor of deviant behavior in adults (Tittle & Botchkovar, 2005a, 2005b; Rebellon *et al.*, 2008; Özbay, 2008) and youth (Vazsonyi & Klanjsek, 2008; Marshall & Enzmann, 2012). Finally, some of the recent research has tested and found support for self-control theory in the East using data from Japan (Vazsonyi *et al.*, 2004), China and Hong Kong (Chui & Chan, 2013; Cheung & Cheung, 2008, 2010; Cretacci *et al.*, 2009; Lu *et al.*, 2013), Thailand (Kerley *et al.*, 2008), South Korea (Hwang & Akers, 2003), Taiwan, Iran, and Singapore (Rebellon *et al.*, 2008).

Only a few studies have investigated the origins of self-control in international settings. Vazsonyi & Belliston (2007) find a modest connection between childrearing and self-control in a study of five countries, Japan, Switzerland, the Netherlands, Hungary, and the US (see also Vazsonyi & Klanjsek, 2008) whereas Brauer *et al.* (2012) also confirm this link in the sample of adults from Dhaka, Bangladesh. Another study by Rebellon and colleagues (2008) links low self-control to parental neglect in 32 Western and non-Western countries. Interestingly, their findings also suggest that self-control, beyond individual circumstances, may be a product of the average level of parenting neglect in the nation. Finally, Botchkovar & Broidy (2013b) and Brauer *et al.* (2012) fail to find a connection between parenting and self-control in samples of adults in former Soviet countries of Russia and Ukraine, respectively. Overall, these mixed findings seem to echo the disparate results of relevant US-based studies (e.g. Morris, Wood, & Dunaway, 2007).

In sum, the relationship between self-control and deviance appears to hold in many countries. However, some findings, particularly those from the non-Western settings, indicate that the power of self-control theory to explain "all crime, at all times" (Gottfredson & Hirschi, 1990:117) may be limited, and more evidence is necessary to establish the generality of the causal mechanism proposed by the theory. In a series of studies of Chinese youth, Cretacci and associates (2009, 2010, 2012) as well as Wang *et al.* (2002) reveal no association between self-control and some acts of deviance. As Cretacci and colleagues suggest (2009), for young adults in China, under some circumstances, factors like social bonds may be more con-sequential for deviance than self-control. Moreover, several multisite studies (Marshall & Enzmann, 2012; Rebellon *et al.*, 2008; Tittle *et al.*, 2010; Vazsonyi *et al.*, 2006) report varying strength of the association between self-control and crime. For instance, using data from 32 countries, Rebellon and colleagues (2008) show that the relationship between self-control and deviance varies by cultural site and specific criminal act (see also Marshall & Enzmann (2012) for similar find-ings), whereas Tittle and associates (2010) find that the link between self-control and criminal behavior may be weaker in Greece relative to Russia. In addition, findings from non-English-speaking Western and non-Western settings show varying relationships between specific dimensions of self-control and deviant behavior (Meneses & Akers 2011, Romero *et al.*, 2003; Rebellon *et al.*, 2008; Vazsonyi *et al.*, 2004), and accumulated evidence is insufficient to resolve existing debates regarding the stability of self-control (Jo & Zhang, 2012; Yun & Walsh, 2011; cf. Hay & Forrest, 2006) or the role of opportunity and other conditioning factors in self-control theory (see Grasmick *et al.*, 1993; Marshall & Enzmann 2012; Tittle & Botchkovar, 2005a).

## Social Learning Theory

Akers' (1998) social learning theory specifies complex causal relationships between misbehavior and social learning concepts, including differential reinforcement and imitation, definitions, and differential association, proposing that misbehavior is more likely "when, on balance, the combined effects of these four main sets of variables instigate and strengthen nonconforming over conforming acts" (50). Differential reinforcement (instrumental learning through a schedule of rewards and punishments) and imitation (learning through observation and modeling of others' behavior and its rewarding and punishing outcomes) are the principal learning mechanisms. Definitions, cognitive elements that include beliefs, attitudes, beliefs, and orientations, constitute the content of learning produced by these mechanisms. Finally, differential association is a process of learning deviance through exposure to conforming and nonconforming behavioral models and sources of various definitions as well as by observing positive and negative consequences of misconduct.

In English-speaking countries, there is a large body of literature confirming substantial associations between various social learning variables (especially differential association with deviant peers and definitions) and many forms of crime and delinquency (see Akers, 2009 and Pratt *et al.*, 2010 for reviews). In the meta-analysis of social learning theory (SLT) studies, Pratt *et al.* (2010) find that two social learning components, differential association with deviant peers and definitions, consistently demonstrate strongest mean effect sizes across various studies, whereas various measures of differential reinforcement have fared somewhat worse with smaller and less consistent mean effects (Pratt *et al.*, 2010). Regardless of some observed variability in the explanatory potential of social learning variables, the results of this research have been interpreted as very favorable to SLT, and the theory has emerged as one of the mostly strongly supported major explanations of crime (Akers, 2009; cf. Pratt *et al.*, 2010).

Yet the body of literature on SLT in non-English speaking countries is relatively scarce, and, with few exceptions, it mostly employs non-random samples of school/ college students. On one hand, the research conducted in European countries, including Austria (Rumpold *et al.*, 2006), France (Hartjen & Priyadarsini, 2003), Germany (Link, 2008; Oberwittler, 2004), and Greece (Tittle, Antonaccio & Botchkovar, 2012), has produced findings consistent with those originating in the United States and other English speaking nations. Most of this scholarship focuses on deviant peer associations and attitudes and their effect on individual behavior. The findings suggest that these variables are linked to various forms of misconduct among young people and that their effects are very robust (e.g., Hartjen & Priyadarsini, 2003; Link, 2008; Oberwittler, 2004; Rumpold *et al.*, 2006). In addition, one study using a random sample of adults from Athens, Greece, also provides evidence supporting significant associations between less explored social learning variables, such as differential reinforcement, various types of definitions, and criminal involvement (Tittle, Antonaccio & Botchkovar, 2012).

On the other hand, the tests of SLT in non-Western contexts are mostly conducted in Asian countries such as China (Friday *et al.*, 2005; Zhang & Messner, 1995), India (Hartjen & Kethineni, 1999), Japan (Kobayashi, Akers. & Sharp, 2011), Taiwan (Wang & Jensen, 2003), and South Korea (Hwang & Akers, 2003, 2006; Kim *et al.*, 2010) provide support for SLT documenting significant associations between different social learning measures, including exposure to delinquent friends and parental deviance, individual and peer delinquent attitudes, imitation of peers and parents, and friends' reaction favorable to delinquency. However, they also reveal several cross-cultural disparities in absolute and relative effects of social learning variables on delinquency. Thus, studies employing comparable samples of American and Indian (Hartjen & Kethineni, 1999) and American and Japanese (Kobayashi, Akers, & Sharp, 2011) students report that exposure to delinquent peers is significant in all samples but it appears to have a stronger association with delinquency among Americans relative to Indians and Japanese. In addition, in the Indian sample, the relationship between exposure to delinquent peers and delinquency appears to be conditional on gender as the effect of this social learning variable is significant only for boys. In addition, Kobayashi *et al.* (2011) investigate sources of individual deviant attitudes and report that, although in both American and Japanese samples peer attitudes are more influential than parental attitudes as predictors of attitudes toward deviance among college students, relative effects of peer attitudes on individual attitudes are larger among Japanese. They argue that such differences are consistent with a more lenient approach to parenting practiced by Japanese. Finally, Kim *et al.* (2010) find that, whereas association with delinquent peers does not predict deviance, intensity of peer association has a significant impact on substance abuse in the nationally representative sample of junior high school students in South Korea. Yet, the effects of the rival predictors, such as parental supervision, are statistically significant and somewhat larger than those of peer variables. Interestingly, this finding of the study stands in contrast not only to the results from the Western-based research but also to the other two studies of SLT conducted in Busan, South Korea (Hwang & Akers, 2003, 2006). Kim *et al.* (2010) attribute this disparity in the findings to a unique socio-cultural environment of the city of Busan that is more westernized and heterogeneous than South Korea in general.

Finally, in spite of the mandate laid down by Hwang & Akers a decade ago calling for additional cross-national research to evaluate social learning theory in "many other societies besides Asia... in Latin America, Eastern Europe, Russia, the Middle East, and elsewhere" (2003:55), to date only three tests of SLT in non-Asian non-Western contexts have been conducted (Meneses & Akers, 2011; Tavits, 2010; Tittle, Antonaccio, & Botchkovar, 2012). The 2011 study by Meneses & Akers compares the effects of social learning variables on deviance in the non-random samples of Bolivian and US college students. The study reports stronger relative effects of peer association and peer imitation in the American sample, whereas definitions favorable to marijuana use appear to be more salient among Bolivians.

The two remaining studies of SLT utilize randomly selected data from several former Soviet Union countries. Using two nationally representative datasets, one consisting of members of general public and the other of public officials in post-communist Estonia, the study by Tavits (2010) examines relationships between individual involvement in corruption and two social learning variables, normative definitions and imitation (defined as pervasiveness of corruption). As expected, Tavits finds that these social learning variables have significant effects on the likelihood of corruptibility among public officials and paying a bribe in the general public. The study also advances SLT research by exploring previously unexamined contingent effects of factors such structural incentives (e.g. extortion or being asked to pay bribe) on the relationship between social learning variables and individual corrupt behavior. Interestingly, the results indicate that social learning influences are not significant among those individuals who have experienced extortion. This suggests that social learning causal processes might be relevant for decision-making regarding corruptive behaviors only in contexts where structural incentives for corruption are absent. Finally, the study by Tittle and colleagues (2012) assesses the underlying causal mechanisms of SLT in Greece, Russia, and Ukraine and finds that, in all three contexts, social learning variables are associated with projected probability of crime. However, this research also reveals some intriguing cross-national differences suggesting SLT mechanisms may not be completely culture-invariant. For example, relative to utilitarian definitions of costs and benefits of crimes, moral definitions of crime are observed to be more potent predictors of criminal involvement and more prominent mediators of reinforcement-crime relationships among Greeks than among Russian and Ukrainians. The researchers argue that, because Russians and Ukrainians live in seemingly more anomic and socially disorganized environments lacking conventional definitions, they may be more often guided by mechanisms emphasizing rational calculations of benefits and costs than the residents of Greece.

Overall, social learning variables appear to demonstrate consistent and substantial effects on delinquency and crime in diverse contexts. However, the strength of their effects is not invariant across contexts and neither are the underlying causal processes, which, again, suggest that the key processes outlined by SLT may be conditioned by various societal characteristics.

## Other Theories

Several other popular accounts of criminal behavior, such as deterrence, rational choice, and situational action theories, have been more or less extensively tested in English-speaking countries but not in other societies. For example, abundant empirical research on deterrence/rational choice theories in English- speaking countries demonstrates consistent significant effects of perceived benefits of misbehavior, whereas effects of sanctions tend to be variable and modest in size (Tittle *et al.*, 2010; Wikström, Tseloni, & Karlis, 2011; see Paternoster, 1987 and Pratt *et al.*, 2006 for reviews).

Only a few studies have examined these theories in other contexts. On one hand, the results of this research suggest the cross-cultural variability of sanction effects on illegal behavior. For example, the study of adults residing in Dresden, Germany shows that perceived probability of formal detection may deter crime (Kroneberg, Heintze, & Mehlkop, 2010), whereas the threat of formal sanctions appears unimportant for crime in Russia and Ukraine (Tittle, Botchkovar, & Antonaccio, 2011). Tittle and colleagues speculate that their finding may be due to the deterioration of the criminal justice system in many former Soviet republics. In line with US-based research, informal sanctioning items have been found to be significantly, although weakly, associated with various types of crimes in one non-random sample of Dutch adolescents (Pauwels *et al.*, 2011), one non-random sample of Russian adults (Tittle & Botchkovar, 2005a), and the random samples of Russian and Ukrainian adults (Tittle, Botchkovar, & Antonaccio, 2011). Unexpectedly, two studies, Grasmick & Kobayashi (2002) and Tittle *et al.* (2011), find no significant effects of informal sanctioning on crime among university hospital employees in Japan and adult population of Athens, Greece, respectively. Tittle *et al.* suggest the observed pattern may reflect greater reliance of Greeks on normative types of controls such as moral constraints rather than on utilitarian considerations of costs of punishment. Somewhat consistent with this explanation, Grasmick & Kobayashi (2002) find that self-shame predicts workplace deviance better than informal sanctioning in their Japanese sample. On the other hand, studies carried out so far in few non-English speaking countries such as Germany (Kroneberg, Heintse, & Mehlkop, 2010; Seipel & Eifler, 2010), Greece, and Russia (Tittle *et al.*, 2010) uniformly support associations between perceived crime-related rewards or its expected utility (benefits minus costs) and various types of crime proposed by rational choice theory.

Similarly, although still scarce in non-English speaking contexts, studies of situational action theory (Wikström, 2006) show that morality has consistent and relatively strong relationships with various types of crime in the samples of adolescents and adults from Belgium, Netherlands (Svensson, Pauwels, & Weerman, 2010), Sweden (Wikström & Svensson, 2008), Greece, Russia, and Ukraine (Antonaccio & Tittle, 2008; Tittle, Antonaccio, Botchkovar, & Kranidioti, 2010). However, even this research reveals some interesting contextual variations. For example, Tittle and colleagues (2010) report that, although both expected utility and morality are good predictors of criminal probability among Greeks and Russians, effects of expected utility relative to morality effects are larger in Russia confirming that, for Russians, instrumental considerations may be more salient than normative factors.

## Conclusions: Cross-National Research and Criminological Theory Development

Tittle (1995) outlines three features of adequate theories – comprehensiveness, depth, and precision. Comprehensiveness concerns the degree of completeness of a theoretical explanation and its inclusion of all necessary causal elements. Depth refers to the extent to which a given theory describes the full causal chain leading to an outcome of interest and does not omit descriptions of how causal elements are linked together in a unified whole. Finally, precision indicates how well a theory spells out all contingencies for its causal processes as well as whether it discusses the type and form of the causal relations. Ultimately, improvement in all of these elements of adequate theories is necessary for successful theoretical growth.

Overall, the reviewed research has been able to attend to each of these elements to a greater or lesser degree. First, by default, one feature of adequate theories tested in all theoretically-relevant cross-national research is precision. As mentioned earlier, empirical evaluations carried out in any context other than those where theories were originally developed always help establish their generality. In particular, extant cross-national research has aided in finding out whether socio-cultural environments may serve as contingencies for causal processes outlined in theories. Yet, the answer provided by this body of research is far from a simple "yes" or "no." On one hand, the good news is that US-based criminological theories including general strain, social learning, social bond, and self-control theories may apply to other contexts and that their main explanatory variables are confirmed to predict crime and delinquency in most locations around the world. On the other hand, the review of cross-national evidence indicates that exceptions to this pattern are abundant and that societal contexts may condition influences of those individual-level variables in various ways. For example, some theoretical predictors of crime show very weak or no predictive potential in some research settings and populations, whereas others exhibit differential explanatory power and varying relative effects across different cross-cultural environments. Yet, to date, virtually no criminological theories have attempted to incorporate potential conditioning effects of societal contexts into their explanatory frameworks (for exceptions see Braithwaite, 1989; Colvin, Cullen, & Vander Ven, 2002; Wikström, 2006). Thus, more work in the direction of further theoretical specification of such influences is clearly needed.

Further, almost all internationally-based research provides at least some evidence that speaks to another feature of adequate theories, their comprehensiveness. At a minimum, most studies that focus on only one criminological theory report the power of theoretical predictors to account for variation in outcomes, thus showing whether the theoretical predictor/s drawn from the theory are sufficient for the explanation of crime and delinquency. Similar to Western research, international studies have indicated that no theoretical predictor/s drawn from a single theory is sufficient for providing an adequate explanation of crime and delinquency, thus suggesting the need to include more causal elements. In addition, those several cross-national studies that go a step further and evaluate relative predictive power or two or more theories (e.g., Antonaccio & Tittle, 2008; Egli *et al.*, 2010; Hartjen & Kethineni, 1999; Hwang & Akers, 2003; Kim, Kwak & Yun, 2010; Link, 2008; Meneses & Akers, 2011; Shoemaker, 1994; Tittle *et al.*, 2010; Wang *et al.*, 2002) find that many theoretical variables predict criminal outcomes independent of each other and that relative predictive potential of different theories varies across socio-cultural contexts. Collectively, the results of the cross-national research are useful for examining comprehensiveness of criminological theories. They demonstrate empirically that none of the so called "simple" criminological theories operating with a single explanatory variable (Tittle, 1995) is adequate as a stand-alone explanation of crime and suggest that some kind of integrated theoretical perspective may be needed to address the issue of crime causality satisfactorily.

Finally, the feature of adequate theories that has received least attention in cross-national research is depth. Likely because of the lack of longitudinal or prospective/retrospective data in these locations, most studies conducted in foreign contexts do not consider full causal chains leading criminal involvement including antecedent and intervening variables. Notable exceptions are several cross-national studies that examine causes of self-control as well as preceding and mediating factors in general strain and social learning theories (Antonaccio, Botchkovar, & Tittle, 2011; Beeck, Pauwels, & Put, 2012; Botchkovar & Broidy, 2013b; Botchkovar, Tittle, & Antonaccio, 2009, 2013; Brauer *et al.*, 2012; Rebellon *et al.*, 2008; Vazsonyi & Belliston, 2007). Empirical examination of extended causal processes such as influence of prior coping strategies on the relationship between accumulated strain and crime as well as associations between prior differential reinforcement, current definitions and criminal probability are rare or non-existent even in the US-based research. These studies, then, are especially likely to contribute substantially to the relevant body of criminological research. Generally, all cross-national studies seem to have added important knowledge regarding one or more features of adequate theories. Yet, much more research in foreign contexts is required to assess further comprehensiveness, precision, and depth of the theories already examined and to conduct evaluations of theoretical explanations that have yet to be tested in international locations.

The conclusions detailed above should be interpreted with some caution as the extant cross-national research on criminological theories is not without methodological limitations. Some of them are actually shared by the studies using data from both English-speaking and non-English speaking nations. For example, most tests of individual-level criminological theories conducted in the US or elsewhere rely on survey data and any international survey-based evaluation of theoretical explanations is thus subject to the same weaknesses as any research based on the US survey data. In addition, similar to North American and other studies from English-speaking countries, most internationally based tests of criminological theories operate with limited and highly variable measures of theoretically relevant predictors of crime and deviance. Curiously, in contrast to the US-based data, data on crime from unusual foreign locations have been generally viewed with suspicion and distrust. Fortunately, in the last few decades, many strides in collecting valid cross-national data have been made, which resulted in well-designed comparative studies of crime employing multiple data verification procedures and indicating that their data are as unbiased as those typically derived from crime surveys in the US (Antonaccio & Tittle, 2008; Bennett, 2004; Junger-Tas, 2010; Tittle *et al.*, 2010). Yet, most empirical evaluations of criminological theories in international settings still draw on youth and student data, which precludes firm conclusions about the potential generalizability of those theories to adult populations (but see, for example, Antonaccio & Tittle, 2008; Botchkovar & Hughes, 2010; Brauer *et al.*, 2012; Tittle *et al.*, 2010; Tittle & Botchkovar, 2005a). Finally, multisite, comparative tests of those theories are still rare and thus direct comparisons across cultural settings are usually impossible (but see, for example, Botchkovar, Tittle, & Antonaccio, 2009; Brauer *et al.*, 2012; Hwang & Akers, 2003; Lin *et al.*, 2014; Meneses & Akers, 2011; Rebellon *et al.*, 2008; Sigfusdottir *et al.*, 2012; Tittle & Botchkovar, 2005a).

Overall, not only do these difficulties further add to the complexity of comparative analyses, but they also slow the process of theoretical improvement. In spite of them and other impediments facing internationally-based research (see Bennett, 2004), it is great to see that theoretically driven cross-national research has been flourishing in criminology since the beginning of the 21st century and that this body of literature is growing rapidly. One obvious benefit of this expansion is that it is going to continue to contribute meaningfully to development of criminological theories in multiple ways. Concomitantly, it will also make it possible for more and more criminologists to embrace a less ethnocentric, global perspective on understanding causes of crime.

# References

Agnew, R. (1992). Foundation for a general strain theory of crime and delinquency. *Criminology, 30,* 47–87.

Agnew, R. (2006a). *Pressured Into Crime. An Overview of General Strain Theory.* Los Angeles, CA: Roxbury.

Agnew, R. (2006b). General strain theory: Recent developments and directions for further research. In F.T Cullen, J.P. Wright, & M. Coleman (Eds.), *Advances in Criminological Theory, Taking Stock: The Status of Criminological Theory,* Vol. *15.* New Brunswick, NJ: Transaction.

Akers, R. (1998). *Social Learning and Social Structure: A General Theory of Crime and Deviance.* Boston, MA: Northeastern University Press.

Akers, R. (2009). *Social Learning and Social Structure: A General Theory of Crime and Deviance.* New Brunswick, NJ: Transaction.

Antonaccio, O., & Tittle, C.R. (2008). Morality, self-control, and crime. *Criminology, 46,* 801–832.

Antonaccio, O., Tittle, C.R., Botchkovar, E.V., & Kranidioti, M. (2010). The correlates of crime: Additional evidence. *Journal of Research in Crime and Delinquency, 47,* 297–328.

Antonaccio, O., Botchkovar, E.V., & Tittle, C.R. (2011). Attracted to crime: Exploration of criminal motivation among respondents in three European countries. *Criminal Justice and Behavior, 38,* 1200–1221.

Bao, W.N., Haas, A., & Pi, Y. (2004). Life strain, negative emotions, and delinquency: An empirical test of general strain theory in the People's Republic of China. *International Journal of Offender Therapy and Comparative Criminology, 48,* 281–297.

Baron, S.W. (2004). General strain, street youth and crime: A test of Agnew's revised theory. *Criminology, 42,* 457–484.

Beeck, H.O., Pauwels, L.J.R., & Put, J. (2012). Schools, strain and offending: Testing a school contextual version of general strain theory. *European Journal of Criminology, 9,* 52–72.

Bennett, R.R. (2004). Comparative criminology and criminal justice research: The state of our knowledge. *Justice Quarterly, 21,* 1–21.

Bernburg, J.G., & Thorlindsson, M. (1999). Adolescent violence, social control, and the subculture of delinquency: Factors related to violent behavior and nonviolent delinquency. *Youth and Society, 30,* 445–460.

Blokland, A.J., & Nieuwbeerta, P. (2005). The effects of life circumstances on longitudinal trajectories of offending. *Criminology, 43,* 1203–1240.

Botchkovar, E.V., & Broidy, L.M. (2013a). Accumulated strain, negative emotions, and crime: A test of general strain theory in Russia. *Crime and Delinquency, 59,* 837–860.

Botchkovar, E.V., & Broidy, L.M. (2013b). Parenting, self-control, and the gender gap in heavy drinking: The case of Russia. *International Journal of Offender Therapy and Comparative Criminology, 57,* 357–376.

Botchkovar, E.V., & Hughes, L.A. (2010). Strain and alcohol use in Russia: A Gendered Analysis. *Sociological Perspectives, 53*, 297–319.

Botchkovar, E.V., Tittle, C.R., & Antonaccio, O. (2009). General strain theory: Additional evidence using cross-cultural data. *Criminology, 47*, 801–848.

Botchkovar, E.V., Tittle, C.R., & Antonaccio, O. (2013). Strain, coping, and socioeconomic status: Coping histories and present choices. *Journal of Quantitative Criminology, 29*, 217–250.

Braithwaite J. (1989). *Crime, Shame and Reintegration.* Cambridge: Cambridge University Press.

Brauer, J.R., Tittle, C.R., Antonaccio, O., & Islam, M.Z. (2012). Childhood experiences and self-control. *Deviant Behavior, 33*, 375–392.

Brezina, T. (1996). Adapting to strain: An examination of delinquent coping responses. *Criminology, 34*, 39–60.

Broidy, L.M. (2001). Test of general strain theory. *Criminology, 39*, 8–32.

Capowich, G.E., Mazerolle, P., & Piquero, A. (2001). General strain theory, situational anger, and social networks: An assessment of conditioning influences. *Journal of Criminal Justice, 29*, 445–461.

Caspi, A., Moffitt, T.E., Silva, P.A., Stouthamer-Loeber, M., Krueger, R.F., & Schmutte, P.S. (1994). Personality and crime: Are some people crime prone? *Criminology, 32*, 163–194.

Chapple, C.L., McQuillan, J.A., & Berdahl, T.A. (2005). Gender, social bonds, and delinquency: A comparison of boys' and girls' models. *Social Science Research, 34*, 357–383.

Cheung, N.W.T., & Cheung, Y.W. (2008). Self-control, social factors, and delinquency: A test of the general theory of crime among adolescents in Hong Kong. *Journal of Youth and Adolescence, 37*, 412–430.

Cheung, N.W.T., & Cheung, Y.W. (2010). Strain, self-control, and gender differences in delinquency among Chinese adolescents: Extending general strain theory. *Sociological Perspectives, 53*, 321–345.

Chui, W.H., & Chan, H.C. (2011). Social bonds and male juvenile delinquency while on probation: An exploratory test in Hong Kong. *Children and Youth Services Review, 33*, 2339–2334.

Cohen, B.-Z., & Zeira, R. (1999). Social control, delinquency, and victimization among kibbutz adolescents. *International Journal of Offender Therapy and Comparative Criminology, 43*, 503–513.

Colvin, M., Cullen, F.T., & Vander Ven, T. (2002). Coercion, social support, and crime: An emerging theoretical consensus. *Criminology, 40*, 19–42.

Cretacci, M.A., & Cretacci, N. (2012). Enter the dragon: Parenting and low self-control in a sample of Chinese high school students. *Asian Journal of Criminology, 7*, 107–120.

Cretacci, M.A., Rivera, C.J., & Ding, F. (2009). Self-control and Chinese deviance: Behind the bamboo curtain. *International Journal of Criminal Justice Sciences, 4*, 131–143.

Cretacci, M.A., Rivera, C.J., & Ding, F. (2010). Tr. *International Journal of Criminal Justice Sciences, 5*, 220.

Doherty, E.E. (2006). Self-control, social bonds, and desistance: A test of life-course interdependence. *Criminology, 44*, 807–833.

Egli, N., Vettenburg, N., Savoie, J., Lucia, S., Gavray, C., & Zeman, K. (2010) Belgium, Canada and Switzerland: Are there differences in the contributions of selected variables on self-reported property-related and violent delinquency? *European Journal on Criminal Policy and Research, 16*, 145–166.

Friday, P.C., Ren, X.; Weitekamp, E., Kerner, H., & Taylor, T. (2005). A Chinese birth cohort: Theoretical implications. *Journal of Research in Crime and Delinquency, 42*(2), 123–146.

Froggio, G., & Agnew, R. (2007). The relationship between crime and "objective" versus "subjective" strains. *Journal of Criminal Justice, 35*, 81–87.

Fukushima, M., Sharp, S.F., & Kobayashi, E. (2009). Bond to society, collectivism, and conformity: A comparative study of Japanese and American college students. *Deviant Behavior, 30*, 434–466.

Giordano, P., Cernkovich, S., & Rudolph, J. (2002). Gender, crime, and desistance: Toward a theory of cognitive transformation. *American Journal of Sociology, 107*, 990–1064.

Gottfredson, M.R., & Hirschi, T. (1990). *A General Theory of Crime*. Stanford, CA: Stanford University Press.

Grasmick, H.G., Tittle, C.R., Bursik, R.J., Jr., & Arneklev, B.J. (1993). Testing the core empirical implications of Gottfredson's and Hirschi's general theory of crime. *Journal of Research in Crime and Delinquency, 30*, 5–29.

Grasmick, H.G., & Kobayashi, E. (2002). Workplace deviance in Japan: Applying an extended model of deterrence. *Deviant Behavior, 23*, 21–43.

Hay, C., & Forrest, W. (2006). The development of self-control: Examining self-control theory's stability thesis. *Criminology, 44*, 739–774.

Hay, C., & Meldrum, R. (2010). Bullying victimization and adolescent self-harm: Testing hypotheses from general strain theory. *Journal of Youth and Adolescence, 39*, 446–459.

Hartjen, C.A., & Kethineni, S. (1999). Exploring the etiology of delinquency across country and gender. *Journal of Crime and Justice, 22*, 55–90.

Hartjen, C.A., & Priyadarsini, S. (2003). Gender, peers, and delinquency: A study of boys and girls in rural France. *Youth and Society, 34*, 387–414.

Hirschi, T. (1969). *Causes of Delinquency*. Berkeley, CA: University of California Press.

Horney, J., Osgood, D., & Marshall, I. (1995). Criminal careers in the short-term: Intra-individual variability in crime and its relation to local life circumstances. *American Sociological Review, 60*, 655–673.

Hwang, S., & Akers, R.L. (2003). Substance use by Korean adolescents: A cross-cultural test of social learning, social bonding, and self-control theories. In R.L. Akers & G.F. Jensen (Eds.), *Social Learning Theory and the Explanation of Crime* (pp. 39–36). New Brunswick, NJ: Transaction.

Hwang, S., & Akers, R.L. (2006). Parental and peer influences on adolescent drug use in Korea. *Asian Journal of Criminology, 1*, 59–69.

Jo, Y., & Zhang, J. (2012). The stability of self-control: A group-based approach. *Asian Journal of Criminology, 7*, 173–191.

Junger, M., & Marshall, I.H. (1997). The interethnic generalizability of social control theory: An empirical test. *Journal of Research in Crime and Delinquency, 34*, 79–112.

Junger-Tas, J. (1992). An empirical test of social control theory. *Journal of Quantitative Criminology, 8*, 9–28.

Junger-Tas, J. (2010). The significance of the International Self-report Delinquency Study (ISRD). *European Journal on Criminal Policy and Research, 16*, 71–87.

Junger-Tas, J., Marshall, I.H., & Ribeaud, D. (2003). *Delinquency in an International Perspective: The International Self-Reported Delinquency Study (ISRD)*. Monsey, NY: Criminal Justice Press.

Junger-Tas, J., Ribeaud, D., & Cruyff, M. (2004). Juvenile delinquency and gender. *European Journal of Criminology, 1*, 333–375.

Keane, C., Maxim, P., & Teevan, J. (1993). Drinking and driving, self-control, and gender: Testing a general theory of crime. *Journal of Research in Crime and Delinquency, 30*, 30–46.

Kempf, K.L. (1993). The empirical status of Hirschi's control theory. In F. Adler & W.S. Laufer (Eds.), *New Directions in Criminological Theory*, Vol. 4 (pp. 143–185). New Brunswick, NJ: Transaction.

Kerley, K.R., Xu, X., & Sirisunyaluck, B. (2008). Self-control, intimate partner abuse, and intimate partner victimization: Testing the general theory of crime in Thailand. *Deviant Behavior, 29*, 503–532.

Kim, E., Kwak, D.-H., & Yun, M. (2010). Investigating the effects of peer association and parental influence on adolescent substance use: A study of adolescents in South Korea. *Journal of Criminal Justice, 38*, 17–24.

King, R., Massoglia, M., & Macmillan, R. (2007). The context of marriage and crime: Gender, the propensity to marry, and offending in early adulthood. *Criminology, 45*, 33–65.

Klanjsek, R., Vazsonyi, A.T., & Trejos, E. (2012). Religious orientation, low self-control, and deviance: Muslims, Catholics, Eastern Orthodox-, and "Bible Belt" Christians. *Journal of Adolescence, 35*, 671–682.

Kobayashi, E., Akers, R.L., & Sharp, S.F. (2011). Attitude transference and deviant behavior: A comparative study in Japan and the United States. *Deviant Behavior, 32*, 405–440.

Kobayashi, E., & Fukushima M. (2012). Gender, social bond, and academic cheating in Japan. *Sociological Inquiry, 82*, 282–304.

Kreager, D.A., Matsueda, R.L., & Erosheva, E.A. (2010). Motherhood and criminal desistance in disadvantaged neighborhoods. *Criminology, 48*, 221–258.

Kroneberg, C., Heintze, I., & Mehlkop, G. (2010). The interplay of moral norms and instrumental incentives in crime causation. *Criminology, 48*, 258–294.

Langton, L., & Piquero, N.L. (2007). Can general strain theory explain white-collar crime? A preliminary investigation. *Journal of Criminal Justice, 35*, 1–15.

Latimore, L.T., Tittle, C.R., & Grasmick, H.G. (2006). Childrearing, self-control, and crime: Additional evidence. *Sociological Inquiry, 76*, 343–371.

Lin, W.-H. (2011). General strain theory and delinquency: A cross-cultural study. *PhD Thesis*, University of South Florida. Available at http://scholarcommons.usf.edu/ (accessed May 3, 2015).

Lin, W.-H., Dembo, R., Sellers, C.S., Cochran, J., & Mieczkowski, T. (2014). Strain, negative emotions, and juvenile delinquency: The United States versus Taiwan. *International Journal of Offender Therapy and Comparative Criminology, 58*, 412–434.

Link, T.C. (2008). Adolescent substance use in Germany and the United States: A cross-cultural test of the applicability and generalizability of theoretical indicators. *European Journal of Criminology, 5*, 453–480.

Liu, R.X., & Lin, W. (2007). Delinquency among Chinese adolescents: Modeling sources of frustration and gender differences. *Deviant Behavior, 28*, 409–432.

Lu, Y.-F., Yu, Y.-C., Ren, L., & Marshall, I.H. (2013). Exploring the utility of self-control theory for risky behavior and minor delinquency among Chinese adolescents. *Journal of Contemporary Criminal Justice, 29*, 32–52.

Marshall, I.H., & Enzmann, D. (2012). The generalizability of self-control theory. In J. Junger-Tas, I.H. Marshall, D. Enzmann, M. Killias, M. Steketee, & B. Gruszczyńska, (Eds.), *The Many Faces of Youth Crime: Contrasting Theoretical Perspectives on Juvenile Delinquency across Countries and Cultures* (pp. 285–325). New York: Springer.

Maxwell, R.S. (2001). A focus on familial strain: Antisocial behavior and delinquency in Pilipino society. *Sociological Inquiry*, *71*, 265–292.

Meneses, R.A., & Akers, R.L. (2011). A comparison of four general theories of crime and deviance: Marijuana use among American and Bolivian university students. *International Criminal Justice Review*, *21*, 333–352.

Moon, B., Blurton, D., & McCluskey, J.D. (2008). General strain theory and delinquency: Focusing on the influences of key strain characteristics on delinquency. *Crime and Delinquency*, *54*, 582–613.

Moon, B., Morash, M., McCluskey, C.P., & Hwang, H.-W. (2009). A comprehensive test of general strain theory: Key strains, situational- and trait-based negative emotions, conditioning factors, and delinquency. *Journal of Research in Crime and Delinquency*, *46*, 182–212.

Morash, M., & Moon, B. (2007). Gender difference in the effects of strain on the delinquency of South Korean youth. *Youth & Society*, *38*, 300–321.

Morris, G.D., Wood, P.B., & Dunaway, R.G. (2007). Testing the cultural invariance of parenting and self-control as predictors of American Indian delinquency. *Western Criminology Review*, *8*, 32–47.

Nakhaie, M.R., Silverman, R., & LaGrange, T.C. (2000). Self-control and social control: An examination of gender, ethnicity, class and delinquency. *Canadian Journal of Sociology*, *25*, 35–39.

Nofziger, S. (2008). The cause of low self-control: The influence of maternal self-control. *Journal of Research in Crime & Delinquency*, *45*, 191–224.

Oberwittler, D. (2004). A multilevel analysis of neighbourhood contextual effects on serious juvenile offending: The role of subcultural values and social disorganization. *European Journal of Criminology*, *1*, 201–235.

Özbay, O. (2008). Self-control, gender, and deviance among Turkish university students. *Journal of Criminal Justice*, *36*, 72–80.

Özbay, O. (2011). Does general strain theory account for youth deviance in Turkey? *Nevsehir University Journal of Social Sciences*, *1*, 107–129.

Özbay, Ö., & Köksoy, O. (2009). Is low self-control associated with violence among youth in Turkey. *International Journal of Offender Therapy and Comparative Criminology*, *53*, 145–167.

Özbay, O., & Özcan Y.Z. (2006). A test of Hirschi's social bonding theory: juvenile delinquency in the high schools of Ankara, Turkey. *International Journal of Offender Therapy and Comparative Criminology*, *50*, 711–726.

Özbay, O. & Özcan Y.Z. (2008). A test of Hirschi's social bonding theory: a comparison of male and female delinquency. *International Journal of Offender Therapy and Comparative Criminology 52*, 134–156.

Paternoster, R. (1987). The deterrent effect of the perceived certainty and severity of punishment: A review of the evidence and issues. *Justice Quarterly*, *4*, 173–218.

Pauwels, L., Weerman, F., Bruinsma, G., & Bernasco, W. (2011). Perceived sanction risk, individual propensity and adolescent offending: Assessing key findings from the deterrence literature in a Dutch sample. *European Journal of Criminology*, *8*, 386–400.

Piquero, A.R., & Rosay, A. (1998). The reliability and validity of Grasmick et al.'s self-control scale: A comment on Longshore et al. *Criminology*, *36*, 157–174.

Pogarsky, G. (2007). Deterrence and individual differences among convicted offenders. *Journal of Quantitative Criminology*, *23*, 59–74.

Pratt, T.C., & Cullen, F.T. (2000). The empirical status of Gottfredson's and Hirschi's general theory of crime: A meta-analysis. *Criminology, 38,* 931–964.

Pratt, T. C., Cullen, F.T., Blevins, K.R., Daigle, L.E. & Madensen, T.D. (2006). The empirical status of deterrence theory: A meta-analysis. In Cullen, F.T., Wright, J.P., & Blevins, K.R. (Eds.), *Taking Stock: The Status of Criminological Theory.* New Brunswick, NJ: Transaction Publishers.

Pratt, T.C., Cullen, F.T., Sellers, C.S., Winfree, L.T., Jr., Madensen, T.D., Daigle, L.D., *et al.* (2010). The empirical status of social learning theory: A meta-analysis. *Justice Quarterly, 27,* 765–802.

Pulkkinen, L., & Hamalainen, M. (1995). Low self-control as a precursor to crime and accidents in a Finnish longitudinal study. *Criminal Behaviour and Mental Health, 5,* 424–438.

Rebellon, C.J., Straus, M.A., & Medeiros, R.A. (2008). Self-control in global perspective: An empirical assessment of Gottfredson and Hirschi's general theory within and across 32 national settings. *European Journal of Criminology, 5,* 331–362.

Ribeaud, D., & Eisner, M. (2006). The "drug-crime link" from a self-control perspective. *European Journal of Criminology, 3,* 33–67.

Romero, E., Gomez-Fraguela, J.A., Luengo, M.A., & Sobral, J. (2003). The self-control construct in the general theory of crime: An investigation in terms of personality psychology. *Psychology, Crime & Law, 9,* 61–86.

Rumpold, G., Klingseis, M., Dornauer, K., Kopp, M., Doering, S., Hofer, S., *et al.* (2006). Psychotropic substance abuse among adolescents: A structural equation model on risk and protective factors. *Substance Use and Misuse, 41,* 1155–1169.

Sampson, R.J., & Laub, J.H. (1993). *Crime in the Making: Pathways and Turning Points through Life.* Cambridge, MA: Harvard University Press.

Sampson, R. J., & Laub, J.H. (2003). Life-course desisters? Trajectories of crime among delinquent boys followed to age 70. *Criminology, 41,* 555–592.

Sampson, R., Laub, J.H., & Wimer, C. (2007). Does marriage reduce crime? A counterfactual approach to within-individual causal effects. *Criminology, 44,* 465–508.

Savolainen, J. (2009). Work, family, and criminal desistance: Adult social bonds in a Nordic welfare state. *British Journal of Criminology, 49,* 285–304.

Seipel, C., & Eifler, S. (2010). Opportunities, rational choice, and self-control. On the interaction of person and situation in a general theory of crime. *Crime & Delinquency, 8,* 167–197.

Shechory, M., & Laufer, A. (2008). Social control theory and the connection with ideological offenders among Israeli youth during the Gaza disengagement period. *International Journal of Offender Therapy and Comparative Criminology, 52,* 454–473.

Sheu, C. (1988). Juvenile delinquency in the Republic of China: A Chinese empirical study of social control theory. *International Journal of Comparative and Applied Criminal Justice, 12,* 59–71.

Shoemaker, D.J. (1994). Male–female delinquency in the Philippines: A comparative analysis. *Youth and Society, 25,* 299–329.

Sigfusdottir, I.D., Kristjansson, A.L., & Agnew, R. (2012). A comparative analysis of general strain theory. *Journal of Criminal Justice, 40,* 117–127.

Sigfusdottir, I.D., & Silver, E. (2009). Emotional reactions to stress among adolescent boys and girls: An examination of the mediating mechanisms proposed by general strain theory. *Youth & Society, 40,* 571–590.

Svensson, R. (2003). Gender differences in adolescent drug use: The impact of parental monitoring and peer deviance. *Youth and Society, 34,* 300–329.

Svensson, R., Pauwels, L., & Weerman, F.M. (2010). Does the effect of self-control on adolescent offending vary by level of morality? A test in three countries. *Criminal Justice and Behavior, 37,* 732–743.

Tanioka, I., & Glaser, D. (1991). School uniforms, routine activities, and the social control of delinquency in Japan. *Youth and Society, 23,* 50–75.

Tavits, M. (2010). Why do people engage in corruption? The case of Estonia. *Social Forces, 88,* 1257–1280.

Tittle, C.R. (1995). *Control Balance: Toward a General Theory of Deviance.* Boulder, CO: Westview.

Tittle, C.R., Antonaccio, O., & Botchkovar, E.V. (2012). Social learning, reinforcement, and criminal probability. *Social Forces, 90,* 863–890.

Tittle, C.R., Antonaccio, O., Botchkovar, E.V., & Kranidioti, M. (2010). Expected utility, self-control, morality, and criminal probability. *Social Science Research, 39,* 1029–1046.

Tittle, C.R., & Botchkovar, E.V. (2005a). Self-control, criminal motivation and deterrence: An investigation using Russian respondents. *Criminology, 43,* 307–354.

Tittle, C.R., & Botchkovar, E.V. (2005b). The generality and hegemony of self-control theory: A comparison of Russian and US adults. *Social Science Research, 34,* 703–731.

Tittle, C.R., Botchkovar, E.V., & Antonaccio, O. (2011). Criminal contemplation, national context, and deterrence. *Journal of Quantitative Criminology, 27,* 225–249.

Tittle, C.R., Broidy, L., & Getz, M.G. (2008). Strain, crime, and contingencies. *Justice Quarterly, 25,* 283–312.

Tittle, C.R., Ward, D.A., & Grasmick, H.G. (2003). Gender, age, and crime/deviance: A challenge to self-control theory. *Journal of Research in Crime & Delinquency, 20,* 426–453.

Torstensson, M. (1990). Female delinquents in a birth cohort: Tests of some aspects of control theory. *Journal of Quantitative Criminology, 6,* 101–114.

Vazsonyi, A.T., & Belliston, L.M. (2007). The family, low self-control, and deviance: A cross-cultural and cross-national test of self-control theory. *Journal of Criminal Justice, 34,* 505–530.

Vazsonyi, A.T., & Klanjšek, R. (2008). A test of self-control theory across different socioeconomic strata. *Justice Quarterly, 25,* 101–131.

Vazsonyi, A.T., Pickering, L.E., Junger, M., & Hessing, D. (2001). An empirical test of a general theory of crime: A four nation comparative study of self-control and the prediction of deviance. *Journal of Research in Crime and Delinquency, 38,* 91–131.

Vazsonyi, A.T., Trejos, E., & Huang, L. (2006). Risky sexual behavior, alcohol use, and drug use: A comparison of Eastern and Western European adolescents. *Journal of Adolescent Health, 39,* 753.e1–753.e11.

Vazsonyi, A.T., Clifford-Wittekind, J.E., Belliston, L.M., & Van Loh, T.D. (2004). Extending the general theory of crime to "the East." Low self-control in Japanese late adolescents. *Journal of Quantitative Criminology, 20,* 189–216.

Wang, S.-N., & Jensen, G.F. (2003). Explaining delinquency in Taiwan: A test of social learning theory. In R.L. Akers & G.F. Jensen (Eds.), *Social Learning Theory and the Explanation of Crime* (pp. 65–83). New Brunswick, NJ: Transaction.

Wang, G.T., Qiao, H., Hong, S., & Zhang, J. (2002). Adolescent social bond, self-control, and deviant behavior in China. *International Journal of Contemporary Sociology, 39,* 52–68.

Wikström, P.-O.H. (2006). Linking individual, setting, and acts of crime. Situational mechanisms and the explanation of crime. In P.-O.H. Wikström & R.J. Sampson (Eds.), *The Explanation of Crime: Contexts, Mechanisms, and Development.* Cambridge: Cambridge University Press.

Wikström, P.-O.H., & Svensson, R. (2008). Why are young English youths more violent than Swedish youths? A comparative study of the roles of crime propensity, lifestyles and their interactions in two cities. *European Journal of Criminology, 5,* 309–330.

Wikström, P.-O.H., & Svensson, R. (2010). When does self-control matter? The interaction between morality and self-control in crime causation. *European Journal of Criminology, 7,* 395–410.

Wikström, P.-O.H., Tseloni, A., & Karlis, D. (2011). Do people comply with the law because they fear getting caught? *Journal of European Criminology, 8,* 401–420.

Yun, I., & Walsh, A. (2011). The stability of self-control among South Korean adolescents. *International Journal of Offender Therapy and Comparative Criminology, 55,* 445–459.

Zhang, L., & Messner, S.F. (1995). Family deviance and delinquency in China. *Criminology, 33,* 359–387.

Zhang, L., & Messner, S.F. (1996). School attachment and official delinquency status in the People's Republic of China. *Sociological Forum, 11,* 285–303.

Zhang, L., & Messner, S.F. (1999). Bonds to the work unit and official offense status in urban China. *International Journal of Offender Therapy and Comparative Criminology, 43,* 375–390.

## 25

# Qualitative Criminology's Contributions to Theory

## Andy Hochstetler and Heith Copes

Most of what is known of crime and offenders was first suspected or hypothesized by a qualitative investigator. Qualitative methods, however, are not the dominant methodology in contemporary criminology. In fact, they may play a relatively small part in the development of the field today as compared to earlier periods. Recent evaluations about the relative distribution of methods in criminology and criminal justice journals certainly bear this out. Currently, somewhere between 4 and 15% of articles in top criminology and criminal justice journals rely on qualitative methods (Copes, Brown, & Tewksbury, 2011; Tewksbury, DeMichele, & Miller, 2005). Nevertheless, qualitative and ethnographic methods remain fruitful and serve essential purposes for the analysis of crime and its sources. Few could question the theoretical advancements in understanding crime and criminals made from employing various ethnographic methods.

Despite being a small percentage of current research in criminology, the sheer number of ethnographies of crime is too great to summarize fully. With this caveat in mind, this review provides a modest detailing of the most important theoretical and substantive advancements made by qualitative criminologists. It includes research on a variety of criminological topics, but focuses on research on those who commit crime rather than on those who respond to it (i.e., police, courtroom actors, correctional officers).

*The Handbook of Criminological Theory*, First Edition. Edited by Alex R. Piquero.
© 2016 John Wiley & Sons, Inc. Published 2016 by John Wiley & Sons, Inc.

# What is Qualitative Criminology?

Qualitative criminology refers to the collection and interpretation of the meaning of textual, verbal, or real-world observational data to shed light on the causes, patterning, and consequences of crime. Investigators who use related methods place an emphasis on the meanings, perceptions, and beliefs held by participants (who are primarily offenders) when collecting and coding their data. Qualitative criminologists also study those who work within the field of criminal justice (e.g., police, attorneys, and correctional officers), and have informed our understanding of criminal justice mechanisms, bureaucracies, and policies. In addition, content analyses, mainly of media depictions, compose a large literature. The focus here is on qualitative research that has led to developments within criminological theories of offending.

When grouping studies into qualitative or quantitative, the categories can blur (Diesing, 1971), but there are differences. For the purposes of discussion, we distinguish quantitative studies and methods, which rely on numeric measurements, derived from surveys, experiments, or codified and counted official records and observations, from qualitative studies, which rely on textual or visual data that is not quantified. Qualitative analysts tend to look for observable patterns and meanings in language or interactions rather than focusing purely on quantifiable measurements. They may aim at samples representative of a population, and, at times, even count appearances of themes or words to form data, but approximation of general thematic patterns from study participants' words rather than statistical generalization typically is the larger objective. While qualitative researchers can increase reliability, say by using multiple coders, their work often is predominantly interpretive.

Qualitative researchers can explore interpretations or observations implementing greater fluidity, mutuality, and depth of interaction with participants than those who analyze official records or conduct surveys with quantitative goals. Therefore, qualitative investigators typically need not narrowly restrict the bounds of their study or set their interview guide in stone. Many prefer loosely structured and evolving interview guides. The advantages of this freedom contrasts with the constrictions on survey research where one must establish parameters early in the study and proceed to construct numeric data representing the entire sample and statistical generalization. Where survey researchers constrain responses *a priori*, qualitative researchers typically are loath to put words in their participants' mouths and prefer free-flowing, participant-generated responses. To get opinions, qualitative researchers eschew an emphasis on ordinal responses focusing instead on explanations and thick descriptions.

The improvisational and mutual analytic approach of constant comparison of what respondents say across interviews or do in natural settings is beneficial to theory development because the researcher can, in a single study, pursue new lines of inquiry as they emerge or check formulations from earlier interviews in later ones with increasingly in-depth inquiry on a topic of interest. Moreover, the collaborative nature of interactions and conversational exchanges with participants allows them to pursue their own meanings and relay their own interpretations of events and interactions as well as to use the linguistic categories that they prefer.

## Legacy of Qualitative Criminology

Qualitative research has a rich history in criminology. Oral history methods were an integral part of criminology in its early development in the 1920s and 1930s (Laub, 1984). Many of the most influential studies of crime have resulted from field work and interviews with known offenders or with residents of the poor places where many street-offenders lived. Henry Mayhew's works in the 1840s on the poor and deviant in London foreshadows this approach. By going to parts of the city the elites avoided, Mayhew was able to shed light on the complexity of thought and behavior of the London poor by giving them a voice.

Perhaps the most influential camp of qualitative researchers was part of the Chicago school of criminology and sociology, which prospered most famously in the first half of the 20th century. These investigators took keen interest in the relationship between spatial and social organization including crime and vice as an outcome. Using both quantitative and qualitative methods, they emphasized how the development of cities and the varying level of organization in neighborhoods contextually influenced community arrangements for living and subsequently individual behavior. Chicago's streets became a character in the ethnographies they produced. Investigators relied on a metaphor of the city as an evolving organism and extended this notion to its smallest parts by observing patterns in how individual residents thought and behaved predictably in their cultural environments (Park, Burgess, & McKenzie, 1925).

The geographer Chauncey Harris argued that Chicago in the 20th century was the most studied city in the world; ethnography and criminology composed a share of the work he referenced. After analysts mapped its ethnicities and spatial indicators of social problems, attention turned to attempts to capture the quality of life in neighborhoods. Some of these ethnographies aimed at understanding the influence of context on crime's occurrence and on more specific endeavors including understanding delinquency, prostitution, gang membership, homelessness and even, in other parts of town, the lifestyles of the wealthy.

The Chicago criminologists were most interested in the industrial city, its immigrants and downtrodden residents, and in social problems of the city (Park, Burgess, & McKenzie, 1925). They were drawn to understanding and bringing to light the goings on and thinking among marginalized and underprivileged populations who were geographically proximate but far from the attention of polite society. They were influential in many ways; including their community activism (e.g., the Chicago Area Project) and commitment to sojourns among the disreputable. One somewhat embarrassing legacy for all qualitative criminologists is the voyeuristic tendency of privileged academics peering into other worlds with pretense of exotic anthropology, however. The saving grace is that much qualitative research gives voice to people who might not be heard otherwise whether they be sex workers, embezzlers, dog-fighters, marijuana cultivators, gangsters, street-criminals, or other outlaws. While critics might aptly describe much qualitative criminology since the earliest days as zoo-keeping of deviants for inattention to grand theory or policy, they should remember that ethnographers must present people in their natural settings and from their own perspectives lest subjects be represented as abstractions or correlation coefficients.

By participating in daily life as an observer, or in some cases by engaging in participatory research by helping, organizing, or advocating for disadvantaged residents, the criminologist gains a sense of the lives of offenders and those who deal with them regularly. Chicago's research revealed that offenders often are not social isolates but part of identifiable lifestyles that can be classed and characterized. These lifestyles vary in their rate of occurrence by place, serve local functions and organize activity among offenders and those proximate to them. A legacy for criminology is found in recognition that criminal lifestyles and identities are associated with local economies, and this often means that they are nested or reflect the goings on in informal or black markets (Levi, 1981; Reuter, MaCoun, Murphy, Abrahamse, & Simon, 1990).

While some of what Chicago school criminologists learned of ties, neighborhoods, and behaviors were characteristics of particular times and places, the influence of their approach to crime and its sources is apparent and lasting and there is consis-tency with contemporary work. For example, it may seem a quaint notion to the contemporary criminologist that the lines between ball teams, semi-formal gang-like playgroups, and neighborhood youth clubs and criminal youth gangs sometimes were difficult for early criminologists to see (Thrasher, 1927). However, youth who belong to today's gangs are not as criminally organized or dedicated to crime as most casual observers suspect (Decker, 1996). Moreover, some things among the population of greatest interest, serious criminals, seem immutable; for example, there is nothing new about the regard for "snitches" or the leveled aspirations of delinquent youth in neighborhoods that produce many street-offenders (Shaw, 1930). No early ethnogra-pher of crime would be surprised that today's most criminally involved youth see prison or death as potential outcomes of their choices or by the somewhat contradictory finding that they still, perhaps unrealistically, hope for the best (Brezina, Teken, & Topalli, 2009; Shover, 1996). It probably is a general truth that many offenders seek a reputation for being bad even to the point of hiding or struggling to explain and justify their better angels (Topalli, 2005).

Early work also taught that the context of an area, and particularly the economic prospects and living conditions there, shapes residents' ideas and thinking in ways that may be difficult to discern from afar. These ways of thinking make sense to those embracing ideologies and systems that are local to some degree (say 1980s gangster culture in large US cities, skinheads in East Germany, or football hooliganism in 1990s Europe) but that sometimes have much in common among those placed in similar social and economic positions worldwide. For example, gangs around the world have similar origins, ways of thinking, and initial organization, but differ by degrees in their institutionalization and activities (Hagedorn, 2009).

# Developments in Qualitative Methods

There are many qualitative studies of crime, especially if one counts ethnographic books and papers. They are too many to document here and certainly they are too diverse to characterize easily. Bolivian cocaine producers are far from Chinese human smugglers and even farther from children in youth gangs, or a study into the categories drug addicts form to understand street status. Across the range of subject matter, the textual data used in qualitative research means that most are better read than presented second-hand anyway. Rather than attempt to summarize or draw what is valuable from such a diverse field, it is more useful to document significant trends among those who have used the methodological approach in recent years to show some of the most important developments in methodology and theory.

## Methodological developments

Not a great deal has changed in the techniques for analysis of qualitative criminological data since the development of the method. The basic idea of getting out of the office and talking to people is still the essence of qualitative criminology. Notably, accessibility of high-quality and portable recording technology and personal computing has eased detailed attention to language and analyses of observational data. Very soon automatic transcription software will surmount the remaining technical barriers and glitches plaguing it, and one of the most expensive and time-consuming tasks of the research (the dreaded transcribing of interviews) will be a thing of the past. Whereas, earlier generations of researchers often had to rely on memory and field notes to capture occurrences on the street or in interviews, today it is more likely to be a matter of direct record. Improved access to archives of electronically stored data also will advance the field, by allowing secondary analyses and data sharing of qualitative data.

Analysis software has become much better, and contemporary coders have layers and layers of options for how to tag their data for search and retrieval. With time and resources, it is feasible to effectively manage and warehouse complex codes for hundreds of in-depth interviews. It is arguable that the intense focus on language in qualitative criminology in recent years is a direct outgrowth of technical developments in recording and coding software in much the same way that developments in statistical analyses have contributed to better understanding of the trajectories and turning-points of criminal careers. Nevertheless, the logic of qualitative analysis generally remains the same as that in analyses of pasted transcriptions on color-coded note-cards. Newer qualitative analysis software developments include ways of visualizing and presenting data and sampling strategies graphically, but as yet they have not changed traditional presentation of findings. With smaller studies, old-fashioned cut-and-paste techniques and simple word-processing and search technologies remain sufficient.

Another development that potentially benefits qualitative researchers is advancement in sampling as illustrated by respondent-driven sampling (RDS) (Heckathorn, 1997). Investigators use these techniques to reach difficult to locate populations based on social networks and chain referral. Investigators recruit a small number of research contacts whom they pay and interview. They give these participants identifiable coupons to pass to friends or others who they know to share a key characteristic (say heroin addiction, or drug dealing) (Curtis, 2010). When recruits show up to interviews and present coupons, investigators pay them. The recruited become the next interviewed class and the study continues until reaching the desired number of participants. By tracking the coupons, statistical analysis and mathematical modeling can be done that correct for selection bias, the tendency of recruiters to recruit persons like themselves, and the ability of recruiters to make effective referrals. Researchers can estimate the size and characteristics of the population of interest. While still infrequently used, this advancement allows for generalization from chain referral methods with an ease and accuracy that could only be imagined a few decades ago.

## Mixed methods and triangulation

Qualitative and quantitative research often was part of the same larger study in criminology traditionally. However, for the period beginning in the late 1980s until the late 1990s quantitative criminology so dominated production and publishing in the field that an outside observer could easily have lost sight of the traditional linkage. One recent development worth noting is the beginning of a resurgence of incorporation of qualitative methods into studies that also collect quantitative data for mixed methods analyses.

The reinvigoration of mixed-methods designs represents an effort to return to the approach that resulted in many of the classic works from the Chicago School and other community studies (Short & Strodtbeck, 1965; Whyte, 1943). While early examples of combining fieldwork and surveys are not rare (Reiss, 1968; Van Maanen, 1975), there appears to be increasing recognition that quantitative analyses are richer when placed into the context of interpretive understandings and verbal explanations offered by participants. In evaluation research, investigators increasingly use the narrations of program participants as supplement to statistical observation of who succeeds or recidivates (Miller, 2014). Sponsoring agencies want to know how administrators and participants experience the programs to understand program fidelity. Interviews with clients and program managers give administrators and funding agencies insight into what is going on in programs. In addition, sponsors have learned that sound-bites, particularly if they are verbal acclamations for programs, make for interesting reports and persuade stake-holders, say the skeptical taxpayer, city councilman or other provider of revenue, as much as outcome statistics.

The fact that books and articles on developmental criminology, where cutting-edge quantitative research occurs, often incorporate interviews into the analysis of primarily quantitative data evidences a resurgence in mixed methods (Carlsson, 2012; Cherlin, Burton, Hart, & Purvin, 2004; Giordano, 2010; Laub & Sampson, 2003; Weisburd & Waring, 2001), as does increasing interest in how to handle such a study methodologically (Small, 2011). Mixed-methods approaches may be particularly relevant for cohort and developmental research. Investigators know that in this type of work a great deal may change between waves of data collection. There is a blank period between contacts with participants that is difficult to capture or detail without doing interviews. The qualitative interview gives researchers the opportunity to fill in gaps of time as well as those significant omissions from surveys that researchers discover only on repeated application of a questionnaire. Interviews also can identify changes in thinking and on-going mental processes that might elude even the craftiest survey researcher attempting to find out what has happened between waves.

Investigators often use qualitative analyses to interview or analyze subsets of respondents in large longitudinal panel surveys in order to contextualize; at times, they target interviews to segments of the data such as residual cases, or two groups to maximize difference on some key variable such as social mobility (Elliott, Miles, Parson, & Savage, 2010) or job stability, or on a subpopulation of particular interest such as those who are most at risk of offending (McAra & McVie, 2010) or at the tail ends of a distribution in opinion (Maruna & King, 2009). Generally, researchers use extensive self-report data from surveys as their main source of information when dealing with large samples and qualitative data for all cases in a sample only in smaller studies, with hundreds rather than thousands of participants. Qualitative analysis of sub-samples often enriches findings efficiently. A large two-wave survey showed that negative school climate and low self-esteem predicted bullying, but in 115 supplemental focus groups the authors learned that bullying was related to emergent sexuality, power dynamics between peer groups, was a means of social control of annoyances, and perhaps most disturbingly, was portrayed as a fun diver-sion (Guerra, Williams, & Sadek, 2011), for example. The goal of triangulation is cross validation by compensating for the weaknesses of one technique by imple-menting another so that convergences support and divergences or inconsistencies introduce skepticism. Mixed methods are particularly theoretically relevant for certain interactional kinds of questions, where survey data does not get at the meat of the issue and vignettes are artificial. Consider theories that rest on premises that offenders call forth attitudinal precursors of crime through interaction in certain set-tings. Criminal codes, for example, might best be captured by observing offenders or those thought predisposed to offend interacting as they consider behavioral options (Sampson & Bean, 2006). The most casual observer knows that the talk is different in tone when one male offender is talking to a criminologist than it would be when a group of his close friends drinks and banters about what to do when insulted. Surveys on opinions about when to strike someone reveal important information (Berg & Stewart, 2013), but to understand the belief systems and culturally proper application of beliefs more natural contexts and exchanges are beneficial. For this reason, on some topics insider key informants might elicit more valuable interviews than outsider criminologists (Copes, Hochstetler, & Forsyth, 2013). Observers can see things in natural settings and interactions that will not show up on surveys, and this is not only due to deceptiveness on the part of subjects but also to the contextual representations they present (Sandberg, 2010).

## Developments and Trends in Theory

Qualitative research can advance theory and be instrumental in initial theoretical development; investigators often ground theory in emergent data and reconstruct theory during a single study. Simply explained, investigators organize data into constructs, discover thematic patterns in data, develop emergent theoretical notions and refine these with more investigation and observation. While this general approach is common, what is discovered in any study is contingent partially on data, and partially on shifts and trends in theoretical approach occurring alongside prevailing approaches to analysis. Three prominent developments in the past two decades in how qualitative investigators approach data, theory, and choice of subject have occurred: increased emphases on details of talk, culture, and gender.

### From facts to language

Arguably, contemporary qualitative investigators in criminology pay greater and more careful attention to language and interpretation of it, than those who conducted such research in earlier eras. Traditionally, qualitative criminologists entered foreign worlds to get first-hand information about criminal decisions and the contexts where they occurred. The goal was to draw out general themes about offenders' decisions as well as to understand the objective facts of how things happen and how decisions are made in offenders' worlds. Analysts focused on having respondents explain their seemingly aberrant behavior to reasonable listeners, but investigators generally accepted explanations either as accurate reflections of the facts or as inaccurate and therefore methodologically invalid deceptions or mistakes on the part of the interviewed (Presser, 2010). Of course, it is difficult to know for sure when offenders are lying, deceiving or bending the truth, but investigators could check for internal inconsistencies or external inconsistencies with other data sources, such as criminal records. The job of the qualitative interviewer was to get the "facts."

Fortunately, in much of this work, the interpretive task was descriptive and light and there was little reason to expect deception or attend to words carefully. If the question is what burglars fear and how this affects their choices, one need not pay precise attention to discerning meaning or intent of language. This is not to demean asking simple questions. All interviewers want to know what their population of interest believes, and it always is important to understand the rudiments underlying choices. With good reason, analysts are curious about the mechanics of crime commission and decision-making, and want to garner general truths about the work involved in crime to aid policing efforts by better understanding how it is mentally scripted and physically accomplished (Decker, 2005).

Nevertheless, in contemporary analyses, there will be greater attention to the specific language used and the meanings an offender intentionally and unintentionally imparts when speaking. This emerging shift in the qualitative approach is subtle and stylistic. There is more artistry, attention to linguistic detail and to the subjectivity of accounts in newer forms and styles of qualitative criminology than in traditional "just-the-facts" forms. More than in the past, offenders' self-conceptions and views of themselves in a larger social world intrigue qualitative criminologists. To understand the difference, the background of literature used to frame qualitative studies is useful; the cultural, phenomenological, and narrative turns in the social sciences represent broad shifts underlying a shift in the style of qualitative criminology toward the interpretive.

Phenomenological approaches vary but generally they focus on how actors make sense of life experiences and explore experience as it is from the actor's perspective, avoiding attempts to view experience in overly abstract, impersonal or predefined categories. Miner-Romanoff (2012) advocates that in this pursuit investigators focus on capturing actors' impressions in their own frames of reference but also engage in meaningful exchange or dialogue between the academic interpreter and the interpreted. Indeed, some researchers notice that the interview itself often is incorporated into the offenders' narrative, with offenders using it to substantiate that they are on the right track and want to help others (Presser, 2009). The interviewer can and should attempt to get the respondent to meaningfully explore what they are explaining. Interviewers should be judicious with questions but need not fear explaining how they interpret a situation from their own knowledge or previous engagements or of introducing developing expertise to the dialogue with participants; there also is great sensitivity to capturing and understanding participants' values and norms.

In phenomenology or existential-phenomenology, there is due attention to physical, and emotional experiences as well as to mental experience. Phenomenology seeks to be a "descriptive science that focuses on the life-world of the individual," recognizing that experiences and perceptions emerge in contextual settings, and that experience and accounts of it contain both reflected and unreflected aspects (Thompson, Locander, & Pollio, 1989:136). The analyst assumes and attends to those parts of decision-making that are less than fully rational and that lie below simple, material, cost–benefit calculations. Such an interviewer should pay great attention to probing and delving into what offenders mean when they claim that crime is a "trip" or a "rush." They should investigate an outlook reflected in offenders' belief that they "must think positive" or the superstition that they sense beforehand when a crime will go badly (Sutherland, 1947). The phenomenologist's ears would perk up and she would probe extensively if an interviewed offender said that they were mentally inattentive to consequences, or "really, in a way, wanted to get caught" or "deep down, always expected prison." Phenomenologists also treat emotional and physical responses as significant; therefore it intrigues that offenders must overcome the body's response to fear and often intentionally surpass or suppress mental barriers to committing reckless acts. Wood, Gove, Wilson, & Cochran (1997) showed in their quantitative exploration that experience enhances intrinsic enjoyments of crime, and affirmed this in interviews with habitual criminals, many of whom were sex offenders that took a particular delight in their offenses. The mental process and distinctive decision-making of offenders who get peculiarly magical, intoxicating, or powerful sensations from crime surely is better seen in what they say than in their tendency to check the last agreement box on a Likert scale. It was a phenomenological bent that allowed Jack Katz (1988) to see the theoretical and empirical importance of acknowledging that crime was "seductive," that being seen as a "badass" had much to do with many crimes, that offender styles were reflected in their preferred symbols and crimes, and that thieves personified stolen objects as particularly alluring. While couched in different theories, similar attention to details of interaction, collected during participant observation as a political prisoner, led another investigator to conclude that much of what prisoners do is ordinarily irrational but occurs in attempt to communicate through subtle and obvious signals and demeanor that they have what it takes to make it in tough institutions (Kaminski, 2004).

Offenders may implement distinctive categories unknown to others as they consider a crime. Certainly, they see criminal opportunity where others do not and have faith in their expertise and criminal sense developed through experience (Shover, 1996). Their larger world-view also enters the self-conversation as they consider the utility of an action. Hochstetler, Copes & Forsyth (2013) revealed culturally shared metaphors of violence, which sometimes drew on primitive man or animals, as a natural event for sorting out conflicts and establishing hierarchy. Offenders interpreted fights as significant indicators of a belief system tied to notions of honor and essential characteristics needed to make it in a competitive world. The fear of expected private shame and negative emotions for refusing to fight was an important motive for fighting. The interviewed portrayed fights according to the degree to which they followed culturally shared prescriptions and proscriptions about when and how one should fight fairly.

The influence of phenomenology on contemporary qualitative criminology is identifiable, but a related strain of qualitative criminology deems itself narrative criminology, and this group in recent years formally identifies with the title (Presser, 2009; Sandberg, 2010). Their work draws inspiration from narrative and cultural psychology as well as phenomenology and traditional qualitative criminology. "The storied nature of human conduct" inspired narrative psychology (Sarbin, 1986). Practitioners focus on meaning and see as foundational the idea that stories rather than logical connections or axiomatic formulations are how humans usually communicate message. Narratives serve as the root metaphor for understanding meaning and are significant for understanding why persons act as they do. Obviously, it is meaningful if someone consistently casts themselves as a prototypical gangster or hustler in their life story or even in an event in their story. Actors rely on narrative devices when explaining an action or pattern of action. We know what to expect as a plot unfolds when an offender begins by saying "where I'm from, everybody is gangster" or "I always looked up to the gangsters" and the offender knows that we know.

Narrative criminology holds that narratives about crime and related narratives (including in criminal justice, psychiatry of misbehavior, of failure and stigma, and deviance) can serve as data, regardless of whether the stories objectively are true (Sandberg, 2010). Lois Presser's (2009) theoretical work on offenders presented a narrative understanding of self-making and established the perspective in the field. Narrative criminologists think not only of criminal situations but also of interviews as performative work (Sandberg, 2008). Self-presentation, shifts in stories, and use of plot devices all intrigue narrative criminologists. Themes of narrative analysis include interest in tone, plotting, multiple and shifting objectives in self-presentation, and inconsistency in presentation or with espoused beliefs. For example, demonstrating that one is dangerous and tough but not insane is a prominent theme of many interviews with violent offenders (Hochstetler, Copes, & Williams, 2010). Lois Presser (2009) noted of her interviews with violent men that they portrayed their stories, typically of disadvantage, as tales of heroic struggles against long odds rather than as moral failures. Narrative criminologists find fascinating that offenders say that they "don't snitch," or "don't give a damn" when other actions and parts of accounts where they explain violations to the snitching rule or how hard they are trying to be good seem to indicate otherwise (Garot, 2010; Topalli, 2005). Lest one think that research on narratives is overly fuzzy or soft, if not outright flaky and unscientific, it may be important to show that analyses of talk and behavior reveals predictive capacity.

In a broad range of contexts, the way that people talk about and present themselves in speech is predictive of subsequent behavior, and this can be quantified. This is not only because of the attitudes that speech and text reveal, but also because of the classification schemes, tone, and word selection that a conversation and resultant text may tap. Campbell & Pennebaker (2003) showed that people who switch from high rates of personal pronoun "I" when writing about emotional turmoil to other personal pronouns showed greater health improvement. Schneidman (1971) used 30 cases with from an existing 40-year longitudinal data set of children with high ability, five of whom committed suicide in middle age, to study suicidal ideation. In a blind study, he rated each person on the level of perturbation exhibited, or how upset they seemed in interviews, and how likely he deemed suicide. Of the five rated most likely for suicide, he was right in four cases. There was stability in perturbation across years and interviews revealed signs of suicidal outcome at age 50 appearing by age 30. That talk reveals significant representations that indicate behavior is old hat to marketing experts who often use focus groups to understand customer desires and representations, at no small expense (Greenbaum, 1998).

Offenders talk reveals something of their trajectory. Shadd Maruna (2001) conducted life-history interviews with a matched sample of desisters and non-desisters living freely in or near Liverpool, UK. All of those interviewed formerly were imprisoned. They were matched on age, criminal records, and basic demographics. He then compared the talk of those who persisted in offending with those who were desisting. He learned that both groups portrayed offending as something that happened to them. However, the persistent offenders had "after years of denying their essential criminality... learned to accept that they would never succeed in life outside of criminal pursuits" (2001:224). Persisters viewed their past history of misfortunes as consistent prologue to their current offending. Desisters denied having ever been essentially criminal, contending that they had never been comfort-able in the criminal lifestyle as they saw themselves as good persons. Desisters portrayed their early struggles as leading to a reformation and rehabilitation and a rediscovery of their innate selves, sometimes via a breaking-point. Desisters tended to exhibit what Maruna viewed as a cognitive distortion with an overly optimistic assessment of what probably lay before them – an unfortunately grim lot in life. Part of this view, was the sometimes zealous opinion that they could serve as example for those in early in criminal careers or help others using experiences. Some acknowl-edged humble circumstances ahead of them, but they portrayed it optimistically relative to the alternatives of crime, addiction, or imprisonment. The desisters tended not to concentrate regretfully on where they had been and the disadvantages it wrought but to be forward looking in their intent to live right.

## Attention to culture and gender

Another development in qualitative criminology reflecting larger academic leanings is increased emphasis in understanding the layering of culture and how it ultimately influences the actions of daily life (Kane, 2004). One typical goal of a cultural approach in qualitative criminology is to understand how large structures (such as economic changes and relations, immigration patterns, waves of crime or deindus-trialization) shape everyday understandings, local arrangements, routines, and calculations to inform how culture operates in particular places and interactions. Bourdieu (1990) gained fame in part from theoretical attention to these connec-tions. His notion of habitus continues to inform criminology. Bourdieu's (1990:53) definition of habitus is:

> Systems of durable, transposable dispositions, structured structures predisposed to function as structuring structures, that is, as principles which generate and organize practices and representations that can be objectively adapted to their outcomes without presupposing a conscious aiming at ends or an express mastery of the operations necessary in order to attain them. Objectively "regulated" and "regular" without being in any way the product of obedience to rules, they can be collectively orchestrated without being the product of the organizing action of a conductor.

Investigators often characterize the subculture of the streets as a response to disadvantage and an effort to distance oneself from drudgery and the mainstream (Willis, 1976). It develops its own cultural assets or cultural capital which people can deploy for advantage in the circumstances of street-life and for trans-situational reputational advantage (see Bourgois, 2003; Jacobs, 1999). Those who have criminal capital, perhaps exhibited in the potential for violence, often do not have considerable resources for success in conventional society (Sandberg, 2008). In this respect, economic positions shape not only economic prospects but what they seek, what they deploy for advantage, and the situations they are likely to face. Sandberg (2008), for example, showed that, in the streets of Oslo, immigrant street-offenders implemented ethnic stereotypes associated with violence to advantage in disputes. They also capitalized on their presumed fearlessness, sometimes bred by upbringing in economically peripheral, wartorn nations. By adopting the role of the dangerous foreigner with little to lose, they gained something – respect and deference.

Attention to gender in qualitative research has burgeoned. The fact that males commit most crime, and particularly felonious or violent street crime, meant that gender did not receive the same attention among criminologists as it did in other areas of social research after the phase of the women's rights movement that occurred in the 1960s to 1970s. However, some of the most important theoretical developments in criminology in recent years result from attention to gender, and qualitative data provide a fountainhead for much of this. For example, Jody Miller's (2001) *One of the Guys: Girls, Gangs and Gender* documented and inter-preted gang life among girls in Ohio and Missouri. She revealed that gang girls perpetuated a myth of gender equality within gangs, but also easily described hierarchies, victimization, and treatment of women that belied this myth. In addition, they often pointed to superiority of males for their admirable attributes like ability to keep secrets, be serious about violence and gang business, keeping calm and on task, and strength and fighting skill. Many girls pointed out that they admired these masculine attributes and personally upheld them when possible. Girls were defensive about their place in the gang and seemingly constantly wres-tled with how to escape gender and ordinary stereotypes of femininity, as well as belief that they are second-class gang-members or likely to be victims. Ways of doing this included participation in belittling other girl gangsters, girls who belong to female gangs, and soft, popular and pretty non-gang girls. Gang life was gendered life.

Most qualitative research drawing on gender literature is not primarily about women. Being an admirable man is a goal that shapes many crimes. Crime often is a masculine performance and gender is done in different ways in different subcul-tures. Analysts can interpret a great deal of street-life and crime through the lens of masculinity – or ways of representing one of the endlessly varied culturally acknowl-edged ways of being manly. Where qualitative subcultural research or theoretical interpretations of subcultures and crime occurs, the theme of being masculine reappears regularly. Skinheads reproduce masculinity in ways that correspond to football culture and fandom and working-class industrial production, such as aggressive physicality and emphasis on toughing-out strife (Clarke, 2006). Others have emphasized the influence of situated masculine performances on offending in places as diverse as clubbing culture (Anderson, Daly, & Rapp, 2009), among inner-city minority street offenders (Katz, 1988), and graffiti crews (Monto, Machalek, & Anderson, 2013).

Street-life contains ideals of manliness and masculinity borrowed from the conventional world, such as conspicuous consumption and leisure. Male thieves often commit crime because they emulate breadwinners. They form their groups and divide tasks so that risky and aggressive acts fall on men. They often see male crime partners as equals or peers and women as tag-alongs, and their belief that one should be loyal and brave in the face of danger leads to acts they would prefer avoid but commit in the interest of not being feminized. One problem with qualitative masculinity literature is that since investigators usually conceptualize masculinity as situational, performative, and culturally varied; it can be used to explain most any outcome. Additionally, the intersections of gender, race, and class influence forms of masculinity, and criminologists have only begun to attend to these. Nevertheless, interest in these topics and gender literature as a lens for interpreting crime grows among both qualitative and quantitative criminologists.

## Key Findings from Qualitative Criminology

The importance of talk and of culture are larger theoretical movements that have influenced the nature of qualitative criminology inquiry, including what we look for and how we make sense of the findings. Within this context, qualitative criminologists have shed light on several key aspects of criminal behavior. Again, a comprehensive list of key findings is beyond the scope of this essay. Consequently, four compelling findings are discussed here. These include the importance of sense-making for crime, the role of street life on individuals' identities and decisions, the implementation criminal calculus, and the importance of culture on shaping violence and crime.

### Street life and identities

The greatest value in qualitative criminology research may be in its ability to capture stories, social settings, and events that compose the lives of offenders. Offenders often cast crimes as very ordinary and understandable culminations to sequences or logical outcomes of events and decisions that started long before a discrete offense. The ordinary, daily lives of offenders are just that, but may strike readers as highly unusual in their lack of structure, future-orientation, and seemingly invulnerability to positive change in the face of inevitable consequence. Many criminologists have at some time spent days drinking and not thinking about work, family or other obligations, but few know anything of the way that those entrenched in serious crime live. As apparent as they seem, revelations and reminders about offenders' lifestyles are relevant for shaping criminology as well as public policy.

Many offenders live a lifestyle that has been characterized as "life as party" (Shover, 1996; Wright & Decker, 1994). They structure their activities around good times in the present with little attention to obligations external to their immediate friends and leisure settings. In some respects, offenders live much like hard-partying college students on spring break. Central distinctions from a young working person's vacation or spring-breaker being that they are not sure from whence the resources to sustain the party will come, know that the party will be interrupted intermittently by catastrophe, and seemingly are committed to continuing for very long periods nevertheless. Many parties of this sort obviously are manifestations of drug and/or alcohol abuse or addiction. Criminal gains are spent on partying, alcohol, other drugs, diversions, and splurges (Cromwell & Olsen, 2004; Shover, 1996; Wright, Brookman, & Bennett, 2006). This lifestyle impedes offenders' relationships with conventional institutions and supportive others. For those who work, their diversions exhaust them physically, become difficult to hide, and often diminish material resources to the point where jobs cannot sufficiently provide and are difficult to sustain. Spurts of criminal activity correspond temporally with periods of work loss and difficulty holding down work. In many cases, the eventual inability to draw on legitimate resources, such as borrowing from friends and family or payday advances, precipitates a crisis that offenders hope to avert at least temporarily through crime. When money comes in, however, it is spent with rapidity due to the addictions, craving for escapist parties, and financial obligations that offenders amass—whether they are debts to dealers or the light company.

Criminals also take on identities related to their lifestyle. Katz (1988) showed how adopting an identity as a "badass" carries certain expectations and failing to live up to these expectations can have a dramatic effect on one's self-identity and how others treat such people. Hochstetler, Copes, & Williams (2010) found that distinctions between "crackheads" and "hustlers" were extremely significant and consequential for a sample of violent offenders and the sense they made of their contexts. Others have shown that addicts were drawn to and utilized images of capable users as opposed to sick addicts to shape their lifestyles and hierarchies (Boeri, 2004; Faupel, 1991). Shover (1996) showed that persistent offenders had incorporated their patterns of mistakes into how they conducted their lives and made sense of crimes. Some viewed themselves as hapless blunderers. Others attributed errors and crimes to addictions. A few embraced the image of intentional outlaws or bad men with little inclination or desire to be part of conventional, constrained lifestyles. Lonnie Athens (1997) shows that violent men often have self-conceptions tied to varying definitions of the appropriate use of violence. Observers may interpret violent acts as actions that carrying through on who offenders intend to be and personal/cultural understandings of appropriate violence.

## Choice and criminals' thinking

Investigators have framed much of qualitative criminology research in the language of various rational choice perspectives. The rational choice or choice approach assumes that humans select behaviors according to incentive structures. Being creatures who tend to minimize pain and maximize pleasure, humans' behavior is predictable. The simplest choice models of crime leave it at that, recognizing that incentive structures shape crime and that the most apparent payoffs (money) and the most apparent costs (probability of arrest and jail time) influence the choice to commit discrete offenses.

In keeping with the idea that risks and rewards determine patterns in crime, investigators have paid a great deal of attention to mapping how offenders mentally and physically achieve their objectives. This is because even with constant ends in a particular type of offense a sequential criminal decision is a complex event to map and the form of offenders' thinking and how it is reflected in plans, scripts, and situational awareness requires observational or interview data that attends to the increments of choice and variation in decision-making. Moreover, the specific considerations (risks, rewards, strategies) of each type of crime are unique; what a drug dealer watches for as risks, as compared to a burglar, identity fraudster, or child molester, is worth investigating. Clearly, understanding how the crime is enacted and how offenders make decisions has policy implications for prevention and potential rehabilitation of offenders' thinking (Decker, 2005).

The task of mapping offenders' thought processes in increments can be extremely complicated even if the goal is only to find a common sequence of considerations for a crime. For one thing, qualitative research has made it clear that criminal decisions begin in "non-criminal" settings, or settings that are not exclusively criminal, and that many of these settings, such as binge drug-using or drinking groups, blend gradually into crimes. From the offenders' perspective such settings almost accidentally turn to criminal planning or crime commission (Hochstetler, 2001). Offenders also make decisions sequentially. They have established practices and sequences for moving toward a crime and for evaluating targets. These include schema for framing situations and scripts (often decision-tree like mechanisms) for selecting behavior. If capturing sequences of decision-making is complex, things get much more difficult when the goal is to garner deeper motives or variety in offender preferences. Interestingly, offenders exhibit considerable variation in what they see as the most effective and efficient means to carry out crime. This is true even when committing the same crimes. For instance, robbers are not in agreement whether men or women, or law-abiding or criminal targets are the ideal victims (Wright & Decker, 1997).

Perceptual choice models use the general depiction of offenders as self-interested, maximizing, or satisficing actors as a point of departure, but approach choice from a more individualistic perspective; most qualitative researchers come to embrace these models of decision-making. This view acknowledges that humans estimate what pays for them based on experience and cultural or personal preferences and have varying decision-making capacities. For example, thieves develop their own strategies for minimizing risks and maximizing rewards such as offending only in neighborhoods they know well or conversely of driving far into the country-side to find burglary targets (Wright & Decker, 1994). Many male robbers avoid targeting or striking women as a rule, but will do so if they encounter a woman accidentally or other circumstances align. Female robbers like to lure victims into vulnerable situations, sometimes under the guise of prostitution (Miller, 1998). Offenders also have stock knowledge, superstitions, and practiced techniques that aid them in deciding when to offend and which targets to select. Moreover, they typically have incomplete knowledge of the incentive structure and incentives at hand. Of course, one often must approximate the potential costs and benefits of discrete actions using a rough calculus. This is even more so for the drugged, impulsive, and igno-rant. Increasingly, analysts also acknowledge lasting influence of narcissistic and hedonistic lifestyles on offenders' legitimate and illegitimate work decisions, noting that many make the choice to commit crime weighed against perceived conven-tional options (Tunnell, 2006). The environment where crime occurs is not the best place for careful deliberations and that too must be considered to understand criminal choice. In many respects, rationality is complex and bounded (Shover & Honaker, 1992).

In large part, qualitative criminology has addressed choice by revealing the complications of simple rational theories when applied to real-world criminal decisions that reveal complexity of choice and decision-making. From a barrage of studies of various types of offenders in the last 30 years that are far too numerous to cite, we have learned that offenders consider the costs of crime, that cost calculations change with age, that offenders develop and refine general and crime-specific strategies to reduce risk and increase rewards, and learn to find criminal opportunities in diverse settings as they become more experienced.

Convenience appears to be of utmost importance in their decisions, which tend to have a spontaneous or improvisational character but are likely based on experience and expertise. They build an arsenal of tricks that they use to avoid arrest, and accompanying confidence in expertise, alongside a somewhat superstitious faith that they can sense the risks of crime in their gut (i.e., larceny sense) (Jacobs, 1999). We have learned preferred techniques and scripts for committing many types of crimes, from telemarketing fraud, to identity fraud, to college and street drug dealing, to robbery, burglary and auto-theft. We can describe how preferred techniques contribute to target selection and related decisions. Qualitative criminol-ogists also have identified key cognitive and practical turning points where offenders move toward or away from sustained criminal careers. In short, by talking to thieves and criminals of varying types we have learned that they have developed a criminal calculus that they use to increase rewards and decrease risks when committing crime. While not always effective, these decision strategies provide them a sense of security that they will be successful, at least for the specific criminal act they are in the midst of committing.

## Making sense of actions through talk

One of the recurrent findings from qualitative criminology is that those who break the law interpret their indiscretions in ways that allows them to minimize damage to their self-concepts and/or social standings. In short, people account for the discrepancy between social expectations and their behavior by providing justifications or excuses (Scott & Lyman, 1968). The amount of research supporting this claim is substantial; appearing regularly with every imaginable wrong-doer being accounted for (see Maruna & Copes, 2005 for review). This literature suggests that when asked to provide motives for their actions, offenders engage in narrative sense-making (i.e., they excuse or justify their indiscretions) to align their actions with personal and cultural expectations of appropriate behavior. Making sense of offending is important because it allows people to manage the potential stigma that arises from violating norms and to continue offending with minimal guilt.

While some may assume that accounts are merely self-serving excuses designed to evade sanctions, this perspective implies that offenders do not believe their stories. But criminologists who study accounts view them as outward manifestations of a person's self- and social identity. When challenged about wrongdoings, the way offenders explain their actions becomes a central way of maintaining a particular sense of self. Those who make claims of being law abiding citizens, honorable men, or respectable offenders must be able to justify or excuse behavior that seems contradictory or they risk losing face. Telemarketing fraudsters often claim that they are business men and not "real" criminals. They argue that they are merely engaging in routine sales transactions and it is the victim's fault for being greedy or ignorant (Shover, Coffey, & Hobbs, 2003). Embezzlers contend they were borrowing the money and would have paid it all back (Cressey, 1953; Willott, Griffin, & Torrance, 2001). Rapists often frame their actions within the realm of hegemonic masculinity and claim they were merely acting out culturally accepted sex roles (Scully & Marola, 1984).

The importance of defining indiscretions in a positive light has implications for criminal persistence. The use of linguistic devices allows offenders to free themselves from the guilt or negative self-image that may be associated with their crimes. Excuse-making may begin as after-the-fact rationalizations, but it can become the rationale or moral release mechanisms that facilitate future offending. As such, accounts can be applied retroactively to excuse or redefine some initial criminal act. If doing so successfully mitigates others' or self-punishment, these accounts facilitate the repetition of harmful behaviors, eventuating into criminal persistence. Thus, by holding onto justifications or excuses and bringing them to the foreground when needed offenders can continue a line of behavior without the corresponding guilt or loss of status. Whether accounts cause people's initial participation in crime is unclear, but excuse-making techniques help many continue with their crimes unabated.

## Mindset as culture

Since the 1970s, sociologists and criminologists have experienced a cultural turn or at least a reinvigoration of an interest in culture and crime (e.g., Anderson, 1999; Horowitz, 1983). Much of the resultant work draws on subcultural theories of the 1950s and 1960s. Adherents of these perspectives in criminology held that there were identifiable cultural differences in both youthful and adult offenders and that many of these derived from social conditions in the lower rungs of the working class. Crime was seen as a form of adventure-seeking, exhibition of desired traits such as toughness, expression of quests for good-times, and as an outgrowth of fatalistic attitudes and frustrated aspirations. Due to their circumstances, offenders adapted an outlook that discounted future consequences and emphasized outlooks appreciated by some peers but costly for legitimate prospects. Work in this tradition continues (e.g., Brezina, Tekin, & Topalli, 2009).

Perhaps the most influential work descended from this tradition is that of Elijah Anderson (1999). Anderson argues that there is a code of the street that thrives among America's poor, inner-city, black communities. The code developed in these places due to indirect pressures of stagnant and declining job markets and from the resultant presence of a few dangerous residents. In neighborhoods, where there are youth who are largely unsupervised and who come from families without the resources to properly provide or socialize them, there will be high rates of victimization, violence, and interpersonal aggression. Those who must live in proximity to the indecent and disorderly families that produce troubled children learn to navigate the environment and behave in ways intended to prevent being marked as a victim or an outsider. Some do so by exhibiting violent self-representations. These people may get street-credit and respect by committing robberies, being drug dealers, or stealing cars. Others, generally from more respectable circumstances, are not entrenched in criminal lifestyles and do not view these representations as primary. This latter group often is composed of code-switchers. They desire to behave civilly in most circumstances, but use representations and adherence to the code of the streets in circumstances where they think they are threatened or company demands it.

The code of the streets is self-perpetuating. It has many elements and can be interpreted through several theoretical lenses, but there is a good deal of evidence for its existence and core claims. Doubtless, those who believe that a person will be victimized if they do not appear capable of violence, who believe that honor demands violent responses to provocation, and that those who are unwilling or unable to use violence or escalate when insulted are not respect-worthy are more likely to strike someone in confrontations. Documenting the code of the streets and how it operates and responding to the work in other ways has led to an impressive and important body of qualitative work, as well as to quantitative support (Berg & Stewart, 2013). In sum, this body of literature suggests that those who value the code of the street are more likely to engage in criminal and violent behavior (and be the victims of such behavior) than those who do not support such values (Brookman *et al.*, 2011; Brunson & Stewart, 2006; Rich & Grey, 2005).

When it comes to the details of offenders' thinking, qualitative researchers often show that much of what offenders believe they hold in common with others. For example, most do not want to be seen as ruthless, mad, or violent and the ethics for choosing crimes that are appropriate derive from general values (Presser, 2008). In many respects, offenders' beliefs reflect the larger goals and imperatives of society, thereby defeating some classist stereotypes of those who commit crime as outsiders. In other respects, hardship, sequential poor decisions, and experiences have contributed to offenders' destructive or hopeless ways of thinking and further diminished their life-chances. Some are entrenched in deeply criminal subcultures. Those who have spent large percentages of their lives in and out of prison, for example, in early middle age may conclude that it is too late and senseless for them to disengage from crime. Curiously, even many of those who reach that decision at mid-life will tire of crime as age slows them and costs of crime accumulate (Shover, 1985).

## Conclusion

This review provides some indication of where one type of research may lead in the immediately ensuing years, but to predict direction in a field is hazardous. One thing is clear: many of the ideas that criminologists pursue will be inspired by qualitative research. A reason is that educations in the field often begin with reading qualitative criminology as students often do not acquire sufficient statistical expertise to consume and fully comprehend contemporary quantitative work early. Certainly, quantitative techniques and quantitative data collection will advance rapidly, and probably faster than qualitative methods. As this happens it will become increasingly important to remind that there are lived experiences, stories, and accounts in each trajectory statistically identified, correlation discovered, or intervention applied. Qualitative research will provide context.

## References

Anderson, E. (1999). *Code of the Street: Decency, Violence and the Moral Life of the Inner City*. New York. W.W. Norton.

Anderson, T., Daly, K., & Rapp, L. (2009). Clubbing masculinities and crime: A qualitative study of Philadelphia night club scenes. *Feminist Criminology*, 4, 302–332.

Athens, L. (1997). *Violent Criminal Acts and Actors Revisited*. Champaign, IL: University of Illinois Press.

Berg, M.T., & Stewart, E. (2013). Street culture and crime. In F. Cullen & P. Wilcox (Eds.), *Oxford Handbook of Criminological Theory* (pp. 370–388). Oxford: Oxford University Press.

Boeri, M.W. (2004). Hell, I'm an addict, but I ain't no junkie: An ethnographic analysis of aging heroin users. *Human Organization, 63*(2), 236–245.

Bourgois, P. (2003). *In Search of Respect: Selling Crack in El Barrio*. New York: Cambridge University Press.

Bourdieu, P. (1990). *The Logic of Practice*. Cambridge: Polity Press.

Brezina, T., Tekin, E., & Toppali, T. (2009). Might not be a tomorrow: A multimethods approach to anticipated early death and youth crime. *Criminology, 47*, 1091–1129.

Brookman, F., Bennett, T., Hochstetler, A., & Copes, H. (2011). The role of the "code of the street" in the generation of street violence in the UK. *European Journal of Criminology, 8*, 17–31.

Brunson, R., & Stewart, E.A. (2006). Young African American women, the street code, and violence: An exploratory analysis. *Journal of Crime and Justice, 29*, 1–19.

Campbell, R.S., & Pennebaker, J.W. (2003). The secret life of pronouns: Flexibility in writing style and physical health. *Psychological Science, 14*, 60–65.

Carlsson, C. (2012). Using "turning points" to understand processes of change in offending: Notes from a Swedish study on life courses and crime. *British Journal of Criminology, 52*, 1–16.

Cherlin, A.J., Burton, L.M., Hart, T.R., & Purvin, D.M. (2004). The influence of physical and sexual abuse on marriage and cohabitation. *American Sociological Review, 69*, 768–789.

Clarke, J. (2006). The skinheads and the magical recovery of community. In S. Hall & T. Jefferson (Eds.), *Resistance Through Ritual: Youth Subcultures in Post-War Britain*, 2nd edition (pp. 80–84). New York: Routledge.

Copes, H., Brown, A., & Tewksbury, R. (2011). A content analysis of ethnographic research published in top criminology and criminal justice journals from 2000–2009. *Journal of Criminal Justice Education, 22*, 341–359.

Copes, H., Hochstetler, A., & Forsyth, C.J. (2013). Peaceful warriors: Codes for violence among adult male bar fighters. *Criminology, 51*, 761–794.

Cressey, D. (1953). *Other People's Money: A Study in the Social Psychology of Embezzlement*. Glencoe, IL: Free Press.

Cromwell, P., & Olsen, J. (2004). *Breaking and Entering: Burglars on Burglary*. Belmont, CA: Cengage.

Curtis, R. (2010). Getting good data from people that do bad things: Effective methods and techniques for conducting research with hard-to-reach and hidden populations. In W. Bernasco (Ed.), *Offenders on Offending* (pp. 141–160). Cullumton: Willan.

Decker, S. (1996). *Life in the Gang: Family, Friends, Violence*. Cambridge: Cambridge University Press.

Decker, S. (2005). *Using Offender Interviews to Inform Police Problem Solving*. Washington, DC: U.S. Department of Justice.

Diesing, P. (1971). *Patterns of Discovery in the Social Sciences*. Chicago, IL: Aldene Atherton.

Elliot, J., Miles, A., Parsons, S., & Savage, M. (2010). *The Design and Content of the "Social Participation" Study: A Qualitative Sub-Study Conducted as Part of the Age 50 (2008) Sweep of the National Child Development Study*. CLS Working Paper Series 2010/3, London: Centre for Longitudinal Studies.

Faupel, C.E. (1991). *Shooting Dope: Career Patterns of Hardcore Heroin Users*. Gainesville, FL: University of Florida Press.

Garot, R. (2010). *Who You Claim? Performing Gang Identity in School and on the Streets.* New York: New York University Press.

Giordano, P. (2010). *Legacies of Crime: A Follow-up of the Children of Highly Delinquent Girls and Boys.* Cambridge: Cambridge University Press.

Greenbaum, T.L. (1998). *The Handbook for Focus Group Research*, 2nd edition. Thousand Oaks, CA: Sage.

Guerra, N.G., Williams, K.R., & Sadek, S. (2011). Understanding bullying and victimization during childhood and adolescence: A mixed methods study. *Child Development, 82*, 295–310.

Hagedorn, J. (2009). *A World of Gangs: Armed Young Men and Gangsta Culture.* Minneapolis: University of Minnesota Press.

Heckathorn, D.D. (1997). Respondent-driven sampling: A new approach to the study of hidden populations. *Social Problems, 44*, 174–199.

Hochstetler, A. (2001). Opportunities and decisions: Interactional dynamics in robbery and burglary groups. *Criminology, 39*, 737–764.

Hochstetler, A., Copes, H., & Williams, J.P. (2010). "That's not who I am:" How offenders commit violent acts and reject authentically violent selves. *Justice Quarterly, 27*, 492–516.

Horowitz, R. (1983). *Honor and the American Dream: Culture and Identity in a Chicano Community.* Newark, NJ: Rutgers.

Jacobs, B. (1999). *Dealing Crack: The Social World of Streetcorner Selling.* Boston, MA: Northeastern University Press.

Kaminski, M. (2004). *Games Prisoners Play: The Tragicomic Worlds of Polish Prison.* Princeton, NJ: Princeton University Press.

Kane, S.C. (2004). The unconventional methods of cultural criminology. *Theoretical Criminology, 8*, 303–321.

Katz, J. (1988). *Seductions of Crime: Moral and Sensual Attractions of Doing Evil.* New York: Basic Books.

Laub, J., & Sampson, R. (2003). *Shared Beginnings, Divergent Lives: Delinquent Boys to Age 70.* Cambridge, MA: Harvard University Press.

Laub, J. (1984). Talking about crime: Oral history in criminology and criminal justice. *Oral History Review, 12*, 29–42.

Levi, M. (1981). *The Phantom Capitalists: The Organisation and Control of Long Firm Fraud.* London: Heinemann.

Maruna, S. (2001). *Making Good: How Ex-Convicts Reform and Rebuild Their Lives.* Washington, DC: American Psychological Association.

Maruna, S., & Copes, H. (2005). What we have learned from five decades of neutralization theory research. *Crime and Justice: A Review of Research, 32*, 221–320.

Maruna, S., & King, A. (2009). Once a criminal, always a criminal?: "Redeemability" and the psychology of punitive public attitudes. *European Journal of Criminal Policy Research, 15*, 7–24.

McAra, L., & McVie, S. (2010). Youth crime and Justice: Key messages from the Edinburgh Study of Youth Transitions and Crime. *Criminology and Criminal Justice, 10*, 211–230.

Miller, J. (1998). Up it up: Gender and the accomplishment of street robbery. *Criminology, 36*, 37–66.

Miller, J. (2001). *One of the Guys: Girls, Gangs, and Gender.* Oxford: Oxford University Press.

Miller, J.M. (2014). Identifying collateral effects of offender reentry programming through evaluative fieldwork. *American Journal of Criminal Justice, 39*, 41–58.

Miner-Romanoff, K. (2012). Interpretive and critical phenomenological studies: A model design. *The Qualitative Report, 17,* 1–32.

Monto, M.A., Machalek, J., & Anderson, T.L. (2013). Boys doing art: The construction of outlaw masculinity in a Portland, Oregon, Graffiti Crew. *Journal of Contemporary Ethnography, 3,* 259–290.

Park, R., Burgess, E., & McKenzie, R. (1925). *The City.* Chicago, IL: University of Chicago Press.

Presser, L. (2008). *Been a Heavy Life: Stories of Violent Men.* Urbana, IL: University of Illinois.

Presser, L. (2009). The narratives of offenders. *Theoretical Criminology, 13,* 177–200.

Presser, L. (2010). Collecting and analyzing the stories of offenders. *Journal of Criminal Justice Education, 21,* 431–446.

Reiss, A.J. (1968). Stuff and nonsense about social surveys and observation. In H.S. Becker, B. Greer, D. Riesman, & R.S. Weiss (Eds.), *Institutions and Person: Papers Presented to C. Everett Hughes* (pp. 351–367). Chicago, IL: Aldine.

Reuter, P., MaCoun, R., Murphy, P., Abrahamse, A., & Simon, B. (1990). *Money from Crime: A Study of the Economics of Street Level Drug Dealing.* Santa Monica, CA: RAND.

Rich, J.A., & Grey, C.M. (2005). Pathways to recurrent trauma among young black men: Traumatic stress, substance use, and the code of the street. *American Journal of Public Health, 95,* 816–824.

Sampson, R.J., & Bean, L. (2006). Cultural mechanisms and killing fields: A revised theory of community-level racial inequality. In R.D. Peterson, L.J. Krivo, & J. Hagan (Ed.), *The Many Colors of Crime: Inequalities of Race, Ethnicity, and Crime in America* (pp. 8–38). New York: New York University Press.

Sandberg, S. (2008). Street capital: Ethnicity and violence on the streets of Oslo. *Theoretical Criminology, 12,* 153–171.

Sandberg, S. (2010). What can "lies" tell us about life? Notes towards a framework of narrative criminology. *Journal of Criminal Justice Education, 21,* 447–465.

Sarbin, T.R. (1986). *Narrative Psychology: The Storied Nature of Human Conduct.* Westport, CT: Praeger.

Schneidman, E.S. (1971). Perturbation and lethality as precursors of suicide in a gifted group. *Life Threatening Behavior, 1,* 23–45.

Scott, M.B., & Lyman, S.M. (1968). Accounts. *American Sociological Review, 33,* 46–52.

Scully, D., & Marolla, J. (1984). Convicted rapists' vocabulary of motive: Excuses and justifications. *Social Problems, 31*(5), 530–544.

Shaw, C. (1930). *The Jack-Roller: A Delinquent Boy's Own Story.* Chicago, IL: University of Chicago Press.

Short, J.F., & Strodtbeck, F.L. (1965). *Group Process and Gang Delinquency.* Chicago, IL: University of Chicago Press.

Shover, N. (1985). *Aging Criminals.* Beverly Hills, CA: Sage.

Shover, N. (1996). *Great Pretenders: Pursuits and Careers of Persistent Thieves.* Boulder, CO: Westview.

Shover, N., Coffey, G., & Hobbs, D. (2003). Crime on the line: Telemarketing and the changing nature of professional crime. *British Journal of Criminology, 43,* 489–505.

Shover, N., & Honaker, D. (1992). The socially bounded decision making of persistent property offenders. *Howard Journal of Criminal Justice, 31,* 276–293.

Small, M.L. (2011). How to conduct a mixed methods study: Recent trends in a rapidly growing literature. *Annual Review of Sociology, 37,* 57–86.

Sutherland, E.H. (1947). *Principles of Criminology.* Philadelphia: J.B. Lippincott.

Tewksbury, R., DeMichele, M.T., & Miller, J.M. (2005). Methodological orientations of articles appearing in criminal justice's top journals: Who publishes what and where. *Journal of Criminal Justice Education, 16*, 265–279.

Thompson, C.J., Locander, W.B., & Pollio, H.R. (1989). Putting consumer experience back into consumer research: The philosophy of existential phenomenology. *Journal of Consumer Research, 16*, 133–146.

Thrasher, F.M. (1927). *The Gang: A Study of 1,313 Gangs in Chicago*. Chicago, IL: University of Chicago Press.

Topalli, V. (2005). When being good is bad: An expansion of neutralization theory. *Criminology, 43*, 797–836.

Tunnell, K. (2006). *Living Off Crime*, 2nd edition. Lanham, MD: Rowman & Littlefield.

Van Mannen, J. (1975). Police socialization: A longitudinal examination of job attitudes in an urban police department. *Administrative Science Quarterly, 20*, 207–228.

Weisburd, D., & Waring, E. (2001). *White-Collar Crime and Criminal Careers*. Cambridge: Cambridge University Press.

Whyte, W.F. (1943). *Street-Corner Society: The Social Structure of an Italian Slum*. Chicago, IL: University of Chicago Press.

Willis, P. (1976/1993). The cultural meaning of drug use. In S. Hall & T. Jefferson (Eds.), *Resistance Through Rituals: Youth Subcultures in Post War Britain* (pp.106–118). London: Routledge.

Willott, S., Griffin, C., & Torrance, M. (2001). Snakes and ladders: Upper-middle class male offenders talk about economic crime. *Criminology, 39*, 441–467.

Wood, P.B., Gove, W.R., Wilson, J.A., & Cochran, J. (1997). Nonsocial reinforcement and habitual criminal conduct: An extension of learning theory. *Criminology, 35*, 335–366.

Wright, R.T., Brookman, F., & Bennett, T. (2006). The foreground dynamics of street robbery in Britain. *British Journal of Criminology, 46*, 1–15.

Wright, R.T., & Decker, S. (1994). *Burglars on the Job: Streetlife and Residential Break-Ins*. Boston, MA: Northeastern University Press.

Wright, R.T., & Decker, S. (1997). *Armed Robbers in Action*. Boston, MA: Northeastern University Press.

# Index

*Note*: Page numbers in *italic* refer to figures; those in **bold** to tables. A lower-case n after a page number indicates a note.

*The Handbook of Criminological Theory*, First Edition. Edited by Alex R. Piquero.
© 2016 John Wiley & Sons, Inc. Published 2016 by John Wiley & Sons, Inc.

Printed and bound by CPI Group (UK) Ltd, Croydon, CR0 4YY

16/02/2023

03192552-0001